The Road from Wigan Pier, Memoirs of a Linguist

First published in 1998 by
Transcreen Publications
Riversdown
Warnford
Hampshire SO32 3LH

Tel. +44-1962 771111
Fax +44-1962 771083
Email richard.lewis@crossculture.com

ISBN 0 9534398 0 1

Printed in Great Britain by
Axis Europe Limited, London.

To Bob, Arthur and Mathias, with whom I shared the years

Contents

The Road from Wigan Pier

If you were born in Wigan in the 1930s, you grew up speaking two languages – North Country and the Wigan miners' dialect. Besides these you could understand a third one – a funny, nasal, heavily diphthongized kind of English emitted daily by our crackling Philco wireless. The people who used it were from the BBC and they all spoke in this strange, affected manner whether they were newsreaders, play-actors or story tellers.

After 1939 they called themselves the Neshenal Sahvice and the accent grew thicker as the war progressed. They didn't seem to be able to handle their 'a's or their 'u's properly and said "cricket bet" for "cricket bat", "batter" for "butter" and "raff" for "rough". They pronounced all their aitches as if their jobs depended on it.

We never actually met anyone who spoke like that in the flesh, neither did we try to speak that way ourselves, as we reckoned we had enough on our hands with North Country and Wigan dialect. But, as I indicated, we understood, which was more than the London evacuees did when they came up and first heard our version. They had a tongue of their own, called Cockney, and a right ear-pounder it was, too. They said things like "apples and pears" for "upstairs" and "trouble and strife" for "wife". We amused ourselves a while with them, then ceased to take them or their speech very seriously and rarely listened when they gabbled away at school lunches. After a few months they could all speak North Country fluently and would have mastered the mining dialect too, only the war didn't last long enough.

Well, to come back to my own mental processes, I was speeding up in both my tongues and could slide into one from the other without even thinking about it. North Country one spoke with teachers at school, with preachers in chapel and with genteel ladies like Mrs Kane and Mrs Marsh, who seemed to be having some trouble understanding pitmen and their relatives. The dialect was what one spoke at home, with one's playmates and schoolfellows, with grown-ups in general and with any animal, bird or fish. We talked quite a lot to fish in those days, both before and after catching them.

I was particularly proficient in the dialect since I had an excellent model in my grandfather, who had been a face-worker down the mine for 60 years and still was going strong in his seventies. He lived with us after my grandmother died, and came home with a sooty face every day at 5 o'clock at the end of his shift. His speech was descended directly from his own grandfather's (born 1795) and when his tea or bath tub were a little behind schedule he ransacked an impressive Viking-Saxon-Celtic vocabulary which had to be heard to be appreciated. Even today I find it useful when missing two-foot putts.

My father, too, spoke dialect with uncompromising correctness and so did my mother, except when she had just come back from one of her elocution lessons, which were popular at the time.

My parents had married late, so I was the only child. The Chinese say that happiness is three generations under one roof; it was certainly true in our case. My grandfather – his name was Jake – had left school when he was nine and had spent his whole life down the mine. He was still a face worker at 74 and his two brothers, Tom and Johnny, both did over 60 years on the same face. Few people today are obliged to contemplate such a hard existence, but I remember Jake as being completely satisfied with life. I suppose now we would call it positive thinking. In winter he saw daylight only on Sundays, as he was invariably on the morning shift, going to and returning from work in darkness. Apart from a Sunday afternoon walk or fishing stint with Tom, the pit was his whole life. Around the mine revolved the hopes, ambitions, disappointments and drama of his youth. Yet there seemed to have been no setbacks. He was physically tough and cut more coal than the other men, which meant he was relatively well-paid. He married a local girl and had five sons, none of whom he let go down the mine. In spite of his aborted schooling he could read, write and calculate and was never known to make a spelling mistake. If he felt he couldn't spell a word, he would use another one. He never read fiction, but he always had his nose in one book or another – a strange assortment – biographies of missionaries, voyages of discovery, life and career of Harry Houdini, Kitchener at Omdurman, Pitman's shorthand, Pilgrim's Progress, Seven Pillars of Wisdom, Encyclopaedia Britannica, Old Moore's Almanac, various essays by Emerson and Max Beerbohm and odd writings by John Wesley and other Methodist luminaries. He would glance briefly at daily newspapers but seemed to give them little credence. After his eldest son Robert became Mayor of Wigan in 1930 and dominated the Borough Council for the next decade, Jake spent every Friday evening for the rest of his life buried in the "Wigan Observer". It was the only night I couldn't get a peep out of him. Otherwise he gave me most of his spare time.

In his late seventies, with his hardened body, craggy features, blue-scarred nose (coal dust under the skin), he ought to have been the strong silent type, but that he was not. He was not really loquacious, but he was sociable and humorous. In those television-less days people talked to each other a lot – men to women, old to young, neighbour to neighbour. We went out and visited for miles around and at home we were visited, too. My father and grandfather both liked walking (at that age I didn't) and they sallied forth on most nights, weather permitting, to call on brothers, cousins, friends and colleagues in the different Wigan districts of Ashton, Garswood, Ince, Platt Bridge and Billinge. They lugged me along with them and I would sit perched on sofas, drugged out of mind with endless cups of tea, listening to their male gossip, mining reminiscences, Rugby League legends and countless stories. Wherever we went, or indeed at home, my grandfather was the great storyteller. His stories were the oldest and the funniest and the ones which seemed to have most relevance to our everyday lives. He told stories about pit ponies and greedy farmers and people getting parts of their bodies stuck in textile machinery. He knew tales about Welsh witches, deaf lions, open coffins and clever parrots and the story about all the dogs in the world going to St Peter to ask him for shoes.

When we were at home and had no visitors he would tell me children's stories – he knew all the traditional ones and several others from Wales. He could not resist giving the tales a little twist of his own, so that the Three Bears sat in the front pew in the chapel, the Seven Dwarfs worked down his own pit and they had names like Tubby and Thrutcher and Cage Winder, while Red Riding Hood's grandmother and the Big Bad Wolf did the football pools together.

All this went on in dialect, evening after evening. As my mother did not let me go to school till I was nearly seven, I reached the age of six without ever having spoken even North Country apart from odd exchanges when we had the preacher for Sunday lunch or Dr Hunter to look at my tonsils. I asked for things in dialect, I dreamt and had nightmares in dialect, I cajoled, connived and complained in dialect, I planned my little revenges in the miners' tongue. When, on my best behaviour, I addressed Mrs Kane or Mrs Marsh in straight Lancashire, it was like slipping into a foreign language.

Lest the reader should underestimate the difference between the two tongues I am talking about, here is a passage in dialect with its translation in standard English.

Tha's bin starvin' it lone agen beht lappin' thisell up proper!

You've been freezing outside again without wrapping yourself up properly.

Ast fert start maitherin' when tha sees us ah'm clemmin'? Wheer's pies? Ast hoven um eht th'oon?

Do you have to start making a fuss when you can see that I'm starving? Where are the pies? Have you taken them out of the oven?

Tha wants um prigmeet dustn't? Howd thi din un cahr thi dehn while ah umbethinks me!

You want them done just right, don't you? Be quiet and sit down while I collect my thoughts!

Aw reet, but hag thee, or ast be eightin' um pindert.

All right, but hurry up or I'll be eating them burnt up.

Harken! Is beht getten wom un is hahmin' un consterrin' when ah've bin powfaggin' misell aw mawnin', sidin' un scratchin' baggin' fer yon lot! Gi' oer bein' so sackless!

Just listen. He's hardly got home and he's snapping and arguing when I've been tiring myself out all morning, tidying up and getting food ready for all of you! Stop being so fidgety.

Worra fililoo! Stop pooin' thi chowf un gi' us a jonock afoor ah' goo slancin'.

What a din! Stop making a face and give me a piece of black bread before I start stealing (something to eat).

Tha pikes off dehnt lone, jaftin' un gallivantin' aw mawnin', tha loyses thi kale at butcher's an comes wom wi powsy meight.

Off you go down the street, living it up and socializing all morning – you're last in the butcher's queue and come home with poor meat...

Tha sez it's powse?

You say it's no good?

Ah metta clod it int flash.

I might as well have thrown it into the lake.

Ditto?

Did you?

Un be beht fert pies? Thall'et eight wot tha browt. Wheer'st bin fradgin' anyroad?

And have none for the pies? You'll have to eat what you brought. Where have you been gossiping, anyway?

Ainscough sez us Coddy's sahned on that fillet Agnes agen.

Ainscough says that Coddy (nickname) has started courting that floosie Agnes again.

Hm! Ah deht is getten aw his cheers awom. Oo met bi brossen, but ooze widdert. An nangy an sauvy, thanose! Ooze norrafe lerron wi yon mon, anter?

Hm! I don't think he's right in the head. She might be bonny, but she's wrinkled. And bad-tempered and deceitful, I can tell you. She's really caught a prize with him, hasn't she?

I reckon oo cun oerfawse im. Ainscough sez he'd not speyk to 'er if he fawd oe'r er.

I suppose she's that much smarter than he is. Ainscough says he wouldn't speak to her if he bumped right into her.

Oose as fehh as a dolly-tub!

She's ugly as sin!

Wheer's Harry and Tom?

Where are Harry and Tom?

They're caw'd elpin' Charlie t'flit. They pole off at ten, beht meight, aw uv a rook, varneer nowt on, hafe frozzen.

They're supposed to be helping Charlie to move house. They charged off at ten o'clock without eating anything – untidy, wearing hardly a thing, half frozen.

They're teed t'go, when tha reckons heh much tronnin' Charlie does up these parts.

They're obliged to go when you think what a handyman Charlie has been for us around here.

Here's thi pies an divilsnose. When tha's etten, tha cun deg t'flehrs.

Here are your pies and currant cake. When you've eaten, you can water the flowers.

Aw reet, burram gooin' fer a pow at two.

OK, but I'm going for a haircut at two o'clock.

Only people born within seven or eight miles of Wigan are capable of understanding anything of this dialect when it is spoken at normal speed. Today not more than ten per cent of the local population can follow it, while even fewer can speak it.

When I finally started school in Ashton-in-Makerfield just south of Wigan, the situation hardly changed. All the boys and most of the girls were dialect speakers; they shunned normal English like it made their jaws ache. We were segregated at playtime and the one hundred boys on our side of the wall were a tough, profane, quarrelsome bunch of working class Lancastrian youngsters, often undersized and pale-faced like their parents, but independent, tenacious and hard as nails. There was the miners' sons' clique, the cotton mill clique and the shopkeepers' clique. I was sort of half in the miners' clique and half a loner, though I was dragged into all the petty disputes and schoolyard fights and got my nose bloodied like everyone else.

The youngsters were all rich in dialect expressions and colourful insults. None of them had a vocabulary greater than mine, but several of the really hard cases were much more foul-mouthed, commanding swear words and sexual innuendo in dialect that made me realize I had been shielded at home. Looking back on those days, I realize the immense strength of oral culture and the unlimited powers of linguistic absorption that a child possesses.

One hears so much today about the dangers of exposing a young child to two languages – it will cause him to stammer, or wet his bed or interfere in some strange way with his identity. I have always held this to be nonsense as I know a good number of well-balanced grown-ups who spoke 3 or 4 languages at the age of six without ever developing squints or limps or ruining their parents' furniture.

The dialect-wielding Ashton schoolboys disliked "posh talk", but any of them could mimic three other versions of English – (BBC, North Country and Cockney) at will, showing a fair mastery of the pronunciation, intonation and different vocabulary of each. If you can mimic another tongue in depth, the fact is that you can understand, and even speak it. There is no undue strain on a child's mind if he uses four languages naturally. One must remember that a youngster's vocabulary is limited to perhaps 500 – 600 words, so that even four tongues would only stretch him to around 2000 items – well under the number he will command as an educated adult in one language. My own daughter, now in her thirties, is still completely fluent in Japanese, the result of attending a kindergarten in Tokyo. Her bilingualism has also given her two separate personalities (and that is another matter worthy of consideration) but as she seems to enjoy both of them it would appear to be an advantage, like possessing two passports might be.

Cancer claimed old Jake at the age of 78 and a few months later, on Sept 3rd, 1939, war with Germany was declared. The lights started going out all over Europe, nowhere more effectively than in Wigan, where the blackout was *de rigueur*. Our location, midway between Liverpool and Manchester, meant that we had bombers passing overhead many nights from 1940 to 1944. The Cockneys were moved on to the Lake District or somewhere safer, but they came back again when the raids abated.

My mother bought two sacks of sugar one week before hostilities commenced. The sugar lasted until Christmas 1944, but otherwise we ate the same rubbish as everyone else who did not have relations in the farming business.

The house seemed empty for a while after Jake's demise and I took to listening more and more to the wireless, where children's programmes made up for the loss of my grandfather's tales. As the Battle of Britain raged, we eagerly awaited the 6 o'clock news every evening, when incredibly cheerful statistics on shot-down German planes were fed to us nightly by Bruce Belfrage, Frank Philips, Alvar Liddell, John Snagge and Stuart Hibberd. They were occasionally interrupted by a spiteful gentleman named Lord Haw-Haw, who shouted things such as "That's a lie!" and tried to give us quite a different set of numbers, but in general old Bruce and Frank managed to shout him down and he got hanged at the end of the war for his insolence, anyway. Stuart Hibberd's Golden Voice used to tell us several times a week how healthy beans and potatoes were for us; everybody in Wigan seemed to be taking his advice, too, for the chip shops did a roaring trade, even after Spam was invented. In the schoolyard the rumour was out that the corned beef was made from dead soldiers.

My fascination for the radio increased in my last year at elementary school (1940). Wilfred Pickles, the first North Country newsreader, was brought in to lend a bit of variety to the Bruce-Alvar-Frank team, but he was a Yorkshireman and we all thought he sounded as funny as his name. He seemed to do better when they gave him the "Have a Go" programme in which he persuaded octogenarians to sing or recite poetry to keep us all amused in those dark days.

For my part, I started listening to the foreign language broadcasts. I couldn't understand them but I thought the strange sounds were more entertaining than some of the stuff coming across in English.

At that time the BBC was putting out the news in nearly every European language, just to make sure that those unfortunate occupied peoples knew that we British were tightening our belts, melting down our iron railings and preparing for the day when we would liberate the lot of them. The Norwegian, Swedish and Danish bulletins used to go out on the World Service in mid-morning. I listened to them regularly on Saturdays and Sundays and on days when I was at home with tonsillitis. The double tones of Norwegian and Swedish, as well as the glottal stops of hot-potato-in-the-mouth Danish, held a particular fascination for me. What was even more intriguing was the fact that after a few months, I began to understand the gist of these broadcasts. The

Scandinavian languages are very close to English as well as being close to each other. I bought a Danish phrase-book-cum-glossary in a second-hand bookshop in Wigan (threepence) and checked some of the most common news bulletin vocabulary such as "news", "army", "planes", "Prime Minister", "attack", "bomb", "shoot down", "advances", "rationing" and so on. War news was very much the same day after day, so after hearing it first in English, I was able to follow a lot of it in my three pet languages. When you know that "news" is *nyheter* (pronounced new-hater) in Swedish, then you can have a pretty good guess what *nyheder* and *nyheder* mean in Norwegian and Danish respectively.

I discovered to my astonishment that many Scandinavian expressions were actually closer to English than the Wigan dialect was.

"Shall we go up there?" in Swedish is *Skall vi gå upp där?* (pronounced "Skal vee go up dare?") which people south of Watford would understand better than "Heh abeht gooin up theer?"

The Swedish pronunciation: "Vee must go noo dare-fore at vee must come-a-hem furry midnatt." (We must go now because we must get home before midnight.) is no stranger than Wigan "Wid beht pike off neh cuz wi mun bewom afoor mid-neet."

Danish *farvel* is nearer to "farewell" than "ta-rah". Swedish *kasta* nearer to "cast, throw" than "clod", *krinklad* nearer to "wrinkled" than "widdert", *hårklippning* nearer to "haircut" than "pow", *trött* nearer to "tired" than "powfagged", *just så* nearer to "just so" than "prigmeet".

In my twenties I was to learn the 3 Scandinavian languages in a short space of time. I am quite sure that my many hours listening to them in 1940 and 1941 greatly facilitated their absorption when I tackled them more than a decade later.

My interest in the Nordic countries had increased in November 1939 when the Soviet Union attacked Finland by land, sea and air. The ensuing bitter struggle became temporarily the focus of world attention.

The BBC commentators, as yet with little fighting of our own to analyse, digressed for a few months from the growing anxieties surrounding Adolf Hitler and his men to sing the praises of this David of the North resisting with unforseen stoicism the Goliath of the East. My boyish imagination was captured by a memorable account of a lone Finnish soldier, clothed all in white for camouflage against the snow, attacked 3 times by a Russian plane. Sheltering behind rock and tree, he was struck twice on the helmet and gasmask case by bullets, but symbolically survived to fight again.

This war, and its sequel, have considerably less romantic connotations for Finns who fought in them, but the thin grey line remained unbroken at the Armistice in 1944, as this upright, dependable people gave new dimensions to the concepts of tenacity and heroism.

Ashton-in-Makerfield, a small, undistinguished market town 4 miles south of Wigan, had in 1939 a wartime population of 28,000. With its numerous slag-heaps, moribund cotton mills, near-exhausted coal seams and general lack of attractive scenery it was just about as dreary a place as you could find to spend a war in, except for one saving factor: it had the Camp. In the south part of the town there was a large, sprawling expanse of partly-forested parkland, formerly belonging to a huge estate. This walled area of several hundred acres was commandeered by the government for the establishment of a military camp. This camp did not possess barracks in the normal sense, housing any permanent regiment of British troops. Instead it was a motley collection of huts, tents and prefabricated hostels which accommodated, as the war progressed, different groups of armed forces personnel from a large variety of countries, ideologies and persuasions.

First, in 1938, we had the Free Czechs. During the six months they stayed with us we invited them for tea, got all their Czech stamps, struggled with their Slavic pronunciation and observed their language had practically no vowels. They taught us how to say *zmrzlina* (ice cream) and I mashed *Strc prst krk* for a while, as it went down well in the school yard.

After the Czechs came the Scots – a roaring, ruddy-cheeked, drinking, brawling bunch of tam-o-shantered Glasgwegians who filled the pubs every night and went out with the local girls, who understood them less than they had the Czechs. The Scots, after ten weeks of this kind of training, went off to France, returning to Ashton via Dunkirk a short time later.

Next were the Free Poles – in Air Force blue this time. They went to tea with the local miners of Polish extraction (we had a dozen). They chatted incomprehensibly to the girls, drank their share, though less than the Scots, and marched up and down Wigan Road twice a day, getting ready for their big revenge on the Nazis who had forced them to flee their country. It is said that they were brave airmen who commanded a lot of respect in the Royal Air Force, though many of their pilots lost planes chasing German bombers so far out over the North Sea that they ran out of fuel and had to ditch. I started learning Polish, but abandoned it after one week partly on account of the difficult nasal pronunciation (worse than Czech) and mainly because from one night to the next the Poles decamped and were replaced by the Royal Australian Air Force.

The Aussies, bless'em, were the best-looking, cleanest-cut, cheeriest young warriors that we had in the whole course of the war. They consumed large amounts of beer, re-conquered our girls and bashed the odd Pom, but they could march, they were smart, they liked our tea and they never stopped smiling. Some of us kids would march alongside them on the pavement and they would wink at us behind their officer's back and throw us halfpennies, sometimes even the little silver threepenny bits. They had their own language too, – a kind of warm-hearted Cockney, without the apples-and-pears bit – and called everybody either "mite", "love" or "cobber". You could see they weren't afraid of anybody; with them on our side I couldn't see us losing the war, even though we were doing pretty badly at the time.

After the Australians went, our girls had a few weeks rest, much needed as it turned out, for next came the French sailors. They had blue and white uniforms with striped jerseys showing a lot of neck and wore tam o'shanters with a red bob on top. They spoke hardly any English at all and very bad French, but the girls seemed to understand what they meant and eventually married quite a number of them. The French stayed well over a year, as France's political situation was becoming increasingly confused; a lot of them didn't seem to have boats to go back to. They did a lot of cooking in the Camp and played their own version of bowls in which they threw their *boules* as opposed to the English manner of rolling them. Sometimes they threw our bowls on the Recreation Bowling Green and left small craters in the turf, which Mr Shaw spent years trying to eliminate.

After Montgomery's successes in North Africa, Ashton's war took a new turn. The visible effect of our Libyan victory was an influx of Italian prisoners-of-war into our Camp, up to now used only for our allies. The Italians came in larger numbers, new huts were erected, the French sailors were transferred elsewhere and I started learning Italian. The prisoners were divided into browns and greens, (we never ascertained the distinction) and after three months they were allowed out in the evenings. They were mainly from southern Italy and Sicily and were a voluble, friendly bunch, clearly much relieved at being able to exchange the Sahara sand dunes for Ashton's slag heaps. They walked a lot, sometimes with girls but usually in pairs. They came to tea with sparse English but willingness to learn and they played football with each other in the Camp, with us peering over the wall, which crumbled more and more as the war wore on. The Italians were good swimmers and used to dive from the top diving board at Wigan and Southport Baths. They entered pubs, but drank very little – I don't think they were very fond of bitter and neither they nor our fathers could afford much whisky.

From 1943-1945 the Italians were dispersed in the countryside to work on the land and our Camp was enlarged to accommodate the increasingly large numbers of German prisoners of war whom we had seen taken in North African newsreels. The first thing we noticed was that the Germans looked very much like the British. There were dark and blond Germans, as well as red-heads – a racial mix as is found in the British Isles – whereas the Italians had been almost uniformly quite short and very dark. The German prisoners wasted no time in integrating themselves into Ashton life. They joined the Choral Society, they played football matches against the local English clubs and many of them went to church, where they read the lesson, sang hymns and even took the collection. They formed their own choir and in 1944 gave Ashton an impressive performance of Handel's Messiah in St Thomas's church.

Their football team beat everyone out of sight and Bert Trautmann, their goalkeeper, later played for Manchester City for ten seasons.

The Germans, too, were gradually sent to work on the fertile South Lancs plain with its Nordic settlements – Ormskirk, Skelmersdale, Kirkby and so on. They were tireless workers who took their agricultural tasks seriously. Some of them married farmers' daughters and are still with us.

The last contingent of foreign troops to occupy Ashton was the largest, most colourful and most charismatic of them all – the American D-Day invasion force. Around the Camp and on manoeuvres they were less than impressive in drab-coloured denims, but in the evening when they came into town in their newly-pressed, well-tailored olive green uniforms, they were the envy of the British civilians and servicemen alike. We had seen these dashing young men in black and white newsreels for two years, but to have them on one's doorstep in full technicolour was indeed electrifying – particularly for the girls. The soldiers, too, came in all colours, shapes and sizes. There were handsome negroes from the South who said "y'all" for "you" even when there was only one of you. There were dark-headed Italians and Jews from New York, Chinese- and Japanese-Americans from Hawaii, gangling hill-billies from West Virginia and Kentucky, sunburned blonds from California and Easterners from Boston and Maryland who stressed their English ancestry.

American troops, even today, usually go in for some kind of embellishment of their uniform and the 1944 crowd was no exception. They wore all kinds of battle memorabilia – Nazi officers' daggers with swastikas carved into the silver hilt, Italian *bersagliere* hats with fine plumes, long beautifully-polished German riding boots, Colt 45s, shoulder-belts with clips of hand grenades, Navajo warrior rings and bracelets – any weapon, medal or insignia which distinguished them from their fellows. They would come to tea with all this gear on. We were allowed to finger the daggers and guns and occasionally bargain for them, but usually in vain. Texans came visiting in ten gallon hats, thong-ties and high heeled boots with silver spurs on. People like that we had thought existed only in the movies. Now we knew they were for real – those invasion troops out-moved the movies.

Although the date and place of the June Normandy invasion were still closely-guarded secrets, Ashton and its troops knew that these men were being held ready for an attack which would be on the mainland of Europe and would take place in the near future. It was understood that many of these young men, so full of vitality and exuberance, would be killed. I remember how the people of Ashton developed feelings of sympathy for the American force during the spring months of 1944 and how the troops themselves occasionally looked sad in off-guarded moments.

They ate cakes by the thousands. Those who were on camp duty in the evening were desperate for cream cakes to supplement their boring rations and we kids did a roaring business shuttling back and forth between the camp and Pilling's Confectionery. Loaded with chocolate eclairs, sponges, cream puffs and currant cakes, we would gallop the mile and a half to the Camp and try to gain access. It was not easy, for the wall was high and those parts which had crumbled were usually reinforced with barbed wire. The guards, too, were supposed to keep us out; those at the main gate, under the eyes of their officers, always did. Others were less conscientious and let us slip through – for a cake of course. The going rate was one shilling for a threepenny cake -a profit of 300%. It was big money for wartime schoolboys – you could buy a new suit for five shillings. But the Americans thought shillings, even pounds, were nothing and sometimes even tipped kids who made several trips in one night with a whole pound note.

*   *   *   *   *

In 1941, when our war fortunes were at a low ebb, I had begun my studies at Ashton Grammar School. It was an old school founded in 1588, which meant that its students at least remembered the date of the Spanish Armada. Its teachers were old, too, as all the young ones had gone off to war. The Headmaster, Frank Gardner Hall (referred to as F.G. by the staff and Lob by the students) was an eccentric martinet from the South who disliked the North and Ashton in particular. Approaching 60, he was six feet tall with a menacing stoop, thinning hair and an Adolf Hitler moustache. School children and staff went in constant fear of him for the seven years I was at school. He castigated all transgressions – laziness, truancy, stupidity, lies – with frequent Saturday morning Detention and a huge cane. Teachers he caned verbally, with a caustic vocabulary and biting sarcasm that none of them could match, or would ever have dared to.

F.G. Hall had a commanding, chilling presence such as I have never seen possessed by anyone else. Vincent Gardner, our popular 60-year old Senior Master, had the job of quieting the 300 children in the Great Hall each morning before the Roll Call began. He was a good disciplinarian and achieved a quiet hum by about one minute to nine. Then F.G.'s first step would be heard on a creaking floorboard fifty feet down the corridor as he approached, hymn book tucked under left arm. Immediately you could hear a pin drop. His next twenty steps were listened to one by one by 300 pairs of ears, attached to now upright, unmoving heads. His entry was signalled by the loud squeak of a third former whipping back the hall door – now his tread was loud and clear, twenty-six more steps to the stage, seven up the stairs, left turn, five across to centre stage, left turn again, then the whispered "Good Morning". Our thundered "Good Morning sir" was always a great relief. Sometimes he would stand there for half a minute, glaring at some miscreant or some innocent sparrow near the ceiling and we would have to hold our breath, like pearl divers.

Gardner told me in later years how he envied Hall this uncanny ability to dominate – so useful in the teaching profession. Hall seemed to have no weaknesses – he was punctual, hardworking, decisive, ruthlessly logical and hardly ever ill or indisposed. Hated though he was, he was an excellent teacher of English – a subject few of us were allowed to fail in. He was a competent administrator and the school's results were good, most of us gaining a university place if we wished to. He had a nice family who lived next to the school – a pleasant-faced wife, a pretty daughter, Sheila, who played a fair game of tennis, and his bespectacled blue stocking Kate, who looked like him and whom he adored. Maybe she was his only *point faible*. She was quiet, modest and bordering on genius. We all called her Congo Maisie, though nobody quite knew why.

Our class of '41 had F.G. to the bitter end – he retired in 1948, the year we left. It was the end of an era, as many of our ageing teachers were being replaced by returning service personnel. I have always considered it good fortune – almost a privilege – to have been taught by our elderly staff. There were two generation gaps between us (some of them must have thought they were lucky to be still working), but they were experienced, equable and wise. Their guidance and F.G.'s discipline produced a special breed of students, to which I belong. We are old-fashioned and fair, have imagination and humour, but respect authority; we tend to believe rigidly in absolute values and are suspicious of compromise; we tolerate fools with difficulty and, like F.G. Hall, many of us are a little mad.

A good number of these teachers, long since dead, live on in my memory. Kind and humorous Welsh geographer Trevor Jones with his rift valleys and cwms and corries. Dry old stick Ernest Roscoe, the living image of Trevor Howard. Beaming gym teacher Ossie Lahive, who gave everybody a nickname on their first day at school (He called me Ringtail). Vincent Gardner who taught us waltzes, foxtrots, veletas and Barn Dances in the lunch-hours. George Mitchell who taught me how to bowl in-swingers to make up for his boring English lessons. Arthur Gee, the woodwork teacher who used to tell me I would be the worst woodworker in Ashton when they had hanged Naylor. Arthur had his own way of saying things ("Keep your wood as long as you can as long as you can" and "Don't bring it to me when you've cut its head off.") When Naylor, in sheer frustration drove 100 nails into a piece of birch on the woodwork bench, Arthur first knew instinctively who to blame ("Come out, Naylor.") and secondly the right punishment ("Pull them all out again").

Whenever I took my latest work out to show him he would hide his eyes with both hands and moan "No wonder we lost Singapore". Arthur lived till he was 96.

My favourite teacher had to be Isabel Chaffer. She taught French and she taught it so well that she really laid the basis for my career as a linguist. She instilled in me not only a love of the French language and way of life, but also of the French people – not everyone's cup of tea. Miss Chaffer was a plump, cheery-faced spinster of 50 with completely unfailing good humour and a firm belief that all English school children could learn French. This belief was shared unfortunately by very few of my classmates, especially the boys. French is a very beautiful language but is considered, through no fault of its own, effeminate by the English schoolboy. There is no way he can say *un bon vin blanc* without feeling silly. Spanish sounds a much more masculine language to him – he will yell *toro* and *caramba!* at will, but that did not console Isabel Chaffer one jot. She charmed, she cajoled, she did everything a teacher should do to motivate her students, but after 5 years' French most of the boys were hard put by to order a lemonade in the language.

At least she had her successes with the girls. Lenora Taberner developed a beautiful French accent and actually understood the grammar. Ruth Bayman, with less talent, struggled mightily with her text books and usually won the annual honour of giving the French Recitation for the Vikings in the House Competitions. Norman Taylor, Jack Lowe and Bert Temple could all handle the language, too, though they never betrayed their secret by opening their mouth in class. But I am forced to confess that I was Miss Chaffer's star. After my humiliations in the woodwork and art classes, I badly needed a win; French turned out to be my opportunity. After my desperate scrambling for words listening to Norwegian news broadcasts, I found French – actually explained by a brilliant teacher – to be ridiculously easy. French had present, past and future tenses, just like English and if they happened to say four-twenties for eighty or wine red for red wine, what was so shattering about that? It is true that the Subjunctive held me up for a few minutes, but give me a *viens/vienne* mutation any day before Integral or Differential Calculus (other battleground defeats of mine).

In short, I spoke French fluently before the end of the first year and Miss Chaffer, who did not know how I had done it, beamed broadly whenever my skinny figure hove into view. The Headmaster, who, like Adolf Hitler, did not trust anybody who spoke two languages, nevertheless set me long essays in English and marked these severely and clinically in neat red ink. It was his way of paying me a compliment and soon my English grammar was as good as my French.

Like Miss Chaffer I, too, had no idea how I had learnt French. Perhaps a better way of putting it is that I could not understand how the others had **failed** to learn something so simple. Once you can swim, it is hard to imagine how anyone else cannot. Later, when learning two or three languages simultaneously, I began to realise that it is like changing gear in a car – once you click in, you stay in, until you decide to move into another gear. I shall have more to say about this phenomenon in a later chapter. Real linguists do not speak a foreign language by stringing some words together into a sentence and then making up one sentence after another. They do a certain amount of ground-work first, like absorbing vocabulary and studying endings and word order. The rest is achieved by memory, mimicry and slipping into a verbal groove or calibration demonstrated to them by the native speaker. A linguist can learn 3 or 4 languages a year in this way, just as a good sportsman can become proficient at soccer, hockey, tennis and cricket during a school year.

Linguists learn languages quickly and effortlessly and each successive tongue is gobbled up more rapidly than the previous one. Intelligent "non-linguists" can learn languages quickly, provided they have strong motivation (girl friend, job needs, etc.). Almost anyone can learn a language to the extent of being able to communicate, but the less gifted just take that much longer. I have only met a dozen people in 40 years who were entirely incapable of learning a language and **they** were all virtually incoherent in their own tongue.

*   *   *   *   *

I have many vivid recollections of those wartime years which would occupy too much space in this volume. I would like to tell of the schoolboy war waged by Arthur Naylor and Archie Tate against F.G. Hall and of the cold fury they produced in him. ("I'm looking amongst you boys for leadership. You, Naylor, will lead them all the wrong way.") Naylor went on to become a headmaster and recently was awarded an OBE. There was the night when Eldon Griffiths, with 3rd former Lewis illegally on his bicycle crossbar, was chased 3 miles by the police (in vain), also on cycles, determined to take us into custody. Eldon's father was the local police sergeant and Eldon himself went on to become Minister for the Environment with special responsibility for Police Affairs.

However, these lines I am writing concern languages and this brings me to the event which was to be the culmination of 5 years of French with Miss Chaffer – our first expedition to France. This may sound trite these days, but it must be remembered that from 1939-1946 no British schoolchild was able to set foot on the continent of Europe. France was under German occupation and Europe to us was as remote and inaccessible as the moon. Even after liberation, schoolboy traffic between England and France only began after considerable delay.

Eventually cooperation between the British and French authorities led to schoolboy exchanges in 1946 and from the Class of '41 Bert Temple, Bob Bradley and I found ourselves in the vanguard of this new experiment. We were all to be packed off to the families of French "opposite numbers", who would come to England the following year. Bert's French had been coming along fine since he had seen a picture of Michèle Morgan and Bob was always good for an adventure, so off we went for a month, £5 in our pocket and "En Route" and "En Marche" in our rucksacks. The four and a half hour train ride from Wigan to London was the longest trip any of us had made in our sheltered lives. The next hurdle was Euston to Victoria by tube. None of us really believed that trains ran underground and the long escalators down reminded us of going down the pit. We sweated it out for 10 stations, gripping our rucksacks between our knees, squinting meanly at Cockney passengers ready to pounce on us should we relax our vigil.

Victoria was bustling and booming. We bought French newspapers, sausage rolls and Vimto before clambering aboard for Newhaven, Dieppe and Paris-St Lazare. The dash from London across the Sussex countryside seemed very brief after our Wigan-Euston leg. The Channel was busy with shipping, plying to and fro, much of it battered and unpainted as it had been during hostilities. When both coasts were visible, Bert fell back on his strategic reserve – four thick slices of toast with melted cheese packed up for him by Mother back in Wigan. At sixteen, Bert already weighed 12 stone. Bob and I hardly turned the scales at 8 stone each.

At Dieppe the French customs men wore hats like General de Gaulle and smoked evil-smelling cigarettes with parchment-like yellowed paper. We had nothing to declare, though we were loaded with butter, sugar and raspberry jam for our emaciated, ex-occupied French opposite numbers and their fathers and mothers. We boarded a French train from a station with no platforms. The first culture shock was a whiff of the French ticket inspector's breath as he squeezed past me in the corridor. I had never encountered garlic before and I really thought I would have to take the next train back to England. I love garlic now, but it took me ten years to get used to it. Bob and Bert weren't wild about it either.

The other shock I had on this trip was that I failed to understand the first question addressed to me in France, even though it was only 2 words long. Rather disappointing after 5 years' preparation. We were met at St Lazare by Serge Morette and Jacques Martin, two of our pen friends, accompanied by Jacques's father, Georges Martin. Monsieur Martin pumped my hand and asked *Ça va*? I had never heard that before in my short life. Miss Chaffer was one of the best French teachers that ever lived, but she never used *Ça va*? (only *Comment allez-vous?*) It was an object lesson to me, borne in mind in later years when I, too, wrote language manuals.

We had four marvellous days in Paris, staying with 3 French families – the Morettes, the Martins and the Tissiers. The grey wartime Ashton schoolboy world was suddenly left behind, and we wandered wide-eyed round the sunlit elegant streets of Paris – a vibrant capital enjoying its first real summer since Liberation. It never rained that July and everything was fun for the cheeky

Parisians – running for a bus, buying a lottery ticket, whistling at the girls, scurrying along with a pair of *baguettes* under the armpit.

A whole new world opened up for us. We drank our first beers, took pictures of the Eiffel Tower and Notre Dame, went to the Folies Bergères and the Grand Guignol, leaned over the platform rails of the quaint,green and white French buses, dipped *croissants* in *café au lait*, took *douches* instead of baths and got so drunk off *vin rouge* at dinner that we could not find Liverpool on a map of England.

"They live, we exist" said Bert, who liked to sum up situations in short aphoristic sentences and who was eating everything they put in front of him. Our modest gifts of sugar and butter, though graciously accepted, seemed meagre offerings for people who laid on for us two six-course meals a day – *soupe à l'oignon, paté de foie gras, biftek aux pommes frites, salade au roquefort, fromage Brie de Normandie, banane flambée, café noir, un petit cognac après* – we went to bed every night stuffed to the gills and woke up every morning at seven with a splitting headache.

French schoolboys seemed to take this gourmet existence in their stride, but we would not have lasted more than a week. Fortunately, though to our great chagrin, we were transferred after four days to our main pen friends who lived in different places far from the high life of the capital. Bert was the lucky one – he had a pen friend in Antibes – James Willard – and there he spent an idyllic four weeks, swimming in the Med, plucking lemons off trees, hobnobbing with *les gens du Midi,* ruining whatever French accent Miss Chaffer had endowed him with. I was despatched to Nevers of all places – the French city which, I am told, is furthest from the sea. It is like an oven in July, and about as interesting as Widnes on a Sunday. My pen friend was Claude Merlot, son of the *chef de gare* in Nevers. He was my age and played the violin. An only child, he spoke no English, though he had studied it two years at school. My hobbies at the time, besides languages, were football, cricket, tennis, table tennis, snooker, photography, chemistry experiments and collecting stamps and birds' eggs. He had no knowledge of any of these delights. His only passion was the violin, which he played night and day. I could knock a few hymns out of the organ and get through parts of Handel's Messiah on a good day, but Claude was a talented and dedicated musician who never seemed to play a wrong note. If he had done, I would never have noticed it. I hate the violin, even more than I used to hate garlic. I would never have made a good spy, for torturers of foreign secret police forces could have made me divulge any secret just by making me listen to violin music for an hour. Claude and I shared the same bedroom. When he couldn't sleep, he used to get up and play his fiddle. Between 11 and midnight was his favourite time, but one to two a.m. was not uncommon. He disturbed his parents' sleep too, but he was their only son and they loved him.

Bob Bradley was packed off to a village 30 kilometres from Nevers called Chateauneuf-val-de-Bargis. It had more animals than people. He stayed with Pierre Thieuleux and his parents. Monsieur Thieuleux was the village barber and sheared sheep in his spare time. Bob, whose family were constructors, often wondered how he had got matched up with a barber's son in a village twenty miles from anywhere, but we supposed the authorities were going through teething troubles after all the bother of the war, so we all made the best of it. Both the Merlot and Thieuleux families were very kind to us during all our stay. At least Pierre Thieuleux did not play the violin at inappropriate hours. He went for 10-mile walks, taking Bob with him. The Nièvre *département* has beautiful, green, undulating hills and Bob got to know them quite well. One day Claude Merlot and I cycled out to Chateauneuf and walked a few leagues with them. Pierre's father had to take Claude and me with our bikes on the back of a lorry back to Nevers, as we were quite poorly come dusk. It was the only night Claude didn't play his fiddle.

At the end of four weeks, Bob, Bert and I spent a final night in Paris with the Morettes. (The Martins and Tissiers had departed, with three million others, for *les grandes vacances*) By now we had graduated to *pernods* before dinner and we sipped these as we compared experiences and took stock of our *séjours*. Each one of us had spoken French non-stop for a whole month and the Morettes were quick to compliment us on our improved fluency, though Madame Morette – a sweet genteel lady – shuddered at some of Bert's *expressions méridionales*. We were no longer the English schoolboys who had boarded the train at Wigan Station a month earlier. Bert, complete with beret and silver chain round his neck, now smoked clandestine *Gauloises* instead of clandestine Woodbines. Bob had fattened up on *baguettes* and *agneau rôti* and could drink a whole glass of *calvados* if they let him put two lumps of sugar in it. I, for my part, felt that my developing affection for the French language and dialects, for the rich and varied aspects of the rolling countryside, for the disarming friendliness of the *paysan*, had added a new dimension to my personality. All three of us felt we could now identify with the French, whom our schoolfriends still saw as excitable, frog-eating Latin lovers who drank tea without milk and drove funny-looking cars on the wrong side of the road.

Serge Morette, Michel Tissier, James Willard and Jacques Martin are still my good friends today and our children often visit each other. Bert, Bob and I go to France almost every year, meeting many French people, but somehow the old saying that there are no friends like old friends holds water. Sadly I have lost touch with the Merlots – they are no longer in Nevers. Returning from a skiing trip in 1977, I passed through Chateauneuf-val-de-Bargis after a gap of 30 years. On an impulse, I parked the car on the main street and resolved to find Pierre Thieuleux. There was only one problem – I couldn't remember his second name. Chateauneuf didn't seem any bigger than it had been 30 years earlier, so I assumed that it would not take me long to track him down. I went from house to house, knocked on doors, asked the good people of the village if they remembered Pierre, now aged about 47, who had had an English schoolboy staying with him 3 decades before. Some of the people I spoke to were from Lyon and Chartres. Others had only been in the village for ten years or so. But several oldies said yes, they knew Pierre, but which Pierre? There were at least 4 of them, but they weren't sure about the English schoolboy. My investigation led me to the doors of Pierre Noël, Pierre Convin, Pierre Bassot and Pierre Levèque, all between 45 and 50 years of age. None of them looked like our Pierre or had heard of Bob Bradley, though they were all friendly and apologetic. Levèque took me to the Post Office where we made further enquiries, but the missing surname blocked our progress. There were no more Pierres in Chateauneuf except a four-year-old.

Finally I hit upon the idea of phoning Bob from the Post Office and he gave me the name of Thieuleux. By now I had a curious gathering of a dozen Chateauneuf citizens all helping me in the Post Office, including three of the Pierres. They looked up at me expectantly as I came out of the phone booth. "Pierre Thieuleux" I shouted, but their faces fell. *"Ah lui, il est mort"*, mumbled Pierre Bassot. The good people around me were touched by a momentary sadness and they smiled ruefully as the sun tucked itself in behind a cloud. Then they said *"au revoir"* and shuffled out of the Post Office, back to their shuttered windows and closed doors.

Levèque told me where I could find his grave on the hillside. Pierre had died at the age of 39, of cancer they thought. It was a neat, marble gravestone, standing out pale pink against the green of the hill which we had climbed together in our teens. The sun came out again and I took a picture of the quiet scene for Bob. As I walked down the hill back to the car I could hear the bleating of a flock of sheep from the slopes across the valley. Suddenly the car was *de trop* and I had an urge to hike in the sunshine for the rest of the day. I didn't of course, but I felt like a schoolboy again.

Chapter 1

University Days

The last 2 years at school passed only too quickly, as we grew 3 or 4 inches more and ate bacon and pork sausages again and studied hard for University entrance. We were distracted from our studies by the shining performances of Wigan Rugby League Football Club which, largely due to the genius of such players as Cecil Mountford, Joe Egan and Brian Nordgren, put our modest borough firmly on the world map of sport. Wigan was truly peerless at that time. Other distractions were Joe Loss, Tommy Dorsey, Artie Shaw, Stanley Matthews, Denis Compton, Jane Russell and several corn-haired girls in the class of '41, among whom I remember Lenora Taberner, Margaret Cottam and Mary Leech as being particularly desirable. Jean Winstanley was the prettiest of the brunettes. They, too, however, were kept nose-in-books by F.G. Hall and Co., so that, in the absence of drugs and hard liquor, I would say we were a pretty strait-laced lot, judged by today's standards.

It was difficult to secure a university place, as most of these were rightly claimed by demobilized servicemen. Oxford and Cambridge were beyond our reach, but Lenora and Bob got into Manchester and I squeaked into Nottingham, probably on the strength of my *patois nivernais*. It was my first choice, as my close friend Arthur Wadsworth had gained a place there the previous year and told me it was the loveliest campus in Great Britain. The creation of Jesse Boot of Boots Chemists, University Park was indeed a felicitous complex of proud buildings, lawns, lakes and trees which remains unspoiled up to the present day. We were hived off from the city in a tasteful, tailormade cocoon of academic activity, with football pitches, cricket grounds and tennis courts for our exclusive use and amusement. Everything was laid on for the students, including good meals, comfortable Halls of Residence and Saturday night dances with plenty of booze. During the week the White Hart and the Trip to Jerusalem were only a mile or so away. Indeed the City of Nottingham, although the student did not depend on it, was one of the liveliest cities in England, with a bustling Town Square, cinemas, pubs and theatres galore and, it was reputed, the prettiest girls in the British Isles, Joan Collins among them.

Nottingham had two fine football teams, Notts Forest and Notts County, so that one half of the city hated the other. The great Tommy Lawton was making goals for Jackie Sewell in the County team and at Trent Bridge Joe Hardstaff and Reg Simpson were hitting double centuries on a wicket that broke many a bowler's heart. Nottingham even had a winning Ice Hockey team

– the Panthers – for whom Chick Zamicke, of Czech extraction, demonstrated sporting talents which heralded those in later years of his compatriots Jaroslav Drobny, Emil Zatopek, Jan Kodes, Ivan Lendl and Martina Navratilova.

In short, it was a great place to be and Arthur Wadsworth was my ideal roommate. A diminutive nineteen year old, five foot three in his socks, Arthur had instinctive sporting abilities and a great Lancashire sense of humour. He was the sort of lad who would ask you if you had finished reading that newspaper you were sitting on. Both his father and mother had died before he could remember them and he had no pictures of either. He had had very kind and understanding foster parents, but at times I sensed his utter loneliness. Yet Arthur was one of the most gregarious persons I have known and everyone loved him on sight. He was chirpy but unassuming, diligent but laid back, canny and street-wise but entirely without malice. At school he had been captain of soccer and cricket, patrol leader in the Scouts and had had a pretty girl called Rita. When he came up to Varsity he was a nobody, just over 5 feet tall and speaking a strange dialect. But he was soon in the first team at football and his frequent goals from the wing quickly established his reputation. He took me under his wing, improving my football rapidly and keeping me on half pints in the pubs, while the "big drinkers" knocked back the pints. Arthur was only eighteen months older than I was, but his paternalistic attitude toward me persisted for many a year.

When it came to buying beer or anything else, it is interesting to look back on the economics of paying one's way through university in the immediate post-war era. Tuition was free, but books, room and board were not. I had taken French, English and Latin as my Higher School Certificate subjects and had won a grant from the county in the French scholarship paper. It was £60. Room and board cost £2 a week either in Hall of Residence or in lodgings. We were at University 30 weeks a year. The couple of dozen books we had to buy (usually second-hand from older students) cost about £5. Bus fares, if you were in lodgings might cost £2 a term – a bit more if you played games and travelled to away fixtures. The problem areas were clearly beer and clothes. Ale was cheap, but students (especially the sporting crowd) visited pubs several times a week. Besides normal clothes, I found I needed football shirt, shorts, stockings and boots, tennis shirt, shorts, socks and shoes, long-sleeved shirt, long flannels, boots, bat and ball for cricket as well as other items of equipment such as table tennis bats, tennis racquets and so on. Some of these things I had brought from school, but I was still growing and all my clothes and shoes were too small. In 1948 a jacket cost about £2, corduroy trousers £1, shirts ten shillings each, shoes nearly a pound. Even these modest prices were beyond our reach. At the beginning of each term there ensued a frantic bartering of clothes and equipment among the students. If you were giving up football you might get a nice pullover for your soccer boots and shin pads. If you were taking up tennis you could get a second-hand racquet for your old size seven shoes and a bike pump.

I noticed that enterprising students often had a good stock of barter goods in their room. The Geordies particularly seemed knee deep in cricket pullovers, packs of cards, bicycle parts, scarves, batting gloves, tennis racquets with no strings, blackened tennis balls, football rattles, German dictionaries, satchels, hip flasks, grey underwear, cigarette cards, scout belts, Parker pens and wrist watches of every make and description.

Arthur guided me through this maze of bargains, so that on the whole we didn't fare too badly, though we always came off worst with the Geordies and the Cockneys. As the grant only covered room and board, whatever else we needed after bartering all we had we had to buy with our own money. The problem was, we had none. My father, being a railwayman working with the mines, was not allowed to change his job during the war. His wages were also frozen at £2-10-6 a week. We envied many of our neighbours who went to Risley to work in the munitions factories, where one could gross ten or even twenty pounds working overtime. One Sunday my father was given a day's overtime unloading heavy cast-iron pipes from a railway wagon. Halfway through the morning a dozen tumbled down on top of him; luckily he escaped with four broken ribs and a fractured ankle, but that was the end of overtime pay for my Dad. Never a wheeler or a dealer, he just went back to doing his job quietly and efficiently and we all simply lived within our means, as he had always taught us to do.

To finance our beer and summer holidays, Arthur and I worked during our Christmas and Easter vacations. This is normal practice in the United States and some other countries, but in post-war England, with hundreds of thousands of servicemen returning to civilian life, even vacation jobs were hard to come by. Arthur delivered mail and painted gasworks, while I cleaned out railway carriages in sidings around the Wigan area. I won't go into the details of hot bucket, cold bucket, hot mop, cold mop, but twelve hours a day of this back-breaking activity brought me in £6 or £7 a week and once I grossed £13 by sleeping in a compartment overnight and starting every day at 5 a.m. Accordingly we would finance every autumn term by using up a good portion of our room and board money and top this up again after Christmas with our earnings.

At the end of my second year at Nottingham, Pickbourne, the Registrar, called me into his office and told me nobody could live off £60 a year and gave me £140 out of a special fund he managed. I had difficulty in breathing for several days after that, but it was no dream and I bought my parents a new suit apiece, two tins of tennis balls for Arthur and me, a second-hand bike to cut down on bus fares, a Full Colours University blazer at long last and a Parker pen from Stan Smith the Geordie. I sent £100 home and still had enough left to live like a king for 4 weeks that summer in Spain. It was like a Monopoly game. You have just won £140; proceed to "Go".

Besides the struggle for survival, there were other things to occupy our minds: lectures and tutorials. I had opted for French and History, but after one look at the Professor of Spanish, I dropped History for Spanish. I could not have made a better decision. Professor Geoffrey Stagg was an outstanding lecturer in Spanish and Italian Studies, but he was much more than that. A small, neat figure of a man with white hair and black eye-brows, he combined a penetrating gaze with a winning smile and read your linguistic mind before you knew it yourself. Like many of the most effective lecturers, he had practised as a schoolteacher before gaining his Chair, which meant he actually taught you things instead of just braying at you. This was invaluable for me, as I had to start Spanish from scratch. I had had an accidental conversation with Stagg as I was waiting to meet my French Professor. Intelligence just oozed out of his aquiline, rather handsome features and when I heard he was a left-handed tennis player of no mean ability, I knew he was the man for me. I asked him if he would take a beginner into his department, as I knew he lectured only in Spanish. When I promised to learn Spanish in 6 weeks, he agreed to accept me, whereupon I dashed across the Hall and sold 3 history books to Brian Derry for ten shillings, snapping up a Hill and Ford Spanish grammar plus dictionary for the same amount.

Professor Stagg taught me Spanish in one month to the extent that I could function in the language almost as easily as in French. Lest the reader should think that I am exaggerating at this point, or that I am claiming any extraordinary abilities, I feel that I should explain how this process takes place. It is true that from the age of 22 I became a professional linguist and eventually earned large sums of money from this activity, but that does not mean that I possess outstanding intellectual qualities or any traits bordering on genius. I find it very difficult to follow any mathematical argument beyond 'O' level and I have consistently demonstrated my inability to cope with any developed theory or practice in Physics, Algebra, Geometry, Biology, Botany, Zoology, Philosophy and Woodwork. I can paint, but I was always bottom of the class in Art at Ashton Grammar School. F.G. Hall knocked into me the basic ingredients of English grammar and punctuation and (like my father and grandfather) I do not make spelling mistakes, but having said that, it is only languages and table tennis that I find easy.

How do you learn Spanish in one month? It is really quite simple, if you have 'O' level French. You already have a vocabulary of 1500 French words, more than half of which bear a strong orthographic resemblance to their English counterparts. Spanish words, especially long ones, are almost identical to their French equivalents (*atención – attention, vino – vin, establecimiento – établissement,* etc.). You can therefore acquire a Spanish vocabulary of 1000-

1200 words in two or three evenings' study. Grammar is strikingly similar in both languages. Like French, Spanish has masculine and feminine nouns; adjectives follow the verb, pronouns precede it; the subjunctive, causative and passive voice are common to both languages. French uses *le passé composé*, whereas Spanish prefers *el pretérito* in the past, but if *Nous avons vu partir le train* becomes *Vimos salir el trén*, what undergraduate worth his salt is going to choke on that? Spanish pronunciation is much easier for the English student than is French and apart from a bit of Arabic influence on Spanish nouns (*alcoba, algebra*, etc.), you can copy French without any undue qualms. It takes a linguist about a month. It would take another month to switch to Italian. Portuguese might take 6 weeks on account of tricky nasalized diphthongs and Rumanian two months because of Slavic loan-words, but that basically is all there is to it. Any linguist will tell you that. Disbelieve us if you wish, but there is no need to be afraid of foreign languages. They can be a piece of cake. I have heard physicists tell me how they have little trouble with maths or mechanics or trigonometry. They are right. One thing just leads to another. *I* never believe *them* either.

The French Department was quite good. Professor Holdsworth was a tall, striking figure in his middle age, striding majestically across the campus with his gown flying in the wind in a manner not unlike that of F.G. Hall. I do not remember a single sentence he uttered during 3 years of lectures, but he had a beautiful, sonorous pronunciation that was a pleasure to listen to. Josie Townley-Smith said the right things about French poets and Lewis Thorpe – the brilliant one – got us interested in everything from Villon to Ancient Paleontology. I remember having long arguments with Miss Daniel about the use or disuse of the Imperfect Subjunctive. I know one of us was trying to kill it, the other to resuscitate it, but I am no longer sure which way round it was. The only Frenchman in the Department, Pierre Jolivet, often got mad with me on account of my Parisian accent, which he said was too strong. He was perfectly right, of course, but it is not easy to specify exactly what constitutes a Parisian accent, so it is hard to give anything a quick chop. I had picked up this way of speech with Serge and Michel in one month. It took me three years to get rid of it.

By contrast I had no problems with my Spanish, as Professor Stagg spoke the purest Castilian imaginable and I followed him like a parrot. There were only seven of us in the Spanish Department, as the language had not become fashionable by 1948; consequently we received maximum personal attention and there was high group morale. The others I remember were Brian Lancaster, the amiable university football captain, who has taught languages for most of his life, Mike Plumridge, who became a Police Commissioner, J.P. Cole who later wrote books on the economics of geography (or the geography of economics) and Monty Maynard, a swarthy twenty-five-year-old from

Hackney whose avowed ambition was to run the East London underworld (perhaps he does!) I think we all got our degrees in the end; we certainly won the inter-departmental tennis championship with Geoffrey Stagg winning all his matches in the first couple.

*   *   *   *   *

By the summer of 1949, I was itching to go to Spain, which was as yet almost unknown to British students or tourists. General Franco was firmly in the saddle, having judiciously steered Spain through the Second World War without getting into too much trouble with either set of belligerents. He was hardly in a mood to rush into Europe, however, and while Schumann, De Gaulle and Adenauer made their plans for an integrated continent, eagerly supported by the Benelux countries and later Great Britain, Spain kept her low profile behind the Pyrenees and remained very much a European backwater.

My enthusiasm for the country, its people, language and literature had infected Arthur, who didn't speak a word of Spanish but bravely volunteered to go with me. We packed our rucksacks, scraped up £10 apiece and hitch-hiked through France to Biarritz, thence to Hendaye and the Spanish frontier. A short bridge leads over the river from Hendaye to Irún and it is here where one gets one's first glimpse of Spain. It is a formidable sight, with the Pyrenees towering 6000 feet up in the clouds as a backdrop to the Spanish customs shed fifty or sixty yards away attended (at that time) by a dozen grim-faced *guardias civiles* with their sinister three-cornered hats and black machine-guns. Arthur and I walked across that bridge like Gary Cooper at High Noon, the difference being we had nothing to grab for.

An unsmiling policeman testily waved us into the shed – we were both wearing shorts, which automatically put us on his lengthy black list. Once inside we were told to put our jackets on. Wear short-sleeved shirt and shorts in Madrid in those days and you were an enemy of the state.

We were ushered to a counter where a sign reading "Pasaportes" made conversation unnecessary. Our passports were inspected at length by a sour-faced sergeant who carefully read every page including all the blank ones. He then went off with them to a back room where he spent a good 20 minutes with our interesting documentation. By the time he returned, a nervous Arthur was ready to slip back into France, where he had been treated like *un libérateur* and my Spanish speech had got cold. The sergeant slapped the passports on the counter along with some long forms resembling a property conveyance.

"Rellenen los trípticos" he said. It was the second time I had entered a country and been defeated by the first sentence. Stagg, bless him, had never told us about *trípticos* and the part they played in your life. They were documents in triplicate which a foreign visitor in Spain had to fill in every

night before going to bed. Having arrived at your lodgings for the night you would get together with your landlady and fill in everything in triplicate for each guest. With Arthur's Spanish in the state it was, I was filling in six a day. The landladies were not much help, as they hated the forms as much as we did, but they had to supply details of the address, their own name and parentage and so on. If you can assemble together in your mind all the questions you have been asked on all the immigration forms of the different countries you have visited and add in a few more useful ones like "names of paternal grandfather and maternal grandfather" or "list all countries visited within the last 5 years giving exact dates of entry and exit", then you will have some idea of the length of a *tríptico* and the tedium involved in filling one out. Once the task was completed, you or the landlady had to trundle off to the local police station where they would stamp all three parts — one for them, one for your host and one for you. Woe betide anyone who retired for the night without doing his duty with the *tríptico*. If the landlady did not haul you out of bed, the police would — regardless of the hour.

In this manner the Spanish police knew exactly where you were every night you spent in Spain. They had maps of the city with coloured pins stuck in them. Your pins came out when you left, but they had to go up on somebody else's board the next night. As if this was not effective enough, your papers would be checked at least once or twice between towns, whether you travelled by train, car or lorry. Arthur and I were usually clearly visible on the back of lorries, so we were favourite targets. The procedure was always the same:

"Bajen ustedes" "Climb down."

"Documentación"

Guardias civiles always travel in pairs (*una pareja*). The Spaniards tell you that one can read and one can write. I do not know whether this is true or not, but in 1949 more than one policeman held my passport upside down till he came to the page with the picture. This he would scrutinize suspiciously and at length, glancing back and forth at you and the photograph. After this diligent comparison he would tap first the picture and then your chest, asking *"Este es usted?"* "Is this you?" When you nodded guiltily to confirm that it was, he would then go off with his friend a few yards, ostensibly out of hearing range, and they would study the pictures anew, shoot a few more glances at you and mutter dark things in Catalan or Andalusian. After returning the passports, they would often re-focus their suspicion on the lorry driver, who would be interrogated and frequently made to unload his cargo with the help of the *extranjeros*. Once we had to pull out 60 boxes of fish for inspection at two in the morning halfway between San Sebastian and Madrid. Arthur has never forgiven me for that.

Lest the reader should think that I am being over-critical of Spain, I should perhaps hasten to dispel this impression. Despite the frosty reception over the bridge at Irún, we were about to enter a country where the warm-heartedness of the people, their sense of honour and their old-fashioned humour would confirm the romantic, idealized concept of Spain and the Spaniards that the writings of Cervantes, Galdós, Blasco Ibañez, Ganivét, Lope de Vega and Guzman de Alfarache had printed on my mind. The Spain of 1949 was a wonderful, unspoiled country to be in. There were no skyscrapers in Torremolinos or Marbella, no traffic jams in Burgos or Seville. The people were poor and often appeared simple and naive, but they possessed an earthy friendliness and an impulsive generosity which has no counterpart in many northern countries. Spaniards living in villages or even small and middle-sized towns had mostly never met anyone English and bubbled over with eager curiosity in your presence. They admired your Army and Navy rucksack, your Swiss watch, your blue and gold passport, your Tootal tie and Marks and Spencers' shirt, even your pale skin. They would drag you into bar after bar to ply you with *tinto*, stuff you with *tapas* and *cordero asado* and send you back to England laden with weighty gifts from their town. Any village fortunate enough to secure a pet *inglés* took very good care of him indeed.

In the light of this ubiquitous open-heartedness and congeniality, even the antics of the police appeared in better perspective. Spain had, in 1936-38, gone through a horrendous Civil War where brother had killed brother and son had fought against father, trapped on one side or other of a horrible divide. Franco won this brutal conflict and showed little compassion for his defeated opponents, but in consolidating his grip on the nation he effectively prevented the outbreak of any further hostilities. He achieved peace – peace at any price – but it was still peace. The Spanish people could not afford any other solution at the time. Again, during the Second World War, more fighting and slaughter would have been too heavy a burden for even the brave Spaniards. Franco kept them out of it and few of them criticise him for that. One has to judge the arrogance and suspicion of the security forces in the late 1940s within this historical framework. Franco's men were still keeping Spain at peace, enforcing their own brand of law and order. Foreigners, who after all were just emerging from the greatest bloodbath that history has seen, were to be kept a close eye on. No drugs, no speeches, no unrestricted travel to spread dangerous liberal ideas. They could visit the cathedrals and the Prado and sit on the beach in Santander, but keep them on a short leash with roadblocks and the nightly *tríptico* and all would be well.

In the end, the foreigners won. The annual invasion of *extranjeros* is now greater than the Spanish population. The south and east coasts have been ruined by tasteless developments and in those parts of Spain foreign tourists are no longer treated with the old-world courtesy that greeted them in the 1940s. Spain is involved with drugs, corruption has been exposed in high places and the rate of crime has risen significantly. The anachronistic behaviour of the *guardias* can now be seen as a period piece, though even today Spanish traffic policemen are much tougher than their Portuguese or Italian counterparts.

In the summer of 1949, the spread of liberal ideas or the decline of Spanish morals were concepts which were very low indeed on the list of Arthur's and my priorities. I wanted to practise Stagg's Spanish on the descendants of Cervantes, Cortés and Goya and Arthur aimed to play football every day on the beach. In these respects we were both successful in achieving our objectives.

After finally disengaging ourselves from the attentions of the frontier police in Irún, we boarded the train to San Sebastián, where we found a room rented out by a widowed *señora* for the tidy sum of 9 pesetas a night. The rate of exchange was 160 pesetas to the pound, so we were paying approximately 6p between us (then 1 shilling a night). The *"señora"* made a deal for us with the restaurant down below for three meals a day at a fixed price of 20 pesetas for the two.

Our room and board, therefore, cost us 15 pesetas each or two shillings apiece per day. If we had remained there, we should have been able to stay in Spain nearly 100 days on our £10 budget! We might have done so, too, had we had such long holidays or had the food in our 20-peseta eating house been a little more appetising. But after one week in San Sebastián, the cathedrals and art galleries of Castile were beckoning, not to mention the bullrings of Pamplona and Madrid. So Arthur and I said *adiós* to our *"señora"* and footballing friends on the beach and headed south for the capital on our fish lorry, as summer rain splashed along the Basque promenades and hastened our departure. But looking back over many years of travel and accommodations, I have to say that our San Sebastián "package deal" beats anything I have ever come across or heard of.

It was also in San Sebastián that I had the good fortune to meet Luis Rueda, who has popped in and out of my life ever since. On our third day in Spain, Arthur and I ran out of pesetas and went to the bank to change a few of our precious pound notes. The bank teller informed us, in voluble and barely comprehensible Spanish, that we could not change foreign currency without the proper *documentación*. San Sebastián is in the Basque province of Guipúzcoa and certain inhabitants of that area speak a Spanish which would not classify as pure Castilian. This particular bank teller also spoke very rapidly indeed, to the point where I failed to comprehend what action we had to take to remedy the situation.

Waiting patiently behind me was a dark, good-looking young man in his late twenties, who seemed to be following the conversation with some interest. When I eventually bogged down, he stepped forward and asked the bank clerk a few questions. Then he turned to me and explained in beautiful, sonorous Spanish what the problem was. We had not picked up a currency declaration form in Irún and had it stamped by the police at the first point of entry. Without such a paper we should not be able to change any money in Spain. We had no alternative but to return to the frontier and get the missing form.

I thanked the young Spaniard, who introduced himself as Luis Rueda y Anta. He then presented his wife, who had been observing the scene from a short distance away and offered to accompany Arthur and myself to Irún, where he would satisfy himself that all would end well. We protested against taking up his time in this way, but he would not take "no" for an answer, saying that he and his wife were in San Sebastián on their honeymoon and really had nothing to do all day. I could not think of anything suitable to reply to this remark and ten minutes later all 4 of us were aboard the train for the half hour ride to Irún.

Once there, Rueda dealt speedily with the matter of procuring our missing papers. He clearly had a way with people, disarming the sullen *guardias* with an old-fashioned, provincial reasonableness and an apologetic smile on behalf of his young, untravelled-in-Spain *ingleses* who would do much better now he had them in tow.

And so he towed us all the way back to San Sebastián where we had *gambas al ajillo* in the Bar El Nido in the Calle Larramendi where he introduced us to his cousin, also Luis Rueda and his cousin's son, Luis Rueda. When I asked him why was it that I was having trouble following local Spaniards, but understood every single word that **he** said, he grinned modestly and replied that it was because he came from Zamora, that ancient and venerable city perched proudly on the dry, cracked, Old Castilian plateau, where they spoke the purest and clearest *castellano de todas las Españas*. His explanation was a serious one and indeed valid, as any Spaniard will tell you. *Zamoranos* speak slowly and sonorously, like they might be rendering a monologue from an epic poem. *Madrileños* look upon people from Zamora as their rather simple Castilian cousins, but the *zamorano* is a Spanish student's dream. On the few occasions when Rueda uttered a sentence that I did not comprehend, he was able to paraphrase immediately, so that the meaning became clear. Everyone in Zamora can do it. Years later, one of my Madrid friends told me that the girls of Zamora were well-known in the capital as call girls, as the high unemployment in Zamora forced them to seek work in the big city. I told him that they had no need to offer such services as they were all potential language teachers of the first water.

We spent many a congenial evening hour with Luis and Nines Rueda in the bars and cafés of San Sebastián. On our final evening together, Luis Rueda invited us to visit Zamora on some future occasion, as in 1949 our route was in another direction.

Two years later I was able to take up this invitation and spend some time in that old city with its eccentric cathedral, twenty-eight dark churches, its ubiquitous widows in black, its deserted water mills on the islands in the middle of the swirling Duero River and feel I had found the real Spain among the red brick bodegas, groves of mushroom-like pine trees and simple shepherds stumbling homewards with their flocks across the dry parched moonlit sweep of the age-old plateau.

*   *   *   *   *

From San Sebastián we went to Madrid, on the back of our fish lorry, courtesy of José María Tellechéa and Luis Gallardo, who hated the police because they were constantly halting their truck. They were mildly conspiratorial, taking Arthur and myself into their confidence, though no thought of violence seemed to have entered their heads. Every two or three hours we stopped and picnicked on *chorizo* sandwiches washed down by *tinto* squirted from little leather bottles. They joked merrily with me in Spanish, though they spoke Basque with each other and often with Arthur, to whom it made no difference. By the time we arrived in the capital Arthur knew the Basque words for bread, sausage, wine, fish, money and women. Learn six words a day and you possess a working man's vocabulary in a year, I reflected, though Basque grammar might lay a few snares along the way.

We spent a fortnight in Madrid and its environs, making day trips to the handsome, unspoiled towns of Castile – Toledo, Segovia, Avila and Aranjuez. For the British student of Spanish language and literature there can be no more rewarding or enriching experience, since it is here on this arid, proud, bleak plateau that he finds the heroic, austere, frugal Spain of his textbooks. The northern coasts of Galicia, Vizcaya and Guipúzcoa are rich in fish, wine and minerals; Catalonia to the east is the industrial powerhouse; Valencia produces its vegetables; even Andalucia abounds in wheat, olives and orange groves. High above it all, in their harsh, barren uplands, sit the proud peoples of Castile, León and Aragón, less diligent and industrious than the Catalan or the Basque, less canny than the Galician or the Valencian, less flexible or content with life than the Andalusian, but descended from the arrogant, generous, often cruel class of aggressive *conquistadores* who regard rule and authority as their birthright.

The Castilian is a charming companion. He tends to be slimmer and sharper-featured than the lowland Spaniard and carries himself proudly with that quick, springy step engendered by long, frosty winters. He takes you by the arm and propels you briskly towards your next pressing appointment – probably the bar or the bullring – and he will let you spend not one penny of your university grant. (*"En España pagan los españoles."*) Less demonstrative than the Andalusian, he nevertheless declaims his way through life, thumping and hugging his friends, quarrelling with them fiercely and briefly about politics, bulls or football, buying them more *tinto* and *coñac* than they can drink, until the advanced hours of the morning. With *los ingleses* the Castilians have a secret pact of dry humour, *machismo, pundonor* and several other values Arthur and I were not aware we possessed. They tapped our chest with the back of their index finger and winked knowingly at us over the rims of their glasses. *Madrileños* were quick to introduce themselves in the bars – in 1949 foreigners were interesting objects of curiosity to be befriended and questioned about the world outside. Hardly anyone we met had been abroad and few people spoke more than a few halting words of English, French or German. Although they were hungry for details of life in London or Paris, I noticed that nobody showed much interest in foreign languages or worried about their inability to speak them. Rather like the English, I thought.

In every bar we had entered in Spain there were two framed photographs displayed in prominent positions. One was of General Franco and the other of Manolete, the leading *matador* of the 1940s. A shy, poor, proud Andalusian, he had won the hearts of all Spaniards with his faultless technique and grace of movement, by his clean living and God-fearing humility, above all by his unequalled bravery when working a bull at close quarters. Alone among *toreros* he ignored the bull as he executed his passes, keeping his gaze firmly riveted on the section of the crowd facing him, chin up, ankles together and back straight. Unfortunately he fought one *toro* too many. One blustery April afternoon in Linares, a gust of wind blew the scarlet cape across his abdomen and the charging bull obediently followed it in and ripped him open. He was 29 years of age and engaged to be married. The country mourned for him like for noone else since the Civil War. Even today in some bars in Madrid the photograph has not been taken down, though Franco's has.

Arthur and I enjoyed our holiday in the Castilian cocoon, for indeed it was a world of its own, in its own time warp. The fierce shoulder-gripping friendliness of the *madrileño* was in sharp, daily contrast with the cold, watchful attentions of the police and his vitality and *individualismo* sat uneasily with the tedium of identity checks, jackets in July and Victorian swimming suits in the *piscinas* At least in San Sebastián we had played football in shorts on the beach and Barcelona later proved to be as European as Bordeaux or Marseille, but in Madrid in 1949 you toed the line, whether you were Castilian, *andaluz* or from foreign parts.

The very anachronisms were part of the regional charm. Few women were seen in the bars (we assumed they were at home in the evenings) but those few who did venture out were treated with old-world deference and gallantry. Compliments were proffered, trunks were bowed, hands were kissed. The *señoras* themselves (there were no *señoritas* at large in the evenings) were elegantly attired and bejewelled, usually wearing handsome eighteenth-century combs of silver and enamel in their long black hair. They looked men boldly in the eye and half-flirted with Arthur and me in front of their husbands, though this seemed to be just a harmless pastime in Madrid and we were good boys anyway. They spoke and ate much faster than the men, though all displayed moderation in their intake of alcohol.

The new, sprawling suburbs of modern Madrid were many years away from construction and the heart of the city was the Puerta del Sol (where we had found the usual cheap, gloomy *pensión*) and the majestic Plaza Mayor. We circulated in a *chiaro-oscuro* world of narrow, twisting alleys, cobblestones, dogs, beggars, cripples, and sellers of lottery tickets, eating a large variety of *tapas* – shrimps, eels, squid – which a few weeks earlier would have turned our stomach. As a treat we were taken to *El Botín,* where we made our début on crisp young suckling pig, cooked so brittle that the waiter cut your slice with a plate. We visited the galleries and palaces and a church or two and at the *corrida* we sat with the poor in the *sol* as we wanted to get tanned and were poor in any case. We made friends in the cafés and the bullring, in the fish market and the Post Office, where sending postcards to England was still something worth talking about. When we eventually left Madrid for Barcelona, I felt we were going back to Europe, leaving behind us a special old-world enclave with its own niche in time, yet doomed before long to integration and dilution of identity and soul.

We were not in Europe yet. We had been spoiled in the capital. The prospect of hitch hiking to Catalonia did not hold much appeal. We decided to make the long trip to Barcelona by train. It was a very slow train making a large number of scheduled stops, as well as numerous unscheduled ones. Such a trip gave us glimpses of a good cross-section of Spanish everyday life. On our 3rd class wooden benches we sat among peasants, dogs, children, chickens, geese, turkeys and cardboard boxes stuffed with fruit, vegetables and old clothes. It was a noisy, friendly, irritating environment, quite unlike the hushed, boring atmosphere of an English railway compartment. Dogs barked, geese hissed, chickens clucked and children stepped on bananas and ran up and down the long aisles followed by elder sisters whose duty it was to stop them falling out of windows.

Noone seemed to know when the train would arrive in Barcelona (time-tables meant very little) and morning, afternoon, evening and night succeeded each other as we read, ate and drank, chatted, dozed and watched the scenery go by. After midnight Arthur and I stretched out in the aisles and slept, using our rucksacks as pillows. People, animals and birds walked round or stepped on us in the darkness. At dawn people offered us hot coffee from flasks and some of the cocks crowed.

Passengers got on and off at the many stops and the menagerie on board changed its composition from hour to hour. Rabbits were added to the menu and at one stage we were heavy on goats. In the middle part of the journey the train was almost empty in the heat of the afternoon. At one small station, we remained stationary for a whole hour and later in another one for nearly two hours. We were not far from a lake, and Arthur and I asked the guard if we had time for a quick swim. He assured us the train would not move for another half hour, whereupon we grabbed our swimming trunks and splashed happily in the lukewarm water. After 10 minutes the train left with our rucksacks, passports and finance on board. We ran dripping to the station master, who laughed at our plight. The only advice he could offer was to walk down the line after the train. We had no alternative and hobbled five miles along the sleepers in our bare feet. We caught the train up at the next station and thanked the peasant who had been minding our bags. Throwing ourselves down on vacant benches, we slept for two hours. When we woke up the train had still not left.

*   *   *   *   *

In Barcelona we spent more time on the beach where the sea was much warmer than it had been in San Sebastián. Most of the signs were in Spanish, but people spoke almost exclusively Catalan amongst themselves. I understood very little of this, though Catalans switched to Castilian when they realized we were English. Notwithstanding their reputation as early risers, Catalans frequent their bars and restaurants with the same enthusiasm as the people of Madrid and we had many a long conversation with the locals until the early hours of the morning. Catalans are more outward-looking than Castilians and I found very little difference between their attitudes and those of the meridional Frenchman. They are interested in food, football, factories and commerce and were quick to express their political opinions about everything from trade unions to cod wars.

After a fortnight in the capital enjoying persistent *madrileño* hospitality, I had come over to the Castilian point of view to some extent and took some satisfaction in playing the devil's advocate when the Barcelonans broached their favourite subject: Catalan Home Rule.

"Are you sure Catalanism is all that powerful?"

"Yes. We only began seriously in 1882. We were making good progress until the present regime."

"You did pretty well in the wars."

"What do you mean?"

"You got on your feet in the war with the United States. You did well during the war with Morocco and the really big Catalan fortunes were made trading with the Allies in 1914-18."

"We are an industrial people."

"You have the industry, but you need Spanish agriculture. Your area consumes far more than it yields."

"We are not after separation. We wish to be independent, not separate."

"A sort of subsidized autonomy" (a phrase the *madrileños* had taught me).

"What do you mean?"

"You want Spaniards to recognize you as a state, give you your own parliament and laws, but at the same time protect your industries with high tariffs, provide you with a rail network and a post office and an army to stop any other country absorbing you until you are strong enough to absorb Castile."

"You have been taken in by the Castilians."

"Let's have another drink", Arthur always said at this stage.

Catalans enjoy arguing, particularly about money and politics and they were quite fearless in their exchanges with the police (who were from other provinces). One night, after a conversation such as the one above, our Catalan interlocutor offered us a ride in his horse-drawn cart. It was cool in the dark streets and the horse's hooves beat out a pleasing rhythm on the cobbles. Our friend pulled up in front of the jail which he said was full of Catalan separatists. Many of his friends had done a stretch, he said. When they came out they worked hard again, supporting the rest of the Spaniards, especially the Castilians, he added. He had it in for the Castilians. He addressed the guard at the prison gate – a young man in his twenties, armed with a rifle.

"Heh, you, how many prisoners have you got in there?"

"Don't know, never counted them."

"Well well, it speaks. Can you read and write, sonny?"

"You can't rile me. Keep moving!"

"Would you like a drink, son? I've got a bottle in the cart."

"You've got one inside you. Get a move on."

"My word, you speak queer Castilian. Are you from the South?"

"Sure, I'm an Andalusian. You can't rattle me."

"Why is an Andalusian keeping Catalans in a Castilian jail?"

"I didn't put them in. I let a few out now and then."

"My God, boy, you speak queer. You eat half your syllables."

"The Castilians don't give us enough to eat. We have to eat our syllables."

Our friend laughed at that.

"That's the style son. You're a good boy, I can see that."

"*Adiós, señor.*"

"*Buenas noches.* And don't forget, let a few out, now."

We trotted down a few more streets and had a night cap with our separatist, leaving our witty *andaluz* to his sombre, lonely vigil.

The next day we were leaving Spain, or so we thought. After some queueing at the railway station, we bought tickets to Cerbère, the first French town over the border as one travelled north. We were due in Cèrbere at 9 p.m. and decided to have dinner there. Lunch we took in the dining car, making the most of our last Spanish meal by using up our remaining pesetas. We ate *jamón de York* for starters, moving on to a fine leg of lamb *(cordero asado)*, goat's cheese from Navarra and *crema catalana* as dessert. When we had paid the bill, we went through all our pockets, seeking any surviving pesetas, which we piled up on the table for Arthur to count. Arthur has this thing about never changing money twice. He calculates in advance what he needs, changes that amount, then metes it out to the last centavo. He seldom runs short, but he hates to be left over with any. He once had ten cents left in Swiss money as his train was about to leave Switzerland and he bought a pair of shoelaces in the kiosk on the platform.

On this occasion he decided we had enough for another dessert (we loved *crema catalana*), coffees and two or three cognacs each to pass away the time as the train crawled towards the frontier. We seemed to halt longer in each station as the afternoon wore on and as falling dusk accompanied our last budgeted drink, we began to realize that dinner might be late that night. In the event, we arrived at Portbou, the Spanish border town, at 10 p.m. and the frontier with France had closed down for the night. We were told that a train would go through the tunnel the next day, Saturday, at noon.

Our problem was that we had no Spanish money left. We had pounds, but the law at the time forbade us to change any, except in the bank, which would be closed the next morning. Portbou banks barely make it on weekdays. Spanish restaurateurs and hotel-keepers were not allowed to receive foreign currency and, even if they had done we would have had problems with the currency declaration. On entering Spain, you filled in a form declaring the amount you had in pounds and francs. That amount you had to take out again, minus whatever a bank receipt showed you had changed officially. It all sounds trivial today, when you can change money freely even on the black market. It was quite a different matter in Spain in 1949 when they checked every document three times and where any petty discrepancy was swooped on by officials desperate to relieve the boredom of their unproductive occupation.

Arthur had got us down to two pesetas and I daresay I was a little cool with him as hunger returned. We went into the Café Central to make our plans.

"What shall we do?" I asked Arthur. We were drinking coffee, so we were already in the red. Arthur stared at reflected lights in the glass-topped table while he considered the alternatives. He had that calm, contemplative look on his face which he wore when he was picking football teams.

"Let's change a pound – enough for dinner, hotel room and breakfast and souvenirs tomorrow morning."

"What about the Customs? No banks, no receipts. No receipts, no leave Spain. You know how it is, Arthur."

"Leave the Customs to me," he said.

Arthur, now in charge, beckoned to the café boot-black, an old wrinkled fellow with a conspiratorial air, to come over and shine my shoes. Catching on quickly, I sneaked a pound note out of my back pocket and slipped it to the boot-black muttering the useful word *"cambio"* He took the money without taking his eyes off my shoes and I stared at the crowd like Manolete on a lucky day. Arthur thought we both did it rather well. The old man went off on his errand and returned ten minutes later to clean Arthur's shoes. Once he had the pesetas Arthur paid him off and ordered supper for two. It was 11 p.m.

I was still worried about receipts, but when two pork chops were put in front of me I decided to give them the concentration they deserved. When I had eaten one, an unshaven character came in from the street and tried to sell us half a dozen Parker 51s for the price of a good meal. I sent him off. Halfway through the second chop another stubbly chin came to the table and offered to guide us over the hill into France for one hundred pesetas apiece. No Customs up there, he explained. We declined his offer.

We were in the middle of our dessert when the police came in and arrested us. There were three of them with guns. One would have been enough. We went quietly. They did not give us time to pay the bill. I thought they would march us up to the police station, but we all did it at a stroll. Once inside, we were relieved of our rucksacks and told to present our passports to the sergeant. He was a mean-looking, bull-necked Galician with the crisp, sing-song accents of that province. Without opening the passports he put them on his desk and charged us with suspected smuggling of Parker pens and trying to make an illegal exit from Spain after the closure of the frontier.

I broke the news to Arthur, who did not take it well at all. If he had not been well-fed I think he would have come out with something which would have got us in even more trouble with the sergeant. As it was, I made no impression on him with Stagg's Spanish and soon he was ordering his subordinates to lock up our rucksacks in cupboards and making us sign slips of paper left and right. When he eventually deigned to look inside our passports he said they were out of order. Tomorrow we would be sent back to Madrid. Nobody mentioned changing pound notes.

They took us across the road to a white building with thick walls and no windows. We were allocated separate rooms, about ten feet by six. My room had nothing in it but a bed, a Bible and a cockroach. At least there were no bars. The room had an ordinary wooden door which our guard closed but left unlocked. We would be questioned further at 8.30, he said.

After lying on my cot for a while wondering who had turned us in, I slept fitfully for a couple of hours and awoke to some sound in the corridor.

I decided I would go and confer with Arthur re the morrow. The door creaked slightly as I tip-toed into the corridor. Facing me was the dim shape of a *guardia* in his melancholy three-cornered hat, a carbine across his knees. He looked at me questioningly. I asked him where the conveniences were. He escorted me there, stood with me, then accompanied me back to my quarters. The next morning, Arthur told me he had gone through the same ceremony. The guard could not have had a very good night, either. Arthur had offered him a cigarette but he had just shaken his head and tapped his gun significantly with two fingers. Arthur supposed he meant he could not smoke while on duty.

Under the circumstances we rose early and our guard took us into a nearby private house where a wizened old woman gave us coffee and rolls for five pesetas. Arthur offered the guard another cigarette after breakfast. This time he accepted it and stowed it carefully in the top pocket of his tunic. He escorted us to the police station at 8.30 for our questioning, but the sergeant was in bed and was not to be disturbed. The young corporal on duty motioned us to sit down and we waited around an hour and a half during which time, the corporal tried four of Arthur's 'sweet Virginias'. "*Muy rubio*", he kept saying – very blond tobacco. At ten o'clock he unlocked the cupboard where our rucksacks were and restituted our property against the usual slips of paper. He then found our passports and, after a brief scrutiny, passed them across the counter. We could go, he said, but there would be problems with the Customs.

Arthur left him the rest of his fags and the corporal saluted us as we made our exit. We walked down the street to the harbour and looked at the clear water sparkling in the morning sunlight. The sun was warm on our backs and Arthur suggested I have a swim. He never swims before noon, so I took him at his word and went in without him. As I swam up and down I could see Arthur sitting there thinking. I remembered his offer to deal with the Customs. At half past eleven Arthur bought three bananas, eating one himself and giving me another. Then he sent an urchin down to the station to see what time the train to France would leave. The boy returned and informed that it would depart half an hour late at half past twelve. Arthur gave him one peseta and the remaining banana.

I was getting anxious to go to the station, but Arthur pulled me the other way up the main street. We went into the bar where we had eaten the previous evening and Arthur paid the bill. The proprietor was so glad to see us that he set out two cognacs on the house. We drank these and Arthur ordered two more and one for the proprietor. After that some of the customers joined in and our pesetas dwindled rapidly. At twenty-five past twelve we heard the engine whistle go and the first laboured puffs of the locomotive. Arthur gulped down his brandy, grabbed me by the sleeve and we ran pell-mell down the street to the station fifty yards away. When we arrived on the platform the engine had just put its head into the black mouth of the tunnel and ten wooden carriages were heading slowly after it. There was no time for passports or currency receipts or dignified embarkations. Customs officials and railwaymen shouted and waved their arms wildly, as they ran along the platform with us. One got a door open, a second pushed us in and a third threw in our rucksacks after us.

"*Gracias*", shouted Arthur as we waved goodbye. I looked at him. As they sometimes say, a little language goes a long way.

*   *   *   *   *

Back at University, Arthur and I continued our comfortable life in the Hugh Stewart Hall of Residence, where we were familiar figures on the snooker and table tennis tables till late every evening. Nevertheless Arthur worked hard at his geography and I sank deeper into languages by taking extra courses in Italian and Danish. I was to take Italian eventually at degree level and studied this language under the guidance of Professor Stagg. I thus acquired Italian fairly painlessly in the same manner as Spanish. Danish was a different matter, as I attended lectures in a haphazard manner, not being officially enrolled on the course. Beegan, one of my friends from the poker crowd, was doing a degree in German and had found that Danish as an extra language in the linguistics stream obviated the need for studying many thick tomes of German literature, which meant more time for poker. Danish was a bit of a lark, so he asked me to join him for company.

My experience in the Danish lectures served to illustrate my belief that while learning a language can be an easy and painless task, in certain circumstances things can go awfully wrong, even with good linguists. Professor Clark was Professor of German, but he was proud of his Danish, too. His enthusiasm infected us and we made good progress in the first term, attending lessons 3 times a week. Soon we were gambolling through Hans C.Andersen's Fairy Tales in the original and by Christmas we were telling each other jokes in Danish. Beegan was using it for poker. Clark was delighted.

For the second term Professor Clark was due to lecture at the University of Copenhagen and the Danes were sending us a Danish professor in exchange. This seemed a good idea to everybody at the time. The Danish professor was in his late thirties, wore a white shirt and bow-tie and exuded Viking energy. He seemed glad to have got out of Denmark. The first day that he took us he introduced himself as Professor Hansen and said that colleague Clark had told him he could conduct the course entirely in Danish since we had already been chatting away in it for 3 months. We all concurred and Professor Hansen continued the lecture in Danish. After 20 minutes Beegan stopped him.

"Hvad er det for noget?" asked the professor

"Please sir, nobody understands a single word."

You had to hand it to Beegan, he wasn't one to beat about the bush. Professor Hansen looked a little upset, but he took it well in the end.

"Not a single word?"

"Not a single one."

"But Professor Clark said you spoke Danish."

"We do, sir. But we can't understand it."

"But didn't you understand Professor Clark?"

"Yes sir. But it isn't the same."

"What isn't the same?"

"It isn't the same Danish, sir."

"Not the same Danish?"

"No sir."

"But surely ... there is only one Danish. I mean, after all ... Danish is Danish."

"Professor Clark has his own, sir."

"But what is this Danish like?"

"Do you wish me to read some, sir?"

"Yes, please do."

Beegan began to read from his Danish book and we all began to understand again. But the professor stopped him after five lines. He looked sorry for Beegan and asked somebody else to read and then a third. After that he couldn't take any more. He suggested coffee for everybody in the refectory and we broke up for the morning.

For the rest of the term he gave us pronunciation drill. It is only the pronunciation that makes Danish difficult. Andersen's fairy tales were familiar to us and we could read them in Danish at will, only rarely having to consult the dictionary for the odd word. But it was all in the mind. It was a phonetic dream. Professor Hansen's Danish from Copenhagen was a new, alien and at times almost terrifying phenomenon. It could have been Martian. What was worse, it was practically inimitable. Some of us were not too bad as linguists go and we were well aware of the value of slavish imitation of a native speaker. I daresay most of us would have made a fairly respectable attempt at *"un bon vin blanc"* . But Hansen said things like *"rød grød med flød"*, and we could not say it like he did for all the bacon in Denmark.

After a while he abandoned the idea of our being able to pronounce whole sentences correctly and started concentrating on short phrases. These, too, proved to be beyond our reach and he soon relegated us to single words and subsequently to separate syllables. The final ignominy came when we were struggling with our vocal mechanism to produce a simple Danish sound. Like "ø" for instance.

There was not, Hansen told us, just one sound "ø" in Danish. There were three. There was "ø" and there was "ø" and there was "ø".

The Swedes tell you the same thing, except that they say there is "ö" and "ö" and "ö". All you have to do is distinguish between them. Professor Hansen could do it. He used to say them for us slowly, one after the other. To make it easier for us, he numbered the three different sounds. This table helped us a lot:

1) ø
2) ø
3) ø

If he had not numbered them there would have been the danger of our not knowing which was which.

If you don't know what "ø" sounds like, Beegan used to say that it was more or less the sound a burly Scot emits when he tosses the caber. Especially ø Nr 2. Number 2 was Beegan's speciality. He could always say Nr 2. I used to be pretty good at Nr 1, myself, and O'Flaherty never failed on Nr 3. This was the sort of conversation which took place during pronunciation drill:

Hansen: Beegan, give us the second ø, will you please?
Beegan: Ø.
Hansen: Excellent! Now give us Number Three.
Beegan: Ø.
Hansen: Tsk, tsk, Beegan, that was Number Two again. O'Flaherty, *you* give us Number Three.
O'Flaherty: Ø.
Hansen: Well done, my boy. Beegan, try again on Number Three.
Beegan: Ø.
Hansen: No, no, you're back on Number Two again!
Beegan: Sorry, sir.

It is hard for anyone who has never heard Danish spoken to imagine just what sounds can be produced by even an average Dane, let alone a professor. I suspect they all have cleft palates or some kind of equivalent. We couldn't hope to match them with our ordinary palates. Beegan made a fair show of counting up to six, but he found *"syv"* (seven) unpronounceable. Hansen had O'Flaherty a whole week trying to say *"Dage"* (days). When O'Flaherty said "days" in English he was nearer to the correct Danish pronunciation than he was when he tried to say it in Danish, so Hansen finally let him say it in English. Beegan just refused the gate with *"halvtresindstyve"*. When Professor Hansen returned to Copenhagen at the end of term he left an unfinished task behind him. He had taken great pains to make something out of us and he had not always seen the fruits of his labour.

The departure of Professor Hansen heralded the return of Professor Clark and the opening of the summer term brought with it a sneaking nostalgia for our old fairy tales. It was like old times when we saw his familiar figure shuffle in through the doorway and pad up to his desk, the beloved book under his arm. We skipped through the pages, expectantly.

As he opened his tattered copy we noticed the tired lines under his eyes and we could detect a new humility in his glance. The poor old boy had had as rough a time of it as we had. He, too, had been through the mill.

Finally he found the right page and he started reading the opening paragraph of the tale. He had a poker face. O'Flaherty looked at Beegan and Beegan looked at me. For some moments the guttural stream of alien syllables swirling around our ears stunned us – numbed our thought process. Then slowly it dawned upon us and, looking at our teacher with new eyes, we knew that the good old days had gone forever.

Professor Clark had gone over to the other side.

*   *   *   *   *

During the summer term of 1950 Nottingham sent me as an exchange student to the Université de la Sorbonne, where I took a special course in French culture and civilization. We were lodged with French families and I had the good fortune to share the home of Monsieur et Madame Quinat in Charenton. The Quinats, who hailed originally from Bessines in the Limoges area, had 6 children – five sons and one daughter. Yves, the third son, was of my age and spoke the best *argot* in east Paris. My Chaffer-Holdsworth-Morette French soon disintegrated under the daily onslaught of this unique tongue which, though obeying the sacred rules of French grammar, substitutes almost the entire vocabulary of the language by one of its own. Thus in Charenton, as in most of the *faubourgs* of Paris, the word for nose is not *le nez* but *le pif*; *les oreilles* are *les pavillons* or *les portugaises; le visage* is *la gueule; l'eau, le vin, le fromage* are *la flotte, le pinard, le coulant; le lit* becomes *le pieu, j'ai peur* is *j'ai les chocottes*. Let's go in normal French *partons!* – is rendered as *on met les voiles* (we put on the sails), *on met les rideaux* (curtains) or simply *on les met.*

I am told there is a whole dictionary for *argot* which runs to over 6000 words. Fables and parables are related in pure *argot* in which all the animals and birds have special names. Thus La Fontaine's celebrated *"Le Corbeau et le Renard"* translates as *"Le Corbac et Le Ragdos"* and can be related, with full literary effect, without any French noun, adjective or idiom:

> *Un piniouf de corbac, sur un touffu planqué*
> *Se carrait par la fraise un coulan baraqué.*
> *Maître Ragdos, qui n'etait pas marle,*
> *N'ayant eu sous la dent que cent clous de bectance*
> *Vint lui tenir la jactance*

"Salut, oh canari, mince qui te dégotte.,
Si tu pousses la gueulante aussi bien.que tu es frusqué,
Tu es le mecton à la redresse des costauds du loinqué.
etc.

I once recited the true French version in House Competitions at Ashton Grammar School. Once I learnt it in argot I could no longer reproduce the original. This is the risk one takes if one becomes reasonably proficient in argot – it drives the language of Balzac and Victor Hugo out of your head. Argot speakers also use too much breath (like Liverpool scousers) so that this type of over-articulated pronunciation creeps into one's normal French. It is hard to get rid of – I think it took me 3 years. Father Quinat himself spoke splendid Limousin, a dialect much closer to that of Marseille than to anything Parisian, though he too could throw in a fair measure of argot in the midst of his languedoc.

The Quinats were a very Catholic family and indeed their first two sons were both priests. One lunchtime, Monsieur Quinat was hosting six priests from Britanny. Though they spoke French, they fell easily into breton, even at the dining table. I think they were encouraged to do this as they understood nothing of what the Quinat children said. It was a strange linguistic situation where I sat in the middle of a dozen French people, six of them chatting in Charentonnais on my right, six talking Celtic on my left, me and M. Quinat exchanging occasional pleasantries with the priests in French.

I had some marvellous social evenings with the Quinats – a boisterous, loquacious, warm-hearted family who interacted enthusiastically with each other and their guests. There is a well-known lunatic asylum in Charenton. When talking to strangers M. Quinat used to say:

"J'habite à Charenton. Pas dans la maison des fous, mais c'est plus ou moins la même chose."

Madame Quinat, a great lady, lived to the ripe old age of 90. Yves Quinat remains my close friend to this day.

*   *   *   *   *

There were some good linguists at Nottingham University, in both the Romance and Germanic departments. Like teachers and scholars today, we often discussed the mechanics of second and third language acquisition. One of the conclusions we came to is that the linguist's mind functions a little like a gear-box. As with cars, there are different types of gear-boxes, each one being designed to cope with the particular languages that the linguist speaks.

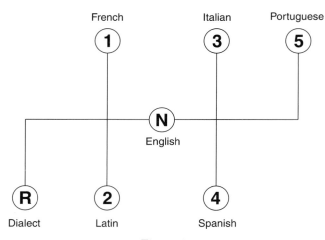

Figure 1

Figure One represents a Romance Languages gear-box for an English speaker. His mind ticks over in English. (N for neutral). He can reverse (R) into his own dialect, if he has one, or he can go forward into French (1) probably his first foreign language. Latin (2) may well be his second. (1) to (2) is not an easy gear shift, but (2) to (3) is easy due to the close affinity between Latin and Italian. The following gear shifts (3) to (4) and (4) to (5) are fairly simple as Italian, Spanish and Portuguese are very similar. As in a car, one sometimes gets into the wrong gear and many a Romance scholar, (switching languages rapidly), has done a (4) – (3) when he intended a (4) – (5)!

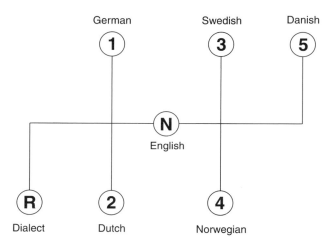

Figure 2

Figure Two shows a Germanic gear-box for the English speaker.

From first foreign language German (1) it is an effortless gear shift to Dutch (2) as grammar, word order and vocabulary bear strong resemblances.

(2) to (3) or even (1) to (3) (if he prefers that) is only moderately difficult as word-order changes, but morphology simplifies. (3) to (4) (Swedish to Norwegian) is the world's easiest gear change (slight vocabulary and tone variations) and (4) to (5) is simple in all respects except for the hurdle of Danish pronunciation.

Gear-boxes become more complicated as further languages appear on the scene, particularly if they come from different linguistic families. In my own case, after spending some time in Germany, Scandinavia and Portugal and also learning Japanese as a hobby, the language mechanics function as in Figure Three.

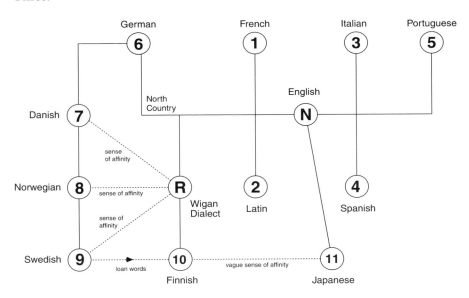

Figure 3

The Romance gears (1) (2) (3) (4) and (5) are normal as with any graduate in this department. I go from (N) to (6) (German) via the North Country "junction" due to strong resemblances in vowel pronunciation (Butter, Banknote, etc.) I find the shifts (6) to (7), (8) and (9) deliriously easy, as one throws off the finicky German word-endings while still benefiting from strong vocabulary clues. When in gears (7) (8) and (9) I feel close to (R) in terms of pronunciation, phraseology, articulation and delivery. To go to Finnish (10) I first reverse strongly into (R) (Wigan dialect) as I learnt Finnish in a manner similar to mother tongue acquisition by working in the fields with Finnish peasants who spoke no other tongue. Thus I do not think about

Finnish grammar, but match phrase for phrase with my own dialect as each situation presents itself. Accordingly *Ah'm pikin'off wom"* sits comfortably with *"Lähden kotiin"* and *"ooze ibed awom"* goes nicely with *"hän on sängyssä kotona"*. A grammatical analysis of the second sentence in Finnish would be :

hän	he or she
on	3rd person singular verb 'to be'
sängyssä	inessive case of "sänky" (bed)
kotona	essive case of "koti" (home)

- a much more laborious process.

The gear change (N) to (11) Japanese is a long push at a tangent and does not go through any other gears, though there is a slight resemblance between Japanese and Finnish.

A certain number of people are bilingual or trilingual from an early age due to the circumstances of their parentage, country of residence or education. These are the only truly bilingual or trilingual individuals and the majority of professional simultaneous interpreters come from their ranks. To give one example, a Japanese friend of mine, a diplomat, has a Finnish wife. Their only son, Fusao, was brought up and educated in English-speaking countries. The boy is equally fluent in Finnish, Japanese and English. His "gear-box" looks like this:

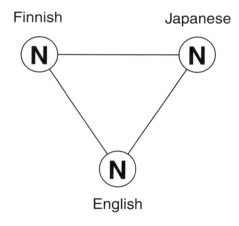

Figure 4

He can switch instantaneously from each of these three languages to another without involving himself in any process of translation or grammatical analysis. Like the rest of us, his mind ticks over in (N) but in his case (N) is the language he spoke last, or happens to be reading in (watching TV, listening to the radio, etc.)

If the boy went on to learn Estonian, Korean and German the gears would probably function in this manner:

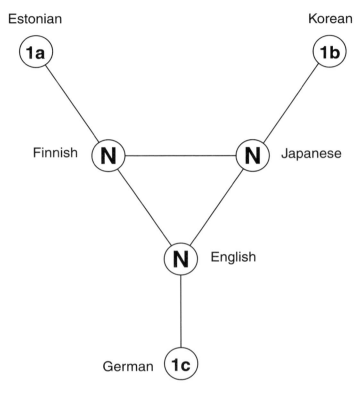

Figure 5

At this stage Fusao is entering into translation processes which were unnecessary when he switched between English, Japanese and Finnish. In his truly trilingual area, no analysis was needed. He simply calls up "situation of his youth" in any of these 3 tongues and they print out automatically like on a computer screen. The rest of us, who have *studied* languages, have to go through our gear changes (though this often takes place very rapidly). Accordingly some languages can be turned to more speedily than others. If we look back to Figure Three, I have little difficulty interpreting for a Frenchman and Italian as my route is relatively simple, but I cannot switch so rapidly from Swedish to Portuguese for obvious reasons. With linguists, like with sprinters, the difference in time "out of the blocks" can be measured in less than a tenth of a second, but it is important for them.

Many of you who speak more than two languages will have noticed that while you can switch quickly from your *own* tongue to any other, it is far trickier to go from one foreign language to another. Some people just cannot do it at all. Others find that after speaking say French for a while, they are quite unable to use, for instance, German, for half an hour afterwards, as a mental block develops.

*   *   *   *   *

Beegan, O'Flaherty, Cole, Lancaster, Plumridge, Maynard and I all got our degrees in the end and some of us went on to diplomas in Education. Arthur qualified in Geography and Education and has spent a good part of his life teaching others how to do the same.

In July 1952, after finishing my exams, I decided to have a different kind of holiday before going out in the world and trying to make a living. The Olympic Games were being held that year in Helsinki and I resolved to attend these and meet the Finns – that calm, unpretentious, heroic band of athletes and warriors whose old-world gallantry in 1939 had sent shudders of admiration throughout the Western World.

My old school friend, Norman Taylor, had found himself a Finnish girl, Nelly Soininen, on a potato-picking camp in Wisbech the previous summer. Not unnaturally, he wished to further his relationship with this dazzling blonde who, he presumed, must now be languishing in dark Finnish forests. We both bought tickets for all the athletics events in the Games and set off for Finland, land of Paavo Nurmi, Jan Sibelius and Marshal Mannerheim, of *sauna* and *sisu,* of a thousand cool lakes lined with forests of pine, spruce and fir, of Lapps and nomadic herds of reindeer roaming the barren Arctic fells under a midnight sun.

Chapter 2

Finland – the indefinable appeal

We knew nothing about Finland except that the men were brave in war, could run like fury in peacetime and the girls were good-looking. These facts alone were sufficient motives for our trip, which led us through Denmark and Sweden.

Swedes and Danes are the smoothest of the five Nordic peoples. Their long history of contact with most European nations has left them cool, worldwise and sophisticated. At the time, they were much better-dressed than the average Englishman (blue blazers and bow-ties were in fashion) and many spoke better English, too. Travelling for a few days through these countries with their neat green fields, well-designed houses and delicate church spires, Norman and I had the impression of journeying in a tidier, cleaner, more affluent England. Sweden in particular, untouched by the ravages of military conflict, seemed like some northern Utopia, on days when the sun shone.

In friendly, red-brick Copenhagen we were model tourists. We went to the harbour to look at the mermaid, watched the changing of the guard at Amalienborg, ate *pølser* and drank Tuborg in the bustling Town Hall Square and finished up dancing and throwing wooden balls at coconuts in Tivoli Gardens. I tried out my Clark-Hansen Danish on girls whom I danced with. They complimented me readily, but could not refrain from giggling. I was inwardly cursing Clark as the Town Hall clock struck twelve and reminded me I had just turned 22.

We had a full day in Stockholm before catching the 6 pm boat to Turku in Finland. The Swedish capital is grey compared with Copenhagen and the people have a grey look about them, too. Often called "the Venice of the North", Stockholm sits around its harbours on a succession of interlinking, windy bridges across which long-skulled, long-legged Nordics scurry briskly to their next appointment. If you can get them to stop for a moment they are politely friendly, but will tell you little except how to find the museums and Post Office. In cafés they rarely start a conversation with you, preferring to stare at the wall. The Stockholmer's speech, whether he speaks Swedish or English, has a harsh, strident beauty. It is dry and staccato, with virile, trilled 'r's and a forthright double tone. Each sentence has force and finality. The crisp delivery reminds one of Scots who went to Oxford.

We spent a fruitful day around the harbour and explored the Old Town with its narrow, cobbled alleys and shops unchanged since the Middle Ages. A few yards from the water's edge there is a story-book Royal Palace where uniformed sentries come and go and important black Volvos bring dignitaries for an audience or take princesses to riding lessons. At the excellent museum of art we saw exhibitions of Munch and Klee arranged in orderly fashion, with the Scandinavian concept of space. Perspex-topped launches shuttled tourists and commuters back and forth between the main harbour and various islands in the inner archipelago. The water was clear and placid, as the port is well protected.

*   *   *   *   *

The best sight in Stockholm, say the Finns, is the departure of the evening boat to Finland. Even in 1952 there were many thousands of Finns working in the Swedish capital and the departing vessels were usually packed with homebound Finns, relatives who had been on a visit, and Swedish and foreign tourists. A huge crowd of well-wishers invariably thronged the quay side, white handkerchiefs on the ready. The boats were smaller in those days and when the passengers packed the nearside rail to deliver their last messages, the liner would tilt precariously. At six exactly the horn would blow and the vessel would slowly back off before making a u-turn in the harbour and heading out towards the estuary. On the u-turn the passengers rushed to the opposite rail and waved their white handkerchiefs at their loved ones, who loyally waved back. The air was thick with faith and friendship, but all took place in near silence, as Finns and Swedes do not shout to each other across the water. Once the well-wishers were out of sight, the decks suddenly emptied. Some passengers went below to organize their cabins, but the majority headed straight for the bar.

Norman and I stayed at the rail, for we were anxious to see the mouth of the estuary and glimpse Stockholm from the sea. We went with our cameras from side to side in vain, however, as island after island flanked our route and Stockholm's spires eventually sank behind them. We learned that the open sea would not be visible for hours.

We retired momentarily to the bar, where the thronged conditions encouraged us to go to the dining room for an early dinner. The dining tables creaked with Scandinavian delicacies – cold cuts, crayfish, pickled herring, beetroot and cucumbers, followed by the hot dishes – Swedish meatballs and Finnish stuffed cabbage. We ate our fill and went back to the bar, contriving to get a seat as the first and second dinner sittings changed round.

Already in the dining room I had heard a strange, new tongue rivalling the familiar rasp of consonant-heavy Swedish, Danish and German. Its speakers were in general shorter and stockier than the lanky Swedes and walked in a different manner. There were now many Finns in the bar and I was able to study them at leisure, as they were in no hurry to leave. They had the Nordic colouring – blond hair and blue eyes, even paler than that of the Swedes. But there the resemblance ended. Many of them were broad-skulled with fine, prominent cheek-bones and firm, resolute chin and jawline. Their eyes were more sunken than Scandinavian ones and surveyed you calmly and steadily from their deep sockets. If they shared a table with you (a foreigner) they did not initiate the conversation, but if you were to do so they were immediately companionable and folksy, crushing your hand in a grip of iron and solicitously seeking to re-fill your glass.

Those who spoke English did so modestly and apologetically, laughing at their own efforts, quite unlike the linguistically confident Danes and Swedes. Many of them did not speak English at all, but this did not preclude their sociability. Finns are able to create an atmosphere of warmth without language and we quickly became aware of their non-verbal understanding skills, feeling more at home with these newcomers from the East than with our Nordic cousins on the adjoining tables.

All around me I was hearing the Finnish language (*suomea*) for the first time – a gripping experience for a sound-hungry linguist. Its abundance of vowels and flowing liquidity at first remind one of Italian or Polynesian, but, as one listens, one detects underlying, vibrant sinews unheard in southern tongues, yet quite unlike tough, thrusting Germanic. The impressive length of its regimented nouns and adjectives, the musicality of its coordinated case-endings, the rippling sonority of its convoluted sentences, all hint at the artistic, tenacious soul of a people come from afar.

The language has in it the swishing coniferous forests and boisterous Arctic streams that we hear in the music of Sibelius, the loneliness and cold melancholy of the northern lakes, the unlimited, invigorating roaming of the Central Asian steppes, the vitality and perseverance of adventurous, hardened, migrant explorers. I sat and listened in awe, understanding not a word, but completely captivated by the unfaltering harmonics of this nimble Asian tongue. For me it was more entertaining than any symphony.

At ten o'clock stewards began to arrange deck-chairs along the rail astern and it was announced that dancing would begin shortly. There was still no sign of the open sea, but the night was brilliant. In mid-July in these latitudes the Nordic sun dips only briefly below the horizon before rising again in scarlet splendour. The Baltic archipelago is the biggest in the Northern Hemisphere, with thousands of small, green, low-lying islands lining the route from Sweden to Finland. Many of them are uninhabited, some are simply huge granite slabs a few feet above water-level, others exist treacherously just under the surface. Here are some of the most interesting sailing waters in the world, for Finns and Swedes map their channels carefully and during the four brief months of the Baltic sailing season they scatter throughout the islands for their scenic picnics and find the solitude they often desire.

Norman and I went out on deck to survey the tranquil, slowly-changing scene. Our new Finnish friends followed us out, hugging their drinks, and soon every deck-chair was occupied as the dance music blared over the ship's loudspeakers. There were Finns and Swedes, Germans and Danes, the odd Norwegian or Brit on his way to the Games. Half a dozen Lapps in their gaudy costumes contributed splashes of red, blue and gold to the pastel shades of the sea, rocks and sinking sun. They were drinking vodka and chatted merrily in their own tongue.

When the music got under way, the Germans danced first, then the Swedes, Danes and Brits. The Lapps joined in in a desultory fashion, but most of the Finns leaned back in their chairs, clutching their glasses and chatting interminably. The middle-aged men ferried drinks from the bar as the need arose and as the bar permitted. They watched the Swedes and other tourists gyrate round the deck with their polkas and fast waltzes for an hour or more. Finns tend to start dancing when others flag or begin to tire. Then they dance all night.

Around 11.45 there was a lot of activity in the area of the bar, which was due to close at midnight. A considerable number of bottles made last-minute appearances on deck and were wedged between chair-legs, briefcases and life-boats. The bar closed down and the Finns began to dance. They were good dancers, too – twisting, swaying and bending to the music more than central Europeans do. The Swedes and Danes competed valiantly for the girls, but did not seem to hold their liquor as well as the Finns, who strode decisively and unerringly towards the girl of their choice as each dance began.

There were girls from Helsinki, Turku and Tampere as well as a few lady tourists, but the great majority were young girls from the islands of Ahvenanmaa (Åland) which lie between Sweden and Finland. Used to the open air, in summer, they are brown-skinned, blue-eyed and straight-limbed – no-one would have called them strait-laced. They danced on and on, though I noticed that they returned to their place after each dance; there was little pairing off, as there would have been in England.

The music went on throughout the night, but there was no night, for the sky remained bright and the seas glimmering. The blue of the waters deepened, taking on an indigo hue, but as the sun settled close to the horizon the low ripples were crested first with gold, then orange, pink and finally crimson. The sheltered waterways between the islands have little turbulence at night and the only sound one heard, apart from the muted throb of the engine, was the quiet hiss of the prow bisecting the mirror-like surface.

At Mariehamn, the capital of Ahvenanmaa, many of the island girls left the ship, as holidaying Finns came aboard. The Finnish language now won a decisive battle over Swedish and, as we continued our journey in brightening daylight, new islands ahead brought with them a change of air, water and sky, imperceptible yet pervasive, heralding transition to a different environment with a subtle, mysterious Altaic appeal which can be neither defined nor summarily described, but which affects every sensitive traveller approaching Finland or Finnish territory.

The open sea was behind us as we continued to thread our way through hundreds of small islets, holms and reefs. The granite seemed pinker now and more exposed. Buttercups and daisies pushed up among clusters of yellow-green moss. The wooden cottages and log saunas were frequently left unpainted, in contrast to the bright yellow, blue or reddish-brown houses on the Swedish islands. The light grey, dead logs of the Finnish dwellings, unattended and deserted in the early morning pale sunlight, lent an air of bleakness and desolation to the simple landscape. No human being or animal moved on shore to lessen the sense of solitude.

Aboard they were still moving. Jenkka followed polka, waltz succeeded foxtrot as the loudspeaker reeled off once more its now familiar repertoire. The music was interrupted by an announcement in English, Finnish, Swedish and German that we should land in Turku in one hour's time. Some danced on, but the Finns went to pack their bags, lined them up on the disembarkation deck and stood with them. It is a Finnish habit; they are well organized luggage-wise. Even today they do it half an hour before docking. In the old days they always stood the hour.

*   *   *   *   *

We were vaguely excited as we stepped ashore in Turku; I noticed the Swedes and Germans were, too. Perhaps it was the long summer night seaward approach, or the strangeness of the signs on the buildings, TUPAKOINTI ANKARASTI KIELLETTY, etc., but we all looked about us in eager anticipation of something new. The Finns were on home ground and, in a business-like manner, led the march into the Customs Hall, serious-faced, carrying briefcases stuffed with bottles. They were braced for the skirmish with their Customs officials, for liquor was an issue in Finland in the 1950s. In England they looked for smuggled dogs and parrots, in Germany for contraband coffee, in Spain for guns and anti-Franco literature, but in good old Suomi you could slip through a tank or a grand piano more easily than a bottle of Scotch.

There were limits to be observed, bags to be searched, fines or duty to be paid and bottles to be confiscated. Tales were told, excuses were proffered, hip-flasks were hugged. Some of the regular commuters seemed to have an in with officials, but in the main, the correct revenue due to the state seemed to be extracted. One saw there was little corruption in this country, or if there was, it was of a moderate, good-humoured variety. Norman and I, without alcohol or predator fish, had our bags chalked fast and were bundled into the bus for Helsinki without further ado.

It was still early and the streets of Turku were deserted. We glimpsed the majestic rough masonry of the 12th century Turku Castle and the equally imposing bulk of the Cathedral right on the river bank. The statue of an athlete flashed by – it was of Paavo Nurmi, Turku's favourite son, muscular and impassive like the man himself. The houses were low and wooden.

The road from Turku to Helsinki undulates gently and the bus kept up a steady 90 kilometres per hour in the sparse 1952 traffic. The road was straight, cutting through avenues of pine and spruce; occasionally one glimpsed through the trees wheat fields, rape, pasture and unspoiled lakes. We stopped only once, at a lakeside cafe. The coffee, we noticed, was very strong, but of excellent quality. The wrinkled driver in his grey, peaked cap drank three cups and winked at us before clambering up to his seat. He tooted the horn twice and the Finnish passengers dutifully emptied the cafe to take their places. We entered Helsinki in mid-morning.

*   *   *   *   *

The Finnish capital is constructed on a narrow promontory pointing south into the Baltic. It has a fine, island-sheltered harbour dotted with holms of light-coloured local granite, which forms the foundation of the city itself. Surrounded by water on the east, south and west, Helsinki was normally entered from the north and our bus ran down Mannerheimintie, the long thoroughfare which bisects the peninsula. Apart from Reykjavik, it is the world's most northerly capital, at 60 degrees North, comparable to the upper Kamchatka Peninsula of the Soviet Union or Nunivak Island off Alaska. We noticed that the old buildings along Mannerheimintie had thick granite walls and small windows. All street signs were in both Finnish and Swedish.

We pulled in at a Wild West style bus station next to a huge outcrop of pink granite, on which stood a few dozen people watching the buses come in. Among these onlookers, looking very Finnish with her striking blond hair and dark blue dress, was Nelly Soininen. When we alighted she climbed briskly down the granite and kissed us both warmly, concentrating mainly on Norman. Jouko Kero, another Wisbech potato-picker, was also there to greet us. As he lived just round the corner in Lapinlahdenkatu, we were quickly spirited off to his apartment where he thoughtfully prepared tea for us. We made our plans. Nelly only had the day in Helsinki – she lived in the country near Lahti. Norman and I had transported a tent from England and we intended to inhabit this during the fortnight of the Games. Jouko was the man who would show us where to pitch it. There was an island called Mustikkamaa (Blueberry Land) in the eastern harbour set aside by the Finns for tents like ours.

We chatted for an hour before going out to look at the city centre. In Helsinki this is not an actual square, but a bustling oblong, which starts where Mannerheimintie widens out in front of the Post Office and runs for a quarter mile as far as Erottaja. The buildings are in an impressive, imperial-and-monumental style of dignified proportions. At the Swedish Theatre the elegant Esplanaadi runs left down to the harbour a stone's throw from the broad expanse of Senate Square with its Cathedral – Suurkirkko – and Helsinki University. Not far from the Square rise the onion-shaped cupolas of Uspenski Cathedral, one of the few recognizable reminders of Russian rule in the 19th century.

We sauntered light-heartedly around the harbour and lunched in the sunlight at one of the stalls on the waterfront. Finns lunch quickly and simply without the fuss attendant on French or Spanish repasts.

Towards the end of the afternoon Nelly had to take her bus to Lahti. Norman was due to go there after the Games. Jouko by this time had discovered that the Olympic tent site had been switched from the quaintly named Blueberry Land to another island called Seurasaari (Company or Companionship Island). There we pitched our tent at around 8 pm and Jouko left us to our own devices. A Danish tent had been erected alongside ours and we spent the evening discussing the prospects of various athletes and teams with three or four young Danes of our age.

It rained hard during the night and Norman and I fared badly. Either there was something wrong with our tent or we did not know how to pitch one. A stream came in at the top and flowed out through the front door. Norman lay on the right bank of the stream and I on the left. We watched it nervously all night, for in Finland in July it is never really dark, even in a tent.

It stopped raining at 7.30 and the Danes breezed out of their tent, well-rested and dry, to cook bacon and eggs on their elegant camp-stove. Our waterproof rucksacks were wet and so were most of the contents. The Danes gave us cups of tea. In mid-morning, as it began to drizzle again, we packed up the lot and caught the No. 4 tram back to Jouko's. We slept on the floor of his flat for the rest of the Olympiad.

*　　*　　*　　*　　*

No-one who attended the Helsinki Olympics can ever forget them. As a schoolboy I had read many books about the history of athletics and was consequently well-versed in the sequence of Finnish triumphs dating from 1912 to the Berlin Olympiad of 1936. They say the Finns ran onto the map of the world. It started with Hannes Kolehmainen, a thin, delicate, smiling figure, who attacked the powerful French favourite Jean Bouin three times going down the back straight before winning in the last strides of the 5000 metres in the Stockholm Olympics.

Paavo Nurmi was then only a boy, but once he began winning races he was to remain unbeaten in a main event for more than 10 years. Nurmi was like a machine. He trained in deep snow to make his legs stronger, developing a new "circular" stride which had not been considered ideal for running. Soon he held all world records at distances from 800 metres to 10.000 metres, breaking records every time he ran, craftily watching the time on a stop-watch held in his left hand. He dominated the 1920, 1924 and 1928 Olympiads and would probably have won more medals at Los Angeles in 1932 had he not been disqualified for taking money.

By then Finland was firmly established as an "athletic power" and they won 8 gold medals in Hitler's Berlin Olympics to finish second behind the United States.

The next Olympics were scheduled for Helsinki in 1940, but Finland and most of the world were at war by then and the Games were cancelled. Impoverished and war-shattered Helsinki was unable to stage the Olympics in 1948, when London, as the only other Western European belligerent capital which had not been occupied by a foreign power, stepped into the breach.

But four years later the Finns were ready. It was an atmosphere charged with emotion. The entire city of Helsinki was a feverish beehive of activity. Everything had to be done just right. The events would start on time, the judging would be fair and the crowd would applaud the foreigners. We all had the feeling that the Games were coming home. Greece, it is true, was the Olympic homeland, but it was almost as if the running of Ritola, Kolehmainen, Lehtinen, Salminen, Iso-Hollo, Hoeckert and the invincible Nurmi had earned for Finland the title of modern custodian of the Games. The Finns talked, breathed and lived athletics. It was their religion.

Norman and I, guided by Jouko, wandered the streets of this young, vibrant, anxious capital for the two or three days remaining before the start of the Games. People from the countryside, smartly turned out for their momentous Olympic visit, stared stolidly at our foreign appearance, serious-faced and shy at first, invariably grinning and friendly when we waved at them. They just loved the English. It was nice for us.

Helsinki has a wonderful department store called Stockmann – right in the middle of town. It ranks with Harrods, Takashimaya, David Jones and Niemann Marcus as one of the great shops of the world. Norman and I went in several times and shopped with our eyes. One morning, with Jouko, we ran into another Finn who had picked the potatoes of Wisbech. He was a young Finnish farmer from the Lapinjärvi district called Mathias Wallen. Tall, blond and handsome, he was himself a fine athlete at local club level, dominating 100 metres and 200 metres sprints and he actually held the Finnish schoolboy record for throwing the javelin. Though still in the process of learning the language, his English was quite good and he greeted us warmly. He was accompanied by an even taller friend, a tanned, smiling matchstick of a man named Hakon Borup. Borup farmed the estate next to Wallen's near Lapinjärvi and they were friends since boyhood. Borup was a Swedish-speaking Finn with little English, but he could follow a conversation, grinning hugely from time to time and making the odd, wry remark in Swedish which Wallen translated.

The two farmers, both aged 25, were in Helsinki for two or three days for the Games and we drank a few beers together. Mathias Wallen was extremely knowledgeable about athletics and we all got on well together. Before they left, Mathias and Hakon invited us to come and stay with them in the country after the Olympics had ended. We were happy to do this, as Lapinjärvi was not far from Nelly Soininen's home and Norman would easily be able to fit this visit into his romantic itinerary. For me the decision was even easier – I had nowhere else to go. I had calculated that my funds would run out on the Final Day and that I would need to work to earn money to return to England. Mathias said I would get 80 marks an hour and my keep. This worked out at about 15 shillings a day (75p). I had no complaints.

*   *   *   *   *

The day of the Opening Ceremony arrived. It had been raining hard from eary morning and the ninety thousand spectators packing the Olympic Stadium were soaked to the skin. Many had umbrellas but often did not put them up, as it would have blocked the view of the people standing behind. Compared with other sports crowds I had seen, this one was disciplined, well mannered and appreciative. Not even the torrential rain could dim the Finnish enthusiasm for the event. President Paasikivi, elder statesman and war hero, had entered the stadium and the moment had arrived for some person – probably a handsome young student – to enter the arena carrying the Olympic torch. The gates opened and lights sudenly began to flash on the electronic scoreboard. Ninety thousand eyes strained to make out the words in the grey gloom. One by one they appeared:

"Carrying ... the ... torch ... into ... the ... Stadium ... PAAVO NURMI!"

The gasp was universal. The teams, already lined up in the middle of the field, immediately broke their ranks and ran to the edge of the running track to get a close look at the living legend. Like Norman and myself they had read books about him since they were children. The tension was electric and the seconds passed slowly .... suddenly he was there, between the gates, then crunching down the track, tall and straight, impassive as always. We saw the familiar blue vest and white shorts, the powerful white legs with their long stride and steady rhythm – only the thinning hair and lined face to tell us that 20 years had passed since he had last been seen on the track. He ran the lap unfalteringly, looking only straight ahead as the rain whipped his features. Athletes young enough to be his children waved at him and tried to touch him as he scraped by. Thousands of cameras clicked in the downpour. Tears of emotion ran down thousands of faces, not only Finnish ones, as the gaunt, unsmiling Nurmi ran at his fifth Olympiad. It was one of those rare moments in the history of sport when ninety thousand people were united by a moving moment and a common emotion.

At the end of Nurmi's lap, he handed the torch to no other than Hannes Kolehmainen, now a very old man, who took it up the Olympic tower to light the flame. The Games had begun.

The 14th Olympiad was exciting in the extreme, though I will not dwell on the results here. Nurmi's successor as King of the track proved to be Emil Zatopek, a Czech soldier, who won 3 gold medals in long distance running. Nurmi was watching from the stands and more than one of us surmised that he must have been reflecting what the scene might have been if he, 30 years younger, could run down to the track, put on the old blue vest and give battle to an opponent who would surely push him to the limit (no one else had done). It is probably better for us idol-worshipping sports lovers that such "races of the century" can never be held. How could Nurmi or Zatopek ever lose a race? They will both be remembered as unbeatable.

Wet weather prevailed for most of the Olympic fortnight and the Finnish athletes failed to win a medal on the track. Finland had lost many fine athletes during the war and Lasse Virén was only 2 years old at the time. The generous, fair-minded, enthusiastic Finnish public went unrewarded by a home victory – sweet though it would have been. By the end of the Games, even the foreign visitors wanted a Finn to win something – it would have been so fitting. Olympiads have come and gone since then, but all who were in Helsinki feel that the Finnish Olympics had that little something that the others did not. Perhaps it was what de Coubertin was talking about when he tried to explain the spirit of athletic competition. You felt it as you watched Paavo Nurmi's feet crunch the wet track. You heard it in President Paasikivi's voice. Whatever it was, it was there in the clean Finnish air.

*   *   *   *   *

Images of the city still remain vivid in my mind's eye. Blonde Finnish girls waltzing wildly with raven-haired Mexican athletes at midnight in Kaisaniemi Park; Bob Mathias – the American decathlon winner – patiently signing

Lancashire infants 1937

Wigan Rugby League F.C. 1948

Old Wigan miners

Miners' cottages

The Olde House at Home

Sea Scouts 1945

Mathias Wallen 1951

Zamora goalkeeper

Luis and Nines Rueda

Kapelle, Loviisa 1956

Gammelgård

Loviisa

Finnish housewives' class

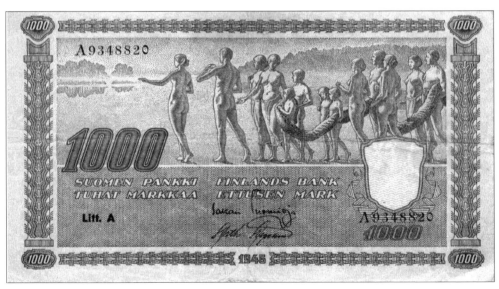

Finnish money 1952.
Finns say it depicts people waving goodbye to the last Russian war reparations train

Major V. Volanen at the front 1943

Göran Boije

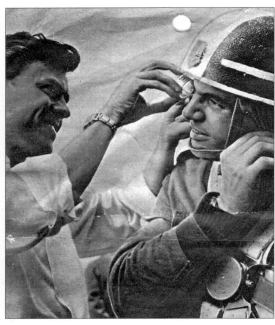

Parachuting, Helsinki 1956

D'Oncieu, Adams, RDL

Berlitz Congress, Paris 1956

Robert Strumpen-Darrie

Jean Piton

Charles Berlitz

Mathias Wallen 1988

Old Berlitz directors 1945 (Gilbert on right)

Berlitz wedding, White Plains, N.Y. 1963

Class of '41

40th anniversary Finnish schools

hundreds of autographs for country Finns in front of the Post Office; Zatopek's hunched walk as he tramped down Mannerheimintie, slapping an occasional Finnish back as people wished him well; crimson dawns over Töölö Bay at 2 am; the gently smiling face of Armi Kuusela – Finland's newly appointed Miss Universe 1952 – as she waved to admirers; Chataway falling on the last bend of the 5000 metres; the thousands-long procession of raincoated, cloth-capped Finnish country folk on their daily pilgrimage to the stadium – all these memories add up to a nostalgic picture of a capital where there were no traffic jams, no pushing, no ticket touts or conning or profiteering, no thieves or pickpockets, no blaring horns or fanatical crowds, no muggers or boot boys or graffiti, no dirty toilets or rubbish on the streets, no political disturbances or death threats or bombing; in general no hassle at all. As the Finns say, athletics are not a matter of life and death. They are far more important than that.

*   *   *   *   *

After Helsinki, a new and interesting experience lay in wait for us – getting to know the rustic and largely undiscovered (by foreigners) Finnish countryside. It proved to be far more fascinating than we would ever have imagined.

The day after the Games finished, the rain stopped and the skies cleared. Jouko accompanied us to the bus station, reluctant to part with his English guests and offering us his floor any time, rain or shine. Our destination was Lapinjärvi in the coastal province of Uusimaa or, more precisely, a village of some notoriety called Pukaro, where Mathias Wallen and Hakon Borup owned their farms. There we were to make our *débuts* as farm labourers, Norman for a week and I for an indefinite period of time.

The journey took two and a half hours, along dirt roads once the Helsinki city limits had been crossed. The road surface was dark ochre in colour and small stones and loose earth on many bends made me wonder if skids occurred frequently. But the driver was competent, belting along happily at 90 kilometres an hour, slowing down just enough on the curves to avoid spinning into the forest. To Englishmen, used to the firm grip of asphalt, the dust-flinging charge of the vehicle smacked somewhat of stagecoach days, but for everyone else it was normal. Most roads in Finland in 1952 were of the same packed earth. In winter treacherous ice and snow added to the hazards, but drivers seemed to go just as fast. It has never been a source of surprise to me that Finland produces the best rally drivers in the world.

We passed through the picturesque market town of Porvoo where reddish-brown mediaeval warehouses huddle together along the river. A charming, tent-like, miniature cathedral dating from the 12th century dominates the old wooden houses, which are painted egg yellow, brick red and bright Russian blue. A narrow, creaking, hump-backed wooden bridge spanned the river and from it one has the best view of the cathedral crowning the array of sloping roofs. Norman pointed at the church and the driver obligingly stopped for a moment while he took a photograph.

At Forsby we left the coast and turned north on even dustier and narrower roads. The area was less wooded than the coastal strip and around Strömfors and Liljendal we saw big open fields of rye, wheat and barley as well as grazing land with Ayrshire cattle. The bus stopped a few minutes in Lapinjärvi; we were unsure whether or not to get off, but were told that Pukaro was the next stop, another 7 kilometres further on. It was sunny now and, as the bus doors opened in Lapinjärvi, a wonderful smell pervaded the air – damp pines drying in the sunlight, the scent of the forest floor with its bright green moss, brittle pine cones and pink granite boulders. The village seemed to consist of no more than a quaint, old white-washed wooden church with a separate bell-tower, a general store with hardware and some tinned food in the windows and a watchmaker's shop with "Antas" over the door. We learnt later that Lapinjärvi was in fact the head village (Kirkonkylä) for the area and many a wooden house was tucked away among the trees in the secluded manner Finns are so fond of.

We glimpsed the lake on our left, then the bus followed the river through open fields till we came to Pukaro, a small village with a fine arched bridge cut out of chunky blocks of pink granite. We crossed the bridge and pulled up in front of Lotila's store – a large white building which dominated the dozen or so wooden houses in the village centre. Lotila himself was there to greet us – a huge, bleary-eyed bulk of a man in his late fifties. The driver treated him with deference and they both retreated into the store for the inevitable cup of strong coffee. The bus line actually belonged to Lotila, a self-made man who had started with one bus and now had the concession Kotka-Kouvola-Pukaro-Porvoo-Helsinki. In the years I knew him I never once saw Lotila stone cold sober, but there was little business in the village that he did not have a hand in.

Apart from the small cluster of houses in the village main street, open farmland surrounded us on all sides and half a dozen farmhouses were visible a mile or so away adjacent to the encircling forest. We asked for directions to Gammelgård – the farm belonging to Mathias Wallen – and were told it was situated a mile to the north of the main road. It was around noon and the day was still fresh. We shouldered our rucksacks and followed the farm roads and cart tracks which had been indicated to us. A field of rye lay on our left; a herd of several dozen cattle grazed on our right. Ahead of us we could just see the red-tiled roof of Gammelgård – a substantial, square timbered construction, cream or buttermilk in colour with elegant porches and verandahs typical of 19th century Swedish-Finnish farm houses. A tall beech hedge, ten feet high and several feet thick assured the manor house and its sizeable garden of privacy. We were a couple of hundred yards away before we saw Mathias Wallen coming to meet us. He greeted us warmly and took us into his home.

Englishmen are unused to buildings made completely of wood. We associate wooden construction with temporary dwellings – summer houses, beach cabins, hunting lodges and Scout huts. Gammelgård had wooden floors, ceilings and walls, painted off white, beige, pale yellow and pastel green. There were four square reception rooms on the ground floor as well as a dining room, a huge kitchen and two bedrooms for guests. There were six bedrooms upstairs, several of them with generous verandahs. Each room had a big stove, tiled attractively in a variety of colours and patterns. The chandeliers were made of wood and had painted motifs in the Uusimaa style. Cupboards, dressers and chests of drawers were in pastel shades of green, grey and pale blue with floral designs in pink, yellow, purple and other colours. The wall rugs and brightly-coloured floor matting had been woven locally. Tables and chairs were functional – rustic style. It was noticeable that no wood was left unpainted. The dining room furniture was a pale grey-green – an unexciting colour – but striped placemats of red, purple and bottle green livened up the table. Gloomy portraits of late Wallens and a painted grandmother clock completed the dining room décor. It was all very un-English and, I reflected, very un-Scandinavian, too.

Hearing our entry, Mathias' mother, Fru Martta Wallen, strode across the dining room to greet us. She was an extremely handsome woman in her mid-fifties – a dark Finn with streaks of grey in her brown hair. Her broad skull and high cheekbones bespoke an Eastern provenance; her widow's peak, deep-set eyes, full figure and vitality of approach stamped her as a Karelian. She was in fact from Sortavala, on the shores of Lake Ladoga and her Russian grandfather had often taken her in her childhood to the island monastery of Valamo, Russian Orthodox stronghold and headquarters for centuries. Her grandparents, like many Karelians, had moved to the Lahti area at the end of the war. Martta, the loquacious schoolteacher from Sortavala, had become village schoolteacher in Pukaro, where she soon captivated Väinö Wallen, a Swedish-Finnish landowner and poet, still a bachelor at 36 and living with 6 sisters at Gammelgård. A whirlwind courtship led to marriage and the birth of 3 children – two boys and a girl – in as many years. The Wallen sisters left for Helsinki.

Väinö was a fine poet, gloomy and foreboding, with a keen sense of life's brevity, tragedy and beauty. His poetry lives on today but his own life was short, a weak heart causing his early démise at the age of 45. Martta, the school teacher, was left to run the farm for 15 years until her boys were able to take over. Mathias, interested in chemistry, science and languages, had little inclination to do so. Kaj, the younger brother, studied agriculture, but was currently doing his military service.

Martta Wallen addressed us in Swedish, as Mathias had told her I understood a little of the language. She herself was Finnish-speaking, but had learnt her husband's language perfectly and used it in the household after his death. After three weeks' exposure to flowing Finnish, I had to readjust to Finnish-Swedish, which I found unlike Sweden's tongue, strange at first yet with a comforting familiarity. After a while I realized that it was real Swedish, but entirely lacking in double tones which make Riksvenska so distinctive. Finnish-Swedish intonation is in fact very close to English, so that Finn-Swedes generally intone our language well and we have little difficulty with their pronunciation and accentuation.

Fru Wallen was briskly talkative, watching your eyes as she spoke. She had the habit of feeding you the practical information you needed, making sure you understood, then turning sharply on her heel and leaving you to your own devices. At other times she would expound her views at length, usually on literary or historical subjects, always adding her personal conclusion or philosophical summary. She was interested in events and stories and above all people and the way they behaved. There were times when I listened to her Swedish for two or three hours at a time, understanding more as the weeks passed by. I was never bored by her.

Lunch was ready and, after we had been shown our rooms, we took our places at the dining table. It was a normal working day, yet an air of formality prevailed. Fru Wallen sat at the head of the table with her guests on her right. On her left sat her son and Gammelgard's foreman, Peltonen, who had bowed stiffly to us as we shook hands. The hostess rang a small bell to summon the maid – a dour, disciplined Tavastian called Hilkka, who smiled only at Peltonen, who was thirty-five and unmarried. It was a three-course meal – our first in a Finnish home. For starters we had a kind of open sandwich on dark sour Finnish bread. It consisted of hard-boiled eggs, tomatoes, cucumber and beetroot all cut into thin slices. The main course was fish in a rather weak dill sauce. Dessert was a thick mousse made from the farm's raspberries. Bland but wholesome summed it all up, even for the English palate. Norman and I, who had lived on pea soup for a fortnight in the capital, devoured everything in front of us, almost producing a glint of approval in Hilkka's pale blue eye. Martta Wallen, who spoke Finnish to Peltonen and Hilkka, announced that coffee would be taken in the sitting room. She led us there, Peltonen bringing up the rear. Again we noticed how coffee was served in a formal manner, Hilkka moving from person to person in prescribed order with coffee, sugar and cream. Everyone had two cups. The whole meal lasted half an hour. As Fru Wallen put down her second cup, Peltonen jumped to his feet, thanked the hostess for the meal, reached for his cap and left the room. A few moments later we could hear him barking orders in the farmyard. He was a good foreman with a sense of urgency which, I suppose, is an important quality in foremen. He had lost some good years in the war and now he was making up for them.

During the next few days Mathias showed Norman and me round the farm. Gammelgård was sizeable, with about 500 acres of cultivated land, some forest and a small herd of cattle. They were due to take in the rye – the first crop to be harvested – in a week's time, so that there was a lull in the labourers' activity and odd jobs were being done. Norman and I helped Mathias cut down some unwanted bushes on the fringe of the forest and put up a few fences here and there, but mainly we talked about the Olympics and Wisbech and Finnish girls. There were none at Gammelgård, that was for sure, except Hilkka and the milkmaid and they were both untouchable. At the end of the week Norman caught his bus to Uusikylä and Nelly Soininen and that was the last Mathias saw of him for 20 years.

The following Monday morning dawned fair and everyone was mobilized to harvest the rye. There were ten of us in all. Besides Peltonen there was the diminutive Martti Roth, 70 and blind in one eye; his giant son Väinö Roth in his mid-forties and Kalle Tähtinen about the same age, who lived in the labourer's cottage adjacent to Gammelgård; Oksanen and Tuominen, two newly-hired hands in their thirties; Juhani Korhonen, a big silent old man who looked after the horses; finally Mathias, myself and the milkmaid roped in specially for the job.

I had been surprised earlier to see Tähtinen and Väinö Roth sharpening the scythes. These were indeed soon put to use. We all climbed into a cart and old Korhonen drove us a couple of kilometres to the rye fields where we chose a corner to pile up our lunch baskets, bottles and extra clothing. Kalle and Väinö then stripped to the waist, took up positions side by side and began to swing their scythes rhythmically. The rye fell. Oksanen and Tuominen followed them, scooping up the stalks to their stomach until they had a bundle, then deftly binding it with a dozen more stalks. The bundles were then thrown down in a line and so it went on. After a while Peltonen started cutting with a third scythe and the rest of us busied ourselves scooping up bundles and putting them where they were supposed to go. I had never done this kind of work and soon discovered the problems, one after the other. The first trick to learn was how to make and twist the binding while still holding the loose bundle to one's stomach. I mastered this after half an hour or so and felt good about harvesting until my back began to ache. Everybody was now working rhythmically and in unison; there was no dropping out or slowing down. My back felt as if it was at breaking point as we maintained the stooping posture for what seemed like hours on end. Finally Peltonen grunted "*Pausi nyt*". I knew what that meant – a break! Mathias grinned as he passed me a bottle of mineral water. We had been working for 45 minutes.

We were soon bent double again, scrambling after Roth and Tähtinen down an ever-lengthening avenue of stubble. My categories of suffering changed as the morning wore on – soon my back ached less than my hands smarted – prickled and stung by broken stalks. Later, when we took our shirts off due to the heat, it was the stomach that suffered most. Later still, in the afternoon, sheer exhaustion obliterated all other aches and pains.

I observed the Finnish labourers as we toiled. Mathias and the milkmaid were as uncomfortable as I was, but Tähtinen, Roth and Peltonen kept going like machines. One felt they could have scythed all day, and indeed they did, but they showed no exhaustion. The new men, Tuominen and Oksanen were clearly not in the same class, eagerly throwing themselves to the ground in the breaks and swigging drinks at every opportunity but they too were good workers according to most standards. Old Martti Roth worked little, just tidying up the lines of bundles, while Korhonen stayed with the horses and seemed to take little interest in the harvesting. I supposed he had seen too many harvests; certainly he spoke only to the horses during the course of the day. He ate lunch away from the others, squatting motionless on his haunches, staring into the forest as his huge yellow teeth crunched the hard black bread.

That night I slept like the earth, as they say in Wales, waking up with an excruciating backache at 7 am. We breakfasted on rye porridge topped with melting butter and creamy milk, washed down by coffee, Finnish strength. We were in the fields by eight and the torture continued. The scything lasted 3 days and the weather stayed dry. By the end of the third day I felt more at home with my new occupation and could only vaguely remember doing any other kind of work. My hands, forearms and stomach were raw as butcher's meat but the sound sleep I was getting every night (I was in bed by nine) revived me sufficiently for the following day's tasks.

On the fourth day the last of the crop fell and we switched our energies to putting the rye up on the carts and transporting it to the barn. Two carts were used and Korhonen selected the best two horses, Humu and Martta, to pull them. Humu was a big, fine-looking stallion with a long blond mane like Väinö Roth whose cart he pulled. Martta, much smaller, was a black-maned mare aged 20. She pulled Kalle Tähtinen's cart. One did not have to work long with the men to notice that there was considerable friction between Peltonen and Väinö Roth. Roth, a competent and immensely strong worker, probably resented the younger man's authority and gung-ho manner. Unlike the easy-going and phlegmatic Tähtinen (a model of efficiency if there ever was one) Roth could be brittle and weasel-worded on bad days, of which he had at least one a week.

Oksanen, Tuominen, Mathias and I pitchforked our sheaves up on the carts where Roth and Tähtinen built their respective loads. The work was tiring (less so than the scooping) but the tempo was steady. We had our "rest" as we walked back to the barn with the fully-loaded cart. Then we toiled again, unloading the sheaves and placing them neatly inside the barn. That was when Roth and Tähtinen smoked and had their rest. The more often during the day you came to the barn, the more rests the drivers got. The smaller the load you made, the more often you came to the barn. On Thursday Väinö Roth's loads became smaller and smaller, while Tähtinen's remained uniform. At 4 o'clock in the afternoon Peltonen let fly at Roth, in the most voluble and high-pitched Finnish I had heard to date. The tirade lasted 5 minutes, interrupted only by Roth's bellowed retorts, flinging of arms and choleric snarls. Peltonen did not flinch one iota; he was half the size of Roth, but he had twice the vocabulary. Old Martti Roth squeaked out a couple of broadsides in defence of his son, but clearly his heart was not in it. Tähtinen, Oksanen and Tuominen lit up their cheroots and scrutinized the forest, their backs to the outburst. Mathias winked at me; Korhonen sneered at Väinö Roth who finally stomped off to a distance of 50 metres and smoked two cigarettes accompanied by three inches of vodka before suddenly climbing back up on his load and heading for the barn.

The next day Peltonen took an hour off from the harvesting to supervise another activity. While he was absent Väinö Roth built the tallest load of rye that anybody had ever seen. Tuominen and I could barely pitch it up high enough; still he beckoned for more. Humu, for all his size, could hardly make any forward progress, though he strained every sinew. At last the load was such that the rim of the cart wheel began to sink into the earth and, as we hit a soft patch, there was a sudden squelch and the wheel went down almost to the hub. Humu took the strain momentarily, then gave up with a snort. Roth shouted at the horse, but it was clear that nobody was going anywhere. Mathias, who was working Tähtinen's cart, came across and gave Roth a piece of his mind.

"He wanted a big load, didn't he?" screamed Roth in reply, referring to his absent friend Peltonen.

When the foreman returned, we had a repeat performance of the previous day's brouhaha, resulting in Väinö's departure for the rest of the afternoon. One third of the load was chucked off again, Korhonen got Humu to pull us out of the rut and normal service was resumed. It was the easiest day I had. The weather was holding so we worked on the Saturday until 3 o'clock and cleaned the fields. Väinö built normal, average loads. He liked Fridays and Saturdays and became increasingly jovial as his weekly booze-up drew near. At the Saturday night dance in the Pukaro Valssimylly (waltz-mill) he was the chummiest character around. Peltonen did not go to these functions, though all the other labourers did, taking their families. Fru Wallen said Peltonen usually had a quiet beer with Hilkka.

During the last days of August and the month of September we harvested the wheat, the barley and the oats. The last got caught in the rain and we put the sheaves up on big poles to dry. The weather deteriorated as the days quickly shortened and the oats stayed up for several weeks, eventually getting caught in the first snowfall on October 26th. One of my jobs thereafter was to go out first at 8 a.m. armed with a long, stiff-bristled broom and brush off the mantle of snow from the clumps of sheaves.

*   *   *   *   *

As my farming experience continued, so did my education in the Finnish language. All the labourers were Finnish-speaking, consequently I was bombarded eight hours a day by this beautiful but entirely strange language in a variety of practical situations. I had never learnt a language in this total fashion and the experience I gained from it led me to apply certain principles when in later years I formulated language courses for others. The process was entirely deductive. As each task was performed I would find myself in a familiar situation, for instance loading a cart with sacks of grain, and I would hear words on all sides referring to this activity. The vocabulary came at me thick and fast, often persistently repeated, but with different permutations of word order that left my analyses floundering. There is an old Finnish joke that foreigners coming to Finland think that all horses are called Perkele*. This is not so unlikely as it may sound, as I too fell into the trap. The first words I heard Korhonen utter were "*takaisin perkele*" (he was talking to a horse, as usual). So what to deduce? Either the horse must be called Takaisin or Perkele. He was tugging it backwards, so which word meant "back"? Hearing these words in other contexts (*menemme takaisin* or *missä perkele rahat ovat?*) eventually enabled one to get a fix on the probable meaning.

It was a linguistic situation where initially there was a tremendous amount of input and almost no output, as my utterances were limited not only by my lack of vocabulary and access to cognates but also by the Finnish case-ending system confusing any clear idea of what the basic word actually was. It is discouraging to know that *pöytä* means table but to hear it almost exclusively in the guise of *poydässä*, *poydällä* and *pöydän*. Even my middle name, Don, by which I was known, was bandied around as Donille, Donilla, Donin and Donista, which is all clear to me now, but led to no little bewilderment in those first hectic weeks on the farm. My occasional brave attempts at expressing myself gave cause to great amusement in our little band. The most common words I heard were all oaths (*perkele, saatana, paska, jumalauta, jumaliste* being the most frequent). One day old Martti Roth decided to teach me some Finnish and, pointing to the darkening sky he said "*sataa*". Thinking he had trotted out the usual "*saatana*", I responded nobly with "*perkele*". The boys guffawed for days over that one.

Gradually the pieces of the jig-saw began to fall into place. *Helvete* was hell, *hevonen* was horse (but they usually said *humma*), *talvi* was winter, *lumi* was snow, *sataa* it's raining but *sataa lunta* it's snowing, *ruoka* was food but *ruoka on poydässä* meant lunch (or dinner) is served, *Anna* was a woman's name but *Anna sen takaisin Donille* was give it back to Don. *Talo* meant house but it changed like lightning to *talon, taloa, talossa, taloon, talosten, talolle, talolla, taloin* and several other forms, all with precise meanings slotted into the right contexts. Mathias told me the Finnish noun had 14 such case endings and I believed him too, though it was a little discouraging especially when Tähtinen's four sons, youngsters all, handled all 14 cases without batting an eyelid.

In 1952 seven per cent of Finland's population was Swedish-speaking. Most of the Swedish Finns lived in Helsinki, Turku, Uusimaa and the areas around Vaasa, Hanko and Tammisaari. These places also had Swedish names so that a visitor to Finland found that Helsinki was sometimes Helsingfors, Turku was Åbo, Uusimaa was Östra Nyland, and so forth. I was fortunate to be located in Pukaro (in Swedish, Pockar) inasmuch as the village and Lapinjärvi (Lappträsk) were inhabited by speakers of both languages. Pukaro sat on a linguistic border or dividing line. If you went a few miles north towards Artjärvi everybody spoke Finnish. If you went south towards Loviisa most people spoke Swedish. Most of the landowners in Pukaro – the Wallens, the Borups, the Boijes were Swedish-speaking, but though most of Gammelgård's labourers spoke Finnish, most other labourers in the village spoke Swedish.

Kalle Tähtinen's wife, Ellen, was Swedish-speaking, although her Finnish was quite fluent. It was a bewildering experience to listen to Ellen Tähtinen and Martta Wallen speak together, since, both being bi-lingual, they could never decide which was their common language. Consequently they said the first word that came into their head in either Swedish or Finnish. Sentences begun in Finnish would end up with Swedish predicates. Monosyllabic Swedish nouns would be embellished by sonorous Finnish adjectives; Finnish case-endings would be deployed in all their majesty even if the root was Swedish. Mathias, who listened to these daily conversations with great amusement, swore that neither woman was aware that she was switching languages in mid-sentence. With any third party they would choose one language and that was that.

Kalle and Ellen Tähtinen lived with their 5 children in a small labourer's cottage in the Gammelgård farmyard. They had 4 fine boys – Tauno, Tapio, Tarmo and Taisto – and one girl, Anneli, the youngest. Kalle and Ellen had to bring up their family in hard times, the husband spending 5 bitter years at the front (commencing with the Winter War) when all the children were tiny. Even in the post-war years they had no resources other than Kalle's wage and whatever little extras his capable wife could earn with her hands. With 7 mouths to feed they were as poor as you could get. I had seen miners' families brought up in similar conditions in Lancashire in the 1930s. One of my schoolyard mates, Billy Johnson, took me home to tea one night and I ate with the nine Johnson children and the mother standing round the dining room table. The Johnsons had all their meals standing up as they could not afford chairs – the room wasn't big enough for them, anyway. The father sat on a stool at one end (he had been cutting coal all day and needed the rest.)

The Tähtinens were better off than that, but they had no luxuries. Kalle was the prototype of the honest Finnish worker – conscientious, hard-working, rhythmic, uncomplaining and highly-skilled within the limits of his activities. The boys were all learning trades, Tauno roofing and carpentry, Tapio forestry, Tarmo joinery – while Taisto, a thirteen-year-old, was said to be the best businessman in Pukaro after Lotila. Mathias and I would often sit in their cottage in the evening listening to Ellen Tähtinen's tales, for she was the talker of the family, when she could keep Taisto quiet. Kalle said about ten words a week. They were visibly a very happy family; Mathias asked Ellen one night how they managed to maintain such harmony, being so crowded as they were.

"Well, it's like this", said Ellen, "a few years ago I used to fly off the handle occasionally and scold Kalle and the boys for being untidy or for smoking or some other reason. Whenever I got too loud, Kalle used to lead the boys quietly out of the house and they wouldn't come in again for 2 or 3 hours. I got fed up with being left on my own, so I gave up making a fuss."

*   *   *   *   *

Most evenings I spoke Swedish, as Peltonen invariably went to bed early and Martta Wallen would spin her yarns, entertain me with her reminiscences and welcome neighbours who very often came over after dinner. Finns eat their evening meal early compared with other Europeans and often dinner would be over by seven. In Pukaro people visited each other regularly between seven and ten. Borup's farm, Pockar Gård, was only a mile away and Hakon would pop in two or three times a week. Nisse Borup, his father, was a wealthy man, owning not only the sizeable Pockar Gård with its big herd of cows but also great tracts of land as well the well-known glass factory in Lahti – Lahden Lasitehdas.

Grandfather Borup had been an immigrant from Denmark and had bought Pockar Gård in 1891 from an old Finlandsvenska Emeleus. He prospered as a dairy and pig farmer in Uusimaa and bought forest whenever he could. Nisse, his son, proved to be an even shrewder farmer and entrepreneur and vastly increased the family's land-holdings and commercial interests.

Nisse was just over 60 when I first met him – a tall, broad-shouldered figure with a toothbrush moustache and humorous wrinkles around his eyes.

He was very fond of Martta Wallen and would come over nearly every morning about 10.30 to have coffee and *pepparkakor* with her. His entry was always formal and dignified with the same ritualistic exchange of remarks:

- *God dag, god dag. Får jag stiga på?*
- *Var så god och stig in. Hur mår Nisse i dag?*
- *Nåja, inte så illa. Inte så illa alls. Och hur står det till med Dej?*
- *Tack bra. Hur skulle det smaka med litet kaffe?*
- *Det ar inte någon dålig idé.*
- *Nå, var så god och ta plats.*

I don't think the wording ever varied on the many occasions when Nisse came. Swedish Finns love these little rituals. Finnish Finns would just say *Terve, onko kahvi valmis* and get on with drinking it, very much as the English would.

Hakon Borup was of Mathias' age and they had been at school together. Other young men in this Swedish-speaking group of friends were Bertel Salenius and the Antas brothers, Gunnar and John. John was a good athlete and rivalled Mathias at the local meets, excelling in the sprints and the high jump.

Gunnar could run too, especially after girls, and had a reputation as a brilliant dancer in all the waltz-mills as far as Lovisa and beyond. Bertel Salenius was a chubby, smiling forestry student who lived with his parents in Solstrand, a cosy wooden house on the river across from Lotila's store. Bertel was a great entertainer, possessing not only a natural bent for music but a strong countryman's sense of humour which bubbled to the surface in almost everything he said and did. He was equally at home with the landowners and the workers, belonging to neither, but able to disarm both groups with his ability to pinpoint quickly a basic truth, hint at any irony or hypocrisy surrounding it, then show everyone the whole thing was a good chuckle anyway.

You had to tread warily with Bertel in the first few encounters, for he spent that time summing you up and you felt that any remark was being quickly annotated. Everybody in the village had been summed up long ago and Bertel was an excellent walking reference book if you wanted to know who was who, what they stood for and how they figured on the Salenius balance sheet. At the end of the day he had his likes and his dislikes, but he spoke, joked and did business with everybody.

At Gammelgård he was the friendly neighbour and valued *animateur*. When Bertel was due, you knew you were in for a good evening of singing, tales and card-playing. After his first cup of coffee he would regale Martta Wallen with all the latest gossip from areas south of Pukaro such as Liljendal and Strömfors. She would then tell him what she had heard from the north side and the village jigsaw puzzle would near completion. Listening to these tidbits over a period of a few months, I daresay I became quite knowledgeable on local engagements, pregnancies, divorces, love affairs, suicides, crop failures, outbreaks of foot-and-mouth disease and other weekly developments of vital importance to people accustomed to the slow rhythm of country life. I found that I, too, lacking my diet of football news, cricket and Wimbledon, BBC broadcasts, strong tea, bitter beer, snooker nights and theatre evenings, looked forward to Bertel's weekly or twice-weekly bulletins. The problems, hopes, ambitions and successes of the Pukaro villagers gradually became my own as well.

*   *   *   *   *

Looking back on these cosy evenings in the autumn and winter of 1952, I have a vivid picture of a Finnish society with a strong oral culture – in this village, both bi-lingual and bi-cultural – excelling in its ability to entertain itself, through the long dark evenings, with its own knowledge, intelligence, originality and resources. At a time when England was turning rapidly towards external entertainment – radio, magazines, cinema, big bands, clubs, professional sport and shortly television, the rural Finns still maintained intact and whole a lively social intercourse which depended almost entirely on the characters and personalities of the individuals themselves. It was the old sit-round-the-fire atmosphere that I had experienced as a boy in Lancashire in the early thirties – even more an environment similar to the village life of my father and mother in the 1890s. But what struck me forcibly as I followed these Finnish conversations was not so much the old-fashioned, anachronistic manner in which they were conducted, but the depth of knowledge that was paraded during the discourse. I had already noticed that the Finns, as a small nation, were well-versed in the histories of the larger European states which had influenced their destiny. But their knowledge of history extended not only to that of Russia, Sweden, Germany and the Baltic and Scandinavian countries, but also to that of England, France, the Mediterranean countries and, quite significantly, the history of the United States, on whose constitution that of Finland had been modelled. Finns know well the adventures of the errant Vikings, whose exploits reached not only British and American shores, but also the Arab Kingdoms of the Mediterranean. The Russian state itself was founded by Swedes in Novgorod and the reigns of many Swedish kings and Russian Tsars are familiar ground for Finns, whose own long, ancient migration led them across lands larger than Europe itself.

If my Finnish friends knew the history of England as well as I did and that of America even more comprehensively, no more less remarkable was their grasp of geography which seemed to include every land and sea on the globe. Englishmen are often unsure where the Kamchatka Peninsula is located or what are the capitals of Laos and Ghana, but my Pukaro Finns scored heavily on such points, for they were interested in the world around them and read avidly when winter came. Another thing I had noticed is that the quality of the Finnish press was far superior to our own. I am not referring to the "Times" or the other British newspapers which approach that level, for indeed we can be proud of some of our reporting. Unfortunately the great majority of the British people, in our busy and pell-mell society, have time to read only the tabloids at the lower end of press coverage. These handy newspapers concentrate heavily on sensation, scandal and events of essentially local (British) interest and often ignore completely significant developments and events taking place in that strange area beyond Calais. In Finland, on the contrary, Helsingin Sanomat, Hufvudstadsbladet, Uusi Suomi and Aamulehti – the most widely read Finnish newspapers, generally gave widespread coverage to world events with an admirable lack of bias. The Finnish worker, consequently, reads daily the same material as the upper and middle classes (such as they exist in Finland) and emerges as well informed as they in politics, economics, the arts and knowledge of the world stage. Differences in education notwithstanding, I had the definite impression that all Finns have this window of opportunity to keep themselves well informed and that the average Finn has a much more balanced view of the world than, say, the typical Englishman, Frenchman or American.

Mathias and his mother were great readers, devouring volumes of history, philosphy, memoirs, war chronicles, voyages of exploration from Marco Polo to Sven Hedin, as well as the classic novels of Finnish, Swedish, English and American literature. I found that most of the books I had read at school and university, including plays, poetry and essays of four different literatures, were readily available in Finnish and Swedish translations. The Wallens, Borups and Boijes of Pukaro were as familiar with the works of Shakespeare, Browning, Emerson, Hawthorne, Proust, Molière and Cervantes as I was and had read most major works in German and Russian (in translation). I discovered that both Finnish and Swedish have rich literatures of their own, even though the former language had existed in written form only since the middle of the 19th century. I felt ashamed at my ignorance of these works, especially in view of my friends' extensive knowledge of my own country's history, literature and institutions. I began to hunt around for translations of Finnish novels and read the originals in Finnish and Swedish as soon as I was able. Only after digesting Marshal Mannerheim's memoirs did I feel comfortable discussing the war period with Mathias, who had read Churchill's works in their entirety.

*   *   *   *   *

Pukaro was full of strange characters, at least it seemed so to me at the time. Perhaps it was simply that I was reacting to a new culture for which I had not been pre-conditioned by my education. We English go to France or Spain with pre-conceived ideas of what their peoples are like. Our ideas may be to some extent exaggerated, but we easily recognize the French or Spanish prototype and we have some knowledge of the background, habits and pressures which make him twist and turn. The life and works of Napoleon and Maurice Chevalier are known to us and we and our kind have interacted with their countrymen for centuries. The Spanish Armada has been to our shores and Ernest Hemingway has told us quite clearly what made Juan Belmonte and General Franco tick. But the only Finns that Englishmen have read about are Paavo Nurmi and Jan Sibelius. One ran very fast and the other composed wonderful music. Beyond that we have had no dialogue with them.

The Englishman therefore sees the Finn or the Finn-Swede as he really is; there are no pre-conceived notions to cloud his vision. The very starting point for our interaction is quite different from that which we adopted with the Frenchman, Spaniard or Italian. When we rub shoulders with the Latins, we are the stolid, calm ones, unflappable while the others grimace and shout and wave their arms. When we meet Finns – friendly but silent – we have to assume a different stance. Norman and I had soon noticed that in rural Uusimaa, even more than in Helsinki, **we** were the exuberant ones. Instead of meeting French brilliance or Spanish ebullience with our customary northern reserve, we now found ourselves having to make the going with people who quickly passed over to us the role of *animateur* . What is more, we were never quite sure how they viewed our efforts to be lively. A Lancashireman in this position feels like a fish out of water – at a certain disadvantage, though he quickly learns to trust the Finns for, at the end of the day, the chemistry between Englishman and Finn is as right as any can be.

But the apparent strangeness of the people of Pukaro was not entirely the product of my cultural adjustment. Some places just are strange or, better said, special, and Pukaro was one of them. I did not find the surrounding localities of Artjärvi or Liljendal or even Lapinjärvi strange, but the people of these villages all considered that *Pukarolaisia* were indeed a different breed. Their attitude was one of mild contempt mixed with great respect, if such a complex feeling is at all possible. I know other places (though very few) which stimulate similar reactions – Zamora in Castile is one of them and the village near Wigan where I was born has a touch of it too. One cannot define the "specialness" of these places, but some vital elements seem to be well-defined borders, isolation, sharp differences in class or religion among the inhabitants, involvement in agriculture, some backwardness or old-fashionedness and adequate facilities for drinking and brawling. Pukaro had all of these and the surrounding communes, as far as Loviisa, Porvoo and Kouvola knew the people of Pukaro as a rough tough bunch of extremely clannish villagers who invaded their territory on Saturday nights, always got drunk and tried to seduce their womenfolk. As this reputation preceded them, it was not uncommon for the

young and even middle-aged men of Pukaro to end up fighting the men of
Loviisa or Elimäki, who often had planned their defence the day before. It was
also a known fact in Uusimaa that if any *Pukarolainen* was attacked, all the
other *Pukarolaisia* in town would rush to his aid. They were a clannish lot. I
became part of this clan, which was just as well, for they came to my aid one
night when a gang of Loviisa youths took me for a Swedish sailor and were
about to throw me into the sea.

*   *   *   *   *

It was not long before I learnt that Pukaro's reputation for violent
inhabitants had something to do with our old worker Juhani Korhonen.
Though he was now approaching eighty, one could tell by the way he handled
the horses and wagons that he was still a powerful man; also it was noticeable
that both the giant Roth and sizeable Oksanen treated him with the utmost
deference. There were stories relating to Korhonen's immense strength as a
younger man, for he, too, was well over six feet and his now slightly stooping
posture failed to conceal the undiminished musculature of his broad shoulders.
He could still pick up a 40 kilo sack of flour with one hand and swing it into
the cart with a flick of the wrist. Feats of his youth had included carrying huge
urns full of milk under either arm and dragging barn doors across farmyards.
In Finland they build wooden platforms by the road to take milk urns or other
heavy items to await being loaded onto carts. Korhonen had once taken horse
and cart to Lapinjärvi to fetch an enormous barrel of cement for the farm. It
was of such weight that the two local men destined to place it on the cart were
unable to handle it, so, after ten minutes' rocking and manoeuvring, Korhonen
lost patience and asked them to take the reins and back the horse and cart up
to him while he took the barrel. Standing on the road, he put his arms round
the barrel and with a loud grunt swung it round to face the oncoming cart.
They handled the horse badly and Korhonen had to hold his barrel for nearly
a minute. Finally they backed the wagon, flap down, under the barrel, which
Korhonen gratefully released. The wagon collapsed.

But Korhonen's reputation did not rest on his strength. He had killed
three men. In the short time I had known him, I had grown to like him
immensely. Silent and withdrawn, with eyes only for what he was engaged in
doing, he had a gentle manner which completely belied the roughness of his
gnarled, brown hands and craggy features. The horses knew his gentleness for
he treated them like favourite children, softly stroking their mane, jaws and
nostrils in moments of rest, feeding them tidbits, calming them quietly when
they were nervous or overworked. Korhonen paid little attention to me, or to
any other human being, but when we sometimes had the occasion to exchange
stiff remarks, his very abruptness had a certain understanding and dignity

about it. He had had his fill of people, preferring horses and other animals, but one had the feeling that nothing passed him by – his blue eyes were keen and his thoughts ran deep.

Two of the killings had been accidental, or at least provoked by the victims. In his late forties he had attended a Finnish country wedding, enjoying to the full the eating, drinking and dancing that took place in the great barn until the early hours of the morning. In a state of some intoxication he had fallen asleep in the hay and snored happily there for a couple of hours till a drunken farmer woke him up in jest with a *puukko* (a Finnish dagger of finest steel normally carried by most countrymen at the time) at his throat. Korhonen was a fast mover in those days and in a flash he had knocked aside the *puukko* at his throat, whipped out his own and sunk it into his attacker's heart.

Under the circumstances Korhonen was acquitted in court. He and his family moved to a different village and he continued his life as a farm labourer for a further ten years. Then, at another wedding, he was taunted and provoked by a very big and very drunken carpenter who drew his *puukko* and announced Korhonen's imminent departure from this world. He advanced upon Korhonen who retreated a good fifty yards, until a wall at his back obliged him to draw his knife and dispatch his leering tormentor with one lunge through the heart. He is said to have wiped his knife carefully in the hay before putting it back in the sheath and asking his wife to phone up the Lapinjärvi police. He fed the horses before leaving in their custody, telling his son how to handle them in his absence. He did three years, on account of the mitigating circumstances.

When he was in his late sixties he killed his third Finn, this time in a straight knife fight, but again after being severely provoked. He sustained minor cuts but again found the heart with unerring accuracy. The message was clear: don't mess around with old Juhani. He doesn't like violence or knives, but when he does fight he goes for the kill. A charge of murder was later reduced to manslaughter and Juhani did five years with a little time off for exemplary behaviour.

Martta Wallen employed him at Gammelgård on the strength of his uncanny ability with horses, also because she quite liked him. He ceased carrying a *puukko* and kept out of trouble for years. In one of the post-war farm workers' strikes, some pickets tried to stop Korhonen taking the horses to Lapinjärvi for fodder. He explained that he sympathised with them, but had to work on certain days to see to the animals' needs. They barred his way on the Monday and the Tuesday and the horses went without their feed. On the Wednesday Korhonen again led his animals up to the picket line and asked for free passage, which was refused. Mournfully he took out his *puukko* and asked the pickets which one wanted to die first. When they didn't quite understand, he mumbled something about three or four or five not making an awful lot of difference to him now, at least not at his age. The horses had no feeding problems after that.

Korhonen suffered his final ignominy in the winter I was in Pukaro when he went to a Saturday night dance in Elimäki, seven kilometres away, for a quiet drink with his friends. A young Elimäki tough, noted for his violence and bad behaviour, took it upon himself to taunt the ageing Korhonen whom he depicted as a spent force – a has-been – calling into question Korhonen's legendary reputation. Juhani ignored him steadily, infuriating the youth by refusing to show any interest in what he was saying. Finally the ill-advised young man, desperate to establish his superiority, took a beer bottle and cracked Korhonen over the head with it. The old man blinked hard, momentarily stared at the youth, then quietly put on his cap, turned on his heel and made his way out of the waltz-mill. The young tough jeered him all the way to the door and when he had gone, boasted to his friends of his victory. One of the Pukaro labourers addressed the youth, saying:

- "Do you know who that is?"
- "Of course – feeble old Juhani Korhonen."
- "Do you know where feeble old Juhani Korhonen has gone?"
- "Who cares?"
- "He's walking the seven kilometres back to Pukaro to get his *puukko* from his bottom drawer. He will then walk seven kilometres back here with it. It will take two hours and a half. If I were you, I would not be here when he returns."

Not only did the youth disappear, but the whole dance hall emptied within the hour, the owner locking it up at midnight. At one o'clock Korhonen arrived with *puukko*, tried all the doors and windows in the darkness, saw that all was abandoned, then trudged another seven kilometres back home to Pukaro.

*　　*　　*　　*　　*

Korhonen was only one of the unusual characters who inhabited Pukaro. Another was Göran Boije, who dropped in twice a week at Gammelgård, always at mealtimes. The Boijes lived at Lumnäs, the farm adjacent to Gammelgård. They were a noble Finnish family whose records dated back to the 12th century. Three sisters lived in the manor house, but not Göran. Though of a noble line, he dressed like a tramp and shaved only occasionally. On my third day at Gammelgård he dropped in for a chat just as the dinner gong sounded. Martta Wallen, who had seen him coming across the fields, already had a place laid, but the usual formalities were observed:

- "*God afton, god afton. Jag var just att sticka förbi och tänkte hälsa på.*"

- *"Nå, god afton. Skall Göran inte ta litet middag med oss?"*
- *"Det var hemskt vänligt."*

Göran would then take his usual place in front of the grandmother clock and Peltonen would reluctantly move one down. Göran always wore a black jacket with frayed elbows, baggy grey trousers and an "off-white" shirt, black on the inside of the collar, without tie. He was about sixty, sallow of complexion and wore thick-rimmed spectacles. Peltonen, who washed every day, did not approve of him, but Martta and Mathias Wallen found him entertaining, welcoming him unreservedly to their table. He spoke mainly Swedish, in view of his lineage, declaiming all he said in a hoarse, rasping voice, as if he were speaking in church, or reading out a list of rules. I found him easy to understand; when he discovered I actually listened to what he said, he would devote at least 5 minutes of every sermon to me.

He was a classic black sheep: the three Boije sisters had little to do with him. I never saw him at Lumnäs: he lived in a wooden shack about a mile from Gammelgård in the middle of open farmland. The shack served as a home and a workshop, for Göran actually worked – he had a trade. In spite of his vagabond appearance, he was a skilled metalworker specializing in wrought iron, though he could hammer brass and copper with the best of them. He would make a variety of articles for the farms of the district – black wrought-iron gates, fancy hinges and door-knobs, metal chandeliers, candlesticks, coffee tables, garden chairs and anything else you could describe for him. Give him the basic idea, he would come back a week later with a drawing and a quotation and the work would be done sometime in the next six months. You could not rush him. He had an impressive waiting list stretching all the way from Pukaro to Lovisa. If you wanted a floral-shaped lamp bracket with the Boije name on it, you waited your turn.

Göran was funny about his name. Though he had in a sense turned his back on his family and lived the life of a semi-hermit, he never quite let you forget his ancestry. It is said that he once visited Savonlinna Castle where the coats-of-arms of all Finland's ancient families are displayed in the Great Hall. He went at an unusual hour and was challenged by an eager young sentry, suspicious of Göran's vile appearance.

"Who are you?" shouted the sentry.

"Who am I?" echoed Göran. "Listen young man, I know who I am. The question is, who are **you**?"

He then is said to have led the boy inside and pointed to the shield bearing the name Göran Boije av Gennäs

"That, my boy, is who I am", said our eccentric *Pukarolainen*.

In 1944 Göran was called up in the Finnish Army – an indication of how hard pressed they were. He was sent to a Swedish-speaking regiment at Dragsvik near Ekenäs (Tammisaari) on the south-west coast. It was not long before the instructors realised that nobody was going to make a soldier out of Göran, who rarely shaved, looked like a tramp in or out of uniform and pretended not to hear orders or simply ignored them.

Whenever he felt like it, Göran wandered out of the barracks and walked to Ekenäs to buy cigarettes, which he smoked on or off duty. One day he was returning from such a shopping trip when he was halted at the gate of the garrison by a patrol of Military Police who were not from the area and did not know him.

"Why didn't you salute?" shouted the sergeant in charge of the patrol.

"What?" replied Göran vacantly.

"Salute!" screamed the sergeant.

"Nå guda, guda," said Göran, which translates roughly as "Tut, tut."

The sergeant went up to him, pointed to his MP badge and shouted:

"Do you know what this is?"

The short-sighted Göran suddenly showed some interest, scrutinized the badge an inch away from his nose and replied.

"It's brass, and pretty poor workmanship, too."

The sergeant blew his top and ordered his men to arrest Göran, but the Captain of the Guard, seeing what was happening, rushed out and whispered a few words in the sergeant's ear, whereupon Göran sauntered off in his usual reverie.

*　　*　　*　　*　　*

As the months went by, I became acquainted with most of the people in the village – my circle of close friends linked to Mathias, Hakon and Bertel; the Gammelgård labourers and their families; other individuals from the neighbouring farms whom I would meet at the Pukaro *Valssimylly*. Some called me Donni or *Gammelgårdin engelsmanni*, all eventually casting off their initial shyness, shouting greetings, getting a kick out of hearing my incipient Finnish, often confidentially taking my elbow to lead me behind some bush or hut where they would produce the ubiquitous hip flask and pour some local hooch of molten fire down my unwilling throat. There were eccentric and quarrelsome characters of all kinds, with fixed ideas, prejudices and grudges, extraordinary streaks of obstinacy, persecution complexes. Yet I noticed that all these strange peasants had a friendly attitude towards me and my country and that in general their prejudices rarely extended to bias against nationality, apart from historical anti-Russian and anti-Swedish sentiments due to Finland's centuries-long occupation. I felt that the Finns, along with perhaps the Italians, were the least chauvinistic or jingoistic of European peoples.

Besides the village drunks, who would soon have included me in their ranks had I accepted each *pieni ryyppy* that was offered, there were rake-like characters such as Malén and Backström who were men of some substance, but always in trouble. Each with a bit of land, they preferred wheeling and dealing to farming and involved themselves in every kind of peddling from second-hand cars to crayfish. The problem was that as soon as one heard that the other had gone into a new venture, whether it were trucking or insulated roofing, he had to go into competition at once, so that, as they were roughly equal in resources and intelligence, they invariably ruined each other's business. The fact was that the village was not big enough for the two of them. They would fight regularly – at the *Valssimylly*, in the street, even in other people's houses. Once a month one would sue the other, though it was never known for one of these cases actually to reach court. One day they set to with the knives (for fists and feet could not do justice to their hatred of each other) and Backström came off worst with Malén's *puukko* in his back, right between the shoulder blades. He managed to stagger to Lotila's store where he phoned the Lapinjärvi police, saying it was Malén who had killed him. The police jumped in their patrol vehicle and were in Pukaro in ten minutes. They found Malén and Backström – the latter with his shirt drenched in blood, swigging beer sympathetically provided by Lotila.

- "What about the stabbing?" shouted the police sergeant.
- "Oh, that," replied Backström. "Just a small misunderstanding."
- "Backström and me are buddies, you know that" said Malén. "Nothing happened really."

And that was all the police got out of them, though the short-tempered sergeant snatched the beer and poured it all over Backström's head.

Then there were the mad Leppänens. Kalevi Leppänen had had six children, three of them blond and three brown-haired. The blond ones were all normal but the brown-haired ones were not right in the head. Paavo was a kleptomaniac, Juha was a recluse who did nothing but fish, while Pirkko talked to trees. She was the only one we saw much of, as she worked on a nearby farm as a milkmaid. She never talked to the cows and only to people when she had to, but her conversations with trees lasted for hours. In Finland there are lots of trees and she knew a great number of them. Some days she would talk to the trees near where she worked, but when she had an hour or two to spare she would chat to Lumnäs trees and Pockar Gård trees and a nice clump of silver birch behind Roths' cottage.

She used to say her piece to Gammelgård trees about six or seven in the evening, usually when we were having dinner. That was frequently Pirkko's complaints session, though sometimes we would be entertained by a modest sermon or her next day's shopping list. If we were unlucky, she would sing, in a cracked, toneless falsetto. When it got too bad, Martta Wallen, who had taught her at the village school 20 years earlier, would grab the long-handled broom from the porch, run out into the farmyard and crack Pirkko over the head with it. If you only tapped her, she would go on addressing the trees. Even after a good beating she would say goodbye to them before she scuttled off.

*   *   *   *   *

Finland in 1952 was in a state of semi-prohibition, that is to say, you had access to alcohol only under certain circumstances. During the Olympic fortnight the regulations had been relaxed to some extent. Visitors could order beer in restaurants without too much fuss or without eating; I noticed that Finns were quick to accompany them. Snack bars, cafes and kiosks sold only soft drinks, however. There seemed to be no equivalent to the English pub, French bistro or Spanish bar. In the restaurants Finns were normally allowed only one drink before eating, then further drinks during the meal at intervals of sufficient length to guarantee sobriety. Neither could you just go in a shop or off-licence and buy alcohol. This was only purchasable at state liquor stores (*alkoholiliike*) and there only with an alcohol-card which could be withdrawn by the attendant if he decided you would be better without for a few weeks. Foreigners, if they looked respectable, could procure liquor against their passport. A friend with a passport was a very valuable commodity indeed in 1952.

These stringent regulations were in force for two reasons. First, a succession of Finnish governments, elected after 1911 by women, remained convinced that if you liberalised the alcohol laws the Finns would drink themselves to death. Second, the production and sale of alcohol was a state monopoly i.e. it would have been a state monopoly but for the ingenuity and entrepreneurial nature of the Finnish peasant, who found ways and means of supplying his own needs and those of his friends on those long, thirsty evenings when his toil was over.

Some nights, half awake in *det lilla gästrummet* I fancied I heard the clink of bottles coming from the forest. On other occasions I heard only the crunch of cartwheels, the creaking of wagons, muted human exhortations and the occasional neigh of a horse. There were mornings when Korhonen's blue eyes had redder rims than usual and more than once I had found him asleep in the stables in the late forenoon. I was careful not to wake him.

The Finnish rural worker's preoccupation with hard liquor has a centuries-long history and even today the national consumption is higher than in most countries. In 1989 Finns drank 6.5 litres of strong spirit per capita as compared with the European average of 3.2. Alcohol distilling has long been a popular activity in the Finnish countryside. In the 18th century, under Swedish rule, permission was granted by the King to nobles, farmers and priests to make spirits from grain and vodka from potatoes. This was most often done in the autumn in huge copper pans. In some years so much grain was used for spirit that more had to be imported from abroad to make bread.

Labourers were not allowed to do their own distilling, but they got a sip every morning before going out in the fields. Landowners noticed they worked better and ate less when they had had their little *ryyppy*.

Towards the end of the century, spirit making became more rampant; priests were found in ditches and the King applied brakes to the system. Nobles and priests accepted the restrictions and foreign wines and strong beer were imported for them. The farmers, however, resisted the braking and were justly chagrined when Russian rule (after 1809) imposed stricter limitations. During the nineteenth century farmers combined with fishermen in smuggling operations around the southern coast. In the archipelago they would go so far as to light fires to lure boats onto rocks, enabling fishermen and peasants to pirate the rum and wines on board. Inland, they had to rely on stills.

The 20th century witnessed no diminishment of the Finns' appetite for liquor, either before or after independence (1919). Prohibition, during the years 1928-32, gave a further boost to smuggling and production of spirits (*salapoltto*) with forest stills. Estonia was one of the main sources of foreign spirit. It was brought out to sea in big boats and then thrown overboard in 10-litre canisters enveloped in nets loaded with salt at the bottom. When the salt melted, the canisters resurfaced, to be picked up by Finnish fishermen in small vessels, then transported to various ports and inlets in the archipelago – Kotka, Loviisa, Pernaja, Porkkala and so on. The smugglers had fast boats (to avoid police and customs officials) and they needed fast cars and good drivers to whisk the bottles to their customers inland. The "taxi" route from Loviisa to Lahti went through Pukaro, hence the high level of interest in such matters in the village. Lorries used to hide in Väinö Wallen's barn. Besides motorized vehicles, horses, carts and bicycles were pressed into service. Many Finnish fishermen got rich and became respectable businessmen.

Later spirit was rationed at 2 litres per month (an extra 4 litres for your wedding) but smuggling continued as before. In the 1950s most of the liquor came from Poland, which gave rise to the term *Varsovan Laulu* or "Song of Warsaw". Polish spirit was tasteless, but very strong (96%) and Finns usually mixed it with grapefruit squash, though some peasants in Pukaro drank it straight.

If one did not have access to a smuggler friend, another way of solving the Saturday night crisis was to know one of the chemists in the central laboratory in Helsinki or, better still, a country vet. Veterinary surgeons had an unlimited supply of alcohol and were constantly pestered by farmers whose "cows were sick" at week-ends. One vet in Lapinjärvi had to disconnect his night-bell, as he got no sleep on Saturday nights.

Distilling continued apace in the 1950s – Finnish home brewed liquor was called *pontikka* (perhaps from the Swedish *bond-drickar* (peasant drink). Unlike the Polish version, it had a strong taste. Local distillers were well-known for their special flavours and were naturally prosecuted by the authorities. The first time they were caught they were fined. The second time the fine was bigger. The third time they went to jail for 3 months, after that 6 months, then a maximum of one year. The Finnish state brooked no competition in this sector of the economy. Meanwhile the position of General Manager of ALKO became a sought-after post by some of Finland's top politicians. A local entrepreneur, Grönroth, heeded the state's exhortations to create more employment and set up a *pontikka* factory, only to wind up in prison.

Distillers naturally tried to avoid incarceration, as it interfered severely with production. On one occasion, Ville Jakobsson from Lovisa, caught for the third time, asked Lakkonen, a fellow-distiller (who had only been caught once) to say he had produced the liquor. Lakkonen responded nobly to his friend's cause and told the court it was his brew. The judge (a Wallen) was suspicious and ordered a recess so he and the clerks of court could sample the offending liquor. Half an hour later Judge Wallen came back into court, pronouncing firmly "It's Jakobsson's". Ville got 3 months.

For someone who had been only a moderate beer drinker at university and been treated to the odd aperitif in France or Spain, this conspiratorial world of moonlight drinking and bootlegging was both bewildering and exciting. It was a novel experience at the Saturday dances to be grabbed by the arm by Roth, Tähtinen or another fellow labourer and dragged into the forest for a quick slug. There we would sit on a fallen log in the moonlight, six of us drinking *pontikka* from the same bottle, savouring the impact of the fiery liquid as it wound its way down our throat, wreathed in "*Työmies*" tobacco smoke enhanced by the forest smells of resin, pine-bark and moss-covered boulders of granite. Occasionally the silver moon sliding out from behind a cloud would suddenly illuminate vividly the congenial scene, or an approaching figure (was he the law or Leivo from Elimäki with another bottle?) A nearby moose would take flight, startling us all. The accordion music emanating from the *Valssimylly* wheezed out rhythmic, age-old Finnish country numbers, by now familiar to me, too. Tapio Rautavaara's strident masculine tones delivered yet another "*Hummani Hei*" to the rustling tree-tops and I was reminded that he had won the javelin at the 1948 Olympic Games in my own country. Finland gets the most out of her heroes.

*   *   *   *   *

The town of Loviisa is situated at the end of a deep inlet on the southern Finnish coast about 100 kms east of Helsinki. It was originally named Degerby and fishing and farming were both practised there as early as the 1500s. Close to the big neighbour to the east, Loviisa people are keenly aware of their geographical position. In 1745, after Viipuri and Hamina had been ceded to Russia, Loviisa became Finland's eastern frontier and was officially founded and subsequently fortified. The fortress on the island of Svartholm at the entrance passage to Loviisa bay still stands, though the mainland fort – Bastion Ungern – became a lovely dance hall until it burned down in 1960.

In 1752, after a visit by the Swedish king, Degerby was renamed Loviisa (Swedish Lovisa) after Queen Lovisa Ulrika of Sweden. In the 1800s it prospered both as a bathing resort and sea-faring town. Today it is a charming, somnolent market town of 9000 inhabitants with a fine neo-Gothic church and an impressive well-proportioned, cobbled market square, where the Finnish and Swedish languages share the Saturday morning hubbub. Loviisa enjoys the reputation of having the prettiest girls in Finland and in 1952 I found no reason whatsoever to quarrel with this assessment. Perhaps it is the admixture of Russian, Swedish and Finnish blood that gives the Loviisa girls their blooming-rose, slightly cosmopolitan beauty.

For the people of Pukaro, Strömfors, Liljendal and Elimäki, Loviisa was also the drinking capital of Finland. *Pukarolaisia* used to call it Capetown and headed for it on Saturday nights; it was half an hour's drive from Pukaro in Hakon's car. During the winter of 1952-3 I got to know that winding road well.   In Loviisa there were five fine establishments which provided refreshments and, at the same time, the company of ladies. These were Skansen, Seurahuone, Kapelle, Bastion Ungern and the Casino before it burnt down. The first task was always to gain entry, for this was by no means automatic. Five sturdy doormen judged new arrivals, many of them already in an expansive mood after one or two Saturday afternoon *pontikkas*. Our group usually let Hakon or Bertel do the negotiating and, more often than not, we were granted admission. Once inside it was easier to get a girl than a drink (hard for a Latin to understand). In Finland eating drinking and dancing usually take place on the same premises, especially in the countryside, where the number of establishments is limited. This system, which obviates the need to go from one place to another in sub-zero temperatures, is both practical and congenial. Loviisa pubs had a swinging atmosphere – convivial, hot and smoky, often noisy in the extreme. In the days before disco and hi-fi, the local musicians played with gusto. When the music started, you jumped to your feet, seized a lady and danced. When it stopped, you escorted her back to her place, bowed stiffly and scuttled back to your table for a quick drink. Whichever male at your table failed to get a girl used his break to cajole the waitress to bring more beverages. At some time between 9 and 11 you ate, perhaps a lot, but eating was low on the list of priorities.

In spite of the rivalry between Loviisa people and visitors from Pukaro, Mathias, Hakon and Bertel had friends among Loviisans. Two of these were Bo Larsson and Henry Widell, both of whom became prominent local businessmen in later years. Henry Widell was a versatile athlete excelling in the sprints and the long jump, as well as being Loviisa tennis champion. Bo

Larsson, blond, red-faced and invariably benign, was the man whom everybody knew, and who knew everybody. There was always a twinkle in his eye and he spoke of his fellow-Loviisans with gentle sarcasm:

"Last night I sat over there with a dozen labourers from Valkom. They didn't half have a skinful. The more they drank, the better qualified they became. When the accordion was playing they had to shout about their accomplishments. By 10 o'clock they were all engineers. One of them clicked with a woman at the next table who had also had a drink or two. He took her home at midnight – by that time she was an ambassadress. The next morning she was a cleaning lady."

*   *   *   *   *

Late summer became early autumn – for a few brief weeks one was treated to the incomparable fall colours of the changing Finnish forest, with its gaudy, coniferous-and-deciduous spectrum – then winter came quickly and the first snow fell on October 26th. Our farming activities changed and we were more in the forest, felling, trimming and lugging timber. The horses again played an important role and I marvelled at the rough-hewn skills of the Finnish peasants working in sub-zero temperatures. I soon felt the cold bitterly, but it was better in the forest out of the wind and with Finnish country clothes and boots I found it bearable.

Finland's winter is long and the season's work hard and monotonous. Consequently the sociability of the evening chats and above all the weekly outings to Loviisa assumed paramount importance. If the car broke down and one missed a Saturday night on the coast, the fortnight seemed an eternity. I realized how English town-dwellers take for granted nightly entertainment just around the corner.

But the experience was enriching and I learned the value of being able to interface with foreign friends or strangers, with the time to do it. In Finland the development of relationships is often slow. The Finns are curious about visitors and wish to find out what drives, motivates or amuses them, but they investigate bit by bit, week by week: they are not in a hurry to assess and evaluate. The result is often an enduring friendship.

At Christmas the other Wallen children came home for a few days. Kaj, the younger brother, resembled Mathias physically, but had quite a different character. He did not smoke or drink and went out with young ladies only one at a time. He had a smiling, laid-back, forgiving nature and was entirely incapable of quarrelling with anybody. Put him between a Greek and a Turk, or a Jew and an Arab, and you had a happy trio. Whenever accusations flew around, he would heap the blame upon himself. When in his company, you could get a cart stuck in the mud, miss an aeroplane or squirt ketchup on the ceiling with absolute impunity. "It's all my fault" he would say, and he would prove it was. Kaj had just spent a year in the United States studying agriculture, so that his English was quite fluent, though some of the Americanisms he had picked up were completely out of character with his angelic nature. He could say "you bet" fifty times in one evening. "Would you care for another cup of tea?" would be followed by "Well, ain't that just one son-of-a-bitch." When he set off for work Kaj was getting the show on the road, when he had no choice it was the only game in town, accountants were bean-counters, lawyers were shysters and sweet young ladies were dolls with class.

Ann-Mari Wallen, his sister, had class. Twenty-one years of age, blonde and slight of frame, she was pale and interesting alongside the typical pink-faced, vivacious, cheeky maidens of Uusimaa. Ann-Mari had delicate hands and ankles and projected an overall impression of fragility, belied by wide, well-moulded cheek-bones and resolute jaw line. Grey-green, sunken eyes watched you carefully, as you said your piece. She was a good, sympathetic listener, imputing the best motives; she was soft-spoken herself, but a compulsive speaker once she had begun, analysing behaviour and seeking the meaning of things; she was well-read and if she was occasionally over-serious for her age she was blessed with tolerance and laughed infectiously. She had a peculiar effect on men, making them behave like gentlemen in her presence. They opened doors for her, even gave up seats in buses, though she herself was entirely unpretentious.

Two other beautiful Finnish girls – close friends of Ann-Mari – were Ulla Antas and Kari Hellner, both aged around twenty. Dark-haired and vivacious, they were seen as very special by Pukaro males (used to blondes) and their frequent visits to Gammelgård certainly livened up my long winter evenings.

Christmas in the Finnish countryside has its traditional features and these were duly observed by the Wallen family. Dinner on Christmas Eve had two main courses – ham and *lutfisk* – Finnish punch (*glöggi*) was drunk by candlelight and each one of us threw a ladle-ful of molten lead into the fire, creating different shapes which told our future. The labourers came round for their schnapps or Jaloviina, the horses were decked out in their best finery and we made the required visits to the neighbours by horse and sleigh. It is a bitterly cold mode of transport, though picturesque in the extreme, especially under a silver moon and stars. We called on the Borups at Pockar Gård, the Boijes at Lumnäs and the Salenius family at Solstrand. They also visited us. It was far more formal than the usual English Christmas, but the warmth of feeling was the same. We all gave each other books for Christmas and I noticed that the Wallens spent some of their holiday reading theirs, so I did the same. It's a sensible thing to do when it's -20°C outside – also it improves the mind.

*   *   *   *   *

In the spring Mathias emigrated to Canada. Kaj came out of the army and took over the running of the farm. I decided to spend a few months in Helsinki as I wished to do some teaching and get to know the capital better. Also I needed my tonsils out, as I had constantly been plagued by a sore throat in the biting cold. The operation was duly performed in Tilkka Military Hospital where Dr. Kalle Pursiainen did it in exchange for 20 English lessons. He was a prankster of the first water and took out one tonsil, tugged at the other and said it wouldn't budge. Finnish humour, I thought. Eventually he removed the second one and we became friends for 40 years. Pursiainen – a highly-respected ear, nose and throat surgeon – was one of the most engaging characters I have ever met. Though at the top of his profession, he had the knack of making every patient his friend, almost his confidant. I suppose it could be described as the perfect bedside manner. He was solicitous and kind, with an inexhaustible store of anecdotes to cheer up even the most morose. The stories were not just plucked out of a vacuum – they always revolved around him. Persons pronounced dead woke up in the middle of the night and Pursiainen would be summoned from his bed to deal with them. In an effort to prolong their resuscitation, he would undo "invisible" throat stitching – proudly completed that very day by a pompous fellow surgeon – and the patient would go on to live – suitably scarred – for another 20 years. Called out on another emergency, Pursiainen could not find his car (buried under a heavy fall of snow) and he would rush to flag down hapless motorists who would skid wildly trying to miss him. He had tall stories of gigantic fish he had caught, mammoth-size moose he had shot. On the one occasion I went fishing with him he pulled out a fish bigger than any that had figured in his stories. God, I should have brought a bigger boat, he cried.

I stayed 6 months in Helsinki, improving my Finnish, teaching English to a couple of dozen people from different walks of life and writing a Sunday morning column for the newspaper "Uusi Suomi".

Bo Larsson and Henry Widell were "mature students" in Helsinki and they introduced me to one of the student clubs which are such an integral part of Finnish university life. I met Olle Sirén, a specialist in history, also from Loviisa, who helped me put my ideas of Finland's history into perspective. I noticed my students all talked a lot about the war and I realised how traumatic those years had been for Finland and her people. Pursiainen himself had been four years in the front line; he introduced me to a former officer, Major Väinamö Volanen, a beaming patriot who always claimed he had shot the last Russian of the war, 30 seconds before the ceasefire.

Other friends included Martti Karttunen and Pekka Lakkonen, who had also picked the peas at Wisbech. They were both English teachers and spoke our tongue so fluently and accent-free that I became convinced that the old Finnish belief that they are poor at languages was a myth. With Bo Larsson,

Henry Widell and Pekka Lakkonen I spent my first Vappu in Finland – the festival preceding the 1st of May – and I had to marvel once again at the Finn's capacity to down hard liquor for 48 hours in a row.

*   *   *   *   *

Finns vacate the capital in July and August and I spent the summer travelling up and down the country, visiting friends in their summer houses and hiking around the many lakes. In the autumn Martti Karttunen and I went to Lapland, viewed the unbelievable colours of the forest and mingled with the Lapps – at that time still ubiquitous.

The Lapps, or Sami, as they call themselves, are an ancient people living mostly above the Arctic Circle, practising a rural economy which is a balanced mixture of reindeer-herding, fishing in the lakes and rivers, berrypicking on the heaths and a little sheep or cattle farming wherever the land allows it. No-one is quite sure how many Sami there are, but a credible total is 60,000 spread over 4 countries – 30,000 in Norway, 20,000 in Sweden, 8,000 in Finland and 2,000 in Russia.

The history of the Sami is one of continuous retreat. They once inhabited almost the whole of Finland, as is indicated by many place names. Pukaro, where I had spent the winter was part of the commune of Lapinjärvi (Lake of the Lapps). My friend Kalle Pursiainen had a summer house in Lappvik or Lapinlahti on the southern shore. Unlike most indigenous people, the Sami have never fought, either against advancing strangers or amongst themselves. Archaeologists have found a plentitude of tools and artefacts, often of beautiful design and decoration, but no weapons. There is no word for "war" in the Sami language. Such innate pacifism is as admirable as it is rare, but it has had a costly legacy of submissiveness.

Martti Karttunen and I were both interested in meeting some of these unique people on their own ground – Martti had often seen them, in full native dress, on the streets of Helsinki, but had never talked to one. We hitch-hiked over large areas of Lapland, as far north as Inari, as well as Kilpisjärvi in the western corner, where we crossed over into Norway and spent a couple of days in Tromsø, climbing the mountains there in brilliant September sunshine. Overlooking Tromsø Sound, one could clearly see the top of the German battleship Tirpitz sticking out of the Norwegian Sea where it had been sunk by the British in 1943. We followed the course of the river Tanajoki to Utsjoki, Finland's northernmost commune, some 1200 kilometres north of Helsinki. Utsjoki was reckoned as 80 percent Sami in the 1950s and Lapps took a rich harvest of salmon from Tana's raging torrent. They showed Martti and me their catches – though normally quiet people, they chattered excitedly when they had a big one on the line. Martti could not understand their language (though it is a distant relative of Finnish), but the younger Lapps spoke Finnish willingly, with a quaint local accent which even I could hear.

The Sami have always been a hunting and fishing people, making use of a natural environment without altering or disturbing it. About 200 years ago they began to herd the reindeer instead of treating them simply as game. The animals spend the winter in the forests or the scrub-covered tundra, subsisting on lichen. In May, soon after the calves are born, they are rounded up and driven to summer pastures. From the plateau of northern Norway they go to the coast. From the Swedish and Finnish forests they go to stretches of open hillside. In September, when we were there, the herds are culled for slaughtering. During this period the men live in traditional wigwam-like tents or in wooden cabins, which they share with their dogs, day and night. Martti and I were welcomed into some of these wigwams, where we were offered primitive coffee, black and grainy, and raw fish. The tents had a pungent smell on account of half a dozen dogs having spent the night there. As the September evenings were getting decidedly chilly, the Lapps didn't seem to change clothes very often; Martti and I also fell into the habit of sleeping fully clothed in our sleeping bags. The men spoke to us in fits and starts – sometimes there would be 5 minutes of silence. This did not bother Martti (Finns like silence) but I was not fully acclimatised to it. In daylight the dogs wandered in and out of the tent door like human beings. They eyed Martti and me warily – I suspect we did not smell right.

I was interested in the way Lapps thought and tried to open various conversations with them. One evening we were sitting in a wigwam with an old Lapp, a young Lapp and five dogs. The younger Lapp spoke Finnish and I was able to converse with him in this tongue. The older man spoke only Lappish. Using the younger nomad as interpreter, I asked the senior Lapp a question: "What are you going to do tomorrow if it rains?" He stared into my eyes, ignored the question and looked away. I repeated my query and again he ignored me. I asked the interpreter if my question had been understood. He nodded in affirmation.

"He understands you, but he doesn't like the question."

"Why not?"

They exchanged a few words in soft Lappish tones.

"He says it is a stupid question."

"Why?"

"He says how can you ask him what he is going to do tomorrow if it rains when he doesn't know if it will rain or not?"

I was not sure what the answer to that was, so I said nothing. The young man went on explaining patiently.

"He will look out of his tent tomorrow morning and inspect the weather. If it is raining he can do this or he can do that. He will decide. However, if it is fair, he will do something else or maybe another thing. Again he will decide.

That was as far as I got in communicating that night. Later in Helsinki, a specialist in Lappish studies told me more:

"The Lapps endure extreme cold, economic hardship and often utter loneliness. Under those conditions they favour doing things one at a time. They do not build on hypotheses."

Never play chess with a Lapp, I thought.

The Lapps are often referred to as nomadic people, but this is not strictly true. They have acquired this reputation on account of the seasonal migration of the reindeer, but they have a strong feeling for their land of lakes, rivers, forests and fells. Most of the land in Sami-inhabited areas is state-owned. When only Sami lived in the north, there was no state-owned land because there was no state. I look back with fondness on my days spent with these simple, hospitable, colourfully-attired herdsmen, joyful when fishing and herding, striking a sadder note as they discussed their future with strangers.

"Our tradition is one of accepting whatever happened to us."

Vivid in my memory is my first experience of the *Revontulet* (the Northern Lights or Aurora Borealis) – a breathtaking display of kaleidoscopic fire and colour in September in these latitudes. We also heard sung the *joiku* – an extremely old form of Sami chanting, where the words are of secondary importance and the melody and rhythm act as descriptive elements, portraying a person's character and emotions. A strident *joiku*, sung by a young girl in full costume, can be a moving spectacle.

Martti and I also walked along the Lemmenjoki river and looked for gold, without any great success. The history of Lapp gold goes back over a hundred years, or even further if one digs into the past. It was already mentioned in a chronicle dating from 1546, though it was not until the 1930s that gold panning really took off there. The story goes that Sauva-Aslak Peltovuoma, a Lapp from Purnimukka, discovered the first gold after a dream. Far from discovering any new nuggets, Martti and I got so lost trudging along the river banks that we ran out of food and, by the time we stumbled across the next village, were much more interested in survival than in riches.

*   *   *   *   *

In December it was time to go home and spend my next Christmas with my parents. Germany beckoned in 1954, for I spoke no German and wished to remedy the deficiency. I had spent 16 months in Finland, a country of which we in England know so little, yet which has an exciting and heroic history and a unique, vibrant culture. I came to realise that small countries – Finland had just over 4 million inhabitants – are not merely appendages to the territory of others, of little consequence in the grand scale of human evolution. On the contrary, they may have been in the past – like Sweden, Holland,

Denmark or Greece – major actors on the stage of history. Finland is the most important place in the world for Finns, who have their own highly-developed and beautifully-wrought language, their intensely original literature and music. This "small" nation "ran onto the map of the world"; it preserved its independence (virtually unaided) against Stalin's hordes; it paid off its "war reparations" on time; it pays its National Debt (other countries don't); it absorbed 400.000 displaced Karelians at the end of the war without any fuss; it transformed an impoverished, war-battered country into one with (in the 1980s) one of the highest standards of living in the world. The Finns achieved all this on inhospitable territory lying above 60°N latitude. One measures the importance of a country not by the number of its inhabitants, but by the stature of its achievements. Many people would do well to get to know Finland as part of their education.

Chapter 3

Post-war Germany

In January 1954 I went to Mönchen-Gladbach in the Rhineland in order to learn German and to get to know the German people. Mönchen-Gladbach is not the ugliest town in Germany, but it would probably make the top ten. The reason for my going to this industrial centre was that I had established contact with a German family who wished to have a young Englishman as a paying guest. The family was particularly suitable, as the husband was a railwayman like my father, they had an only son about my age, and they spoke no English. Like many working people in post-war Germany, they found it hard to make ends meet – a situation with which I had been only too familiar since 1935. The Schlössers were honest, kind and hospitable and the rent, including food, was a friendly 40 marks a month – an amount which I could not pay. I had 25 marks, of which I advanced them ten, leaving me fifteen marks for rail fares to enable me to look for a job. My host family agreed that I need not pay them any more until I had found employment.

I find it interesting to look back on these minor financial details, firstly because it is incredible to see how cheap life was in Europe at the time and secondly how trivial such budgetary worries appear in view of the considerable amounts of money I was about to make in the near future. The Schlössers, too, were soon to prosper greatly and now we all look back with a smile on those days when 10 marks passing between us represented a major transaction.

For my own part I was getting vaguely tired of 20 years of hand-to-mouth existence and had started to lay my plans for an improvement in the family fortunes. Already in Finland I had sensed the great opportunities that awaited a professional linguist who had the ability to organize. In the mid-1950s countries such as Germany, Italy and France were achieving full recovery from the war and turning their thoughts from sheer survival to economic planning, international trade and education. They found themselves in an American-dominated Europe. English was the language of the Americans, as well as that of science and technology, air and sea communications and world-wide commerce. Half a million English-speaking soldiers were on Western European soil; IBM, General Motors and Coca Cola were names on everybody's lips; hundreds of thousands of jobs were available for English speakers. The Swedes, Danes, Dutch and Swiss, moreover, seemed to have learnt English during the war, which accentuated the deficiency in the 3 major European countries. Germans, French and Italians needed to close the war-time gap in their English instruction and their sons and daughters would need English for their careers. In countries such as Spain, Portugal and Finland, for various reasons a few years distanced from Anglo-Saxon affairs, the desire to learn our language would be just as great. In all these countries English courses had been introduced in state schools and universities. Instruction was however, bookish, theoretical and old-fashioned. German grammar schools (like the one attended by Paul-Heinz Schlösser) produced no more fluent speakers of English than England's grammar schools produced good speakers of French or German. In Germany, France and Italy good native teachers of English were few and in Spain, Portugal and Finland they were almost non-existent. It was to this last country, now close to my heart, that I had resolved to return to embark on a career which would serve humanity and at the same time make me rich. What a splendid combination of objectives!

But to make money you have to work very hard and provide the goods. In my case, providing the goods meant being a fully-rounded linguist with an in-depth knowledge of not only those languages in which I intended to organize instruction, but also of those of my future students. Language is not only a tool of communication, but it is inextricably bound with the cultural outlook of its speakers – it is the key to their mentality, the particular strait-jacket inside which they organize their aims, feelings and expression, it is the mould into which their thoughts are poured. Understand and feel the language of your student and you understand his difficulty or facility in learning another, the cultural ease or trauma he experiences in the process, his peculiar strategy in organising his study, his likes, dislikes and sensibilities when confronted by a particular linguistic challenge. To use a modern expression, some languages are more user-friendly than others – Italian and Indonesian are good examples – but one's gut-feeling attitude to a foreign tongue emanates mainly from the entrenchment characteristics of one's own and is often decided by the degree to which the two languages can be calibrated, harmonized or synergized. There is cultural empathy, and there is such a thing as linguistic empathy, too.

German was the one major Western European language I did not command and its acquisition I regarded as essential. In the long Finnish evenings I had kept up my French, Spanish, Italian and Danish; my Swedish and Finnish were now reasonably fluent. Norwegian I could also get along in without difficulty. The German language, so admired by Mark Twain, is truly a formidable and worthy opponent. A tightly-disciplined, no-nonsense entity with three genders, four cases and numerous declensions, it takes on where Latin left off as present-day Europe's linguistic crossword puzzle – a splendid mental exercise in logic, consistency, discipline and organization. There are a few exceptions here and there, but these add to the excitement and therapeutic value of the study.

To the Englishman, German is user-friendly up to a point. Butter is *Butter* and finger is *Finger* but *Fingerspitzengefühl*, still amicable, begins to introduce a word-building tendency which rings alarm bells for John Smith and which culminates, a little further down the line, in

Oberammergauerpassionsfestspielealpenkräuterklosterdelikatfrühstückskäsesc hnittchen

English and American people, as anyone who has read Dickens or Faulkner will know, prefer long sentences to long words, and our word-building usually hits its zenith with Master-builder or Assistant Company Secretary. The Germans would put a body like Accrington Stanley Association Football Club Members' Supporting Committee Brass Band into one word, without the slightest hesitation or remorse.

The German language has various idiosyncrasies of word order which cause considerable difficulty to its learners, not the least of which is the verb-at-the-end-of-the-sentence phenomenon. Simply, "I must drown the cat tomorrow" becomes "I must tomorrow the cat drown." English, French, Spaniards tell you immediately what they are going to do with the cat. The Germans delay Pussy's fate till the end of their utterance. It's one way of making you stick around until they have finished speaking. If you are into cats, you will wish to know if the animal is going to be fed, brushed, let in, kicked out, taken for a walk or castrated. This delaying-the-action trick affords the German various advantages. Apart from commanding your attention for the entire sentence span, he creates suspense, increases curiosity, plays with the element of surprise and can in fact change the verb completely at the end depending on the feedback he gets from your facial expression as he feeds you the secondary details. A clever, well-educated speaker can procrastinate indefinitely. Even news editors do it, though you would think they would try to bring you the news as hot as it can be served up. I once had to translate this sentence as a news broadcast item:

In der dreiunddreissigsten halbjährlichen sozialpolitischen Sitzung der jugoslawischen Nazionalversammlung, hat der Auschuss für Innenpolitik in Belgrad gestern Nachmittag um 3h, mit 320 Stimmen, gegen 144 die von dem kroatischen Regionalparlament neulich umstrittenen Vorschläge für höhere Staatsautonomie ABGELEHNT.

This sentence takes about 20 seconds to read clearly. For that amount of time the proposals might have been approved, rejected or shelved. An average news broadcast contains approximately 15 items of news. Should each item be presented in the same manner, you have 20 X 15 seconds = 300 seconds or 5 minutes of suspense. It might not happen that way but, as every learner of German knows, you have to listen carefully right to the end. It's like an athlete who has to run through the tape.

My tussles with this magnificent tongue gave me great satisfaction and enjoyment. It was a process which took more than a year; of more pressing concern was my need of employment. My travels around the world have taught me one thing about getting a job. You may have made your reputation or niche in one country (in Finland I had dozens of friends and connections and a name as a newspaper columnist) – when you move to another country, you start from scratch. I knew nobody in Germany and in 1954 work in the Rhineland was not easy to find. As far as schools were concerned, I was in mid-year and there were no immediate vacancies. Travel bureaus, hotels and advertisement agencies interviewed me politely, but (rightly) turned me down as I spoke little German. My 15 mark rail budget dwindled rapidly as I shuttled between Mönchen-Gladbach, Düsseldorf, Neuss, Viersen and Krefeld.

The failure of state schools to teach language in any manner other than writing emanating from the mouth was not reflected in the private sector. There were excellent individual teachers of English and French and some private schools whose fate depended on the fees of their students actually devised ways of producing some kind of oral fluency. One of these organisations was the Berlitz School of Languages. This chain of schools had been in existence since 1878 and had branches in most sizeable European towns between the two world wars. They taught languages using the Berlitz Method, which had been invented by Maximilian D. Berlitz in Rhode Island in 1878, originally conceived to teach French to Americans and subsequently adapted to teach English, Spanish, German and most other languages. It is often described as the Direct Method, as the teacher uses only the target language from the very beginning and prohibits entirely the student's own tongue during instruction and conversation. If you imagine yourself learning Lithuanian or Tibetan without a word of explanation in your own or any other common language, you may envisage a situation where difficulty, misunderstanding, even incomprehension would reign. This is not, however, the case. Once the student has survived the initial culture shock of being addressed in Tibetan and has perceived that he actually understands, the resulting gain in confidence enables him to deal directly with the language instead of discussing it for hours in another. Everything naturally depends on the skill of the teacher in correctly perceiving and then adhering to the almost fool-proof progression of vocabulary items and grammatical structures that M.D. Berlitz had so painstakingly worked out. In my experience, only about 10 per cent of language teachers are able to do this, though the approach is not difficult to learn, provided that the teacher himself is properly trained. It takes 100 hours of theory and practice – mainly the latter – under the guidance of an expert. Then you can do it for the rest of your life. Most new teachers are subjected to hurried or inadequate training and emerge from their method course "half-baked" and somewhat confused. Their confusion is small compared to that which they will shortly impart to their students. A competent Direct Method instructor, on the other hand, can give his student oral fluency and a working knowledge of any language in a few weeks.

I was offered a ray of hope by the French Directress of the Berlitz School in Düsseldorf, which enjoyed a prominent location half way along the Königsallée. She indicated she might need another English instructor soon, and allowed me to observe one or two classes. The students were young and middle-aged Germans of both sexes, keen, attentive and clearly making progress. The weeks went by, however, and the vacancy failed to materialize. One evening after a fruitless day in Düsseldorf, I noticed a new sign "Berlitz School" over a building opposite the railway station in Mönchen-Gladbach. On the off chance I mounted the stairs and edged my way into the school office. I was greeted by a tall, handsome American woman of middle age, Mrs Stevenson – the woman who shortly introduced me to her German husband Wilhelm Hermann – they were the owners of the establishment. It was a brand new school – they were only in their second week of operation. They had few students and no vacancy for a new teacher, but they interviewed me courteously and I left them my name and address for possible future contact. I caught the local train on to Schlösser's, a journey which took twenty minutes. When I arrived home Frau Schlösser, was excitedly waving a piece of paper on which she had jotted down the contents of a telephone telegram. The Berlitz School of Mönchen-Gladbach, on reflection, had offered me a job. Hallelujah! Solvency was on the horizon and the Schlössers had a paying guest who would now be able to pay. We celebrated with a glass of something.

My job turned out to be 2 hours a week at 2.60 DM an hour. I seized it with both hands. If you begin at the very bottom you end up at the very top. In those days, young people were not offered indefinite employment with guaranteed rates of pay, fixed term contracts, four weeks' holiday, sick pay and pension schemes. You were paid by the hour and you worked every hour you were paid, which, I suppose, is what real life is all about. There are no free lunches. My first month's earnings were 17.60 DM after some small deduction. I gave ten marks to the patient Schlössers and began collecting students like an ardent stamp collector collects stamps. The Hermanns, who had given me two hours training in the method, were delighted as my classes doubled in size and had to be divided. Soon I was doing 4 hours a week, then 8. My second month's cheque was 56 DM! The Schlössers started planning a holiday by the sea. At the end of the third month I was the recipient of 200 DM – a princely sum for a pauper. I bought a new jacket and Paul Heinz got a pair of shoes. As spring nudged its way into the Rhineland, pale sunlight filtered through the windows overlooking Hindenbergstrasse, stimulating our rapidly burgeoning morning classes. The Hermanns, too, clambered to solvency and other teachers were engaged in different languages. A Scot, Ian Mackay, became second teacher of English and an attractive Italian lady, Anna Candiago, appeared to teach Italian and French. Madame de Bournonville, who claimed to be a relative of Tolstoi, gave lessons in French "conversation" and regaled us during lunch hours with dozens of Tolstoi's letters which she carried around wrapped up in newspapers. There was a Spanish teacher called Martinez who appeared to be not very fond of Franco and another Italian – a man called Virzi – whose students occasionally fell asleep during lessons, or so he claimed. He took this as a sign of German indolence. We were a pretty mixed bunch.

The students, too, were far from uniform, differing greatly in age, profession and outlook. Morning and afternoon classes consisted largely of young people 18-25 years of age seeking an extra qualification or the ability to use English meaningfully in a new job. The evening classes – 10 to 12 in a group – were much older, many of the participants were of the previous generation. They had been deprived of English during the war and now wanted it for travel, job betterment or as an evening hobby. Many of the men were ex-soldiers. One of these, Karl Olberts, has maintained his friendship with me for nearly 40 years and still shows up on birthdays. Another genial student, Max Fritsch, had been a bomber pilot in 1940-41. His favourite line delivered to me at least once a fortnight, was, "I often visited England, but never stayed for tea." This unfailingly produced a roar of laughter from the class, even more amused when I battered poor old Fritsch with phrasal verbs for the rest of the period. He was a great ice-breaker and our evenings were full of mirth.

*   *   *   *   *

These happy days drew to a close at the end of the summer when I applied for a job with the German radio in Cologne and was appointed for the coming September. By this time Berlitz in Mönchen-Gladbach was well-established and would be able to take on 3 or 4 new teachers for the following autumn term.

The position I had applied for held a great deal of interest for me, as Germany had just been granted permission by the Allies to commence short wave broadcasting in English and three other languages. In other words, they were about to launch their post-war World News Service, a luxury they had been deprived of up to now. The head of this new organization – called *Die Deutsche Welle* – was Doktor Hans-Otto Weseman, who was in charge of news services and other feature programmes in English, French, Spanish and Portuguese, put out from the sixth and seventh floors of the *Funkhaus* in Cologne. This fine building, which also housed the *Westdeutsche Rundfunk*, (then called the *Nordwestdeutsche Rundfunk*) was located a stone's throw from Cologne's imposing Gothic cathedral, framed by my office window.

My job was that of English news announcer, but in fact it was combined with the function of news editor, since we had to write our own news bulletins prior to reading them. Applicants being interviewed were subjected to a sudden-death test. A wadge of news items, mainly in German, but occasionally in French, Italian, Spanish or Swedish, was slapped on your desk. You had one hour to translate the bulletin (with the help of a German dictionary) but it was tacitly understood that if you did not do it in under 45 minutes you were hardly likely to be appointed. There was also a voice test, during which you read the material you had just written. I managed to complete my translation in 44 minutes, not without difficulty, as my German was still rather sketchy. Fortunately my university days had taught me how to thumb through dictionaries at a fair number of w.p.m. I gabbled off my virgin bulletin down a mike they put in front of me, trying to remember how old Brucie Belfrage had delivered his goodies in the dark days of 1940-41. The Head of the German News Service, a beaming, bespectacled giant named Dr Rudolph Böhringer, gave me tea and some sympathy before sending me off to Mönchen-Gladbach with instructions to ring him in two weeks' time. When I did so, he said there was good news and bad news. The good was that I had been chosen for the job, the bad was that it paid only 700 DM a month. As that represented double my current earnings, I was not unduly dismayed. After some warm-hearted farewell parties with my colleagues and students, I said goodbye to the Schlössers, found an indifferent lodging in Cologne and began work in September.

$$* \quad * \quad * \quad * \quad *$$

The *Deutsche Welle* put out 4 English news broadcasts daily to coincide with peak listening times in different parts of the world. The first was at 12.30 for the Far East; the second, at 4.30 in the afternoon was for the Middle East and Eastern Europe; the third, for Western Europe and Africa, was at 8 p.m.; the last one, for the Western Hemisphere, was at 3.30 in the morning. Three announcers divided this work between them. My two English colleagues were Barry Jones, a brilliant linguist and broadcaster who could translate and edit a news bulletin inside 15 minutes and invariably delivered it without any error of pronunciation or phraseology and Freddie Adams, an eccentric, ambling giant of a man who had spent the post-war years living in Germany and was fluent in the language as well as in several local dialects. Both men were in their mid-forties and married to German women.

The original plan was that the work would consist of three shifts. In the first, one of us would cover the 12.30 and 4.30 bulletins; the second would be the 8 p.m. bulletin; the night shift announcer would do the broadcast at 3.30 a.m. After some discussion we decided that one of us would do the night shift 10 days a month while the other two did all the day broadcasts for 3 1/2 days, leaving each one 3 1/2 days free. The system worked well, for it meant that one could take on extra work for the 3 1/2 days as well as during the 10 days a month that one was on the night shift. This we all did without hesitation or exception. No-one took the free days off for rest or leisurely pursuits. This was post-war Germany and the atmosphere was one of hard work and rapid recovery. All the German news editors did the same thing, grabbing every minute of overtime they could get their hands on. By taking on teaching hours, translations and interpreting work, Jones, Adams and I were able to double our income without difficulty. We slept very little for 10 days a month. I found it was almost impossible to sleep after a night broadcast anyway. However sleepy one became between 1.30 and 3.30 a.m. as one prepared the (double) bulletin, the very sight of the huge, shining microphone and the ten-second countdown woke one up like a cold shower. Ten minutes of concentration for the reading and you would not sleep a wink for two or three hours afterwards. Barry Jones, who had been broadcasting fifteen years, told me he was affected in exactly the same manner. The only solution was to go down to the Rhineside *Gaststätte* with the German crew, down a few enormous beers and go home at 5.30. After a few days I fell into this system and was able to sleep soundly from 6 till noon.

After a couple of months my comprehension of German improved rapidly and my bulletin translation time came down from 44 minutes to 30, then 25 and eventually 20 minutes. This meant that even on a day when I did three broadcasts, my actual working time did not exceed two hours, though we all tended to come in before the news was ready and exchange gossip with our French, Spanish and Portuguese colleagues on the same corridor. There were 2 Frenchmen – D'Oncieu, a tall, reserved distinguished scholar with a permanent cold and Réne Leurquin, a small bounding Parisian, never completely drunk or sober, murdering both the German and English languages every day. The Spanish announcer, who did night broadcasts only (for South America) was actually Peruvian – Dr. Alberto Montani. He looked so Indian one would not have batted an eyelid had he arrived to work on a mule or a lama. Dr. Schmidt, the Portuguese announcer, was a competent Brazilian of German origin who arrived every night about an hour before his broadcast, translated, edited and read his bulletin and promptly disappeared for the next 24 hours. No one ever saw him outside the office or outside these working hours. Montani, on the other hand, almost lived in his office, translating South American novels into German and combing his drooping black *bigotes* every hour on the hour.

There were 6 German news editors, led by the incomparable Böhringer, who wrote the best German, spoke the best English and was well-versed in both English and American literature. We worked with each editor on a rotating basis, soon becoming familiar with their work-style, idiosyncrasies and personal details. It was the first time I had worked with Germans at such close quarters and the difference between them and the Finns or English was noticeable. Hard-working and competent, their chief preoccupation was to avoid making mistakes, as this would provoke comment from their colleagues. They were quick to spot others' mistakes and pounced on them immediately. We foreigners were not exempt from this vigilance and had to be very careful how we rendered their news items. If we erred, the question that came up would not be that we had made a mistake, but **why** had we made a mistake? I always found this a difficult question to answer. The Germans are not more unkind than anyone else – they are just hot on constructive criticism. They proved in fact to be loyal colleagues and never hesitated to help each other or us over difficult patches.

Böhringer and Barry Jones never made mistakes, so they commanded maximum respect from the German staff. From our point of view it was noticeable that some news editors were easier to translate than others. We compared notes with the Frenchmen and their reaction was the same. A Böhringer bulletin could be rendered into English or French in 20 minutes. News items written by the other five took 25-35 minutes according to the individual. Böhringer wrote more elegant and penetrating German than his colleagues – he had clarity of style. One editor had a genius for making at least one sentence in each item completely ambiguous; we were constantly nipping across the corridor to ask him what he meant – and this in a news broadcast, mind you. It was just a particular talent he had. He could have made a fortune writing clues for crossword puzzles.

Other colleagues with whom we came into contact on a day-to-day basis were the German technicians. These men sit at a console behind a glass screen, monitoring and recording your broadcast in your cosy, sound-proof studio. Theirs is a job with limited creative requirements and the repetitive nature of their activity is extremely monotonous. They are consequently very bored and constantly seek escape routes out of this boredom. One outlet is the pastime of teasing or tormenting the news announcers, preferably while they are in the process of reading a bulletin to millions of listeners. The teasing assumes many forms, beginning with pulling faces or making semi-obscene gestures through the screen, pressing the cut-out button and shouting insults at the announcer in between his items, even entering the studio quietly and combing the announcer's hair as he reads. The technicians had been playing these tricks on the German announcers for years. We foreigners enjoyed a honeymoon of about two months while we were new, after that we were tormented like everybody else. The big problem, of course, was how to refrain from laughing in the middle of the broadcast. This occasionally we did, covering up our giggles with coughing or hitting the cut-out button. Leurquin, when he did this, used to scream back insults at the technicians, who would respond by donning carnival masks or waving tricolores at him. The German news editors, who were on the floor above and did not witness these antics, nevertheless heard of them and were not at all pleased. Nothing seemed to deter the technicians from entertaining themselves in this way, though what would have happened had the austere Dr. Wesemann walked through one day is questionable. On one occasion a technician lowered the microphone to six inches above the floor during a broadcast and the unfortunate German announcer had to read most of the bulletin on his hands and knees.

Other catastrophes were of one's own making. One night I translated Herr Pfefferkorn's ten-minute bulletin between 2 and 3.15 a.m., then fell asleep on my desk. Pfefferkorn woke me in a panic at 3.29, shoving my translated items, each on a separate green slip, into my hands as I hurtled down the stairs to the studio. Recovering my breath, I was half way through the news when my green slips gave out. Where was the other half of the news? Five minutes to go and all of the Western Hemisphere anxiously waiting. The other half was upstairs still on my desk and there was no way I was going to get my hands on it. The technician behind his screen had seen the problem and was conducting an imaginary orchestra for my amusement. I took a deep breath and said: "This is the Deutsche Welle bringing you world news on the 10th of February 1955. Here are the main headlines once again." It took another 5 minutes as I read the same items, in their entirety, all over again. I tried to get out of the building quickly, but Pfefferkorn was too fast for me.

"What about the second half?" he screamed, coming clattering down the staircase. "You must have dropped it", I yelled, somewhat unfairly – Pfefferkorn was a person who really worried about responsibilities and things like that. It was a scandal the next day at the office, though Böhringer laughed it off – he had seen that sort of thing happen before. Pfefferkorn and I kept out of the building till the following night, when he entered my office every five minutes between 2 and 3.20 to see if I was still awake and carried my green slips down personally at twenty-five past three. It was not long before he forgave me, but it was a month before his nerves stopped jangling.

*   *   *   *   *

Other amusing incidents occasionally took place. Adams used to eat an apple five minutes before each news bulletin. Someone had told him it had a calming effect on the nerves. It became a habit with him and after a while he could not broadcast without one. He used to keep them in a big brown paper bag in the cupboard by the door. He never had fewer than six in reserve and the whole office used to smell of apples.

One night Jones got hungry on night shift and ate them all up. He didn't know how much Adams relied on them. On the morning shift Adams didn't find out they were missing till 5 minutes before he had to go on. He sent a secretary scuttering to buy some but she got stuck in the lift and didn't get back in time. He said he wouldn't go on the air but they made him and the bulletin was awful. Every time he made a mistake he coughed, and he coughed so much that his mother wrote to ask if he was all right. Whenever you hear a news announcer cough, you must not think that this means he has a cold. It means that the technicians are flashing the sun into his eyes with a mirror or taking his shoes off or combing his hair in the middle. It is the only fun technicians get.

Dr Weseman was not fond of announcers making mistakes. When Adams came up from the studio he found a note on his typewriter:

"An apple a day keeps the Doktor away."

It was not a kind note under the circumstances and everybody kept out of Adams' way during the morning. He weighed 14 stone.

When Adams had gone home to sleep, I came on to do the 4:30 bulletin. Leurquin, the French announcer, was in the adjoining office. We wrote our bulletins as the stuff came in and went down at 4:25 to wait for the red light. It was then we all noticed Leurquin was drunk. This had happened before and he was a good announcer when he was drunk, so we carried on with the news and he was all right. Every time he hiccoughed he did it at the end of a paragraph and cut himself off the air on each occasion with the press button.

We were due on again at 8: pm and I went up to the office to get some letters off. At 6 they rang up from the canteen and told us that Leurquin had passed out over his fifth *Steinhäger*. They carried him to his office but couldn't bring him round. D'Oncieu was on his holidays and Jones had gone to Hamburg for the day, so we had to ring Adams up to help us out. He had just eaten a dozen apples and gone to bed.

I started doing the French news and Adams took a taxi in and got going on the English. He had an apple in either pocket and was in a vicious mood. I had heard Leurquin and D'Oncieu drone away in French for a year so that I knew all the French words, but the French typewriter was unfamiliar and Leurquin snoring a few feet away distracted me. I had just got it finished when Leurquin came round and said he was going to read the news. He could hardly stand up and his eyes were crossed. The German editor tried to restrain him, so Leurquin went beserk and started wrecking the office. He was only a small chap, but it took four of them to lock him up in the lavatory. The din was terrible.

When news time came I was feeling pretty nervous; Adams made a big sacrifice and gave me one of his apples. As we were going down in the lift one of the editors shouted that Leurquin had broken loose, so we locked the studio door from the inside.

It was my turn first and while I read we could hear Leurquin thumping on the studio door demanding entrance. Then he shattered the circular window in the door and tried to climb through, cutting his hands on the broken glass. After that he ran round the front and beat up the technician who was regulating the bulletin. Listeners in France must have asked themselves what all the strange noises were. I was glad when my five minutes were up.

While Adams read the English news there was a full-scale battle going on on the other side of the glass panel between Leurquin on the one hand and the technician, the assistant technician, a German news announcer and the German news editor on the other. We had ringside seats. It was the second awful broadcast Adams made in one day.

We were all Short Wave men and Wesemann was proud of us. There was a bitter feud going on at the time with the Medium Wave Service. It was all about studio rights and rehearsing facilities. There had been a lot of snooping. All the Medium Wave men were reporting the Short Wave men for this and that and we were all reporting them. You had your work cut out to keep your record clean.

When Adams and I came out of the studio the fight had just moved over to the corridor. There was a scarlet trail along the linoleum from Leurquin's cut hands; two pictures had been knocked down from the wall. Leurquin was sitting on top of the technician strangling him; the news editor and the assistant technician were trying to pull him off. The German announcer was sitting on the floor with his nose bleeding profusely; all five men were covered in blood. Leurquin was screaming at the top of his voice. The technician was desperately trying to free himself because he had to put on another tape to follow the news. The station signal had been repeating itself for a full three minutes. Adams wouldn't help because he said the news editor had taken his apples. While all this was going on the Medium Wave Cultural Exchange Chief happened to pass by.

It just shows you can't be too careful.

*　　*　　*　　*　　*

Besides housing the Deutsche Welle, Funkhaus Köln was the headquarters of the NWDR which eventually became known as the West German Radio. It was not uncommon for people in the building to do some work for both organisations and I was engaged from time to time by the NWDR for a variety of assignments. These proved a welcome change from the daily treadmill of news and included visits to fairs to interview foreign exhibitors, writing education playlets for English by radio and even commentating (in German) international football matches. Germany had the previous year beaten the 'invincible' Hungarians to win the World Cup, It was a victory not infrequently brought to the attention of the English trio of announcers during the winter of 1954-55 and it was not without some satisfaction that I was able to summarize on the NWDR England's 3-1 defeat of the World Cup holders in April. Stanley

Matthews and Len Shackleton were at their dazzling best and I daresay my commentary gave birth to a few brand new German verbs and adjectives as I tried to find an adequate description for their artistry.

During this time I became friendly with Kurt Brumme who eventually became the best known sports commentator on West German Radio and Television and with Dietmar Schönherr, a smiling Austrian announcer who doubled up as a heart-throb film star in his native country. He used to walk his huge Alsatian dog up and down the Höhestrasse for exercise, stopping to oblige autograph-hunters, more numerous on days when he left the dog at home.

Occasionally I worked on speeches for German politicians such as Gerstenmaier and Franz-Joseph Strauss who from time to time sought to convey a message to British or American audiences. Once, for German-American Day, I had the thrill of helping to compose an address for Bundeskanzler Konrad Adenauer and met the great man himself, then in his late eighties. The over-riding impression he gave was one of excellent health, energy and vitality. Newspaper picturees of him always showed a broad, very white, owl-like face. In real life he had a lovely pink complexion and twinkling eyes, while his handshake was a grip of iron.

*   *   *   *   *

During the course of the winter I had developed friendly relations with Emil Jungfermann, the director of the Berlitz Sprachschule in Cologne. Already in his sixties and heavily dependent on his ear trumpet, he was of the old-style generation of Berlitz directors who had known Maximilian Berlitz personally and who had helped to pilot the organisation through the twenties and thirties and even to assure its survival in the hectic days of wartime. The Cologne school was now booming again and old Emil had begun to groom his nephew who would eventually inherit the business. Herr Jungfermann kindly arranged for me to meet Roger Montfort, the President of the Société Internationale des Ecoles Berlitz, who was scheduled to inspect the Cologne School in the near future.

Roger Montfort was a charismatic Frenchman of about forty, corpulent of figure with quick, darting, rather beady eyes which told you he was summing you up in the first ten minutes he scrutinized you. The next half hour I spent with him in fact decided the course of my life. I told him I was interested in applying for a Berlitz franchise for Finland, where there was no branch of his organisation. All other countries in Western Europe with the exception of Norway and Portugal had Berlitz Schools. He discussed my qualifications, which were satisfactory and asked me how much capital I had. I was saving fast at the time, but I didn't know what would impress him, so I added on a little bit. He nodded silently and queried me on Finland, a country about which Frenchmen know even less than the rest of us do, if that were possible. I gave him some basic historical and geographical background and touched on the potential of the market, being careful not to make it sound too good, in case he had some spare capital himself.

After thirty minutes he declared himself willing to grant me a franchise on condition that I would attend a two-week training course at the Paris Berlitz School. The contract would be for 5 years renewable with a 3% royalty on turnover payable to the Société Internationale. This sounded reasonable to me and I shook hands on the deal. He rushed off on other business, leaving me to sort out details with his accompanying assistant, Monsieur Guy Berthier.

Berthier was a pleasant young man of about thirty, of French nationality but linguistically and psychologically German. His father, many years dead, had been French but Berthier had been brought up in Germany by his German mother. At the end of the war, when privation and chaos reigned in Germany, he had claimed his right to a French passport and, having obtained it, made his way to Paris to seek employment. After considerable hardship he found a job with Berlitz, where his fluent German made him useful. He had to learn French the hard way, but spoke it quite well when I met him. As the majority of Berlitz Schools in 1954 were located in Germany, Roger Montfort spent a large proportion of his time inspecting these schools, whose combined royalties constituted the major contribution to the Berlitz coffers. Since Montfort's German had such a strong French accent that you were never quite sure which language he was speaking, he quite sensibly took Berthier around with him on his tours of inspection. Berthier, who later learnt excellent English and dabbled in other languages, fulfilled this role of special assistant for many years. Montfort once told me quite seriously that he was going to give Berthier a school "when he was ready" (this after granting me a franchise after half an hour's interview). Berthier, who 15 years later was still waiting, consequently became, after hundreds of inspections the length and breadth of the organisation, the most knowledgeable and competent Berlitz administrator, mastering the method completely in five or six languages and troubleshooting for Montfort in Germany, Italy and Spain. On the occasion when I first met him he was not a little envious at seeing a franchise awarded to a 25-year-old (I was to become by far the youngest Berlitz director in the world) but he was then and later invariably courteous and helpful. He indicated various pieces of documentation I would have to get together and agreed to take me under his wing when I came to Paris to be trained and that was that.

*   *   *   *   *

The rest of my time in Germany passed quickly. In spite of a heavy workload I was able to visit the Hermanns, Schlössers and Karl Olberts on occasion, I sailed down the Rhine to Boppard, Koblenz and Rudesheim, I had a delightful week-end in Heidelberg and I explored Altenberg and other bewitching spots in the neighbourhood of Cologne itself. My relations with Barry and Gretel Jones became particularly close, for I much admired this essentially professional man who had spent most of his life in Germany, but, at the flick of a mental switch, was tranformed into a humorous, big-hearted tea-drinker from Warwickshire. Back home, my parents were receiving our broadcasts loud and clear – my mother even used to get up ten times a month to listen to the night bulletins, father sensibly stayed in bed. The voices of Barry Jones and Freddie Adams were now as familiar to them as my own. Whenever we coughed to disguise our laughter, a letter would arrive three days later from my mother, worrying about the state of our health. In the summer my parents came over to meet everybody and we all had a good time.

Much as I enjoyed my work and the *Kameraderie* of Böhringer, Bruehl, Gentz, Pfefferkorn, Paschold, Kerneck and other colleagues, I felt that 12 months of reading the news was about right. It had taught me the value of discipline, exactitude, speed of action and teamwork. I had learnt German, I had seen the workings of an efficient and powerful organization and I had forged bonds of friendship with many kind and resourceful German people. There were now other countries to visit, other peoples to explore. I had an urge to go to the Far East, but first I had to make some money in Finland – and before that I had to unlock the secrets of M.D. Berlitz in Paris. I had enjoyed lovely summer days with the French as a student. Now I would see how they worked.

Chapter 4

The Paris Berlitz School

In June I took some leave and skipped over to Helsinki for four days. During that time I founded a company with Kaj Wallen as my partner, rented 120 sq.m. of space in the Bensowin Talo in the middle of Helsinki, hired a temporary secretary and a bookkeeper, made arrangements for the premises to be partitioned into 6 classrooms and an office, placed a series of ads in Helsingin Sanomat, Hufvudstadsbladet and Uusi Suomi for the following August and got back to Cologne just in time to read the 8 o'clock news.

If you were to say to me that I made an unbelievable amount of progress in four days, I would certainly agree with you. Today, after 40 years experience in business, I would be totally incapable of doing it. Certain things are achieved only by youth: a poignant poem by Keats or Shelley, a blistering century on a sticky wicket, a contemptuous disregard for red tape in starting a business. I shudder to think of the legal pitfalls, intricacies of accounting, employer's obligations and requirements of officialdom that were later to encumber the running of a school in a foreign land – I knew little of these niceties. What I did know that June was that if you united a keen student and a competent teacher in one room with a chair for the former to sit on and a ceiling over their heads in case of rain, then success would follow automatically. Students' fees would have to be fixed to cover the teachers' wages and other costs of the establishment, but the more facilities you provided other than the dynamic teacher, the less chance you had of either making a profit or improving the student's lot. The essential equation is a comfortably-seated receptive student exchanging guided remarks, in a cultural-context situation provided by a native teacher, who for best effect should pace up and down. This intensive oral communication in a semi-physical ambience is what hurries the student along the path to spoken fluency. Other aids may be utilized to stimulate, consolidate or refine his/her grasp of the language, but the two-way, sociable contact is the main thing.

*   *   *   *   *

Having set the wheels in motion in Finland, I took my 10 days remaining vacation and enrolled on a method course at the Paris Berlitz School. There I was greeted by Montfort and Berthier and introduced to Michael Watson, the Method Director, an ageing, bald-headed Englishman with a humorous twinkle in his tired red eyes and a low threshold of tolerance for fools. It was a special course being held for new Berlitz directors, some of them already running schools. There were seven Germans and myself.

The Paris Berlitz School was a large triangular building on the Boulevard des Italiens, a stone's throw from the Opéra. The isosceles triangle was divided into many rooms – reception and administration being located at the front on the short side of the triangle and about 60 classrooms extending back along the other two sides. Busy at all times of the year, Berlitz Paris could well have been the largest language school in the world in 1955. It was also the headquarters for most European Berlitz Schools.

Maximilian Berlitz was not, as people often believe, a German, but a Frenchman who emigrated to the United States. The organisation was originally American, as he wrote the Berlitz Method there and founded the first school in Providence, Rhode Island, in 1878. His purpose was to make a living teaching French to Americans, but the Method proved so effective and popular that he wrote manuals in several other languages and opened schools in New York, Boston and other American cities. Before the end of the century Berlitz Schools had been founded in London, Paris, Berlin and a large number of European centres of culture. It is not generally known that there was an enormous boom in language learning at the turn of the century and this continued right up to the First World War. In 1955 I met an old Frenchman, Monsieur Delon, who had been director of the Palermo Berlitz School in 1902 when it had had 2000 students!

Berlitz was an academic rather than a businessman and the administrative problems of the huge empire he had spawned eventually proved too much for him. In 1921 a consortium of Paris teachers bought the rights to the Berlitz name in all parts of the world except North America. Thus two companies came into being – the Berlitz Schools of North America, based in New York, and the Société Internationale des Ecoles Berlitz, based in Paris. These two separate organisations went their own way, sharing a name and almost identical method, though their business styles differed more and more as the United States prospered and developed its own approach to salesmanship, advertising and service industries.

A joint Berlitz Congress was held every four years, usually in Europe, attended by all school directors. The American contingent on these occasions generally numbered around fifty. Charles and Victor Berlitz, the grandsons of the founder, eventually lost control of the American company, whose President, Jacques Strumpen-Darrie, was the majority shareholder. His son, Robert Strumpen-Darrie, was President at the time I joined Berlitz Europe. Robert Strumpen-Darrie and Charles Berlitz, Vice President, led the American delegations to Europe and maintained close contact with Roger Montfort, though there was a certain amount of rivalry between the two companies.

All the American Berlitz Schools were company-owned and each director was a paid manager who shared profits and was moved regularly to a larger or a smaller school depending on his degree of success in his current one. In Europe the French Company owned only a handful of schools – Paris, Bordeaux, Marseille, Lyon, Strasbourg, London, Manchester, Glasgow and Vienna, later on buying Stuttgart and Düsseldorf. All other schools in Europe were franchise operations generally run by directors native to each particular country but sometimes, as in my case, by foreigners. The Société Internationale derived its income from the profits of the 9 schools it owned outright, the 3% royalties paid by the franchise operations and the sale of Berlitz textbooks throughout the whole organisation. As there were about 200 schools in Europe in 1955, one could say that the Société had a nice little business. The majority shareholder emerging from the 1921 consortium of French teachers had been a certain Madame Delpeux. Childless, she had eventually left her shares to Roger Montfort, the nice little boy next door, who inherited not only a valuable piece of equity, but also the myriad problems that had driven M.D. Berlitz to distraction.

*   *   *   *   *

Michael Watson was a reassuringly eccentric English bachelor in his mid-fifties rarely separated from his rolled-up umbrella, soiled mackintosh and the previous day's "Daily Telegraph". He had spent most of his working life amongst Parisians, whom he did not like, inspecting teachers, whom he occasionally despised and instructing novices with whom he had little patience. In spite of these considerable frustrations, he carried out his mission with the utmost conscientiousness and (if they survived the course) provided bumbling trainees with a cast-iron formula for teaching their own language.

Most English graduates in French, German and Spanish are perfectly able to teach these languages to the next generation of students, using the same grammar-based method by which they themselves were taught. Employing the same terminology as was invented for describing Latin, they discuss Preterites, Subjunctives, Causatives and the Passive Voice in the common language (English) that they and their students share. Only a small proportion of the time do they actually speak in the target language, but, in the main, the method works, though the process is protracted (months or years) and the student's spoken ability is rarely satisfactory.

The same English teacher is, however, generally incapable of teaching his own language in this or any other manner. To begin with, people who left school after 1950 have not been taught English grammar in the way previous generations were and have only the vaguest notions of how the language works. In method courses I have given over the last decade, most trainees, when asked to put a sentence into the Passive Voice, unhesitatingly put it into the Past Tense; very few indeed know what you mean by conjunctions, prepositions, relative pronouns or reported speech and a good proportion fail to identify adjectives, adverbs or even nouns.

All this is sad enough, but when they realise that they may be asked to teach their language, of which they know very little, to some foreign chap who may not speak one word of English, they tend to become anguished in the extreme. There are two possible reactions: one, that the task is perhaps impossible, certainly unfair; two, that one does it in a natural manner, through **conversation**. I have had so-called language instructors, who had had some brushing acquaintance with the "notional-functional" approach, attempt quite seriously to teach me (playing the part of a complete beginner) with opening gambits such as:

"Good morning, my name is William Potts – no, don't get up – I believe you're from Indonesia – lovely country I'm told. You understand "lovely"? No? Well it's not lovely weather today. In fact it's raining. You understand "rain"? No? Well don't worry, it all seems a bit difficult at first, but after a while you'll find it's quite easy. Now, open your exercise book and copy these words I put on the blackboard: rain, lovely, easy, difficult ...."

When I tell them one can't teach a beginner in this arbitrary, unstructured manner, they laughingly assure me that it works, whereupon I make them sit down and give them the same treatment in Japanese – ten times for clarity – after which they concede that the only thing they understood was "William Potts", which I had kindly thrown in instead of Yoshi Fujitani. At this point they either declare that English can only be taught to foreign beginners by other foreigners or they embrace humility and ask you to give them a method course.

Watson's course in the Berlitz Method served two purposes. First he showed trainees how difficult it is to teach complete beginners at the outset – how warily one has to tread the minefield of unfriendly vocabulary and prematurely-complex structure. Second, he showed how a carefully-conceived progression (that devised by M.D. Berlitz) could not only pave the way for rapid and confident progress, but could be applied to any language – Finnish, Georgian, Mongolian, Chinese or any other. It is all a question of training in technique. As a teacher of mathematics must guide his student through the ordered concepts of arithmetic, geometry and algebra, eventually progressing to calculus, so must the language instructor steer his charge through that infinitely more complex and labrynthine phenomenon – the English language (or Japanese, Algonquin or Aranta, as the case may be). Watson illustrated perfectly how a beginner, when confronted with unambiguous, visible objects or people and clearly demonstrable verbs (he loved to teach "hit"), felt firm ground under his feet and responded readily, quickly progressing to an intermediate stage where he absorbed simple abstract concepts such as "always", "never", "tomorrow" and eventually became advanced enough to understand and use complex terms through association of ideas. The adult student has the maturity and mental equipment to follow a path of programmed learning (in a language) just as he perhaps did in sales techniques or computers. He will not reach his goal through aimless or imperfectly-structured "conversation". The programme happens to be the English language – changing, fluctuating and permutating certainly – but nevertheless a relatively finite and clearly-defined target for the foreign learner, its vocabulary varying little decade by decade, its grammar and genius hardly at all. The trick is to present this phenomenon to the student in the best-ordered manner. That is all you can do for him – the language will not modify itself for your or his benefit. The Berlitz Method – and one or two others devised in recent years – are effective, because of this required logic and clarity of presentation.

Most French, German, Spanish or Italian teachers know the grammar of their own language well. And as they are generally confronted by students (often American or British) who are actually **learning** their language, starting as beginners, semi-beginners or at a lower intermediate level, they tackle the task of introducing German, Spanish etc. step by step in digestible portions. English teachers are often in a different position, inasmuch as many of their students have had English as first foreign language at school and put up a pretty good show, wielding a vocabulary widened by watching English or U.S. films on television or memorising forever the endlessly repeated lines of pop songs. The teacher may then make the assumption that his charge has not come to **learn** English, but to brush it up. What he must need, therefore, is **conversation**. Thus a substantial percentage of those Anglo-Saxons who travel the world for the very valid reasons of broadening their mind, or to take judo, karate or zither lessons – and particularly those who do not have qualifications in languages (as plumbers or biscuit-oven technicians they do not need them) – proclaim themselves to be **English conversation teachers**. Indeed some perfectly qualified instructors prefer to join this category, feeling perhaps that the label lends some aura of Victorian refinement or genteel superiority (over us ordinary grammar teachers). The English **conversation lesson** becomes not only a handy bread-winner, but can be served up as a social highlight, a moment when both student and (especially) teacher can **relax** and find passing solutions to environmental problems, economic and technological revolutions and the dilemmas of the foreign policies of their respective governments.

As real language teachers know, and as perceptive students quickly realize, there is no such thing as a **conversation lesson**. What takes place is either a **conversation** or a **lesson**. Either the learning process has stopped or it has not. If it has not, a lesson is required. If it has (and this is a rare case) then a conversation is in order, but it is questionable if the teacher should be paid for it. Learning a language is an endless process: a corollary of this is that the avenues for instruction are endless. Random conversation, even with a very advanced student, merely indicates that the instructor is not able to locate and identify these avenues. It requires a competent professional to raise the level of a fluent advanced speaker, yet it is not difficult to do. The complexities of English idiomatic usage, nuance and even grammatical subtlety are infinite. These are just the phenomena that the intelligent student wishes to examine. The native instructor is the person ideally suited to steer him through this maze, either by dint of his/her own cultural refinements or by sheer technical competence (idioms, phrasal verbs and vocabulary enrichment can all be organized, parcelled and to some extent rationalized). What **appears** to be a conversation going on is, under the guidance of the true professional linguist, a craftily constructed and tightly disciplined series of ordered concepts introduced to the student in conversational form.

*   *   *   *   *

The two weeks spent in Paris were most enjoyable. It is always an elucidating and often invigorating thing, in later life, to go back to school for a while. I was still young; I noticed that some of my older co-trainees got an even bigger kick out of it. With Watson the kick could be more than figurative if you did not pay attention. I, like most of my generation, knew English grammar fairly well; I was not slow to realize that my German colleagues were equally familiar with it. Watson hardly needed to spend any time describing the grammar itself; what he taught us to do in that fortnight was to introduce all English grammatical structures to the student (in an easily digestible order) through guided conversation which hardly ever made reference to grammatical terminology. Once you can do that, you have the best of both worlds. The student who "doesn't want to slave away at grammar" is not shown it, but he is dosed with it just the same. One who "insists on grammar" is fed with it, spoonful by spoonful, but he has to talk and listen to get it. The end result (with a cunning instructor) is the same. Watson was as cunning as they come.

His tactic was to half show you how to teach something, then make you come out to the front and do it. The other half had to come from your imagination, inspiration or simply powers of deduction based on the clues that Watson had provided. If you erred, or failed to observe principles he had been hammering home, then he would ridicule you without mercy. There were two German walk-outs and at least three or four by Watson when someone challenged his ideas too vigorously. The walk-outs served as coffee-breaks; at the end of two weeks we were all united in friendship and budding competence. Watson always won the argument – he was immovable as a stone wall, but invariably rational and **right.**

"Yes, Doktor Schmidt, I know you want to introduce "soul" in that way, but the student won't **understand** you."

He would then apply Schmidt's approach to the introduction of something relatively simple like "perhaps" in Guaraní or Nootka and we would all sit there gaping at him. Then he would introduce "sensibility" (the Watson Way) in East Greenlandic and everything would be as clear as an Arctic morning in spring. Good old Watson – now dead many a year. If he had made his career in the army, he would have been another Montgomery.

*   *   *   *   *

Paris Berlitz was more than just a school. It had occupied its building – Le Palais Berlitz – for many decades. It contained a cinema of the same name and of course Le Café Berlitz, which did a roaring trade resuscitating shattered Americans after two or three hours immersion in French. The school's strategic location on the *boulevards*, its large and variegated student body and its continuous record of instruction since the end of the 19th century lent it an old-world, cosmopolitan atmosphere which the introduction of "modern methods" entirely failed to dispel.

This venerable institution had its many legends and annals, which included the tantrums of famous film stars, scandalous romances among eminent figures of society, comings and goings of princes and princesses with their bodyguards, fabulous sums spent on lessons by American millionaires and a host of other minor excitements which seemed to occur every week. In the fortnight our training group spent there, we were not disappointed.

Berlitz, after a long period of agonizing, had finally invested in some language laboratory equipment. As the shape of the building did not lend itself to the creation of a large actual laboratory, Montfort had had installed, in the quieter back part of the school, half a dozen small, individual booths where students could don their earphones and listen to their tapes undisturbed. Each booth was curtained off to ensure privacy.

In a school the size of Paris one always needs a handyman; since the advent of electronic equipment it had become important that this person had the capability of keeping the lab in good shape and fixing broken machines when necessary. Luciano Stagnaro was such a man. A dark-skinned, gnarled Sicilian of middle age, he resembled a Mediterranean goat-herd more than an electrician, but he came cheap, was devoted to the school and prowled the dark corridors ten hours a day.

I have mentioned earlier the triangular shape of the establishment. One entered the school through a well-lit area which served as reception, waiting room and general rendezvous point for students and teachers finding each other before or between lessons. Departing students would often hang around here to discuss their experiences, pay their bills and briefly socialize. Classrooms were aligned along the sides of the triangle, the language lab booths being furthest from reception. To inspect the school, you went round the triangle, returning to your starting point in due course: there was no other way out. The cashier was strategically placed closest to the exit.

One morning as we underwent our training in one of the bigger classrooms, an intruder made his way into the school. This was not difficult, as in mid-morning the reception area was thronged, and his arrival went unnoticed. We did not learn much about him except that he was French, fairly well-dressed and was a sex pest. After some time he discovered the language booths, peered through the curtains and found a young, blonde Californian girl in deep concentration on her exercises. He tried to assault her. You can well imagine the effect of the student's screams as she struggled to free herself. Stagnaro (I believe the name means "pond-minder") heard them first, as he was not far from his precious booths. He ran to the scene, whipping open the curtains of each one till he found the intruder. The latter, after one look at Stagnaro's craggy weather-beaten features, abandoned his Californian prey, smashed his way past the hesitating Sicilian and ran pell-mell down one of the long corridors of the isosceles triangle. Stagnaro, recovering quickly, went off in hot pursuit screaming fearsome oaths in Corleone Sicilian.

The fugitive reached the reception area, which was packed with students and Berlitz staff. What this body of people saw was a well-dressed Frenchman, looking fearful in the extreme, being desperately chased by a mean-looking, stubbly-chinned, rampageous hobo screeching hysterically in a weird, cacophanous tongue. Two sizeable Americans, men of action as they were, quickly took in the scene and jumped on Stagnaro, pinning him to the floor. Other students piled in to help immobilize the Sicilian while a French student ran outside to find a *gendarme*. The sex maniac, given a moment's respite, was nevertheless unable to force his way through the thronged exit, so he ran into an adjacent office and jumped through the window, cutting himself seriously in the process. He then fled across the busy Boulevard des Italiens and disappeared down a side street.

After some frantic explanations on the part of the Berlitz office staff, the American Good Samaritans reluctantly released Stagnaro, by now frothing at the mouth and about to be arrested by the newly-arrived *gendarme*, who felt he had to start taking notes, instead of chasing the fugitive.

It appeared that the intruder had made good his escape, but it was not to be. When the police eventually initiated pursuit, their task was easy, as the badly-cut miscreant left a trail of blood right across the boulevard and down several side streets. As they followed the gory tracks the amount of blood increased until finally, after one kilometre, they came to a veritable pool of blood where the Frenchman had lain, now unconscious, for 20 minutes before being taken to hospital by an ambulance. Back at school the Americans took Stagnaro out for a couple of stiff drinks – he liked *grappa* – though he normally abstained till seven in the evening.

*   *   *   *   *

Before leaving Paris I had a formal meeting with Montfort and the company lawyer, Maître Denoyer, during which I signed various documents – a franchise contract and a *"cahier des charges"* (at twenty-five one will sign anything). This thick bundle, which I still keep in some bottom drawer, gave me exclusive authorization to use the Berlitz name in Finland for the following 5 years in activities relating to the teaching of languages and the sale of educational aids (books, records and wall charts) provided to me by Paris at a discounted price.

The founding capital, running costs and subsequent risks were my responsibilities. No financial help was available from the Société – all one got free from Paris was a send-off lunch. Montfort's lunches were good ones – so I had no complaints. After all, the profits, should they accrue, would be mine.

Chapter 5

Taking the Plunge

Setting up a business on one's own, in a foreign land and with limited resources, is a challenging and exhilarating experience for a young person, matched by few others in life. The exploration of a remote part of the earth, the conquest of a mountain peak, the breaking of a world record – all these bring their supreme thrill – but the variegated nature and changing complexity of business dealings over a protracted period are paralleled perhaps only by war.

War is a terrible, fascinating game which all known generations of men have taken to quite naturally, played with great energy and skill – only too often with dedication and enthusiasm. It may occasionally bring the worst out of a people, but not infrequently it brings out the best – history bears witness to countless examples of heroism, self-sacrifice, endurance, camaraderie, stoicism in defeat, generosity in victory and powers of recuperation after near-annihilation.

War, it seems to me, might be all right, were it not for two nasty side-effects: killing and suffering. As the second is largely a result of the first, if we could find a substitute for killing, we should make a lot of progress. Civilized society continues to experiment with possible substitutes, where a brush with danger or near-death might encourage young men with superfluous aggressive instincts to leave it at that. Such pursuits are boxing, karate, lion-taming, motor-car racing and crossing the road in Istanbul.

For me, starting a business with your own money beats them all. Business reflects war (or is it the other way round?) There are risks to be taken, resources to be managed and utilized, attacks to be planned and launched, "enemies" to be out-manoeuvred. As the chairman of Olivetti said when contemplating the formation of the EC, "European companies are marching off to war – a war that will have its dead and wounded; a war from which not everyone will come back a winner." I agree with this, but isn't it much better than a real war with spears, bullets, and bombs? I am often irritated when people moan about the Japanese or the Germans taking over the world through their economic might. They had far more reason to squeal when there were real armies in the field. Let's get out there and compete, like the Koreans, Taiwanese, Dutch and Italians have done. Business is a series of many battles, some of which are lost, some won, a few drawn. One can lose many battles, before winning the last one which wins the war and, it is hoped, the spoils of victory. It does not do you any harm, however, to win the first battle, as I was soon to discover.

*　　*　　*　　*　　*

In the autumn of 1955 Finland was a nation still in its infancy. Independence from Russia had been achieved in 1917 but in the 38 years of its existence the country had suffered the enormous setback of 5 years of warfare, during which the mighty Soviet Union had been the principal adversary. But the intricacies of politics had led to Finland being at war with virtually everybody else including most of the Allies and its erstwhile comrade in arms, the German Reich. Heads, however, were still held high. Apart from London, Helsinki was the only capital among western belligerent powers not to suffer a foreign occupation; war reparations had been paid off; the shattered parts of Helsinki had been re-built; 400.000 Karelians had been absorbed from now-Soviet Karelia. Though many limbless and maimed ex-soldiers were still to be seen, the new generation of Finns was beginning to look to the future offered to them by peace – a future of unwonted travel, foreign experience, cultural diversity, universal popularity and, it would be hoped, increased prosperity.

Economically, Finland was in a weak position. The long war had sapped her manpower, materials and financial reserves. Reparations had delayed recovery and the obligation to create new industries to service the payments had been costly and frequently irrational. Of the four Nordic countries, her lot had been the least fortunate. Norway and Denmark benefited from Marshall Aid and pre-war friendships. Sweden, the only neutral, had strengthened her industry and economy during the war years and had become very much the Big Brother (though not in the sinister sense) of the Nordic family. Finns and Norwegians resented to some extent this Swedish pre-eminence. As far as Finland was concerned, another Big Brother to the east had to be placated and managed regularly, thereby delaying the benefits that increased trade contacts with the West would bring.

It was, nevertheless, to the West that Finland turned her face and it was this eagerness of the Finns to intermingle with peoples west and south of Sweden, to participate in that thrilling world which vibrated and hummed west of the Oder-Neisse line, to plunge their own Finnish originality and genius into that sea of excitement uniting Europe and the United States, that I counted on to facilitate my début in business. Finns wanted to learn everybody else's language and culture at once – French, Spanish, Italian, German (not Russian) – but they sensed that the key which fitted most locks was that strange, hybrid, easy-but-difficult, rambling, undisciplined tongue which had been exuberantly manufactured in ever-increasing richness since the turn of the century by the men-in-the-street, journalists, film-makers and play-wrights, novelists and orators of the British Isles and their flamboyant cousins in North America.

*   *   *   *   *

The economic and political situation in Finland imposed certain formalities and restrictions on the importation of foreign capital and labour in the area of education. These formalities, while reasonable enough, could delay the start of a business by several months. One could, however, import a car without much difficulty. Accordingly I bought a Volkswagen in Cologne and subsequently sold it to Kaj Wallen in Helsinki, paying the duty. We therefore used Finnish money to start the Finnish company. Teachers I recruited from the limited availability in Finland and trained them there. I was in immediate need, however, of experienced aides, so I chose my Heads of Department in Germany and took them with me. For French, I selected Claude Hubert, a volatile Belgian, who was one of the best teachers in the Cologne Berlitz School. For German I chose Reinhold Dey, an economist and former student of mine from Mönchen-Gladbach, who knew the Method well by dint of having been on the receiving end. They were both in their late twenties and anxious to seek excitement and fortune in a far-off land. One fine day in September, Dey and I drove the Volkswagen across Germany and Denmark and took the steamer to Helsinki. It was the perfect trip with sunny weather, convivial on-board atmosphere and time for thought as our ship skimmed the calm, grape-gin-coloured waters of the southern Baltic. It was Dey's first time out of Germany and he much admired the blonde Scandinavian girls – particularly one who sat in the prow of the boat during the daylight hours of the voyage. She was so good-looking and remote in manner that he never plucked up the courage to speak to her, but he looked quite a lot.

Our vessel docked in Helsinki at 9 a.m. in beautiful sunshine. Entry by sea from the south is inevitably spectacular in good weather and as we glided past Suomenlinna fortress I heard Dey's gasp of admiration as the market-place, Suurkirkko and Uspenski Cathedral revealed themselves. A smiling curly-haired Swede-Finn friend of mine, Robert Ehrnrooth, waved from the quay in greeting. Robert owned a small plastics business and as we shook hands he exclaimed "Welcome to the world of private enterprise." When we had extracted our precious VW from the bowels of the ship, we went with him to Fazers for coffee. Robert had promised, on my previous visit, to collect the 20 students I felt I needed to cover basic expenses at the start. He beamed as he told me he already had 12. He knew from experience how important a little nucleus can be. We were joined in the next couple of hours by Pekka Lakkonen, Martti Karttunen and Kaj Wallen, who drove down from the farm. The news was nearly all good: the ads had brought in 1500 enquiries on coupon, the partitioning had started, the brochures had arrived and we had been given a sexy telephone number: 66 66 96, which rang most of the day. The bad news was that the carpenter was off sick, the temporary secretary had collapsed and that all enquiries were going unattended.

Tidings of such chaos made me dash over to Helsingin Sanomat and place another ad for an efficient secretary/receptionist **IMMEDIATELY**. My visceral tuggings would have been so much less savage had I known that a large number of businesses operate in this way most of the time. The God of Finland smiled on me and the next morning the first applicant for the job strode imperiously, yet elegantly into the school – the tall, flaxen-haired, green-eyed beauty whom Dey had so admired in the bows of our ship. Her name was Sinikka Sarkama, she was qualified in secretarial skills, accounting and languages. She had just returned from one year in England – her English was perfect – and she was looking for a position where she could use it. The telephone rang ten times during the time it took to interview her. She got the job. After a quick sandwich, Sinikka addressed envelopes to those people who had enquired by coupon; I folded brochures and stuffed them into the envelopes, Dey put on stamps and ran out and mailed them. Whenever the phone rang, Sarkama picked up the receiver and answered questions about our organisation, which she had never heard of before reading the advertisement that morning. The three of us worked until midnight, when we ran out of stamps. By ten o'clock the next evening we had answered all the enquiries. Dey's tongue was like leather – he insisted on licking all the stamps. I told him he was lucky it was not Italy, where stamps tasted like mothballs, or Spain, where they did not stick to the envelopes.

On the third day, matters became more complicated, as the sending out of our brochures brought large numbers of people into the school. This not only interfered with our answering the phone, but these would-be students wanted to see our books, which were still on the way from Paris, our teachers, most of whom had not yet been appointed, and our classrooms most of which had not been built. Sarkama's cool efficiency and Dey's obvious German-ness in his fine leather coat lent us a certain amount of credibility, but it was a difficult month. Eventually the carpenter was resuscitated, partitions were completed, new teachers were trained, furniture and carpets were installed, students were tested and divided into groups, schedules were established and pinned up on the wall. We opened in grand style on the 26th of October 1955 with 1600 students enrolled. They had all paid, by the way – one month's fees up front. The fees were 1600 (old) finnmarks per month for two hours a week and 2400 fmk a month for four hours a week. This meant we had 3 million fmk in the bank. The only people we had to pay were Sarkama (40.000) Dey for licking the stamps and the carpenter. Printers, newspapers, furniture suppliers gave us several weeks' credit and electricity and phone bills did not come till the end of the following month. We had a normal teacher payroll at the end of November, but by that time our students had paid another 3 million on November 26th. By Christmas we had retained earnings of over 5 million (about £10.000 at the official exchange rate), which, although appearing insignificant today, represented a tidy sum in 1955. We did not, of course, maintain this level of profitability over the long haul, as payment of start-up costs, accountants and lawyers took their toll, but the Helsinki Berlitz School – the first of over 90 institutions that I was to found – proved to be the fastest-growing of them all, eventually reaching a peak of 4000 enrolments in one year, thereby laying the basis for the establishment of further schools in other Finnish cities.

*   *   *   *   *

I spent the next 3 years in Finland, setting up schools in Tampere, Kotka, Lahti and Turku, besides organising various courses in the Finnish countryside. As I have devoted a previous chapter to Finland, I will not describe these operations in detail – I have already chronicled my deep admiration and affection for the Finnish people; the many encounters and experiences which ensued as a result of our teacher-student relationship did nothing to diminish my regard for Finnish determination, originality and fidelity. There were amusing moments, minor setbacks, unusual situations, some competition, intriguing characters and personalities. Claude Hubert, the strong-willed temperamental Belgian, showed up on time and taught French with flair to Finns at all levels. Dey was a reliable and competent colleague, never failing to appear for his lessons in the thickest of snowstorms. The itinerant language teachers of Helsinki gradually joined our fold – Franco Moccia, a handsome, melancholic Napolitan; Bertolo Amodeo from Venice; Pedro Calvo, an anti-Franco Spaniard from Palencia; Heinz Hammer, as Bavarian as they come, from Garmisch; Valentina Krugloff from Tsarist St Petersburg; Luciana Escobedo from Buenos Aires, bilingual in Spanish and Italian.

Among the most eccentric, naturally were the English, –– Cherrington, an ex-commando from the war in Malaysia, who used to jump out of old Finnish planes at Malmi airport on Saturday afternoons with even older parachutes. I used to go with him to see if he survived for his Monday lessons. The other English teachers were Mrs Wadsworth, a lovely old lady from Oregon who delivered her lesson like a sermon; James B. Patterson from Vancouver British Columbia, an inquisitive person who taught mainly through asking questions, which, (knew he it or not) was sound pedagogy, and finally David Alexander Willey from Manchester, who lived up to the standard I expect from fellow Lancastrians. It was, all in all, a good staff and we ploughed through 1955 and 1956 with this combination of talent from various countries. In December 1955, Anna Candiago, my former colleague from Mönchen-Gladbach, tired of diplomatic duties in Rome, came out to join us. She spoke Italian, French and English all fluently and she was possessed of a

Latin vitality and extroverted charm seldom seen above 60 degrees North. One could say Finns liked her.

Many of our students, too, live in my memory. One spring morning in 1956 we had two of the country's leading singers – baritone Matti Lehtinen and tenor Veikko Tyrväinen studying German and Italian in separate classrooms. As they were studying pronunciation, Lehtinen began to sing – his voice rose from an experimental hum to a throaty full rendering. Tyrväinen, hearing him, responded with equal volume from his classroom – I think they both finished up in operatic Italian. All lessons stopped, the students and teachers spilled out into the corridor – finally the two singers emerged, still singing, and advanced down the corridor to meet in full crescendo.

Foreign Minister Johannes Virolainen also came occasionally – I used to help him with speeches he had to make in front of the United Nations. He was a hard-working, humble student, who always did his homework on time, in spite of his many commitments. It was no surprise to me when this practical, intelligent man later became a long-standing Prime Minister. Other busy people, who worked hard at their English were Timo Sarpaneva – the country's leading designer – Väinö Leskinen, Minister of Commerce and Industry and Pirkko Mannola, then Miss Finland and later film star and stage actress. The luminaries from the business community are too numerous to mention – and many studied incognito – at one time we seemed to be teaching all the top officials of the Bank of Finland. The army also sent officers in large numbers – most of them spoke only German – I remember them as being the most humorous, teasing and convivial of our students.

The Russians, too, came to study English and Finnish. I remember the cultural attaché in Helsinki, Oleg Pirsikov – a charming character, who knew 136 different uses of "would" and "should" and ended every lesson inviting me to the Soviet Union. Sergei Makulov – the KGB man – was far less sophisticated, though he possessed a certain engaging jocularity. He used to begin every lesson by taking his revolver out of his shoulder-holster and putting it on the table next to the dictionary. Sometimes I had to tell him to point the barrel away from me. His lesson was usually followed by that of a certain Mr Uitto, a former Finnish high jump champion, who disliked Russians. Makulov tended to run over his lesson time (why go back to the embassy?) and Uitto used to rap on the door one minute after time was up. They hated each other. Uitto often appeared ready to hit the Russian. I told him about the gun, but he didn't give a damn.

Finland's two national languages – Finnish and Swedish – were in great demand. Not only the Russians, but British, German and other diplomats studied Finnish. There existed no Berlitz manual in this language, so it fell to my lot to write one with a Helsinki professor, Dr. Kajava. Our book was later used by Finnish universities. Swedish was required by the Finns themselves.

Though not a world language, Swedish can be understood in all three Scandinavian countries and in many coastal towns in Finland and is therefore a useful Nordic *lingua franca*. Kaj Wallen, my partner, eventually sold Gammelgård, took degrees in languages and became a first class teacher of Swedish. Our Finnish staff included well-known writers such as Pentti Holoppa and Olli-Matti Ronimus.

The Finns' appetite for language instruction seemed insatiable. Officially we opened the school every morning at 9.15, but many businessmen took lessons at 8.30 and some as early as 7 a.m. Reinhold Dey found nothing unreasonable about tramping to work through deep snow to work in pitch darkness, but Hubert, new to Nordic habits, was a reluctant performer before 9 o'clock. In the evening our largest classes were from 6 to 8 and 8 to 10 p.m. All our teachers of English, German, French and Swedish were busy during these hours. Everybody paid cash in those days, so Sarkama counted the takings and balanced the books between 10 and 11 p.m. The staff used to eat sandwiches in the teachers'kitchen at 8 o'clock. At 11 Sarkama, Patterson and I used to have pea-soup or *lihakeitto* at the railway station. The day's takings would be in my briefcase, which we took turns to watch.

People do not seem to work such long hours these days. Dey and I, used to German working habits, found little unusual about it. The Canadian Patterson, a businessman at heart, was fascinated by the rapid development of the operation and lived in the school. Sarkama, beautiful creature that she was, had that physical and mental stamina that the Finns call *sisu* – she never flagged. Language teaching is very much a people business and I suppose we were all stimulated by the contact with over a thousand people a week. Our students, too, showed amazing durability. After a normal day's work, some of them took 2 hours English and two hours German, or vice versa. One old lady – a fishmonger named Hyöti – began learning English at the age of 80 and was in good command of the language at 83.

*   *   *   *   *

In the winter of 1956 there was a general strike in Finland and most forms of transport ceased to function. This did not do our business any good, as many students were unable to attend classes. Some of our teachers lived a long way from the school. (I was 5 km away in Lauttasaari) and it was hard to get to work on time, particularly as the temperature had dropped to -20 degrees on most days. Our Mediterranean teachers suffered particularly. One night when a howling wind caused the thermometer to descend to -30 degrees C, seven of us were unable to leave the school at 10 p.m., as our clothing was simply inadequate. We eventually left around 2 a.m. when the wind had dropped. I don't recall ever being so cold in Helsinki before or since. Kaj told stories of Lotila in Pukaro giving all his bus drivers one share each in the bus company during the strike so they could continue driving as "owners". The day the strike finished, he took the shares back.

*   *   *   *   *

In the summer of 1956 Helsinki Finns bolted the capital, as they usually do, and stared happily into their lakes for two months. A handful of students continued to study during the summer, but we were all able to take holidays ourselves, either in Finland or abroad. I spent a couple of weeks at the sports training centre in Vierumäki, near Lahti, running in the forest and playing a little football and table tennis. During lunch on the first day I found myself sitting next to a small, wiry, melancholic-looking foreigner with pale hollow cheeks and a black moustache. He spoke only French, so I helped him with the menu, feeling that I had met him somewhere before. He was in fact Alain Mimoun, the silver medallist in both the 5000m and 10.000m at the Helsinki Olympic Games. He was training for the 1956 Olympics held in Melbourne, where he was to compete in the marathon.

This brooding but likeable and modest athlete became my table companion for the next fortnight and I was able to study his training and personal habits. He had no coach with him, but disciplined himself severely, running at varying speeds for 4-6 hours a day. He ate very little, and sensibly, saying that the blandness of Finnish food suited him. Every day he dragged me out to the forest nearby where he had discovered a cold spring. He was convinced that Finnish water was the purest in the world and he made two or three visits daily to the spring, each time drinking a litre or more from his cupped hands. He exhorted me to do the same and I obeyed him, though I have never liked water from any source whatsoever. On some days he would run a 5000m on the Vierumäki track and invited me to run behind him. I could never stay for more than 2 laps. He was 36 years old at the time and went on to win the Gold Medal at the Melbourne Olympics. There were a couple of hundred Finns on various courses at Vierumäki at the time we were there. They all knew who Mimoun was, but they appeared to ignore him completely, not wishing to intrude upon his privacy. In most other countries he would have been constantly pestered by autograph hunters, journalists and other admirers.

*   *   *   *   *

In the autumn of 1956, I opened a second school in the city of Tampere, 200 km northwest of Helsinki. Tampere, sometimes referred to as Finland's Manchester because of its many chimneys, was the second largest city in the country with about 120.000 inhabitants. It is the capital of Häme – that Finnish region notorious for its reticence ("even other Finns think they are quiet"). I had reserved a 10 classroom space in the new Stockmann building, but that was still under construction in the autumn, so we functioned for the first year in a beautiful all-wooden house I rented in Palomäentie on Pyyniki ridge. It was big enough for our purposes and had accommodation for four teachers as well.

Sinikka Sarkama, Anna Candiago and Heinz Hammer transferred to Tampere and two new teachers were imported from England to complete the staff. It was soon apparent that teaching in Tampere was quite different from Helsinki. There had been virtually no language teaching in the area since the war, so most of the 600 students we enrolled understood some German but were beginners in English. Furthermore the population of the surrounding market towns and villages in the Häme region, completely deprived of local language instruction, came to us in Tampere once or twice a week. In the days before television, many of these rustic *Hämäläisiä* had never heard a word of English, certainly never seen an English person. At least seventy per cent of our students were in English beginner classes – it was a hard slog for our teachers. For a beginner to make quick progress, he really needs access to a teacher several times a week, at least two hours each time – then there is no backsliding. Many of our students from outlying districts were not getting enough exposure. Nevertheless, some of these Häme classes continued for years – Finns don't give up easily.

It was around this time that I made the acquaintance of a very fine Hämäläinen – a certain Erkki Mattila from Kangasala. He possessed all the Häme characteristics – shyness, taciturnity, a closed, enigmatic exterior concealing warm, deep feelings and an incredibly dry sense of humour. His uncompromising external pragmatism and sheer common sense stood him in good stead in business and he ultimately became Managing Director of Kauko-Merkinat, one of Finland's two biggest import-export companies. Erkki had a multitude of hidden talents – he was a good skier, an even better painter in watercolour and quietly mastered 6 languages without telling anybody about it. Taciturn in Finnish, he was more talkative in Swedish, English and french. Very much a "doer" he had a healthy disregard for people who perorated – especially marketing consultants who came to analyse projects he was working on. As warehousing was an important factor in the import / export business, one such consultant did a year's "research" on best methods of warehousing. What were the conclusions, I asked Mattila. "He concluded (after 12 months) that the heaviest goods should be kept nearest the door," replied Erkki with a straight face.

*   *   *   *   *

In 1957 and 1958 we opened further schools in Kotka, Lahti and Turku. All these towns supported our organisation readily and we established a virtual monopoly in each area. Our credit was such that in one instance – Kotka – I was in danger of opening a school with no capital at all. A friendly landlord offered us partitioned space with the rent payable in arrears. Furniture, carpets and curtains had been supplied on 60 days' credit and books and stationery had been shipped in from Helsinki. *Kotkan Sanomat* would send their bill for advertising in due course. We were ready to open on the first Monday of October and by six o'clock on the previous Friday I had not spent a penny on the venture. Suddenly there was a sharp knock on the door and a young man strode in waving an unpaid bill and demanding prompt settlement. It was the deposit on the new school telephone -18.000 fmk or about £20.

Roger Montfort honoured us with a visit once – he knew little or nothing about Finland and, as a gourmet Frenchman, found the rarity of *haute cuisine* and fine wines somewhat distressing. He was surprised at the size of the market, as the only other Berlitz school of note in Scandinavia was Copenhagen. Stockholm and Malmö had been tiny dead-end schools for years and in Norway there was nothing at all, Oslo having collapsed years earlier. It was during Montfort's brief visit that we decided I would be given a franchise for Portugal, but that I would scout Norway out for him first.

Chapter 6

Fjords and Fells

Norway was a country unknown to me. I had only ever met one Norwegian, a 30-year-old printing ink salesman based temporarily in Helsinki. His name was Terje Riise – he was 6 feet 6 inches tall and he was studying Spanish with us.

Riise advised me against opening up a school in Norway. Firstly, he said, I would never find space in Oslo for an office. Secondly, even if I did, I would never make any money because of the *fri-undervisning* – the free evening school education provided by the state. Thirdly, if I did make money, the state would take nearly all of it away in taxes. He was right on all three counts. Unfortunately I did not take his advice; instead I persisted with the Norwegian venture.

After two winters in Finland, Anna Candiago was ready to try a warmer climate, though Oslo turned out to be colder than Helsinki on days when the winds whistled down the *Karls Johans gade.*. She went on ahead to look for premises, but fortunately for her she was unable to find any. The renting situation at that time in Oslo had to be seen to be believed. Space was at a premium and even with ready cash you could not secure even a hundred square metres. The method of seeking space was as follows: you first found a new building under construction. There you had no chance, as it would have been booked by another firm months or even years in advance. If, however, you were able to find out the name of the firm going into that building, (let's call it Company A) you could visit them and see what was going to happen to their old office. Invariably this would have been reserved by Company B. When you visited Company B, they would tell you that their space had been booked by Company C, which you also could approach. If you persisted in this game for a few weeks you might find that Company L, M or N had not finalized their arrangements with an incoming tenant, this giving you a chance to compete with the offer. If you were lucky, Company R, S or T might have no incoming tenant, though in these cases the rooms would usually be unattractive. In any case you faced a time lag of several months before the first new building was completed and the game of musical chairs began.

In these circumstances we decided to forget about Oslo and see how things looked in the country's second biggest city, Bergen. Bergen was a bit bigger than Tampere – it was a bit wetter, too. Statistics tell me that it rains 290 days a year in Bergen, but I consider that to be a conservative estimate. At all events Candiago charmed a hotel owner in Bergen who was instrumental in finding us 150 sq. m. space in the building next to his hotel. This was the Nordenfjelske Byggning, located right next to where the boats left for Newcastle. We took the space immediately -for better or for worse – in fact the rent was very reasonable. We set up the school in much the same manner as we had done in Tampere, transferring books and teachers – in this instance it was Manchester's David Willey – as Head of English – and we painted the classroom doors orange or yellow to combat the grey skies without.

The first problem we had was to find a name for the school. Berlitz was OK, but what was Norwegian for "School of Languages?" Educated Norwegians swore on their mother's bible that the correct version was:-

(i)   *Sproginstitut*
(ii)   *Språkinstitut*
(iii)   *Sproginstitutt*
(iv)   *Språkinstitutt*

I am not kidding you, or trying to make this chapter any more ridiculous than it already is. I never even discussed it with Montfort, who thinks all such matters are decided by the *Académie Française.* The problem with the Norwegian language, is that there isn't one. that is to say that there isn't **one,** there are four. Now, in most countries you have an official language, which is diluted, or tweaked, in various areas – north, south, east and west, – by different dialectal forces of varying importance. Thus we have northern and southern English, Castilian and Andaluz, Prussian and Bavarian, Yankee and Southern and so on. In Norway, however, they don't arrange things like that. Firstly they have *Riksmål* which is spoken in the **cities.** Secondly they have *Landsmål* which is spoken in **country districts.** This means that people in Oslo, in the south, speak in a very similar manner to the inhabitants of the city of Narvik, nearly a thousand kilometres to the north. Persons who happen to live in a village just outside Oslo, or just outside Narvik, all speak a similar tongue – *Landsmål–* in spite of the distance between them.

All this is misleading enough, but in 1957-8 Norway was in the throes of a multilingual, multicultural and social controversy where *Bokmål (*the written language) and *Nynorsk* (modern Norwegian) had entered the fray. People had strong feelings about these things. There was no way we could choose a name for our school without losing three-quarters of our friends (and we didn't have many).

The students came in any case. Bergenske people had close links with England and, as former members of the Hanseatic League, were internationally-minded. They cared little for Oslo people or other Norwegians and it was easy to see why: before the advent of the railways it had been virtually impossible to reach Oslo in winter whereas the sea links to Gothenburg, Copenhagen, Hamburg, Danzig, Lübeck and particularly north-eastern England were always open and offering lucrative trading opportunities.

It is said that the fishermen of Bergen and Newcastle understand each others' dialects. I cannot comment as I am unable to understand either.

I spent about three months in Bergen, which I consider an extremely beautiful city. I cannot understand how anyone – given nearly 300 days of annual downpour – can live there. The fjord is magnificent, the drier hinterland majestic, but life in town was puddles, puddles, puddles. A local shoe factory manufactures footwear with a special glaze or plastic veneer, which prevents your shoes deteriorating in the constant wet. You had better buy some, for your Italian ones won't last long. Willey, who was born in Manchester, and liked wellingtons and duffle-coats, weathered well in Bergen, but he was the only one of our staff who did.

The students were lovely – painstaking, honest and friendly as Norwegians usually are. Only one gave me trouble – he could not pronounce anything correctly. After 2 months I asked the secretary – a Norwegian named Wenche Garmann – what was the matter with him.

"He's stone deaf" she replied. When I said she might have warned me, she just shrugged. Norwegian humour, I supposed.

Riise had warned me back in Helsinki, "Don't tell jokes about Norway to the Norwegians, they just don't understand them." He was right as usual – Riise is as intelligent as they come. I tried only one joke in Norway – it was a Finnish one. It goes like this: –

A Swede, Dane and a Norwegian are riding a tricycle up a hill in Austria. It was very hard work. When they reached the top the (Socialist) Swede said "Together we managed it." The (practical) Dane said "If we had picked the bike up and carried it, it would have been a lot easier." "Maybe," said the Norwegian, "but if I had not stood on the brake the whole time we should have slid backwards."

When I told this story to a Norwegian he asked "But why should the Norwegian brake when they were going uphill?"

If you had substituted 'Irishman' for Norwegian he would have laughed his head off.

*   *   *   *   *

If I have said earlier that Norway at that time had 4 languages, I have forgotten to tell you about the fifth, which was the speech of Bergen itself. With its Parisian 'r' and lack of double tones, it is quite unlike the Norwegian of Oslo and sounds more like the rough Swedish spoken in Skåne. I had some trouble adapting my knowledge of Scandinavian languages to this dialect, but after a while I was satisfied I could give a fair rendering of it. The day came, about 6 weeks after we had been teaching, when we had to give the inaugural party, during which I would address the good people of Bergen. We eventually mustered about one hundred citizens, including the Mayor and some luminaries from the Chamber of Commerce. After some wining and dining I delivered a ten-minute speech in my best Bergenske Norwegian. It must have been an unusual event for them, for they listened attentively. I was gratified by the round of applause which greeted the end of my address, until the Mayor stepped forward and congratulated me on my "excellent Swedish".

*   *   *   *   *

Life in Bergen was pleasant enough, but hardly exciting. Kirk Douglas and Tony Curtis came to stay at the Slottsgården Hotel for a couple of months while they made the film "The Vikings". Willey locked himself in the school walk-in safe one evening (we used it for book storage) and he had to spend the night there, sleeping on one of the shelves. Candiago was burgled, losing most of her clothes and had the novel experience of chasing a Norwegian prostitute wearing her best dress along the *Bryggen*. (She caught her as the dress was too tight to run fast in). Otherwise life was uneventful with cod every day for lunch and *lapskaus* for supper. Willey and I skied at weekends – if you took a bus thirty miles inland the climate changed completely. Bergen is on a latitude level with the Shetlands and is constantly buffeted by strong Atlantic winds in winter. More often than not planes coming from the east could not land there and had to put down in Stavanger until the storms abated. It always paid to have a good book to while away the hours of waiting in Stavanger airport.

By the summer the school was well established with three or four hundred students and five teachers. Willey and I were planning a tour of the United States; Anna Candiago stayed on for another six months, at which time we handed over the management to Wenche Garmann who, two years later, bought the school from me. It continued in business for many years, paying its taxes, recruiting new teachers each year as the rain drove the old ones away. As far as I know it is still in existence, though it is no longer a Berlitz School.

Chapter 7

USA – Languages and Business

In the late spring of 1957 I contacted the management of the Berlitz Schools of North America Inc. with a view to touring a selected number of schools in their quite sizeable chain. I received a warm response from both Robert Strumpen-Darrie, the then President and Charles Berlitz, the grandson of the founder. As it was my intention to buy a car in New York and drive round the edges of the United States in a clockwise direction, Strumpen-Darrie very kindly scheduled visits for me at the schools located in New York, Philadelphia, Baltimore, Washington, Miami, New Orleans, Houston, Los Angeles, San Francisco, Seattle, Chicago, Detroit and Boston.

We were still in the days when one could enhance the thrill of one's introduction to the American continent by making a five-day Transatlantic crossing on one of the dozen or so luxury liners which left French, British and other European ports several times a week bound for New York. David Willey and I embarked in Le Havre on board the *"Flandre"*, a popular and well-used French vessel somewhat smaller and less glamorous than the "Queen Mary" but with a definite edge in succulent cooking, full-bodied reds and crispy bread. Our crossing was uneventful, except inasmuch as we enjoyed to the full the epicurean, yet strictly organized routines of liner life, putting our watches on one hour each day at midnight, doing one's two mile walk round the upper decks, fighting for the best deck chairs, trying one's hand at deck tennis and clay pigeon shooting, stuffing oneself at mealtimes, surveying the half-empty dining-room on rough days, betting furiously on the evening "horse races", looking over the shoulders of the expert bridge players, scrutinizing our wads of crispy, new dollars – all coloured green whatever the amount, marvelling at the cheapness of the duty-free whisky and ordering doubles, conversing interminably with Americans of our age who, returning from Europe, had the advantage of comparing our two continents, generally smoking, drinking, and dancing our way to comforting exhaustion sometime around two or three in the morning.

Many of the waiters and stewards, *d'un certain age*, had seen it all thousands of times before – they were laid back and cynical at the same time, doing all the little things they could to facilitate our enjoyment just as long as we remembered that the going rate tip was $3 per man on disembarkation in New York. We must have seemed so naive, predictable, probably boring to these gentlemen, who no doubt would have welcomed bed-time at twelve. But the well-worn routine had hidden added value for us, for, though we were unaware of it at the time, we were catching the tail-end of a social era – five swinging decades of flappers, jazz, Charleston, Louis Armstrong, Mrs Simpson, Princes of Wales, Blue Ribands, white ties, champagne breakfasts, Fords, Rockefellers, Roosevelts, two World Wars, Glenn Miller, Ted Heath and Joe Loss, Cary Grant and Bob Hope, black jack, roulette and caviare on toast. And no jet lag, either.

The experience was capped by the unparalleled sight of the Empire State Building rising out of a crimson ocean at 6 a.m. New York time. It was soon joined by dozens of smaller, though hardly less imposing structures and soon the familiar Statue of Liberty – gift of the French nation – welcomed us and our cameras to the Land of the Free. On shore, everything was strangely familiar. The yellow cabs, predatory cab drivers, soaring sky-scrapers, steaming streets, side-walk diners, Irish cops, ubiquitous shoe-shine boys and nasal tones of New York have been screened for decades in every cinema in Europe, particularly England. It is all there to greet you, right down to Gene Krupa playing in person on 42nd Street at $10 per admission. In Harry's Bar you look around the dark corners to see if Bogart or Hemingway are in tonight.

Instead of these celebrated Americans, we met up with the other members of our party, who had arrived in America by different means: my old school friend Bob Bradley, escaping from his construction company, and two of our teachers, Warwick Rathgen from New Zealand and Jean-Paul Schilling from French Switzerland, all eventually made the rendez-vous. We had three months before us to purchase an automobile, buy a few shirts and tour the States "from coast to coast, from the Lakes to the Gulf." It was an exhilarating prospect.

* * * * *

During the next few days we ascended skyscrapers, flipped through museums and art galleries and walked round Brooklyn, Broadway, Greenwich Village and Central Park. New York invariably makes a big impact on the first-time visitor: it is all you expect it to be, only more so. My personal touring was interspersed with daily visits to Berlitz, where I was engaged in a lively exchange of views with my American colleagues. Strumpen-Darrie, the President, was accessible at any time, an open-door, feet-on-the-desk American CEO with an endless barrage of questions about Berlitz operations in Europe and an inexhaustible supply of statistics and details of his own company's activities. The US schools, unlike the European ones, were all company-owned, as the franchise system had been discontinued several years earlier. Strumpen-Darrie's father, Jacques, had welded the language institutes into a cohesive, strictly-monitored organisation. At the time of my visit, Robert Strumpen-Darrie controlled 53 schools the length and breadth of the nation.

They were very different from the Berlitz schools in Europe. Most of the European directors, like old M.D. Berlitz himself, were genteel, often absent-minded linguists whose schools constituted an integral part of their lives. It was indeed a life-style in itself. The Berlitz director in Bologna or Berlin had been around for years, his father and mother for a generation before that. Several government ministers. perhaps a prince or two, had studied French, Italian or Russian under his tutelage and the local barons of industry entrusted to him their fourteen-year-old sons. His wife gave teas for ladies of society; if the school made money, they perhaps owned a modest villa in Antibes or Benidorm (then unspoiled) and once every summer a fleet of hired coaches would take the entire body of students out to a splendid picnic in the Vienna woods, the Tuscan hills or the Bois de Vincennes. Some of these men had written books, which did not sell very well, and more than one had published collections of poems. Every four years this gracefully ageing generation celebrated another *étape* of Berlitz existence at the *Congrès*, to which they flocked in new clothes and old cars – many Rovers and Citroens, not a few stately Mercedes and Lancias and at least one black and yellow Rolls Royce.

In the United States the Berlitz organisation was a well-oiled machine that made money. This is not to say that it did not adhere faithfully to the worthy principles that had served as a basis for world-wide success. In many respects Berlitz teaching in America was more thorough, conscientiously applied and certainly more rigorously monitored than was instruction in Europe. The difference was that in the US everything was on a strict business basis, as opposed to the European style of pursuing a life's hobby, and hopefully getting paid for it.

In Europe one discussed the student's wishes and needs, the twists and idiosyncrasies of the target language, a mutually convenient time-table and selection of teachers, a suitable break in instruction to accommodate holidays and family weddings – rarely did one talk about money or dates for payment. One sent a bill, after a decent interval, to the company, the parent, the ministry or the Palace. In America it was cash up front, as much of it as possible, please. One did not sell lessons 20 or 30 at a time, one sold them in hundreds, maybe a thousand, if Chinese or Tibetan was required. I cannot sell you 50 lessons, madam, you have to buy two hundred – that way you make a commitment to learn the language. If you have paid for these lessons in advance, you will take them and you will learn. We cannot afford failures, Madam, we have a reputation to protect.

In every American Berlitz school the director was the chief salesman, and sell he did. The most important piece of equipment on his desk, along with his telephone, was a small manual typewriter in which was always inserted, for the duration of one month, the same piece of paper. This was the famous Cash Report – fifty-three of them sitting round the nation, all up-to-date on money taken that month. Strumpen-Darrie, on phoning a school, would expect the figure to be given to him in seconds – it invariably was. On the day I first met him he genially informed me that his company had taken $3,220,000 by eleven o'clock that morning and that that represented an increase of 17% over the corresponding figure for 1956. He was mildly surprised when I could not whip out exact statistics for the Finnish and Norwegian schools, let alone the turnover for all of Europe. Strumpen-Darrie, who generally wore a suit, never went anywhere without a single sheet of A4 paper which he carried folded in his inside pocket. It was the current Berlitz "league table" which ranked the 53 schools according to revenue year-to-date, showing income, increase or decrease on the previous year and change in ranking achieved the previous month. All school directors received a copy of this shortly after month end – they would rip open the envelope in the back room and gloat or brood over the figures according to whether they had passed a rival or slipped further down the ladder. Those in the top six, or a director who was climbing rapidly, would rush to the telephone and call each other, sharing the current euphoria. At directors' meetings they would form their élite little clique and dine out together. Those directors in disgrace in the bottom six hastened to phone clients on the following days, though they also had their own bleak dinner clique at sales conferences.

Those directors who dramatically improved the fortunes of their school were rewarded by being assigned to a school in a bigger city. If you doubled the take in Detroit, you were in line for Boston. If you did well there you might get Chicago or L.A. Such a promotion usually involved a shuffle of four or five people, so that every year or so a game of Berlitz musical chairs took place. If you were stuck at the bottom of the table, this game did not concern you – you were in Cincinnati for life.

Like the European Directors, those in the United States were a motley bunch. Few had English as their mother tongue, only two had English-sounding names. There were several supple, flexible Italians, the same number of hard-working Germans, various Hispanics of Cuban or Puerto Rican extraction, a couple of sharp North Africans and one Japanese-American. But the majority were Frenchmen who had emigrated to the United States. In a sense they were maintaining the Berlitz tradition and following in old M.D.'s footsteps. Strumpen-Darrie, for his part, was convinced that the French accent and Gallic charm combined to make the best sales approach as far as Anglo-Americans were concerned. The best ones I met could have passed for Maurice Chevalier anytime on the phone, unless asked to sing. Madame, you are a lovely lady – how can you do this to me? What do you mean, a refund? You want to throw away all you have achieved just because your husband has been a little sick? Finish your French lessons quickly, Madame and take your husband to Nice for six weeks. January in New York is enough to kill a man with a weak chest...

The American Berlitz directors were, on the average, about 10-15 years younger than their European counterparts and had a tendency to look upon the latter as a bunch of old fogies who would not stand a chance of surviving in the American business world. The Europeans, for their part, saw at every congress a cliqueish contingent of glib young men in shiny suits reeling off sales figures, quarterly results and three-year rolling forecasts in the manner of people who sold encyclopaedias, vacuum cleaners or soap powder. These two very disparate groups of people secretly (sometimes openly) despised each other, yet they shared a common bond – they all loved the business they were in. Berlitz in those days was a world of its own with its own particular fascination. Whether in Europe or America it was a milieu where you could combine the twin attractions of academic excellence and commercial success. You could make half a million dollars **without** having to sell soap powder or pork belly futures; you could make your quarterly forecast by signing up Marlon Brando or Princess Anne or Fernandel. In Europe, especially, the balance sheet of the school often depended on the qualifications and erudition of the director/owner.

For my part, I enjoyed belonging, in a sense, to both groups. The Americans I identified with because of my youth and mobility, the Europeans, on account of my linguistic abilities. I felt more old-world European, though as an Englishman I probably leaned instinctively towards the special relationship with America. At any rate after my first few days with Strumpen-Darrie I felt I had a foot firmly in both camps – a feeling which was borne out several years later when I opened up Japan for the Americans. I also noticed that the most successful American directors – André Pacatte, Max Besenbruch and Pierre Bordes – were older men who had brought their talents with them from Europe and blended them with the more aggressive business methods used in the United States.

Robert Strumpen-Darrie was the ideal leader for this collection of intelligent, motivated professors and salesmen. In his mid-fifties he stood six foot three in height, had iron grey hair and a rose complexion and sprouted ideas in a booming baritone from 9-6 every day through the open door of his office on the 14th floor of the Manhattan Center on Fifth Avenue. Himself a salesman through and through, he masterminded a persuasive, yet subtle marketing campaign which depicted Berlitz as the only credible language school in North America on account of its 80-year historical record and uncompromising strictness of method. Berlitz was top-of-the-market and you paid top dollar. Strumpen-Darrie's institutes had the thickest carpets in the United States. His school directors followed him because he or his father had picked them and he could market and sell the product better than any of them. He was a humorous and thoughtful leader, spoke beautiful French and was unquestionably the chief architect of Berlitz's almost unassailable position in the market.

The other secret of Berlitz success in the United States was often overlooked by the directors – this was the existence of Charles Berlitz himself. There were actually two of M. D.'s grandsons alive in 1957 – Victor Harrison-Berlitz and Charles. Victor dealt mainly with publications and was not strong on charisma, but Charles Berlitz was. In his early forties, he was of medium height, had an enigmatic smile and was already beginning to resemble his grandfather. He did not look American at all, nor any other nationality, either. Like Orson Welles, he was hard to classify.

Charles was a brilliant linguist, having got off to a good start with an English speaking mother, a German father, a Spanish maid and a Gaelic nanny. He was reputedly quadrilingual at the age of five. When I first met him we spent a couple of hours fencing in about ten languages, establishing where each one's superiority lay. Eventually we settled for English with Swedish swear words, a combination we have used up to the present day.

Charles added that extra shade of mystique to the Berlitz enigma – a living legend with an American passport, incontrovertible proof that one could be bilingual or trilingual or any class of polyglot provided one devoted the necessary time (and money) to the study of languages. As an American polyglot – rare creature indeed – Charles was immensely popular on television shows – he even dragged me into one during the brief time I was in New York. He also wrote interesting articles about the world's different languages and their idiosyncrasies and these, along with innumerable interviews he granted newspaper reporters, were of enormous publicity and public relations value to the Berlitz organisation. His ability with the pen was only too obvious, when, years later, Charles turned to full-time writing and made millions of dollars with "The Bermuda Triangle" and many other books.

*   *   *   *   *

When I told Strumpen-Darrie that I intended to buy a second-hand car, he insisted I take one of his assistants with me to afford me some kind of protection in the jungle of New York car showrooms. He assigned to this task a young man named Nino Huarte, an American of Hispanic extraction. Nino, who in later years became director of Berlitz New York, did not succeed in helping me to buy the right car, but he certainly prevented me from buying at least a couple of dozen that we looked at up and down Manhattan. In those days $3,000 bought a two-year-old Ford or Chevrolet – they were all big sedans by European standards – in 1957 America did not know the meaning of the term "compact" car. I would have been easy meat for the fast-talking salesmen we encountered. All the cars they showed me were clean and shiny and looked fine to me, though some of them might not have had engines inside for all I knew. But Nino prowled round them with a look of intense hatred in his black Spanish eyes, kicked all the clean white-walled tyres and sneered as he wrenched steering wheels from side to side. Just when I was pulling my $3,000 out of my back pocket to make the purchase, Nino would drop to his knees, take a sight along one of the wings, fling his right arm up in the air and scream "It's been hit!" He and the salesman would then exchange insults of increasing intensity to such an extent that I finished up defending both of them out of sheer embarrassment.

It was no deal that day, or the next, after which Nino was reassigned to selling language instruction and I went off to Hoboken, New Jersey, where the first salesman who took my elbow sold me a turquoise-and-cream 1955 Ford with white-walled tyres and a tank full of gas for exactly $3,000, which, he reliably informed me, was far less than the actual value of the car, which he was letting me have cheaply as I was one of the family and he knew that Europeans coming over on first papers had it tough until they got a break, so he was giving me one hell of a break right now – sure this car'll get you to California, kid. I needed a car that would also get me back from California and I wasn't sure what first papers were, but as it turned out the car was a good one and took us round the States without a hiccup, apart from the overdrive, which my friend stressed as an invaluable feature on a long trip, not working at all. I sold the car 18 months later in Finland for $5,000 and saw it occasionally eating up the kilometres between Helsinki and Tampere for another 3 years, so there is something to be said for Hoboken car dealers.

*   *   *   *   *

During the next 3 months I toured a selection of schools in Strumpen-Darrie's far-flung empire and, with my companions, had the exhilarating, once-in-a-lifetime experience of driving, in a leisurely manner, through 40 states of a vast magnificent country, then still unspoilt and uncluttered, possessing a variety of breathtaking landscapes and awe-inspiring geographical phenomena unmatched anywhere in the world. The Everglades and white beaches of Florida, the bayous of Louisiana, the Texas cattle-country, the deserts and Grand Canyon of Arizona, the Indian settlements of New Mexico, the golden hills of California, the natural beauty of Yosemite and Yellowstone, the Badlands of Dakota, the incomparable autumn colours of New England were just a few of the unsurpassable beauties that unfolded themselves as we drove from state to state. We saw the Wild West, the cowboys, the Indians, the fishermen of Monterey, the rodeos of Montana and Wyoming, the taciturn yokels of Vermont and Maine in all their rustic magnificence. We recorded with our still and movie cameras a beautiful old-time America that to-day hardly exists. The people, too, were friendly, hospitable, natural, even naïve. In New York and Los Angeles we felt green and gullible, but the cynicism and dog-eat-dog way of life of those cities disappeared as we got into the countryside and there was plenty of that still left in 1957. The further west one went, the warmer was the welcome, but everywhere outside the big cities one met open solid honest Americans reminiscent of the colourful characters we had encountered earlier in the writings of Steinbeck, Dos Passos, Dreiser, Hemingway and Mark Twain.

The Berlitz directors around the country were warm and enthusiastic hosts, keen to hear how the organisation was faring in the "new" countries, Finland and Norway, and happy to talk shop with a colleague. They were not on fixed salaries, but drew a monthly allowance against the profit, of which they were entitled to 50%. On this basis they entertained lavishly, calculating that New York always paid half the restaurant bills. This profit-sharing system worked well in the Strumpen-Darrie era and probably was one of the secrets of the organisation's prosperity.

The directors I remember best were Max Besenbruch (Philadelphia) and Peter Haase (Chicago) both genial, methodical Germans always well up in the league table; Rodriguez (New Orleans) who laid on a magnificent tour of the city in an open red Oldsmobile, took us to five different jazz clubs in one night and gave us the First Lesson in Arabic with bacon and eggs at 6 in the morning; Drex Gibson (Boston) formerly Havana, who had spent 2 years in a Cuban jail when gunmen had fired on revolutionaries out of the Berlitz school windows; Stieglitz (Seattle) a gentle professor who constantly refined the Method; André Pacatte, the fiery charismatic Frenchman in Los Angeles who fathered us all for several days and made me speak at the L.A. Rotary Club lunch; finally Pierre Bordes (Houston) whose finest sale that year had been 1000 lessons to a Texas cattleman to be taken by his daughter in **New York** to learn **English!**

Our tour of North America would not have been complete without two incursions into Canada, the first to spend a few days with Mathias Wallen in Vancouver and the second to see Norman Taylor, now married to Nelly Soininen, in Montreal. Both these friends were making their life in Canada, but were eager for news from Finland. My last port of call before Boston and New York was Friendship, Maine, where Professor Geoffrey Stagg, now Chairman of Italian, Spanish and Portuguese at the University of Toronto, had a summer cottage. Apart from the warmth of his friendship, I remember the biggest and best lobsters it has ever been my good fortune to eat.

Bob Bradley and Warwick Rathgen had returned home from Vancouver, Jean Guy and David Willey remained in Montreal, so I finished the tour alone. Robert Strumpen-Darrie and Charles Berlitz, hardly able to believe that we had actually driven through 40 states in 3 months, gave me a splendid farewell lunch preceded by the three largest and driest Martini Gibsons I have ever downed. That same evening I walked somewhat unsteadily aboard the "SS United States", having seen the old Ford safely hoisted and deposited into the hold. She had done California and back. The icy roads of Finland awaited her.

Chapter 8

Salazar's Portugal

With the opening up of Finland and Norway, there were now Berlitz schools in every western European country except one: Portugal. As a Lancashireman, I have never been particularly fond of cold weather, having had my fair share of it in my youth. My involvement with the Nordic countries was due more to my affection for their inhabitants, rather than any enthusiasm for the meteorological conditions. After two weeks of Californian sunshine I developed a compelling interest in the map of southern Europe, noticing that Lisbon had approximately the same latitude as San Francisco.

On my drive back to Helsinki from Le Havre I called in on Roger Montfort in Paris and negotiated a five-year renewable franchise for Portugal. He did some grumbling about the considerable distance between the Finnish and Portuguese capitals and in his hesitation I detected the first signs of nervousness over my now controlling seven schools when he himself owned only nine. However I was in a strong negotiating position – I had good qualifications in three Romance languages, I had the capital to invest and, already paying dues on 6 schools, I was one of his best customers. In the end his love of royalties won the day.

Running two sizeable companies at opposite extremities of Europe was not without its problems, but I now had capable managers in Finland and Norway and, among the teachers who had wintered twice or thrice in the north I had a ready-made staff for the Portuguese school. In the years that followed there was a regular annual transfer of English instructors from the Nordic countries to Lisbon.

In December 1958 I flew to Hamburg, bought a new Karmann-Ghia – a new-look sports car just introduced by Volkswagen – and drove down through Cologne, Paris, Bordeaux, San Sebastián, Burgos, Zamora and Salamanca to cross into Portugal near Guarda. Guarda claims to be the highest city in Europe and the temperature there was the same as in Helsinki. The men sat in cafés huddled up in thick sheepskin coats and trilbies. There were no women to be seen in the cafeterias or bars; the coffee, served in tall glasses with milk and sugar (*um galão*) was excellent. There were a few shafts of sunlight as I drove through Coimbra, but when I reached Lisbon it was pouring down. There was no shortage of office space in the Portuguese capital and it took me one week to find a suitable building, during which time it never stopped raining. Lisbon is, for me, Europe's most beautiful city, but rain there looks the same as it does in Manchester. On two or three occasions I was within an ace of packing my bags and leaving. A maverick ray of sunshine, a glass of Alentejo wine, a glimpse of the Castelo, a glistening palm tree, the crash of a wave retained me a moment longer. On such tenuous slender threads hang the fateful decisions of our lives. At the end of the week I went home for Christmas with a Portuguese rent contract in my brief-case to keep Montfort's *concession* company. Little did I know that the tiny school I had situated in a humble back street would eventually outgrow the Paris Berlitz school itself.

*   *   *   *   *

At that time the Portuguese system of government was a dictatorship. Some say that Salazar was a benign dictator; at all events it was obvious that he held the country in a grip of iron. A former university professor, called to power to rehabilitate a tottering economy in 1933, he was by 1958 a self-perpetuating institution in Portuguese life – an old man in total control of the police, the armed forces and what could be called the establishment and with no inclination whatsoever to abdicate his powerful position.

An ascetic, he had never married, ate and drank sparingly, in general shunning the many luxuries often indulged in by dictators around the world. He rarely appeared in public, worked a long day and was, in principle, married to the Portuguese state. The idea that the Portuguese people had long been wishing for a divorce was not a subject of open discussion. Political meetings were not allowed; the feared secret police, the PIDE, were everywhere. Given the natural Latin tendency to rebel and conspire, there were of course thousands of active dissidents, but their efforts made little or no headway until 1974, the year of the Portuguese Revolution. As the last-named event was to show, Portugal is a country where intense struggle can take place without violence. Few of the opponents of Salazar were executed, though opposition leaders were forced into exile. The small fry dissidents at lower levels were periodically clapped into jail for a few weeks at a time. Their absences showed on our class registers. When they returned to their class after such "holidays" they smilingly avoided any explanation. We were warned that there was probably a PIDE representative in each class and we instructed our teachers never to discuss religion or politics in or out of school. As a consequence we never had any problems with the authorities. If there were secret policemen in the groups, they paid their fees regularly like everybody else.

*   *   *   *   *

Salazar, though an academic, had proved to be an astute politician. Like Franco, he had kept his country out of the war, balancing his traditional alliance with the British against his identification with Europe's other dictatorships. As the belligerent powers maintained embassies in Portugal during the war, Lisbon was a hotbed of spies from both sides. Salazar himself never left Portuguese territory, a trick he had learned from Franco, with whom he conferred occasionally. The neutrality of Spain and Portugal meant that they avoided the horrors of global conflict. The continuing isolation of the Iberian peninsula from the mainstream of European affairs, when the democracies boomed, resulted in both Spain and Portugal falling behind in modern developments. In 1958 Portugal seemed incredibly backward in many social aspects. Women packed the cinemas and restaurants with their husbands and friends, but were barely seen in Lisbon's many cafés after ten. Widows wore black for life, single Nazaré fishing girls wore seven petticoats and even foreigners were forbidden to wear short bathing costumes in public swimming pools. This rule was not often enforced on the beach itself, but one of our teachers who lived one hundred yards from the sea was frequently turned back by an unfriendly (PIDE) neighbour and made to "dress properly" for the hundred metres dash to the water. Another teacher, sun-bathing in a deckchair on the back patio of the school, was pelted with tomatoes by neighbours because he was wearing swimming trunks. Middle-aged men, presumably secret police, patrolled all the beaches between Lisbon and Estoril the year round, dressed in dark suits, collar and tie and black trilbies. They were not hard to spot in July and August.

There was no inflation, the escudo being as hard as a rock at 80 to the pound. This defence of the Portuguese currency, the major goal of the economist Salazar, was achieved by the maintenance of huge gold reserves. This large amount of wealth lying idle meant that little was ploughed back into the economy. Roads were poor, there were only two tiny stretches of motorway about 15 km. each, buses and especially trams were ancient, there was no welfare state and the plumbing left a lot to be desired, though the country, thanks to the industriousness of the Portuguese housewife, was generally clean and tidy. Portuguese wives were not allowed to leave the country alone unless they could produce written permission from their husbands at Customs; young men who had not completed military service were confined to Portugal.

One often refers to Salazar's Portugal as being a country of only very rich and very poor – this was not strictly true. A small class of very rich people existed, living in a completely different world from the desperately poor fishermen's families, farmers, peasants and country folk in general. In Lisbon itself large numbers of destitutes were clearly visible, but between these extremes there existed a very sizeable lower middle class of people who led decent lives, largely due to their own strenuous efforts for self-betterment. These people – bank clerks, teachers, technicians, civil servants, grocers, postmen and shop girls – prized education, clothes, travel, the arts and progress as much as any other Europeans; their aspirations and intelligence of application were as high as those of any German or Scandinavian. They were paid so little – many of them held down two jobs to maintain their precariously decent standards. The lower classes, including some of the city people I have mentioned, were lucky if they had a salary of 1000 escudos a month. This was about £12 in English money. Our first school secretary, whom we paid 1500 escudos monthly, considered her ship had come home and we often had to drive her out of school at midnight.

Life was, of course, unbelievably cheap for anyone coming from Northern Europe. Coffee was one escudo, a simple meal 10 escudos, taxis started with only 2 1/2 escudos on the meter, a suit cost 500 escudos, the school rent was 3000 per month (£35). Teachers earned about 4000 escudos a month (£50) whereas in Finland they grossed about £120 at that time. Income tax was virtually nil. A teacher paid about 500 escudos a month (£6) for room, full board and laundry! Many of our staff, though earning at such a low rate, managed to save about half their salary – in Scandinavia they saved maybe 10 per cent.

Student fees were, of course, very modest. Those in groups, (the majority), paid 10 escudos an hour or 80 – 120 a month depending on whether they came twice or three times a week. Private students (the rich) paid 35 escudos an hour. All types of students paid regularly and willingly once a month – the fixed sum they had set aside in their humble budgets. In several decades of business in Portugal I can hardly remember a bad debt.

*   *   *   *   *

The tight political control also extended to the press and other sources of information .The "Diario de Noticias" was the national newspaper, read by virtually everyone. If you rose late, you might try the "Diario Popular" – the evening paper. The other two newspapers, with a much smaller circulation, were the church-influenced "O Seculo" and the "Diario de Lisboa". When you had read one, you had read them all – there was only one line to follow. When one sees the liveliness and variety of Portugal's newspapers today, it is hard to remember or even imagine how utterly boring and ingratiatingly platitudinous Salazar's editors were. In a post-war Europe of seething political activities and exciting economic transformations, the "Diario de Noticias" waxed hysterical about the opening of a new Fire Station in Cartaxo by the Minister of Public Works, the list of government dignitaries received by Admiral Amerigo Tomas on his 70th birthday, or the accreditation of the new Chargé d'Affaires from Rwanda-Burundi. The poor Portuguese public had to turn to the Death Notices for interesting news or, even better, to "Bola" the football newspaper, where occasionally something unforseeable might take place. We foreigners scoured Lisbon for English newspapers which were allowed in as long as they contained nothing uncomplimentary about the Portuguese *régime*. On many days they would be banned on account of some reference to dictatorships or some imagined slight. It could be particularly frustrating during the Wimbledon fortnight or Test matches.

The strict control of the media and political affairs did not apply to the world of business, where freedom of action was quite astonishing. One simply went into the country on a tourist visa, founded a company (which could be 100 per cent foreign-owned) paid in the capital and got on with it. I discovered that I needed no special permits to import funds, rent a building, found an educational establishment, employ staff and bring in foreign personnel. Work permits were required for aliens, but were generally obtained in one month. Apart from losing half a day at Police Headquarters procuring a *bilhete de identidade* and getting fingerprinted and photographed, there was little red tape to go through. By February 1959 my initial staff of six teachers – three English, one French, one German and one Portuguese – had access to the minds and opinions of a hundred or so Portuguese citizens and their children – a paradoxical situation in a police state! To my knowledge, my staff never abused this privileged position (and we shall never know to what extent we were being monitored) but to this day I marvel at the flexibility of the *régime* – tough and spiteful in many aspects, but essentially Portuguese in its capacity for tolerance and accommodation. It is also true that Portuguese of all classes have a genuine fondness for the British, jokingly referred to as *"Os Bifes"* (the Beefs). Many of our English teachers stayed on for years.

*   *   *   *   *

The first three Englishmen to transfer from Helsinki, George Pearson, Kenneth Crossley and Martin Dahlgreen were excellent instructors and the school expanded quickly. Teaching was very different from the way we did it in Finland, where we would charge into class bubbling over with extroversion and enthusiasm to draw some response from the shy, introverted Finns. It was not unusual for a live-wire like Crossley to fling open the door, throw his arms up in the air and shout "Here I am again, you lucky people!" Finns like being woken up in this way and grin back at you and sometimes even speak. We had all developed this theatrical teaching style in our years in the north. If you walked into a class of Portuguese and flung up your arms everyone would jump to his or her feet and come around the table to pump your hand. After that they would babble excitedly for ten minutes. They are sociable people. Whereas in Finland we employed every subterfuge to make our students speak, in Portugal, we had to strain every sinew to keep them all from talking at once. One of my first advanced classes contained Carlos Baleia and Mario Cardoso, two well-known amateur actors, a voluble lawyer named Antonio Osorio, two car salesmen from Mercedes and General Motors, two pretty, talkative girls and a doctor. There was more shouting than in the House of Commons and there were evenings when I hardly got a word in. Baleia and Cardoso were brilliant orators and the latter's English was so good that he used to correct some of our younger teachers, who soon dreaded having him on their programme.

We used to teach two or three hours every morning, mainly to private students and groups of youngsters. From 12 to 5 the school was to all extents and purposes closed; we soon developed the habit of lunching by the sea and spending the afternoons, even in winter, on the beaches of Carcavelos, Parede, Estoril and Cascais. There would be a few classes at 5 o'clock, but the evening programme really got under way at 6. The last groups finished at 11 pm. The day did not end there, for we had to eat. This in itself posed no problem, for the Portuguese dine late and many of our students would invite us out after lessons. Before the Revolution, Portuguese restaurants used to stay open till the last customer left. I have seen as many as 300 people in the Cervejaria Portugal still ordering food at 3.30 am. In 1959 we rarely went to bed before 2 am. making up for lost hours of sleep by snoozing on the beaches in the afternoons. The lawyer Osorio was Portuguese national table tennis champion and I used to play with him in the Sporting Club. One night our team had a match in Caldas da Rainha due to start at 10 pm. Someone else took my last two lessons so that I could make the start of the match. I drove one hour and a half to Caldas where the proceedings had not yet begun. The match eventually started at 1 am and finished at 5. We had "dinner" (huge beefsteaks) from 6-7 am. Our hosts felt we had not eaten enough (everyone was starving) so they served another main course – pork chops with two fried eggs on top, to fill us up. We left at 8 and I got back to school just in time for my first lesson at 10. It was definitely a change from Finland.

*   *   *   *   *

The opening of the autumn term in October 1959 saw a large increase in the number of enrolments. The original nucleus of 100 students swelled to 300 and, as the winter progressed, topped 1000 and kept going up. The first floor of the premises on the Rua Sociedade Farmaceutica was soon bursting at the seams. Private individuals occupied the second and third floors, but our problem was short-lived as, not surprisingly, they were not long in moving out. In the spring of 1960 we were using the whole building.

Although the academic year 1959-60 was a very hectic one in terms of growth and development, it was a period when I had the opportunity to relax and pursue a few hobbies. Anna Candiago came down from Norway to help with the management of the school and at this time my father retired at the age of 66. This enabled my parents to come to Portugal for an extended stay and we rented a cosy little apartment on the Avenida de Roma. Soon the aromas of my mother's age-old Lancashire recipes permeated the blocks of flats around us and after years of eating foreign food I was back on a diet of Hot Pot, Bacon and Egg Pie, trifle, Egg and Marmalade Pie, tripe and onions, lobscouse, black puddings, Lancashire stew, raspberry blancmange, bubble-and-squeak, red currant jelly and bread-and-butter pudding.

Portugal is a wonderful country to winter in. Not only is the climate mild enough to enable you to plan attractive excursions every week-end, but one can buy a large variety of fruits and excellent vegetables the year round. The little corner grocers' shops fairly bulged with merchandise and, even better, one could buy fresh vegetables directly from farmers at the roadside as one drove to Sintra, Ericeira, Obidos, Sesimbra or Nazaré. In some of these places, as in Cascais and Setubal, one could also buy fish straight from the fishermen. My mother, a villager herself, loved to buy food from direct sources in this manner and enjoyed mixing and making friends with peasants and vendors of all kinds in the many attractive villages and fishing harbours around Lisbon.

Between the ages of 25 and 30 I had worked hard at creating an international organisation which already taught thousands of people. I had not been able to do this without neglecting some of the pursuits of which I was very fond – particularly sport. Now I began to play regular tennis again, travelled around southern Portugal with the Sporting Club table tennis team and made friends with Victor Barna and Alec Brook when they visited Lisbon. Barna, Hungarian, had been world singles champion 5 times and Alex was a former English champion. My friendship with Alec Brook, the most unfailingly cheerful person I have ever met, lasted until his death in 1988. I also took up a new sport – Judo – at a club in the neighbourhood of our apartment.

The Judo Club was in the strong, capable hands of Masami Shirooka, former major in the Imperial Japanese Army, 8th Dan Black Belt at the Budokan and (though he did not know it at the time) future Mayor of Sapporo City, Hokkaido, Japan. He was the first Japanese with whom I came into close contact (physically and mentally) and, looking back over my many years' experiences in Japan, I realise that I could have not had a better man to hurl me around the *dojo* and initiate me in all things Japanese. He was a fascinating prototype – strong, proud, impassive, utterly confident of his abilities, careful not to attempt anything beyond his control. Like many Japanese, he seemed to be an island unto himself, volunteering little information except that required to carry out his job and using his simple but effective English to answer direct questions or to make polite but firm requests, the latter always well within his rights. His knowledge of Portuguese was limited to "push", "pull" and "harder". Otherwise his students communicated with him in English. Completely at ease in the *dojo*, he was like a fish out of water socially. We would all go out to eat together after training, as we did at Berlitz. The

Portuguese habit of pushing dinner back till 10 or 11 pm. was clearly
discomfiting for Shirooka, whose Japanese stomach was synchronized for
attention at 6. He would fill in the time with a few beers, at a loss with the
endless small talk which the Portuguese engage in between the hours of 8 to
10. Recognizing in my relatively controlled English utterances a manner of
communication somewhat closer to his own, he quickly latched on to me as a
conversation partner during these twice weekly outings. He would sip half a
glass of beer, stare at the ceiling or his feet for a good half minute, then come
out with some pronouncement or judgment to be delivered to me with the
utmost politeness, but with a clear ring of finality:

"This man Joaquím – very intelligent, but no common sense" or

"Portuguese tell you one thing on Tuesday – only once – not enough.
Then Wednesday they forget it themselves". or

"Vitor he come so late for Tuesday lesson, I tell him he come early for
Thursday lesson, – Japanese feel bad, but Vitor he laugh and feel better" or

"In Japan when we have different opinion we speak with low voice; in
Portugal they shout and wave arms, like they hate and will fight. Then they kiss
on both cheek before go home." or

"Portuguese very personal – invade privacy. Rodrigues he stare at my
suit long time, he feel material with fingers, he pat me hard on back and tell
me I got better suit than him, good cut. I tell him both suits same, only my
body better."

Masami Shirooka, first time out of Japan and separated from his family
and peers, was experiencing culture shock. In fact his view of the Portuguese
was not unlike that held by Finns who lived in Portugal. My background in
Romance studies enabled me to explain some things to him: that Latins often
make tentative arrangements which they later change out of sheer flexibility;
that they use pitch and tone in conversation for more expressiveness and add
to this with body language; that punctuality is not the cult that it is in
Germany, England or Japan; that personal comments are often made out of
kindness and Portuguese like to compliment strangers in any way they can. At
the same time Shirooka's reactions were giving me the first inklings of Japanese
mentality and world outlook – the months I spent with him were excellent
cultural training for my eventual work in Japan.

In the spring, a diplomat at the American Embassy in Lisbon asked me
to arrange a Japanese language course for him, as he was to be transferred to
Tokyo. After some hesitation, I asked Shirooka if he would be willing to teach
this course, provided that I trained him in the Berlitz method. He spent three
or four weeks wrestling with his conscience before finally agreeing – I assured
him that the American knew his background and was quite happy with the
arrangement, as he insisted on a Japanese national instructor. I feared that I
would have a formidable task training a 50-year-old Japanese army major in

new classroom techniques, but to my surprise Masami Shirooka took to it like
a duck to water. He listened carefully to all that I told him, made copious notes
in neat, flowing *kanji* and imitated my teaching style faithfully and without
demur. After he had taught me the first ten lessons in Japanese, I let him loose
on the diplomat.

The course was one of 300 lessons taken over a ten-week period. As the
student was very motivated (and Shirooka, anxious to prove himself, certainly
was, too), the end result was highly satisfactory and we received compliments
from the embassy. My lasting impression, after many years, is the sight of
Major Shirooka marching back and forth along the width of the classroom,
singing out new vocabulary loud and clear, signalling accentuated syllables by
crashing his impressive right fist on his desk, inspecting the hastily scribbled
notes of the student on each item and nodding sharply with a loud grunt of
approval before resuming his march.

*   *   *   *   *

The academic year 1960-61 saw school enrolments top 1500. We were
now using 3 floors at the Rua Sociedade Farmaceutica and there was just no
more room. I decided to open a second school in the residential area of Lisbon
known as the *avenidas*. In the autumn of 1961 I rented two floors in a good
building in the Avenida Guerra Junqueiro near the Praça de Londres. My old
friend Mathias Wallen, now married to a German girl, Helen, decided to leave
Canada and take up the post as director of this school. It was an immediate
success. In those years Portuguese parents were very protective of their younger
children, particularly daughters between 14 and 19. There were not allowed
out alone in the evening and, when they enrolled for English classes with us
they were invariably accompanied to the school by one of their parents and
picked up again at the end of the lesson. We had not had large numbers of
youngsters in the Rua Sociedade Farmaceutica, which was rather "dangerously"
close to downtown. As soon as we opened in the middle of the *avenidas*
residential area, teenagers began to attend our evening classes in droves. Many
of their parents also took advantage of the convenient location to study before
or after dinner. Mathias – tall, blond and handsome – was immensely popular
with the Portuguese. The actors Carlos Baleia and Mario Cardoso became his
close friends. Great conversationalists as they were, they were fascinated by the
Finn's encyclopaedic knowledge and command of languages. We had some
very late evenings. Two other, slightly older, benign Portuguese – Fernando
Jorge de Silva and Ruy Cunha Tavares – used to lie in wait for us after their
lessons from 10-11 pm and insist on taking us out to dinner. Silva was an
engineer and constructor, well-off with, a big house near the Torre de Belém.
Tavares, who owned a dark little grocer's shop near the school – nothing more

than a hole in the wall – seemed to have even deeper pockets. My mother swore that pokey little dens like that, with rock bottom prices, always made a lot of money. At all events Silva and Tavares loved to rush us off to Vila Franca da Xira, a town on the Tagus 20 kilometres upriver from Lisbon and feed us *perdiz na pucara* (partridge in the pot) well after midnight, followed by the inevitable pork chops and two fried eggs. You needed quite a lot of red wine to get that down.

We suspected that Alberto, another middle-aged student who had been studying a couple of years, was PIDE. Fellow students didn't talk to him much, but he was courteous and often affable to us and frequently took us out for a meal. Officially he had a job with one of the airlines; he used to drive round a lot in a Volkswagen. One incident confirmed our suspicions of his real power. A well-known Portuguese broadcaster, whose name I do not recall, was very interested in the career of Marshal Mannerheim, the former President and Commander-in-Chief of Finland. I had a copy (in English) of the Marshal's autobiography and I lent it to the broadcaster. He did not return the book and, as it was out of print, I rang him up a couple of months later asking him if he had finished with it. He said he was still reading it, so I forgot about the matter for another month or so. Then I asked the school secretary to phone him and have it sent back. To my astonishment, she reported that he considered I had made him a gift of the book and had no intention of returning it. Subsequently I called the broadcaster several times, but he refused to send it back and eventually became quite irate on the telephone. There did not seem much I could do after that – he was supposed to be a powerful man – and I reluctantly decided to drop the matter. A few months later, during a dinner with Alberto, I happened to mention the incident, as we had been discussing the Russo-Finnish war. Alberto said nothing, but the next morning Marshal Mannerheim's Memoirs were on my desk. Alberto disappeared from sight after the Portuguese Revolution of 1974. I often wonder where he went.

*   *   *   *   *

As I relate in the chapters that follow, I spent the years 1960-63 shuttling between Finland and Portugal. In Lisbon I had an apartment in the Campolide district, in Finland I shared a flat with Kaj Wallen, the brother of Mathias. After getting married in the autumn of 1963, I moved to London, as described in Chapter 10. I had enjoyed my years in Europe's only Atlantic capital. Lisbon in sunshine, is, for me, the most beautiful city in Europe and the quaint, twisting, cobbled streets of Alfama huddled round the ancient Castelo de São Jorge, remain today my favourite European haunt. I was to resume my profession in Portugal in later years, when it would be dramatically transformed by revolution, modernisation and entry into the European Community.

Chapter 9

Walter and Connie

Lisbon and Helsinki are the two most widely separated capitals in Western Europe and commuting between these two cities entailed a great deal of time and effort. The size of the Finnish operation required, however, my presence there at least six months in each year. The efficiency of my Finnish administrative staff at this time enabled me to concentrate on pedagogy. The Berlitz Method, though 80 years old, was still, in my opinion, superior to any other for teaching oral skills to beginners and lower intermediate students. It was less attractive in its usefulness to more advanced students who had already mastered the structures of the target language and who in essence, would benefit principally from communicative practice in the cultural environment of the country where the language was spoken. Gifted language teachers are able to re-create this environment in the classroom. This is done by the use of newspapers, photographs, recordings and other realia, but most of all by the gradual, almost confidential revealing of the instructor's native personality and driving force by the eager sharing of his or her cultural baggage with the pupil.

Unfortunately some teachers are less gifted, or more introvert, than others and tend to fall short in their ability to portray adequate visions of their cultural heritage. There had been little new in language teaching in the 1950s apart from the spread of the language laboratory facility, based largely on repetitive (often unimaginative) audio-tape drills with a minimum, if any, visual stimulation. In the second half of the 1950s, television was rapidly replacing radio as the most popular source of information and entertainment in households from Liverpool to Leipzig. Though rare in Portugal, TV sets were common in Helsinki homes in 1960 and Suomen Televisio (Finnish Television) and the commercial channel, Mainos TV were producing ambitious home-grown programmes as well as showing old films and TV series made in the USA and the United Kingdom.

Among our students in the Helsinki School were two well known television executives, Nils Holm, a producer, and Ossi Harkimo, a film director. I was friendly with both these gentlemen and opened a dialogue with them on the subject of making a TV series for the teaching of English. English by Television was as yet an undiscovered or at least undeveloped concept. It was not until 1962 that the BBC brought out their mammoth series "Walter and Connie", which was ultimately screened in 74 countries.

Holm and Harkimo were all ears. In Germany or Portugal the bureaucracy involved in processing a new idea in education would have taken months. In Finland, where people love things that are new, wheels can turn much more quickly. It took me a couple of evenings to knock out one or two trial scripts and within a week Holm had me sitting in the office of Zilliacus, the Director General of Finnish Television. This perspicacious and extremely personable man, having read the trial scripts, took less than half an hour to authorize the production of a six-episode TV film series "Englantia Hauskaa ja Helppoa" ("English Can Be Fun").

In the course of the next few weeks David Willey and I completed the scripts for six 20-minute episodes. A budget and shooting dates were arranged and the programme was filmed in various locations in the south of the country, during the rather severe winter of 1960-61. The series was almost entirely in English, with occasional introductory remarks or side comments by Finnish presenters. Each episode was freestanding, but the general thread was the theme of two typical Englishmen battling Finnish culture shock in the shape of hot saunas, cold lakes, wild bears, runaway skis, black bread, raw fish and taciturn peasants. Humour, to some extent inherent in the screenplay, was enhanced by the dry, but imaginative character of the director Kauko Vuorensola and the impish antics of the chief cameraman, Antti Ruuhonen, later to become a well-known film director for Suomen Televisio. Willey and I had to do most of the acting, aided by a gentleman from Nottingham called Geoffrey Mason, who made an admirable judge with the right wig on. Deficiencies in acting ability were offset by the firm grip kept on us by the experienced Vuorensola, who often made us carry on till 3 or 4 in the morning. One night Willey had to make an entrance 19 times before Vuorensola would can it. We had some interesting Finnish extras including one rock star and one Miss Finland, as well as Tomi Gallen-Kallela, (grandson of the famous painter) who actually broke his leg during one of the skiing scenes, but carried on anyway until the sequences were completed. Such is Finnish *sisu*.

In the spring the series was screened and was well received by the Finnish public. The level of English was lower intermediate, which meant that more than half the viewers could follow the dialogue. The series was repeated after a few months' interval. Thus began the huge industry English by Television, not in England or the United States, but pioneered, with no fuss or high profile, by humble Finnish Television, in black and white.

The BBC was, however, quick to react. A few weeks after the first screening of "English Can Be Fun", I received a phone call from Christopher Dilke, Head of BBC English by Radio and Television. The British Broadcasting Corporation, which frequently describes its educational service as "the biggest English language classroom in the world" had for some time been planning an ENGLISH BY TELEVISION series and Christopher Dilke, in charge of the project, was anxious to exchange views. We arranged an appointment in Lisbon for the following month. Our first discussion was over beer and sandwiches on the sands of Cascais.

Dilke was the grandson of Sir Charles Dilke, a prominent Victorian Cabinet Minister who aspired to the premiership in the late 19th century, but was unfortunately frustrated in his ambitions on account of a scandal involving a famous actress. The BBC Dilke was an engaging character, huge in stature and sense of humour, casual in manner and style of dress, incomparably witty and articulate in self expression. He had an endless store of anecdotes, most of which were connected with his experiences with a varied assortment of BBC agents all around the world. He often used to visit Europe to see them. He never failed to get through his appointments in Denmark and Germany, but always had trouble in Greece. The Greek agent was a popular man in Athens and had to see so many people each day that he invariably ran over time. So Dilke usually missed his appointment or waited 3-4 hours for him to turn up. Finally, after several trips, he adapted to the multi-active culture. He simply went to the Greek's secretary in late morning and asked for the agent's schedule for the day. As the Greek conducted most of his meetings in hotel-rooms or bars, Dilke would wait in the hotel lobby and catch him rushing from one appointment to the next. The exuberant Greek, happy to see him, would not hesitate to spend half an hour with him and thus make himself late for his next appointment.

The story I remember best was about his Turkish agent, a strong-willed gentleman possessed of a violent temper when he felt the occasion warranted it. One evening the agent was driving Dilke to dinner when a lorry collided with his car, badly denting his left wing. The lorry driver jumped down from his cab, cursing the BBC agent in rasping Turkish, whereupon Dilke's man promptly beat him up, then left him dazed by his lorry and drove Dilke to dinner .After a a splendid repast, accompanied by suitable wines, they emerged from the restaurant to be confronted by the irate lorry driver, who had thoughtfully brought along five cronies. The six of them set on the BBC Turk, who gave a good account of himself before finally being knocked down and "trampled" by the six (a kind of insult in Turkey). At this point, the sizeable Dilke did what any English gentleman would do for a friend who has just bought him a good dinner; he took his jacket off in order to sail in. Fortunately for the Head of English by Television, a policeman arrived on the scene and the tramplers all jumped up into their lorry and drove off. The bleeding agent, ignoring the policeman, grabbed Dilke and his jacket, threw them into his car and chased the lorry for five kilometres through the sleazier streets of Istanbul. Happily (for Dilke) it escaped.

"Walter and Connie", still in the planning stages, was to be a 39-episode, structure-based course pitched initially at semi-beginner level with a view to attracting a maximum number of viewers. It differed from "English Can Be

Fun" in its length, scope and rigidity of structure, but resembled the Finnish product in that it was in black and white, low level, dealt with certain "stereotyped" aspects of the English character and was driven by tongue-in-cheek humour.

Each episode was to deal with a different topic, e.g. Walter and Connie on the Farm, At the Bank, At the Races, etc. and was to be linked to a main structure e.g. the Present Perfect Tense, plus two secondary structures, for instance, comparative and superlative adjectives. The task facing the scriptwriter was to match up structures and topic so that the former were not only smoothly integrated with the latter, but would often appear as essential for dealing with the topic. If the subject and the grammar did not suit each other, stilted English would result. If we take the episode At the Races, the most appropriate main structure would be the Future Tense (Will he win, or won't he?) whilst the secondary ones might well be adverbs of probability (perhaps, maybe) and the Present Perfect (Thunderbird has won!). Not the least difficult duty of the scriptwriter was the injection, in each episode, of the humour which was to drive the series. Dilke and I discussed this at length. Humour, as we all know, crosses frontiers with difficulty, particularly when heading East. The BBC were targeting a large and disparate audience, including sensitive Arabs, volatile Latin Americans and bewildered Chinese. Jokes and punch lines were out of the question. Humour would have to arise from the situation, be easily (and universally) recognised and give no offence to the viewer whatever his or her sect, creed or culture. It is not easy to find 39 different items that Chinese will laugh at. The low level language strait-jacket helped in a way, for if we had been allowed more subtlety, we would have lost our audience. In the end I settled for Connie dreaming winners, jockeys falling off horses, Walter breaking jewellers' windows with a brick wrapped up in old brown paper with his address on, and similar inoffensive subterfuges.

In the event, the series proved immensely popular and was shown (often repeatedly) in most countries of the world. The only (inadvertently) offensive item turned out to be the choice of the name Connie, which has unfortunate connotations for speakers of Spanish, Portuguese, Italian and French. In due course I was allowed to attend the shooting of some of my scripts and had the pleasure of meeting that charming couple, Walter and Connie, who, seemingly, had forgiven me for the many inanities that I had caused to pass their lips. On location, it never ceased to amaze me how the British seemed to need three times as many people on the set as were used in Finland. I had the pleasure of meeting the fascinating Dilke on many occasions and became acquainted with other stalwarts in BBC English by Television such as René Quinault, Barbara Goldsmid, Joe Hambrook and Barry Tomalin, some of whom I remain in contact with up to the present day.

English by Television eventually developed, then mushroomed, into a very large industry indeed. The BBC followed "Walter and Connie", with "Slim John", "The Bellcrest Series", "The Sadrina Project", "The Lost Secret", "Person to Person", "Follow Me" and several other series, made available not only to national broadcasting corporations, but also to organisations and individuals world wide in video format. English by Video has indeed become an essential feature of modern language teaching; its inter-active applications and integration with computer-aided learning will undoubtedly ensure its retention for language study where immediacy, reality, appeal and cultural input are increasingly demanded.

Chapter 10

The Archaic London Berlitz School

During the Second World War, the Nazis occupied a large part of Europe including those countries where the large majority of Berlitz schools were located. The headquarters of the Société Internationale des Écoles Berlitz were housed in 31, Boulevard des Italiens in Paris and it was here that Berlitz policy was directed, new franchises were granted and, most importantly, royalties were collected. As in most French organisations, centralisation of control was a primary objective and, though the Berlitz Empire was spread over a motley collection of nations, Paris was able, in the main, to keep tabs on their disparate subjects and maintain a respectable degree of uniformity and fiscal benefit.

It was obvious that the Germans would seek to control all educational institutions in France as elsewhere, and indeed Europe's Berlitz schools, while being allowed to continue their activity, gradually became part of the training facilities of the Third Reich. In order, however, to protect the theoretical autonomy of the Société Internationale des Ecoles Berlitz, not to mention its financial resources and royalty-collecting privileges, the HQ of the Société was moved, for the duration of hostilities, to the country most likely to remain out of the Nazi clutches - Britain.

The director of the London Berlitz school in 1940 was a middle-aged retired army officer, John Gilbert. Gilbert - one of those forthright, no-nonsense Englishmen instrumental in building the Empire, was aided in his duties by his former batman and devoted disciple, William Myers, slightly younger than his commander. When Gilbert was approached by Paris on the subject of transferring the Berlitz HQ, he unhesitatingly shouldered the burden, on condition that the London school should remain his property not only for the duration of the war, but during the rest of his lifetime and should be passed on to Myers for as long as he lived, too. Such was loyalty and faith between brother ex-officers. Paris, though reluctant to hand over the sizeable company-owned London school, had no option but to comply and the contract was signed.

Few European royalties were paid to London during the years 1940-45, though Spain contributed the odd amount and there were some touching instances of faithful German *concessionaires* trying to maintain tenuous contact with the Société. Many French Berlitzers wound up as prisoners of war, in German concentration camps. One of them, a middle-aged director called Durand, had a most uncomfortable experience one winter's day when the prisoners, as part of a disciplinary measure, were forced to lie face downwards on the wet ground and be harangued, in this supine posture, by the camp commandant. To make matters worse, a new adjutant to the commandant strode up and down among the prostrated Frenchman and eventually put his foot on the back of poor Durand's head. As he pressed the Berlitz man's face into the mud, he whispered into his ear:

"It's Schneider here. Berlitz Karlsruhe. Don't worry, everything's going to be OK. I'm moving you to a better block – the warmest – and I have a couple of big food parcels for you, as well as cigarettes and cognac. See you in church."

Gilbert and Myers continued in good health, ran London according to their own lights and were exempt from paying royalties as per the 1940 agreement. I had called in on them on various occasions between 1955 and 1962. Though of different generations, we invariably got on well together. They fathered me a bit.

In the spring of 1963, while I was in Lisbon, I received a rather agitated phone call from Roger Montfort late one Saturday evening. He told me the following: it appeared that Gilbert, who had been in robust health, had suddenly dropped dead the previous Saturday. A very dejected Myers had moved into his office and helped the distraught widow to make arrangements for the funeral, which was for the following Saturday (the day Montfort rang me). That very morning two Berlitz employees, Mrs McLeod and Mr Fletcher, went round to the apartment of Mr Myers, who was to drive them to the internment. They rang the bell, but nobody answered. They knocked on the door several times to no avail. Going to the nearest phone box, they rang Myers again with no reply. They checked with the widow, he was not there either. As the hour of the funeral ceremony approached, they became increasingly anxious and finally located spare keys to Myers' flat in the school and entered the dwelling, where they found Myers dead in bed. The doctor's examination revealed that he had had a heart attack in the early hours of the morning. The fact that he should pass away on the very day of his mentor's funeral was regarded by the administrative staff of the school - most of them were in their fifties and sixties - as the ultimate proof of his loyalty and devotion.

Montfort wished me to take over the school immediately. It was a sizeable operation, having recently expanded. The Head Office was at 321 Oxford Street - a highly visible location in the middle of the Golden Mile. A short time earlier Gilbert, through a useful connection, had secured an inexpensive lease at No. 1 South Audley Street - a fine, rambling red-brick Victorian mansion just behind the Hilton Hotel. Student numbers were however well below those required to fill both Oxford Street and the new premises. Montfort wanted someone to organize a Big Push to double the number of students and, it was to be hoped, the profits of the business. He personally had not the slightest idea how to do this. From distant Lisbon and with no experience of the British market, neither had I.

I was reluctant to take the position, as I was enjoying life in Lisbon and had my hands full with eight schools of my own. Neither did I wish to relinquish the franchises which I had spent 8 years establishing and developing. Montfort, however, persisted in his request. There was absolutely no-one on the London staff of managerial material or potential. All decisions, both major and minor, over the last 20 years, had been taken and implemented by Gilbert and Myers. It appeared that nobody on the sizeable Paris staff was suitable either. London still used to have fogs in those days. Take the job for 2 years, pleaded Montfort. You can keep all your franchises as long as you see to it that they are run properly.

I suppose it was the prospect of sipping real English bitter ale at Lords again that proved to be the final enticement. Also I had a certain fondness for London, where I had spent a heady fortnight among the delirious crowds celebrating the end of the war in 1945. Tackling a completely different market would broaden my experience. Mainly, however, I did it for Montfort, who had after all entrusted three countries to me and who clearly wished to have an Englishman in place to deal with the eccentric British, whom he never really even half understood. In the event, the people in the office all turned out to be foreigners: Mrs McLeod was German, Fletcher was Yugoslav, Poulier was Indonesian, Picasso was French-Italian, Mrs Mulholland was Russian, Dr. Dobreziniecki was Hungarian-Czech - only the book-keeper - Captain Woodward he used to call himself - had been born on the island and he had spent his best years in the Raj.

Although I made several sorties to London in the summer, I did not take up the post as director until the following November. Not only did I have various things to tie up in Portugal and Finland, but I became engaged in June to Jane Garst, a young American working for the BBC. Jane, like myself, was a graduate in Spanish, a trained teacher and loved travel, so that the somewhat unusually peripatetic life I led held fewer terrors for her than for other young ladies of the more domesticated variety. We had a marvellous honeymoon in Mexico City and the Yucatán and rented a flat in Campden Hill Towers, the high-rise structure overlooking Notting Hill Gate tube station. Anna Candiago remained in charge of the Portuguese schools and those in Finland were entrusted to a German baroness, Dana von Uexkull, who had worked for me for five or six years.

* * * * *

It was a brisk 40-minute walk to 321 Oxford Street through Hyde Park. In those days it was the fashion to wear a white shirt to the office; I was astonished to note that on arrival at the school there would be a black rim on the inside of my collar. The smoggy air of the British capital was in sharp contrast with the purer atmospheres of Helsinki and Lisbon, where pollution by industry is virtually non-existent. Apart from the obvious change in environment, however, the sharpest contrast I felt was in the nature of the work itself, since the archaic London Berlitz School seemed like a period piece from days long gone by. In Finland emphasis is on modernity, in Portugal the pursuit of English is feverish, in the United States Berlitz had run like a well-oiled machine. In London walk-in customers were greeted with stares of astonishment by the elderly, kind-hearted receptionists, who found it hard to believe that even well-dressed citizens would be willing to pay £3 an hour for foreign language instruction. This view was conditioned by the abysmally low level of the salaries of the office staff, which ranged from £9-11 per week according to length of service - and most of them had been there a long time. The working week was 40 hours; nobody arrived late, left early, or even conceived of overtime with pay. The regulations were Victorian, the furniture was Dickensian, there were even inkwells, for those who wrote with real pens. The two typewriters - ancient Remingtons which would have fetched a price on Portobello Road - were used almost exclusively by the two translators, Mrs. Picasso and Mrs. Mcleod. The office walls, painted grey to match the hair and some of the faces of the staff, had acquired in the previous decade a film of grime thick enough to prevent any peeling of the Dulux. The lighting, as in the classrooms on the two floors above, was of the bluish, fluorescent type which killed any hint of cosiness or quaintness that the age-old desks and misshapen floorboards might have offered. The main office was long, narrow and gloomy, with Fletcher, Poulier, Mrs Mulholland and Dr Dobryziniecki lined up behind the counter, Picasso and McLeod glared over their Remingtons at the far end. Woodward was encapsuled in a tiny smoke-filled cell near the entrance, where he relived campaigns of better days long gone, and occasionally made entries in Edwardian cash books on the basis of volatile, ambiguous statistics pushed through his door at regular intervals by the tremulous Fletcher and the gentlemanly, egg-domed Poulier.

Such were the foot soldiers of Colonel Gilbert - a motley collection of displaced foreigners, turned into Londoners through marriage, revolution or exile, harassed misfits in a changing Britain, underpaid, exploited, often bullied, but with a remarkable loyalty to the company and the men who had employed them, obedient, dutiful, anxious to please, if only someone would show them how to do it. Only Mrs McLeod with her German thoroughness and mental toughness could really fend for herself. She was an excellent translator - she and Mrs Picasso always turned in a monthly profit - and she

Arriving in Japan with Rafael Alberola

The Emperor and Empress visiting
the UK

Japanese school group 1966

Inauguration of Tokyo school, September 1966

First day in the office

with Geoff Mason

K. Haraguchi

Japanese teacher in Karuizawa

Tokyo Lawn Tennis Club

Japanese wedding

Party in Shibuya

Leslie Perkins

One blonde amongst brunettes

Family group Shibuya, Tokyo 1969

Children in Japan

Soccer in Japan

Being presented to Sir Stanley Rous, FIFA President
Yokohama Olympic Stadium 1967

Parents in Nara

Caroline, Princess Mikasa, Mrs Yamashita, Mr Y. Miyake

Crown Prince Hiro and Hisashi Ito at Riversdown

Hotel Caravelle, Saigon 1967

Wartime view from Caravelle

Saigon panorama

Saigon rickshaw

Young couple, Saigon

Street scene, Saigon

Child by the Mekong

Vietnamese girls

Cercle Sportif, Saigon

Colette

General William Westmoreland

Cathedral

Cycling down the Yangtse

Pit stop

Caroline and friends

Wuhan, China

Professor Yeh and grandson

Shanghai

Professor and Mrs Yeh

On the wall

understood the mechanics of business. The other four, who met the public, did not understand that they had to sell! The word "sales" never passed their lips, as it had rather shady connotations. They discussed group lessons, which incurred only low fees, in relative ease, but were the enquirer to contemplate taking a private course, they felt it their duty to warn him of the astronomical cost. Mrs Mulholland, the most honest soul of them all, having sold a private course, had a stock question she always put to the customer at the very moment his pen hovered over the dotted line in the contract. It was "But can you really afford it?"

The six front office staff all did general duties as required, though Picasso and Mc McLeod would only leave their typewriters in case of someone being ill or in a very busy period (rare, this). The four leading dogsbodies, who covered all duties from interviewing prospects to making tea and fetching sandwiches, each had a speciality. Fletcher's was weighing things, whether it was a book-parcel to be sent to a student in Manchester, the day's outgoing mail to calculate the postage, or tea and coffee he kept in canisters bearing coloured portraits of King Edward VII and Lily Langtry. If you didn't assign other tasks to Fletcher, he would weigh all day. Approaching sixty, he was the epitome of the broken man, a latter-day Uriah Heap who twitched when you addressed him, hopped like a wallaby when he crossed the office and, once summoned to your presence, would not go away until you actually dismissed him. Fleeing Yugoslavia at the outbreak of hostilities there, he had served as a private in the British Army during the war, this making him more than normally vulnerable to the barking regime of Gilbert and Myers. Yet this poor-looking creature, with little grey tufts sticking out on either side of a bald head, permanently poised in a subservient, marsupial crouch, had hidden reserves of efficiency, talent and culture. You could address him in English, French, German, Italian, Russian, Czech, Polish or Serbo-Croat and find him fluent in them all. He once gave me a dozen lessons in Serb or Croat - I was never sure which - and proved to be an excellent teacher. Later, worried about the greyness of his complexion (he never took time off) I took him along on a one-week summer course at Barton-on-Sea where he astonished everyone by going for a half-hour swim every morning before breakfast, participating energetically in all the group activities and entertaining all of us in the evening after dinner playing the grand piano like a concert artist.

Poulier, whose age no one ever got to know, looked even worse than Fletcher. His face was not grey, but parchment yellow. His skull, egg-shaped, had four or five hairs at the pointed end, otherwise he was an emaciated Yul Brynner. He spoke all the languages Fletcher did, plus Spanish, Indonesian, Malay, Hindi, Bengali and Gujerati. He knew the grammatical secrets of another dozen tongues including Japanese. He was perhaps the most gifted linguist I have ever met. His speciality, in the Gilbert order of the day, was counting books.   Gilbert and Myers, perhaps on account of difficulties involved in the publication or transportation of books during the war, had amassed a huge stock of Berlitz books.   In 1963 there still remained thousands of them, all out of date and selling at the rate of about ten a week.   Gilbert had been determined not to order any new editions from Paris until his entire stock, paid for in good English pre-war pounds, had been sold in its entirety. This mountain of books, neatly piled in packets of twenty, was hidden away in the dimly-lit, cavernous cellar below the huge South Audley Street Mansion.

Inspecting the stock one day with Poulier, I walked down avenues, turned corners and lost myself in mazy alleys of brown paper parcels.   There were labels on the packets which said "20 English Books" or "20 Livres Français". Occasionally Poulier and I would open a packet, say "20 Nihongo Hon" only to discover that it contained Spanish or Polish editions, usually 1925 vintage. Poulier kept the inventory - a fine-sounding, business-like word - the statistics of which he entered into a thick red ledger printed in the reign of Queen Victoria.   One week he was missing 3000 books, most of them French.   The next week he had 1500 too many.   The figures seemed to vary according to the weather, Poulier's disposition or the number of burnt-out bulbs in his subterranean retreat.   It was a tricky, full-time job, but he managed it by absenting himself from Oxford Street just two mornings a week.   On these days he would bring back with him the five or six books required for the new students of the week. It happened sometimes that he would leave South Audley with two German books, two Spanish and one Czech, but would arrive at Headquarters with three German, one Polish and two Portuguese. When this occurred, he would scuttle back across Mayfair to rectify his errors. It was a much better system than keeping two separate stocks. (I agreed).

Elena Mulholland, a Russian lady of generous proportions, was the dominant personality in the front office. Her speciality, apart from that of discouraging people from taking private lessons, was to mother everybody else (except Mrs McLeod, whose countrymen had invaded Russia) and see to it that neither Fletcher nor Poulier died on the job by obliging them to drink tea or eat apples at regular intervals. Though untrained in business, she had a tremendous capacity for work and was always in a good mood unless somebody put her in a black one, when she would bristle and literally shake with rage. For the most part her beaming Mother Russia smile and genuine concern for students and colleagues gained her great popularity and affection. When later I transferred her to the front desk at South Audley Street (where we taught only English) her booming voice reverberated through all five storeys of that gloomy, venerable mansion, as she bossed little Japanese, Algerians, Iranians and Italians, sending them scurrying to their classrooms if they arrived late and scolding them mercilessly if they dared light a cigarette in no smoking areas.

Dr. Chistine Dobryziniecki, the fourth office dogsbody, should never have been in anybody's office in the first place. A shy, retiring Czech-Hungarian, soft of voice and academic in outlook and appearance, she was in an understandable state of bewilderment amidst the mixture of duties she struggled with – accounts and statistics one minute, sales the next, helping with Slovak or Rumanian translations, rushing upstairs to give a Hungarian lesson, she never knew what the next day would bring. Of sweet disposition, she had one or two doctorates and was, like Fletcher, one of those erudite, polyglot Central Europeans, well versed in literature, opera and ballet, forced by turbulent events to flee their native Vienna, Prague or Budapest and live in a bedsit in Fulham or Finchley. In the classroom, where I put her, she was fully in command, teaching German or any required central European language to a whole string of British executives for the next decade.

*   *   *   *   *

If I have painted a picture of an old-fashioned teaching institution, it was hardly less archaic than the approach adopted at that time by British companies to the problem of training their staff in foreign languages. I was accustomed to dealing with Finns, Norwegians and Portuguese, who not only pursued the study of English with great energy and enthusiasm, but regarded its acquisition and that of other foreign languages as an essential element in their basic education. A Nordic, Dutchman, Swiss, Belgian or Portuguese who does not speak English plus one other foreign language is simply not educated. Most of my collegues in German broadcasting had possessed fluent English and few Austrians, Italians and even Russians were restricted to one foreign language.

In 1963 only the citizens of the former great empires – British, French and Spanish – evinced reluctance to acquire fluency in foreign tongues. Within the sprawling reaches of these empires, one language had been enough, whether for administration, trade, diplomacy or social intercourse. *El Mundo Hispánico* was vast, the French language was taught with great efficiency in their possessions in Africa and the Far East, and in the British Empire the sun never set on someone speaking English, somewhere.

Today, people speaking English, French or Spanish as their native tongue have come to terms with the necessity of learning the languages of their trading partners or for use in the United Nations or the European Union. Yet there is still a gap to be closed between the attitude of these three peoples and say, the Danes, Dutch and Portuguese. The French use English `a contre-coeur. Spaniards who wander the streets of Madrid muttering to themselves "*Tengo que hablar inglés.*" are not quite sure why. The British, with their Anglo-Saxon cousins, Americans, Australians, New Zealanders, are still the most inept. It is a question of stance, not of talent or aptitude.

In 1963 only a small number of British companies – Unilever, Shell, Lloyds and ICI among them – had systematic programmes in foreign languages for their expatriate staff. Most companies hit the panic button a few weeks before the unfortunate employee was due to depart. Mr Thompson, headed for Turin, would need to be comfortably fluent in Italian. His Training Officer generously allowed him two mornings off each week in March. We were asked by another Training Officer to teach his export manager Arabic in two weeks. A Mr Clegg was donated to us for a week to learn Spanish, only for us to find out he was being posted to Rio de Janeiro. Some Personnel Officers would plan long term and ask us to teach their men the required language over one or two years. This type of student would be sent **once a week** for two hours. Often they would cancel owing to illness, holidays, too much work in the office or lack of interest or motivation. Occasionally, but not often, the Training Officers would wonder why they made little or no progress. Some students flirted with a language in this way for 5 years or more, during which time many of the teachers assigned to them would re-emigrate, retire on a pension or simply die. Other students died in mid-course, relatively confident in their use of *le passé composé* but never to discover the delights of *le subjonctif* and became history themselves before reaching *le passé historique*...

This had been going on for many years and the London Berlitz School was the main stage on which it was enacted. It was only natural that the Berlitz name in Europe should be associated with regular, leisurely, rather genteel tuition in foreign languages. Since before the turn of the century Dutch princesses, French bourgeois, young ladies from Belgravia and ballet dancers from Dresden, Munich, Prague and Budapest had faithfully attended their weekly lessons in whichever language it was fashionable to learn in a particular decade. This instruction was often oriented towards the arts, where certain expressions in French, Italian or German were most appropriate in delivering one's opinion on painting, opera or ballet. The acquisition of selected phraseology in a foreign tongue was a social asset, a useful card to play now and again; there was no sense of urgency involved.

Languages for business is an entirely different ball game. The German executive does not learn English for 15 years in order to quote Shelley or place a bet on a horse at Ascot. The Dutchman's mastery of our language enables him to negotiate for hours, haggle without the embarrassment of an interpreter, detect subtle changes in an Englishman's stamina or anxiety to conclude a deal – his skill in finalising a unit price or comprehending muttered asides among his opponents may save his company thousands or millions. The Swedes' social graces in English or German make their partners feel that they are dealing with people who do things right, who are almost like us, whom we can trust.

In the 1960s, British businessmen, with their schoolboy howlers' French and *Donnerwetter* German, just did not understand the role of languages in international trade. It is questionable if they really do today, though there are some admirable exceptions. They cannot see that bumbling Jack Smith, with his smug jovial ignorance of any foreign tongue, may be viewed in the same poor light as we would see a foreigner who had no knowledge of maths, or physics, or even British history. We pity people who do not share our delight in cricket or rugby. How would we look upon a Japanese who could not form the letters of our alphabet?

The fact that "other people can speak English" is often used as an excuse. Until 1939 England was a world power and English was (and still is) a world language. If linguistic arrogance is still available to us (what else is there for us to be arrogant about?) should we persist in continually playing this card? In the current global village situation, there are no points scored by insularity, yet failure to learn foreign languages inhibits our ability to penetrate foreign minds. The Europeans know us (and the Americans) much better than we know them and soon the Japanese, Koreans, Taiwanese and Indonesians will also know what makes us tick, how far they can go with us, whilst our ignorance of their language, (therefore of their culture) will still cause us to see them as "impassive" or "inscrutable".

At the end of 1963, full-time intensive language courses were unknown in London. Progressive training officers would often send us their staff for full days, but this was usually from 9 to 4 and a lunch break of one and a half or even two hours was often taken to allow the student to recover from the shocks of the morning. The lessons themselves, moreover, would frequently be interrupted by phone calls from the office and long conversations in English would ensue, completely derailing the train of thought in the language being studied.

*   *   *   *   *

In January 1964 a well-known insurance company hauled before me two forty-year-old gentlemen, who, they said had an urgent need to be fluent in French. When they told me they were leaving in two weeks I lost my temper and said if they were going to learn anything at all in a fortnight I would have to lock them up with two Frenchwomen and have them completely *incomunicado* from their office, friends and families. To my great surprise the training officer took me at my word and said I could have the two gentlemen (who also looked very interested) on those conditions. With such a mandate, I drove an hour out of London and rented four bedrooms and two seminar rooms in the CHA (Cooperative Holidays Association) hostel in Hindhead. It was hidden in a wood, extremely quiet and secluded and in fact closed for the winter. I bribed the warden and his wife, who lived on the premises and saw to the food, to make the facility available for 2 weeks. I persuaded two experienced French teachers to do the job (an unusual assignment for them). One was an extremely attractive Frenchwoman in her late twenties, the other (one could not go too far) was a lively male of the same age. The hours of instruction were 9-6 with one hour for lunch, taken with the teachers, in French. In the evening after dinner French would continue to be spoken. They could discuss homework, French crosswords, play cards or snakes and ladders, chess or dominoes, but not a word of English was to pass anybody's lips for 14 days. I paid the teachers 12 hours a day, the insurance men were motivated and cooperative and the company paid double. The results were excellent and both students spoke reasonable French **without inhibition or embarrassment** at the end of the period. The CHA warden thought we were all mad. Thus Total Immersion was born.

The concept was not readily accepted by British companies. The training officer involved recommended the method strongly and in 1964 and 1965 I repeated the experience a dozen times, nearly always with impressive results. But the idea of completely immersing oneself in a language, of deserting one's family while still living in England, was too revolutionary for British business. The Americans, however, took it up quickly. I was in regular touch with Charles Berlitz and it was not long before he developed a course along the lines I had indicated. He, I believe, invented the term **Total Immersion**. In a few months this type of instruction was being marketed across the United States with typical American marketing muscle and flair. It was a Berlitz product, though it was rapidly imitated by other schools and training organisations. Sales of these courses in the 1960s ran into the tens of millions of dollars. By 1970, total immersion courses were becoming common in London and Europe, though often on a day basis (9-5) with the student escaping homewards in the evening. Such non-residential courses are less successful but of course vastly more effective than the stop-start approach of five years earlier.

Back in 1964 I was still wrestling with the problem of how to convince English corporations that they should carry out more language training. In most of Europe and even Asia, the customer is already convinced. It is not a question of "should we learn foreign languages?" but rather "which languages should we learn?" As I continued to run schools in Finland and Portugal, I could not cease to be astonished by the differences in attitude and (by comparison with Finland at least) by the incredible backwardness of some British institutions. My dealings with the Kings Court Hotel was a case in point.

In order to secure accommodation at a reasonable price in London every summer (the months of June, July and August always produced a student "bulge") I had been negotiating a special tariff with this hotel based on guaranteed numbers each summer for the next two or three years. The Kings Court was a pleasant little 2-star establishment in Bayswater, unpretentious in the extreme, but conveniently located for shopping and sightseeing and not too far from our South Audley Street school. The then owner, a gentleman from the south of France named Crespo, told me about some of the problems he had encountered when he had purchased the property the previous year. The building had been in a general state of disrepair and the key employee, around whom the events of each day seemed to revolve, was an ageing caretaker named Simm. Crespo took over the management himself, but he noticed that the reception staff, chambermaids, waiters and kitchen staff always checked with Simm before they did anything. The hotel was unremarkable as far as the reception and bedrooms were concerned, its only notable feature being a fine, square dining room with a huge, multi-panelled window (occupying virtually the whole wall) at one end. One stuffy evening, Crespo asked one of the waiters to open the central section of this fine window to let in a little air for the guests. The waiter protested that the window had never been opened during the years he had been employed by the hotel and ignored Crespo's exhortations to open it until Simm was sent for. When the septuagenerian caretaker arrived, his face also registered horror at Crespo's proposal and he swore the window had not been opened for 30 years. Crespo was, however, a true son of the *midi* and was not to be disobeyed. He forced Simm to go through with it. The latter fetched a ladder and, climbing up it, tugged with all his strength at the catch on the central panel. Nothing happened for a minute or so, then suddenly, on further exhortation from Crespo, Simm with a superhuman tug flew backwards from his ladder and brought the whole window (i.e. the wall) down into the dining room. Diners were cut by flying glass, one of the waitresses had to be treated for shock and Simm was taken to hospital for concussion.

The new window cost Crespo the year's forecasted profit; his increasing irritation with Simm led him to fire the caretaker against the earnest advice of the entire staff. The problem seemed to be the cellar, where the controls for water, gas and electricity were located and where only Simm had operated for more than two decades. The cellar was criss-crossed with wires to such an extent that one could not cross from one side to the other without twisting, turning, bending and contorting oneself in a manner which only Simm seemed able to handle. On the morning after he was fired, Crespo went down to the cellar with a young electrician and spent a few hours rearranging the maze of wires in a more rational and orderly fashion. After that nothing in the hotel worked properly. Toilets flushed with hot water, emergency lighting woke everybody up in the middle of the night and the fire alarm went off three times a day. The cellar had to be "re-done" at further great expense.

In order to meet his rising repair bills, Crespo lowered his room charges to attract a greater number of guests. He had little success, so he lowered them even further. Eventually the advantageous prices attracted customers from two organisations – the Women's Church Guilds and the American army. The Church Guilds had frequent conferences in London and, being short of cash, were desperate for low-cost accommodation for visiting delegates from the provinces. American soldiers, on a few days leave in the English capital, were also on the look-out for cheap rooms. For a while Crespo filled his hotel. The ensuing problem was what one today might call client synergy, or more exactly, lack of it. The GIs naturally brought up girl friends (often prostitutes) to their rooms. They would have parties in the middle of the night and stagger round the corridors from room to room, often in a drunken stupor. Church Guilds women on the way to the toilet might be grabbed by a myopic corporal or confronted by a naked call girl. Sometimes the soldiers burst into the Guild women's rooms (by mistake). Crespo rarely slept. Eventually he banned all US soldiers, but the Church Guilds opted for alternative accommodation and Kings Court found peace again.

By the time Crespo had found us, he had completed his repairs, mended the hotel's reputation and slightly raised his prices. We used the hotel for several summers and never had a serious problem with the establishment. I recount these events, as Crespo related them to me, to give an example of the lack of professionalism I encountered in many instances in dealing with British firms in those years. I am English and happy to be so, but as it was the first time I had worked in an English business environment, I could not help but feel that Britain was being passed, in terms of efficiency, clear goals and modern approach, not only by the Americans, Germans and Scandinavians, but possibly by the French and others as well.

*   *   *   *   *

As far as *the Société Internationale* was concerned, however, there was little modernity in their approach to solving the problems of their London offspring. Setting aside for a moment the ageing staff and the lack of any clear goals for marketing, the initial and most important task was the refurbishing of the Oxford Street school. My experience with US Berlitz left me in no doubt as to what the Americans would have done – that is, rip out the guts of the old building, re-partition, re-decorate and re-furnish. The teaching was in fact not bad, so that a plush environment would have enabled us almost to double our fees, which were ridiculously low. I proposed this course of action to Montfort, who would not even consider it, in view of the investment involved. His suggestion was that the school should be made profitable and leasehold improvements could then be paid for out of profits.

At that time Berlitz was facing rather stiff competition in Oxford Street itself. LTC (Language Tuition Centre) had just leased a shiny new building on the other side of Oxford Circus. Their rent was rumoured to be £15,000 per annum (a huge sum in those days) and their marketing was vigorous. Once or twice I took up a position opposite this school and was impressed by the teeming numbers of students entering and leaving at bell-times. The gleaming white façade of the premises looked magnificent. Many other schools were also providing services, though LTC was at that time our chief rival, due to its proximity and its ability to teach all languages. The Paris Berlitz School, though in an old building, had reasonable décor. I had seen, however, German Berlitz schools that were measurably more attractive, not to mention our own Finnish schools and the plush establishment of the Berlitz Schools of North America. I likened the London School to an old, decrepit, leaking boat which needed to be repaired in order to win a race. The French attitude was win the race and we'll do the repairs with the prize money. In the end I spend a week-end in the school with 10 Australian students, washing the walls and repainting them in light beige – the cost was £100 and several rounds of bitter in the nearest pub.

Paris's shortsightedness with regard to marketing one's image and return-on-investment principles was in direct contrast to the kaleidoscopic world of ideas which was revealed to our Board members on the occasion of each board meeting. The board consisted of Montfort, Chairman, Mr Betts, Finance, Mr Parker, the company lawyer and myself! Betts and Parker both worked in the City, were calm, friendly, rather traditional Englishmen, no doubt appointed many years earlier by Gilbert and used to attending meetings where decisions and courses of action were generally dictated by Common Sense. If there were 10 items on the agenda, they discussed the first item till it was settled, then proceeded to item 2 and usually finished item 10 at 4:45 in the afternoon, leaving quarter of an hour for relaxing small talk or a dash to beat rush hour. They had had little to do with Frenchmen before and were less prepared for what was to come than I, who had attended many management and editorial meetings in Paris.

Montfort was no better or worse than the average French company president who chairs a meeting in the manner to which PDG's are accustomed. French people, in their communicative style, are essentially Latin and polychronic, that is to say that they have a tendency to think about, discuss and even do many things at the same time, instead of proceeding along a linear mental path more popular with Germans, British and Scandinavian people. The role of a PDG is to define *"Les Grandes Lignes"* that is to make participants in a meeting aware of the Grand Strategy and then to initiate animated and thorough discussion of all aspects of the plans in a manner designed to throw maximum light on the issues and to consider them from every possible angle. It is supposedly an empirical approach which will lead to a perfectly logical conclusion. The problem with a polychronic speaker is that while he is discussing item 8 on an agenda, he will be simultaneously considering the implications it has for items 2 and 5 dealt with earlier and which are now seen (by the Frenchman) in a different light from that in which they were discussed before. He will then go back to items 2 and 5 with the intention of revising, re-negotiating or changing them in some way. This tactic or habit can be very disconcerting to Anglo-Saxon or Germanic people who consider that previous items, once dealt with, have been "settled". Another problem with French speakers is that their superior imagination causes them, during discussion, to introduce a profusion of ideas, in the order they occur to them, and which may or may not be related to the subjects under discussion. Parker and Betts, during the first meetings, innocently began taking notes of Montfort's remarks. After several pages of increasingly hesitant scribble, they would abandon the task and just sit back in their leather chairs. The patient Betts, who attended all meetings, invariably asked the same weary question at four o'clock in the afternoon: "Well, gentlemen, could we perhaps summarize what we have agreed?"

We never did.

*   *   *   *   *

Montfort's inability to tune in to the same wavelength as the English was demonstrated by his relations with the Head of the English Department at South Audley Street, Scott-Clark. This young man, a rather portly figure in his late twenties and not unlike Montfort himself in appearance, had been spotted by Montfort as a likely lad about the time I took over. He was one of the best English teachers at South Audley and the Frenchman felt that there was a need for a Head of English to provide leadership for the dozen or so instructors, many of them part-time, whom we had on the staff. They were an exceptionally talented bunch, most of them being actors between plays or broadcasters temporarily without a programme. Lavinia Tauwhare had been a renowned broadcaster in New Zealand, David Berlin and Martin Scott, actors, had wonderful presence in the classroom and Sixsmith went on to read the news for the BBC. The irregular availability of these teachers eliminated them as possible heads of department or managers; Montfort concluded that the more solid figure of Scott-Clark, with a double-barrelled name to boot, would give us the continuity of leadership that was required.

I liked working with Scott-Clark, who, though he had no experience of management or leadership, was more than usually intelligent and possessed a fine sense of humour. It was a pleasure for me to escape for an hour a day from the HQ grind in Oxford Street and exchange anecdotes with him. He was a very literary person with a ready string of quotations from the best writers, especially Kipling, and knew a lot about the history of the British Empire. None of these attributes were likely to endear him to Montfort, who had had an initial meeting with him on his promotion explaining *les grandes lignes*.

It is not only in France that the boss or a managing director may indulge in giving a "pep talk" to someone taking up a new appointment. Indeed German employees require this in order to have their tasks "put into context" and it is a weekly or sometimes daily occurrence in Japan. American bosses do it – they call it "pumping someone up". Montfort spent more than an hour pumping up Scott Clark, who, with his aphorisms from Samuel Johnson, knowledge of the workings of the Empire, affiliation to the Establishment and double-barrelled name, had a natural inclination towards pomposity which needed little encouragement at this stage in his career. He interpreted Montfort's rhetoric as a prelude to a situation in which he, Scott-Clark, would be the chief architect of the Master Plan, which might need the occasional nod or slight modification from Paris, but which he would be allowed to develop in unfettered freedom. What I should have told him there and then was that when a PDG spells out *les grandes lignes* they are **his** *lignes* and that he expects a manager or department head to roll up his sleeves, put his head down and devote ten hours a day making sure they are implemented in the manner prescribed.

The following Monday morning, however, I had too many pressing tasks of my own to cross Mayfair with such cynical advice, so the pumped-up Scott-Clark picked out a nice big office (there was plenty of spare room at South Audley) went out and bought a nice red leather-topped desk and a neat little Afghan rug to spread in front of it. Half a dozen fine reference volumes completed the scene and Scott-Clark, taking himself off the teaching programme, seated himself carefully behind his antique desk and embarked on the planning of the Grand Strategy.

He had good ideas and I have no reason to believe that, in the fulness of time, they would not have been successful. He had a fertile imagination and could put two and two together as well. Mrs Mulholland, once she had made it clear that she ran the front office, tolerated his whims reasonably well and occasionally beamed at him when he sweetened her with quotations from Dostoievski and Gogol. A group of middle-age ladies from Cadogan Square, who preferred to study French at South Audley as Oxford Street was too far and a bit dingy, got on well with Scott-Clark, who persuaded them to buy another fifty lessons. They all agreed that the most prestigious French was Parisian spoken with a Belgravia accent.

Scott-Clark excelled himself one Friday morning answering a phone call in the front office while Mrs Mulholland was interviewing a walk-in. I was standing next to him and saw his jaw drop after his initial "Berlitz, good morning." What he actually heard was "Is that Berlitz? Just a moment I have the Queen on the line." There was a hiatus of half a minute, during which Scott Clark frantically gestured for everyone in the vicinity to keep quiet. The next thing he heard was a plummy "Good morning". Watched by all of us,

Scott Clark straightened his back, took a deep breath and intoned, heavy with respect:

"Good morning Your Majesty."

"Actually this is **Queen Magazine**, not Queen Elizabeth. We were wondering if you would like to place an advertisement in our next issue."

"Oh, I am so sorry, we get so many calls from the Palace", snarled Scott-Clark pompously, then adding what the good lady might do with her advertising. We all thought he handled it rather well.

Scott-Clark's mental nimbleness and social poise did nothing to endear him to Montfort, who considered one portly gentleman doing a prima donna behind a small desk was enough for any organisation. The arrangement of a couple of theatre outings for students with a generous school subsidy increased our President's hostility; the unauthorized purchase of another Afghan rug (a mere fifty quid in those days) led to an inevitable explosion of Gallic wrath and the sudden curtailment of Scott-Clark's career at South Audley Street. I was instructed to fire him with one week's pay and a two-line reference. I broke the news to him as a rare midday sun picked out rich glowing reds in his Muslim carpet. He was in the act of drawing up a short list of Japanese students he planned to take to Ascot and did not take the tidings well. He stuck around, Humpty-Dumpty like, for a couple of days, clearing out his four drawers and mentioning two or three famous lawyers. Mrs Mulholland and I gave him a quiet farewell tea party on the Friday afternoon at which he delivered a witty piece about the characteristics of French shopkeepers. I was sorry to see him go; after he left we turned his office into a dance floor.

*   *   *   *   *

One day I received a phone call from a certain John Ambler, who wished to learn Swedish. He turned out to be a wealthy, landed Yorkshireman, who had just got engaged to Princess Margrethe, the eldest daughter of the King of Sweden. Preparations for the wedding that summer were well advanced. Ambler, naturally, would have to speak on Swedish Television. Showing admirable initiative, he had resolved to make a speech in the Swedish language (which he had yet to learn). The whole thing, however, was to be kept secret from Her Royal Highness. He swore me to secrecy.

Fortunately I had a really good Swedish teacher up my sleeve. Eva Cormack was an elegant and extremely well-qualified Swedish lady in her late twenties, married to a man who, at the time of writing, is British Ambassador in Sweden. for the job – proficient, well-mannered and, above all, discreet. The gossip columnists of the Daily Express and the Daily Mail had been harassing Ambler ever since the announcement of the engagement and he was determined to maintain a cloak of secrecy around his language study until after the wedding. For this reason we decided that he would take his lessons not in the school, but at his apartments in Wilton Crescent. The instruction (3 times 3 hours a week) commenced.

Swedish is not particularly difficult for Yorkshiremen. Ambler was delighted to hear that the Swedish for "to play" (*leka* was the origin of the Yorkshire word "lakin" (as in "What are tha lakin here for?" He made reasonable progress and Eva's cloak-and-dagger entries and exits at Wilton Crescent passed unnoticed by the tabloid press. Ambler congratulated us on our discretion.

One afternoon I went round to his dwelling to watch a lesson in order to monitor his progress. It went well. After an hour or so, Ambler summoned his butler (a Jeeves clone) to bring in tea and scones for the three of us. I had to admire the magnificent silver tea pot and we said a few words about it in basic Swedish. Our pleasantries were interrupted by the harsh shrill of the old-fashioned sitting room telephone. Jeeves answered it of course.

"John Ambler's residence".

A look of horror then monopolized Jeeves' plump features. He put one hand over the mouthpiece of the telephone and turned to Ambler.

"It's the Daily Express – they want a progress report."

Ambler was at a loss for words, in either English or Swedish. He gaped at me, I squinted at Eva Cormack, she stared helplessly at Ambler. There are some Yorkshiremen who would have told the journalist to bugger off at this point, but Ambler did not belong to that category. When he had recovered his composure, he instructed Jeeves to say he was out of town and the receiver was gently replaced. The rest of the lesson was less of a success, though Ambler did his best to concentrate. He absolved Eva and myself from any blame – the tabloids just hounded him constantly, he confessed. I suppose it is a kind of compliment. The next morning the gossip column headlines were JOHN AMBLER LEARNS THE LANGUAGE OF LOVE. I suppose Swedes around the world were rather flattered at this description of their language – a distinction usually reserved for French, or perhaps Italian. We never discovered who at Berlitz had leaked the secret – no doubt for a few bob – but Ambler **did** eventually make his Swedish speech in Stockholm and, by all accounts, did not disgrace himself.

*   *   *   *   *

It would be nice to relate that in the two years I ran the London Berlitz school I was able to awaken British industry's interest in, or in some cases awareness of, the advantages of possessing staff who spoke foreign languages. These hopes did not materialize. Lack of adequate promotion, not to mention well-paid staff, made penetration of what could certainly be described as a sluggish market well-nigh impossible. The only way in which I could reach out towards the target of doubling the business was by concentrating on the English in England division. At least foreigners were interested in what we were doing. Methods of promotion were highly visible. Berlitz had nearly 200 schools on the European continent and each of these establishments was a potential agent for sending students to us. Imagine an organisation with two hundred ready-made outlets all with the same brand name and with customers who were likely to want to study in the British Isles in any case! It should have been an in-house jamboree. In fact there was hardly any inter-school movement. Gilbert-and-Myers insularity combined with a graying population of European directors had led to a diminishment of interest in Berlitz cross-channel activity. London had done nothing to encourage their small student body to take part of their courses on the continent, neither had they begged their European colleagues to send them business. The Paris school sent annual groups to Roman Catholic Ireland, whence they returned with rich brogues picked up in Cork and Limerick. I was recruited twice by Montfort to shepherd over sizeable batches of French school children, all travelling on July 31st (*le Grand Départ*) and returning home on the last day of August. We used to arrive in Cork around 11 pm after a bout with Aer Lingus and a long drive from Dublin in two busloads. Try matching up 96 squealing Parisian 15-year-olds with 96 Irish landladies in the dark streets of Cork some time and you will really get to know why Guinness is good for you.

I promised our European colleagues attractive commissions, Bayswater accommodation, trips down to Greenwich, in-house dancing and – oh yes – good lessons. The last was of little interest to the kids, but parents responded well (keep them off the London streets) and a mixture of nationalities was an extra bonus. Helsinki and Lisbon kicked in with 50 students a year each and our teaching standards eventually attracted executives, especially from northern Europe. Two lively Italian teachers, Sandro d'Addario and Nicola Castoro, organised the social events, especially in summer, and our dance hall would have been sold out, had we been selling it. Sandro eventually became the Berlitz supremo in Canada (after a few years in Japan) and Nicola is still one of the best teachers of Italian in the United Kingdom.

My first two children were born during this period and my parents moved down from Wigan to London to help with the baby-sitting. The cavernous basement in South Audley Street had a self-contained flat which they utilized. There was ample space for recreation and I had an Alec Brook table tennis table installed. Alec himself used to come to play and Tapio Penttilä, the then Finnish champion, spent a couple of months with us in the spring of 1964. I also made the acquaintance at this time (when attending the World Table Tennis Championships in Llublyana) of Ladislav Moudry, a famous Czech veteran who was a member of the Czechoslovak wartime squad of Vana, Andreadis, Tereba, Stipek and Moudry. Ladislav was the fourth best player in the world in 1940 and even two or three decades later was capable of thrashing the national champions of several countries. This incredible Czech sportsman (proficient also at tennis, volleyball and soccer) still, at the age of 73, beats anyone over 60 in the Czech Republic at either tennis or table tennis! He spends a month with us every summer.

The English department prospered. Two efficient secretaries, Jennifer Stratton and Agnese McDonald, aided the amiable Elena Mulholland, as student numbers grew. My mother became friendly with Lord Fraser, the kindly President of St. Dunstan's who occupied the second floor of the mansion. He was soon eating stew and Lancashire Hotpot. Three of my Finnish TV colleagues, Harkimo, Vuorensola and Ruuhonen took a 3-week English course at Berlitz in the summer of 1964. The perennially wise-cracking Ruuhonen claimed he could say "There you are!" in 18 different ways and with 18 different meanings. David Willey, my former colleague from Finland and Norway, joined us as Director of Studies, also taking charge of summer courses which we held not only in London, but also residentially in places as far apart as Bangor, Ambleside, Barton-on-Sea and the Highlands of Scotland.

The two years I spent in London were pleasant in as much as we enjoyed our private life, our loyal colleagues and some of the attractions of the capital, but from the work point of view there was no incentive to increase my tenure of the London management. The Paris yoke was heavy, their vision myopic. Huge opportunities beckoned for an organisation which would demonstrate efficient marketing methods, improved facilities, an innovative approach to learning. Instead we spent hours discussing whether books should be sold at eleven shillings or eleven and six and our Oxford Street school – in one of the world's prime locations – continued to resemble a musty museum. It is true that Princess Anne signed on for a month's intensive French – the upstairs toilet had to be hastily spruced up and reserved for her.

I gave notice in March 1965 and left London in September. The summer of 1965 showed a substantial increase in business, almost exclusively in the English department. My wife and I were ready for another spell abroad – the Far East appealed to us. But first I wanted to carry out a publicity stunt which involved a little adventure. Helsinki was about to celebrate its tenth anniversary and I wished to mark the occasion with something novel. This was the Language Bus.

Chapter 11

The Language Bus in the Arctic

I have never quite made up my mind about whether the Language Bus rates among the best or the worst of my ideas. I was thirty-five at the time and ten years in business had taught me some rudiments of pragmatism, but I suspect the unrelenting mediocrity of the Paris management engendered in me an unstoppable impulse to do something different, or original, or at least to make a gesture in that direction.

It was mid July, the English had left town and the foreign hordes thronged Oxford Street and prowled round the speakers at Marble Arch like lions round a lame zebra. One night I shared the front seat on the upper deck of a London bus with three tipsy Finns. They giggled with glee at the "roller coaster" ride – no double-deckers in Finland, you know. As I was a bit tipsy myself, I had a sudden glimpse in my mind's eye of me driving a London double-decker around Lapland. That night I dreamt about the same thing.

Now, I have always had a weakness for double-deck buses. We had a lovely fleet of them in Wigan where I grew up. They were sensibly painted cherry-and-white – the same colours as the shirts worn by Wigan Rugby League players – they were familiar, cosy vehicles used extensively by the local populace. Downstairs they would be crammed with housewives and their bulging shopping bags, upstairs packed with black-faced pitmen and grammar school boys with their surreptitious fags. Like many other schoolboys I had a period longing to be a bus driver. Of course I went to university and all that, but I never really got it out of my system.

September 1965 marked the 10th anniversary of the founding of the Helsinki Berlitz school – my first business. Though I was rarely there, I still ran it at a distance, along with the four other Finnish schools and, surprisingly enough, they enjoyed continuing prosperity. In 1965 language laboratories were right in vogue and every language school in London except Berlitz had one. Suddenly three things came together in mysterious coalescence: I would create a mobile language laboratory in a London double-decker bus and drive it over the Arctic Circle and then down to Helsinki as a stunt to commemorate the founding of the Finnish Berlitz schools.

Well, as a stunt, it worked – the press coverage was tremendous – but as I began to take the first steps to implement this wild scheme, a second, and unexpected, agenda began to develop. The world did not have any mobile language laboratories. As I canvassed various purveyors of equipment (there were many in a very competitive market) word got around in the trade and elsewhere about what I was trying to set up. I had of course, to buy a bus. This did not prove to be difficult, as in fact London Transport had a sizeable rest home for retired double-deckers somewhere out in Redhill. Buses are not quite the same as people. It is true, that many of them take up retirement while they are still in relatively good health, but, unlike humans, their condition does not deteriorate (if they are well-looked after) and they do not die. As they cannot be buried – dead or alive – they tend to accumulate in ever-increasing numbers, too good for the scrap-heap but for some reason unwanted on London's streets. Consequently the Transport Authority is very anxious to sell them to anyone crazy enough to drive one away, whether to adorn his back garden, use as a retirement caravan, go joy-riding round the British Isles, lay on excursions for the local Labour Club or (you've guessed) to turn into a mobile language laboratory.

I got one for £550. I don't remember why it had been withdrawn from the roads, but it was authentic, painted a nice green, cheap and (I was assured) was good for another 50,000 miles.

By the time the equipment had been installed (upstairs) and we had made an audio-visual "classroom" on the lower deck, a certain buzz of excitement was discernible among various people who had come into contact with the project. The tenth anniversary of my little schools was of no import to them; what now stared us in the face was a new and perhaps viable business.

The main reason why many people are unsuccessful at learning foreign languages is lack of motivation. This applies particularly to Anglo-Saxons, whose language currently dominates five continents. The second most important reason for failure is a general lack of receptiveness. When we are in receptive mood, we can imbibe and learn most things quickly and easily – the words of a song, the gist of a story, the ability to swim etc. If we are in a non-receptive mood (frustrated, distracted, too hot, too rushed) then our capacity to learn something new is reduced almost to zero. Many under-achievers in the language learning field enter the classroom suffering from one distraction or another. A really fruitful attention span is often thought to be between 45 and 90 minutes, depending on the learner. Most students, especially adults, arrive for their language lesson having spent 45-90 minutes travelling to it, sometimes in difficult conditions (Tokyo underground, London taxis, etc.) I had often thought that for adults it would be better if the classroom were taken to them, rather than their having to make the trip. A mobile language laboratory (in a bus) could be driven right to their office door. It could, moreover, be timed to arrive just as they finished their office day. And it could bring the teacher, too.

Various London businessmen saw the viability of this concept and I received not a few offers with a view to setting up a joint venture. It was, however, a difficult moment for me. As I was just working out the last days of my notice with London Berlitz (and needed to be in Helsinki with the bus not later than the 26th of September), any immediate participation on my part was not feasible. It would have been possible to exploit the project on my return, but mentally I was already heading for Japan. Montfort had hinted that I would not be allowed to retain my European franchises if I were ever to join the Americans. Dana von Uexkull, the German baroness who managed the Finnish schools, was, I knew, anxious to buy them. At any rate, I was all set for my long bus ride. I consequently did not exploit Mobile Language Laboratories at that time.

*   *   *   *   *

There were various things to organize regarding the trip. Once the bus was fully equipped, I had "Berlitz for Languages" signs made for each side of the vehicle. On the front we painted LONDON TO LAPLAND. I had a team too. Vince Canty, an Australian teacher, wanted to go for the ride and was proficient in operating the language equipment. In view of the considerable distances involved, I engaged Ernie Taylor, former Liverpool bus driver, to make up the trio. The paper work for taking the bus to the continent and securing the necessary insurance papers took less time than we expected. Once I had learnt the art (with Ernie's assistance) of backing a double-decker round right-angled corners, I felt we would make our destination. Ernie said the bus was in first class shape.

The route was Dover-Boulogne, then through Belgium and Germany, Denmark and Sweden, right round the top of the Gulf of Bothnia to the Finnish border, thence up to Rovaniemi, the capital of Lapland. After that there would be the 1000-kilometre descent to Helsinki. In 1965 Sweden still drove on the left, as we do in the UK. France, Belgium, Germany, Denmark and Finland have driven on the right since Napoleon made all of Europe switch in 1805. The Swedes betrayed the English in 1967 and started driving on the right, but we have held firm. Ernie, proficient driver though he was, developed a gnawing sense of anxiety as we approached France, as he had never in his life driven on the right. In fact he had never before left Britain, where he was mainly seen on the streets of Liverpool.

I assured him that driving on the other side of the road was an easy transition, especially for a man of his competence and experience. Yet in the back of my mind there lurked the memory of what had happened on the Caribbean island of St Thomas a few years before. Most English-speaking island nations in the Caribbean drive on the left – a legacy of their colonial past. But St Thomas is located in the American Virgins and the US government switched the traffic to the right hand side to be in conformity with the USA. Unfortunately this resulted in a catastrophic increase in accidents involving donkey carts. This continued to such a degree that the authorities were obliged to rescind their decision and go back to the left hand side of the road – a regulation which is in effect today. The cause of the accidents was a by-product of the hot and humid St Thomas climate, which led to many cart drivers falling asleep, whereupon the donkeys crossed automatically to the left and promptly collided with oncoming vehicles.

With all this in mind, I drove the first 30 miles in France before handing over to a nervous Ernie. He was, however, somewhat emboldened by seeing me do the trick and held the right hand side fine for 10 miles before hitting the first roundabout and going round it **clockwise** `a l'anglaise* and finishing up on the left in due course, head to head with a French farmer on a tractor of all things. The farmer hurled the abuse customary in such *imbecilités* in that country – it was all lost on Ernie, though the level of his self-esteem had sunk to such a nadir that no reprimand was even needed.

*   *   *   *   *

I will not bore the reader with a mile-by-mile account of our progress or routing. We demonstrated our laboratory in German grammar schools, ran over a few Belgian rabbits who were crossing the road looking the wrong way. The wheel-on-the-right-pavement-on-the right combination led to my unseating a red-jacketed Danish cyclist postman whom I gently brushed on the shoulder in passing. Danish subjunctives flashed like knives for a while, but we finished up sipping Carlsberg together. We gave him a ride in the bus, in return for his not reporting us to the police.

From Copenhagen we drove up to Hamlet's castle in Elsinore and took the ferry to Helsingborg in Sweden. Ernie was now happy again and did a lot of rally stuff across to Stockholm and up the north-east Swedish coast. It is 1320 kilometres from Helsingborg to the Finnish border and Ernie certainly earnt his wages. Canty was fascinated by the trees and lakes – apparently they are both in short supply in the part of Australia he came from.

We were staying at small hotels and bed-and-breakfast houses along the route. Parking (even a double-decker) is less of a problem in the Nordic countries than it is in London or Hong Kong and some of the establishments we stayed at seemed quite pleased when our vehicle attracted the usual crowd of curious onlookers. A succession of local newspapers interviewed us each morning, or whenever the bus came to their attention. The drive up the western side of the Gulf of Bothia is pretty boring, mainly trees on both sides and the same kinds of conifers all the way. One night we arrived late in a small Swedish town – Umeå – and were unable to find any lodging. The hotels were all full and the landladies were either fully booked or didn't like the look of us. At nearly midnight we gave up and drove north out of town. After 10 minutes a Volvo flashed past us doing about 60 miles an hour. When he was about 50 metres ahead of us, I saw his brake lights flash, heard a loud **splat** and watched him veer from side to side and wind up in the left hand ditch. I braked hard to avoid hitting him before he lurched to the side. We got out in a hurry to see if anyone was hurt. The two people in the Volvo were OK, but a huge bleeding hulk lay all across their bonnet with its head and antlers in the ditch. They had hit an elk crossing the road. The men were shaken, but unharmed apart from bruises. The car was a write-off. The elk, which weighed about 400 kilos was unfortunately still alive, though obviously moribund.

A driver coming in the opposite direction took in the scene and drove into Umeå to alert the police. The two Swedes went with him; we stayed with the poor animal, though there was nothing we could do. When two policemen arrived, they first produced a long knife and gently probed the elk's heart which quickly caused it to breathe its last. After that they took some measurements and asked us a few things. Their English was not very good and, as they seemed to find the investigation tedious, they soon abandoned it. Apparently collisions with elks in September happened every day, so few people were prosecuted. When they had erected some warning signs around the stricken vehicle and animal, they returned to town.

By this time, we had felt it imprudent to drive any further, so we continued another mile till we found a grassy lay-by, parked the bus, went "to bed" and fell asleep. Around 1 a.m. I was awakened by a sharp rapping on the window of the bus. It was the police again – the same two who had dispatched the unlucky animal. They seemed less friendly now and resurrected some mean phrases in English. What did we think we were doing? Hadn't we heard of the Swedish vagrancy laws? This was not Albania, you know. Why were we not spending the night in a proper establishment? When I told them Umeå's inns were jammed to the rafters, they snapped a few things in Swedish to each other and then informed me that we should have to go to the police station. We followed the police car for the ten miles back into town and they motioned us into a parking place outside their precinct. They ordered us to pack our night things and took us into the station, where we had to fill in some forms. We were then led to the cells, assigned one each and promptly abandoned. Ernie was not used to jails, or even the idea of them, but I pointed out that we had warm accommodation for the night – blankets, pillows, towels, central heating – two stars better than half the hotels in Russell Square and much more welcoming than the seat of a London bus. Canty, with an air of unconcern no doubt born of good Australian ancestry, simply lay down fully dressed and snored seconds after his head hit the soft grey cushion.

The Swedish police, non-communicative in the extreme (as seemed to be general in that part of the country) woke us up at 6:30 and served us hot oat porridge with melting butter and thick cream on top. Ernie, delighted with this home-like outcome, drove happily away at sunrise, not sure whether he had been arrested or not.

*   *   *   *   *

We had been told that Lapland abounded in mosquitoes the size of prawns and Ernie, who was used to eating paper pags full of the latter on Blackpool and New Brighton sands, was developing a new form of trepidation. It was, however, late in the season for these insects and early frosts had in fact finished them off before our arrival. More problematic was the routing as we kept having trouble with low bridges in northern Sweden where the information provided by the authorities frequently turned out to be inaccurate; on one occasion we had to take a 60-kilometre deviation to be able to proceed north-east as was required.

After nearly a week en route we crossed the Finnish frontier at the Lapland town of Tornio and continued north, on the right hand side of the road now, towards Rovaniemi. Ernie and Canty (used to kangaroos) were intrigued to see the odd reindeer and Lapps in their colourful red, blue and yellow attire. The Lapland press had been alerted and we knew that a small press reception had been arranged at the Hotel Pohjanhovi in Rovaniemi. A formidable obstacle barred the way, however. Rovaniemi, at that time a small provincial capital of 5000 inhabitants, is approachable from the south only by a long metal bridge, consisting of steel girders top, sides and bottom. Our bus was six inches too high to pass under the overhead girders. Studying our maps, we were unable to find another route in, as the Kemijoki River cuts right across Lapland and other low bridges cut off our access to Rovaniemi even if we made detours of over a hundred kilometres. So near, yet so far.

We had been facing this impasse for a couple of hours, during which time some journalists and a cross-section of the Rovaniemi public had crossed the bridge to see us, when the local headmaster found the solution. He brought forty schoolchildren over and piled them in the bus, while Ernie carefully let half the air out of all the tyres. In this way, we crawled under the girders, at two or three miles an hour, with an inch to spare over our roof. We got to the half way point when a large central girder scraped the top of the bus and Ernie had to stop again. Another twenty children and more airletting finally did the trick. We entered the Lapland capital just before dark.

The next day we demonstated our technology at the local grammar school, not least to thank the resourceful headmaster who had contributed the useful scholars. The press took a lot of pictures and wrote nice things about us. We ate reindeer stew with mashed potatoes followed by Arctic cloudberries with whipped cream. Later in the afternoon we drove ceremoniously over the Arctic Circle and took some more photographs.

After repeating our tricks on the bridge, we left friendly Rovaniemi and headed south. The rest of the trip was something of an anti-climax, though grammar schools along the way, such as those in Oulu and Tampere, showed great interest in both our vehicle and its contents. More than half a dozen newspapers recorded our progress to Helsinki, where we paraded the bus up and down the main streets and held a lively 10th Anniversary Party on the 27th September 1965.

I was never able to exploit the commercial possibilities of the Mobile Language Laboratory, as I accepted an assignment in the Far East shortly after I arrived back with the bus in the UK. The venture was a lot of fun. Besides benefiting from the promotion it offered, it was exciting in a way to have pioneered the world's first mobile language laboratory, though for all I know, it might well have been the last. I sold the bus, years later, to a collector of double-deckers. Apparently it was a rare model, though it looked the same as any other to me. When you've seen one London bus, you've seen 'em all.

Chapter 12

Japan 1966

The successive atomic bomb attacks on Hiroshima and Nagasaki in 1945 had sealed Japan's fate and made the immediate cessation of hostilities virtually inevitable. For a nation that had never suffered a major defeat in her proud, warlike history, surrender – for so long an unthinkable concept for a Japanese – suddenly loomed up as the only alternative to complete annihilation. Emperor Hirohito intervened with decision and un-God-like Common Sense. The Japanese people must bear the unbearable. The war could not go on. The Americans had won.

The humiliation of Japan would have been complete had it not been for the generous, unvindictive attitude of the conqueror. The shattered economies of Europe were to receive Marshall aid; Japan would be totally reorganized by the Americans in nearly every field of activity: the war machine would be dismantled, the *zaibatsu* broken up, the economy re-built, the armed forces restructured, the legislature re-written, a new constitution compiled and imposed. This gargantuan task was given to General Douglas McArthur, the United States Commander-in-Chief in the Pacific. He was an excellent choice for the job for reasons that had more to do with Japanese historical tradition than with American intuition.

The figure of the Emperor has been ever-present in Japanese history since the 6th or 7th centuries and has had a significant influence on Japanese thinking, attitudes and behaviour. For centuries he has been seen as the undisputed symbol of the Japanese nation – descended from God and the personification of unity. All-powerful he has never been; power in the Japanese islands has traditionally been shared by the *daimyo* – warlords – commanding allegiance and obedience in their respective fiefs according to the strength and aggressivity of their own band of *samurai*. The numbers of powerful *daimyo* fluctuated wildly, depending on military success or re-groupings, but not infrequently a particular warlord would be seen as dominant, or even supreme, and at such times he would guide Japan's fate both militarily and politically. Such a supremo would be known as the *shogun* ; Tokugawa Hideyoshi was the best known of them all. *Shoguns* would rarely conflict with the Emperor and the Court, using them instead as a cloak of respectability.

The xenophobic Tokugawa closed Japan to foreigners in 1600 and it was not until Perry's Black Ships in 1853 that the Americans were able to prise open the oyster and force the Japanese to trade with the rest of the world. In the years that followed, *shogun* power declined and Emperor Meiji (1878) took the forestage in the succeeding decades as the guiding hand on his people. During this period and up to the First World War, Japanese were sent to the United States and Europe in large numbers to study commerce, technology and all Western institutions.

In 1946, when the Emperor shouldered responsibility for the defeat and denied his divinity, it was not unnatural that the confused Japanese people should look left and right for the new leader. And there he was, standing next to Hirohito in the well-known photograph – General Douglas McArthur, 6 feet 2 inches tall, strong-willed, mature, all-powerful – the new *shogun* of Japan. McArthur, like previous *shoguns* before him, was clever enough not to destroy the concept or institution of the Imperial dynasty. Divine, no, but unifying factor, yes. The readiness of the Japanese people to accept this duality – historically so familiar – that of the undisputed conqueror and the enduring face of Japanese unity and uniqueness – made the "reconstruction" of Japan a relatively easy task for American administrators and a digestible prescription for Japanese society.

Post-war rebuilding and change in Japan was protracted and often tortuous. In the aftermath of defeat food was scarce, life was spartan and frustrating for millions of Japanese, but American aid was generous and ever-flowing. The traditional Japanese qualities of collectivist effort, sacrifice and co-operation played their part. Once the big wheel began to turn, the momentum gradually increased to become unstoppable. The US-Japan alliance became a reality and, aside from the political implications, a commercial bond was forged which led to the greatest bilateral trade that the world has ever seen.

The alliance with the Americans meant, as far as our profession was concerned, that Japan would soon emerge as the biggest single language market anywhere. The world at large does not speak Japanese. To trade with other countries and to communicate with them to an extent commensurate with Japan's size and importance, Japanese people in many fields of activity would need practical abilities in English and probably other languages. As well as businessmen and politicians, the entire youth of the nation would be interested in the language of the conquerors and would perceive English as the key to an understanding of the ways of the (successful) West. English would be a mandatory subject throughout the Japanese educational system. This would provide familiarity with grammar but, in all probability, precious little spoken fluency. The opportunities for an experienced language school entering Japan were almost limitless.

And this is how it turned out to be, but not without a lot of spade work. The main problem was that the rights to exploit the Japanese language market belonged not to the American half of Berlitz, but to the French. As early as 1960 I had intimated to Roger Montfort that we ought to be making definite plans to open up Japan. My Finnish and Portuguese schools were well-established and I was ready to have a go at the Far East. My relations with

Shirooka had stimulated my interest in the fine qualities of the Japanese people, which I was anxious to experience at first hand. Also I was fascinated by the strange, subtle language. Above all there was a huge market beckoning – and clearly under-serviced.

Montfort indicated some interest, but exuded caution. After all, the war had only been over fifteen years. What would be the size of the investment? I suggested I make a quick trip to Japan to find out. Ah, but that too would cost money. How about doing a month's survey on a total budget of £2000 ? He went pale. I re-did my sums, cut the stay to 2 weeks and switched from Air France to Aeroflot. A thousand pounds. It was still too daunting a sum. Staying at the YMCA brought it down to about £900 or so, but at that stage I gave up. A few years passed.

In 1964 Tokyo hosted the Olympic Games, the Japanese economic boom was evident to all, and an even bigger boom was on the way. Robert Strumpen-Darrie had, a couple of years previously, departed from the US Berlitz principle of concentrating activity in the United States and had founded a few schools in Canada, where change in legislation had made it important for Canadians to develop bilingualism. The outstanding success of these new Canadian schools encouraged Strumpen-Darrie to think about other non-US markets and it was hardly surprising that Japan entered into focus. We had maintained close relations since 1957 and he had visited some of my schools. He knew of my interest in Japan, shared by his assistant, Rafael Alberola, whom I had interviewed for a job in Europe some year earlier.

In 1965, Strumpen-Darrie negotiated with Roger Montfort for the transfer of the rights to use the Berlitz name in Japan from the French to the American company. I was not privy to these negotiations or to the sum involved, but Americans usually get what they want and it was not long before I received a phone call from Strumpen-Darrie to confirm that the Japanese rights had indeed been acquired. Would I accept the post of General Manager of the newly formed Berlitz East Asia if it were offered to me?

It was not difficult for me to reply affirmatively, since I had decided not to renew my contract with London Berlitz and had already given 6 months notice to end in September 1965. I had accepted the London job just to get Montfort out of a hole; the salary I was being paid was a mere fraction of my remuneration from my own schools; the absence of investment in the operation did not allow the school to shed its Dickensian atmosphere; urging reform simply meant adding further strain to my relations with the parsimonious French president; apart from my developing fondness for Mrs Mulholland, Poulier, Fletcher and Dr Dobryziniecki, there was no reason for me to stay.

*   *   *   *   *

As soon as it was confirmed that I would go to Tokyo, Montfort insisted that I sell all my European schools. They belonged to me, of course, but he threatened to cancel the franchises. Ten years' hard work had gone into building up these businesses; they were market leaders in all three countries My instinct was to tell him to cancel and be damned, for well-established schools can survive a change of name and continue to thrive, as my later experience showed. However, within three or four months I was able to negotiate the sales to colleagues who had been working with me for some time. The Norwegian franchise was sold to Wenche Garmann, the Finnish schools to the German Baroness Dana von Uexkull and the Portuguese schools to Anna Candiago. These good ladies, armed with shiny new franchises and bustling schools seemed to have their future assured, but Berlitz politics and clash of personalities led to the gradual withering away of these establishments. Five years later, when I returned to Europe from Japan, only three of the nine schools still existed and they were tiny. The precious royalties, so coveted by Montfort, had dried up. Today Berlitz has one surviving school in Helsinki and one in Lisbon – they are both insignificant.

*　　*　　*　　*　　*

Strumpen-Darrie and I began to make our plans. Although I was already rather familiar with the American Berlitz system, it was decided that I should go to New York and take a Total Immersion course in Japanese there, before going on to tour the prolific Canadian schools. I enjoyed this period of preparation, which took place in February and March 1966. My Japanese teacher Nishino had been well-trained by the Americans. It was interesting for me to be on the receiving end of a T.I. – entirely in Japanese, of course.

My trip to Canada was no less interesting. The Canadian schools were headed by a remarkable individual called Jean Piton, a short, stocky, impeccably-dressed Frenchman from Tours who had spent some time in Algeria and trusted only *pieds noirs*. Starting with Montreal, he had soon added Toronto and Ottawa, going on to establish a string of a dozen schools in the small towns of provincial Quebec. They all made money. Riding the wave of favourable legislation, it seemed that Piton could do no wrong. Paid a percentage of profit, he had earned $80.000 personally in 1965. I thought this compared rather well with Fletcher's twelve pounds a week.

Piton was a man of ideas. Besides opening one school a month, he had just rented a spanking new headquarters in the best location in Montreal and furnished it like an Arabian palace with Berlitz money. He had also opened a residential training centre in the Laurentian mountains and at the time of my visit was planning the building of a small airstrip so his students could fly in directly.

Strumpen-Darrie, who tended to give his directors a free hand as long a they turned in regular profits, was beginning to get nervous about these grandiose plans and profligate spending; he lent me a Minox camera to take pictures of Piton's "furnishings". I had a good time snapping Moroccan rugs and interior fountains, though Piton himself was far from pleased, asking me to give him copies of all photographs.

Strumpen-Darrie had instructed Piton to "show me everything", which meant I could attend management meetings. These were often held late at night, over and after dinner in dimly-lit hotel cabinets. Piton, flanked by half a dozen *pieds noirs*, sat at one end of the table with the main light behind him – a handsome, if somewhat sinister figure with his prematurely white hair, black eyebrows, grey suit and pale blue tie. He seated me at the far end of the table, with a couple of empty chairs between me and his henchmen. The food and wine were first class, the *pieds noirs* mumbled reports on their operations over *couscous* or *tournedos*; Piton snapped orders in soft, decisive tones; I strained my ears to catch their particular jargon. The conversation was purely business, nobody mentioned the delicious food and my few attempts at levity were greeted with polite smiles. When Piton had finished his coffee and stood up, all rose with him and melted away, instantly, with a quiet "*Bonsoir, Monsieur*". Nobody thanked Piton for the dinner, no-one seemed to pay the bill. We all went home to catch a few hours sleep before executing Piton's orders at 8 a.m. His men were devoted to him; they were all making money. My friend Mathias Wallen, who was later appointed director of the Vancouver Berlitz school and attended many such management meetings, inherited my lonely chair at the end of the table. As the only English-speaking director in the Canadian Berlitz set-up, his presence went a long way towards disturbing Piton's carefully constructed ambience.

Piton was friendly enough towards me and I admired his courage and style. Properly controlled, he would have been a great asset to Berlitz North America for many a year. As it turned out, his flamboyance exceeded Strumpen-Darrie's patience, or pocket, or both, and a couple of years later neither he nor the majority of his disciples were with the company.

*   *   *   *   *

In April 1966 Strumpen-Darrie packed me off to Tokyo in the company of Rafael Garcia Alberola, who was to stay a couple of weeks to settle me in. Alberola was a former French teacher at the Berlitz school in Pforzheim, Germany, who had decided to emigrate to the United States in search of the American Dream. Blond and humorous, he was a man of my own age and we made a good team. Born and raised in Casablanca, his mentality was more Arab than French. A canny negotiator, he trusted no-one, despised laziness and hypocrisy, worked hard himself at all hours of the day and night. During his five years with Berlitz North America, he had been put in charge of various schools – usually ailing ones – and had doubled the business in nearly every case. With his reputation as a trouble-shooter established, he was appointed special assistant to Strumpen-Darrie, who used him in a variety of roles. Most often this was one of hatchet man, a role he was quite fond of. This was not required in Japan as we had no staff and nobody to hatchet. Alberola and I always saw eye to eye about the business and I still enjoy good relations with him.

*   *   *   *   *

We arrived in Tokyo one sunny April morning at 10 a.m. after an overnight flight via Seattle. Haneda airport was a bustling microcosm of Japan – politely smiling but watchful officials, clean counters and stalls, a stream of instructions emanating from the loudspeakers, dozens of bowing young women in white shirts and blue tunics, money changers pushing plastic trays full of yen at arriving passengers, everywhere people scurrying back and forth in a controlled, muted hubbub. The delicious smell of *teriyaki* pervaded the golden morning sunlight. Alberola and I took a Toyota taxi with a door that opened by itself; the taxi-driver wore white gloves. It was half an hour's drive to the Okura Hotel.

The Okura, next to the American Embassy in the centre of the Akasaka district, was in those days rated by many as the best hotel in Tokyo. Strumpen-Darrie had generously booked me in for a month, Alberola for the duration of his stay. After that I would have to find more modest accommodation. In 1966 the Okura cost 6000 yen a night for a big single room with bath. At that time the yen was 1000 to the pound, but even at £6 a night it seemed horribly expensive to me. London hotels were then £3 to £4 a night. Alberola and I went down to the coffee shop for a snack before going to bed for a few hours sleep. At eleven in the morning the hotel cafe was packed with smartly-dressed men and elegant women nibbling toast or cakes. The quality and tasteful nature of their attire – so much more attractive than daytime apparel in London or New York – made us wonder if there was some special event taking place.

*   *   *   *   *

Later that afternoon and during the next few days, Alberola and I addressed ourselves to two important issues which demanded immediate attention. One was the structure of our company in Japan; the other was the location of premises from which we would operate. As far as the first question was concerned, Strumpen-Darrie had had several contacts with the Ricoh Company – a conglomerate producing mainly cameras, watches and sewing machines. It had been suggested that the best way to gain a quick foothold in the Japanese market was to form a 50/50 joint venture with a well-established Japanese domestic company. Strumpen-Darrie had only a vague idea of what Ricoh was; in fact it was a huge and very rich firm and a household name in Japan.

Strumpen-Darrie had had direct correspondence with Ichimura, the octogenarian president of Ricoh. Our access to him was through a go-between, Mr Akai. We contacted Akai, who said we could meet Ichimura the following day. We had dinner with Akai the same evening. He was a diminutive, dapper executive in his mid-forties, spoke in a soft voice with his finger tips placed together, never looking at you directly, preferring to concentrate on a blank spot on a nearby wall. In the Japanese manner (with which I was later to become so familiar) he never actually proposed a course of action, only hinted at what might be possible. President Ichimura **might** be interested in entering the language field, but would have to give the matter serious thought after meeting us. Ricoh could of course open many doors for us in Japan. One must bear in mind that during his long life President Ichimura had never been associated with failure. On another tack, Akai pointed out that Nippon Express might be a more suitable partner. Nippon Express, which we had never heard of, was Japan's second largest travel bureau, dwarfing most European and American ones – another household name in Japan. Akai was well-connected to decision-makers in Nippon Express, who might be interested in forming some link with us. They would want 50 per cent, possibly a controlling interest.

We knew that Strumpen-Darrie had more or less made up his mind to go it alone, but the next day, after forty minutes in a waiting room with Akai, we met President Ichimura. The aged chief executive, who did not seem to be in the best of health, sat in a tall, black leather armchair behind a huge rosewood desk. He spoke no English, addressing all his remarks to Akai via the ceiling. He was courteous and kind, as most Japanese are, but whatever hints he might have dropped as to our eventual co-operation were lost in a fog of impeccable politeness and subtlety. Akai was a skilful interpreter, which meant that he could convey Ichimura's tortuous platitudes and generalizations to us in an equally impenetrable fog of English vagueness, under-statement and imagery. The meeting ended in typical Japanese fashion with both parties expressing their thanks for being granted the valuable time of the other, all doors remaining not quite closed, but not quite open, either.

It was not the type of situation that Alberola relished. Roundabout, nebulous discourse suited neither his French logic nor his American bluntness, let alone his Arab scheming. I was more comfortable since. Portuguese indulge in courteous, indirect proposals and the Finnish use of discreet silence seemed not unlike the Japanese manner. At all events, the Ricoh connection was not pursued by either party, neither did we actually meet anyone from Nippon Express, though Akai mentioned them on several occasions over the next few weeks.

The next Japanese executive he introduced us to was, however, a horse of a very different colour. On the evening of the day we met Ichimura, the Sony Corporation was opening its new building on the Ginza. Akai, once again demonstrating his impeccable connections, not only secured invitations for us, but was able to arrange a half hour meeting over coffee with Akio Morita, the President of Sony. Morita, at that time 49 years of age, was arguably the most successful and dynamic chief executive in Japan – a reputation he enjoyed for more than two decades until his cerebral haemorrhage in 1993. As far as international outlook and Western-style charisma were concerned, he had no peer among Japanese businessmen. In 1966 Sony, though not among the largest of Japanese companies, was just entering a phase of driving international entrepreneurship and expansion which would make it a household name in the United States, Great Britain and most of Europe and Asia. Morita, silver-haired, quick-thinking, original, magnetic, was the brains behind Sony's unparalleled marketing expertise in the 1960s and 1970s.

He greeted Alberola and myself with kindness and enthusiasm. He spoke fluent English, so that Akai's interpretation of opinion was rendered unnecessary. Morita, who already ran a flourishing US operation, knew the Berlitz name well. He was very interested in language instruction, as Sony was involved in the manufacture of various products used in teaching, particularly VCRs, television receivers and language laboratory equipment. Sony was about to get involved in the teaching of English in Japan. They had the hardware and plenty of ambition, but they had no method. Morita was very interested as to how I would go about assembling a staff, training teachers and implanting the concept of the Direct Method in the Japanese psyche. Language instruction in Japan at that time was almost exclusively grammar-based. I outlined my plans to him, pointing out that an important element of our strategy was to train a considerable number of Japanese teachers, too, and promote Japanese as a useful language in Asian business.

I met Morita on several occasions in the next couple of years as well as some of his brilliant lieutenants, such as Yoshi and Shu Nishiura. He was invariably friendly and full of life, with a very positive attitude to English people, as well as to Americans. With the benefit of hindsight and the familiarity I have gained with Japanese manners, I have little doubt that Berlitz could have entered into a joint venture with Ricoh, Nippon Express or Sony. The meetings arranged by Akai and the hints so delicately expressed constituted a typical Japanese approach which tacitly offered further discussions.

Whatever the case may have been, Strumpen-Darrie was not the man for conducting courtships of this kind. He was one of those forthright Americans who liked to spell it all out and tell it the way it is. After one or two long telephone calls with Alberola, who had even less sympathy for Oriental circular thinking than his boss, Strumpen-Darrie decided he would go it alone and told us to get on with it. Instead of having the mighty assets and virtually limitless connections of a famous Japanese *kaisha* at my disposal, I was left, after the departure of Alberola, with $50.000, my bare hands and the lease of a basement in Akasaka. Strumpen-Darrie would never know what he had missed out on. And yet the decision he made was the right one.

*   *   *   *   *

Alberola and I busied ourselves looking for space. We had had a meeting with a lawyer, Yamada, who got us to sign a paper and vaguely assured us that we had a licence to operate. Yamada was cheap as lawyers go and when Berlitz engaged a much more famous and expensive American lawyer three years later, it turned out that we had been illegal all the time. By then we were getting rich. Alberola just loved lawyers like Yamada.

There was plenty of space available in Tokyo. We looked at floors in the Ginza, Akasaka, Yuraku-cho and Otemachi. Rents were high, though they later became much higher. The most interesting experience for me at this time was to observe how Alberola negotiated with Japanese landlords. He knew nothing about Japanese negotiating principles, so he applied Arab ones. The conversations usually went like this:

Alberola:	This building is totally empty.
Japanese:	You see, it is a new building.
Alberola:	There seem to be so many in Tokyo. Who'll rent them all?
Japanese:	This is a very good location.
Alberola:	We need a big sign on the front of the building.
Japanese:	We are quite happy to let you put one up, but you may have problems with the authorities.
Alberola:	It's a major condition for renting. What's the rent for the first floor?
Japanese:	700.000 yen.
Alberola:	Far too high – we have much better offers.
Japanese:	This is an excellent location.
Alberola:	What's the real rent?
Japanese:	I beg your pardon?
Alberola:	What's the rent for me? Just be realistic – I can walk away from this.

Japanese:	I can discuss the matter with my colleagues. Perhaps we could reduce the rent by 5 per cent on certain conditions.
Alberola:	Let's use 500.000 yen as a base figure for the time being. But in fact I only need half the floor.
Japanese:	Which half?
Alberola:	I guess more people will see us if we take the front half on the main street.
Japanese:	Naturally.
Alberola:	I take it the front half would cost exactly half of the total.
Japanese:	This we must discuss.
Alberola:	If we base our figure on 500.000, the front half should cost 250.000.
Japanese:	However the front half is better space. There must be a premium for this.
Alberola:	Then how would you split the rent?
Japanese:	Something like 60% for the half on the street and 40% for the back half.
Alberola:	I'll take the back half. (the quiet half he wanted all the time).

This particular landlord was so miffed that he didn't rent to us at all. He did, however, prolong the dialogue for a week or so. It was quite a different situation when we tried to negotiate the Monte Carlo building in the Ginza. The president of the company which owned the building had checked on the Berlitz name back in the US and kindly agreed to give us an interview. He was in his late seventies, spoke no English, had provided a timid interpreter. The old gentleman spelled out, in the correct, prescribed manner, the attributes and benefits of the building. It was almost new, had an impeccable address, enjoyed a good reputation, was conveniently located for all kind of transport, was, in short, a **prestige** building and had many facilities such as restaurants, a travel bureau, a bank and others which he proceeded to list. His well-balanced account took 10-15 minutes. When he had finished, Alberola asked him what the rent was. One million yen a month, replied the president through his young interpreter. Offer him half a million, snapped Alberola to the hapless translator. The young man swallowed hard and took some time to muster up the courage necessary to intimate Alberola's proposal. When this had been done, the president rose from his chair, placed his hands on both knees, bowed slightly as he said *Domo, arigato gozaimasu* and left the room followed by his nervous subordinate. "He'll come back with seven hundred and fifty, you'll see" confided Alberola to me.

The president did not come back, neither did the interpreter. We sat there alone for half an hour until a young girl popped her head round the door and asked if we had a problem. No problem, said Alberola. Ten minutes later she beckoned to us from the doorway and asked us to follow her. She took us to the lift, pressed the button designating the ground floor and took the ride with us. As we departed, she bowed much lower than the president had done.

*   *   *   *   *

We eventually settled for the basement in the Kowa No. 2 building right next to the American Embassy. It was big enough for 13 classrooms, relatively cheap and certainly quiet. As it was in a back street, we did not have a sign. It was an inauspicious beginning and there were some problems in constructing 13 classrooms plus three offices in a basement where proper air-conditioning would be vital. Kowa, however, proved to be an excellent firm of constructors and we were never other than comfortable in the building.

Once we had decided on the premises, Alberola's main task before leaving was to fix the fees, for instruction. This was a tricky job, since the Berlitz name was unknown in Japan and local schools charged much less per hour than Berlitz in the US. We played around with the figures, assuming various scenarios, different student numbers, best and worst cases, and so on. The current US fee was $16 per 45-minute lesson. There was little price resistance in America, where Berlitz had been in existence since 1878. What were the Japanese, more used in any case to group instruction, prepared to pay for a private lesson? In the end Alberola decided to start with American fees – about 6000 yen in Japanese currency. Don't worry about the basement. Good lessons and opulent furnishing will see us on our way, said Rafael.

*   *   *   *   *

That was in early May. Alberola wished me luck and took his plane back to New York. We planned to open the school at the beginning of September, so I had four months to get everything into shape. There was plenty to do, but the most time-consuming tasks were those of partitioning and furnishing our empty basement space and assembling and training a staff.

American firms abroad generally prefer to sub-contract to other American firms when this is possible. After some shopping around, I entrusted the interior decoration and furnishing of the school to Herman Miller, represented by a friendly Eurasian lady named Lily Strand. Kowa themselves saw to the partitioning and air conditioning. About $30.000 were committed in these areas. The basement was going to look good.

At the end of May I carried my bags out of the Okura and took a room for 8 weeks at the Asia Center, a humble concrete block hostel between Aoyama and Roppongi. The rooms were narrow and tiny; minuscule bathrooms separated each pair of units with access from either side. Once the other person was in occupation, he or she could lock your door from the inside. A lot of one-upmanship went on between 7 and 8 every morning. There must have been about 100 people staying at the Asia Center which cost only 1000 yen a night. Some were Japanese, though the majority were youngish people from abroad – students of the martial arts – judo, karate, aikido, as well as others needing a month's pied-a-terre while they toured the Kanto area. There was a modest restaurant and lounge where we sat in the evening, watching television in fast Japanese or trying arm-locks or karate routines on each other. It was far from dull and one met a much bigger variety of people than one did in the Okura lobby. The guests staying at the Asia Center were also adept at living on a shoe string; they showed me all the cheap eating places and Happy Hour haunts in the Roppongi area.

My old friend Alec Brook, former table tennis champion of England, had given me an introduction to two Englishmen working for NCR – Chris McDonald and Mike Williams. The NCR building was located 200 yards from our school, and I met these two men – of my age – over lunch at the Okura. They were well placed in NCR, both having been in Japan for about 15 years. Not only did they become close friends of mine, but proved to be of great help in my work, as they knew everybody that counted. McDonald, at the time of writing President of Rolex in Japan, is almost certainly the best-known Englishman in Tokyo, having hob-nobbed with a long line of ambassadors and company Number Ones for over 40 years. He was recently awarded the OBE for his services within the British community. McDonald introduced me to the YCAC – Yokohama Country and Athletic Club, where we played on the same soccer and cricket teams for several years.

One of Strumpen-Darrie's old friends, John Emerson, was Minister at the US Embassy. Emerson – tall, hulking, very American in appearance – was an ardent Japanophile, with the ability to speak the language fluently and bow lower than any Aryan I have ever seen. He kindly invited me out to dinner one night and proved to be a charming and knowledgeable individual – one of those rare diplomats who really possessed the skills for doing his job. The then US Ambassador was the famous Edwin Reischauer, the American envoy most liked by the Japanese. Emerson introduced me to Hartzell Lincoln Dake, a former assistant to Reischauer. Dake, who was running Tupperware at the time, was fluent in Japanese and Spanish. Still in his mid-thirties, he was, like Emerson, one of half a dozen Americans in Tokyo who impressed by their knowledge of Japanese language and culture. Dake was very valuable to me during my first few months, instructing me in Japanese ways and attitudes, often explaining in a perfectly logical manner examples of apparently enigmatic behaviour. At the time of writing Dake still lives in the Shibuya district of Tokyo.

*   *   *   *   *

As far as the recruitment of staff was concerned, I had already lined up my English staff before leaving Europe. The best teachers in Finland and Portugal were all anxious to spend a year or two in Japan. The following months saw the arrival, in ones and twos, of Ed Wilton, Geoff Mason, Vince Canty, Hazel Blick, Jean Mair, Mike Barmby, Ken and Joan Crossley and Margaret Ridgewell. They were all first class instructors in whom I could have complete confidence.

As we intended to make Japanese our second biggest language – there was an easily identifiable market among the many expatriates in Tokyo – I decided to train about 20 Japanese teachers, on the assumption that about half would drop out. First I employed a secretary – Miss Sato – who had good skills in English and typing. We placed ads in the "Japan Times" and "Asahi Shimbun" for teachers who would be willing to work either on a full-time or part-time basis. A large number of people sent in their CVs, which we vetted. Eventually I interviewed about 40 persons, from whom I selected 20 for training.

The people I chose were between 25 and 30 years of age and possessed university degrees, mostly in foreign languages. Some of them were actually teachers in the Japanese state system; all of them spoke good or fluent English. I can see their eager faces today: the men – Haraguchi, Okada, Komine, Matsuda, Miyamoto, Koichi Sato and Masami Sato; The women: Yamane, Tanaka, Yamazaki, Enomoto, Fujishima, Hashimoto, Fujimura, Kuwata and Nakayama. Miyamoto, in his early fifties, was the only one of the previous generation. He, Tanaka and Nakayama spoke almost perfect English. None of them had ever heard of the Berlitz or Direct Method and found it hard to believe that one could teach Japanese without explaining everything in English. I told them the training would take 2 months at 4 hours a day from 6-10 p.m. They would neither pay nor be paid for the course. Those who were holding down full time jobs could just make it by 6 p.m. I could not guarantee them employment at the end of the course, but what lessons the school was able to attract would be shared among those who completed the training.

Nobody found these conditions onerous or unreasonable. There was only one drop-out over the two months. By the end of October all the others had started work for us full-time or part-time according to their preference. Some European people think they should be paid during training. The attitude of the Japanese is quite the opposite. Their hunger for learning – especially something new or unusual that westerners possess and they do not – is such that a free training course appears an incredibly lucky opportunity. They regarded two months of evenings as a sound investment to acquire a valuable skill. In fact most of them are still practising what I taught them, either for Berlitz or on their own account.

The only person to drop out – a Mr Shimizu of Miyamoto's age – did not desist for lack of interest or stamina. He simply could not learn the Method;

thirty years of reciting grammar rules set up a mental block which he was unable to surmount. After 3 or 4 weeks of struggling with him, I was approaching the point where I would have to find some kind way of encouraging him to discontinue. I need not have worried – the gradual loss of face inspired Shimizu to seek recourse to that fine old Japanese institution, the ailing grandmother, who suddenly needed his help in the evenings.

The rest were unbelievably good. I had given thirty or so Method courses to more than a dozen nationalities, but the Japanese were something else. Firstly, they put themselves one hundred per cent in the hands of the instructor, showing complete faith in him and the method they are being shown. Secondly, they are good listeners, drinking in advice rather than looking for other options, never interrupting the trainer. Thirdly, their visual memory is acute, enabling them to observe with great perspicacity and imitate their instructor with astonishing fidelity.

At times I found it uncanny. The way I give a method course is to demonstrate the whole lesson from beginning to end, then ask trainees to take the floor and do exactly what I did. By this time I was able to do the first 25 lessons in Japanese. I would demonstrate Lesson Six, for example, taking 20-30 minutes to cover the teaching points. Then Haraguchi would come out and give a well-nigh perfect imitation. All teachers, whatever method they are using, have their personal mannerisms, oratorical style, little idiosyncrasies. I am no exception. English, French, German and Spanish teachers normally ploughed through the teaching points I demonstrated, but injected, during their exposé, their **own** mannerisms. Not so the Japanese. They imitate, very faithfully indeed, **the mannerisms of the teacher.** Haraguchi could clone me so accurately that even my mother would have looked twice. For the twenty minutes or so that I let him off the leash, a Japanese Richard Lewis paced up and down in front of the audience putting across concepts such as *hanasu koto ga dekimasu* and *nomanakereba narimasen* with the cocked eyebrow, the prodding forefinger, the knowing look that I had treated classes to for over a decade. Then Yamazaki would take the stage and a female Richard Lewis would go through the eyes-raised-to-the-ceiling, bent-knees, whirling-round routines to complete the evening's cloning. I was, in a sense, on the horns of a dilemma, since, while one has to encourage trainees to imitate technique, my Tokyoites were injecting my body language and facial expressions into a tongue which does not normally require them. At all events, the extra emphasis seemed to work well with American and other students in later months, especially when expressions such as *hara ga tachimasu* (my stomach rises = I get angry) were being taught.

The Method Course was completed without a hiccup; I could not fail to be impressed by what I had seen of the Japanese capacity for dedication to a subject, single-mindedness and stamina. The trainees even had meetings on their own at week-ends to discuss the week's progress. The group spirit, for which Japanese are so famous, was reinforced on several occasions when we had meals together at 10 p.m. or a picnic on Saturday or Sunday. I saw that Japanese do not strictly separate their working and private lives. When everybody works as a team, work is fun and social pursuits are easily intertwined any time from 9 a.m. to 11 p.m. You don't get much sleep at home during the week, but a doze in the office is OK, almost any time.

Foreign languages other than English were in little demand in Japan in 1966, but I covered most eventualities by engaging, on a part-time basis, teachers of French, German, Spanish, Chinese and Korean among foreign residents in Tokyo. Outstanding among them was a young Frenchman, Jacques Meon, who a decade later headed Berlitz East Asia and held the position until 1993.

*   *   *   *   *

In June I was invited to lunch by Dr Masatoshi Matsushita, the Dean of Rikkyo University. An ardent Anglophile, he was concerned at the pathetically low level of oral fluency in Rikkyo's Department of English. He asked me to put together an intensive summer course to be given during July and August on the university campus at Ikebukuro. This was aimed at first, second and third year students, who would be divided into groups of 15 according to their level of oral proficiency. I was surprised at the prospect of university students giving up their summer holidays to remain in class for such a course, but Dr Matsushita said that he intended to push strongly for this with the parents of those undergraduates who needed it. He assured me that a significant number would enrol. In fact 120 did so and spent from 10-12 each morning and from 2-4 each afternoon for six weeks of Tokyo's sweltering summer in Rikkyo's non-air-conditioned classrooms. Thinking of the useful connection with Dr Matsushita, who at the time was also running for the Governorship of Tokyo, I somewhat unwisely agreed to give the course myself. After the arrival of Ed Wilton and my wife in July, we shared the teaching, taking the Yamanote line out to Ikebukuro at 9 a.m. and getting back about 5 in the afternoon. The students were keen and made good progress; the work was exhausting on account of the heat. Tokyo is incredibly humid in summer and while nearly all offices had air conditioning in 1966, universities did not. Normally a lover of heat, the only way I could keep going was to open all windows and stand framed in the open doorway as I taught, desperate for the slightest current of air. Jane and Ed Wilton did not fare any better; students perspired freely, though they seemed used to the conditions. I was surprised at the lack of facilities and teaching aids at the university as well as at the spartan aspect of most of the lecture theatres. Japanese universities take a lot of wear and tear and I learnt that some of the bigger ones – Waseda, Keio and so forth – might have as many as 60.000 students.

*   *   *   *   *

In mid June, after some hunting around, I found a house which seemed suitable for my family. It was located in Shoto-cho, a quiet, highly-rated part of Shibuya. It was a wooden structure, part Japanese style, part western, with a lovely, big living room, three bedrooms and a maid's room. The garden was minuscule, but pleasantly planted with bamboo. It was next to the official residence of the Governor of Tokyo; unfortunately Dr Matsushita lost the election to Ryoichi Minobe, otherwise we should have had a familiar neighbour from the autumn. The rent was 200.000 yen a month – good value as it turned out. This amount ($550) made quite a hole in my basic salary of $1200 but I have always found that if you have good living accommodation it is easier to solve life's other problems. There was an excellent Japanese Kindergarten just round the corner – Shoto Yo-chen – where my children were to receive their first education; from Shibuya I could get to work in half an hour; I took a deep breath and signed a 3-year contract.

*   *   *   *   *

I bought two mattresses and Wilton and I slept on the floor for a few weeks – nothing unusual in Japan. We were invariably woken up by bright sunshine at 6 each morning, though no Japanese in Shoto-cho stirred at that hour. I began the day by reading the Japan Times – pushed under the door – and was able to wake Ed up one morning with the astonishing news that the England soccer team had won the World Cup. We celebrated with bacon and eggs. Jane and the children were about to arrive; I had to look for furniture. Tokyo has wonderful department stores with a lot on view and in the days that followed I frequented the home furnishing floors of Mitsukoshi, Takashimaya, Seibu, Hankyu and Matsuzaka. It was while I was looking for a table that I gained my first insight into the nature of Japanese courtesy. I had spotted a lovely Danish teak dining table, just the right size for our house, in the Takashimaya department store. I asked the shop assistant how much it cost – it was 66.000 yen. I was eager to snap it up, but the assistant explained that he could not sell it to me, as a certain Mr Kishi had "reserved" it. I accepted this explanation, but was surprised, when still hunting around Takashimaya two weeks later, to see the table still there. I approached the same assistant and enquired about the fate of the table. Mr Kishi had still not made up his mind, was the answer. Had Mr Kishi put down a deposit on the table, was my next question. No, he had not. Then how do you know he is serious about buying it? Mr Kishi is a valued customer. Could I put down a deposit on the table, in case Mr Kishi decides not to buy it? That would not be necessary, my interest had been registered.

The following week, I tried again. Could the assistant please ask the invisible Mr Kishi to fix a date for a decision, as I was holding off buying another table until the fate of this one was decided. He was afraid that was not possible; Mr Kishi should not be pushed into making hasty decisions. How long had the table been standing there? I asked. Three months, was the reply.

The days passed, the weather got hotter, my determination to secure the table increased. I tried out a variety of strategies with the gentle, but firm, store assistant. Could he give me Mr Kishi's telephone number so that I could ascertain his intentions personally? Unfortunately that would not be possible; besides, he was not sure the store had the number. Then how did he communicate with Mr Kishi about the table? From time to time Mr Kishi would come into the store and look at it, I was told. Could I waylay him in the store one day? That would be difficult, as one never knew when he would come and inspect. I have 66.000 yen here in cash in an envelope, will you take it now and make sure of the sale? The assistant smiled a smile of embarrassment – he could not take the money. Knowing the Japanese as I now do, I reckon I broke every possible social convention surrounding the delicate rules of Japanese customer relations, exercise of patience, practice of courtesy and avoidance of direct propositions. In later months I shuddered at what must have seemed, in Japanese eyes, my uneducated bluntness, even brashness. My humiliation was complete one morning when, as I gazed at the coveted teak top, the assistant sidled up to me and informed me of Mr Kishi's decision. Though he greatly prized the table, he had decided, in view of the foreign guest's persistence and eagerness to purchase it, to renounce his right to buy. He was very pleased to let me have it in the hope that it would bring me many years of enjoyment and aesthetic pleasure. I felt like a heel, paid like a shot and scuttled off with my prize. Twenty-five years later the admirable table is still in use and looks like it did the day I bought it. So much for Danish workmanship. I never met the honourable Mr Kishi, but still think of him with fondness and admiration. He and the shop assistant were true Japanese gentlemen.

This was only one of many encounters I had with Japanese persons in professional and social situations. During the 5 years we spent in Tokyo I found the high moral stance assumed by Mr Kishi and the shop assistant to be typical of the careful standards of Japanese social behaviour. Courtesy is mandatory in Japan, bluntness, opinionated or argumentative discussion avoided, rudeness unthinkable. As far as business was concerned, I found Japanese, especially the classes we were dealing with, to be utterly reliable and considerate. Misunderstandings were frequent, on account of differences in cultural background, but Japanese always seemed ready to pay off any kind of debt, to compensate quickly for any misdemeanours or mistakes on their part. Perhaps we were lucky, but in the 5 years I ran Berlitz in Japan, neither the company nor my family experienced any unpleasant incident at the hands of these smiling, dependable people. Though the Japanese have an ambivalent attitude towards the Americans, the basic feeling is one of respect and admiration for US achievement and generosity. As far as the British are concerned, they still preserve a positive image of the English gentleman and place a definite value on our traditions, institutions and way of life. I have always felt that, given a little more effort from our side, the Japanese could be our best friends.

*   *   *   *   *

At the beginning of September we were nearly ready to open. The basement had been partitioned, air-conditioned, painted, carpeted, furnished and decorated. We had a telephone number (*go-hachi yon no yon ni ichi ichi*). I had had letter-heading and administrative stationery printed and a sign put up by the front door. The Japanese staff were all trained, the first English teachers had arrived by train through Siberia. At this stage I ran out of money. I had done my best to manage the whole project on the budget Strumpen-Darrie and I had calculated, but could not quite make it, as some items just cost more than expected. I asked for a further $5000 on top of the original $50.000. It was sent at once and I paid off the last outstanding bills. I was determined not to ask for more and our expenses would now have to be met out of income. It's a wonderful principle in business.

I had placed three or four ads with different newspapers and Jane Rees gave us a short write-up over the weekend in the "Japan Times". Our fees were fixed, as agreed with Alberola. On the Monday morning we opened our doors and manned our telephones. They did not ring very much. Wilton and I answered queries in English, Miss Sato in Japanese. There were a few walk-ins. I suppose we had a total of a dozen leads on the Monday, but we took no money. Everyone was very polite and seemed interested, but no one signed on. Tuesday was the same. On Wednesday and Thursday we had up to 20 calls or walk-ins a day, but nobody committed themselves to lessons. Friday was less busy and we finished the week with nil income. Wilton and I debated whether or not we had over-priced our services. Neither the Japanese nor the Americans complained about the fees, but everyone held off. Monday and Tuesday of the following week brought no change in the situation. We had $1000 left in the bank, pay day for the 4 English teachers and rent were 18 days away and income was still nil.

On Wednesday I almost phoned Strumpen-Darrie half a dozen times, then decided to give it another couple of days. That day brought 10 enquiries but no money. Thursday was the same, though we stayed late in the office. At 9 p.m. Wilton and I put all the lights out, locked the door and began to climb the stairs to the ground floor. By mistake we had turned the light out on the stairs, so we ascended in the dark. Halfway up the stairs I bumped into a soft, perfumed figure. There was a little cry of embarrassment, Wilton ran down and found the switch. When the light came on we saw a lovely, elegant, kimono-clad Japanese lady clutching her handbag. She asked in Japanese if this was the Berlitz School. It was, I said. We let her in, seated her comfortably and asked what we could do for her. She wanted language lessons. She had seen the advertisement, she had spoken to Miss Sato.

When would she like to start? I asked hesitantly (all this was in Japanese). The following Monday would be fine, she said, that is if we could take her. I assured her we would fit her in. She went on to say she would like 200 lessons in English and opened her handbag out of which she took 240.000 yen (exactly) in cash. I counted it while Ed scampered off to find the enrolment forms. The lady's name was Mabuchi – I shall never forget it. She was the first student of Berlitz Japan, which went on to open 75 schools and turn over one hundred million dollars a year. She was a beautiful, kind lady who actually learnt very passable English over the next 3 months. She always wore a kimono to her lessons, gave little presents to her teachers and drove away in a large, black chauffeured Toyota. She was a lovely lady of Japan.

*   *   *   *   *

The following morning I was able to report $3200 of income to Strumpen-Darrie instead of suggesting that we revise our fees, as it looked as if no one was going to enrol. If we had not stayed late in the empty school that night, Mrs Mabuchi would have gone away disappointed, Strumpen-Darrie and I might have got cold feet and the whole Berlitz story in Japan (the creation of the most successful language teaching operation in history) might have been quite different. But Alberola had been right: the Japanese **were** prepared to pay high prices as long as they were convinced about the quality of the product.

Between the middle of September and Christmas, enrolments came in steadily. Not only were we in the black from October onwards, but we were establishing a reputation with the Japanese. (The Americans in Tokyo already knew us). British, German, Italian and Australian executives also supported us, as well as some South Americans.

From the very beginning we offered Total Immersion, which the Japanese had never heard of. This type of course did, however, suit their general mental attitude to study – one of complete dedication, long hours and stamina. The first Japanese executive to take a one-month Total Immersion was a senior manager from Mobiloil named Yamashita. He was in his mid-fifties, soft-spoken, could handle English in most business situations, but had big holes in his grammar. We arranged a suitable daily programme from 9 a.m. to 5 p. m. A lot of Japanese close their eyes when concentrating and Yamashita was no exception. The only difference was that he closed them quite a lot – like half the time you were talking to him. It was sometimes disconcerting for teachers newly-arrived in Japan.

At the end of the first week, Yamashita and I reviewed the results. He was quite happy with his progress, but had one request. As he was concentrating on pronunciation as well as grammar, would it be all right if he closed his eyes all the time the following week? He was the customer, so we readily agreed, though I had to revolve a team of four teachers on him, as it started getting on their nerves. However all went well and at the end of the second week he had another request: would it be all right if he turned his chair round and faced the wall during lessons. Again we acceded to his request, not quite following the logic. I just knew there would be another condition for the fourth week – and there was: did we mind putting the lights out so his concentration on sound, undisturbed by the sight of gesticulating teachers, pens, books or even light passing through his closed eyelids, would be complete? So Mr Yamashita, our first Japanese TI student, spent his fourth week of instruction with eyes closed, chair facing the wall in a darkened classroom with a team of disgruntled teachers stumbling over chairs and emerging blinking from their lessons after 45 minutes like coal miners coming to the surface after a long shift.

I must point out that no other Japanese student put such conditions to us, though we got used to 15-minute spells of eye-closing. Yamashita was very pleased with his lessons and at the end of the course gave fine presents to all his teachers, some of whom he barely recognized.

*   *   *   *   *

The first students to take Total Immersion courses in Japanese presented an interesting comparison. One was Luciano Cohen, President of Olivetti Japan. Cohen was Italian, an accomplished linguist already fluent in English and French. He tackled Japanese in an orthodox manner, mastering the grammatical rules as well as benefiting from the 100% direct approach. His progress was steady, measurable and foreseeable. After 6 weeks he could use Japanese smoothly in most social situations.

The other student was a very different type of individual. Costello, American, was a young Coca Cola salesman who had just arrived from the United States. About 25 years of age, he had never heard about grammar, neither the Japanese nor the English variety. This suited us perfectly, as he would certainly have struggled with the terminology. Haraguchi and Okada started on Lesson One and carried him as far as Lesson 12 in four weeks. It was slow work as he was an absolute beginner and was not academically inclined. He was, however, very interested and motivated and could imitate well, though half the time he didn't know what he was saying. After a month the result was average, or slightly less.

At this point he was packed off to the provinces to visit Coca Cola dealers and we did not see him again for some time. About six months later I was having lunch in the Press Club when Costello walked in, greeted me heartily and sat down to eat at the next table. He was in the company of a Japanese businessman and I was pleased to hear them conversing in Japanese during their meal. I was astonished at Costello's level in the language, shaky grammar to be sure – but fast, fluent and rich in vocabulary. After lunch I had the opportunity of speaking to him and congratulating him on his progress. He told me what had happened. With Lesson 12 Japanese he had been catapulted into rural Japan where hundreds of Japanese Coca Cola dealers awaited him with their complaints, problems with deliveries, breakages, above all dispensing machines that were out of order. It was Coca Cola Immersion all along the line. Very few of the dealers in the small towns and villages spoke English, so Costello had to deal with it all in Japanese. Out in the sticks, he spent weeks staying in small hotels and *ryokans* where only Japanese was spoken and even the "Japan Times" was unobtainable. Deprived of the interference of English, Costello had begun to think in Japanese and he naturally acquired the idiomatic style of his disgruntled dealers. Costello's success with the language secured for us a whole string of students from Coca Cola, a huge company in Japan. No other American that I can recollect, however, achieved Costello's fluency. There is nothing like being thrown in at the deep end.

*   *   *   *   *

In the following months we enrolled interesting students of different nationalities and from all walks of life. Our Japanese department functioned well and students were delighted to see that it was possible to use the language from the very first day. Steve Parker, the husband of Shirley Maclaine, took a 4-week Total Immersion and made huge progress. Later he brought his daughter Sachiko, (the spitting image of mother Shirley) to take a French course. Prominent businessmen included, besides Cohen of Olivetti, Australian Leslie Perkins of Japan Upjohn, Robert Parker of Texaco, Joe Guilfoyle of Lubrizol and various top managers from Shell, IBM, Dodwell, Nestle and other multinational firms. Meeting these men, – often getting to know them and their wives socially as the months passed – made me realise what a dynamic world the Tokyo business community was. Japan was burgeoning as a hugely exciting market in which fortunes could be made and foreign companies were sending their best men to Tokyo. Intelligent, go-getter executives usually have intelligent, often charming, wives, so that the social circuit was brisk, lively and entertaining, contrasting sharply with that of some other capitals, such as Lisbon, which in the 1960s was an economic and social backwater as far as the foreign community was concerned. The Perkins in particular were a genial, energetic couple who fully understood the value of entertaining at home where clients and friends were concerned. Les and Esther were typically uninhibited Aussies, emanating unfailing cheerfulness, uncomplicated warmth of feeling and genuine homespun hospitality. During Leslie's tenure of his post at Upjohn, his company achieved a high profile among Japanese and the foreign community which it has rarely achieved since. Chris McDonald was another who understood fully the keen interest that Japanese businessmen and women have in experiencing hospitality in a Western home. Chris gave up to a dozen parties a year, attended by the cream of Japanese executives. His fluent Japanese, allied to his boyish enthusiasm and sporting prowess, enabled him to move with virtual freedom inside the Japanese establishment, rubbing shoulders with presidents of companies, such as Nissan and Sony, on a basis of equal intimacy. He is one of the few Englishmen ever to achieve this in Japan, even being accorded the honour of cutting the topknot of an eminent sumo wrestler on the occasion of his retirement. No wonder, when NCR used McDonald at less than his full potential, Rolex snapped him up and made him president of their company in Japan.

Our Japanese students were even more distinguished. One of the first to enrol for English was Dr Mitarai, President of Canon Camera. Dr Mitarai was in his late seventies, but learnt easily and quickly. About the same age was Prince Takeda, a good speaker of English who brushed up his skills a few hours a week over a one-year period. Some lovely middle-aged ladies graced the school two or three times a week with their smiling, scented presence. Mrs Yokogawa and Mrs Yamashita, wives of the presidents of the shipping lines of the same name, were among the most charming of them, as was Miyoko Kato, the well-known Noh actress.

An outstanding student was Prince Mikasa, the younger brother of Emperor Hirohito. I had met Princess Suga, the Emperor's youngest daughter, in Washington a few months earlier and had been impressed by the high level of internationalism of the Imperial Family. Prince Mikasa was (at the time of writing, still is) an incredibly talented individual whose interests range from languages and literature to the history of ancient religions and even ice dancing, at which he is personally proficient. When he visited London a few years later to spend 6 months studying rare books and manuscripts in the British Museum, it was apparent that he was one of the world's leading authorities in ancient religions.

In spite of his immense erudition, Prince Mikasa had, like most scholars, a humble approach to learning. He came to us to brush up his French – one of six or seven languages he could handle. I taught him for a lesson or two for assessment purposes, after which Jacques Meon continued the instruction for many months. Prince Mikasa walked in and out of the school like any other student, expecting no fuss or special conditions; most people were unaware of his presence. Soon afterwards I arranged courses for his two daughters – Mrs Konoye, who had married the son of Prince Konoye (Japan's foreign minister in 1941) and Princess Masako, who also studied French. My wife began to teach Princess Mikasa, Prince Mikasa's charming wife, who was in the process of perfecting her social English. Though we were invited many times to lunch with the Mikasas in their home inside the palace grounds, all members of the family took their lessons in our Akasaka (and later Shibuya) schools.

*   *   *   *   *

It was probably on account of our deepening familiarity with the Mikasas that I received a request, a few months later, to teach Crown Princess (now Empress) Michiko in the Togu Palace. First I was requested to prepare a detailed CV, attaching copies of my various qualifications. Three months passed, after which I was asked to visit the Palace to meet the Princess for a prolonged interview, during which we discussed how I might best prepare a course for a student with such a high standard. In such cases, where grammatical accuracy and polished pronunciation are already in place, it is largely a question of distinguishing between nuances of speech, especially in the area of idioms, and fine-tuning the psychological impact of certain phraseologies and approaches. Such instruction is not easy to programme, especially in view of the social importance of utterances emanating from a personage of such eminence.

At all events we made certain decisions and I had the pleasure of teaching this wonderful lady, on and off for a period of three to four years, during which time I often met Crown Prince (now Emperor) Akihito. The lessons always took place inside the Palace in a pleasant Japanese style sitting room with huge plate glass windows overlooking the beautiful silver birches of the Palace grounds. Out of respect for the Imperial Family's privacy, it is inappropriate for me to comment on the instruction. Suffice it to say that Empress Michiko, as it is widely-known, is an incomparably accomplished linguist, avid for learning and, like most busy people, she always conscientiously found time for any learning assignment. In their own home, the Imperial couple are among the kindest people one could ever get to know. I will give a few examples of their consideration when I later describe our eventual departure from Japan.

*   *   *   *   *

The school continued to progress well during the winter of 1966-7 and my family and I were able to organize ourselves socially. Chris McDonald was a great help, introducing us to many members of the foreign community, particularly among those who were involved in sport. At Chris's suggestion we joined two well-known clubs - Tokyo Lawn Tennis Club and Yokohama Country and Athletic Club, usually referred to as the YCAC. The latter organisation, which had started life as the Yokohama **Cricket** and Athletic Club in 1887, was for expatriates only, running cricket, football, rugby and tennis teams as well as providing facilities for squash, bowling and swimming. It is a venerable institution, recalled with great affection by untold thousands of non-Japanese who have practised sport and been entertained there for over a century. At the time of our joining, the YCAC President was Manny Guterres, a personable Yokohama executive of mainly Portuguese extraction, beloved by all who knew him.   There must have been thirty or forty nationalities among the membership. In the football team, for which Chris and I played, there was Jakobsen (Norway), Bielous (Russia), Bernie and Fisher (Scotland), Bisang and Boillat (Switzerland), Jones (USA) Stanninghauser (Germany), Tanner (England), Hoppe (Holland) and Jensen, Holtegaard, Harrit, Haagensen and Krabbe (Denmark). Although most of the team were in their mid-thirties, we were consistently successful against top Japanese universities and many of the industrial teams, even though they were much fitter, faster and more skilful than we were. Japanese, who are wonderful ball players, have one great defect: they panic in front of goal. McDonald, an enormous goalkeeper at 6 foot 3 inches, seemed to frighten the life out of them. In 1967 we won the Kanagawa league, only losing two or three matches the whole season. We were certainly outplayed by many of the Japanese teams we defeated, but our centre forward that year, Nils Rudi, never seemed to miss in front of goal and actually equalled the club record with 36 goals.

The cricket team, which I was later to captain, had a sizeable fixture list, playing against the Embassies of Britain, Australia and New Zealand, as well as Shell, the Press Club, Ceylon Students, the India-Pakistan XI and a motley selection of visiting warships, particularly Australian cruisers. Mel Guest, former captain of Oxford, and Simon Clark, who had played for Kent, were amongst our stars.

The Tokyo Lawn Tennis Club was considerably more difficult to get into, as it has membership split 50/50 between expatriates and Japanese. The waiting list for Japanese stands currently at 25 years: expatriates are more fortunate in that departing executives make room for newcomers. Jane and I got our membership cards during 1967. Tokyo Lawn Tennis Club is located in the heart of one of Tokyo's top residential districts - Azabu - and enjoys a delightful atmosphere. Not only is the standard of tennis high (most of the Japanese Davis Cup players belong to it), but the social ambience in the pavilion is rather special. Many of Tokyo's top Japanese families hold memberships - the delightful wives seem to manage to play several days a week - and it is a wonderful place for expatriate wives to make good friends. Crown Prince Akihito and Crown Princess Michiko used to play regularly, as did Prince Hiro in later years.

Jane and I also joined the American Club and I became an associate member of the Foreign Correspondents' Club, known as the Press Club. On leaving Japan we took the necessary steps to secure life memberships in all these clubs: the staff are invariably most welcoming when we have re-visited in later years.

In Tokyo in those days there were so many social activities to pursue that one had some difficulty in fitting everything in. In my Wigan days I had played snooker and table tennis at Ashton YMCA. I soon found myself linked to the Japanese YMCA and eventually became Chairman of the YMCA Expatriate Supporting Committee, a fund raising body consisting of 6 ambassadors and various businessmen from Europe and the USA. Prince William of Gloucester, then resident in Japan, was also an enthusiastic member and I had the pleasure of making the acquaintance of this very modest yet perspicacious Royal at our bi-monthly meetings. His untimely death in an aeroplane accident in the early seventies robbed our country of one of our most personable princes.

As Berlitz East Asia was an American company, I had naturally joined the American Chamber of Commerce in Tokyo where Carl Boehringer and Bart Jackson were legendary figures in assisting US firms to establish a foothold in the Japanese market. I later became very friendly with Bart and wound up as Chairman of the Chamber of Commerce Programs Committee, which was a much more interesting job than it sounds. One of my duties was to arrange, with the help of the American Embassy, a sequence of speakers for Chamber of Commerce lunches, usually held at the Press Club. Hubert Humphrey, Ed Muskie, and George Brown were some of the US politicians who honoured us with their presence at this time, though none could hold an audience like Danny Kaye, who had us in such stitches with his antics that many of us did not get through our lunch.

In spite of indulging in all this social activity (which is largely a key to doing business in Japan, in any case) there remained much work to do. Haskins and Sells were our auditors; we had secured the services of a good no-frills, inexpensive Japanese accountant named Yamamoto, who dedicated one of his assistants, Kazumi Kitamura, to work full time for us. In December 1966 my parents, anxious to see their grandchildren again, flew over to Japan for Christmas.

They liked it so much they stayed 4 years. My father had always had a bent for mathematics – he was particularly good at arithmetic and could add up long columns of 3-digit figures just by running his pencil down them once. Yamamoto took one look at him and suggested I engage him as an extra assistant in the accounts department, which was already begnning to creak under the load of so many enrolments. My father slotted in nicely next to Kitamura, who soon became devoted to him. His Lancashire taciturnity sat well with Japanese shyness and the two of them enjoyed quiet lunches together. Once they had a competition to see who could add up a long column of figures fastest. Kitamura used his abacus, Geoff Mason a calculator and my father did his trick with the pencil – he won easily. He liked the Japanese very much.

My mother, who was perhaps even fonder of them, often used to say she wouldn't mind being buried in Japan, though not just yet. She was 73 – one year younger than my father – but anxious to start a new career. I put her on a teacher training course, after which she gave tea-party lessons to groups of Japanese ladies and to one or two high school students who had failed their exams. She coached one of them to success – Edo his name was. The day after passing his exam he arrived at the school loaded down with presents for my mother – chocolates, rice cakes, fancy handkerchiefs, flowers and so on. One night my mother stayed late in the school kitchen marking some exercises when there was a knock at the door. A dignified bespectacled gentleman in his early sixties asked if I could be found. I was out to dinner with some Mitsubishi Bank people, but my mother dragged the gentleman into the kitchen, made him a cup of tea and regaled him for a couple of hours with tales from her Victorian childhood in the north of England. He showed great interest in all her stories, conversed in excellent English and had several cups of tea before departing. He left his visiting card, scribbling a private number on the back for me to ring him the next day. It was Prince Mikasa, the youngest brother of Emperor Hirohito – a historian of some stature who loved old stories.

We had been fortunate in the autumn to engage a wonderful Japanese maid, Haruko Sahashi, a country girl with a very pleasant appearance, amiable manner and a great zeal for work. She became very fond of Richard and Caroline who were very small at the time – Caroline was 2 years and Richard, not quite one. Her devotion to them manifested itself occasionally in novel ways. One evening the house began to shake in one of the frequent minor earthquakes that Tokyo experiences each year. As the glass rattled in the kitchen and Jane and I sat stunned into immobility, Haruko snatched up the two children, put one under each arm and ran out with them into the street. There she remained in the middle of the road till the tremor subsided. Apparently that was routine procedure for Japanese maids caring for small children when an earthquake strikes. When I think of the recent destruction in Kobe, with thousands buried under the rubble of collapsed buildings, I have all the more reason for admiring the presence of mind of this sagacious country maid.

A strange incident occurred on the night my parents arrived in Tokyo. After a late family dinner we all went to bed, Jane and I, the children, my parents in the three main bedrooms and Haruko to her own room. At eight the next morning we assembled for breakfast and Haruko did us proud serving bacon and eggs in the prescribed English manner. As we were finishing breakfast, she suddenly burst into tears. We were astounded, as she was normally a most equable girl, but at that point I noticed a cut on the side of her nose. At the very same instant I caught a glimpse of my brief-case lying on the grass in the middle of the garden! Haruko sobbed away for five minutes or so and then, in Japanese, told her story. About 4 am a burglar, wearing a mask, had entered her room. As she awoke, he held a knife at her throat and threated to kill her if she made a sound. When he was satisfied that she was too terrified to betray him, he went through the items in the living room. There was little to steal apart from a small amount of money in my briefcase, which he took out with him as he went. As a further precaution he returned to poor Haruko's room, deliberately gave her a small nick on the nose with his knife and told her he would surely disfigure her if she raised the alarm in the next couple of hours. The poor girl cowered in her room for 3 hours or so, then got up and prepared our breakfast as it had been ordered, finally she broke down.

The event revealed so much about the Japanese character, especially the girl's fortitude. The police were called – seventeen of them arrived, seventeen pairs of shoes were lined up outside our front door. The house was fingerprinted from top to bottom, Haruko was cross-examined and re-cross-examined. The rest of us marvelled at the manpower involved. They came again, three or four days in a row. Haruko had a band-aid on her nose for a couple of weeks. We felt for her and loved her. The story had a happy ending: not only did they catch the burglar (6 months later) but the bright-eyed 25-year-old sergeant in charge of the investigation later proposed to Haruko and they were married in 1968, when she had given the matter due consideration. They have 3 children. That was my parents' first night in Japan. I had to assure them that it didn't happen every night.

*   *   *   *   *

Our first full winter in Japan made me appreciate the lovely Tokyo climate. It hardly rains at all from October to April. The autumn months up to Christmas are what English people would call an Indian summer – dry, cool, and sunny. The time zone is such that Tokyo is bathed in brilliant sunshine every morning from 6 am. The sunsets are glowing vermilion, perhaps enhanced by the effect of smog, but unforgettably colourful none-the-less. January and February are a little cold, but it is nothing serious – March, April and May bring warmth again. The trouble starts in June, when hot days and humidity herald torrential rain in July and stifling heat in August. Anyone who stays voluntarily in Tokyo in the summer months should know better. Those who can, escape to the mountains or high resorts, such as Karuizawa or Hakone.

Berlitz Tokyo was clearly an all-the-year-round school, like most Berlitz schools around the world. Yet many of our students and certainly most of our English teachers did not relish July and August in the capital. Recalling the success of our summer courses in the UK, I decided to launch something similar in Japan. In May I paid a trip to Karuizawa and inspected the motley collection of villas in the middle of the forested plateau. Karuizawa, a famous summer mountain resort 200 kilometres west of Tokyo, is a favourite retreat of high society Japanese families during the Tokyo heat. It was not cheap (today it is horrendously expensive) and I was not sure that we could afford to house a summer school there. Most of the villas and cottages (all wooden) were booked up in advance from year to year. Others were simply used each July and August by their private owners. There were, however, one or two very large villas (ten rooms and up) which were rather difficult to rent out. These were suitable for us as we needed not only bedrooms for students and staff, but also bigger rooms to use as classrooms. I was lucky enough to find an enormous villa, owned by Mr Nakasone (later he became Prime Minister), which was available for the season. It was a seasonal price of 400.000 yen – there was no bargaining. In fact it was reasonable, as it was ideal for our purposes. I rented two smaller cottages for my family and my parents and we were set up till the last week in August. The students were no problem – we filled Nakasone's villa with a combination of Japanese businessmen learning English and American, British and Swiss (Nestle) executives learning Japanese. Our English teachers revelled in the cool air. Our Japanese teachers (who would normally never have been able to afford more than two or three days in Karuizawa hotels) were even more delighted. In typical Japanese cooperative fashion they established a rota so that more than a dozen or them were able to spend a few weeks in the resort.

In the end the number of students exceeded the capacity of the villa and we rented several rooms in the Seizan Hotel to take the overflow. Prince and Princess Mikasa spend part of their summer in Karuizawa, so that the Princess resumed her instruction with Jane. As in Tokyo there was lively social activity, centering mainly round the picturesque tennis club. The Crown Prince and Princess Michiko played there; it is said that they first met in Karuizawa. Most of our lessons were given out of doors in the gardens of the villa. Geoff Mason in particular liked to work in the open air. He would park his student against the trunk of a leafy tree, put on his straw hat and then pace up and down in the shade as he delivered his lesson. One day I made a quick sketch of him doing this and made the drawing the basis of an ad we placed in *Asahi Shimbun* the following summer to advertise our Karuizawa courses. In November we were informed that the ad had won an Oscar from the Japanese Advertising Association as the best educational advertisement in 1968. Mason, Haraguchi and I attended an enormous prize distribution in the Ginza where I was presented with the statuette and a cash prize of 40.000 yen. The three of us, along with another couple of Japanese Karuizawa teachers, promptly went to Akio Morita's Maxim's restaurant and had a sumptuous dinner. (40.000 yen went a long way in those days.)

The Karuizawa courses became a feature of Berlitz instruction in Japan. We rented Nakasone's villa year after year and one or two others as well. The only time we had a problem was when Ernie Grossmann gave a party. Ernesto was the only businessman from San Salvador in Tokyo apart from the Ambassador and was one of those engaging characters who excel in one-upmanship and are always one step in front of everybody else. For instance when he furnished his apartment in Tokyo with Chinese furniture (which he bought in Hong Kong) he gave the ambassador's name instead of his own for shipping so that the entire consignment came in tax free. Ernie was an expert on pesticides and roamed South East Asia from his Tokyo base advising governments on agricultural matters. It was thirsty work, so Ernie gave big parties when he came home, at which large quantities of wine and spirits were consumed. For some reason he was studying Japanese in Karuizawa and one night he gave a huge party for all teachers and students, about 30 of us in all. Like most Latin Americans, he was fond of rumba and samba music and had his own amplification equipment with him for the purposes of the party. After dinner people danced merrily and the sounds of revelry penetrated the leafy surroundings of our area. Nakasone's villa is located on the bank of a delightful, fast-flowing stream. On the other side of the stream stood the villa of the then Prime Minister, Eisaku Sato. Sato, unfortunately, was in residence on the night of Ernesto's party. A reasonable man, he suffered the hubbub without complaint until 11 pm. At this point he sent a couple of police officers across the stream to ask us to turn down the music so that neighbours might sleep. I was naturally on the receiving end of the complaint and assured the officers that this would be done. I regulated the volume accordingly – much to Ernie's consternation – and people generally kept their voices low and all was well. The party proceeded quietly and I felt I could walk home to our own cottage about half a mile away. I had covered about half this distance when the decibels hit the roof again. I dashed back to find that Ernie had turned the tape recorder up to full blast again. The police arrived a few moments after I did. This time the conversation was more serious, though still couched in conciliatory terms. After they left I told Ernie off and closed down the party. By the time I had got home he had started it up again, as most of Karuizawa could hear. Subsequent visits by the police, now in groups of three and four, took place well after midnight. I am not sure at what time Ernie went to bed, it was one of those situations which could only have been solved by an outright arrest (Ernie's) though the police did not go so far. The next day I spent the hours from 9 to 5 filling in forms at the Karuizawa police station. Komine, Ernie's teacher, spent the same amount of time interpreting and translating the forms. Ernie spent most of the day in bed – he was not required by the police. As I was ultimately responsible, I could not complain – the police, though niggly, were invariably polite and courteous. Goodness knows how Komine's translations of my explanations, excuses and apologies came out in Japanese. The police captain on duty went through everything ten times. Komine and I had lunch at six in the evening. I confiscated Ernie's tape recorder. Mr Sato had had his revenge. I am sure that in many other countries it would have been much worse.

Chapter 13

Assignment in Vietnam

In June 1967 the United States Army asked Berlitz to find 150 Vietnamese language instructors to embark on a major teaching programme in the military language training centre in El Paso, Texas. These instructors were to be recruited on the ground in Vietnam, Laos and Cambodia and they were required immediately, or as soon as possible after that. Robert Strumpen-Darrie phoned me to ask if I would take on the job. I did not speak Vietnamese, but he thought I could swing it with English and French. I was relatively mobile, I was the Berlitz "Eastern expert" and I was vaguely considered by New York to be "in the area". (The actual distance between Tokyo and Saigon was 4000 Kms.), but the assignment appealed to me, so I readily concurred.

Later the same day Alberola rang with further details. The U.S. Army were training infiltrators, intelligence officers and various other types of support personnel to speak near-perfect or at least fluent Vietnamese. These trainees would in some circumstances have to be able to pass themselves off as natives of a particular area or district. The people I would recruit therefore would have to include teachers with different South Vietnamese accents, North Vietnamese dialects and also those dialects spoken in the Vietnamese communities in Cambodia and Laos. There were large numbers of North Vietnamese in South Vietnam, so these I could recruit in Saigon along with the Southerners. For the others I would have to go to Phnom Penh and Vientiane. It was important that the instructors sent to the U.S. should be people who had actually been living in Vietnam, Cambodia and Laos in the previous ten years, as the languages were undergoing certain changes in vocabulary and turn of phrase due to wartime conditions. Vietnamese living in the United States no longer qualified, as they did not have sufficient contact with current parlance.

Alberola had no fixed ideas as to how I should contact or interview candidates. He and Strumpen-Darrie had been informed of the project only the previous day and the rushed nature of the requirement had given nobody time to think the thing through. The army itself was not very forthcoming with advice as it did not wish to be seen involved in the matter – hence the delegation to a private institution. No one in Berlitz had ever set foot in Indo-China, not even in peacetime, if there ever had been a peace-time. The army had asked Berlitz to request me to keep a low profile, but to expedite things as quickly as possible. How I managed this was up to me, said Alberola, who added that he had wired me fifteen thousand dollars and that I should leave within two days. In other words I had *carte blanche* to organize my activity and I would be pretty much on my own after setting foot in Saigon.

These conditions suited me fine, since I felt that flexibility of role and relative freedom of action would be valuable in getting the job done quickly. The less I had to consult the army or other authorities the better, though clearly I would get involved with the American Embassy and the South Vietnamese Immigration Service regarding the question of entry and exit visas.

Departure in two days I felt was unrealistic, since I had to get visas for myself, not only for South Vietnam but also for Cambodia and Laos. At all events it was obvious that I had to drop everything in school and concentrate on preparing for the trip. The next morning I went to the office, dictated replies to all unanswered correspondence and informed Ed Wilton that I was going away for a while. I put all outstanding matters in his hands and told him he would have to save the company for the next few weeks.

Checking with the embassies, I discovered that I could obtain entry visas for Vietnam and Cambodia in Tokyo, but that I would have to get a visa for Laos in Thailand. I therefore applied also for a Thai visa in Tokyo and found that I would have all the necessary stamps in my passport within four days. This gave me a little time to make a few preparations. At Tokyo Tower Clinic I was vaccinated against cholera and typhoid. I changed ten thousand dollars into travellers' cheques – a decision I was to regret later – and put the other five thousand into my money belt. Sasaki's Travel Agency provided me with an open ticket Tokyo-Bangkok-Saigon-Phnom Penh-Vientiane-Saigon-Tokyo. At Mitsukoshi I bought a light blue linen suit and half a dozen white sleeveless shirts of the same material. In Maruzen I purchased concise histories of Vietnam, Laos and Cambodia in English and I read these quickly during the following evenings.

My chief problem was that I had no real contacts in Indo-China, so I resolved to try to dig a few up before departure. First I phoned Chris McDonald at NCR. As I expected, it was only a few hours before he got back to me with some positive information. The NCR manager in Saigon was a Dane called Paul Rasmussen. He and his second in command, Pip Powell, would give me any assistance I required while in Vietnam. Mr Jan Crevels, the NCR manager in Bangkok, would lend me a car and anything else I needed while in Thailand. Unfortunately Chris had no really solid contacts in Cambodia or Laos.

Some months earlier I had arranged a French course for Shirley MacLaine's 12-year old daughter, Sachiko, who spent part of the year in Japan with her father, Steve Parker. Steve, who worked as a film director in Tokyo, had also studied Japanese with us for six weeks. I recalled that he had worked in Cambodia and that he knew Prince Norodom Sihanouk, the then ruler of that country. I called Steve to tell him of my assignment and he came round to dinner that same evening to give me some advice. In 1967 the Indo-Chinese war had not been extended into Cambodia and he warned me that I should have to be careful in initiating any activity in that country which might be seen as being too closely involved with the war effort. Furthermore the Cambodians were of a different stock from the Vietnamese and Laotians and were a touchy bunch in the prevalent conditions.

However he knew Prince Sihanouk well because of his film work and said he would be happy to give me an introduction to him. The Cambodian ruler was a remarkable man. Not only was he the country's political leader, but he was a great patron of the arts and involved himself heavily in all branches of Cambodian culture. His favourite hobby was the cinema. Sihanouk produced and directed Cambodian films, wrote the scripts, played the leading roles and gave supporting roles to various members of his family. He often used the magnificent backdrop of the temples of Angkor Wat in his films and gave full scope to the richness and variety of Cambodian music, song and dance. Steve had helped the prince on various occasions and he assured me that he was a charming, considerate man who could be approached with a view to facilitating my somewhat delicate task in Phnom Penh.

Other friends in Tokyo gave me personal introductions to people in the British and Australian embassies in Vientiane, Laos, as well as to the Director of the Lao-American Association in that city. By the time I had collected all my visas I felt that I had sufficient information and contacts to give me a reasonable chance of seeing the project through.

Berlitz were phoning every day, asking if I had left, so I did my final packing and booked a JAL flight into Bangkok. It was impossible to travel light. Besides packing a lot of spare underwear and shirts so as not to have to depend on laundries during the trip, I had several kilos of application forms sent on by Berlitz (about 1000 in all) as well as other documentation relating to the assignment. I also took my reference books on Indo-China as well as the mandatory bottles of whisky for my contacts in the four countries to be visited. My last minute personal check-list, in addition to the above-mentioned items, read: passport, travellers' cheques, cash, credit cards, airline tickets, vaccination certificate, visas, re-entry permit into Japan, toilet articles, pyjamas, aspirin (for hangovers) milk of magnesia tablets (for stomach upsets), British and American driving licences, letters of introduction, diary and address-phone book, camera, ten rolls of film.

On June 22nd I took a taxi to Haneda to board JAL flight 105 to Bangkok. It was with some trepidation that I hauled my two suitcases onto the scales, knowing that the application forms and documents alone weighed 15 kilos. The total weight of my baggage including hand luggage was 35 kilos, but for some reason the JAL clerk proved to be sympathetic and charged me only 5 kilos excess. I clambered gratefully aboard with my five bottles of whisky procured in duty free – four Chivas Regal for my contacts and one Old Parr for me to spike my lemonade en route and thereafter.

The flight was the usual cheery JAL jumbo outing – new plane, smiling hostesses fussing around in kimonos, mouth-watering sushi and tempura tit-bits, muted Japanese pop music and smooth take-off and landing. I arrived fresh and content but soon deteriorated rapidly under the impact of Bangkok in June.

In 1967 the airport building still lacked air-conditioning and by the time I had hustled my luggage into the small, hot taxi my new linen suit was beginning to crumple fast. The headlong charge to the Oriental Hotel took 30 minutes along the dead-straight, colourless concrete highway between the airport and downtown. I gave the small, taciturn driver ten dollars from my money belt whereupon he suddenly became sunny and animated, chattering away excitedly to me in Thai as he voluntarily carried my heavy load right up to the front desk.

The word must have got around the lobby, for there was lively competition among the bell-boys as to who should have the honour of carrying my bags up to my room. The ultimate winner of this contest received a further two dollars on the Berlitz expense account and flitted happily around the room, opening shutters, indicating the switches for lights, radio and television, hanging up my jacket and trying to read the combination on my brief-case which I had kept firmly in my clutch since setting foot on Thai soil.

Bangkok is noted for its opportunistic bell-boys and chambermaids who collaborate cleverly in relieving you of any extra unwanted cash you leave locked up in your briefcase. Having parted with 100,000 yen in banknotes on a previous visit to the Thai capital (though not at the Oriental Hotel) I was determined not to fall prey to this manoeuvre again. The trick is performed in the following manner: the bell-boy stands close to you while you open your briefcase to extract your passport for check-in. He memorizes the open combination number and subsequently informs the chambermaid. She then memorizes the numbers you have twiddled to, sets the combination to "open", removes some cash (but not all), closes the case and sets again the scrambled numbers you have so much faith in. In this manner she removes a little cash each day, hoping you do not count it daily, and takes most of what is left on the last day about an hour before you check out.

On this occasion, however, I had produced my passport from an inside pocket and had entered the hotel with twiddled combinations. The young entrepreneur finally left and I was able to devote half an hour to the river scene, soothed by a happy combination of Old Parr and Thai ginger ale. Even before its re-building, the Oriental was a beautiful hotel and has one of the best locations in the Far East. It overlooks the Chao Phraya River —about quarter of a mile wide at this point. At all times of the day and night, particularly early morning, there is an industrious coming and going of picturesque river traffic – ferries, motor boats, junks, punts, paddle-steamers and large flat bottomed canoes or dug-outs plying their way to and fro between different landing points or exiting from the mainstream into narrow tributaries leading to the Floating Market and beyond. My room was high up and my window seat dominated the view splendidly. I could see at least a mile and a half up river and by half opening the window I could hear the muted, turbulent cries of the river pilots and quayside vendors as well as benefit from the slight breeze coming off the water.

Jan Crevels, the local NCR manager, phoned me at 6 and proposed to pick me up in the lobby in an hour's time. This kind suggestion enabled me to pour myself another ginger ale and watch the startling sunset over the river. All the vessels now displayed yellow, orange or red lights and these combined with the crimson-flecked ripples on the surface to produce a colourful ever-changing kaleidoscope of oriental splendour. When the sun was really gone and the river had turned grey-blue, I took off my travelling clothes and spent 10 minutes under the shower, first hot, then cold. My suit, now hanging complete in the cupboard, reminded me irresistibly of ones worn by characters in Bogart's "Casablanca" or that worn by Sidney Greenstreet in "The Maltese Falcon" (though several sizes smaller). I resolved therefore to go for dinner in one of my new Mitsukoshi linen shirts and, as it turned out, this proved to be perfectly acceptable attire at the pleasant Thai restaurant that Jan Crevels took me to.

He was a typical NCR Far Eastern old hand – 50 years of age, hard drinker, albeit ostensibly tanned and fit, originally from Holland but speaking fluent English, German, Cantonese and Thai, with a good smattering of Indonesian, Tagalog and Japanese. He had done 25 years time on the Pacific circuit – Manila, Hong Kong, Djakarta, Kobe and Bangkok – and he ran a highly successful local operation. He had not been to Indo-China, but he knew Paul Rasmussen, his opposite number in NCR Saigon. Jan was kind enough to entertain me until midnight or so, over dinner and at a couple of bars after that. We ate a tasty fish caught in the mud at the bottom of the Bangkok bay and had several whiskies afterwards to help us sleep properly in the oppressive climate. Bangkok I have always found to be even muggier than Tokyo. Jan tended to agree with me, although he said that after seven years in Thailand he found he could stand the humidity much better than previously. He advised me to visit Southern Thailand only in December or January, were I in the future to have any choice in the matter.

The next day I was provided with an NCR car and driver, so that I was able to secure my Laotian visa in the morning and thereafter see some of the sights of the Thai capital. The driver spoke good English and he graciously acted as my guide, showing me the Royal Palace and the many impressive temples and monuments immediately adjacent to it. There was so much to see that the afternoon sped quickly by. At six o'clock I invited the driver to a Mai Tai (his suggestion) in the Writer's Bar in the Oriental and after half an hour or so he departed for home to his wife and five children, while I went up to my room, threw myself on the bed, counted the cash in my briefcase, spiked another ginger ale and watched my second Thai sunset.

My plane to Saigon was due out at 9 the next morning, so I spent the evening quietly, being somewhat shattered by all those temples at 30° C in the shade. I went down to the coffee shop for a quick snack, bought half a dozen postcards which I wrote and mailed to England and Japan, watched Thai Boxing on television for two hours or so and had a hot bath to make me sleepy. Kick boxing, as it is often called, has always appealed to me as a spectacle, though I have no particular desire to try it out in person. One is allowed to attack one's opponent with one's hands, feet or knees, making it pretty much a genuine, no-holds-barred contest, where the weaker fighter usually ends up unconscious for a spell, if not stretchered away with a broken jaw. For all its viciousness, however, kick boxing is highly technical and is gaining appeal in several Asian countries, including Japan, where I had first got hooked on it. In spite of my hot bath I was unable to sleep very much, as the boxing had set my nerves on edge and I twitched restlessly around the bed for most of night, almost welcoming the early oriental dawn and the squawks of the pedlars below my window just after six.

*   *   *   *   *

I checked out early and arrived at the airport just after seven. I was anxious to secure a window seat so that I could take some pictures of Vietnam from the air. There were already a couple of dozen people forming a queue at the Air Vietnam desk and I took my place in this line. Most of the passengers were orientals, ostensibly businessmen or government officials, but there were four or five American officers in uniform. There was no one manning the desk at that hour and the queue soon lengthened behind me. It was hardly likely that many of those embarking had had their coffee and they constituted a grim, unsmiling bunch, their luggage a motley assortment of suitcases, duffle bags, metal boxes, crates, rucksacks, briefcases and kit bags. Nobody conversed, except the Americans and even they were unusually quiet. It was no holiday crowd. Around 8.15 a thin, harassed-looking ticket clerk began to take our tickets and I was assigned a window seat just in front of the wing, though I was told it was forbidden to take any photographs. No one took any notice of this rule once the plane was in the air, consequently I was able to get some good shots of the Mekong in due course.

I found myself sitting next to a diminutive, sallow-cheeked Vietnamese diplomat who exchanged a few pleasantries with me in good French before fastening his safety belt, after which he closed his eyes and slept for the rest of the journey. The atmosphere on board contrasted sharply with that of the JAL flight the day before. The Vietnamese air hostesses were pretty in the extreme, but they looked strained and nervous as they went through the motions of announcing the safety regulations in English, French and Vietnamese. The plane was full, although the back six rows on either side of the aisle were stuffed with bulging gunny sacks – possibly mail bags which had already been silently in place, duly buckled up, when we embarked. I noticed that some of the Americans were already drinking before take-off, passing round Scotch and guzzling it straight from the bottle. Once we were airborne, the orientals lit up cigarettes almost to a man, apart from my dozing diplomat and a female American stenographer across the aisle, who complained several times about the fug that soon thickened around us. After half an hour we were served tepid orange squash and small square, unidentifiable sandwiches by the good-looking hostesses with their worried smiles.

As we left Siamese air space one could almost feel the transition into a wartime economy: the uniforms, spartan rations, heavy smoking, grubby cabin interior, lack of conversation, the unsmiling faces of the passengers, the litter and and kit bags in the aisle, – all brought back to me strong memories of the tense days of England in 1940. This impression was strengthened by the interest shown in the next item on the programme – obviously the highlight of the trip – the sale of duty free items. In thirty years of flying I have never seen a lolly scramble time like it. Orientals and occidentals in concert bought cigarettes, perfume, chocolates, whisky and cognac to the limit of their carrying ability. I saw the stenographer purchase six bottles of perfume along with a huge armful of chocolate boxes. My Vietnam diplomat, awakening hurriedly, produced a wad of traveller's cheques looking like the Bible in Viet translation and filled the area around our feet with bottles and cartons of his choosing. Trade was such that the trolley was emptied before it had reached one third of the way down the aisle, and two of the hostesses shuttled back and forth with fresh supplies, so that in the end nobody was disappointed. These planes were obviously specially stocked.

The Americans opened up one or two bottles, the Viets smoked on and munched chocolates and in a while the ambience livened up a trifle; one sensed a feeling of relative enjoyment. I climbed over my Viet friend and threaded my way through ground luggage towards the rear toilets, which were now doing brisk business. After five minutes staring at the mail bag passengers I gained entrance to one of the lavatories. It functioned well enough, but there were half a dozen cigarette butts crushed into the floor, and the toilet paper was brown and grainy. The confined space reeked of smoke and cheap carbolic soap.

Someone had scrawled HO CHI MINH RULES on the back wall in indelible red ink and the airline had made a half hearted attempt at obliterating it in black. I did not stay long.

Back in the cabin passengers had finished stowing away their newly-acquired purchases and were settling down to one activity or another. Two Koreans were tucking into a dish of fish, rice, vegetables and garlic which they had brought on board in black, lacquered boxes. The Japanese sitting next to them was trying to avoid their breath and concentrated on the window and his camera. Two or three Thais – the only ones with current newspapers – were reading, while most of the Vietnamese sat quietly smoking, eyeing the increasingly voluble American servicemen who had now added popcorn to the menu.

The distance between Bangkok and Saigon, about 450 miles as the crow flies, would normally be about one hour's flying time. In wartime the journey took nearly two hours as the pilot flew south-east along the Gulf of Thailand to avoid overflying Cambodian airspace until he was well south of Phnom Penh, then flew due east over the island of Dao Phu Quoc and across the Vietnamese mainland towards Saigon. After passing over the city of Long Xuyen we were afforded an excellent view of the wide, flat, platinum surface of the Mekong, meandering lazily 25,000 feet below us through the rich delta riceland as far as the South China Sea. Through towering banks of cumulus cloud we could see the silver sunlight brilliantly reflected in thousands of rice paddies, ox bow lakes and ubiquitous tributaries. Interwoven into this drenched landscape was the green of the jungle, turning blue as one squinted further ahead. In spite of the high population density of the Mekong Delta, few dwellings were clearly visible from the aeroplane. The intense, throbbing undercurrent of Vietnamese life and habitation was not in evidence from our height. I wondered what activity lay enshrouded below the blue-green treetops. I knew that the jungle areas even in the vicinity of the capital were dark, humid battlegrounds thick with Vietnamese, Viet Cong, Korean, Australian and American patrols. Thousands of American lives had already been claimed in the war, which showed few signs of ending. It was hard to believe, surveying the silent, rural landscape below us, that a human tragedy of such enormous proportions was inevitably being enacted even as we peered out of the plane window.

I took a few pictures, as did most passengers seated next to a window. The sprawl of Saigon became visible ahead of us on the left hand side of the aircraft and the "Fasten Seat Belts" and "No Smoking" signs came on. It was announced that we should shortly be landing at Tan Son Nhut airport, but no decrease of altitude was noticeable. The plane began to circle, maintaining its height, and we flew round the perimeter of the city for fifteen minutes or so. Everyone on board was now quiet and those who could surveyed the scene below. The Viet official gathered his bottles more closely around him and wedged some of his purchases tightly between his feet.

Suddenly, and sickeningly, the pilot pointed the nose of the aircraft down at an angle of 45 degrees and the engine screamed shrilly around our ears as the blue-green vegetation rushed up at us at a speed of three hundred miles an hour. I realised afterwards that most of the passengers were used to this system of re-entering Saigon airspace, but for me it was a completely novel and somewhat un-nerving experience. Apparently a normal, low approach would attract small arms fire from Cong units or snipers hidden in the Saigon periphery. Many aircraft had indeed been shot down in this manner. The solution was to fly high until one was virtually right over Tan Son Nhut, which was well protected by U.S. forces. Then you went straight in and banged the aircraft down on the tarmac.

Bang it down our pilot did, with each individual scrambling to cushion his bottles or his coccyx, whichever he prized most. We screamed along the runway at 200 miles an hour plus, engines reversing piercingly, brakes a-screeching, nerves a-jangling, palms pressed open and up against the back of the seat in front. I have been crunched unceremoniously onto concrete runways several times in my globe-trotting career, memorably at least twice courtesy of Iberia, whose pilots seem to have the procedure in their manual, but the thumping down in Saigon makes all other landings, Tenerife, Madeira and Bergen included, seem gentle by comparison. Our plane finally stopped at the end of the runway as a fire engine and an ambulance roared up alongside to check that no harm had been done to plane or passengers. Apparently it was standard security procedure.

Before we were allowed to disembark, South Vietnamese soldiers boarded the aircraft and examined our passports, visas and hand luggage. They were armed to the teeth, but matter-of-fact and polite. It was noticeable that the Vietnamese passengers came under much closer scrutiny than the rest of us. The garlic-breathing Koreans received the briefest of inspections – I made a mental note of this for future occasions.

*   *   *   *   *

When the check was complete, we were permitted to disembark. We clanked our way down the steps, some of the shorter passengers hardly visible under their purchases and cabin luggage. It was only mid-morning, but the air was thickly humid, heavily redolent of both the jungle and the sea, though the latter was over 50 miles away. The airport building was two hundred yards ahead of us and we slowly followed two soldiers like a procession of heavily-laden mules. It had been raining earlier and we zig-zagged to avoid steaming puddles. The sun was hot on the back of my neck and I felt the sweat trickling down between my shoulder blades under my wrinkled linen attire.

The terminal building was low and dingy, propped up by khaki sand-bags and devoid of any decoration or advertising billboards. It was no bigger than a provincial airport and its size seemed entirely inappropriate to the scale of the war effort, as already in late 1967 there was a massive inflow of war material to support more than 400,000 U.S. combat troops active in South Vietnam. I learnt later that huge quantities of material and supplies reached the country by water, where 3 miles of quays along the Saigon River could unload boats in a port accessible to vessels of up to 30-foot draft. In spite of the tiny airport building, however, one was left in no doubt as to the value of Tan Son Nhut as an airbase; as one crossed the tarmac one could perceive long lines of camouflaged military aircraft of all descriptions, stretching in both directions as far as the eye could see. Two more supply planes came screaming in as we entered the terminal, while a huge crowd of troops milling around the exit gate on our left indicated that a major embarkation was imminent.

The customs formalities were slow and ponderous. All our bags were opened in our presence before we went through immigration. I presumed this was a precaution against admitting persons who might leave a lethal item of luggage revolving on the baggage belts. A South Vietnamese soldier dealt with my two suitcases, closely examining such objects as my camera, electric razor and squeezing half an inch of toothpaste out of my Colgate tube. He tasted a little on the tip of his tongue – I have never been able to figure out why – and seemed fairly satisfied. He looked at my guide books, commenting only with a grunt and ignored my one thousand teachers' application forms, about which I had expected to be questioned. I supposed they were all sick of paper work connected with the war.

We were allowed to re-pack and re-fasten our luggage which was then whisked away to be given to us later, on the other side of Immigration. Our passports were checked by South Vietnamese regulars, but I noticed that there were several American NCO's also checking papers. My Vietnamese visa granted me a 10-day period of authorised stay and the Viet official who looked at it asked me what I intended to do in Saigon. I had rehearsed two possible answers in advance: one, that I was visiting friends; two, that I was looking for a couple of teachers for Berlitz. We had considered that these replies would be the ones least likely to make any waves at minor official level. The second reason had already been given as my purpose of stay at the Vietnam Embassy in Tokyo. As I felt that my application forms had "passed" unseen during the Customs inspection, I decided to switch to the first reply and said I was visiting friends. He asked me who they were and I gave the names of the two NCR men whom I hoped to see later. Address in Saigon? I had already booked a room at the Hotel Caravelle. He had a good look at the Cambodian, Lao, Yugoslav and Czech visas in other parts of my passport, then rubber-stamped the Viet one and motioned me on.

I retrieved my two suitcases from the baggage conveyor belt and looked around in vain for a trolley. There was no shortage of porters, however, and a middle-aged coolie with the traditional cone-shaped straw hat shouldered my 35 kilos and staggered towards the exit with me in tow. The concourse was thick with onlookers, chattering and curious, much more demonstrative than the wooden-faced Japanese throngs I was now used to, but more disciplined and less excitable than Filipinos in the mad-house they call Manila Airport.

We threaded our way through, bodies brushing ours, and as we came once more into the sunlight I was again conscious of the thick treacly air and pungent Asian odours so different from the familiar cooking smells on the streets of Tokyo. The bus stop was 50 metres away and when we reached it my porter put down the bags and sign-languaged me to wait. There were people everywhere, most of them looking in our direction. Women squatted on the pavement selling rice cakes, and hard-boiled eggs. Men stood around in small groups, idle for now but with an air of wanting something to do. They were small and neat, in spite of their humble attire, with sharp, questioning, intelligent eyes. Half a dozen of them only a yard or two away stared at me intently. Their nearness and the directness of their gaze disconcerted me slightly, as I was now acclimatized to being among Japanese, who keep a comfortable body-distance away and stare at your feet as they mutter their pleasantries. I soon realized that these onlookers were in no way offensive, but simply inquisitive. I probably looked out of place amongst the Asian businessmen and the other roundeyes clearly connected with the military.

A battered old bus rattled up – a short, squat thirty-seater with about a hundred people inside. Giggling children hung from the exterior and as the vehicle came to a hissing halt two brown chickens flew out of the open windows. They were chased by the youngsters, quickly secured and hauled back to the bus stop to be handed over to a fat peasant woman. The bus disgorged its contents – a mixture of peasants, vendors and townies, all short in stature and mainly on the thin side.

When the passengers around me began to organize their luggage, I realized that this was the airport bus. My porter began to chatter excitedly and I gave him three dollars. He stowed my suitcases in the rear of the bus. Once I had seen them safely buried under dozens of others, I sought a seat at the front to get a better glimpse of Saigon on the way downtown. After forty or so airline passengers had piled in, the driver jumped aboard and signalled to those remaining on the pavement that another rattletrap was about to come. He gunned the engine with a deafening roar, the vehicle gave a mighty shudder as he let out the clutch and we lurched forward, did a U-turn to the left and commenced our itinerary.

*   *   *   *   *

I was sitting on the front row across from the driver and I had an unrestricted view of the street scene all the way from the airport to the Hotel Caravelle. It was an unforgettable sight and one which will remain indelibly engraved on my memory. Saigon, sometimes referred to as "The Pearl of the Orient", was in 1967 the tinder-box of the world. The ravages that the Viet Cong were in the process of inflicting on the countryside were driving thousands of refugees each week to seek refuge in the capital. The population of Saigon had quadrupled during the period 1960 -1967 and there were now over 2,000,000 people living in an area of 20 square miles. Owing to the rapidly increasing significance of the war, pictures of Vietnamese life were appearing almost every day in both the Japanese and western press and Saigon featured regularly in newsreels in most countries around the world.

Yet nothing I had seen in the media prepared me for the actuality. As we began to enter the main thoroughfares the density of the traffic increased, so that shortly the road itself was no longer visible. I was used to heavy traffic in Tokyo and London, but in these cities it consists almost exclusively of four-wheeled vehicles. In Saigon there were one and a half million motor cycles of various types. These two-wheelers packed in around the cars, buses and lorries so tightly that the tarmac could not be seen. Our bus was completely hemmed in, swept along in a slow-moving tide of sputtering vehicles and perspiring bodies, heading inexorably towards the central district and the Saigon River. Another tide, equal in volume and appearance, flowed sluggishly in the opposite direction. It is appropriate to mention the bodies, since most people were being transported by cycles, motorized or otherwise. There were few motor scooters which did not carry two passengers, the pillion rider often being a woman. Females invariably rode side saddle, or even faced backwards so that from my vantage point in the bus I could see a sea of faces – feminine ones staring back at us and masculine ones belonging to the oncoming tide on our left.

Although cars were heavily out-numbered by bikes, there was a goodly number of small blue-and-white Renaults, which appeared to be taxis, and several big black Chevrolets mostly occupied by Americans. Besides the Lambrettas and Vespas (Italian-built but assembled in two plants just outside Saigon) there were thousands of light motor-bikes with the engine fixed over the front wheel. These, too, carried two passengers. The most traditional type of transport, however, was the "cyclo" or pedicab, where either one or two passengers braved the oncoming traffic in front, while a coolie, often with extremely limited vision, pedal-powered them from behind. I was to try them later and found them neither safe nor expensive.

The boulevards of the downtown area were wide, straight and tree-lined, – obviously designed by former French city planners nostalgic for Paris. On

Riversdown

First students at Riversdown

Ed Wilton and RDL

Country life

Charles Berlitz at Riversdown

Prince Mikasa, Emperor Hirohito's brother, at Riversdown 1974

Crown Prince Hiro at Riversdown with Ladislav Moudry (left)

Prince Hiro at Riversdown 1984

North Korean peasants 1979

North Korean school

National day

North Korean boys marching to school

RDL with minders, Pyonyang 1979

The Beloved Leader

The steps at Panmunjom

with Captain of the Guard,
Panmunjom

Peace treaty room

Plenty caviare

Mother Russia

Volgograd with Alexander Kosov

"Eisenhower's Villa"

Mr and Mrs A. Kosov

Robert Sirabella

Marie-Claire Berte

Cambridge School, Lisbon

Masami Shirooka

with Pele

Stanley Matthews

Alec Brook

Interpreting with Pele, Thailand

Empress Michiko and Caroline

Christine Dobryziniecki
and Elena Mulholland

Mother and friend

Pak Cook (Mr Chips)

either side, there were many fine public buildings and I noticed several leafy gardens and attractive, shady squares. We passed the beautiful Romanesque Cathedral, stamping the city centre with its French heritage and I was reminded that France had ruled Saigon from 1883 to 1954.

There were men in uniform everywhere. Those Americans who were mobile could be seen only in cars, but Vietnamese soldiers rode every kind of bike. I saw captains and even majors in the South Vietnamese army chugging away on their Vespas flanked by coolies, rice vendors and newspaper boys. The sidewalks were thick with soldiers in groups of four or five, smartly-uniformed air force personnel and American commandos in camouflage battle dress. They mingled with shoe-shine boys, peasants, housewives and street hawkers of every description.

After half an hour of such observations, I began to suffer from sensory overload. One over-riding impression, however, remains with me for always: in the midst of this wartime spectacle, with its choking diesel fumes, its frustrated ferriage, its tense unsmiling faces, its bullet-scarred edifices, one thing stood out calm, serene and indestructible – the unequalled, unrivalled beauty of the Vietnamese women. There they sat on their pillions, heading goodness knows where, half shrouded in the diesel haze, probably trapped in a tragic cul-de-sac of history, bitter-sweet figures wearing the traditional *ao dai* – wispy clinging pantaloons under a long-sleeved, high-necked dress slit to the hips – arguably the most enticing item of feminine attire in the whole world : a unique combination of allure and virtue.

The women were slender and raven-haired, high cheek-boned and haughty, round enough in the eye to bespeak an admixture of French blood. They were delicate, wasp-waisted, small-boned creatures who stared you boldly in the eye if you as much as gave them a second glance.

                    *   *   *   *   *

They were still on my mind as I was delivered to the front door of the Hotel Caravelle, a centrally-located and renowned 10-storey building in white stucco on the Tu Do Boulevard. Two bell-boys rushed out to greet me and, as they milled around with the bags, I resolved to concentrate on checking in and preparing my day's activity, for it was still only 1 p.m. My resolution faltered almost immediately as I entered the hotel lobby, where I was met by a delectable young lady, in high collar, snug bodice and slit skirt, by the name of Tran Thi Mai, whose black hair reached her waist. Her job was to welcome new guests to the Caravelle and make them feel at home. She certainly succeeded with me. Shepherding me smilingly to the front desk, she took my passport and gave me my room key along with her name card in exchange. If I had any problems, I was to ring the number on the card.

I went up in the lift with one of the bell-boys; my room was on the 4th floor. It was light and airy with modern, functional furniture and a good view over the square in front of the hotel. When the bell-boy had gone I went to the bathroom and ran a lukewarm bath. After soaking for ten minutes I finished with a cold shower and put on fresh underwear, a clean shirt and my only pair of uncrumpled grey gaberdine trousers. It was two o'clock and I was starving. I took my room key, banged the door hard and went down to eat, using the stairs in order to learn the way down in case of fire. The Caravelle, which had been built less than 10 years before, had already been blown up twice.

The snack bar at the Caravelle had Vietnamese, French and American dishes. I usually try the local food, but as I had a lot of work to get through in the next few days I decided to play it safe and lunched on steak and chips. I had already given some thought as to how I should go about recruiting teachers. The Army had said 'low profile' and Berlitz New York advised me to proceed cautiously, first asking Americans in the Embassy or the Vietnamese-American Association if they had friends who knew friends who might be interested, and so forth. But time was not on my side. My visa was for 10 days only, 150 instructors were required at once, I had an awful lot of screening to do if I did not wish to send to Texas a batch of Viet Cong sympathizers and I still had to go to Cambodia and Laos.

All my life it has been a firm belief of mine that if you want to get hold of something or someone real fast, the best thing you can do is bang a solid ad in a widely-read newspaper. It is not very low profile, but it gets results. Also I figured I could word the advertisement in such a way that it would appear that only one or two persons were required. As I tried out a few drafts on the paper tablecloth I eventually settled on the following version:

WORK IN THE USA

Wanted immediately: Educated Vietnamese with Baccalaureate and knowledge of English for teaching Vietnamese in the U.S.A. Men or women accepted aged 22-55. Apply at once to Richard Lewis, Room 404, Hotel Caravelle.

It was three in the afternoon. There seemed little activity in the square outside the Caravelle and I supposed it was siesta time in these latitudes. The average temperature in Saigon in June is 82° F and the humidity hovers around 100 per cent. I assumed that newspaper offices would be open in the late afternoon and that I might succeed in getting my ad published the next morning. I signed for my steak and chips and made my way to the Front Desk. The Chief Reception Clerk was a calm 40-year-old named Hoang Tien Manh, with whom I had quite a lot to do in the next few days, as things turned out. I asked him which was the most widely-read newspaper in Saigon and he informed me it was the "TIN SOM" DAILY. He confirmed that if I took in my ad at 5 pm it would appear the next morning. I almost jumped for joy, but remembered my Japanese manners and gave him a little bow. This clearly amused him and I reminded myself that Vietnamese did not bow and neither did occidentals in Vietnam. I thanked him and went up to my room. There I printed the advertisement neatly on a sheet of paper and made another two copies for myself. I took one thousand dollars out of my money belt, ten bills of one hundred each, and stuffed them into my trouser pocket. Then I went back to the front desk where Hoang had written out for me the address of the newspaper, along with the name of the editor – Nguyen Kim Cang, – who reputedly spoke good English. Hoang also advised me to put an additional ad in the "Saigon Daily News", an English-language publication read by large numbers of Vietnamese who were interested in American affairs.

I followed my street map to 225, Pham ngu Lao Street and met Mr Nguyen Kim Cang, who indeed spoke a reasonable facsimile of the English language, US version. I wanted a big ad – two days in a row. He agreed and he relieved me of six hundred dollars US. This fee included the translation into Vietnamese, which I asked him to do on the spot. Ten minutes later I left his offices armed with a receipt for 600 dollars, the Vietnamese translation of my ad and the address of the "Saigon News." I deposited my advertisement with this journal – one hundred and fifty dollars' worth – and made my way back to the Caravelle. There I asked Hoang to translate my Vietnamese text back into English. He came up with the following:

WORK IN THE USA

Wanted quickly. Cultured Vietnamese with Baccaulaureate and English course to teach English to Vietnamese people in the USA. Men or women suitable 22-55 years apply immediately to Richard Lewis, Room 404, Hotel Caravelle.

In five minutes I was back in Nguyen Kim Cang's office and we straightened it out together. Forty is a difficult age for translators, I told him. At twenty-one or thirty they still checked carefully with grammar and dictionary. At sixty they didn't need to. He was very apologetic. Yes, I would have been interviewing the wrong people. He offered me a glass of ginseng. Nguyen had a permanently sincere smile – one you couldn't wash off. He probably slept in it. I told him I wanted my money back if I found myself dealing with jockeys or opticians. He promised he would get it right this time. I walked back to the Caravelle in the gathering twilight. The evening was no cooler than the afternoon and I was relieved to enter the blue grotto of room 404 where the air conditioner was going full blast. I undressed, put on a pair of shorts, lay on the bed for a while and soon fell asleep.

*   *   *   *   *

After about one hour I was awakened by a CRUMP sound and the windows vibrated and rattled slightly in their frames. Half a minute later there were three more crumps, two or three seconds apart. I remembered what I had been told in Tokyo: from dusk till dawn the Viet Cong rule nearly half of South Vietnam. I assumed that what I had heard were rockets landing inside the city perimeter. I went to the window and looked out onto the square. Darkness had descended and bright lights from the restaurants on the other side illuminated the evening scene. There were lots of people walking about, but no one seemed to have paid any attention to the explosions. As I stood by the window there were two more thuds, louder this time, but people just went on with what they were doing – strolling, chatting, eating, drinking and reading posters. It occurred to me that war had been Saigon's staple industry for 30 years. The present situation, representing a desperate crisis for the Americans in Saigon, was a way of life for the Vietnamese.

In any event I dressed quickly, left my room and took the lift up to La Terrasse, a cocktail bar on the top floor. It was a small, intimate establishment where one could not help but meet people. There were four men drinking Scotch and by the time I had got my drink I knew that three of them were American and the other was British. One of the Americans said hello and introduced himself as Don Jones from USAID. He was blond and freckled with a pleasant open face and the easy social graces of Americans from Washington State. The other two Americans were Joe Willard, a data processing advisor, also with USAID and John H. Toole, an auditor with RMK-BRJ. The Englishman was Mark Frankland, correspondent from "The Observer." When they heard that it was my first day in town they grinned and asked me if I had heard the rockets. Nothing to worry about, they said.

Don Jones took me out on the roof and pointed in the direction of the river where the sky seemed unusually bright. Flares, he explained, dropped by planes on the VC. We could also see searchlights, which he said were directed from S. Vietnamese river patrol boats sweeping the waterfront of the guerrilla-infested villages of Xom Thu Thiem and An Khanh Xa on the opposite bank to Saigon. From there the VC set up hit-and-run raids with mortars and rifle grenades. Even as we stood out there another rocket exploded and in the distance we could hear the frantic jingling and wailing of a fire engine.

We rejoined the others who asked me laughingly if I had enjoyed the show. It was even better from the top floor of the Majestic they said. The Majestic Hotel, which had also had its share of plastiques, was right on the river. The three Americans had been in Vietnam for several years and they were all interested in hearing about Tokyo. They managed to get there occasionally for their R and R, as they called it. They marvelled at the Japanese economic miracle and asked me to explain it, as if living in Tokyo qualified me to pronounce on such matters. I said the usual things about ten-hour days, fifty-one week years, all pulling together, spending one per cent of budget on defence, and so on. Everybody nodded sagely and we had another drink.

The phone on the bar counter rang — the barman said it was for me. It was Pip Powell from NCR. He and Paul Rasmussen would like to invite me out to lunch or dinner the next day. I suggested dinner, as I expected the daylight hours to be hectic, so he agreed to pick me up at the Caravelle at 7 pm. Pip sounded young, bright and cheerful. My four companions were all in their late thirties. The Americans smoked incessantly as they downed one Scotch after another. It was clear that they were not going anywhere that evening and they settled down in a cosy corner of the bar. Mark Frankland ordered bacon lettuce and tomato sandwiches – no doubt a journalist's standard supper – and I followed suit.

"What y'all fixin to do in Saigon?" Willard asked me. He was from Texas. I explained my mission, playing down the numbers. Toole gave a low whistle and Willard clucked like they do down there in the south-west.

"You're sure gonna stir up a lot of local interest," said Jones. "How're you planning to make your enquiries?

"I've put an ad in tomorrow's newspaper." I didn't see any point in keeping it back. Mark Frankland laughed out loud, losing some of his sandwich.

"English-language or Vietnamese?" asked Jones.

"Both."

"Y'all sure as hail don' beat about the bush, do you, boy?" commented Willard, who might have been a year older than I was.

"Thought I might as well get on with it."

"You checked with the Embassy and the Nam Ministry of Security?" asked Toole.

"I intend going there tomorrow morning."

"You see Ralph Essling, US. Consulate, on Norodom. He's your man."

"You'd better rise at cock-crow", said Mark Frankland. You'll be interviewing at breakfast."

"A hell of a lot of people are trying to get out. You might find yourself popular." said Jones.

"Watch for goddam VC among your teachers." growled Willard.

"How will I spot them?" I asked. Again Frankland gave his hollow laugh and this time Toole and Jones joined him.

"That's the sixty-four dollar question round here," said Jones, more kindly.

"Buying a haircut from a VC that's one thing. Sending him Stateside is another," grunted Willard.

"Where are you going to do your interviewing? asked Toole.

"Here in the Caravelle."

"A bit public, isn't it? Why don't you use one of the U.S. offices?"

"I've got to keep it private."

"Does the hotel know?"

"The man at the front desk does."

"How did he react?"

"He didn't blow his stack."

"Hoang doesn't flap." said Frankland.

"You got a big room?" asked Toole.

"Yes. Very nice."

"I mean for seeing applicants you might need a banqueting hall."

"I take your point. I'll have a word with Hoang before I go to bed. "

"How many people are you looking for?" asked Frankland.

"Depends on the quality of the candidates," I lied.

"You see two or three jobs in the U.S. advertised from time to time. Ten or twenty would really make people sit up." reflected Jones.

"You think the VC read the newspapers?"

I felt foolish immediately after asking the question.

"How do you think they get their war news?" remarked Willard. He was the cynic of the gathering. "You don't think they're all sitting over there in An Khanh looking at us through binoculars, do you? They're here, right among us, every day that Ho Chi Minh sends. He could well be one." He jerked his thumb in the direction of the smiling bartender.

Toole took up the theme. I felt it was one they discussed every night.

"Joe's right, Richard, they're all over. We had a million refugees pour in from the north after partition. It had to be the easiest infiltration in history. And once they're in they're here to stay. Unless they get stopped at a checkpoint with their pockets stuffed with grenades. Happens now and then."

"Do they shoot those caught?"

"The next day. But there are thousands who don't get caught, even after they've killed."

"They are not the killers?"

"Of course not. Most of them do their job quietly. They propagate against Americans, they collect information, some even collect taxes."

"Where?"

"Here in Saigon. It's a kind of protection racket. You pay so much, nothing happens to you. No bombs in your restaurant, no remote control devices in your flower pot."

" It sounds like Chicago."

"The machinery is the same. Only there's supposedly a noble principle involved. Very convenient. They even issue receipts."

"The Cong do?"

"Indo-China's receipt crazy. It's something they learned from the French."

"Look, I've just arrived. I'm leaving next week. You're here all the time – years at a stretch. How unsafe do you all feel here in town? It sounds worse than being in the army."

Don Jones took over. He was obviously the one with knowledge about security.

"The Army and ourselves have basically the same problem. This is a war with few fronts and many ambushes. There are snipers in Cholon and just over the river same as there are in the jungle. That's only one way to get killed."

"What are the others?"

"Well a rocket might land on you, somebody might toss a grenade in a cosy little restaurant you choose one night, or you might even be kidnapped if you walk the same way to the office every day."

"Only Americans?"

"Hell no. If you're European, they think you're a Yank anyway. But Vietnamese get killed all the time. Most of those kidnapped or assassinated are Viet officials."

"Go on, please." I wanted to hear it all.

"Then you might get blown up starting your car, or some nice fella can stick a hypodermic needle into your arm at a football match, or you could get an exploding cigarette lighter from your secretary."

"It's happened." interposed Frankland from the depths of his tumbler.

"Don't you ever get nervous?" I asked in the lull.

"Not much" grinned Jones. "Fright is as heady as booze – you develop a taste for it. I've been here six years. Once saw them find a grenade in a girl's handbag as she was coming into a USO dance. Place emptied like magic. Don't like going out to Bien Hoa air base or Tan Son Nhut, on account of the mortar fire. Makes a mess when a plane with a full tank gets hit."

Willard was more cynical.

"Biggest risk you run is being knocked flat by a bloody Lambretta or getting shot by the police for being out after curfew. If you really want to live dangerously, go for a drive in the country – our B 52's will get you."

"And you can catch cholera down by the canal," grinned Toole.

We carried on in this vein for another hour or so, quietly and competently served by our barman of undetermined allegiance. The three Americans were old Vietnam hands and it amused them to give me a few words of friendly and sagacious advice. It was a role they were not unused to playing and it passed away an evening. Mark Frankland, like most successful journalists, was a better listener than talker. In the ten days I spent in Vietnam I had the good fortune to be in one kind of social gathering or another each evening and observed that no one talked about anything other than the war for more than 10 minutes at a time. The Vietnamese discussed it less than the Americans, for it had been a topic for them since at least 1946, but the outcome of the current hostilities was of such import to their lives that all normal activities, though carried on every day, were almost exclusively subordinated to and coloured by the latest political developments.

We broke up around eleven, as the three Americans had to beat the curfew. Frankland was staying in the Caravelle. He and Jones said they would see me sometime the following evening in the bar; they were curious to see how my campaign would proceed. Toole said he would give me a call and invite me to the Cercle Sportif later in the week. I descended to the ground floor to have a few words with Hoang, but he was off duty. Back at 6.30, said his deputy. Going up to my room I realised that I had not heard any thuds for half an hour. I concluded that the VC slept too, at least some nights.

*   *   *   *   *

I got up at six and peeped out at the square. Immediately below me two street vendors were setting up their stalls; one of them was selling soap, the other vegetables. In the open-fronted Continental Palace restaurant across, a waiter was rearranging metal chairs while another was having his shoes shined by a thin, brown-faced youngster. It looked like the best hour of the day.

I took a shower and was about to shave when the phone rang. It was a Miss Ngo Thanh Nguyet who had seen the advertisement and wished to present herself for interview. In rather difficult circumstances I wrote down her name and fixed an appointment for 2 pm. At twenty past six a Miss Thuy Nguyen-Thi rang me up with a similar request. I put her down for 2.20. Before anyone else had time to ring I got hold of Hoang who had just come on duty and asked him to stop all calls till 1.30. I explained that I would have to spend the morning contacting the authorities. He was very helpful, offering to make a list of people ringing him about the job.

In this manner I was able to shave, get dressed and have breakfast. It was obviously advisable to have a chat with Hoang about the interviewing facilities. He took me into a little office behind reception to discuss this. I showed him the application forms and he suggested that I leave a pile with him in Reception, so that he could ask people to fill them in while they waited. Those who did not bring photographs, he would send out to get some. He would dispatch candidates to my room as he saw the previous one descend. I said I would interview from 2-6.30. Hoang confirmed that he would be on duty the whole time. Would it be too much trouble?, I asked. I was willing to pay for an extra girl to do the work, but Hoang would not hear of it. It was something he preferred to handle himself, he said. Did he think there would be a lot of applicants? Definitely, he replied.

Back in my room I emptied my briefcase of unnecessary objects and made sure I had what I needed for the morning – passport, letter of introduction to the U.S. Consulate, addresses and street plan, half a dozen application forms, typed statement of intent for the Ministry of Security and my own qualifications, CV and job description in Tokyo in case they should wish to check on these.

Before leaving the hotel I deposited the bulk of my cash and travellers' cheques with the cashier, who put them in the safe and gave me a receipt (presumably a normal one). If persons were going to be streaming in and out of my room for the next week, I would have at least one problem off my mind.

I left the Caravelle at 8 sharp and walked up Tu Do Boulevard towards the Cathedral. The sun was already warm on my right shoulder but there was still a freshness in the morning air and a spring in the step of the three *ao-dai*-clad beauties at the corner of Norodom. Where they were going at that time of the morning I could not imagine, unless it was home.

I turned left into Norodom, or Thong Nhut as it was otherwise called, and looked for No. 4, where the Consular Section of the U.S. Embassy had its offices. I was wearing one of my white, short-sleeved shirts, carried only my briefcase and seeing the girls had lent a certain jauntiness to my stride. This disappeared very suddenly indeed as I came to the Consulate. This lay back about twenty yards from the road and had to be approached along a short drive, at the end of which stood two Vietnamese sentries armed with sub-machine-guns. As I set foot on the drive, one of the sentries pointed his gun at me and took sight along the barrel. I remembered Don Jones's words of the previous evening: "When approaching a public building, don't make any sudden movement or the sentries will cut you in half." Too scared to stop, I walked forward with zombie-like step, holding my brief-case well away from my body. Things got worse before they got better, for the soldier kept his weapon trained on me as I walked up to him and past him – at one stage I could see right down the barrel (and believe me, you look down it). Don said that one gets accustomed to this situation, as every public office in Saigon had a sentry with a finger on the trigger (that was the only way to deter bombers), but in a week in the capital I personally did not get used to it. The sentries always looked real mean (they probably just furrowed their brow in concentration) and stories I had heard of innocent Koreans and Thais being riddled with bullets because they did not understand the command "Stop where you are" in English or Vietnamese did nothing for my self-assurance.

Ralph Essling also liked to take advantage of the unwilted, early hours; he had already been at his desk for some time. Once I had been let into the building without getting shot, only a rapid check on the harmless contents of my brief case stood between me and his office. He asked me to sit down, heard my story and looked at my papers. He reflected for some time before commenting:

"Some job you've got here."

"Do you foresee any problems?"

"How will you select?"

"I want good teachers. I'll look at qualifications and personality. I'm used to doing that. Don't know about the politics."

"They'll all tell you the same story: One hundred per cent pro-American."

"Will it be difficult to get visas?"

"Not particularly. The first hurdle is the Immigration and Naturalization Service in New York. The Army will say their piece over there. No need for low profile as here."

"And then?"

"INS will notify this Consulate that so many have been approved. We issue entry visas."

"And exit visas?"

"You'll have to go and see the Ministry of Security. I'll give you the name of the man to talk to. We pressure them to issue a passport to anybody New York has okayed. We also send the applicant to the Director General of the National Police with a letter of introduction. That way the candidates don't have to post a bond."

"How long might all this take?"

"Two months, maybe longer."

"Will they all go through?"

"Should do, but some people will get passports faster than others."

"How?"

Essling shrugged, French Indo-China style.

"Influence?"

"Uncles, lovers, money – you know."

Everything I had heard seemed too good to be true.

"I can start interviewing then?"

"Good luck. How many people are you after?"

"One hundred and fifty."

"Holy Mary Mother of God. Get out of here. You never even saw me." He was kidding – at least half of him was.

"Go and see this guy. See what he says." He wrote the details on Embassy letter-heading:

Mr Pham-Van-Hiep
Assistant for Planning
Department of Security
No. 2, Nguyen-Han, Saigon.

I thanked him and got out of his office before he found reasons why I should not go ahead. In fact he proved very helpful both then and later. The sentry had a bead on the small of my back as I trudged stolidly down the drive, holding my briefcase well away from my legs, like so much wet washing.

Pham Van Hiep, though harder to get at, was equally helpful and agreeable. I had to sit more than an hour in a waiting room, also under a gun, with half a dozen other petitioners, all of them orientals. Pham said no passports could be issued until his Department heard from the Embassy, but foresaw no difficulties once approval had been obtained. I had the feeling that at this stage of the war, with nearly half a million U.S. combat troops in the country and America already several billion dollars in the hole, South Vietnamese officials did more or less as they were told. Pham was less optimistic about the time-table. He felt September or October was the earliest anyone would get out, unless of course they already had a passport. What kind of people had passports? Government officials of course; many businessmen – especially those dealing in goods contributing to the war effort; also a goodly number of persons with enterprise and foresight who had had the initiative to obtain one in one manner or another. Could people pull strings? Frankly, yes, they could, with certain pre-requisites. It was a most un-Japanese conversation.

Back on the streets I walked along Cong Ly and turned into tree-lined Le Loi Boulevard. Here I entered a bookshop where I bought a large scale map of Vietnam, North and South, a box of coloured pins and two felt nib pens – one red and one green. At eleven o'clock I returned to the Caravelle, where Hoang seemed glad to see me. There had been thirty-four phone calls and he had asked everyone to come after one-thirty. Six candidates, four women and two men were already sitting in the foyer. I decided I would start interviewing them before lunch in order to gain time, but first I needed another talk with Hoang.

We retired to his cubby hole and I spread out my big map of Vietnam. South Vietnam was divided into 44 provinces, the North into 23. These divisions were too numerous for my mind to cope with. I asked Hoang to divide each half of the country into 5 rough regions, lending particular consideration to well-known regional accents. He was as bright as a button and, using my felt-nib pens, soon had split up the North into 5 red-lined areas and the South into 5 green ones. He also wrote in the name of each region.

Next I asked him where he was born. He had always lived in Saigon. Did he have any colleagues from Central and North Vietnam? Yes he did; one of the waiters was from Hanoi and the beautiful Tran Thi Mai herself was from Da Nang – a city in Central Vietnam. Did they speak dialects very different from his own? Yes, very much so.

Hoang asked the waiter and Tran to join us and we put together a sentence in Vietnamese which would be pronounced quite a different way in the north, south and centre. It was a bit like asking a Scot, a Yorkshireman and a Cockney to give their rendering of "It's a rainy day today lady, but it'll be a bright night tonight."

I forget the exact phrase they settled on, but it was something like "Bullfrogs croak louder in the rainy season than in the dry." At any rate the difference in pronunciation was loud and clear. Hoang, Tran and the waiter each repeated the sentence several times while I wrote down the 3 phonetic versions. After some practice in my room, I felt confident that I could distinguish clearly between Northern, Southern and Central Vietnamese. It was important for my purpose that my candidates had the accent of the region they said they came from. Many of them (the refugees) would be without original birth certificates. What I really needed was a Vietnamese to assist me in my interviews – for instance a language professor – but I could not take the risk. He would undoubtedly have influenced my choice. Suppose he was VC?

I began interviewing at 11.30 and spent nearly 20 minutes with each candidate. They had already filled in their application forms and Hoang sent them up one by one in the order they had appeared. After each interview I had two or three minutes to scribble my impressions on the back of the form while one person descended and another came up. In each case I opened the conversation by asking them, in English, where they were born. They indicated their place of birth on my map which was now on the hotel room wall. I marked the locality by sticking in a pin. I then asked them if they wished to be interviewed in English or French. Most of them chose French and I would switch to this language after I had satisfied myself that their English was good enough for the job.

The people I saw in this first session were typical of the many that were to follow. They were, in the main, well-educated, cultured men and women who had an excellent command of French, both spoken and written. Unlike many Japanese I had interviewed who tended to be impersonal, factual and modest, the Vietnamese were tense, persuasive and emotional. If you say no to a Japanese he takes no for an answer. Say no to a Chinese and he will smile wisely and come at you again. A Vietnamese will argue with Gallic verve. Of course the people I saw wanted desperately to land the job and under the circumstances it was hardly surprising that they persevered to the limit. The women particularly were difficult to get out of the room, even when I had indicated that their chances were good. Most of their school and college records were impeccable. All had brought their diplomas, testimonials and photographs. Only one of the first six failed my region test. He claimed to be from the North but said the bit about the bullfrogs in strong Saigon. Neither could he change it when I pointed this out. It was like a West Countryman claiming to be a Geordie in a Zummerzet burr. I took his pin out when he had gone. By lunchtime I had two South, two North and one Central.

I decided to have a quick lunch in the Continental Palace, just across the Square. There were thirty people in the Caravelle foyer and beads of sweat on Hoang's brow. After a quick pow-wow we decided that I would have to see them three at a time in order to get through the numbers. I don't recall what I had for lunch at the Palace, but I remember staring at the huge lizards on the walls of the restaurant. They were about a foot long and for a while I thought they were ornaments, until one moved. Even then you can miss them if you blink, as they move about three inches only, and like lightning.

In the afternoon I saw twelve people per hour, that is, three every 15 minutes. Their forms were completed and I was able to economize on time by saying my piece only once. By quarter past six I had forty pins on my map, having removed about fourteen, belonging to candidates who failed to fulfil our requirements. I was doing well in the North and the South; the Central region was thin, probably because there were fewer refugees in Saigon from that area. Two thirds of the applicants were women, half of whom showed up in *ao dai*. The men wore neat blue or grey suits or appeared in clean well-ironed shirts. Most of them were in their thirties or forties and showed me their military records or exemptions on grounds of insanity or something likewise. The women were much younger on the average, usually in their middle twenties – some of them outrageously attractive. They flirted unashamedly when alone, somewhat less when seen in threes. I had to keep reminding myself that it would be unfair to hold physical attractiveness against any applicant.

At 6.30 I tripped down to the lobby and took the names of the dozen or so candidates still hanging hopefully around, fixing them up with the first interview the following morning. Hoang went off duty looking pretty beat – he told me later that people had been pumping him continuously throughout the day while waiting their turn in the foyer. The phone had rung non stop and callers were simply told to show up with two pictures and fill in a form.

I, too, was getting a trifle light-headed at this stage, so we called it a day and I had ten minutes under the shower. I put on my sixth linen shirt and was just ready for Pip Powell who knocked on my door at 7 sharp. He was a short, stocky, smiling young man of thirty with pleasant, open features and completely unfailing good humour. Paul Rasmussen was outside with the Land Rover. They would give me a swing through Cho Lon before dinner.

*   *   *   *   *

Paul Rasmussen, the NCR manager in Saigon, was a handsome Dane in his early forties with the blond hair, blue eyes and easy-going English that one expects from Scandinavians. He invited me to sit next to him at the front and Pip squatted in the back of the Land Rover. He had seen the view before.

"Twilight's a good time to go round Cho Lon" said Paul. "The place is just coming to life at this hour." We proceeded south-west along the broad Tran Hung Dao Boulevard. As we approached the Cho Lon district the streets became narrow and haphazard, the buildings dwindled in size and soon we were passing along an endless line of stalls, small, open-fronted shops, tin lizzy factories and lean-to dwelling houses. Suddenly it was no longer Saigon – or not the one I knew.

Cho Lon, – the name means Big Market – is predominantly a Chinese district. The Vietnamese had settled the Saigon area in the 1670s, spreading down the coast from the north. The region remained extremely strife-ridden for more than one hundred years. In 1773 a large colony of Chinese traders who had made their base in Bien Hoa were routed by warriors and fled to Cho Lon where after 1789 they were able to live in relative peace alongside their Vietnamese neighbours. Cho Lon is in effect Saigon's Chinatown, but after partition the massive influx of people from the countryside led to the district absorbing many of the newcomers, including thousands of Cambodians and Laotians. This human beehive had achieved, by 1967, a population density of more than 12,000 persons per square mile.

By the time we had entered Dong Khanh, Cho Lon's main shopping street, our speed was down to two or three miles an hour. The streets of the southern downtown area were usually choked with thousands of small motor bicycles, the fumes of which competed with the malodorous canals to persuade you to cut short your stay and turn back to French Saigon. But there is no turning back. You are jammed tight by egg-beaters on all sides, so you follow the current, slow as it is, with ample time to take in the sights as you go along.

By now the area had degenerated into an undisguised, unvarnished shantytown; wooden, sheet metal or cardboard shacks hugged the edge of murky, sewage-contaminated waterways where women washed clothes and youngsters splashed and swam. The thronged thoroughfares and alleys of Cho Lon brimmed over with a colourful miscellany of human activity – pavement dentists and barbers drilled and clipped away amidst crowds of vendors of parrots, soap, combs, rope, ointments, dried beef, red and green peppers, kites, candles, fruit, vegetables, duck eggs and everything else imaginable. Old couples squatted on straw mats in front of the stalls and chewed on chicken tidbits. Others barbecued shrimps and crabs on small charcoal stoves. Children scrambled after tennis balls, candy floss and coloured comics and made faces at the polite, serious-countenanced policemen, searching people at the checkpoints.

In mid-1967 street killings were on the increase. Though no one knew it at the time, this was the period leading up to the Tet offensive and the Viet Cong were in the process of destabilizing the situation in Saigon itself by spreading terror at every turn. Only two weeks earlier they had introduced a new way of dispatching the enemy: a girl facing backwards on a motorcycle pillion in Cho Lon had suddenly produced an automatic rifle from under her skirt and shot an American soldier in the vehicle following. Her boy friend then opened up the throttle and zoomed away to safety. This type of killing had repeated itself three times in the following fortnight. There was even speculation that the same girl was involved in each case.

As we crawled along Dong Khanh, first one bike then another with rear-facing girl passengers slipped past us and then led our vehicle. Pip whispered to Paul, who kept his eyes glued on the seductive skirts. For all their breeziness, the two NCR men were alert and on guard during the whole ride, as it was from the Cho Lon district that the VC launched most of their attacks. I wondered how the motor bikes in front of us would be able to accelerate away, as the traffic was quite solid ahead. Paul gunned his engine constantly, warning any would-be sharpshooters that he was ready to smash the vehicle into them should a weapon appear. But the dark eyes of the girls showed no malice as they stared back at us impassively, almost fatalistically, certainly reading our thoughts with greater facility than we read theirs.

For an hour and a half we crept along in sluggish procession, criss-crossing the notorious 5th District, passing the Cong Hoa Stadium, the Phen Tho Race Track, the Buddhist Institute, HEDSPPACT, (Headquarters, Support Activity, Saigon) and other Cho Lon landmarks which Paul and Pip wished to include in the tour. Rasmussen's stubby fingers twitched on the steering wheel like an expressive bunch of bananas while Pip seemed to be gripping a huge gun between his feet. Wondering why they had brought me to Cho Lon at all, I guessed that it was part of the act of hardened residents to do a tour of the danger spots with incoming males. This western show of bravado was both commendable and foolhardy, for the security situation was without parallel. Nobody knew where or indeed who the enemy was. Saigon, and Cho Lon in particular, were surrounded by rural areas – largely rice fields and swamps – which afforded effective cover for the Viet Cong guerrillas. From these sanctuaries, they could slip into Cho Lon in a matter of minutes, carry out their sabotage or murderous assignment and then simply blend into the faceless throngs of the 5th District. Helicopters, marines and the South Vietnamese army patrolled the outskirts and large parts of the Delta, but the ring of security ended where the green fields began and snipers brought down many choppers even while they flew over the city. In most areas you walked about at risk, with your back unprotected. Westerners could trust only each other. Vietnamese could not even do that. It is an old aphorism that taxi drivers everywhere are conservatives. In Saigon one could not be so sure, even less with the pedicab boys.

We hit the Rainbow Bar around nine and drank beer after beer as we talked about Chris McDonald, NCR business in Tokyo and Saigon and my recruiting experiences of the day. Rainbow had no great selection of food since its last bombing, so we ate hamburgers along with all the GIs, politely declining invitations from interested girls and trying to catch what each other said above the blare of the jukebox.

They took me back to the hotel around ten and I thanked them for the evening, promising to report back to them in a day or so. They kindly offered me a car and secretarial support, but I felt that both were superfluous at that juncture. I took a raincheck on the stenographer and went up to the "Jerome et Juliette" Bar on the 9th floor, where Don Jones and Mark Frankland bought me another two beers. I gave them an account of my day and they laughed their heads off for some reason. Don said he was sending me a girl the next day and without entirely comprehending what he meant by that I took my leave and went to bed. I was asleep two minutes after my head bisected the lovely, voluminous, freshly-laundered French pillow.

*   *   *   *   *

The next day I shall always remember as the Day of the Girls. During the first day of interviewing, two out of three applicants had been women, but they had rushed to the hotel half-prepared, no doubt thinking that first come first served might be one of the deciding factors. Probably a lot of would-be candidates did not see the advertisement until the evening and were unable to get ready in time.

By Wednesday, especially with the repeat appearance of the ad, the word had really got around town: there were jobs available, they were in the U.S. and the interviewer was male. The women who came on the second day were anything but ill-prepared; rather were they prepared for anything. On the Tuesday about half of them had been in Western dress. Now they were almost exclusively attired in *ao dai* of the most delicate fabrics and gorgeous hues – turquoise, beige, pale yellow, violet and so on. Many of the girls had come straight from the hairdresser and were exquisitely made-up and wore haunting perfumes of every fragrance and bouquet. Their soft fine-boned hands were pliant and creamy to the touch and dainty, pink-nailed toes peeped modestly out of crisp white sandals. The glamorous pictures of themselves which they attached to the application forms did credit to the photo studios of war-torn Saigon.

Eighty such attractive, single-minded young women, along with twenty or so hopeful men, populated the foyer of the Caravelle when I descended at eight for my morning strategical pow wow with Hoang. He pulled me into his little cubby-hole before anyone could nail me and suggested a change in the interviewing procedure. There were simply too many girls to take up to my room. He indicated that interviews could take place in the lobby (he had checked this out with the manager) and he was arranging for extra seating to be brought down. I would say my piece to a whole lobby-full at a time, thereby avoiding repetition. After that they would come to a corner of the foyer in fours and I would proceed as before. Everybody had completed forms. Some had been there since half past six.

Under these circumstances I decided that further attempts at secrecy were pointless. All Saigon knew what was going on. The only low profiling I could do was to hint at a limited requirement and get on with it as fast as possible. It was clear to me that certain people would hardly approve of the project and I was rapidly getting apprehensive about the eight windows around the foyer, all wide open to create additional ventilation. It had not escaped my notice that the three bars and restaurants of the Caravelle (which had been bombed twice) were on the 8th, 9th and 10th floors of the building. It took no wild leap of the imagination to anticipate a grenade sailing through a window and landing amidst a rather dense gathering of ostensibly pro-Western interviewees and their interrogator. I taxed Hoang with this hypothesis, but he shook his head vigorously. It would not happen, he replied.

Firstly, there would be several VC among my candidates. Secondly he knew how much money the hotel management paid the VC daily to be guaranteed against just such a contingency. He was confident on both counts. Funnily enough, after this information, so was I.

I gobbled down a nervous breakfast and started at half past eight. Hoang organized things smoothly and I found myself liking and respecting him more and more. He was one of those people who thrive on pressure (probably why he was Chief Receptionist at the Caravelle), and I resolved to offer him a good job provided I could get him out of Saigon and assuming he wasn't VC.

He kept good discipline in the lobby and trundled forward the applicants in fours, making sure that there was one man in each quartet. This stratagem kept personal remarks down to a minimum, as the girls were obliged to demonstrate a modicum of restraint in the presence of a man of their own nationality. They all interviewed straight-forwardly and efficiently as I went through their qualifications and background experience, but once it was established that they were eligible, few of them would let the interview be terminated without trying to involve me personally in their hopes, fears and well-being. It was hard to be unsympathetic – so hard in fact that I didn't always quite manage it. I listened to their oriental sob stories, reeled under the impact of their French logic and warded off invitations for later in the day with some difficulty.

The men were tense, earnest and fiercely competitive. Mentally I accepted a dozen of them, aware that some teachers had to be male. At least six I identified as manifestly Cong – or I thought I did. I stuck their pins in the map but pulled them out again later, making appropriate notes on the back of

their forms. It was harder for me to envisage any of the delectable *ao-dai*-clad
applicants as VC sympathisers, but some of them, regrettably, had to be. I
eliminated from my possibles a dozen girls who had pushed too hard, as well
as one or two who seemed to be linked to some of my male rejects. I was
getting a stiff neck trying to observe who was glancing sideways at whom.

I took only half an hour for lunch and carried on till eight o'clock. The
lobby was full the whole time; some of the younger girls were accompanied by
one or both parents. For eleven hours one hundred pairs of eyes were riveted
firmly on me. Hoang ignored his shift and stayed to the end. By evening I had
one hundred and thirty forms to add to those of the previous day. My map
bristled with ninety pins, representing probables and possibles. I had
candidates from all ten "regions" and I was light only in the centre. My forty
rejects for the day were divided into 9 not sufficiently qualified, 7 inadequate
personalities, 5 pronunciation test failures and 20 Cong suspects.

On the bright side I had identified in the two days 70 or 80 people as
being personable, well-qualified teachers or linguists who gave every
appearance of being suitable for the job. Among these, and high on my list of
probables, were 3 girls who had been sent to me with strong personal
recommendations – one from Don Jones and two from John Toole. By a
fortunate coincidence these three well-educated young ladies also happened to
be the most beautiful that I met in Saigon. Collette and Albertine, sent by
Toole, claimed to be cousins. They also had Vietnamese names, but John had
problems pronouncing them. The French names seemed more appropriate
anyway, since both girls had a strong admixture of Gallic blood. They were
small, neat and shapely, dressed in expensive Western clothes, wore pearl ear-
rings and knowing smiles. Each girl was 23 years of age and had a degree in
English language and literature.

Van Pham Khanh, sent by Don Jones, possessed a completely different
allure. Though discernibly one quarter French, she cultivated her eastern
appeal both in demeanour and dress. Tall for an oriental – she was about five
foot six – she walked with a rhythmic flowing stride, her long, turquoise *ao dai*
swirling round her white *cuan* or pantaloons. Her rich black hair, piled up high
above her sculptured forehead, counter-balanced the challenging width of her
rounded cheekbones. There were soft hollows in her cheeks; her shy smile had
the radiance of the moon.

The way she crossed the hall and took her seat was the event of the
morning. The dignified approach, the curtsey-like bow of greeting – she
dropped her chin slightly as she demurely raised her eyes to mine – the delicate
manner in which she perched on her chair with a dainty gathering of her
gossamer skirts around her long, slender legs, – all combined to produce an
aura of softness, translucence and subtlety which made her academic
qualifications an irrelevance. She could have taught Vietnamese to a Texas

mule. As it was, she had a degree in French and German and had written a thesis on Joachim du Bellay. I could see why Don Jones thought she might do.

Collette, Albertine and Van Pham Khanh were not the only people to arrive with letters of introduction. Joe Willard sent one of his secretaries, the bartender in La Terrasse a niece, the lovely Tran Thi presented a school friend, the editor of the Tan Som recommended two journalists, Pham from Immigration gave two of his clerks the day off to come to see me and Hoang himself entrusted me with his half-sister. All of these persons had baccalaureate or a higher diploma, spoke good English and were devoted to the American cause in their country. How could I go wrong?

By eight o'clock I had sensory overload, a splitting headache and a stomach which thought my throat had been cut. I made a sign to Hoang, who gratefully lowered the curtain on the day's proceedings, ushering all unseen candidates out onto the street with the promise of cool-in-the-air interviews the following morning. It remained for me to cart my now voluminous documentation up to my room, add my final impressions re diplomas, charisma and loyalties, readjust my red and green pins and head for the shower.

*   *   *   *   *

At 8.45, dressed in my pale blue linen suit, I descended once more to the lobby, where John H. Toole awaited me, accompanied by Collette and Albertine, both determined to keep me firmly in their sights for the rest of the evening. They wore silk evening gowns, twinkling necklaces and high heels. John suggested we should have a bite to eat at the Cercle Sportif. Collette took my arm and said I looked a little tired. Tran Thi, hovering around the front desk, gave me a black look. We went out onto the street where John's driver was quietly revving an old Packer. It was just a few minutes' drive to the club.

The Cercle Sportif was an affluent sports club originally exclusive to French *colons*, now the domain of ranking South Vietnamese officers, American military and civilian high-ups, European businessmen of standing, odd visitors like me and lovely creatures like Collette and Albertine. Besides the usual reception rooms, the Club boasted a fine restaurant, two bars, a piscine and half a dozen tennis courts.

We had a passable meal. I had begun to realise that although Saigon menus were just as impressive to read as those in Tokyo, Paris or Bangkok, the quality of the food served – particularly meat and vegetables – left a lot to be desired. There was, after all, a war going on. I was again reminded of England in 1940-45.

Collette and Albertine were delightful companions. Looking at their shining faces, listening to their spontaneous laughter and the vitality of their conversation, one could easily forget that they were young, vulnerable members of a desperate society in the penultimate throes of defending its last strongholds in the beleaguered capital and the surrounding guerrilla-ridden Mekong Delta. I wondered how these girls really felt, at bottom. We could hear the rumble of artillery as we dined, yet they giggled and joked as if defeat, occupation and death were far away.

My conversation with Hoang concerning the protection money paid by the Caravelle left me in little doubt as to the eventual outcome of the war. What use the American billions if such internecine complicity took place on a daily basis under the very nose of the authorities? The management of the Caravelle had to be seen as completely pro-Western. Occidental firms and the Australian Embassy occupied several floors of the building, yet their security and the lives of their employees depended, already in 1967, on a timorous financial accommodation with a terrorist arm of the enemy forces, operating with boldness from the heart of the South Vietnamese capital.

"Collette, don't you ever worry a little bit about how this whole thing will end?"

"*Et pourquoi s'ennuyer?* Did the American army ever lose a war?"

"Japan never lost a war until 1945. They thought it couldn't happen, too."

"The Americans are not the Japanese."

"You're damned right we aren't" interposed Toole. He was an accountant, not a soldier. "The Japs would handle the VC a lot better in the jungle than our boys do."

"There are no jungles in Japan", I reminded him.

"We'll win from the air," said Albertine. She had picked her side.

After a while it became clear that both girls thought the war was already going against the Americans and the Tet offensive, eight months later, would confirm this. But a large number of girls in Saigon had put all their eggs quite demonstrably in the American-South Vietnamese basket. The bar girls were a case apart, for they were simply plying their trade. The pillion riders, the Chinese women of Cho Lon, innumerable girls in the outlying suburbs formed another enigmatic class whose ultimate loyalty would be revealed only when North Vietnamese troops marched into Saigon. Yet as the fortunes of war ebbed and flowed, as the position of the Southern coalition appeared less and less tenable each month, hundreds of thousands of Collettes, Tran This and Albertines affirmed their belief every day in the validity of what the Americans were fighting for. While military men and politicians in South Vietnam and the U.S. fretted, hesitated and faltered, these young women, on the surface at least, lived their adolescent lives to the full, talked about exams and marriage and holidays like anyone else with a rosy future, demonstrated a vitality and a life force that I have seldom witnessed in more robust societies and put aside all thoughts of failure, defeat, humiliation and eventual ruin.

One hears a lot about the fatalism of the East and I had sensed this occasionally in my dealings with the Japanese. Perhaps the women of Vietnam, used to centuries of foreign domination and seemingly incessant warfare on their doorstep, felt that all they could do was just get on with their lives. Mortars to the left of them, rockets to the right of them, a fancy dress ball was still a fancy dress ball.

"What are you doing tomorrow, Collette?" I was curious.

"Coming to see you again," she giggled.

"Be serious now. You're a teacher, aren't you?"

"Out of work for a while. School got hit by a rocket. Nobody hurt – it was at night. Blast the VC!

"And you, Albertine?"

"Translate for USAID. I'm busy till around four".

"Beauty sleep for me in the morning," chimed in Collette. "Tennis and swimming in the afternoon. I gotta look good when I go to the U.S."

"Don't count your chickens before they are hatched," said Toole.

Collette grinned. "We say 'don't sell the bearskin until you've shot the bear'. *Ma foi, Albertine et moi*, we must be in with a chance. We got beauty and brains and we both come from Hue. Mr Lewis is short of people from the central provinces, aren't you, Mr Lewis?"

"How the heck did you know that?"

"Hoang told me. He's cute, that Hoang."

"You think Collette and I can get to the States?" asked Albertine.

"I don't know yet. Are you keen?"

"You can say that again." Albertine and Collette had picked up a few Americanisms.

"Do you want to get out of Vietnam?" Albertine shrugged.

"It would be a change. But it's OK here too. Don't you like Saigon?"

"I do, actually."

"You Englishmen are always saying 'actually'. Well, I'd like to leave here for a bit. A job abroad is exciting, you know. As it would be for English girls. We want to travel like everybody else."

"I wanna see the Grand Canyon", said Collette.

"Are you willing to leave poor old John here, all on his own?" After all the serious questioning of the day, I felt like being facetious.

"Oh, he'll come after us. He'll find an audition to do in Dallas."

"An audit", corrected Toole.

"I wanna eat some proper steaks," chirped Albertine. "T-bone, charcoal, off the rib – real steers too, not Cho Lon dogs – deep in the heart of Texas. Attaboy!" She was bubbling over.

"We got some nice beaches up in Nha Trang", said Collette, somewhat irrelevantly. "You oughta stick around a while – you'd probably have a good time."

"Come and swim here in the Club on Saturday", said Toole. "You wanna hit some tennis in the morning?"

"You bet", I replied, slipping into their talk.

"Collette and I'll swim and get brown. We can wear bikinis in here, you know," added Albertine.

"I didn't know Oriental girls wanted to get brown. Japanese girls like to stay pale and interesting."

"Our grandfather was French," said Collette. "We gotta get the French part brown."

After a while the girls had ice creams and Toole talked to me about the war for a bit. He probably wouldn't have been able to sleep if he had not engaged a little in his favourite therapy. The girls evinced no interest at all in the subject and even began chattering away in Vietnamese as John droned on. Around 11.30 we had a last drink and Toole deposited me at the Caravelle a quarter before midnight.

"Don't forget Saturday," shouted Collette as I walked through the doorway.

I took my key from Hoang's deputy and went up to my room. There was a small scented envelope under my door. I turned on the bedside lamp and opened it. It contained a single card which read:

I'm having a party at 108, Phan Thanh Gian, commencing at 8. p.m. Thursday, June 22nd 1967. Wish you will come so it will be really enjoyable. Informal.

Van Pham Khanh

I did not need to check her green form or refresh my memory by looking at the photograph. The reality was recent enough. I undressed quickly, got into bed and put the light out. There was an orange glow over Cho Lon and intermittent gunfire punctuated the more continuous hum of aircraft. It must have been two before I fell asleep.

*   *   *   *   *

I awoke at seven and tried to phone Strumpen-Darrie in New York. I was 12 hours ahead of Eastern Standard time, which meant I had a chance of catching him at 7 in the evening either at the office or at home. But the phone lines were blocked. It was not an unusual situation, as apparently the military often occupied them all. Hoang said six in the evening was better, but by then it would be 6 in the morning in New York. In the end I sent a telegram:

ONE HUNDRED AND SEVENTY CANDIDATES INTER-
VIEWED BY WEDNESDAY NIGHT STOP HALF SUITABLE STOP
SEVENTY PER CENT WOMEN STOP VISAS PROBABLY TAKE 2
MONTHS STOP CANNOT PHONE YOU STOP IMPERATIVE YOU
PHONE ME SOONEST CARAVELLE SAIGON 25712 REGARDS
LEWIS.

As I felt I needed to check back with Essling and Pham Van Hiep, I
arranged to interview from 8.30 – 11.30 and 3 – 6. Don Jones phoned at 8 to
say he was taking me to Van Pham Khanh's party and would pick me up shortly
before 8 p.m. Pip Powell called to invite me to lunch at one. I breakfasted on
grapefruit, mango and papaya, which seemed like a good idea and took a hot
coffee with me to my place in the foyer, as I was running a little late. The place
was packed as usual, a sea of nervous, smiling faces, some already beaded with
perspiration. It was a humid morning and the hot coffee added to my own
discomfort. As I surveyed the morning assembly – sixty or seventy of them in
six disciplined rows, each one clutching forms, diplomas and testimonials under
his or her arm – my feeling was one of sympathy and understanding. They were
fellow linguists, like me, hoping to put to good use the degrees and certificates
they had worked so long to obtain. They had devoted their young lives to
language and literature, not business or politics. Caught up in the maelstrom of
Indo-Chinese intrigue, they still hoped innocently that their hard-earned
qualifications would bring them the respectable pursuit they deserved.

There were more men that morning, many of them already working with
the U.S. forces or auxiliary organisations. Some had cajoled their American
colleagues into letting them apply even if they were not easily replaceable. One
after the other put down before me glowing references, the ink still fresh,
which their superiors had written for them. I wished I could have said "yes" to
them all and whisked them away from the impending debacle.

The morning passed quickly and at half past eleven I hurried along Tu Do
to the U.S. Consulate. It was eyeball to eyeball again with the sentry – an even
meaner-looking one this time, but at least he refrained from pulling the trigger.
Ralph Essling studied the half dozen filled-in application forms I had brought
as samples, as well as the attached diplomas and character references.

"How many you got?"

"Ninety, maybe one hundred."

"Fifty to go, then?"

"Fewer than that. I need twenty or thirty from Cambodia and Laos."

"It's a lot of people. Better you put all of them in one visa petition."

"In one batch?"

"Yeah. Make a joint petition and send it to INS. They'll take longer
over it, but not so long as if you do them all separately. That way it
could take a year."

"All right. Anything else?"

"You know anybody at INS. New York? or in Washington?"

"No."

"Somebody ought to put a word in. Speed things up. Probably the army will."

"I'll mention it to Berlitz."

"Call me if you need me."

"I will, thank you."

"We'll back it up here."

"Thank you again. Goodbye."

At Pham's office, I was permitted instant entry. He asked how I had got on with his two candidates. I replied they were fine. He said they were good boys. And he could get them passports, just like that. How was I getting on in general? I told him the hotel was being very helpful and that I had really liked most of the people who I had seen. He asked me to phone him before I left and gave me his home number. Also if I would send him a list of probables, he would vet it for VC connections. I wondered about that. Suppose he was VC... Toole had told me I could trust nobody.

Pip was waiting for me in front of the hotel, prancing around like a colt in a pasture. He thumped me gleefully on the back, grabbed my arm and dragged me into a little Vietnamese restaurant he knew just round the corner. It was cool and dimly-lit. I could just see fish swimming round in greenish tanks. Pip picked out a couple for us to eat and the waiter carried them off for prompt execution.

"How goes the selection process?"

"Most of them seem fine."

"They are all honest men, but my cloak is not to be found."

"Is that an Eastern proverb?"

"Spanish, old boy."

"How's Paul?"

"Working his bloody head off. Smoking like a chimney. Eating like a pig. Dane, you know."

"Business good?"

"Not bad. Selling stuff to the Yanks, of course."

"War good for business?"

"Christ, without the Army here, this place would be a doldrums. Might be a nice doldrums, though."

"You like Saigon, Pip?"

"Sure. Hate cold weather. I'm on the Eastern circuit, you know. And you've seen the girls."

"I have."

"Me, I'm twenty-eight, unmarried, unattached – all that jazz. Pity we'll all have to leave."

"When, do you think?"

"Oh, not yet. A couple of years, maybe five."

"They can't be stopped?"

"No. Oh hell, we'll give it a bash."

For me the fish was inedible. Pip ate his all right. He said it was fresh enough; it was just the stuff they cooked it in. He was used to it. They brought me eggs on toast and that was fine. Pip asked if I needed a secretary.

"In fact, one at six this evening would be very useful. I want to get off a letter to New York. An hour will do."

"I'll send Jill round. Her shorthand's good. Yank. Do you have a typewriter? "

"No, sorry."

"She'll bring a portable. Fixed up for this evening?"

"Kind of. Fellow called Don Jones taking me to a party."

"I know Don. He's a nice chap. What are you doing at week-end?"

"Playing tennis with John Toole at the Cercle Sportif Saturday morning."

"I know John, too. An accountant. I might drop by and watch – maybe play. Eleven o'clock OK?"

"I think so. I'll ask John and phone you."

Back at the hotel, I spent forty minutes drafting a letter to Berlitz, then resumed interviewing at three. One unpleasant forty-year-old grilled me more than I grilled him. I put him down as genuine – no VC would have shown his aggression like that. I collected a few more girls from the Central provinces and a couple of sharp schoolteachers born in Hanoi. By six in the evening, I was reasonably satisfied with my haul.

Jill came round with an old Olivetti. She was very professional, though she sipped gin tonic while she typed. I got the following message off to Strumpen-Darrie:

June 27, 1967

Berlitz Schools of America
866 Third Avenue
New York 10022, New York

Dear Mr. Strumpen-Darrie and Raphael,

Here is the gist of the situation as I would have explained it by phone, had we been able to telephone each other.

I arrived here Monday, placing advertisements in the newspapers and opening up other sources of teachers. I was able to interview Tuesday, in the hotel lobby. On that day I saw about 40 candidates more than half of whom were qualified and suitable for our purposes. I interviewed again on Wednesday, all day, and the number of people interviewed rose to 100. Thursday has brought me another 50 so far and by Friday evening I will have seen 300. Since

100 at least and probably 120-140 of these are acceptable, I am terminating the interviews on Friday night.

I have interviewed each applicant thoroughly and have made out an application form in each case. The candidates have given full details of their education, references, military status and other personal particulars. Photographs are attached to each application form and in many cases copies of their diplomas. In all cases I have said that we shall require to see their diplomas eventually. On the back of each application form I have made my own comments, which will give a good indication as to whether or not I think the applicant should be accepted. We have applicants from all parts of Vietnam. Most of them are in the age group 22-32, but there is a sprinkling of older men, who are often free from military problems.

I have also visited the U.S. Consulate and the Vietnamese Ministry of Security to check on the procedures when bringing these candidates to the United States. If you are able to take measures which will facilitate these matters, all the better.

The American Embassy here does not think it will be a good idea to bring out people on tourist visas and in any case this would slow up the process, since Vietnamese do not get a visa quickly unless they have good reason for traveling abroad, tourism not being one of these.

The recommended procedure is as follows:

A.   I send you the application forms of the 150 best applicants.

B.   You apply for a temporary working petition for the whole batch of applicants, or alternatively you have to make and have petitions for each.

C.   It is possible that you can make one petition for the whole batch of applicants, or alternatively you have to make separate petitions for each one.

D.   INS will in due course notify the U.S. Consulate in Saigon.

E.   The U.S. Consulate will issue a letter to the Vietnamese Ministry of Security to help these people secure passports and exit visas.

F.   Berlitz should send a note to Ralph Essling, U.S. Consulate, Norodom, Saigon, saying that the petition has been filed for so many names and sending application numbers of the petitions.

G.   All this can take two months or much more.

If this procedure has to be followed there are obviously two things which have to be done.

1)   Our New York office would have to speed things up as much as possible with INS in New York.

2)   Some pull is needed with the Ministry of Security here in Saigon despite upgrading of passports and exit visas. If anyone in Washington is able to intervene, then this would be the answer.

As things are now, it is likely that some of the applicants, who seem to have influence in political and civil service circles, would get their visas quickly and arrive in the United States in late July. Then I think you would have a steady trickle, with the more unfortunate cases arriving perhaps at the end of the year. While this may help, it appears unlikely that it would meet your requirements and the best solution seems to be to try to get the whole batch approved at once. It is not unknown to give a bonus here to people who are able to expedite things promptly.

I am sending my dossier of 200 forms to New York. I am leaving copies with Mr. P. I. Powell of NCR (National Cash Register), Saigon, telephone No. 24471. He is a very trustworthy and responsible person and will keep things confidential. If you send someone later, he will be able to contact all applicants, since their addresses are on the application forms. I think another recruiter ought to be Vietnamese, as I could not judge their language. By the way, the majority of the applicants were women.

As regards Cambodia and Laos, it seems that the only improvements we can hope for are speedier exit visas. Obviously the best source of Vietnamese teachers is here in Saigon. I think most of the applicants, although young, were well educated, enthusiastic and potentially competent. I have my doubts about Cambodia, where it may be politically incorrect to attempt to recruit Vietnamese teachers for the United States. Laos may be better in this respect. My reports will follow in due course.

Further people with whom I have established contact in Saigon and who will be helpful to our organization are:

Mr. Don Jones, JUSPAO, Saigon, Phone: 92026
Mr. Joseph Willard, USAID, Saigon, Phone: 93083
Mr. Hugh Sponsel, USAID, Saigon, Phone: 93083
Mr. Ralph Essling of the Embassy was also very cooperative and sympathetic.

That is about all I can do for now. Best of luck.

Sincerely,

Richard D. Lewis

Jill finished typing the letter and gave it to me to sign. She offered to get it off for me using either NCR or U.S. Army facilities, I forget which. I gave her thirty dollars whereupon she drained her second glass and took her leave. It was nearly eight. Tran Thi Hoa had arranged my laundry, bless her, and I had 4 clean shirts, crisp as new bank notes. It was still steamy outside so I decided against the suit. A quick shower refreshed me and when Don buzzed from below I grabbed my last Chivas Regal and tripped down four flights feeling as frivolous as an April morning.

*   *   *   *   *

Don pumped my hand with his wonted geniality. He seemed like he was in a party mood and eyed my bottle.

"For the girl?"

"I thought I'd better take something. Can't carry chocolates around in this weather."

"That will do fine."

"Is it near here?"

"Fifteen minutes. You eaten?"

"No."

"Good. She sets out a good table."

"Do you mean she can cook, too?"

Don grinned and pushed me into his battered car.

Van Pham Khanh lived on the ground floor of a grey, two-storied house in a pleasant, tree-lined avenue about ten minutes to the other side of the cathedral. The small, neatly-kept front garden contained several trees – palms, rubber, orange and lime – which provided adequate shade during the day. A narrow crazy-paved path bisected the garden and led up to the heavy, carved door. We knocked and a young girl in Chinese dress admitted us. We found ourselves in a dimly-lit hall, where we waited for a moment. Van Pham Khanh emerged from the drawing room and greeted us. She was wearing a translucent pale mauve *ao-dai* over a white *cuan* and her raven-black hair was down to her waist. A diamond flower-cluster brooch was pinned just over her heart. Diamond ear-rings and a solitary ruby on her right hand completed the jewellery. She kissed Don lightly on the cheek and turned to shake hands with me with an effulgent smile.

'It was so nice of you to come."

"It's a pleasure. It was quite a surprise." I held out the bottle, awkwardly.

"I'm sorry, that's all I could scrape up."

She laughed, sweetly."

"It is appreciated."

She took us into the lounge where the guests who had already arrived were drinking, smoking and conversing. There were two middle-aged Vietnamese couples, another Vietnamese girl about Van Pham Khanh's age, two American men and an American woman of around thirty. Van Pham Khanh introduced me to everyone; Don seemed to know most of them already.

"What would you like to drink?" asked Van Pham Khanh. "There is beer, rice wine and some French white wine of doubtful vintage."

The Vietnamese were drinking rice wine, so I decided to try it. It stood in a large, earthenware jar on a side dresser, just as one would keep punch. Van Pham Khanh served it into tumblers with a wooden ladle. Rice husks floated on the surface of the beverage. I found it pleasant-tasting and not too strong, though it bore little resemblance to Japanese rice wine (sake).

The lounge was spacious, airy and cheerful. It was my first glimpse of a Vietnamese home. At one end was a dining table, heavy with deeply carved legs. The accompanying chairs, as well as the side-board and a huge dresser were also carved and of the same dark wood, obviously of Vietnamese origin In a corner was a three-tiered altar decked with offerings of fruit, small wooden statuettes, candles and some framed photographs. The dining area had multicoloured hand-woven rugs on the floor and the walls.

The other end of the room was more western in appearance. An upholstered sofa and lounge chairs surrounded a low coffee table. Book-shelves lined the walls and a green-leather-topped desk stood under a heavy brass floor lamp. The wallpaper was pale green and yellow, with a bamboo design. Half a dozen paintings, French impressionist style, completed the decor. There was no air conditioning, but some windows were open and two large fans turned slowly above our heads, creating a gentle, welcome movement of air. Half of the dining table was covered with a red-and-gold woven tablecloth on which lay an impressive array of cold dishes and tid-bits.

Nobody was eating yet and Van Pham Khanh and the other single Vietnamese girl circulated among the guests, filling up glasses and passing round nuts on small wooden plates. Both Vietnamese men were academics from the Buddhist Van Hanh University in Saigon. The older one of the two, Sinh Vinh, was Professor of History, the younger, Tuan Dam Quang, Lecturer in French language and literature. The latter had been one of Van Pham Khanh's tutors. All three Americans, Henry, Carl and annabelle, like Don Jones, were attached to the U.S. forces in one way or another. The young Vietnamese girl, Kim Anh, was a schoolmate of Van Pham Khanh. She was another slender, long-haired beauty, darker-skinned than Van Pham Khanh and wearing a beautiful orange-hued *ao-dai* covered in white blossoms.

The conversation was spirited but muted. Professor Sinh Vinh in particular was interesting to listen to. He was holding forth on the social and sociological changes then taking place in South Vietnam. The country could never be the same again. Death and destruction in the countryside had resulted in the dislocation of large segments of the population. In some rural areas whole communities moved into safer urban centres. They were joined by others from the countryside seeking better employment opportunities. Previously the majority of the Vietnamese population had been rural. Now it was urban. Over-crowding was endemic, crime and pollution were on the increase.

Yet there would be no return to the countryside, even in peacetime. The war boom had made available a whole range of consumer and luxury goods which people now took for granted – motor cycles, radios, television sets, and so on. Furthermore, those farmers, notably from the Mekong river Delta, who were able to market their produce and livestock in the cities, now profited from high prices and were accustomed to a high standard of living.

But could the cities continue to support such overcrowding? What about agriculture? Sinh Vinh said that in 1955 85% of the people lived on and cared for the land. Now it was probably no more than 50%. The resources were there – the rice fields of Indo-China had been coveted by neighbours and invaders for a thousand years – also the country was rich in rubber, coffee, tea, hard-wood forests, sugar-cane and fishing. But the war had badly disrupted agricultural activities in many areas. Rubber and rice production had dropped markedly and in 1967 Vietnam was actually importing rice, of all things, from the United States! The cities could support large populations as long as the war boom and foreign aid continued. But shifting from a wartime to a peacetime economy would be a daunting task. The trade imbalance would have to be corrected, Vietnamese would have to invest the war-generated capital in Vietnam. Everything depended on political stability. Instability would cause a flight of capital from the country. And how good were the chances of political stability? It was almost a mocking question.

There we were, talking about the war again. The men kicked it back and forth, the Americans said their piece; Don Jones, less serious than some, moaned about the curfew. Once again I noticed how the women had the ability to ignore the war situation when they pleased, discussing animatedly their own personal problems – children's schooling, the price of cosmetics, their painting classes, the coming vacation and their husbands' salaries. They formed their own chatty little circle round the coffee table, lapsing occasionally into Vietnamese, then switching back to English for the sake of the American woman, or using bursts of French to talk about food, clothes and art. The men, apart from Sinh Vinh, drank a lot and the French white of dubious vintage was soon attacked when the jar of rice wine had been emptied.

Van Pham Khanh called everyone to the table where we took lacquer ware plates to sample the dishes. I could recognize the barbecued chicken and shrimps, which were quite delicious. Van Pham Khanh recommended that I try some fried river fish, thickly covered in a strong-smelling sauce. This, she explained, was *nuoc mam* – a sauce made from fermented fish, rich in nitrates, calcium and iodine. The Vietnamese people put this on all kinds of food, just as other Asians use soya sauce. I think if I had stayed in Vietnam a few more months I would have got used to it. Van Pham Khanh next put on my plate delicious strips of pork, sweet, spicy and covered with a lacquer-like coating. There was also *sibi*, a spinachy salad that I did not go wild about. Van Pham Khanh explained this was a Montagnard dish – the Montagnards are semi-wild people who live in Vietnam's central Highlands. She said her maternal grandmother was originally from that area. She was familiar with many of their dishes, also the beautiful rugs and blankets about the house had been woven in the Highlands.

"So you are one quarter Montagnard?"

"Yes. And one quarter French. My mother's father was a French settler named Ferrier. He married the Montagnard and brought her to Saigon."

"And on your father's side?"

"Pure Vietnamese."

Van Pham Khanh did not discuss her interview with me or her prospects of going to the United States. Tuan Dam Quang, however, put in a few quiet words for her later in the evening. He said she had been an excellent student, with a deep love of literature. She had obtained a good degree and in spite of her inordinate beauty had always been diligent and unassuming. He hoped that she would obtain employment in the United States. The possibility of travel, and to a country with such splendid opportunities, was exactly what a young woman of her age and education needed.

Later, I was able to talk to her alone. We sat at her desk, under her books and I asked her what she thought of Sinh Vinh's rather gloomy prognostications.

"He is a very learned man. We must believe what he says."

"Do you think Vietnam is in a hopeless position?

"Yes. We are a strong people, but we are trapped in a struggle bigger than ourselves – bigger than the whole of South-east Asia. *Nous sommes des pions.*"

"Pawns."

"Yes, pawns in a game played by two opponents who do not understand our country at all."

"The Americans and the Russians?"

"Yes. At least the French were here a hundred years. They were beginning to know us."

"And the Chinese?"

"They were here for 1000 years. Chinese influence dominates traditional Vietnamese culture. But they are our enemies, too."

"You are not of Chinese stock?"

"The Vietnamese became a separate ethnic entity in the Red River Delta, around Hanoi, in the years between 200 BC and 200 AD. We were a fusion of Austronesian and Mongoloid races as well as some Chinese refugee scholars."

"It's a wonder China never absorbed you."

"First they made us the most advanced people in the Indo-China peninsula. Then they spent 900 years trying to Sinicize us. We accepted their culture, some of their language and Confucianism. But we often rebelled. About 1430 we threw them out for good."

"You are very resilient."

"We always have been. In this peninsula we dominate the Laotians and the Cambodians. The problem for South Vietnam is that many Vietnamese see the presence of the Americans as a continuation of foreign rule. Because they are here. It makes it easy for the North to talk about the struggle to get rid of the foreign invader. First the Chinese, then the French, now the United States."

"But the Americans aren't trying to colonize you."

"I know. But many people don"t. They do not know about the Domino Theory, either."

"The war's a shame."

"In Saigon people live in relative calm. But in the countryside every night brings terror. Sometimes as many as 50 people can die before the dawn."

"You must often despair, even here."

"All the years of my childhood, of my education have been war-torn. I know nothing else. You just go on planning. Our nerves are, how do you say, cauterized."

"All your people seem to love learning."

"It is very true. The Confucian tradition is of respect for learning. The French, too, went on educating us."

"Dam Quang said you love poetry. Especially Joachim du Bellay."

She smiled.

"Do you like him in England?"

"He is very personal and virile. I think he appeals to Englishmen more than do many French poets. You can follow his melancholy and despair. He never tries to be clever."

"He can be ironical."

"That's true and he was good at it. But he was really very gentle."

"*Vous le connaissez bien.*"

"I had to wade through French literature too."

"You don't like other French poets?"

"I've had to read them all. Lamartine, de Vigny, de Musset, Hugo. I don't believe they could use language like Keats and Shelley could. And there's Browning and a man called Shakespeare. But I am English and it's hard to compare poetry in different languages.

"Your Keats is *fantastique*. But such rich language is sometimes difficult for me to understand. *Les nuances.*"

*   *   *   *   *

After eleven o'clock some of the guests took their leave. Midnight was curfew hour and it was strictly enforced. Nobody was allowed on the streets after 12 either in a vehicle or on foot. Sinh Vinh, Dam Quang and their wives bade everyone goodnight and Van Pham Khanh accompanied them to the door. When she re-entered the lounge she surprised me by announcing that if anyone didn't beat curfew they could stay the night. The others seemed to accept this as a matter of course and we all paid another visit to the table for a second round of food. One of the Americans was decidedly tipsy and Kim Anh's olive skin had taken on a rosy hue. Don Jones had gone on to drinking beer, but there seemed to be plenty of wine left for the rest of us. By now the white wine could have been Puligny-Montrachet and the humidity made drinking all the more enjoyable, along with the strips of lacquered pork that I nibbled at.

Van Pham Khanh, though she drank sparingly, with elegance, holding her glass of white wine by the stem, uninterruptedly toasted all her guests in what I thought was rather a Scandinavian manner, looking you right in the eye before raising her glass and again before putting it down. The alcohol did not seem to affect her at all, unless it added a slight air of mystery to her limpid beauty. Her French blood had obviously bequeathed to her a certain affinity to the juice of the grape.

I took another look at the rugs in the dining area; she drifted silently after me, then beckoned me to follow her into the hall. From there she led me into another room which seemed to be a combination of bedroom and den. On the floor were more rugs of many colours, usually with a red-and-black base interwoven with stripes or geometric patterns of pink, orange and yellow. On the walls were four blankets, two of them vermilion with a black and yellow diamond motif. The others were chessboard-patterned, red, blue, mauve and white squares on a mustard yellow background. On another wall was a tribal dress of some kind made of navy blue heavy linen with bright red and yellow arm bands and shoulder trimming similar to designs I had seen on Lappish costumes.

"This was my grandmother's room", said Van Pham Khanh simply.

She showed me more dresses which were kept in drawers as well as clay pots and a couple of baskets which she indicated had been made by her grandmother. Over the bed hung a big knife in a decorated scabbard – a *chang*, she called it. Plaited bamboo matting on both sides of the bed completed the highland decor.

"Your grandmother is dead?"

Van Pham Khanh nodded wordlessly. She had obviously been very fond of her grandmother and touched lovingly the objects which she had so thoughtfully shown me. She volunteered no information about other members of her family. She stood there, motionless for a moment in front of one of the tribal wall drapes. The dim, bedside lamp half illuminated her form, lending a faint golden hue to the mauve of her dress against the crimson backdrop. It was a one-time picture – a momentary ethnic cameo in *chiaroscuro* – an unforgettable blend of exuberant oriental colour and gilded duskiness. I felt the eastern part of her – that which belonged to a hemisphere that was not mine.

"Do you know the Vietnamese poets?" What are they like?" I hoped that the question would extend our moment of privacy. She smiled.

"Nguyen-Du is the most famous. Eighteenth century. He wrote "Kim Van Kieu" the first major work in Vietnamese. He described the beauties of nature and of women and many other things."

"Was he good?"

"Yes. Even in translation."

We crossed the dark hall and re-entered the drawing room. As we did so, Van Pham Khanh shed some of her gentle Eastern esoterism and assumed her semi-western veneer for the guests, though she was far from attaining the easy occidentalism of Collette and Albertine. Them I could see in El Paso without having to overwork my imagination. Van Pham Khanh seemed by contrast irrevocably enracinated in Vietnam.

In the lounge they were playing records – Sinatra, Nat King Cole, Ella Fitzgerald.

"Would you like to hear some Vietnamese popular music? " asked Van Pham Khanh.

I said I would. She picked out a disc from the rack and put it on. It was a woman singing — shrill, soprano, aggressive. The music was repetitive and melancholy but with a compelling forcefulness. I looked at the record jacket which sported a colour photograph of the singer – My Chau – a young raven-haired beauty in a clinging turquoise *ao-dai*. The strength of character evident in the voice also showed in her direct gaze and broad cheekbones. The song was called *Ai Xuoi Van Ly*. When it ended Van Pham Khanh laughingly gave me the record as a souvenir. I still play it sometimes, though it crackles a fair bit now. I often wonder who the vivacious My Chau sings for these days.

Curfew time came and went and nobody showed any signs of going home. Henry and Carl danced slow foxtrots with Annabelle and Kim Anh. Don opened more cans of beer. Van Pham Khanh made me a special drink – part white wine, two different fruit juices, slices of pineapple, papaya, kiwi and lime, liberally iced and topped with a maraschino cherry.

I am not sure whether it was intended to finish me off or sober me up, but as tropical beverages go, it was one of the best.

For half an hour or so Van Pham Khanh asked me about England – its sights, its traditions, its landscapes. She knew our poets well (she liked Pope, Wordsworth and Elizabeth Barrett Browning), and had read some of the easier novelists – Maugham, the Brontes, Jane Austen, parts of Dickens. Her knowledge of British history and geography were slight; her familiarity with all things French was readily apparent. She talked at length about Alfred de Vigny, about whom I know very little, though I have read *"L'Esprit pur"*, and compared his absolute Romanticism with both Wordsworth and Nguyen Du.

At no time did she give the impression of showing off; poetry meant an awful lot to her. She lived in a world far removed from jungle skirmishes, napalm bombings, torture, political intrigue, mortar fire, rockets and summary executions. And yet she lived right in the middle of Saigon – the eye of the storm. Notwithstanding all the pressures, her sanity and culture remained palpably intact. She was what she was.

Collette and Albertine were composed, too, but in their case they had thrown in their lot with the Americans; they were defiant, optimistic and uncomplicated. Van Pham Khanh represented everything that the Communists were trying to destroy – regional tradition, individualism, Romantic sentimentality, sympathy towards Western cultures, possibly proper-ty and wealth as well – but she remained enigmatically calm and discerning. She was aloof and uncompromised, possessed of her own passions and judg-ments, totally committed to no one – essentially indigenous, Vietnamese.

As if to emphasize this she picked up a kind of drumstick and beat a Montagnard brass gong on her desk as the clock struck one. Quietly she told everyone where they could sleep – there were several rooms on the ground floor – adding that she and Kim Anh would make breakfast at six-thirty. The three Americans trotted off without further ado to the sleeping stations to which they had been assigned. They were obviously accustomed to failing to beat curfew and accepting overnight hospitality in this manner. Don Jones and I were given sofas in the drawing room – he indicated that we might leave before breakfast. The two Vietnamese girls hovered around for a while, ensuring that we had sufficient blankets and pillows. Van Pham Khanh gave me a light, brightly-coloured Montagnard covering; there was a suppressed gleam in her eye – of amusement, I supposed. She had sensed my love of ethnology, folkways, rude art, richness of colour.

"Bonne nuit, dormez bien." – The two young women slipped away gracefully, extinguishing lights as they retired. I was tired, but lay on my back with no wish to sleep. The house was quiet except for the soft hum of the fan slowly revolving under the dark ceiling. I had so many impressions to digest that I suspected I would stay awake until dawn.

As it turned out, it was not necessary. Don got up after half an hour and announced a change of plan. He had to get to the office early; he needed some things from home. We'd take the risk and go. He wrote a short note for Van Pham Khanh, but she heard our movements and came out of her room to join us; she was wearing a silk maroon dressing gown. Don said a few words and she nodded understandingly. We went together to the door which she opened stealthily. Noiselessly she padded down the garden path and looked in both directions along the boulevard. I saw her white wrist signal that all was clear; we quickly followed her as far as Don's car. She pressed our hands briefly and melted away in the darkness. Clearly one did not use speech on the streets after curfew. Don started the car and drove off as fast as he could. He explained the form:

"This is illegal. Army or Police will stop us if they see us. We'll be in big trouble if we're caught. The trick is not to get caught. There's no traffic, so I'll be doing eighty or more. If we don't stop when hailed they will shoot, but usually we have gone by the time they've seen us. They're nearly always parked, so we have the jump on them. If they shoot, lie down."

"What about you, you can't lie down?"

"Don't worry, I do this three times a week – I know the game. When we get to the Caravelle, I'll stop for two seconds. Jump out and go straight in."

It was like he said. He drove like a madman, we saw two military jeeps parked with lights on in side streets, but he was gone before they could pursue. I was scared stiff well before he careened into Tu Do at fifty miles an hour where the darkened façade of the Caravelle Hotel loomed up compassionately against the dark-orange sky. I was home again. He braked hard and I hop-skip-and-jumped into the lobby. I heard the screech of his tyres as I reached for my key. Ignoring the lift, I ran up the dimly lighted stairs before the MPs got me. Once inside my room, I locked the door and slipped over to the window, lights still out. There was no sign of Don, but a police car slowly patrolled the square. I undressed in the dark and slipped gratefully between the sheets, reflecting that Don Jones need never go hungry in Hollywood.

*   *   *   *   *

Hoang pushed a telegram under my door at 6 in the morning. It was from Strumpen-Darrie, replying to my earlier cable.

RICHARD LEWIS HOTEL CARAVELLE SAIGON

PHONE SERVICE BLOCKED PLEASE SEND COPIES GREEN FORMS RE BEST 120 CANDIDATES FROM VIETNAM STOP SAVE 30 PLACES MINIMUM CAMBODIA AND LAOS STOP CHECK QUALIFICATIONS CAREFULLY STOP LEAVE ORIGINAL FORMS IN TRUSTED HANDS SAIGON STOP PLEASE REPEAT QUALIFI-CATIONS IN YOUR CABLE RUSH.

ROBERT STRUMPEN DARRIE.

I had breakfast at 7 and did my sums with reference to candidates I had approved and the distribution of pins in my ten recruitment areas. I was reasonably satisfied that one hundred and ten of the applicants I had seen would be excellent instructor material, whatever else they might be. Eighty of them were women. I was still low on recruits from 2 of the central areas and I resolved that on this last day of interviewing – Friday – I would aim for ten men from the centre, bringing the total from Vietnam up to 120. I would also seek out the ten best girls as replacements for drop-outs.

The day was just as busy as the others. No further advertising had been done. The source of supply was apparently endless. By 6.30 I had chosen ten men and given them reasonable grounds to suppose that they would eventually be selected. Each one showed his elation. The many girls in the foyer looked on enviously and strained to catch every whisper of conversation. I told them in due course that there were still some places open. Hoang stopped people joining the queue at 5 and by six thirty I had seen everyone who had been admitted. It was time to wrap up the operation, for I was convinced that, had it continued, thousands of people would still have come forward.

Willard, Toole and Don Jones came round for a drink at 7 – Berlitz bought 3 bottles of champagne – and I was able to persuade Hoang to have a glass with us as he came off duty. Later I had a quiet dinner with Paul Rasmussen and Pip, who took me out again, to a French restaurant this time. We had a lot of common acquaintances in NCR and we talked about some fine characters in that reputable company for most of the evening.

They returned me to the Caravelle at 10 and I sent a telegram to New York:

ROBERT STRUMPEN DARRIE
BERLITZ
FIFTH AVE NEW YORK
SAIGON INTERVIEWING COMPLETED STOP 130 INSTRUCTORS IN THE BAG STOP ALL WITH BACCALAUREAT AND PASSABLE ENGLISH STOP AT LEAST NINETY FULL UNIVERSITY DEGREE STOP PROCEEDING CAMBODIA MONDAY STOP ORIGINAL APPLICATION FORMS BEING LEFT WITH PHILIP POWELL, NCR ASSISTANT MANAGER SAIGON STOP MY LETTER ON WAY EXPLAINING IMMIGRATION PROCEDURE STOP
LEWIS

Five days and five nights of high humidity were beginning to get to me. For the first time since leaving Tokyo I felt utterly drained. As I had arranged to play tennis at 10 the next morning, I went straight to bed, too tired to pick up fifty green forms I had spread all over the bedroom floor. Muffled mortar fire coaxed me to sleep. It did not take long.

*   *   *   *   *

I was fully rested at 6.30 when another telegram arrived – it was from Raphael Alberola.

MR RICHARD LEWIS HOTEL CARAVELLE SAIGON
IGNORE IMMIGRATION PROBLEMS STOP SEND GENERAL PICTURE AVAILABILITY SAIGON STOP GO TO CAMBODIA AND LAOS SOONEST STOP NEED ONLY PROFESSIONAL COMPETENCE AND QUALIFICATION ASSURANCE NOW STOP VIETNAMESE RECRUITER WILL SCREEN AFTER YOU STOP THANKS STOP
RAPHAEL

Our telegrams had probably crossed, but his message left me less worried. I was more at home judging teachers than processing paper work in ministries. It made sense for a Vietnamese to deal with these formalities as well as to provide a second opinion on the reliability of the candidates I had selected. I just hoped Berlitz picked the right Vietnamese to do the job. I decided the cable needed no reply and ate a hearty breakfast of bacon, eggs and hash brown. Hoang took time out to have coffee with me and I assured him that his half-sister was as good as in. I also slipped him two hundred and fifty dollars cash in a plain brown envelope without asking for a receipt. He did not open the envelope but protested weakly before stuffing it into his inside pocket. He had more than earned it. I would happily have given him a thousand had I not known that Ralph Poses would have me beheaded on my next visit to New York.

I spent the next two hours typing up a summary of the week's interviewing. Borrowing a typewriter from the hotel office, I divided the application forms of my preferred candidates into ten piles corresponding to the regions and made out a top sheet for each pile. This specified the ten best candidates, two probables and three reserves. These one hundred and fifty forms with their top sheets I put in a green dossier (A). I had a yellow dossier (B) for another fifty candidates who were worth a second interview if there was a high mortality rate from dossier A. The third dossier (C and red) contained the details of those people who had proved unsuitable for a variety of reasons.

Rather than put the dossiers into the hotel safe, where they no doubt would have made good week-end reading for the hotel staff, I rang Pip Powell at home and asked him if he would bury them for me in the NCR archives, at least until Monday.

In fifteen minutes he came grinning into the hotel lobby, ruddy and fresh as the waking morn. It was nearly ten and he drove me to the Cercle Sportif where John Toole, Collette and Albertine were half way through three tonic waters on the terrace overlooking the tennis courts. Toole was in tennis gear, ready to play; the girls wore cute little sun dresses. Pip had things to do; after a quick beer and ten minutes ogling Collette and Albertine he forced himself to continue with his errands, declining Toole's offer of a set of tennis. John lent me a racquet, shorts and shoes and we played a couple of sets on the adjacent court.

The girls watched us play, smiling ingenuously all the while. They did not clap or applaud winners (we didn't hit many) as Japanese ladies do, but continued to beam quietly, which made me suspect that either they were reserved, discerning spectators or did not understand the game at all. The humidity took its toll of both John and myself and after an hour we were happy to share the honours and join the girls for gin tonics.

Our place on court was taken by a stocky grey-haired American of middle age, immaculate in white tennis strip, partnered by a tall Vietnamese a few years his junior. I had heard Collette chirp "Morning, General", and seen her exchange a few words with the American as he went on court. It was indeed General William Westmoreland, the Commander of the U.S. forces in Vietnam.

I watched him play as I quenched my thirst. He played a good game of tennis. Properly trained, he had a nice style and controlled power. He knew when to attack and when to defend. Pugnacious at the net, he was also a dogged retriever of the ball at the baseline. He did not like to lose and was prepared to conduct long rallies rather than concede a point through impatience or attempting impossible winners. His opponent also played correctly – probably he had learnt the game in the days of the French. His strokes were graceful, his shots cunningly placed. Of slighter build than

Westmoreland, he did not have the General's punch or dynamism, but his economy of movement and staying power were there for all to see. They were evenly matched.

What astonished me was the apparent lack of security at the club. Here we were, approaching the culmination point of the longest and one of the most damaging wars in American history, right in the middle of a city notorious for its assassination ratio, watching the U.S. Commander-in-Chief (who, would shortly ask his President for an additional 206,000 soldiers) enjoy and concentrate on his Saturday morning tennis, completely unprotected, as far as I could see, front, back and sides. I looked in vain for guards or plain clothesmen among the score of spectators along the four courts. The only possible bodyguard within 50 yards of the General (I discounted Toole, Collette and Albertine) was his slender tennis partner. How he would have dealt with the sudden appearance of a would-be assassin I do not know, unless he planned to brain him with his tennis racquet.

We spent the whole day at the Cercle Sportif. Unused as I was to lazing around, I found the procedure considerably less burdensome than I had imagined, given the attractive neo-colonial surroundings, the unrelenting heat and the decorative, congenial company. The girls took off their sundresses – they wore bikinis underneath – and swam up and down the pool for a while. John found me some swimming trunks and I did a few lengths. He put his gin tonic at the edge of the pool and joined us stopping every two lengths for another slug. The girls giggled and prattled in French, splashing water at John who stood upside down in the water, dived for bottle tops and performed other antics that men often do to amuse girls in swimming pools.

We lunched on the terrace in our swimming attire. The sun soon dried us after coming out of the water, though one's skin retained a thin film of moisture due to the humidity. We had shrimps and salad washed down by an indifferent white wine, then switched back to gin tonics with slightly more tonic in than before lunch. The afternoon passed pleasantly – a relaxed *pot-pourri* of good-humoured teasing, greeting acquaintances, restrained quaffing and occasional observation of exciting rallies on the many courts. We swam several times and ordered coffee in the middle of the afternoon.

Collette and Albertine were the easiest of day-long companions. They talked neither too much nor too little – sometimes modifying a male remark, but never arguing. They willingly discussed any topic John and I raised, but took nothing too seriously. They flirted selectively with most of the men who stopped by our table to exchange the time of day, giving me afterwards a humorous rundown of the characters as they departed. For long periods the two girls would just sit there in Eastern silence. When they did not talk they smiled at their pretty feet. They seemed to have an unlimited supply of inner amusement.

At six Toole signed all his chits and we left the club. From the back window of his car I stole a last look at the tasteful, pink-roofed façade of the Cercle Sportif. I suspected many years would pass before I saw it again or would witness such a graceful, untroubled scene in its nostalgic, old-world atmosphere.

John dropped me off at the hotel and we arranged to meet again at eight-thirty. I had a shower and then snoozed for two hours, hoping I could sleep off the effect of the gin. I felt much more alert after a second shower on awakening and dressed just in time to greet Toole in the lobby at the appointed hour. He had arranged a get-together with a dozen or so of his friends in a USAID club and we drove there with Collette and Albertine in tow. There was a lot more drinking – scotch now – and I remember that we ate pork and danced with the six girls in our party until half past eleven. I recognized another girl I had interviewed – My Dung Hoa – in my yellow folder, if I recalled correctly. I danced with Collette and Albertine in turn – the music was slow and seductive, exclusively American. Both girls danced in the same way as they talked – committed to the Western way, intimate but not pushing, smooth and humorous, quietly pliant, closely following the man's lead. Neither girl could have weighed more than 45 kilos; I have never danced with anyone so light on her feet or on my arm as Collette or Albertine. Yet one felt the latent strength in the delicate frame, female power in the daintiness, maturity and stamina in their cool smiles.

Toole had me home before curfew. He did not share Don Jones's healthy disrespect for the Military Police. When I alighted, Collette and Albertine stuck their pretty heads out of the car windows and I kissed four scented cheeks. They kissed me back and murmured sweet things in French in my ear, whereupon John drove them off into the night.

*   *   *   *   *

Sunday I had reserved for traipsing round Saigon on foot – my favourite way of getting to know a city. Fortunately the day was cooler than most and I set off at nine, armed with my camera and a city plan in excellent spirits. I took in the sights systematically – Saigon Cathedral, Central Market, City Hall, Presidential Residence, National Museum and Botanical Gardens. Near the river were the Majestic Hotel and the United States Embassy from the roof of which Ambassador Ellsworth Bunker would make his dramatic, last-minute take-off in a few years' time.

I walked along the Saigon River, seen silver from the air but, like the Mekong, muddy brown at ground level. Shabby barges, sampans, junks, battered open boats lined the waterfront and riverside piers. One huge vessel, shining white and spotless, stood out from the motley array of craft near the

Majestic Hotel. It was the German hospital ship "Helgoland" from Hamburg — West Germany's contribution to the war effort. I took a picture as a gleaming ambulance drove up the quay and deposited another war victim with the waiting attendants.

The busy river life, though not attaining the intensity of that of Hong Kong, reminded me of the importance of waterways in the south of the country. The Mekong, starting in Tibet, flows more than 2500 miles before emptying itself through its five-mouthed delta into the South China Seas. The port of Saigon was able to handle the vast amount of war *matériel* flowing in at the height of the hostilities. The Viet Cong, for their part, were adept at using waterways of all kinds for their own purposes. Everything seemed peaceful on the river that Sunday morning – men mending nets, quay vendors pushing their wares, old women squatting round their cooking pots, a small brown-skinned girl clutching possessively at a half-nibbled piece of maize, eying me suspiciously as I took her picture. A five-minute rowboat's ride across the river I could see the tin roofs of An Khanh Xa from which snipers downed Bell helicopters with depressing regularity.

Leaving the waterfront, I walked around the streets of the 1st and 2nd districts, choosing my route at random, taking photographs of anything that struck me as being representative. The traffic was lighter than on weekdays, but still moved at a snail's pace. Whenever they could go forward, drivers took no notice at all of stop signs. Pollution was bad – I always associate the pungent smell of diesel with Saigon's main thoroughfares, invariably cloaked in a light blue haze. The parks and quieter avenues were pleasant enough; the constant humidity protected the capital's greenery. One saw lovers everywhere, sitting on benches, under trees, around the edges of fountains, on canal banks, even on stationary motor cycles. I supposed that in this overcrowded city they had nowhere else to go.

Americans, too, were visible on all the streets. Many had become nervous about going to public buildings after the attacks on restaurants, hotels and cinemas, but their presence was very much in evidence along the main boulevards. There were still 20,000 Americans in Saigon, plus soldiers in town on leave from the front. Soldiers fresh from active duty tended to be noisy on the streets and wore all kinds of military or semi-military clothes of a flamboyant nature, from Texan stetsons to Mexican Pancho Villa style cartridge belts and swastika-crested SS daggers sheathed in silver scabbards. One was reminded of their right to use extrovert dress and behaviour as a means of escaping from battle-line tension by the slogan many of them carried on the back of their tunics, "You don't need to go to hell if you've been in Vietnam."

Sandbags, barriers and fences were ubiquitous. It was common VC practice to lob grenades through open doors or over the garden wall. I saw dozens of fences over 25 feet high. If the grenade thrower did not clear the fence in the first attempt, the wire might bounce the grenade back at him.

I passed three Ministry buildings – Justice, Interior and Social Welfare. Each one had a pair of Viet sentries on Sunday duty, all taking spiteful aim at passers-by of any type or nationality. I never saw their trigger-fingers uncrooked. They must have ached terribly at the end of a shift. The off-duty GIs, clearly used to being shot at, shouted contemptuously at some of the sentries, failing to give them the wide berth that the rest of us did.

I went to a soup parlour for a late lunch and in the afternoon took a long loop into the 5th District to peep into the Cong Hoa stadium and the Phu Tho race track, both in the Chinese quarter. It was a tiring 3-mile plod back along Tran Quoc Toan Boulevard as the bleached bright sky began to soften into friendlier twilight and the stall-keepers plugged in their coloured lamps early as if to show there was no power cut that day.

The sociable dusk emboldened me to do a back-of-the-shop currency deal with one of the many Indian-run establishments along the way. Travellers cheques brought you only the official rate of 80 piastres to the dollar, but with dollars in cash ("green" as the G.I.s called it) one could negotiate something much more worthwhile. After some perfunctory haggling, I bought $500 worth of piastres to take care of my last day expenses and the same amount in Cambodian riels. There was always the risk of being handed fake currency (indeed I had previously never even seen any Cambodian money) but while counterfeit dollars were fairly common I could not imagine anyone trying to start a business in counterfeit riels!

In the evening I had a quiet dinner with Don Jones who came round to say good-bye. He was going "up-country" early the next day. I brought him up to date on the week's events, though he had heard most of it on the Saigon grapevine. I was sorry to take my leave of Don who, like Pip, bubbled over with perennial good humour and took everything in his cheerful pounding stride.

When he had gone I did my packing, laid out my travelling clothes for the next day and stuck $20 worth of piastres for the maid under the often useless telephone so that I would not forget in the rush the following morning.

Before I went to bed I sat by my window for a few minutes to have a last look at the cosy square. Three young women emerged from the damp portals of the Continental Palace and strolled lazily down Tu Do, arm-in-arm. One was in Western dress, one in Chinese, the third wore a white *ao dai* and black *cuan*. They shared a private joke which made them all burst out laughing as they passed out of sight under my window. In the distance the muffled thump of a rocket punctuated their laughter. Again I heard them giggle, faintly now as they went on their way. I went to bed aware of some vague symbolism, anxious to think it out, but my tired limbs won the day and I was soon in slumber, changing piastres in my dreams at thousands to the dollar and rowing a white skiff down the Saigon River.

*   *   *   *   *

I had booked a plane to Phnom Penh leaving at 12 noon and was supposed to be at the airport at 10 a.m. Pip came round at 8 and we breakfasted   together. We had agreed that he would keep all the original documentation in the NCR safe for the second recruiter to have access to. Pip had kindly photo-copied every single application form (each had 4 pages) as well as my summary lists. He brought with him a sheaf of paper over 6 inches thick. This I checked briefly and asked him to get it to New York via NCR channels. I was not keen to go through Cambodian customs with a bundle like that to explain.

Hoang had bought several bottles of wine on my behalf for the waiters and junior clerks as well as a large box of chocolates for Tran Thi. They all saw me off with what appeared to be a genuine show of affection.

"Come back soon", shouted one of them as I climbed into Pip's Land Rover.

We crawled to Tan Son Nhut in just over an hour and Pip helped me through the throng and got my luggage checked in. Toole, Collette and Albertine rolled up with half an hour to spare and together we all drank a very powerful beer which Tan Son Nhut was accustomed to serve up to nervous departing passengers. It was certainly the strongest brew I have ever tasted in my life and when my plane was called I felt I was leaving in the middle of a party.

"Good hunting" said Toole.

"See you in Tokyo" said Pip, who planned to visit Japan in September.

"See you in El Paso" said Albertine, meaningfully.

Collette gave me a flower and a kiss. I wasn't sure what to do with the flower. I proceeded through Immigration, had my hand luggage searched, drank another beer at the gate and boarded the Royal Air Cambodge flight without a care in the world.

*   *   *   *   *

Cambodia

In June 1967 Cambodia still enjoyed peace. The American bombing of that country did not start till 1970. Between 1970-73 more bombs were dropped on Cambodia than on Germany during the whole of the second world war. We had the usual vertical take-off from Tan Son Nhut, the plane vibrating shrilly as the engines strained against gravity, but the rest of the one-hour flight was marked by a gradual decreasing of all-round tension as we left the war zone. Once out of the reach of sniper fire, we trundled along happily at 600 kilometres per hour, mainly following the lazy course of the Mekong upstream to Phnom Penh. The Cambodian capital, which is situated at the junction of the two huge S.E. Asian rivers, the Mekong and the Tonle Sap, presented an attractive spectacle from the air. The Phnom (Royal Palace) was clearly visible with its blazing golden, sapphire and emerald roof, as were the big monastaries with their numerous slim *stupas* pointing towards the sky. Our descent was comfortingly gentle (no snipers here) and, as we taxied easily towards the white airport building, one was aware of the relaxed movements and unweary faces of the ground staff as they greeted our arrival. The men were small and brown in comparison with the Vietnamese and they chattered busily in strange, high-pitched tones – it sounded like the chirping of sparrows fighting for crumbs.

We went through customs like lightning – just a few flimsy forms to fill in – and we soon poured out of the light airy building onto a sun-drenched boulevard where lines of *cyclo-pousses* waited cheerfully to transport us into town. In these tricycle-rickshaws the passenger sits in front of the driver, as in Saigon. This is much less daunting in Phnom Penh, however, since traffic was light and consists largely of other *cyclo-pousses*. My driver, a young man in his mid-twenties, could speak no English, but his French was reasonable and we had a pleasant 20-minute spin into the city centre where I had reservations at "Le Royal" – reputedly the best hotel in Indo-China. This building was the last refuge of besieged Western officials and holed-up journalists when the Khmer Rouge entered the city in 1975, but eight years earlier its welcoming peach-coloured portals presented a haven of peace and tranquillity in contrast to the taped-up windows and bullet-scarred facade of the war-weary Caravelle. My room was solid five-star – everything worked except the telephone. I lunched in the restaurant where the unmistakably French nature of the smells emanating from the kitchen made me order *bifteck avec pommes frites* preceded by a juicy *salade aux tomates*. The meal was indeed authentically French, the quality of the food immeasurably superior to the wartime fare of Saigon, the immaculately dressed waiter attending every need and hovering anxiously for his tip as I downed my first decent coffee in a week.

*   *   *   *   *

It was really hot now – approaching 35 degrees centrigrade and I took out a map after lunch. I had ordered my *cyclo* at 4:30 pm and he drove me round the capital, pointing out the chief places of interest in his twittering French. I was fascinated by my first exposure to the Cambodian language which, unlike

Vietnamese, Lao and Thai, is unrelated to Chinese and is not tonal. The tongue is actually Khmer and has Austro-Asiatic origins enriched by terms derived from Sanskrit. The provenance of the Khmer race is in itself uncertain. There are marks of a remote mixture with Indians and Malays. The short stature and brown faces of Cambodians lends some credence to the theory that they entered Indo-China through Indonesia and perhaps earlier from Australia itself. If you hear Cambodian spoken by men in the next room, you may well believe they are women speaking, so high-pitched and squeaky is the tongue. The people seemed to me to be very hospitable, cheerful, peaceful and hard-working. They obviously were relieved at not being involved in the war, though one could detect some nervousness when Vietnam was discussed. Yet in 1967 they could hardly have suspected how terrible a fate awaited them, when two million Cambodians would be killed or die of starvation in four years of Khmer Rouge tyranny.

Such dark times were well into the future as Henry, my driver, pedalled me energetically along the flowered promenades of Phnom Penh, with their jacaranda trees, fresh lawns, fountains and pink sandstone paving stones. There were gay, multi-coloured birds everywhere as well as elegant, slender women wearing the traditional *sampot* – a long skirt down to the ankles, narrow, made of a single piece of richly-coloured material folded over in front. In Phnom Penh the men wore European clothes but in the countryside they remained faithful to the *sarong*. The mellow Asiatic twilight brought some relief from the heat of the afternoon and, as the dusk deepened, the inhabitants came out to stroll along the Tonle Sap, stopping to greet acquaintances with the traditional *choumreap sour* greeting, joining both hands in front of the chest and bowing with a deferential smile. Shaven-headed monks clad in brilliant orange paraded in groups of half a dozen. People peddled food and handicrafts on grassy patches by the river. It was noticeable that they were poor bargainers, not in the least pushy, taking no offence if you handled their products without purchasing them.

I hardly needed any dinner that evening and had a quiet chat in the Royal bar with a New Zealander and two Cambodian clerks who spoke reasonable English. The French had withdrawn from Cambodia in 1953 after 90 years protection. General de Gaulle, in the days before independence, had withdrawn all French teachers of English from Cambodia, so now there was a severe shortage of English speakers. The British Council barely functioned in Phom Penh. The Cambodian clerks said people were worried about being (with Laos) the only French-speaking enclave in S.E. and E. Asia. They exhibited negative attitudes towards the Thais and Vietnamese – stronger neighbours who had often dominated Cambodians.

*   *   *   *   *

I had not forgotten that I had come to Cambodia to work and the next morning I made an appointment to see the First Secretary at the Australian Embassy. They handled all American affairs, as Prince Norodom Sihanouk had preferred to be without a US Embassy in those troubled times. Wayne Elliott received me cordially, somewhat curious as to my mission. I outlined the course of events so far and he listened carefully. His first comment was that Phnom Penh was a tight little backwater compared with sprawling Saigon and that any moves I made along the lines I had discussed would draw much more attention from the authorities than in Vietnam, where the Americans were calling the shots anyway.

When I mentioned Steve Parker's letter of introduction to Prince Sihanouk, Elliott showed clear signs of alarm.

"Do you know who Charles Meyer is?"

"No".

"He is Sihanouk's private secretary. All correspondence and appointments with Sihanouk pass through his hands first."

"And?"

"He is a rabid communist."

"What will he do in my case?"

"Put you in jail".

My experience with 3-star Swedish and minus -1-star Spanish prisons made me suspect that Cambodian jails would be of the non-stellar variety. Elliott warned me strongly against going anywhere near Meyer or even trying to advertise as I had done in Vietnam. Phnom Penh was not free-wheeling Saigon.

"I have 3 days to spend in Cambodia. What do you suggest I do?"

"Go to Angkor Wat – it's unbelievable."

It was somewhere I had always wanted to go. Without further ado, I abandoned my Cambodian mission, *cyclo-poussed* back to the Royal, grabbed the *concierge* and booked an afternoon flight to Siem Reap. It was one of the wisest decisions of my life.

*   *   *   *   *

Cambodia, which in 1967 had about six million inhabitants, is an ancient kingdom dating back to one century before the birth of Christ. Its culture was unremarkable for eight centuries, but achieved eminence with the foundation of the Khmer monarchy at the beginning of the 9th century and witnessed some of the world's most impressive monumental constructions until the abandoning of Angkor in 1432. These monolithic temples and edifices were swallowed up by and completely lost in the humid devouring jungle for 4 centuries, before being discovered by accident by a French scientist in 1860 . They constituted one of the wonders of the modern world until their sealing off and part destruction by the Khmer Rouge in 1975.

We flew up-country, along the whole length of the Grand Lac, glimmering and dazzling us as it reflected the afternoon sunlight. Leaving the lake to our left we flew low over tree-tops for half an hour. The vegetation, thick, humid, dark green, reminded me irresistibly of the jungles of Yucatán. The densely packed trees seemed to be of even height as we skimmed over them. As one looked ahead out of the left hand window, the lush foliage stretched endlessly into the distance and then, suddenly, one saw the tips of a wide array of spires emerging from the sea of green. In seconds, an impressive battery of massive greyish-brown towers leapt up from the jungle, barring the path of our small plane as we hurtled towards them. Moments later we zoomed upwards as jungle glades appeared and we saw the full façade of the monolithic temples, their rich *bas-reliefs* strikingly visible even from the plane. As we skirted the mammoth central temple of Angkor Wat, we were aware of other spires, of almost equal stature, rising out of the forest around us. The majestic stone witnesses of a centuries-old civilisation lay spread out in all its riches below us.

It is beyond the scope of this work to provide the reader with an adequate description of Angkor Wat, Angkor Thom and the numerous edifices in the surrounding area. The temples were erected in a period of religious fervour, similar to and contemporaneous with the era which was giving Europe its magnificent cathedrals. Few European churches can begin to compare with Angkor Wat. The religious thoughts and mythology had come from India, where Buddha's words were first heard, but the Cambodian architects and sculptors expressed their belief in a new and sensational style. Using sandstone, lateite, brick and wood, they created a multitude of temples of gigantic dimensions, covered with statues and engravings which have produced arguably the finest temple-rubbings in the world.

I stayed at the Auberge des Temples, a delightfully frail, wood and glass construction a stone's throw from the main temple. I had two wonderful days, exploring the ruins, taking photographs and buying every huge temple-rubbing that I could get my hands on. One was not supposed to export the big ones, but I rolled them up tightly like newspapers and smuggled them out in my suitcase. They are on the walls of Riversdown today. On my second day at Angkor, Prince Sihanouk led a political rally at Angkor Thom. I watched him silently from twenty yards. He was dapper, tiny, smiling and solicitous, chirping like a bird like the rest of them. Steve Parker's letter burned a hole in my pocket. I took the great man's picture – nobody seemed to mind.

The last night, I stood alone under the giant conifers, quivering with forest sounds, surveying the giant temples resplendent in the evening sky and in their magnificent jungle solitude. My unforgettable impression was that of suddenly being transported back several centuries in time to spend a few fleeting seconds in the company and splendour of the God-Kings.

*   *   *   *   *

Laos

After returning to Phnom Penh, I boarded a Royal Air Cambodge plane to Vientiane, the capital of Laos. My trip there was more memorable than my actual stay in that sleepy city. The aeroplane was of the Tiger Moth vintage and had only 12 seats. These were occupied by myself, an English diplomat, an American and nine orientals. The first thing the diplomat did on coming aboard was to chain and handcuff himself and his briefcase to the metal leg of his seat. After that he fastened his safety belt. Though still on the Phnom Penh tarmac, we were somehow in the war zone again. Everybody on board looked preoccupied – I had no idea why. At that time Laos was like half-in and half-out of the war. Just before take-off, half a dozen ground staff came on board and placed a brown paper parcel, about eight inches by four and three inches deep, in the aisle beside each seat. I prodded mine, it was hard. It looked like a big brick. I tried to lift one edge with my forefinger; it was very heavy. At least it did not tick, so I left it alone. The diplomat and the orientals ignored the mysterious parcels; the American, like me, was mildly curious.

We took off in normal fashion and I noticed that the parcels did not slide backwards. During the trip I went up front to have a peep in the cockpit. Both pilots were fast asleep, we were on automatic. I told the American, he said "Good joke, man." We did a Saigon-style landing in Vientiane, as the surrounding jungle housed sharp-shooters. The brown paper parcels slid forwards a yard. I got the one from the diplomat behind. I gave him a questioning look and he mouthed "gold" at me without showing any further inclination to pursue a conversation. After all, I could have been anybody. On landing the plane did not go anywhere near the airport building. Instead it waited on the runway while a jeep sped towards us, spilling out half a dozen orientals in military uniform who rushed aboard and speedily relieved us of our brown paper parcels, which they loaded into the jeep.

Later we taxied in to the customs building and entered the country after some examination of luggage and objectives. I had an appointment with the Chairman of the Lao-American Association and simply said as much. Through this gentleman – Le Thong Thap – I was eventually able to recruit seven or eight Vietnamese speaking the local dialect as well as a few from Cambodia. My mission was thus complete. I got stuck in Vientiane for four days, as it was the policy to overbook planes at that time and non-military personnel were the ones that got bounced. I found the Laotian capital one of the doziest cities I have ever spent time in, though I met the British

Ambassador and swam in his (hot) pool and was introduced briefly to the Prime Minister whom I encountered by chance at a party staged by the Vientiane Karate Club. The only other thing I remember well was my hotel which was state-run, had terrible service and had no telephones in the rooms. It was called the Lane Xang, which meant the Hotel of the Million Elephants.

*   *   *   *   *

All in all, the recruiting mission was a relative success. In spite of a few strikes organized by the Cong infiltrators in El Paso, a lot of solid teaching was done after the troublemakers were incarcerated. Many of the Vietnamese girls married American soldiers, a few slipped into prostitution. At least I had sent educated ones. The whole scheme didn't help the US much in the end – we all know what eventually happened.

I met some Vietnamese last year, former northerners and communists.

"Who are your favourite foreigners?" I asked them bluntly.

"The Americans" they replied without hesitation and with one voice.

It's a funny world we live in.

Chapter 14

Expansion In Japan

During the summer of 1967 we had started to look for premises in Osaka, Japan's second biggest city. We eventually settled on the Hanshin Hotel building at the terminal of the Hanshin railway line linking Osaka with Tokyo. It faced one end of the main station in Osaka and proved to be an excellent location. Ed Wilton transferred to Osaka to manage the school. He and his wife Marja decided to live in Kobe, about 40 minutes away by train. Kobe, with its mountainous backdrop and its pleasant airy streets was much more cosmopolitan than Osaka. It rivalled Yokohama as a port and nearly all the important US and European shipping and trading companies had big offices there. Nestlé, using Kobe as a base, had captured 93 per cent of the Japanese instant coffee market. Our Osaka school was an instant success. Our reputation from Tokyo had preceded us. Marja Wilton, born a Finn, had that innate Nordic knack of picking up languages and was so proficient in Japanese that she was able to run the office and actually deal with enquiries in Osaka-*ben*. Our early clients in Osaka included Mitsubishi Heavy Industries, Asahi Kasei Chemicals, Nestlé and Sumitomo Heavy Industries.

*   *   *   *   *

Towards the end of 1967 the Arsenal Football Club sent a team to tour Japan. This was an exciting occurrence in Japanese soccer circles, since the Match of the Day had been shown regularly on Japanese TV for several years and the fans knew the stars of the Football League better than I did. Chris McDonald held an important position of influence with the Japanese F.A. and was asked to look after the social side of their visit as well as many technical and logistic matters. He asked me to help him and in fact we ended up shepherding this fine bunch of young men around Japan for the best part of two weeks. It turned out to be an interesting experience, not only as far as the football was concerned, but also from the cross-cultural point of view.

The officials in charge of the team were Bertie Mee, one of the more intellectual of British football managers, Bob Wall, the long-time Arsenal club secretary, Don Howe, coach, and Leslie Taylor of Hunting Lambert, who handled the travel arrangements. Frank McLintock was the team captain, just having superseded Terry Neale, who was also in the party. Other famous figures were George Graham (later Arsenal manager) . Bob Wilson, goalkeeper, (now BBC commentator) and well-known players such as Peter Storey, Bob McNab,

Geordie Armstrong, Peter Radford, Peter Simpson and so on. Sir Stanley Rous, the President of FIFA, also accompanied the group. The securing of such a prestigious club to tour and the presence of Sir Stanley, the world's most important football official, represented a great public relations success for the J.F.A., who bent over backwards to see that everything ran smoothly. There were well-organised training sessions, a reception at the Embassy, visits to shrines and temples, introductions to top *sumo* wrestlers, a musical evening in our home in Shoto, (McLintock and George Graham were great crooners) and a lavish, quasi-all-night party at Chris McDonald's home in Den-en-chofu. On the field Arsenal scored in the first 10 seconds of their first match against Japan, though the final result was a hotly-contested 3-1. Japan had a really good team at that time, spear-headed by their celebrated centre-forward Kamamoto, who could have walked into any English First Division team. Arsenal were in fact interested in buying him, but he politely declined the opportunity to play in the United Kingdom.

The party at McDonald's turned out to be a memorable event. Chris had invited not only a dozen or so very attractive Japanese girls, but also four or five top *sumo* wrestlers in their splendid dark blue kimonos. Several of these men weighed over 150 kilograms – about twice the bulk of the average Arsenal footballer. They were invariably dignified and withdrawn, with their splendid blue-black top-knots, hooded eyes and ham-like hands. They could not, of course, speak any English, but as the evening progressed they established a friendly dig-in-the-ribs rapport with some of the more outgoing Arsenal players - Neale, Graham and McLintock in particular – and downed a considerable number of beers with them. Under a certain amount of intoxicating influence, one or two of the Arsenal players began to fancy their chances of throwing one of these sumo wrestlers in man-to-man combat. The sumo champions laughingly refused contact, but in the end one of them – Yama we called him – agreed to have a few friendly tussles with some of the footballers. A space was cleared in one of Chris's large *tatami*-mat rooms and some good natured jousting began. One or two of the bigger Arsenal players – Furnell and Radford I believe they were – were gently deposited on the tatami after two or three minutes mock struggle by Yama. Finally Frank McLintock, the not-so-heavy but certainly athletic club captain, strode forward to take up the challenge. After what seemed to be a fierce encounter, Yama was suddenly thrown backwards down on the mat, defeated by a jubilant Frank. The Arsenal players cheered their skipper to the rafters, even Bertie Mee looked impressed. Chris and I tried to keep straight faces, it was harder for us than for the impassive blue-clad row of wrestlers looking on. Yama was a warm-hearted gentleman of Japan.

We were eating Japanese style, sitting on *tatami* – the house had big square rooms; about twenty of us surrounded one particular table covered in dishes of all kinds, including mountains of fruit. By midnight the main dishes had been consumed – one had to marvel at the capacity of some of the wrestlers. Rice dishes would be piled one foot high for them and would quickly disappear. Finally only bananas were left and most of us had one. Everyone sat around quietly for awhile, drinking beer and *sake*. Then Takanohana, the most celebrated Sumo champion present, picked up the big bowl containing twenty-one bananas and went round the table to each guest in turn offering the fruit. He knew the operative word in English. To each person he said "Banana?". In each case the answer was a polite "No thank you." Takanohana deposited the bowl on the table again, contemplated the scene for another 30 seconds, then ate the 21 bananas in one minute flat.

*   *   *   *   *

A few days later Arsenal were due to play an All-Japan XI in the city of Fukuoka on the island of Kyushu. The team was housed in a local hotel. Hotel staff in Fukuoka are much less used to foreigners than their counterparts in Tokyo or Kobe and there was some nervousness about the preparation of food for the footballers. Arsenal, in fact, had a set, pre-match meal which apparently had been prescribed 30 years earlier in the days of George Allison and which never varied. It consisted of 2 courses: a thin beefsteak and chips, followed by rice pudding. This meal had to be consumed exactly 3 hours before kick-off. The match was scheduled to begin at 2 pm so everyone assembled in the dining room just before 11 in the morning. A large hotel kitchen was adjacent to the dining room and we could see a dozen or so cooks scampering around through the open hatches. The beefsteak and chips appeared in fine style and were devoured by the players among murmurs of appreciation. The empty plates were removed by the hotel staff and replaced by a large bowl of rice for each player. Japanese eat their rice boiled, white and sticky with no additives of any kind. That is how they like it – hot, pure and tasteless. There was some perplexity, then howls of protest from the Arsenal team: "This is not rice pudding!" One of the assistant managers came running along to see what could possibly be wrong with the beautiful rice and Chris McDonald tried to explain to him, in fluent Japanese, the concept of English Rice Pudding. Now "pudding" is not a word that translates readily into Japanese. When they use the English word themselves (sometimes they write it "puddy") they could mean trifle or cake or almost anything sweet. Rice pudding in Japan is simply an alien concept. They would no more pour milk, cream and sugar on rice than we would put jam on chips. Chris did very well explaining what was required and the assistant manager trotted off to the kitchen to issue further directives. When he came back, it was with bad news. The chefs had refused outright to cook the rice with milk and sugar. Chris reasoned with him, but distressed though he was, he was powerless to sway the cooks: they were adamant. The fact is that Japanese people attach much more symbolism to rice than English people do to fish and chips. Both are national institutions, but good Japanese – and professional cooks at that – do not tamper with a 2000-year-old culinary tradition, with all its religious implications, for the sake of a miserable football match against uncouth barbarians.

Bertie Mee and Don Howe were now glancing nervously at their watches, for the holy three-hour digestion period had now been eroded by a good 20 minutes. Mee muttered something about cancelling the match, which sent the 4 JFA officials present into transports of untrammelled panic as the stadium was already half full and people were still pouring through the gates. The JFA men dragged in the hotel manager and reported to him the seriousness of the situation. He rushed off to the kitchen with a worried look on his face; he looked even more careworn when he came back: he was not able to budge the chefs.

By now we had all the ingredients of an *impasse*. No rice pudding, no match, said Bertie. Loss of face on the English side now equalled that of the faithful-to-tradition Japanese cooks. It was a lose-lose situation, especially for the JFA. "How about some nice bananas?" suggested the JFA vice-president. Don Howe laughed derisively. All the Japanese tittered, too, only in Japan tittering means extreme embarrassment. It was nearly half past eleven.

Chris found the way out. Rushing to the kitchen he grabbed bowls of sugar and jugs of milk. The rice was still there, luke-warm in the bowls on the table. Everybody, Bob Wall and me included, began to spoon sugar and pour milk into the rice bowls. The players stirred it all up with the chopsticks, the JFA men fetched spoons and soon there was pleasant chomping all round. In the middle of all this I happened to glance towards the kitchen. There, through the open hatches, were lined up all the chefs and their staff, arms defiantly folded, watching, open-mouthed, the sacreligious, unhallowed ritual. Arsenal won 1-0.

The Japanese people are the most hospitable one can find anywhere, moreover they are inordinately kind and thoughtful in arranging outings, meals and gifts for visitors from abroad. The problem for Japanese who do not live in Tokyo, Kobe or Kyoto is that they are simply unused to foreigners and their ways. This was certainly the case in the 1960s, especially when we went to the smaller towns. The YCAC football team went on tour to such places as Kofu, Shizuoka and Shimizu, where we were accommodated overnight and fed several meals. In Kofu we ordered tea, bacon and eggs for fifteen people at eight in the morning. When we came to the table at the appointed hour the tea was green, the eggs unbroken and the bacon piled up raw in generous three-inch heaps beside each plate. In Shimizu, at a post-match cocktail party, because one of our group mentioned Scotch, each member was quickly served a tumbler full of whisky, neat. Some of our hosts, who were manfully bracing themselves to accompany us drinking nearly half a pint of neat Scotch, were visibly relieved when we told them we preferred *sake*. The lasting memory of such tours was certainly the painstaking diligence and courtesy of our hosts, as well as the gentlemanly conduct and sense of fair play on the field. There are no soccer hooligans in Japan, either on the pitch or on the terraces. Cheering or shouting is very restricted. Good play, on the part of either side, is generally appreciated by hand-clapping. Were it still so in the rest of the world!

*   *   *   *   *

The next British football team to visit Japan was Coventry City. Again Chris McDonald and I accompanied the players and officials and I became better acquainted with Sir Stanley Rous, who was usually able to coordinate his FIFA duties in Japan with the visit of an English team. Sir Stanley was arguably Britain's best known after-dinner speaker at the time – certainly in sporting circles – and we were regaled evening after evening with a seemingly limitless supply of anecdotes. Sir Stanley told me that he had all his stories nicely filed at home under separate categories. If you said "elephants" or "mothers-in-law", he could pull out half a dozen anytime, usually with a sporting twist. A few years later Sir Stanley was to inaugurate one of our schools in London. He told our audience:

"One of the courses here is called RLC 2000. I don't know if this means there are 2000 words to learn, or if the course costs £2000, or if it will take you 2000 years to learn the language."

I went on with Coventry City F.C. to Bangkok, where I was still trying to get my Berlitz colleague Pierre Conhagen to open a school. He had been trying for 2 years and was still collecting permits. He never did open. Coventry played Thailand and won, in a triangular contest which included Santos of Brazil. I acted as interpreter for the Brazilians who were remarkably ungifted language-wise and were having all kinds of misunderstandings with the Thai football authorities. None of the officials spoke anything but Portuguese. Among the players only Pele – the most famous of all – could speak English. He was grateful for my help in Portuguese and we became quite friendly. In spite of his great fame, he is straightforward and humble, always seeking to help others. We talked about football greats – Stanley Matthews, Bobby Charlton, Garrincha, Beckenbauer – we shared many memories – not least the ecstasy of Brazil's first World Cup victory in Sweden in 1958.

*   *   *   *   *

By the end of 1967, both the Akasaka and Osaka schools were full most of the time, so we had to expand. This was easy to achieve in Osaka as the Hanshin Hotel had adjacent space available and we simply continued partitioning till we had about 20 rooms. In Akasaka this was not possible; in any case we were now interested in above-ground locations and wished to reach other parts of town as a large number of our students were businessmen from the Yuraku-cho, Ginza and Ohtemachi districts. After some hunting around, I rented part of the 12th floor of the Yuraku-cho building overlooking the station. Mitsubishi were the landlords and, though inflexible as to rent, they were quite helpful in all other ways. Again we furnished luxuriously – we had such good cash flow by now that this posed no problem. As the address was prestigious, we moved headquarters to Yuraku-cho. The book-keeping department moved into the new building. Eleanor Kalmanasch, Jean Piton's former secretary in Montreal, was recruited as an administrative assistant and Geoff Mason was made manager of the Akasaka school.

In the Yuraku-cho building my father and Kitamura shared an office overlooking the railway track emanating from Tokyo Station, a few hundred yards to the left. Along this line sped the famous blue-and-white *shinkansen* bullet trains to Osaka – one departure every 20 minutes. As my father had spent 45 years of his life along the London-Wigan-Glasgow track, this daily spectacle had a comforting familiarity about it. Some of the goods traffic he handled had ended up at Wigan Pier (it really exists, though many English people think it is fictional.) It was a long Road from Wigan Pier to Tokyo, for my father, as well as myself.

Six months later we opened a branch in Shibuya, which is actually the geographical centre of the Tokyo Metropolitan Area. Sandro d'Addario, the ebullient Italian social organizer from London, arrived to manage Shibuya, where we constructed 20 classrooms. It was ground floor with a huge plate glass window on the street. There were of course a lot of walk-ins and our public changed slightly. Although there were still a lot of businessmen, well-to-do Shibuya housewives and a substantial number of students between high school and university enrolled for longish courses, taking 4-6 hours a week in the main. It was almost unknown for a Japanese to take just one or two hours a week, as had often been the case in Britain. Languages were taken very seriously indeed, though progress was not always rapid.

For the English staff in Shibuya I recruited three outstanding English teachers – Paul Snowden, Frank Moorhead and Michael Buckley. All stayed on in Japan for many years and eventually obtained influential positions in Japanese universities and other institutions of higher learning. The landlord in Shibuya – it was in the Asia Building near Shibuya station – was a benign, one-armed, old-fashioned Japanese called Endo. He could speak no English, but communicated very well with my mother, who could speak no Japanese. When he heard that my parents had to move from where they were staying, he promptly built them a ground floor flat just behind the Shibuya school! This type of spontaneous generosity and consideration is observable very frequently in Japan. Though a frugal and thrifty people, they can be incredibly altruistic and considerate towards someone they like and trust.

We opened further schools in Kobe and Yokohama, again with noticeably friendly landlords. Ed Wilton ran the Kobe school as well as Osaka– he had excellent connections there as he lived in the city centre. Nestle in particular became one of our big clients, though he was able to sign sizeable contracts with Japanese giants such as Mitsubishi Heavy, Kobe Steel and Kawasaki.

Ken Crossley, a Mancunian, who had taught for me in London, Helsinki and Lisbon, was appointed manager of the Yokohama school.

*   *   *   *   *

Although we taught several European languages as well as Chinese and Korean in our schools, about ninety per cent of our lessons were in English or Japanese. In Akasaka at times the number of expatriates learning Japanese was greater than the number of Japanese learning English. As my wife and I both did some teaching, we met a lot of people both from the expatriate and Japanese communities. Teacher-student relationships often become very close and this is especially valuable for teachers of English in Japan, since they have opportunities to penetrate Japanese social life and make friends, which would be denied to people in other professions. We soon developed a wide circle of Japanese friends from many walks of life. I taught Hanae Mori, who later became a world-famous fashion designer. Jane taught Mrs Tange, wife of the country's leading architect. Shoto is a very Japanese area; it also has one of the best kindergartens in Japan – Shoto-yo-chen. Caroline and Richard were enrolled there as soon as they were old enough. All the other children were Japanese; after 6 weeks in this play-school both our children understood and spoke the language. After 3 months they dominated our TV set, watching endless children's programmes in Japanese . Tokyo, even in those days, had about 17 channels. Caroline and Richard, who conversed rapidly (and incomprehensibly to us) with Haruko, soon developed two personalities (each) – a soft-spoken, courteous, deferential one for Japanese elders and a much louder, outspoken, uninhibited one for their parents and other English speakers. Caroline, now thirty, has retained both personalities up to the present day. I prefer the Japanese one, but it has the wrong face! A tallish girl, she shrinks a couple of centimetres when she switches to Japanese. It is a lovely language and a wonderful attribute. The headmistress, a well-known personality named Mrs Hayashi, welcomed Caroline back to visit the school many years later. We laughingly recalled the two blond heads, among dozens of black ones, bobbing up and down in coordinated dance routines on Parents' Days.

*   *   *   *   *

My recollections and impressions of the enigmatic Japanese people would fill a book on their own. I never ceased to be intrigued by how their behaviour varied so much from European or American. One day in Akasaka we had a visit by the tax inspector – he looked pretty grim and business-like, so that Misses Sato and Yamane panicked as they scrambled to produce the necessary papers. They begged for him to wait for Mr Shirai – one of our assistant accountants – who quickly came over from Yuraku-cho. He patiently dug out the vouchers that the tax-man wished to see. Suddenly, there was a problem – our books showed that Akasaka rents were 850.000 yen – paid out each month, but we had receipts from Kowa for only 650.000. How could this be? Shirai looked perplexed and took down more files. He ploughed through voucher after voucher, receipt after receipt. The tax-man paced up and down. Just before lunch Shirai confessed that the missing documentation must have been taken over to Yuraku-cho. But that was a different tax district, snapped the inspector courteously, the papers should be kept in Akasaka. An apologetic Shirai rushed off in a taxi to Yuraku-cho.

He was away a long time. Miss Sato made the tax man nice sandwiches and Mr Okada, one of our teachers, said he believed one of his cousins had studied at Waseda with one of the inspector's cousins. That seemed to mollify the tax man for a while. About 3 o'clock a sweaty Shirai came back with reports of traffic jams, but no receipts. They must be somewhere in the building, he said. About 4 o'clock, stupid old me figured it out. I ran into their room to throw light on the whole affair.

"Shirai-san" I exclaimed, "the 200.000 yen difference – it's my rent. Remember, the school pays it and then deducts it from my salary!"

Shirai slapped his forehead like a Polish pitman.

"Ah, so!"

He soon found the receipts in the RDL file and the tax man scrutinized them one by one. Then they fiddled with their abacuses a bit, and got it right. Add 200.000 to 650.000 and you get 850.000. It was ten to five. The inspector put his papers back into his brief-case, as I wondered how Shirai could be so thick. After all, I had other things to think about. It was so **obvious**. What on earth were we paying him for?

After Miss Sato had bowed out the inspector, five minutes later, I went to Shirai and looked him in the eye, or tried to. He was tying one of his shoelaces.

"Shirai-san, how could you have missed it? I mean..."

He looked at my neck, spoke patiently to me:

"Lewis-sensei, these tax people, they come to visit us, we never know when they come. But we know when they go home! 5 o'clock. They go home at 5 o'clock, whether they have seen all our papers or not..."

One more lesson learnt in the East.

*　　*　　*　　*　　*

Other little cameos come to mind: the night when Nakata, my friend from the *Yomiuri Shimbun,* came knocking on our Shoto door at midnight asking me to write a letter for the newspaper to Ho Chi Minh. The *Yomiuri* had been offered a slight possibility of placing a correspondent in Hanoi about the time of the TET offensive and they had been told that a respectful letter in French to the Vietnamese leader might clinch the deal. I had not written a letter in French for 5 years, let alone to Ho Chi Minh and it was 3 in the morning when we had finished the second draft. Nakata's French was about as good as my Japanese, so the letter finished up with a lot of English loan-words in it. Apparently the *Yomiuri* didn't want the French to know about it, hence the midnight call. It was no surprise to me when they didn't get to Hanoi, anyway.

Mishima's *hara-kiri* shook us all, Japanese and *gaijin* alike. He was a wonderful writer – a candidate for the Nobel Prize – the ritual suicides and lopping off of heads jolted us with the realisation that loss of face for a Japanese, especially an eminent one, can still produce this reaction. A few weeks later, at the Swedish Embassy, Jane and I met Yasunari Kawabata, an elderly Japanese poet who had in fact received the Nobel Prize for Literature in 1968. It was not long before also this smiling, humble genius was to take his own life, though in a less dramatic manner. Kawabata, when accepting the Prize, had delivered a mystical speech full of readings in Japanese from mediaeval Zen poetry. He was the epitome of Japan's traditional mystics. Kenzaburo Oe, the Oriental novelist who won the Nobel Prize in 1994, gave his speech in English and French, showing an impressive universalism, though he, too, dwelt upon Japan's "ambiguity" – the clash of technological westernisation and traditional, inward-looking, mystical culture.

*   *   *   *   *

By 1969 we were working with most of Japan's large companies, either in Tokyo or the Kansai area. The Japanese banks and securities companies were preparing to launch an attack on Europe, especially Britain, where Sony and other forward looking firms had already established themselves. I met regularly with the training and personnel managers of such companies as Kanebo, Marubeni, Asahi Kasei, Toshiba, Sanyo, Nomura and various divisions of the Fuji, Sumitomo, Mitsubishi and Mitsui conglomerates. Some of these personnel managers had only very vague notions of the problems and implications of language training. In this respect they were as woolly as their British counterparts, though in their case they realised the importance of language proficiency. Others were very perspicacious indeed and made elaborate plans for improving the overall level of English throughout their company or group. One morning I was visited by three training managers from Hitachi who asked me, in all seriousness, to put together a 15-year English programme for future overseas managers! This was indeed forward planning. As I outlined some of the problems in making such long-range plans, with their attendant difficulties of variable human factors, forecasting of potential and achievement and so on, they explained to me why it was important for them. They had 50 young men, all aged 25, whom they had selected as potential future overseas managers. They had planned the various aspects of management training and development of these men, within the framework of the usual Japanese job rotation system, until they would be 40 – the youngest age that a Japanese company will bestow overseas manager status on an employee. Accordingly they wished for a "language course" which would culminate just in time (JIT) for the candidates to achieve the fluency required for the fulfilment of their tasks. This programme, in their view, could be intertwined in the management development syllabus, so that progress would be steady, periodically monitored, and systematically recorded. I pointed out that even if each student took 750 hours' instruction (normally enough for reasonable fluency) this would work out at only one hour a week – useless for visible advancement; that it was almost impossible to maintain motivation (often vital for success) over a period of 15 years; that our teachers, not used to lifetime employment in a foreign company, would come and go every two years or so, retire or perhaps die; that each student might get through 40 or 50 instructors in the period; what if a candidate flagged after 7 years? Would he be removed from the programme? These were only a few of the drawbacks of such a scheme. Learning a language in my eyes is an intensive task, one which will dominate every other activity while it is being tackled. If you are learning Greenlandic, then you should speak, hear, think, eat, drink and live Greenlandic right down to fishing through the ice and eating whale blubber. Anything less than 6 hours a week is a waste of time and even this minimum frequency requires you to be self-disciplined and well-organized, spending more time reviewing the material on your own than you spend in the classroom. Most people are not able to do this. Gifted linguists are exceptions – most people are not gifted linguists. Many Japanese show that they can commit an enormous amount of material, in English, to memory. This is a great help and I have seen some impressive performances by people who use this trick. Yet, lack of flexibility of expression or reaction to others' responses, are obvious problems.

I eventually planned a 3-year syllabus for my Hitachi friends and this was well under way when I left Japan. Those young managers of 25 will now be well over 50. I often wonder how they got on.

*　　*　　*　　*　　*

By 1970 the Berlitz Schools of Japan were firmly established as the market leader in executive language training. Our connections with Japanese industry were secure and in many companies in considerable depth. We were no longer merely giving language lessons; we were formulating and organising entire language programmes for an impressive selection of large companies and conglomerates. These ancillary services involved in planning, adjusting and report writing swallowed up many of the leading teachers I had brought out to Japan. Many of them later secured promising careers in Japanese business and university circles.

The need for staff expansion drove me to Australia and New Zealand to recruit teachers with Downunder accents. It was the beginning of the period when both Japan and Australasia started to realize that they, to some extent, shared a common economic future. This has since become a visible reality, but even at the end of the 60s Australian schools were beginning to teach Japanese and I had no shortage of applicants when I interviewed in Sydney, Melbourne and Auckland. I chose about 35 candidates, who moved to Tokyo over the next 3 months. It was my first trip to Australia and New Zealand and my impression of both countries was unquestionably very positive. New Zealand and her people resemble the British Isles more than Australia does, but I was astonished to see how British the Australians have remained despite 200 years of separation, considerable Asian and south European immigration and no small degree of Americanisation in business. Never discount the bonds created by cricket, rugby, lawn bowls, strong tea, warm bitter and fish and chips.

In Melbourne I met up with my old friend Les Perkins, who had just returned home. This most humorous of men showed me the city's principal attraction, the Botanical Garden. Les, besides being a first-rate executive, had a deep and lasting passion for plants and flowers. In New Zealand I was able to track down that golden-haired genius and greatest outside-half of all time, Cecil Mountford. He had won every Rugby League honour there was in the UK and had captained Wigan in the year they won the Challenge Cup at Wembley in 1949. I also had a long chat over the phone with the other star of that team, Brian Nordgren, now a successful barrister in Hamilton.

On the way back to Japan I was able to take a short Pacific tour which included the islands of Fiji, Tahiti and Hawaii. The air over large parts of the Pacific Ocean must be the freshest and least polluted anywhere, contrasting strikingly with the Tokyo smog awaiting me on my return. Jane and Mathias Wallen rendezvous-ed with me in Honolulu on the last leg and we had four lovely days apart from Jane nearly killing herself while surfing.

*   *   *   *   *

Back at Berlitz HQ, things had changed. Crowell Collier Macmillan, the giant publishing group, had bought the company lock stock and barrel.

Robert Strumpen-Darrie, though beseeched by many of his ageing colleagues to resist the temptation, decided to divest himself of his shares for a reported 6 million dollars. In the turmoil which followed, a lot of Berlitz old-timers lost their jobs, most importantly Charles Berlitz himself, the surviving grandson of the founder. CCM and Charles were subsequently locked in a protracted legal battle, which apparently he ended up winning, but the lawyers took all the money anyway. Strumpen-Darrie stayed on a couple of years as president, but he was no longer the decision-maker.

My own position was not threatened, as Berlitz East Asia had become the most profitable part of the Berlitz empire. Geese that lay golden eggs have a few more Christmases to go. From my own point of view, however, an indefinite stay in Japan no longer appealed to me. Jane and I were not tired of Japan – on the contrary, we were really enjoying it and have returned there many times since. Our son, David, born in Tokyo in March 1969, was being happily whisked round the streets of Shibuya by my father (in a push chair). Caroline and Richard spoke Japanese like natives, dealt with plumbers for us and were fully integrated in their school activities. I felt, however, that their education would be best carried out in their own country. As a family we are not the type that packs their children off to boarding school, to see them only 3 times a year. When our sons played cricket, we wanted to be there to watch. Also I felt less close to the company, now that Strumpen-Darrie and Charles were gone. It wasn't the old folksy Berlitz any more. The exigent monthly reporting system of a big American company began to bite. I accepted it of course and did what I had to do, but the less paper I have to push around in life, the better. CCM were quite reasonable in many ways, though my initial terms of contract were no longer honoured. I had made quite a lot of money by my standards and I felt I could well move on after my 5 years were up. Besides, I had a plan.

I had noticed that Japanese businessmen in Tokyo were a pressured lot. They would arrive late for their lessons, sweating after an hour and a half in the underground, harassed and unreceptive to language tuition for the first hour or so. When they began to settle down, telephone calls from their office would disturb their concentration and start them thinking in Japanese again. It is true that many of them studied 8-9 hours a day, for a full month or more, but the results were rarely commensurate with the effort involved. They needed to be **buried** in English, away from their Japanese-speaking wives, kids and colleagues, far from their tinkling telephones. I had a plan to bury them.

*   *   *   *   *

In the summer of 1970 we took a long-awaited home leave in England. After a few days I bought a copy of "Country Life" and looked at the pictures of estates currently for sale in the southern part of the country. What I sought was a beautiful house, tranquil and in a rustic setting, which would provide an oasis of Englishness for foreign executives to study in. After seeing various properties, I came across Riversdown House, a 14th century Mediaeval Hall which combined all the factors I was looking for – age-old beauty, peace and quiet, a cosy oak-beamed interior, forty acres of land and forest, completely isolated (3 miles from the nearest village) yet only 55 minutes from Heathrow airport. Besides the main house there were two labourers' cottages, various outbuildings, including a stable block, a rose garden, a grass tennis court and a swimming pool. The large chicken shed I earmarked for 20 classrooms; the 30 acres of pasture would do for a golf course. The then owner, Tom Farmiloe, was having some trouble divesting himself of the property for £40,000 freehold. I gave him the asking price on the spot.

*   *   *   *   *

The last year in Japan passed quickly. Strumpen-Darrie resigned early and my old friend Rafael Alberola became President of Berlitz. He kept this post for several years, but his heart was no longer in it and, like me, he eventually left the company to go into business on his own.

Not long after CCM had acquired the American half of Berlitz, they began to negotiate with Roger Montfort for the rights to the name in the rest of the world. This turned out to be a very complicated matter. As I have described earlier, Paris did not own most of Europe's Berlitz schools, which were largely franchised, as mine in Finland, Norway and Portugal had been. The Americans were eventually able to settle with Montfort for the 9 schools owned by the Société Internationale (for a reported $2 million), but they acquired only the royalties as far as the remaining 200-odd schools were concerned. The CCM plan was to buy the other schools one by one.

It was an attitude typical of many medium-size to large US corporations. They had bought the Berlitz name, now they wanted the biggest possible piece of the action. They did not want anybody else fooling around with the name and clearly did not trust the motley European collection of old Berlitz fuddy-duddies. They began to buy. One or two small schools were purchased, but when the first big one – Frankfurt – came up, they found they were talking about half a million dollars and up. With other huge schools like Barcelona, Hamburg and Cologne around, the ultimate buying price promised to be astronomical.

At this juncture, CCM took what I have always believed to be a very unwise step. They gave all franchised schools one year's notice of their concessions. Albert Schwarz, the owner of the Frankfurt school, promptly called a meeting of the franchisees to make Plan B. This ultimately resulted in the formation of the *Société Internationale des Ecoles* INLINGUA, headquartered in Bern. It was a franchise organisation resembling in many ways the old Berlitz structure. My old colleague, David Willey, was given the task of writing the Inlingua English books One and Two and the supervision of other materials. Schwarz showed considerable ability in setting up the new *société* which overnight became the largest language teaching organisation in the world, simultaneously depleting the Berlitz empire by approximately 200 outlets. CCM had obviously expected many of the European schools to negotiate favourable selling prices. In the event, nearly all of them plumped for Inlingua. My old schools in Finland, Norway and Portugal all did. Of the big schools, only Milan stayed with Berlitz.

CCM probably did some fuming, but they had certainly shown little foresight. The 12 months' notice gave Schwarz and Co one year to make their plan. By the time the franchises expired, Inlingua was well organised. To achieve their former size, Berlitz was faced with the task of setting up new schools in over a hundred and fifty cities – places where Inlingua rivals were already entrenched. The fight continues today – truly a Thirty Years War.

* * * * *

I kept out of such squabbles as I had friends on both sides. We made our preparations to leave Japan, saying *sayonara* to many friends, fitting in a tour of Shikoku and arranging for the shipping of our furniture and new Toyota Autoglide to Europe.

The night before our departure we were invited to dinner at Togu Palace by the Crown Prince and Crown Princess. It was a private family affair with their three children romping around as usual as we ate. Princess Michiko had always insisted that they should be brought up in the most natural manner possible – answering telephones, making a noise as they played, talking to and teasing guests as all children do. At that time the eldest – Prince Hiro – was seven. Aya was an exuberant 5-year old and Sayako, shy and tranquil at one. It is probably hard for many to imagine how natural and affectionate this family scene was. There we were in a far-off land, sitting among the heirs to the mighty Chrysanthemum Throne, yet one simply felt at home. It was a long road from Wigan Pier, but family is family everywhere.

It was snowing heavily as we left. There was a minute's delay as the chauffeur brought the car, and Akihito and Michiko, kimono-clad, stood snow-covered, waving gently as we drove away. It kind of sticks in your memory.

Chapter 15

Riversdown – The Paradise

We arrived in Portsmouth on the morning of June 6th, 1971, the anniversary of D-Day, a recollection not entirely devoid of symbolism. The joint Anglo-American-Japanese invasion force consisted of Jane and myself, Caroline, aged 6, Richard, 5, David, 2, and Fumiko our maid. Our equipment filled six suitcases, all in the boot of our assault vehicle, a 1970 Toyota Crown Autoglide. Enemy resistance (customs) was stiff at first and there were some critical moments when I began to doubt our ability to establish a beachhead. It seemed that ours was the first Autoglide to enter the UK and as such had not been successfully identified by the spotters. It was clearly an Intelligence failure again and the enemy was in disarray. No specifications available! No specifications meant no identification, which meant no permit of entry. As the battle raged, reinforcements were brought up -our shrinking beachhead was surrounded by navy blue uniforms. Several high-ranking officers – probably generals – were involved. Behind us, our landing craft spouted more and more suntanned troops who fanned out towards other beaches, leaving our platoon to its fate.

Late in the morning it transpired that no specification, which precluded classification, meant no entry, but no capture either. If it could not be classified it could not be confiscated, as the enemy's ledgers did not contain the appropriate columns to enter it up. So the issue was fudged and a "temporary" breakthrough was allowed, authenticated by a "provisional" document which, as far as I recall, lasted another five years (the life of the car).

And so we advanced on the capital, the navy-clad figures breaking ranks to let us through. It was the **old** capital (Winchester, 901 A.D.) we had set our sights on, only 15 miles away. We encountered no further resistance as we rolled on through rural countryside basking in golden sunshine. Our maps were old and many of the road signs seemed to have been swivelled by the enemy, but we reached our objective, Riversdown, around high noon. It had been abandoned by the opposing forces and we took it in less than an hour, when I found the key. It was a Saturday and by the time we had unpacked our equipment and reconnoitred the terrain the local shops in the village three miles away had closed. It looked like our troops would go unfed until Monday.

It was a memorable, unreal weekend. We had no furniture, no food, no neighbours and twenty rooms to sleep in. The resident gardener had gone away for the weekend; we couldn't turn the water on. We managed to turn on the electricity after a few hours spent locating the mediaeval fuse box tucked in among the rafters. Our crates from Japan had arrived and sat, monolithic, in the tractor shed. We could not open them. We drove around a few miles and found a Garden Centre, where we bought mattresses and plums. In the warm weather we managed without blankets and used suitcases and teddy bears as pillows. At night it was so quiet the children could not sleep.

On Sunday afternoon the vicar came round as I was shaving in the bird bath. He brought a cyclo-styled information sheet on the history of Warnford church, but no loaves or fishes. As we could not make tea, he did not stay long. Later in the day the village policeman, Bill, arrived with a big smile and two dozen eggs. He has been bringing them ever since.

Though temporarily devoid of human beings, Riversdown was by no means unpopulated. Three pairs of pigeons had permanent residence in the cypresses; innumerable pheasants, secure in out-of-season June, gobbled up seeds in the gardens; five thousand chickens squawked and defecated in the chicken shed. We peeped in at one stage, but 30 seconds were enough. Mrs Benham, the "chicken woman" returned Sunday evening from an outing to Birmingham. Judge, the gardener, rolled up in time to say hello before he rushed off to the "Fox and Hounds" for opening time.

Riversdown House, one of the oldest and most beautiful dwellings in central Hampshire, was built in 1341 and is classified as a Mediaeval Great Hall. It stands on an elaborate, timbered frame and many of the original oak beams are exposed throughout the construction. The building is tent-shaped and the curvature of the blackened beams in the third-storey bedrooms indicate that they were taken from the hull of a ship of the period. The outer walls, originally of mud and wattle (still visible in parts of the interior), are now encased in old, weathered brick. The inner partitions, bookshelves, heavy doors and door frames are of the same pale, local oak. The steeply-sloping roof, with its tall Tudor-like chimneys, is of old red tiles, many of them now moss-green and eaten into on the garden side by a huge wistaria tree. The garden itself, planned over centuries, has flowers at all times of the year, sculpted hedges with lovers' seats, a daffodil patch, an ancient grass tennis court and an unused fish pond. The trees, many of them hundreds of years old, are exceptional in their variety. Besides the many oaks, elms, ash and beeches, there are Japanese cherry trees, a towering English yew and even a fig tree. The perimeter of the garden is defined by a ring of magnificent, velvety cypresses, home of the turtle doves, wandering pheasants and numerous smaller birds, not to mention resident squirrels and hedgehogs. Beside the tennis court is a beautiful tea-house-shaped construction in dark red brick with a dignified clock tower spire of weathered copper – now pale turquoise. We called this bulding the tennis pavilion for several years until study of old documents revealed that it had been built as a piggery.

Besides the Manor House, the Riversdown estate consists of the Old Stables (now a dwelling), two cottages, a chicken shed, a huge garage-cum-utility building, various out-houses including a fruit shed, coal lockers, wood stores, pump room, saw shed, and gardener's sheds. In the pump room there is an ancient well, nearly 100 metres deep, from which the estate obtains its drinking water (there is a fast-flowing underground river). The water, which we also bottle, is the purest imaginable. Riversdown originally had 400 acres of land and in mediaeval times collected tithes and duties from the numerous dwellings in the area. At the time I purchased it, only 40 acres were left – almost entirely pasture and woodland. The big field at the front commands views over miles of rolling countryside. A Roman house stood in the middle of it and evidences of the drainage system are seen in a deep, triangular depression round the location of the site. A copper beech tree – the only one at Riversdown – was planted there about 1955.

It was in such a beautiful and historical setting that we began to make plans, on the morning of Monday the 8th of June 1971, to convert this sleepy rural seat into a very special, hopefully unique, residential school of languages. We assembled the whole staff – George Judge, head gardener, Gladys Benham, chicken woman, Fumiko Kawahara, au pair. George and Gladys were already in their sixties – Judge announced his retirement on Monday night. Mrs Benham, faithful soul, stayed on for many a year, though we soon deprived her of her beloved feathered friends. Looking after 5000 chickens was no mean task. They were bought in at a few weeks old and reared for four months before being sent off for slaughter and exchanged for another batch of 5000. The treadmill chores of feeding such a community and cleaning their temporary habitat were ones that only a patient, conscientious, bird-loving character like Gladys Benham could go through with. Her remuneration was pitiful, her holidays severely restricted. When I discovered that the total profit for the Riversdown estate varied between £700 and £900 per annum, I announced that the current batch of chicks would be the last. With school fees estimated at around £500 per month, I intended to fill the chicken shed with chickens of an entirely new strain and nationality.

There were many things to be done. Gladys was dispatched to announce the bad news to the fowls, Judge was told to contact local farmers to ask who wanted free hay (the grass in the big field now stood five feet high); Fumiko, Caroline and Richard were instructed to play in the garden and keep speaking Japanese to each other; Jane autoglided to West Meon to organize food and other supplies; I phoned electricians, plumbers, carpenters and drapers to set in motion the various repairs and embellishments that required attention. David staggered around the grounds in a daze.

I will not bore my reader with a detailed description of the numerous measures and developments which occupied the summer months. In general things went well and the rather felicitous summer weather of 1971 was an unexpected bonus. We saw off the chickens and Mrs Benham began the onerous, protracted chore of ridding their dwelling of all signs of previous occupation. Various local experts offered their advice on methods of cleaning and eliminating the odour of chicken dung. The most effective method in the end proved to be scrubbing, which, fortunately, Mrs Benham was good at. The long grass in the big field was cut and removed by a grateful farmer and we could at last see our borders. The pump was fixed and we had water from our underground river. A new boiler and septic tank assured us of better services for our hypothetical students. Judge served out his month with a minimum of enthusiasm and effort and we engaged a lively local 40-year old bachelor called Bob who soon transformed the garden into something pleasing to the eye. We decided to discontinue the kitchen garden, as its yield would be insignificant when faced with the prospect of feeding 40 people a day. This proved to be a good decision, as the gardener was able to concentrate on the rose beds, borders, lawns, hedges and general beautification of the property, while vegetables could be obtained locally at a reasonable price.

The local suppliers of provisions were, in the early days, less than helpful. Riversdown is very isolated – three miles from Warnford and four from West Meon. West Meon had two grocers (now only one), Warnford had a small shop attached to the Post Office selling fish-fingers. They just did not deliver to strangers – not bread, nor milk, nor newspapers, nor anything else. When our numbers mushroomed, attitudes changed. (soon they were happy to deliver **everything**) But to begin with the only local tradesman who cooperated was Derek Gibson, the publican at the "Thomas Lord". This pub, the only one in England with this name, was called after Thomas Lord who built Lords Cricket Ground, home of the MCC. The worthy gentleman is buried in West Meon churchyard. Derek Gibson was himself not a local – he hailed from London – so he knew what business was all about. In return for some custom at his pub (and the prospects of much more to come when our students materialized), Derek went into the stores across the road, loaded up with sacks of potatoes, flour, rice – whatever we needed – and supplemented these with crates of beer and other beverages at any time of the day or night. During the period of two or three months when we had only one car in operation – and this frequently scouring the district looking for suitable furniture – the friendly publican's support was invaluable. Bill Wall-Palmer, the West Meon policeman, was even more active in his support and without asking for anything in return, turned into a regular conveyor belt of goodies – fresh eggs, pheasants, trout and honey. When our foreigners eventually turned up, Bill ferried their passports back and forth and none of our students ever had to worry about visas or residence permits. Bill is a benign Geordie, with all the nous and native friendliness of the people of that region.

The contents of our Japanese crates furnished four or five rooms at Riversdown. Fortunately, good antique furniture was still to be had at reasonable prices in 1971 and we drove up and down the Meon Valley looking for suitable items. Gradually the main house began to look inhabited. We intended to accommodate nine students in the building; they would all require a private bathroom or shower. Mediaeval Great Halls did not know about showers; there were 3 ancient bathrooms. By some judicious repartitioning and conversion of attics we were able to create 8 attractive units with bath or shower (one with ghost) and a spare bedroom for Fumiko. We named the rooms after places with sentimental connotations – Billinge, Pukaro, Lovisa, Valhalla, Skansen, Lisboa, Shibuya, Kyoto and Nara.

We resuscitated the grass tennis court, filled the swimming pool with water from our underground river, mowed a putting green, bought croquet and volley ball equipment and marked out routes for jogging, which had just come into vogue. We bought a beautiful 13-foot oaken table for the brick-floored dining room, which we decorated with Japanese prints and the huge temple rubbing that I had smuggled out of Angkor Wat. By the middle of July we were ready for the students. The chicken shed, with its lingering agricultural odours, would not be ready for several months, but as there was an abundance of spare rooms in the main house, we had ample teaching facilities.

*   *   *   *   *

We had good connections with several Japanese firms, but, as most Japanese book well ahead, there were no prospects of business from that quarter the first summer. Indeed the summer was already half over; I resolved to do some quick advertising to attract enough students for a pilot course. Residential courses throw up problems which do not arise in normal day-schools; it was as well that we should gain some experience before the hordes descended upon us.

The horde that July and August consisted of two students – Anita, a Swedish girl from Stockholm and Javier, a young Spaniard from Zamora. They made a group of two, the income was quite modest. However, humble beginnings are the best kind; one maintains a sense of proportion. With no teachers to pay and Jane doing the cooking there was no danger that we would over-extend ourselves. Our first customers at least got a good deal.

When Anita and Javier returned to their native countries at the end of August, pickings looked rather slim. English language schools traditionally fare badly in winter and Riversdown House was as yet unknown both in the UK and abroad. In early September I went to London for the day, soliciting business from a couple of companies – both interested in using us, but only in several months time. On the 5.45 train back to Winchester I had the occasion to sit next to a plump, dark-haired young lady who was mumbling the vital parts of English irregular verbs to herself with something less than supreme confidence. After introducing myself, I corrected her gently from time to time. When we arrived at Woking she had mastered put, take, give, catch, go and bring and as we proceeded to Basingstoke she was doing quite well on come, buy, enrol, study and learn. She told me she was Mexican and one of a group of seven who had come to spend 6 months in England to learn the language. The bad news was that they were already enrolled at a language school in Bournemouth. However, they were lodged with indifferent families and the food was *muy mala*. I left her my telephone number, just in case.

By Saturday, we had seven hungry Mexicans, three guitars and a disgruntled Colombian in the house. They stayed six months and ate chilis evey morning for breakfast. One of them – Daniel -was the director of the Mexican National Theatre in Guadalajara where Matt and I had watched the World Cup the previous year. I organised the lessons, Daniel organized the entertainment. They never went to bed before one and often sang and played guitars in the lounge until two. Lessons began late (or on time, Mexican time, depending on how you look at it) – on some days they did not begin at all. Our Latin Americans devoured huge quantities of food, but often helped with the cooking and periodically made trips to London to fetch more chilis. We lived in the same house; we had never eaten such spicy food or slept so little in our not inexperienced lives. Fumiko and the kids, used to cosy snacks of sushi, seaweed and bland rice, found the Mexican diet quite a revelation. Three or four nights a week Daniel and his crew would take their guitars down to the Thomas Lord and put on a show for the locals. Word got around fast. Entertainment for the regular beer swillers in the Meon Valley had hitherto consisted of darts and dominoes; the Mexican national theatre was several steps up from that. The Red Lion wondered where all its customers had gone. Closing time at the Thomas Lord became an empty formality as curtains were drawn and the *mariachis* got under way. It was not unusual for Guadelupe and Maria to be dancing on the bar at two in the morning. As Derek Gibson told the Meonites, they had never had it so good!

So you could say that we were fully booked the first winter, at least until February with the *Latinos* in the house. There was little room for anybody else, the scheduling would have been chaotic, anyway. The income we generated, though hardly astronomic, gave us breathing space during which time we printed our brochure, opened an office in London and partitioned part of the chicken shed. The Mexicans left en bloc in the middle of February. Pub life in West Meon has never been the same since. Daniel and his entourage have their place in the history of the Meon Valley and Riversdown. They even all paid, except one.

*   *   *   *   *

During 1972 we widened our sales base. I was able to secure a ten-year lease on well-located offices at 53, Pall Mall and soon afterwards we took space in both Helsinki (Eerikinkatu) and Tokyo (Nogizaka). In this way I was enabled to revive my contacts with Finnish and Japanese industry as well as to take another look at the foreign language market in London. I founded a company with Ed Wilton and called it Linguarama – a name which Jane dreamt up one evening over cheese and biscuits. We did not use it in all countries, but I would say it did quite well as a brand name for the emerging group. Only Berlitz could claim a 100-year history (by 1978) but "Linguarama" rolled off the tongue somewhat more easily than "Inlingua" which was often confused with "Interlingua" or Interlang".

The Residential Concept at Riversdown sold well. A foreign executive wishing to arrange, say, a one-month language course in England, faces several problems. Most important is the tuition itself, but he also has to have somewhere to stay (hotel? family?) and he has to eat three times a day. At weekends he probably wants to go on a few excursions to see the countryside or interesting historical spots (Stonehenge, Oxford, Winchester, Salisbury, Blenheim) or see a play or musical in the capital. There is also the question of a social programme in the evenings, each week-day. At Riversdown all these problems are solved simultaneously, even the pick-up from the airport and the eventual return to Heathrow. We streamlined the enrolment procedure to the point where the executive's secretary need only confirm the flight arrival; after that we made all the arrangements. Our fees always covered everything: English breakfasts, morning coffee, afternoon tea, wine with dinner, excursions, incidentals and of course all meals and private room with an international telephone. In due course facilities for tennis, golf and a fitness centre were also included. Businessmen and women from all over the world have gained their green card on the scenic and full-size 9-hole Riversdown golf course, where a resident professional assures expert tuition.

*   *   *   *   *

In 1972 and 1973 the Riversdown clientèle became truly international. Japanese and Finns came regularly as well as more Mexicans and a goodly number of Arabs. Prominent among the latter were Prince Azodeen, the son of King Ibn Saud of Saudi Arabia, Dr Khan, the Minister of Works and OPEC representative for Algeria, Dr Francesco Ingrassia, Bank of Sicily director, Abdullah al-Badi, director of the Abu Dhabi National Oil Company (ADNOC) and several influential Kuwaitis including Mohammed al-Dakheel, Waleed Nusf and Al-Nashari. Inlingua Spain, lacking a residential centre in England, sent us numerous Spanish businessmen and by the end of 1973 we were being supported strongly by French companies – Société Générale, BNP,

Michelin, Rhône-Poulenc, Banque de France – and German firms such as Deutsche Bank, Mercedes-Benz, BASF, Hoechst, Klöckner and Krupp. German parliamentarians also began to use Riversdown, often incognito; Manfred Gentz, the Daimler Benz board member and Jan Boetius of Allianz were among several distinguished visitors during this time.

Apart from tailoring courses for specific individuals – most of them sent by business – we also entered, to a limited extent, the field of contract teaching. We created special courses for the Iranian Navy (pre-Ayatollah), the Algerian Navy and the Iraqi army. We were sometimes dealing with 60-70 students at a time in 6-month batches. These men could not be accommodated at Riversdown, or in London. We developed a special division – Linguarama Services – in premises in nearby Fareham, to deal with tuition for military personnel. The Iranians we taught at a naval base way out in Suffolk. This division was ably managed for over a decade by Don Mills and Richard Bassett, former officers in the Fleet Air Arm and RAF respectively. The Iranian ratings seemed to have little motivation to learn English and Mills in particular used to bully them mercilessly in true military fashion. They got their revenge by beating our staff at football   (10-1).

Our most important and interesting contract at Riversdown in these early days was with the IVECO division of Fiat. This truck and fire engine division had united 3 national companies to form the biggest single group in the European market. These were Fiat of Italy, Unic of France and Magirus-Deutz of Germany. There had been some dispute over what should be the company language – Italian, French or German. English was finally decided upon as a compromise and 300 executives were selected to go on a language course.

We tendered for the contract, which was sizeable, and had prolonged discussions over several weeks with Dr Maurizio Ragazzoni of Fiat and Manfred Krips of Magirus-Deutz. Riversdown eventually won this contract on the basis of our whole-in-one concept, where carefully tailored tuition and easy logistics would enable IVECO to turn their language programme into a team-building exercise. We interviewed and assessed the 300 executives, one hundred from each country. They were classified and divided into 100 groups according to linguistic ability and professional area. These groups came to Riversdown, in rapid succession, for two-week stays. Each group consisted of one Italian, one Frenchman and one German. They might be engineers or accountants who had often spoken to each other by phone and worked on joint projects, but never met. During their stay at Riversdown they not only progressed together in English, but got to know each other well.

The success of this programme, carried out over a 3-year period, led IVECO to ask us to write a special course for exclusive use by their organization. This was to be an A-Z progression in the English language structure, but couched in IVECO industry-related vocabulary and realistic situations. The eventual work emerged as two weighty volumes – "The VIP Project" and which, as far as I can gather, are still in use in Turin today. We also carried out a similar programme for KONE, the international lift and crane manufacturing group, though on a smaller scale.

*   *   *   *   *

I mentioned earlier that some European parliamentarians came to Riversdown incognito; this also applied to high-ranking businessmen who, probably for reasons of prestige, wished to conceal the fact that they were still in some stage of learning. The secluded aspect of Riversdown's isolated location and the discreet individualism of its programme took on a new significance in the middle of the 1970s when famous executives and politicians ran a grave risk of being kidnapped, held to ransom, even murdered, especially in Germany and Italy. The shooting of Aldo Moro and the abduction of the children of several prominent Italians led to stringent precautions being taken concerning personal security. During this period several teenage children were tucked away at Riversdown on courses lasting up to six or twelve months. It was not unusual for them to be sent subsequently to the United States. One Italian businessman maintained such a degree of secrecy that even **we** were not allowed to know his real name. Two others, apparently taking the rap for the financial collapse of a large industrial group, spent hours every day on the telephone conducting labrynthine, multinational negotiations. Some high-powered executives, unwilling to reveal plane arrivals, have turned up at Riversdown in bullet-proof cars.

*   *   *   *   *

In 1974 Prince Mikasa, Emperor Hirohito's brother, came to England, accompanied by Princess Mikasa for a visit which was to last 6 months. The Prince, a leading authority on ancient religions, had got to the point in his research where he could further his knowledge of the subject only by reading books and documents which were unavailable in Japan. A large number of these were in the British Museum. Prince Mikasa had made arrangements to study this material over a period of several months. The Princess was to attend our school in London during that time. Jane was pleased to renew her association with this gracious lady who had maintained her fluency in English to an admirable degree.

As we had been entertained by the Mikasas on several occasions in Japan, it was not unnatural that they expressed keen interest in seeing Riversdown House – not only our 14th century home, but a building visited by Jane Austen (on horseback) and reputedly associated with the Bishops of

Winchester. I made arrangements for the Imperial couple to visit Winchester Cathedral and Winchester College, before lunching at Riversdown. We met the Mikasas in our Toyota Crown at Winchester station, where the station master had laid out a fine red carpet on the platform. It was a perfect summer's day. The Dean of the Cathedral, looking splendid in scarlet ecclesiastical attire, escorted us round the church and the crypt, showing us rare documents including a beautifully-lettered and illustrated early Japanese translation of the Bible. The visit to Winchester College, founded in 1383, was equally interesting. The quadrangle is one of the finest in England, while the Chapel rivals that of King's College, Cambridge as a gem of 14th century Gothic. The Prince was also impressed by the wide expanses of the playing fields belonging to the College. Sporting facilities of this nature, if located in Tokyo, would have astronomic value. The considerable grounds of the Imperial Palace in the Japanese capital are said to have a real estate value greater than that of Canada!

Lunch at Riversdown was on local fare. We polished our huge oaken dining table and laid it with English pewter. The first course was watercress soup, as the nearby village of Warnford has the largest watercress beds in the United Kingdom. The main course was pheasant, shot at Riversdown. We served Hambledon wine from a vineyard nearby, and followed the meal with a dessert of local strawberries.

Prince and Princess Mikasa, always good mixers, mingled enthusiastically with our students of assorted nationalities, including one or two Japanese. Once again, one could not fail to be impressed by the engaging nature of the Emperor's brother, his keen interest in the activities and aspirations of others, his encyclopaedic knowledge of many subjects, his infectious laughter and sense of humour.

*   *   *   *   *

Ten years later Crown Prince Hiro, son of the present Emperor, visited Riversdown for a day's tennis. He was on a two-year course at Oxford studying Mediaeval Transportation. My daughter Caroline was reading Japanese at Balliol at the same time. Prince Hiro, like his brother Aya, is a very good tennis player, equally adept on the forehand or backhand and possessing an accurate, penetrating service. He had not played on grass before, but soon adjusted to the lower bounce. We played doubles, in various combinations, from eleven in the morning till nearly seven. It was sunny and warm and our European students enjoyed the spectacle of seeing the eventual heir to the Japanese throne play marathon tennis with a variety of German, French and English partners. Hisashi Ito, head of Japan Air Lines, and Yoshio Miyake, head of Sanyo Securities, came down from London for the day, along with their families. Mr Ito's daughter was a skilful player and together with Kimi

Morizane, our student from Shikoku, they provided ample evidence of the growing Japanese proficiency in lawn tennis.

Prince Hiro, neat and courteous, is thoroughly Anglophile and was enjoying to the full his stay in England. Like his mother an eager and charming conversationalist, he has his father's sharp eyes and impressive recall of detail. He communicated easily and naturally with our German bankers and French industralists, no less than with my ageing mother. You would have thought he chatted to 90-year-old Lancashirewomen every day of the week.

The following summer he came again for more tennis. On the second occasion the weather was not so kind and we were on and off the court between showers. When it rained more we went down to the chicken shed and played table tennis. Fortunately my Czech friend, Ladislav Moudry was in attendance. Ladislav used to be number four in the world at this sport, in the heady days of Czech supremacy with the likes of Bohumil Vana and Ivan Andreadis. Prince Hiro, with his Japanese pen-grip style, had a good knock with Ladislav, showing us his versatility and competitive spirit.

Executives who have passed through Riversdown, when asked which aspect of the course pleased them most, mention the tuition, food and comfort as important elements, but frequently comment that what makes Riversdown different from anywhere else is the friendly, convivial atmosphere which permeates all activities. This is of course partly due to the beautiful location and cosy 14th century environment, but in the main, the ambience is the product of the enthusiastic interaction of the students themselves with each other, their instructors and domestic staff. In over 25 years of activity, the mix of nationalities has almost invariably produced a harmonious combination. Traditional rivalries are forgotten as Germans hobnob with Russians, Japanese with Koreans, Jews with Arabs. The stiffest test was an Iraqi major alongside an Iranian, but even they got on.

Another pleasing aspect of Riversdown life is the way high-ranking executives quickly accept the fact that they are in a learning situation – once more behind the school desk. Many of them seem to welcome the temporary reversal of roles, to enjoy the freedom from having to make endless decisions, to be able to relax within the confines of a new discipline. Those further up in the hierarchy often wish to be driven hard by demanding teachers, but they are also amongst those who enter most enthusiastically in the social activities, frequently showing glimpses of their organising skills in the process. Italian engineers cook for *pasta* parties at midnight, French accountants arrange wine-tasting contests and jive sessions, German board members invent new perfumes or beeping golf balls in business simulation games. One Japanese manager even organised a two-hour lecture on the history of English pubs, delivered one afternoon during closing time in the "Red Lion" by the publican himself.

The vibrant community spirit at Riversdown is all the more remarkable in view of the fact that the courses are individual, tailored to the level of the participant and catering for his or her specific requirements when using the language. Two or three times a week, however, communication sessions are set up between students of equal ability, consisting of a lively debate on current or relevant business topics. The stimulation of joint debate raises the communicative ability considerably, whatever the actual level may be. These exercises, the common social programme and the discussions at the dinner table not only provide Riversdown students with an extra dimension in their application of expressions and structures they have learnt, but build bridges and cement friendships in rapid fashion.

The similar goals of language enrichment, temporary immersion in the English way of life and cross-cultural experience among many personalities and nationalities produce a great unifying and levelling effect where differences of status disappear in an atmosphere of congeniality. It was both revealing and comforting to observe that this participative spirit and refreshing informality adopted by most high-ranking personalities was at no time more amply demonstrated than by the members of the Japanese Imperial family.

Chapter 16

Revolution in Portugal

We had returned from Japan via Portugal where we spent the months February to May before going to England to take up residence at Riversdown. There were seven of us, including my parents, and we rented a big flat on the Avenida de Roma. The Berlitz School in Guerra Junqueiro had passed into the hands of a Portuguese lawyer who understood little of the business. Anna Candiago still ran the school in the Rua Sociedade Farmaceutica, but she had converted it to an Inlingua school. Both establishments were moribund. The Guerra Junqueiro school, situated a few hundred metres from our apartment, welcomed me with open arms. Mathias Wallen had returned to Canada in 1966 and student enrolments had declined from over 1000 to a mere handful. I spent the four months in Lisbon resuscitating the fortunes of this school, which was happy to pay me a good salary to save it from collapse.

There were only 4 English teachers. One was Irish, one a Scot, the other two were Goanese Indians. The only competent person in the school was the French teacher, a young Belgian named Marie-Claire Berte. She was far too entrepreneurial to be left entirely hidden away in a classroom, so I made her chief secretary and put her on the front desk. A few advertisements in the newspaper brought in a goodly number of walk-ins. I told her that nobody was to walk out alive without having signed on for a course. Nobody did. Marie-Claire was a born businesswoman, a person of incredible stamina and loyalty, who was determined to find a worthwhile niche in life to which she could devote her immense energy. She was married to an extremely likeable and intelligent Portuguese banker, Mario Henriques. I told the lawyer who owned the school to call it Cambridge School and to give Marie-Claire a free hand to run it. He gratefully acquiesced and the student numbers grew. When I left in May we had a trained staff of new Brits who spoke real English and the school began to resemble the thriving establishment that Mathias and I had created in the heady, pioneering days of 1962-3.

*   *   *   *   *

Cambridge School prospered to such an extent that new branches were opened in the outlying districts of Benfica and Almada, as well as in Oporto, Coimbra and Madeira. A new HQ was secured in the middle of Lisbon's Champs Elysées, the Avenida da Liberdade. First it occupied one floor, then two, then eventually all five. Another big school was established in the Campo

Grande near the football stadium of the Sporting Club de Portugal. Mathias Wallen returned to Lisbon in 1973 and worked in association with me until his death in 1994. He was a wonderfully versatile character, now speaking 5 languages fluently – English, Finnish, Swedish, Portuguese, Spanish – and having a reasonable command of French and German.

In April 1974, I was skiing with my family in Suommu, Finnish Lapland. We were having lunch on the 25th when the radio announced that Portugal was in revolution. The news staggered me. The country had obviously been ripe for revolution since the early 1960s, when the protracted colonial wars in Angola and Mozambique sapped Portugal's energy and gold reserves and increasingly troubled her people with the loss of many sons. Salazar's regime had to be overthrown, but, like many dictatorships, it was hard to dislodge and the news that it had actually, finally, happened was hard to believe. It was true, nevertheless, as phone calls to Mathias and Marie-Claire soon confirmed.

In order that the reader may have a better understanding of the origins of the Portuguese Revolution and of the background which defined its character, I will add a few details to the picture of Portugal that I outlined in Chapter 8. The regime of Salazar was very much in keeping with the political tenor of the 1930s and while it had few of the ideological pretensions of a Fascist state, it had many of the trappings. Members of the National Assembly were chosen from the one permitted political association, the National Union (UN); "workers organisations" were set up, but run by their employers; education was strictly controlled by the state to promote Catholic values; and censorship was strictly enforced. Opposition was kept in check by the PIDE – a secret police force set up with Gestapo assistance – which used systematic torture and long-term detention in camps on the Azores and Cabo Verde islands to defuse most resistance. The army, too, was heavily infiltrated by PIDE and none of the many *coups* mounted against Salazar came close to success. Despite remaining formally neutral throughout the Spanish Civil War, Salazar had openly assisted the plotters in their preparations and later sent unofficial units of the Portuguese army to fight with Franco. Republican refugees were deported to face certain execution at Nationalist hands.

At home, Salazar succeeded in producing the infrastructure of a modern economy but the results of growth were felt by only a few ; agriculture, in particular, was allowed to stagnate. Internal unrest, though, while widespread, was surprisingly muted and apparently easily controlled; The Government's downfall, when it came, was precipitated far more by external factors. Salazar was an ardent imperialist who found himself faced with growing colonial wars – costly and bringing international disapprobation. India seized Goa and the other Indian Portuguese possessions in 1961 and at about the same time the first serious disturbances were occurring in Angola and Mozambique. The regime was prepared to make only the slightest concessions, attempting to defuse the freedom movements by speeding economic development.

In 1968 Salazar's deck-chair collapsed, and he suffered brain damage. Incapacitated, he lived for another two years, deposed as premier – though such was the fear of the man, no one ever dared tell him. His successor, Marcelo Caetano, attempted to prolong the regime by offering limited democratisation at home. However, tensions beneath the surface were fast becoming more overt and attempts to liberalise foreign policy failed to check the growth of guerilla activity in the remaining colonies, or of discontent in the army.

It was in the African-stationed army especially that opposition crystallised. There the young conscript officers came more and more to sympathise with the freedom movements they were intended to suppress and to resent the cost – in economic terms and in lives – of the hopeless struggle. From their number above all grew the revolutionary *Movimiento das Forças Armadas*. (MFA).

By 1974 the situation in Africa was deteriorating rapidly and at home Caetano's liberalisation had come to a dead end; morale, among the army and the people, was lower than ever. The MFA, formed originally as an officer's organisation to press for better conditions, then increasingly politicised, was already laying its plans for a takeover. Dismissal of two popular generals – Spínola and the defence minister, Costa Gomes – for refusing publicly to support Caetano, led to a first chaotic and abortive attempt on March 16. Spínola was a charismatic figure who a few weeks previously had been sacked from his post as vice-chief of staff on account of his book "Portugal and the Future", in which he maintained that no military solution was possible in Africa, only a politically negotiated one.

Finally on April 24, 1974, the MFA was ready to make its decisive and irrevocable move. The signal would be the playing of the song "Grandola" on the national radio. This led to the troops occupying Lisbon during the night. Mathias was awoken around seven by a loud banging on his door. An agitated cleaning lady told him that soldiers were in all the main streets, that the bridge over the Tagus had been closed and that all ferry traffic had been cut. Mathias threw on some clothes and went out of doors to see for himself. There was a market nearby where, in spite of the news, everything seemed calm. Incredibly a farmer offered him oranges and Mathias bought half a dozen, went home and had breakfast, then caught a bus, full of workers going to their jobs, to the Avenida da Liberdade. People were discussing the situation excitedly, but were so used to reporting for work that it had not occurred to many of them that normal economic activity might be disrupted. The Portuguese were not used to any change in political structure, let alone revolutions!

In the Avenida there was a goodly number of soldiers and military vehicles, but the atmosphere was calm, relaxed, almost as if the army had come to town to celebrate a bank holiday. Some junior officers had a wary look, but the rank and file were smiling at the people and many of them had carnations poking out of their gun barrels. Mathias found the school completely bereft of students, though gradually one teacher after another began to turn up to find out what was going on. Mathias tried to make some international phone calls, but was mainly unsuccessful. He then heard that the papers were coming out with extra editions and rushed out to buy them. For the first time since 1933 the country's newspapers actually related what the political situation was! Now perhaps we would not have to hunt around for English newspapers to find out what was happening in Portugal and the world. Around 4 pm Mathias heard the sound of submachine-gun fire from the direction of the Rossio, but it soon died down (to his great disappointment) though the school cleaners were very alarmed.

The next day, Friday, everyone, by reading the papers and listening to the radio, got a better grasp of the situation. The Revolution was perceived as a reality, and not something that would evaporate in the morning sunlight. This realisation prompted an enormous sense of release on the part of the populace, for so many years downtrodden and exploited. They poured out on the streets in large numbers. The area in front of the Avenida school was packed with demonstrators, carrying placards, singing and dancing. No demonstrations had been allowed in Portugal for 40 years! Tanks, armoured cars and jeeps careened up and down the boulevard; many of the troops jumped off their vehicles and mingled with the crowds, even dancing from time to time. That evening the TV showed the *Junta* to the nation. Spínola was in prime focus, though it was becoming clear that he was only a figurehead and that the chief architect of revolution had been Major Otelo Saraiva de Carvalho, who headed a group of junior officers with political views far to the left of Spínola, who was only marginally left of Caetano.

*   *   *   *   *

The next two years were perhaps the most extraordinary in Portugal's history, a period of continual revolution, massive politicisation and virtual anarchy, during which decisions of enormous importance were nevertheless made – above all the granting of independence to all of the overseas territories. At first there was little clear idea of any programme, beyond the fact that the army wanted out of Africa. Though the MFA leadership was clearly to the left and at first associated with the PCP (Portuguese Communist Party), the bulk of the officers were less political. General Spínola strongly opposed total independence for the colonies. Spínola's dream was clearly to "do a De Gaulle" in Portugal, while the army was above all determined not to replace one dictator with another.

In the event, their hands were forced by the massive popular response and especially by huge demonstrations on May Day. It was clear that whatever the leadership might decide, the people, especially in the cities, demanded a rapid move to the left. From the start every party was striving to project itself as the true defender of the "ideals of April 25". Provisional governments came and went but real power rested, where it had begun, with the MFA, now dominated by Saraiva de Carvalho and Vasco Gonçalves. While politicians argued around them, the army claimed to speak directly to the people, leading the country steadily left. It was a period of extraordinary contradictions, with the PCP hoping to consolidate their position as the "true" revolutionary party, opposing liberalisation and condemning strikes as counter-revolutionary, while ultra-conservative peasants were happily seizing land from its owners.

The first crisis came in September 1974, when Spínola, with Gonçalves and Saraiva de Carvalho virtual prisoners in Lisbon's Belém Palace, moved army units to take over key positions. The MFA, however, proved too strong and Spínola was forced to resign, General Costa Gomes replacing him as president. By the summer of 1975 more general reaction was setting in and even the MFA began to show signs of disunity; the country was increasingly split, supporting the revolution in the south, deeply conservative in the north. The Archbishop of Braga summed up the north's traditional views, declaring that the struggle against communism should be seen "not in terms of man against man, but Christ against Satan." Nevertheless the revolution continued to advance: a *coup* attempt in March failed when the troops involved turned against their officers. The Council of the Revolution was formed, promptly nationalising banking and private insurance; widespread land seizures went ahead in the Alentejo; and elections in the summer resulted in an impressive victory for Mário Soares' Socialist Party.

*   *   *   *   *

To go back to the days and weeks following April 25, 1974, the students resumed their lessons as usual after the May Day celebrations, shortly after which I arrived in Lisbon. Once the excitement had died down, it was possible to perceive a slight increase in student enrolments as opposed to the same period the previous year. This was not so surprising, since many young people and elements of the clerical working classes saw the change in political climate as the key to upward social mobility and international opportunities. Rich Portuguese, for so long protected by Salazar, were going around looking decidedly morose at this time. As far as we were concerned, we carried on with our work as before – we had never been political in any sense – but we were realistic enough to foresee some kind of upheaval in our own organisation. Revolution would entail wide-sweeping changes in the education system, in regulations for foreigners and employees' conditions. Our teachers were far better paid than Portuguese state teachers, but we suspected that a political element would be introduced in our schools.

It was not long in coming. As Spínola's star waned, the communist-leaning Vasco Gonçalves was elected Prime Minister and for the next 12 months Portugal tottered on the brink of communism. It was an unlikely long-term scenario, but 1974-75 proved a difficult period for us, as not a few of our employees took advantage of the changes to cause unrest among our staff. Declared communists came out of the woodwork on all sides. In the Avenida school, three non-Portuguese took it upon themselves to lead the "workers" against the management. They were, somewhat surprisingly, a Swiss, an Austrian and a Norwegian. They were all part-time teachers, but quickly developed into full-time political activists. They made little impression on our full-time Anglo-Saxon staff – British, American, Canadian, Australian, New Zealand and South African – but several of our Portuguese teachers followed them, starting to call themselves *"trabalhadores "* instead of *"professores."*

It was at this delicate stage of Portuguese political development, when apolitical companies such as Cambridge School were being victimised and disrupted by peripheral employees pursuing their own political aims, that management needed a strong figure who would unrelentingly resist a communist attack and continue to conduct business along common sense, pragmatic lines. Such a fearless figure, ever-present and completely incorruptible, was the Belgian manager, Marie Claire Berte.

Her husband had, like many perceptive Portuguese, been opposed to the excesses and suppressive nature of the Salazar regime, neither had Marie Claire herself any fondness for the upper class cliques which had supported it. But she ran a business which had been an outstanding success for the last seven years under her supervision and which had never had any help from the bureaucratic state. This business provided really good jobs for a couple of hundred individuals, many of them Portuguese nationals. There was no way in which she was going to stand aside and watch this institution defamed, reviled and dismembered by born-yesterday communists who happened to have given the odd lesson for Cambridge when regular teachers were sick. As for the impressionable and deluded Portuguese instructors who had jumped on the communist bandwagon, she would tell them a few things straight from the shoulder and maybe save their precious jobs for them in the process.

One of Marie-Claire's chief characteristics is that once she has decided her course of action, she goes through with it whether she has any support or not. Of course Mathias and I were behind her, but it would have helped if several of the *trabalhadores* had come out openly in her favour. Only three dared do this – a diminutive Portuguese secretary in the Avenida school – Ilda Benoliel

– a German teacher named Dieter Vogel and the sternly principled chief secretary of the Oporto school, Isabel Horta. Everybody else sat on the fence, though many rushed to our side when winds began to blow in another direction.

We experienced little disruption during the summer months of 1974 – it was a period when a multiplicity of political groups and factions were making platforms to present to a bewildered Portuguese public. In September, however, there was an important business decision to be made. This was the month when we normally conducted a massive advertising campaign to attract student enrolments which would carry us through the academic year. Many language schools had folded up in the face of teacher militancy. These included Anna Candiago's Inlingua School, which she first sold to some English people, received her down payment, then saw them decamp as the Revolution hotted up. Many British-owned businesses foundered, a large proportion of them being restaurants and bars in the Algarve, where leftist waiters took over the establishments and dictated new rates of pay to the hapless owners. They all went bankrupt in due course. The question facing us was: should we invest in the usual advertising campaign in view of the unstable political and economic climate? Would the autumn rush occur as usual or would an unsettled public hang back in investing in more language instruction?

I was always in favour of advertising; Marie-Claire took the plunge. The previous September she had spent 200.000 escudos. Now she slapped down 400.000 for the campaign to be run in half a dozen grateful newspapers. The other schools did not advertise. Within a fortnight we had more than 5000 enrolments. Parents in the cities saw this as the time when proficiency in two or three languages would open up huge opportunities, in an increasingly Europe-oriented Portugal, for them and their children. Many of them signed up for English, French and German simultaneously. We scrambled for new classrooms; in fact, we had effectively killed the competition. In later years Cambridge enrolments touched 10,000-12.000 annually, making it the biggest private language teaching organisation in the world – in Portugal itself a virtual monopoly.

But in the late autumn of 1974 we were simultaneously heading for trouble. The resignation of General Spínola and the cosying up to the world's communist parties by new premier Vasco Gonçalves encouraged our militants to challenge the management. Marie Claire was denounced as an agent of capitalism by one of the school secretaries; a radio programme attacked her savagely as a reactionary and witnesses (our staff) declared she had taken all the student records home. (This was in fact true, as she was determined that they should not fall into the hands of others, should there be a leftist takeover of the school). Other *trabalhadores* declared her to have been a former PIDE informer, others said she smuggled money out of the country for her foreign masters. A Hungarian girl, who had been giving the odd lessons in Russian (now temporarily a popular language) joined our Swiss-Norwegian-Austrian *troika* as a leading activist. The Norwegian organized a sit-in strike for teachers, but this fizzled out when several dozen students helped us by constantly coming in and out of the school. All the students seemed to be on our side and they saw it as a huge joke to disrupt the disruption in this manner. Some of them must have made 50 entries and exits in the same evening. The Norwegian, who could not be seen to block the way of the **Portuguese,** was beside himself in rage. Some of the sit-in teachers complained of the constant draught.

All our cleaners remained faithful to the management, with one exception. She said Marie Claire had forced her to work 11 hours a day. A Workers Council was formed to deal with this and other abuses. Marie-Claire, having read some of the new laws, discovered she (as an employee) could also form a Workers' Council, so she set up a rival one, consisting of Anglo teachers, cleaners, coffee girls, security guards and most of the wavering secretaries. The two Councils disputed power inside the school and we had lots of meetings with various Lisbon authorities and judges (many of them not sure of their own powers and objectives in a rapidly-changing legal situation). At these meetings (some of which lasted for hours) the air was thick with accusations, counter-accusations, conflicting ideologies and kaleidoscopic interpretations of political directives and announcements. The newly-appointed judges and commissioners were not sure what to do with our bickering councils and finally ordered an all-round vote to set up a definitive "workers' commission" which would run the school. The militants wanted a secret ballot, but Marie-Claire insisted on a hands-up vote of the 34 people who had, in one way or another, been selected as the representatives of our large staff. She took out a notepad and scrutinized every face as the hands went up. Some, seeing her look, went up and down. There were clearly going to be scores to settle in the future. Marie-Claire's union won 18-16 — it was a close shave. An Australian teacher, Joe Tierney, was put in charge of future meetings. He was a sensible lad who always wore a Davy Crockett hat in between lessons and he was determined that this was going to be no Maoist Alamo.

We were still not out of the wood, for political activists were pouring into Portugal from all European countries. The German Embassy referred to them as "revolutionary tourists". Many of them found their way into our school buildings, spreading their ideas among our staff. Our leftists tried to organize union meetings inside the school. Marie-Claire refused. They claimed that any teacher who had worked for the school 15 days (perhaps an hour a day) was unsackable. We did not recognize them. Teachers normally took staggered holidays, as Cambridge was open all the year round. They tried to organize a general summer holiday to ruin our special courses in June, July and August. Marie-Claire made them abandon this scheme by importing new instructors.

As far as wages were concerned, we had no problems. When the Gonçalves government brought in the new minimum wage for teachers, it was fixed at 7,000 escudos per month for 22 hours a week. We paid double that and teachers scrambled for overtime to earn more. They tried to freeze management salaries, but were not able to achieve that. The country was finding that, whatever political changes took place, it still needed managers. Many company owners had fled to Brazil, leaving their middle managers to face the music. Carlos Baleia, my old actor friend, was a senior mnager at the C. Santos firm which represented Mercedes Benz and other companies of that ilk. He suffered the usual abuse and was stripped of his company car and other privileges, though he had been openly anti-Salazar for years. Contemptuous of "sudden" leftists, he stayed on and, with 3 other middle managers, continued to run the sizeable company. Their value was soon realized, as the political luminaries had no idea how to run a business. Carlos ran his own car and charged them murder for it. Cardoso, my other actor friend, (working for General Motors) went from right to left. It was all very confusing.

The countryside, with the exception of the poverty-stricken Alentejo province, remained relatively conservative throughout the revolution. So did the islands of the Azores and Madeira, as well as most of the north of the country. The land-holding small farmers had no wish to see their farms collectivised, neither did the fishermen wish to surrender their boats. Communists made determined attempts to commandeer the fishing boats in the harbour in Oporto, and perorated authoritatively and at length to sullen groups of fisherfolk as they stood with their catches. Then one night two fishermen threw a communist spokesman into the harbour, causing spontaneous mirth among the curious onlookers. That incident settled the collective boats issue.

Three officials of the Oporto branch of the PCP walked into our school one night at 7 pm – peak hour. They confronted Isabel Horta, who was taking enrolments and asked her to hand over the management of the school to a couple of dithering part-time teachers whom they had in tow. Isabel, a tough young woman of working class origins, listened to their spiel for a while, then went to a typewriter and typed out the contract which she had with Cambridge School. When she had completed this, she held it in front of the officials and the two teachers.

"This is the contract I have with the school. It is guaranteed by the present management. As you see, I enjoy a salary of 14,000 escudos a month with four weeks' holiday a year. I have left a blank space here for you (the officials) or these two teachers to sign. You will guarantee these conditions for the next 5 years. When you have signed this we will go to the notary public round the corner and have it notarised. Who is going to sign?"

This little drama was watched by about one hundred students in the school reception area. Nobody would sign, of course – they soon left.

When Eanes was elected President in November 1975, Marie-Claire summoned the militant teachers of Portuguese before her and asked them whether they wanted peace or war. Those who chose peace are still with the organisation. Some (declared Maoists) had of course to choose war and in due course they lost many battles to the unflinching Belgian.

Portugal has come a long way in its political development since then. One always felt that neither NATO nor the neighbouring Spanish state would have permitted, in the long run, a communist government on the Atlantic seaboard. In fact the route chosen was unquestionably decided upon by the Portuguese people themselves. Fiercely independent, basically conservative and largely Catholic as they are, the role of a moderate, centrist member of the European Union was one which most suited this calm, perceptive, internationally-minded people. Their revolution had been achieved bloodlessly and characterised by carnations in the muzzles of the guns. What an object lesson for more violent peoples! What a triumph for common sense and gentle change!

At the time of writing Marie Claire Berte still runs the nation-wide language organisation. The former Maoists are treated even-handedly like everyone else. But sometimes, on bad days, they detect a gleam in the Belgian's eye.

Chapter 17

North Korea, the Closed Country

At various times in recorded human history, some countries have been closed to outsiders, often for quite long periods. The most significant example in recent times is perhaps the isolation of Japan from 1600-1853, initiated and enforced by the Tokugawa dynasty. This self-imposed quarantine led to the Japanese developing a singular, almost unique type of society whose disciplined, collective and moralistic behaviour is without parallel in the modern era.

Since the Second World War, access to certain states has been restricted, in varying degrees, to visitors from the West. Burma-Myanmar, Cuba, Vietnam, large areas in Siberia and China come into this category. There is no doubt, however, that in the post-war period the hardest nation to penetrate has been North Korea.

My rewarding years in Japan and other eastern countries engendered an ever-growing desire to get to know and familiarize myself with the social customs and subtle mentalities of all the East Asian peoples. When I returned to Europe in 1971, the two Koreas constituted a gaping hole in my experience. I had met many Koreans in Japan, enjoying their barbecues and their odd humour, admiring their scything tackles on the football field. My friendship with Seung-Pyo Huh of the Lucky-Goldstar family resulted in my visiting South Korea twice in the mid-seventies where I was able to gain a nodding acquaintance with Seoul, the capital. In its physical appearance, Seoul appeared to me as a twin to several Japanese metropoles such as Osaka or Tokyo, though I was well aware that its temples and monuments, not to mention its teeming people, did not share a particularly close cultural alignment with the Japanese. At all events, South Korea was capitalist, confident, busy and booming and, if not quite westernized, certainly modernized. The hate for the *régime* in the northern half of the country was almost palpable; it was constantly encouraged by the Seoul government.

There were, of course, no border crossings and it would have been less than courteous to my South Korean hosts even to suggest that I had the slightest inclination to sample the "workers' paradise". But naturally I was curious. Could the northern *régime* be as bad as the south painted it?

In 1979 an opportunity came up to enter the Korean People's Republic. The World Table Tennis Championships were scheduled to be held that year in Pyongyang. The North Koreans, though reluctant to open their borders, could not hold the event without letting in the world's table tennis players, their managers, coaches and – horror of horrors – Western journalists. That is how I suddenly became Assistant Coach to the Finnish table tennis team, just as Ian Wooldridge simultaneously became the Table Tennis Correspondent of the Daily Mail. My Finnish friends were only too delighted to join in this mild conspiracy and various other British and Western European individuals who had never seen a table tennis ball smashed in anger in their entire lives, penetrated Kim Il Sung's steely borders under the guise of similar subterfuges.

It was not easy to get there. In April 1979 I was attending a conference in Poznan, Poland, a city which possessed most unreliable air connections with its own capital, Warsaw. Officially bounced off the plane, I managed to squeeze into the "last seat" by turning up at the airport at 6 am and reached Warsaw, whence I flew to Geneva – the starting point for Western Europeans going on the North Korean Odyssey. It was a charter flight – North Korean – and was packed to the rafters. After close scrutinization of our special visas by North Koreans in army uniform, we were allowed, after lengthy drawn-out and tedious formalities, to board the rickety-looking Ilyushin which was to transport us to our remote destination. It is a long way from Geneva to Pyongyang in an aeroplane that does not go very fast. It was a long way, conceptually and culturally, from the hostile screening and nit-picking inspections of the uniformed orientals to the urbane, smart, Swiss officials who supervised – probably out of sheer curiousity – this unusual operation.

We were guests bound for their country, but it was not left to our imagination to see that we were unwanted, decadent, only temporarily-tolerated guests. The Koreans glared at each passport photograph, then at our real faces, then at the picture again. Resemblances were grudgingly conceded. The baggage handling was a grim pantomime. Though put on the conveyor belts in the Swiss departure hall in the usual manner, it waited for us in a cold jumbled pile a few yards from the plane. One by one we had to identify our bags, several of which were opened and rummaged in. Then we had to put them personally into the hold under the nose of a Kim-il-Sung trusty. We were then almost shoved up the stairway to the plane. There was no getting off after that.

Once aboard we sat like stuffed ducks for half an hour listening to the safety instructions bequeathed upon us by a caring People's Republic. When these drew to a close we were suddenly disappointed in our belief that take off was imminent. Surprise, surprise, there was news of a bomb scare. South Korean agents had smuggled explosives on board, their northern cousins were interceding at the last moment to save our lives. This, not unsurprisingly, meant immediate and laborious disembarkation. The hold was reopened and we all had to unload the precious baggage, re-identify our pieces, throw all the contents onto the cold tarmac – women's underwear and all – then stuff everything in again and re-load. The bombs were not found, but re-embarkation was permitted (passports checked at bottom of steps, again at the top, finally a last time after we had buckled up). We were relieved to be spared the handcuffs, though the food we were ultimately offered – over the Urals, I believe – might have disappointed English convicts.

I had the good luck to be seated next to Ian Wooldridge, who proved to be a genial and lively companion on the long, boring flight over Siberia. Our route was Geneva-Novosibirsk-Irkutsk-Pyongyang, which is not the most enticing or relaxing of itineraries. Flying east, the cold Swiss morning turned rapidly into Russian steppe afternoon, glum Urailian twilight and dark Siberian night. At an unearthly morning hour, we were banged down on the Novosibirsk tarmac and herded ignominiously into a grim, prefabricated hut which served as a waiting room. I suppose the stop was for re-fuelling, though they might well have been sticking wings on again. Coffee was obtainable if you had roubles (unobtainable) and proved undrinkable to those unfortunate enough to secure a cup. It was forty degrees below outside, slightly warmer in the hut. After that even the plane seemed hospitable.

Our stop in Irkutsk was no more appealing except the temperature seemed to have reached the mid-thirties (below) in the yellow-grey Siberian spring afternoon, and it looked considerably nearer Pyongyang on the map, heralding a much longed-for disembarkation.

The Pyongyang April climate had been described as agreeable, and this it turned out to be, when we eventually touched down in early evening. Indeed the relatively cool, sunny weather conditions were the only source of continual consolation for the other privations we were subjected to during our 3 weeks in the workers' paradise.

*   *   *   *   *

Our reception was impressive. We were not allowed to disembark until our documentation and faces had once more been eye-balled by a fresh gang of home-grown trusties who boarded the aircraft for this purpose. While this examination was taking place, I managed to sneak a couple of highly illicit photographs of the scene outside while our official had his head under Ian Wooldridge's seat. There were at least 50 figures in military uniform as well as a sizeable assortment of grey-suited officials, guides, stone-faced maidens in colourful national costume, plus a line of blue-uniformed men looking like Rear-Admirals, who turned out to be chauffeurs of the state-owned cars assigned to our transportation needs. This army of special hosts greeted us as we descended the plane steps, bowing stiffly in puppet fashion, shaking hands only if we preferred ours first and forcing thin-lipped smiles as they said "Welcome to the workers' paradise". (They actually said it!) They escorted us into the terminal building, a white marble affair quite upmarket from the

Siberian huts we had experienced only a few hours before. It was a beautiful evening, the temperature was a comfortable 25 degrees and eveything looked spotlessly clean. Those officials wearing suits clearly had been to better tailors than their Russian colleagues or their boiler-suited Chinese protectors. Among all Asians, Koreans – both North and South – are among the most smartly-dressed. We were waved through customs speedily (they had opened all our bags anyway) and we were interviewed in ones and twos at pleasant tables in the concourse. At this time, when we identified ourselves and our position/function, we were given an identification tag – a label with our photograph on it – presumably to help them to distinguish us one from another as we circulated around town.

At this point I was queried about my real profession, apart from my dabbling in table tennis officialdom. I saw no harm in revealing my connection with adult education, though I was slightly nervous about losing status as a coach, which gave me privileged access to ringside seats in the stadium and other useful things. Indeed when I heard them say "special category – official-cum-educated tourist, I was on the verge of lodging some vague form of protest, but they quickly informed me that this category would entitle me to the exclusive use of a Mercedes-Benz 220, aboard which I would be accompanied by **two** personal guides at all times – one man and one woman, both English-speaking. This did not sound like an unreasonable deal at all. As I boarded my shiny new vehicle, I saw Ian Wooldridge out of the corner of my eye inspecting a huge black Volvo, which high-ranking journalists got. The table tennis officials got cars too, but they had to share three per vehicle. The poor players (the real performers) got Russian mini-buses.

*　　*　　*　　*　　*

It was a five-mile run into town where the pristine portals of the Hotel Potong-gang awaited us. It was an interesting ride, in a way. The countryside, mainly rice paddies, was neat, flat, undistinguished. The road was good, seemingly new and straight. As we approached buildings – extremely large blocks of flats lining the road at regular intervals – I was stunned by the absence of any signs of habitation. The edifices – enormous, square, of white stone – seemed to have been recently constructed, but were shuttered, opaque, mute. We did a couple of miles without seeing one human being or other terrestrial animal. The place could have been atom-bombed or gassed – there was no life.

Then suddenly there was. The central entrance to one of the blocks opened and a line of Koreans emerged. Twenty to thirty in number, they were all male, blue-uniformed like Japanese university students, wearing flat blue caps with a red star and the ubiquitous Kim-Il-Sung button-hole badge-portraits which adorn every North Korean breast. They did not walk or stroll – they marched smartly and in rhythm – unsmiling and unswerving towards some unrevealed ideological destination. Our car zoomed closely past them, but not one eye was turned in our direction. We must have been a convoy of thirty-odd Mercedes and Volvos – hardly the normal traffic in Pyongyang – but we made no impression on those citizens. They were going somewhere and were dressed for the part.

The trip to town took not more than 20 minutes, but during this time we observed not fewer than half a dozen of these "exits". Apparently orchestrated – and for what purpose we could only hazard a guess – they were off to join the army, or collect the dole or pursue some common goal which meant a lot more to them than a line of cosseted, decadent aliens, whatever make of vehicle they were carried in.

The hotel was spanking new, on the banks of the river Potong-gang. It was clean, sterile, the rooms were airy and spacious. The radio and telephone did not work, a couple of bulbs were missing, the toilet was temperamental, but for anyone who had experienced a variety of Russian or Rumanian hotels, it was relative luxury. The river had the stench of stagnant water, but the cherry trees which lined its banks were as lovely as any in Japan. The Pyongyang skyline, viewed from the 10th floor where my room was located, was startlingly modern, almost futuristic. Buildings were high, mammoth statues and monuments dotted the scene, most of the city was grippingly decorative and seemed to have been constructed almost entirely of marble. The town silhouette, in the crimson rays of a slowly setting sun, was stunningly colourful, yet sterile and soulless. They could have hired it out to Hollywood as background to Star Trek.

The food on the plane had been dismally unsatisfactory, both in quality and amount offered. They had only one meal and they had served it twice. Once would have been enough. The menu was rubbery chicken, doubtful apples, black bread and coffee. The bread was the best, with a bit of Swiss butter on it. Those who could not drink the coffee bought "soft drinks" – they were North Korean – then went back to attempting the coffee. Ian Wooldridge and I, on entering our pseudo-respectable hotel, looked forward to at least a different menu, hopefully of a higher standard. We were soon disillusioned.

Evening dinner, taken early as is usual in North East Asia, consisted of Korean food. Even in South Korea I had had some trouble with *kimshi* and other strange delicacies, though Korean barbecued meat, both in Seoul and Tokyo, is invariably delicious. Ian and I could not recognize the couple of dishes that were placed before us. We certainly could not eat them, or tolerate them on our table for long. Finns and Germans on the next table were experiencing similar difficulties. We asked for barbecued meat; we were told that it was not on the menu. In fact there were no alternatives to what we had rashly sent away. I will not bore the reader in describing the various arguments we had with the waiters at the hotel, with the manager and ultimately with our interpreter-guides. In the end we found that the only things the hotel possessed that we could eat were tomato soup and boiled or poached eggs. We had these for breakfast, lunch and dinner most days. Roberts, from the Daily Telegraph, ate nothing else for 3 weeks. I was worried about him getting scurvy and catching it from him. Ian and I, considerably more travelled, were adventurous at times and at least were used to filling up with rice. But it is true to say that most of our courageous attempts to eat the hotel's fare resulted in summary failure and loss of face.

That first evening I joined the Finnish players and officials and we traipsed round the majestic avenues of downtown Pyongyang, marvelling at what all the marbled edifices must have cost to build. The Palace of Children alone, where youngsters were allowed to play in a kind of opulent toyland Utopia, made the Finnish parliament look somewhat staid by comparison. The wide boulevards, untroubled and unpolluted by many vehicles, were as impressive as the Boulevard des Italiens or the Avenue de l'Opéra in Paris. But, in contrast to Paris or Rome or Lisbon, the ample pavements (also marble in many cases) sported no outdoor cafés. Perfect for roller-skating, they remained without kids of any kind and of course skate-boarding or roller-blading – not invented at that time – would hardly have been allowed anyway. The gleaming sidewalks, ideal for strolling, seemed to have no strollers either. We had them to ourselves, a motley bunch of aliens, followed, at an appropriate distance of twenty yards, by our guides, interpreters, minders. In North Korea you are never lonely, except in your inner being. The minders mind, from 8 am to your chosen bedtime, with a dedication and thoroughness rarely displayed by "workers" in the west. They were not easily shaken off. They had the last drink with you in the bar at night. They hung around the lobby an extra half hour after you retired, just in case you changed your mind about sleeping or attempted to sally forth unminded. It was dangerous to do that, they said. There was much hatred around. People might think you were American and duff you up, even maim or accidentally kill you. But what about the American table tennis players? The minders frowned. Well, they had special bodyguards to protect them, was their eventual reply.

It was just as bad in the morning, for they waited for you, sunk deep in the red velvet armchairs of the hotel lobby. I used to run every day before breakfast, but my male minder was there at 7.30 and stopped me. Then they gave me a younger male minder who let me run, but ran with me. They were boring runs, I can tell you, past all Kim Il Sung's most imposing edifices (commentary provided). I was finally able to defeat this system by running out of the lobby at 6 am, when I discovered that even the most assiduous minder was not able, or willing, to make it before 6.30. There are limits to human devotion, I found, even to the Beloved Leader.

The World Championships themselves were well organized. Not only had the Koreans constructed a gleaming, spacious stadium, with seats for all, but the general administration, punctual starting times, competent umpiring and so on left little to be desired. Uniformed ushers were ubiquitous, our minders dutifully took their seats behind us – even our toilet needs were properly anticipated and supervised. A welcome feature of the games were the large crowds in attendance. Several Korean players had good chances of reaching the finals and thousands of peasants had come from the countryside to support their stars. These spectators, though naturally partisan, lent an exciting air of expectation to the stadium, They were, moreover, dressed in their Sunday best, the women attired in the colourful Korean national costume.

*   *   *   *   *

The following morning I was re-interviewed by a more senior official who informed me that I, as an official-cum-educated-tourist, would enjoy several additional privileges. He handed me a form to fill in which asked me to request what aspects of Korean life I wished to familiarize myself with. There was a suggested list, which included visits to factories, power stations, dams, farms, universities and so on. I filled the form in eagerly, requesting visits to a school, a university, a farm, a Korean family at home. The official politely added the Museum of the Revolution, the Museum of Korean National History, the Children's Palace and the birthplace of Kim il-Sung at Mangjong-dae. Two out-of-town excursions were permitted. I chose the ascent of Kumgang-san, a beautiful mountain on the east side of the peninsula, and, to my great excitement, an inspection of the frontier with South Korea at Panmunjom.

The Koreans were as good as their word in terms of complying with these requests. I never managed to see a university, but the rest I got. Of course there was a price to pay – everything was meticulously stage-managed – but these forays about town and across the countryside allowed one insights into the actual state of affairs in North Korea that could never have been gained sitting in a stadium. Our minders pounded our ears with propaganda on all these outings – a political doctrine and string of incredible assertions which made Russian or Chinese dogma relatively modest and liberal by comparison – but nevertheless they could not deny us our eyes to see, our judgement to discern, our stomachs to rumble.

Let us take our visit to a Korean school. We were driven ten miles out of town to a suspiciously new-looking building which housed a dozen classrooms filled with a couple of hundred of the cleanest kids that I have ever seen. Their faces were a well-scrubbed reddish-brown, their eyes – which never left us – bright but glazed at the same time (if you can imagine that). They were dressed in neatly-pressed uniforms, sat upright at tiny wooden desks and chanted periodically in uncanny unison whenever teacher gave subtle signals. They were about ten years old, the teacher about seventy. After witnessing some art classes, where the children showed considerable talent and dexterity, we were treated to a music class where an eight-year old Rubenstein gave an impeccable rendering of Chopin's Preludes, followed by the whole class singing a few stirring songs dedicated to the Beloved Leader.

The headmistress, perhaps in an unguarded moment, had let it slip that the school taught English from the age of twelve – so I asked to see an English class in progress. This was clearly not in the script and my minder was tic-tacking full-time behind my back, but eventually, with some un-Asian insistence, I was able to corner them into letting me enter the English class. This was allowed only after some 5 minutes frantic preparation, which resulted in the entire class chanting "Good morning, dear Visitor" as I entered the room. I suppose I stayed about ten minutes, walking round the classroom and inspecting an assortment of English pieces pinned to the walls. They were strictly revolutionary – anti-American songs and quotations from the Beloved Leader – but at any rate they had got the language right. It was the only English around, nobody spoke any. I asked the teacher, a young man in his mid-thirties, where he had learnt his English. I might as well have addressed him in Martian. He tittered nervously, as Asians do when they are on trial for embezzlement or their life, and kept switching his head from-me-to-my-minder-back-to-me-back-to-my-minder till I thought he would swoon out of dizziness. I talked to the children too, but apparently they had not quite reached that particular lesson. "What is your name?" proved exceptionally difficult for them, though one bold youngster did say "yes".

Kim, my minder-cum-fellow-jogger, was fairly ratty with me for the rest of the day, but had recovered some Asiatic composure when, on the following morning, I was taken to see "the typical Korean family at home". Again it was a (seemingly mandatory) ten-mile drive out of town, before we came upon a very small development of a dozen flats or so – white, compact, brand new or newly painted – with a smiling "caretaker" to greet us and show us round. I was somewhat surprised that North Korean janitors looking after modest apartment blocks in a remote suburb of West Pyongyang should be equipped with flawless English, but we took what we could get. Since our arrival in the country, we had been told repeatedly that every family in North Korea enjoyed the amenities of a 3-bedroom flat (unlike the ten-in-a-room situation in the smelly slums of South Korea). We were indeed shown into a small but satisfactory sitting room to meet Mr and Mrs Sam – the prototypical Korean family with their two kids aged around four and six. This nuclear family, well-dresssed and smiling, shook hands with us somewhat awkwardly and then stood to attention while Kim described the flat. We saw the kitchenette and toilet and bedrooms One, Two and Three. Kim counted them on his fingers. Mr Sam, dressed up for the occasion, spoke a little English until I asked him what his job was and had he taken a day off work. After some discussion with Kim in Korean, it appeared he was an engineer. The director of his factory had given him a couple of hours off to meet important foreign tourists. He would work overtime that evening so as not to disrupt production.

The bedrooms had beds, but no bedside tables, lamps or cupboards. In the sitting room there was nowhere to sit. The kitchen cupboards, which I naughtily opened, were bare. Kim, who had some difficulty in restraining himself from spanking the back of my hand, explained that the Sams were just moving in. The state was about to transfer their belongings from the 3-bedroom apartment which they had previously enjoyed. Perhaps that was why there were no bulbs in the hanging sockets, I said. Everybody agreed, the Sam couple in sign language.

The next day we visited a farm. It was a farm unlike any other I have ever seen. It was a farm without animals, crops, workers, or even fields. But it did have a shop, in the middle of nowhere, selling the farm's products. The shop had no customers, but there were five cheerful shop girls in starched white aprons and Beloved Leader badges. The shelves of the shop were stacked with tins, not just here and there, but along their entire length. The number of unsold tins matched to a centimetre the measurements of the shelves. I asked Kim how often they did inventories, but was not able to get across the concept. On request, one of the girls put six of the tins on the shiny counter in front of me. I could not read the labels but coloured images suggested tinned meat, fish (sardines?) corn and an asparagus-like vegetable. It was a very successful farm, said Kim. Where were the fields and the workers, I asked.

"Over there" replied Kim, pointing vaguely to a blue haze in the north, away from Pyongyang. I tried to buy my six tins, but it was not appropriate, said Kim. Everything by quota, you understand.

*   *   *   *   *

My next outing, however, gave me a much clearer picture of North Korean farming. On the first Friday after our arrival we were scheduled to make the excursion to Kumgang-san where we would climb the mountain. For some reason the only people to volunteer for this excursion, apart from myself, were seven officials of the French contingent. We were assigned to a Russian minibus, which we shared with a driver and three minders – two male and one female. The girl, who spoke reasonable French, was interpreter-guide.

My friend Kim was left behind. We left at 5 am and drove across the peninsula to the port of Wonsan where we stopped for breakfast. The route then took us along the east coast of North Korea, heading south into the mountainous region. Rattling along the coast road, we were not more than thirty metres from the sea. Between the road and the sandy shore there were two parallel fences, about 6-feet apart. These were 3 metres high and clearly electrified. There was no break in this barrier, apart from gates at regular intervals. The gates were manned by armed guards.

My companions, being French, were considerably less inhibited than I was in the realm of asking awkward questions and making sceptical comments. I suppose I have lived in Japan too long to be able to match the biting satire of a Parisian who has been eating Korean food for a week. What was the fence for? For safety, replied the poor interpreters. Whose safety? The safety of the people. Safety from what – crocodiles? Sorry, why do you speak of crocodiles? Who is the fence meant to keep out? South Korean fascist pig invaders. When are they coming? They could arrive any day. We must be prepared to repel the invasion of the fascist pigs. You don't think the fence is there to stop your people leaving the country? Of course not, we live in paradise. Where did you learn your French? At University. Have you ever been to France? No. Wouldn't you like to visit Paris? I would go there if requested to do so by our Leader. Wouldn't you like a holiday in France? I have my duty here.

The French gave her a hard time all the way down the east coast. The two male trusties were hamstrung as they didn't speak any French. From time to time they interrogated the hapless maiden in guttural Korean, occasionally shouting at her out of sheer frustration. The French laughed, jeered and sneered at will – I thought we were all going to wind up in a Korean clink. My own behaviour was so gentlemanly by comparison that the minders ignored me and I was able to sneak a couple of pictures of the electrified fence.

Late in the morning, as the road took us inland, we suffered a puncture. This turned out to be an incredible piece of luck, as it happened adjacent to a large open area of rice paddies in which laboured scores of peasants. We poured out of the bus like cons in a jail-break and spread across a few fields before the trusties could stop us. Most of the peasants stopped working and gaped at us in sheer amazement. The French bombarded them with Parisian *argot* and offered everybody *gauloises*; the interpreter scuttled from one to the other like a hen marshalling wayward chicks. One trusty helped the driver change the wheel with a rusty old Russian jack. The other stuck to me like glue as I tried, in vain, to make conversation with a young labourer. The man I had selected to talk to did not look at all like a peasant and I pointed this out to my minder. He spouted out the explanation proudly. The labourer concerned was a bank clerk who gave his services free of charge to the beloved Leader every Friday, helping Korean agriculture recover from the previous year's drought. All office workers did this, he boasted. You too? Of course, when I am not engaged in matters of national importance.

It was now clear to me why all office workers in Pyongyang had faces burned by the sun and why, that Friday morning, we had seen dozens of lorry-loads of people being driven into the countryside at 6 am. I told my trusty I was moved by this proof of loyal patriotism. He thanked me, dewy-eyed. I was really scoring points against the French that day.

Then suddenly we witnessed something very (North) Korean. As we surveyed the rice-planting, we were vaguely aware of some music, heard from a distance. This now grew louder; we turned our heads to seek out the source. On the road adjacent to the rice paddies, and approaching our stricken bus, came pedalling a female cyclist in a red blouse and flowing black skirt. She seemed to find the cycling laborious and no wonder, for the pedalling powered a loudspeaker attached to the back mudguard, just as a dynamo provides power to a bike headlamp. Revolutionary songs blared out from the speaker, over the fields, where the peasants and their part-time colleagues bent their backs. "Victory is ours under your guidance, dear Beloved Leader", was the introduction, and ending, to each piece. If the woman had wind against, or if she tired at intervals, the music slurred. If she was assisted by a stiff breeze, the rhythm picked up again. What a job, I thought – hard work, low pay, no applause. I was wrong; my Gallic friends lined her path, clapped, cheered, shouted in sheer Latin exuberance. Eyes fixed on the road, she ignored them entirely – just pushed on along her allotted stretch. She was doing her bit.

We reached the foot of Kumgang-san about noon. After an indifferent snack – the French had contrived to bring their own sandwiches, which they shared with me – we began the four-hour climb. It was a perfect spring day, cool, sunny, the sky azure and cloudless. It is hard to imagine a more beautiful mountain. The highest peak in a mountain range stretching for thirty miles, Kumgang-san rivals Yosemite National Park in the variety and luxuriance of its scenery. As we climbed, we brushed through colourful shrubs and ferns of many species; majestic cedars, cypresses, maples, chestnuts and sycamores, as well as conifers of all kinds afforded us welcome shade and splashes of colour. Half a dozen exquisite waterfalls punctuated our route, one of them more than one hundred metres high – soaring chimneys and dark spinneys surrounded the summit, where rocky crags enabled us to squat and contemplate a breathtaking panorama. The range stretched endlessly inland, disappearing in a dark blue haze on the western horizon. The afternoon sun filtered through a myriad leaves and foliages, allowing the keen photographers among us a rich harvest of subjects.

On such a climb, arduous, but in no way risky, the excitement of the ascent, the welcome physical exercise and exertion, the stunning loveliness of the environment, the common innocent goal, bonded the French, the minders, the girl and myself in the most comforting manner. One gave one's hand to

Hong Kong seminar

Mathias, Paivi, Lasse Virén, Lewises in S. Africa

French residential school, Burgundy

Stockholm school

Seminar in Turku

Ericsson seminar

Cold seminars in Lapland

Finnair address, opening Gateway Terminal 1996

Crown Prince Hiro's wedding

Knighthood ceremony 1997

Emperor's reception, London 1998

Ambasador Pertti Salolainen and wife Anja at Riversdown

Wigan Pier

Tokyo nightlife

Blackpool, Lancashire's playground   Off to work 1933

Riversdown 10th anniversary

Akasaka

by the Danube

Finnish archipelago

Language Bus

Cologne 1964   Mahlzeit

Miguel Baez Litri

another across swirling streams, helped the older members up the more difficult spinneys, shared the chores of leading, carrying and picture-taking. For four hours we were all friends suspended in time in a real paradise where dogma, revolutions, victories and defeats, Beloved Leaders, presidents and monarchs held no sway, where the only ideology was the one of the moment – the reaching of the summit which would bequeath us an incomparable vision of nature and the quintessential landscape of the Land of the Morning Calm.

How nice this land could be, I thought as we rested at the top and drank in the spectacle. They have it all right here. The minders smiled at me, aware of my delight in the environment. The girl suddenly looked feminine and approachable.

The congeniality of this *entente cordiale* dissipated fast as we descended. The French, who became increasingly peckish, talked incessantly of *bifteck avec pommes frites*, a topic which reminded my stomach to churn and lessened some of my own cordiality towards our Korean hosts. The long trip back along the same route afforded us numerous glimpses of toiling bank clerks, post office employees and shop assistants doing their Friday diligence until darkness engulfed them. The lorry-loads of weary volunteers accompanied us along the highways as they returned to Pyongyang and other towns along the way.

*   *   *   *   *

There was no let-up in our indoctrination. In between the table tennis events, which took place mainly in the evening, we were carted off by the busload to the mammoth, opulent museums of the capital. These all-marble edifices, occupying thousands of square metres of prime downtown real estate, took 3-4 hours each to get through. Though huge in size, they seemed to have only two doors that would open – the entrance where you were pushed in and an exit which turned up half a day later. There was no lateral escape, neither from the building nor from the ministrations of the earnest guides. The history of the Koreas was spelled out for us in several languages from the prehistoric era to 1979. The Korean War of 1950-52 was naturally in greatest focus. World War Two was a skirmish by comparison. No one that I met in North Korea had heard of George Washington or the Battle of Britain, or the moon landing. The world's greatest philosopher, scholar, military genius and supreme statesman was – you've guessed – Kim-il Sung. His philosophy or ideology – the solution for the world's ills – was **JUCHE** – a national spirit of independence and self-reliance which conquered all when the rest of the world abandoned you (as seemed to be the case). This inner, fiery discipline sounded like a combination of British guts, American true grit, Finnish *sisu*, French *panache* and Japanese *yamato damashii*. In fact it was all these and more – it incorporated in addition the redoubtable Korean quality of **HAHN**, that pent-up well of hatred that resulted from two thousand years of oppression, injustice and exploitation. Korean **HAHN**, historically often directed against the Japanese or Chinese, had reached a temporary zenith in the 1970s in its intense focus on the Americans.

One of the most common sights which greeted our eyes in North Korea was that of smartly uniformed children marching to school. They seemed capable of doing this from the age of five or six, always led by a young teacher, usually female. Their uniforms were normally deep blue with red trim, their ruddy countenances well-scrubbed and earnest. Swinging their arms high, they really **marched,** singing lustily along the way. The singing was generally pretty good and we watched these daily processions with grudging admiration, until one of the minders told us what they were singing. "May our country's streams flow red with the blood of shot-down fascist American pilots" was one of the milder lyrics. This routine took place tens of thousands of times daily, to and from school, all over the country. God knows what they sang **in** school.

Our guides – in reality secret police – told the same story to us as that they fed to their own populace. One would have thought that "educated tourists" would have warranted a slightly more sophisticated approach.

Kim-Il-Sung's name was never actually spoken. He was always referred to as "The Beloved Leader" and in a hushed voice. His face looked out at you from every button-hole. Thankfully they did not try to press them on us – perhaps they thought we didn't deserve to wear them. Park, my first and older minder, was the most dogmatic of all. I had the 3-bedroom chant so many times that I finally showed him a picture of Riversdown with its twenty rooms. He asked if it was a ducal palace, I said no, just an ordinary English home. I had already embarked on a counter-propaganda campaign and, though he showed no signs of wilting, he was unable to conceal his frustration. That was probably why he was changed for Kim the Jogger. Ian Wooldridge, fine speaker and journalist that he was, seemed to be getting the better of **his** minder and swore he would make a good Conservative out of him. He had already given him a free subscription to the Daily Mail.

One night in the hotel bar, we had drinks with two Swedish engineers who were working on some project near the Chinese border. Sweden had contributed funds and these men had permanent working visas. They came down to Pyongyang once a month to change scenery. They told us that the two months prior to the championships had seen a frenzy of activity in the capital. Every building in the centre of the city had been washed, air-blasted or painted. Broken window panes had been restored, streets had been swept, doors had been varnished. Kiosks, garbage skips, telephone boxes, lamp posts, fences and water hydrants had been hastily painted; the innumerable marble surfaces had been polished, gravel paths had been re-laid. Thousands of peasants had been drafted in from the countryside to perform this labour.

All the cars we were using were state-owned and most of them had been imported a few months earlier. I didn't see any with more than 10,000 km. on the clock. There were no private cars or bicycles in North Korea at that time. When we asked why people were not allowed to own cars, we were told they were dangerous for bicycles. Everybody in the country except officials went everywhere on foot. There were **no** fat people in North Korea.

Our cars were available for us at all times, though the trusties gave all the directions. The drivers never spoke to us or looked us in the eye. They didn't seem to like us much. Our female minders, mainly girls in their mid-twenties, spoke reasonable English and accompanied us on most trips. As far as I could gather, none of them made any advances to any westerners; those players or officials who playfully attemped to flirt with them, were coldly rebuffed. You didn't fool around with the Daughters of the Revolution. Most of them were basically good looking; all were impeccably dressed. None that I met exuded any measurable degree of femininity. Probably they, too, were secret police; certainly they chimed in with the hackneyed political slogans whenever the male trusties had a rest.

The Pyongyang authorities were not lacking in their provision of spectacular social events for the foreign visitors. One night there was a great banquet in one of the cavernous halls, followed by a mammoth open-air dance in the main square of the city. It was a huge-scale affair, reminiscent of similar events organized at Chinese state-run shows. But the North Koreans were at a big disadvantage *vis-à-vis* the Chinese. Chinese food is good, Pyongyang fare is atrocious. All the more reason to look forward to the dance. Hundreds of girls had been brought in from the countryside, all decked out in their finest dresses. There were at least 5000 people in the square – it could have been a real rave-up. But there were no foxtrots, tangos, rhumbas or even waltzes. The dances were strictly Korean folklore – the smiling maidens pirouetted at a metre and half distance from lusting Frenchmen and Italians. Those Brits who were familiar with Lancers and Cotillions did quite well; the Japanese performed their social duties, though they knew the maids hated them; the grey-suited trusties took care of the foreign women. It was a fine spectacle on a balmy spring evening. Not much atmosphere, though.

In the second week we had a national public holiday. There was no table tennis that day; instead we were conscripted to attend the various celebrations which marked the occasion. In North Korea "celebrations" meant mainly parades. We watched these most of the morning. Seemingly endless, the procession consisted of delegations from every part of the country, each following a red banner indicating their provenance. There were workers, university students, schoolchildren, teachers, farmers, firemen, soldiers, sailors, airmen, youth movements and some sections comprising septuagenarians and even older people whom we supposed to be pensioners. It was good parade weather – the spick-and-span boulevards of Pyongyang were bathed in brilliant sunshine, it was pleasantly cool at around 22 degrees. The smartness and impeccable attire of the participants made one wonder how a people who ate so badly could afford to dress so well.

When we could not take any more parades, we were treated to a public display in one of the city parks. There were dancers and the usual child pianists, but the stars were undoubtedly the acrobats. Korean acrobats have a world-wide reputation for their agility and spectacular performances and Kim-Il-Sung's boys were no exception. At last the westerners had something to enthuse about; cameras clicked, there was generous applause, we were all in a good mood until we were shepherded into huge marquees for another depressing lunch.

In the afternoon we were to experience what had been billed as the cultural highlight of our stay in Korea – a visit to the birthplace of the Beloved Leader. Our convoy of black cars and mini-buses threaded its way out of town to the "village" of Mangjong-dae, a collection of half a dozen reed huts about 20 minutes from the city centre. The huts, which looked like they had been woven the previous day, occupied the top of a charming hill overlooking the Taedong river. In Indian file, we were shepherded past the particular hut where Kim-Il-Sung's mother was supposed to have given birth. There, on a *tatami*-style floor, we evinced great interest inspecting the Leader's little chair, his first toys, a picture of his parents, his early school exercise books. The tones of our guides were more hushed than usual in this Korean Bethlehem. There was not a speck of dust anywhere; lovely pink cherry trees completed the idyllic scene. There were a few speeches by ageing trusties – I think one was the Mayor of Pyongyang. Later each educated tourist and senior table tennis official planted a cherry tree for future generations. The fact that Kim-Il-sung was born hundreds of miles away in another part of Korea was hardly a subject to bring up on such a sunny, harmonious afternoon. A brass band gave us a stentorian send-off as we climbed back into the waiting transports.

*   *   *   *   *

The Central Post Office in downtown Pyongyang seemed to function well. The building was of high quality and seemed very new indeed. It was stuffed by a large number of smiling maidens in national dress. North Koreans were not allowed to send letters abroad, certainly not to their fascist cousins in the South; as far as their fellow-countrymen in the North were concerned, there was probably very little to write about. Consequently queues were very short, in fact they consisted only of foreign visitors.

There were plenty of shiny postcards available in the capital. These showed the imposing edifices of Pyongyang, the mountains in the north, Korean peasants in national dress and of course portraits of the Leader and pictures of his humble birthplace. The Swedes had warned us that all letters were opened, so we opted for postcards to save everybody a lot of trouble. The question was, what should one write? One had certain feelings about the situation, but there was no point in writing anything which would not get through. Our one refuge was, however, irony, which does not register with most East Asians. I wrote, therefore, the same simple message on all my postcards: "Greetings from the Workers' Paradise". The attendants positively beamed at me as they stamped on the postmark.

The stamps themselves were special issue, commemorating the world championships. They were well-designed and pretty enough, but I noticed that the few Koreans who bought them licked the postcard (or envelope) instead of the stamp. The reason for this became evident when one had licked one stamp. Apparently civil servants were known to lick passports and other documents before affixing visas and other official stamps. Journalists complained of problems in getting their telegrams out on time, but on the whole the Post Office was one of the happiest places in Pyongyang.

Our trips to the Post Office, the stadium, the odd park and all the official excursions were facilitated by our fleets of Volvos and Mercedes. But the routes were curious. Leaving our hotel it was only a few hundred yards to one of the main avenues of the city centre. This we invariably drove along, the entire length. At the end of the avenue, we turned sharply left and drove along another wide boulevard for about half a mile. Then we did another sharp left and drove along another majestic avenue which completed the triangle and returned us to our starting point. After that we went where we were going. About the third day we started asking the minders about this strange procedure. They seemed not to understand our puzzlement. That's the route, they replied. That was as far as you got. According to our Swedish informants, the three boulevards in question had had a super-duper sprucing up. Whether you wanted a postcard, an aspirin, a pee in a cafe or an audience with Kim himself, that was the Route.

North Koreans must believe deeply in foreign credulousness, for our gullibility was tried to preposterous limits. One Australian journalist, interested in golf, was told that Kim Jong-Il, the son of Kim-Il-Sung, had shot the 18-hole Pyongyang Golf Club course in a startling 34. The club pro, who volunteered this information, and who had never heard of Jack Nicklaus or Arnold Palmer, said the good score was attributable to Kim having 5 holes-in-one during the round. "He's a fine golfer" added the pro.

*　　*　　*　　*　　*

If one thing stands out in my memory more than anything else about my visit to North Korea, it is the trip we made to Panmunjom. This was one of the optional excursions offered to educated tourists. I had urged Ron Crayden, one of the senior British officials (who had also received a special classification) to take advantage of this opportunity to witness a real piece of history. He took my advice and came with me; we were the only two foreigners to do this.

At the end of the bitterly fought Korean War in 1952, the American generals Matthew Ridgway and Mark Clark concluded and signed an armistice on the mutually agreed frontier between North and South Korea. The armistice was followed by "peace talks" aimed at stabilizing and normalizing relations between the two Koreas, at establishing a no-man's land five hundred yards wide between the two territories, and ultimately at working towards an eventual reunification of the country through the electoral process. This last objective was hardly considered to be attainable in the foreseeable future and the talks soon developed into vicious bickering sessions where each side accused the other of violations of the armistice terms. These regular meetings, now numbering in high hundreds, took place in a long dismal Nissen hut in no-mans-land slap on the frontier in the previously undistinguished village of Panmunjom. Grim-faced delegations from North and South Korea (with US participation) face each other at regular intervals on opposite sides of long, narrow, green-beize-covered tables. At the end of the room stands a leather-topped desk where Mark Clark signed the historic document. The meetings are not for the faint-hearted. Hostile in the extreme, they have been noted for their irascibility, petulance, vindictiveness and pugnacity. In 45 years the progress towards any form of amity or *entente* has been virtually nil. Two American officers who foolishly went crawling round in the barbed wire of No-mans-land were seen, attacked and **hacked to pieces** by North Korean guards armed with hatchets. The pieces were returned to the South side in brown sacks.

We could hardly believe that we were going to be allowed to "inspect" this notoriously dangerous boundary and we could not conceive what form this exercise would take. We were in for a lesson in North Korean stage management. The 150 km. journey to the frontier took 3 hours. Ron Crayden and I were accompanied by an older minder whom neither of us had seen before. His English was excellent, but he was unsmiling and seemed to brood a lot. It was Friday again and Ron and I waved at lorry loads of bank clerks off to their weekly rice business. They ignored us; by contrast groups of school children at the way side cheered our car vociferously. (They have been told to cheer all cars. All cars are government cars).

In the neighbourhood of Panmunjom we were shown some Stone Age monuments. They were impressive and we took some nice pictures. Later we were taken to a giant statue of Kim-Il-Sung, situated on a green hill overlooking, at a distance of less than one kilometre, the undulating fields of South Korea. It is an impressive statue. It is the third biggest in the world after that of Mother Russia in Volgograd (formerly Stalingrad) and the Statue of Liberty in New York. Kim, in black marble, surveys with bulging eyes the territory which he has vowed he will re-incorporate into the homeland. South Koreans can see the statue for miles off. It is so big, you almost have to back off into South Korea to get it all into your view-finder, when taking a picture.

We of course had our ears pounded for some time as we gravitated round the sculpture, but after that we were taken to a house where we sat in red velvet armchairs for four hours without much to do or any intelligent conversation. Apparently there had been a hitch in the arrangements and it was no longer sure that we should be allowed to see the frontier. The spring sun threatened to set and the shadows of some nearby poplars began to lengthen. When the evening light was really nice and mellow and we had given up hope, we were summarily and peremptorily whisked off to the frontier post. This proved to be a fine marble and concrete building, about 40 metres long, aligned along the North Korean side of No-mans-land. Once inside, Ron and I were introduced to 6 military personnel – a colonel, a captain and 4 privates. The privates formed a square around us, the colonel led from the front and the captain stood behind us. We were marched off to a well-furnished waiting room where we were served tea. We were then subjected to 45 minutes indoctrination by the captain, who was competent in well-versed, rhetorical English. He described the events of the 1950-52 Korean War, from his own point of view, of course. He then asked Ron and myself a series of questions, which required "yes" or "no" answers. It was cleverly done, as soon one found oneself endorsing the North Korean position:

"In this internal Korean dispute, were the South Koreans the ones who first called in foreign interventionists?"

Yes".

"Did Japan, supposedly neutral, allow the United States to use their country as a supply base against the North Koreans?

"Yes".

"Did the Japanese supply the American army with *matériel* for the duration of the war?

"Yes".

"Did Japan make a lot of money out of the Korean War?"

"Yes".

"Did North Korea accept any outside help until the Americans bombed the Yalu River frontier with China?"

"No."

I cannot remember all the questions – they did not allow us to take notes – but there were many much cleverer and more subtle than the ones I can recall. I found myself saying all kinds of things I didn't mean. Poor Ron sounded like Karl Marx. After a while I played the game according to their rules and feigned some sympathy for the North Korean cause. The captain was not stupid, yet I detected a gleam of interest in his slant eyes. When I had used the term "Leader" a couple of times (I could not bring myself to say "beloved") his solidarity quickened. His reasoning, previously pompous, became more empirical and appealing. He suspected I might be on his side. He was wrong, but even Wiganers can flatter to deceive. Ron joined in a bit, too. The captain snapped orders to the privates and we were all on our feet. The colonel, mute all the while, took up his vanguard position and led us off on the double down a short corridor. We had to march in rhythm with the six of them –all in full red-trimmed khaki uniforms, of course. At the end of the corridor it was smart left turn and we faced two huge doors. The captain asked us to stand still and the two leading privates stepped briskly forward and flung the two doors wide open. Facing us, at a distance of 20 metres, were two South Korean soldiers with rifles pointed in **our** direction, bayonets fixed. Twenty metres behind them, up a control tower, was an American officer with a sub-machine gun. As our colonel took a well-rehearsed step to one side, the extrovert captain flung out his arm in a southern direction, sighted the US officer with his index finger and screamed:

"There you see foreign occupying troops on Korean soil!"

Neither Ron or I felt like arguing at this point. The American – he seemed to be a lieutenant – took out a telescopic lens camera and calmly photographed Ron and myself. For some reason this irritated me momentarily, so I raised my camera and took a shot of him taking me. The North Korean captain howled with delight:

"Yes, take the pig's picture!" he screeched.

I took a couple more for good measure, wondering if I would ever again be allowed into the United States to visit my wife's parents. The American officer seemed unmoved. His photography done, he put down his camera on the parapet of the gun-tower and picked up his arm again. I winked at him, but nobody noticed. After that we were taken down to the actual border line and were within 10 metres of the South Korean bayonets. The two sentries were as impassive as those Horse Guards in Whitehall. They could have been waiting for a train.

The descent of the fine marble steps was followed by a right wheel which led us to the long Nissen hut where the peace negotiations took place. Once inside, you really felt history lean on you. I was allowed to sit in the chair where Mark Clark signed the treaty and the captain obligingly took my picture. Ron struck a few poses and we were given the North side of the peace talks for the previous two decades. The colonel had accompanied the captain and ourselves into the hut, where we stayed a good 20 minutes. The four privates eye-balled the South Korean sentries outside. Nobody looked like they were going to shoot, but I thought of the hatcheting and shivered a bit.

It was getting dusk, but the captain finished his piece without switching on the lights of the hut.

We were escorted back to the bright lights of the big building, given various propaganda leaflets in English, and marched off to our cars. The captain shook my hand firmly and not unsympathetically as we said good-bye. I think he had hope – he allowed himself a half-smile. Back in England, I received glossy books from North Korea until the end of the 1980s. I am no longer on their mailing list, but I have quite a collection of expensively produced volumes. I suppose that is what they spend their money on.

*   *   *   *   *

As the championships progressed, so did our indoctrination programme. Besides a gushing, conducted tour of the Palace of Children we were treated to a lengthy demonstration of Korean folklore – dancing, singing, playing of a variety of instruments, accompanied walks through one or two parks and, to our utter boredom, a 2-hour inspection of 48,236 gifts presented to Kim-il-Sung by foreign dignitaries during his long reign. I read recently the total eventually reached 73,035 and are housed in a specially constructed 8-storey building to the north of the city.

My female minder was changed in the middle of the second week, as relations between us had deteriorated after she had called Winston Churchill a fascist. I went to great lengths to tell her about a tussle he had had with a real fascist called Adolf Hitler and irritated her further by referring to Winston as our great leader. Her successor, Yuk Mae, pretty, thirtyish and sexless, had obviously been warned about me and quashed any adventurous remarks I made with her two favourite phrases:

"I do not understand you" and "That is dirty American propaganda". Ex-jogger Kim maintained a veneer of friendliness at all times, though he had obviously written me off as a convert. Many of the minders felt they were scoring well on the political front, but they did not realise how much depended on nationaliy traits. Czechs, Rumanians, Hungarians and other East Europeans were pastmasters in pretending to agree with everything: it cost nothing to please the trusties. Some of the Brits and Scandinavians were too polite to disagree violently. Italians were quite capable of hoodwinking the Koreans. With the Americans, and particularly the French, the minders had a rough time and gave up after a few days, though they were still condemned to traipse around with them.

Brainwashing of the insidious type we were subjected to causes sudden irritations: often I would get back at Kim through petty misbehaviour, even though I knew the man was only doing his job. For instance in North Korea you may only cross the road at zebra crossings which are spaced 500 metres apart and supervised by a policeman. Traffic was almost non-existent in Pyongyang, yet you were not allowed to cross any empty road except at the designated points. Walking along a leafy avenue, I spotted a small museum of some interest across the road. I suggested to a pleased Kim that we should visit it. Before he realised what I was doing, I stepped off the pavement and headed across the road. He launched himself after me, grabbed me fiercely by the arm and dragged me backwards just as the policeman 250 metres further down blew his whistle shrilly at the transgression. A second later, the policeman on duty in the other direction, hearing his colleague's blast, joined in the condemnation with his own instrument. Kim, upset and nervous, took me firmly up the road to the first officer of the law, seemed to beseech understanding from him in flowing, staccato Korean, then took me back 250 metres on the other side of the road, where we carried out the visit. The eyes of both policemen followed us right up to the entrance and scrutinized us again when we exited some time later. By these subterfuges many of us managed to make the minders' lives something of a trial.

*   *   *   *   *

I have said that the table tennis events progressed with some normality: one acceded to a world of sporting sanity each time one entered the stadium. In a way, the table tennis matches provided lucid intervals between the sessions of doctrinal conditioning that we experienced outside. And yet it was a scene in the stadium which, in the end, provided us with the deepest insight into North Korean behaviour and organisation. North Korea had a good table tennis team. They did quite well in these championships, though their best chances for medals lay in the individual events. They had two strong men in the singles, while Li Song Suk, their star female player, was fully expected to win the Women's Singles. The stadium was packed each evening by Koreans, most of them drafted in from the countryside to give maximum support to their stars. They did not seem to understand the game, but they applauded vociferously as each Korean player won a point and hissed loudly when an opponent scored. This behaviour put us all off at first, but we got used to it and put it down to partisan enthusiasm. We had seen similar crowd comportment in Yugoslavia. The two Korean male stars were knocked out in the quarter-finals, but the brilliant, scowling Suk got through round after round in convincing fashion and eventually made the final of the Women's Singles.

The Finals, for men and women, were due to be played on the last Saturday. There was not a single seat vacant in the stadium – the crowd was more than 90 per cent Korean. The prospect of a Suk victory – and a gold medal – had raised Rent-a-crowd's expectancy to fanatical heights. The rustic masses waited impatiently as the Women's Doubles, Men's Doubles and Mixed Doubles finals were played. There were no Korean participants. The last two finals scheduled were the Women's Singles and, of course, the Men's Singles.

There was a great hush as Suk took the table against a Chinese opponent. Suk was a sturdy figure, rather tall for an oriental, with long black hair, fine wide cheek-bones and a perenially frowning expression. The Chinese girl, by contrast was diminutive, dumpy and bespectacled. The stage was set for the **JUCHE** heroine, who won her first game comfortably. The crowd nearly raised the roof off. The Chinese girl, amid great hissing, unexpectedly won the second game. The crowd went deathly quiet as the Chinese led throughout the third and decisive game. Pak, though attacking brilliantly, was off her timing. Time and time again she stamped her foot in rage as smashes missed the table. She lost.

The Chinese victor went up to the umpire for the usual handshake. Her coaches rushed to congratulate her. All Korean eyes were on Suk, who, hanging her head and ignoring her coach, walked slowly out of the arena. A new umpire arrived to take the Men's Final, which was to follow immediately. And then a strange thing happened. As Suk exited, the entire crowd rose quickly and evenly to its feet and vacated the stadium. One moment we were 5,000 spectators, the next we were 300 foreigners. I had never witnessed anything like it at any sporting event that I had attended. Sports journalists of 40 years experience said the same thing. Seichi Ono of Japan and Guo Yuehua of the People's Republic of China played the Men's Finals of the Pyongyang World Table Tennis Championships of 1979 to an empty stadium. It was exciting in the extreme, with Guo three times falling on the floor with violent stomach cramps and Ono eventually triumphing to end 12 years Chinese domination in the event. Not one Korean was there to see it.

*   *   *   *   *

We left Pyongyang in mellow evening sunshine with our minders, male and female, and the Mayor of Pyongyang waving us an elegant adieu with little pink handkerchiefs. The Beloved Leader was not present, but his chubby features peeked out at us from 200 buttonholes. We endured the Siberian ordeal once more and some nasty things were spat out by normally phlegmatic West Europeans as our plane circled safely in a holding pattern over Geneva. The flight attendants, male and female, gave as good as they got – I have never witnessed such hostility exhibited within the confines of an aircraft cabin.

They threw our luggage off the plane. We grabbed it fast as it hit the tarmac, zoomed through Swiss Customs and headed without delay towards beefsteaks and *rösti* potatoes.

Chapter 18

Linguarama – 1971-1988

The unique and stunningly beautiful location of the Riversdown estate is undoubtedly one of the major factors contributing to its success. The other is the kaleidoscopic nature of the nationality mix. Many a language school in the UK is dominated by groups of students from one or two countries where they have active agents. In some, Germans preponderate, in others, French, Italians or Swedes. Some institutions deal almost exclusively with Spaniards or Arabs. If one nationality dominates, there is a general air of frustration, both on the part of students and management alike. The preponderant group tend to talk their own language the moment the teacher's vigilance is relaxed. Certain elements of the students' culture, whether it be a preference for certain types of food, social activities, sports events or subjects for common debate, may take over the general ambience. This state of affairs is the last thing mature executives want. They wish, during what may necessarily be a limited stay in England, to extract the maximum of Englishness from their surroundings. This involves not only maximum use and absorption of the language, but being immersed, as totally as is possible, in the national culture, with its stereotypical **and** original twists and turns, its local colour, its sometimes idiosyncratic train of thought. Speaking English 12 hours a day is a species of torture, but it brings its own catharsis. Germans love to be beaten around the head with irregular verb parts, French and Spaniards alike are innately desperate for a few Pygmalion-like phrases, Japanese "salary-men" burst with pride in their ability to reel off a string of idioms or, better still, to relate an English joke. Executives, used to making (often difficult) business decisions on a daily basis are gratified to be on the receiving end for a change – to be guided, monitored, perhaps admonished or chastised – but to improve in the end. ESP for them indeed signifies English as a Special Punishment.

But improving their command of language is only half of the story. Knowledge of linguistic structure or anything else for that matter – is of limited use unless you can impart it to others. Imagine a market consultant marooned alone on a desert island. After linguistic proficiency come communication skills. Businessmen need to make presentations, to negotiate, persuade and cajole, be effective on the telephone, reply to complaints and criticism, articulate strategies, debate policies, perhaps motivate a multi-national work force. In the last instance the issue is complicated by different audience expectations.

It is said that surveys have shown that the third greatest fear that adults have, after death and serious illness, is public speaking. I cannot vouch for the accuracy of this assertion, but, in my experience, the act of getting out to the front and addressing a sizeable group of fellow humans often involves more stress and requires more resolve than actually structuring what one wishes to say. Much of business activity does in fact belong to the sphere of public speaking. The mountain to climb is all the steeper when one has to use a language other than one's own. Such skills can, however, be taught and practised (in front of small groups) in 2 or 3 weeks. The fear can be overcome – fellow students whose turn it is to speak next hardly comprise a critical audience! The cross-cultural element also enters into the equation. German, French Japanese and Nordic listeners, however friendly, will react in different ways – adding to the experience of the trainee speaker.

There are approximately 200 countries registered with the United Nations. Most of them have sent their nationals to Riversdown. On occasion we have had fifteen nationalities present in a body of 20 students. The richness and variety of this cosmopolitanism produces an excitement – an air of expectancy of dialogue – which is rare in creation. One week one has a German-French debate at centre stage with Danish arbitration and Thai onlookers. Another week spotlights a Japanese executive striving to explain the intricacies of the Tokyo Old Boy Network to interested Europeans. Two Tajiks spent a week uncovering the train of thought of ex-Soviet Central Asian Muslims to Finns, who absorbed most of it and to Italians who did not. One memorable week we were treated to fierce sales presentations by representatives of 4 leading tyre companies – Michelin, Pirelli, Nokia and Deutsche Goodyear. The Nokia man complained of being at a disadvantage; the other three were salesmen, while he was only an accountant! In recent years the addition of businessmen and women from Russia, Uzbekistan, Kazakhstan, Hungary, Vietnam and other former Eastern bloc countries has enhanced the variety of discussion and social activity.

*   *   *   *   *

For the reasons quoted above, it became essential for us, as early as 1971, to provide sources of executive students in as many countries as possible. This cannot be done, quickly at any rate, by simply using agents. Such people, often in the travel business, are mainly interested in getting bums on seats. The easiest way to do this is to sell cheap language courses to large numbers, often to teenage students. This was not our market and never would be. Accordingly most travel agents and indeed those language schools abroad which themselves taught largely adolescents, could not be effective partners for our purposes. In the case of several organisations sending huge groups to study

English in the UK, it was hard to know whether they were schools adding on travel or travel agencies adding on "English study". Such organisations employed fleets of landladies each summer in resorts such as Brighton, Hastings, Eastbourne and Bournemouth and hired church halls, YMCAs and other social centres to give their lessons.

We found one or two reputable language schools abroad which specialised in students from the business community. Shenker in Italy was one of them and they were happy to send us Italian executives for a finishing course at Riversdown. Ultimately, however, there was only one solution to providing self-perpetuating sources of the type of student we wished to attract – that was to set up our own executive language schools abroad. We had in fact made a good start in 1971 establishing direct contact with several leading companies in Europe and the UK – Unilever, Deutsche Bank, Barclays and Fiat were among them – but the firms in Europe would inevitably need service on the ground and we could expand our connections much faster by having bases in the major European countries. Such expansion required capital. We were well able to increase the numbers of our schools by two, three or four a year with the income that Riversdown generated. In order to set up a real **language school chain** in double quick time, we would need more money. This was not difficult to find. I had Swiss acquaintances who were only too anxious to invest and remain as sleeping partners; other people appeared from time to time with various proposals and different amounts of cash.

We rented a London office at 53 Pall Mall; our landlords were the then Dunbar Bank with whom we enjoyed excellent relations for over a decade, though they had no shares in our business. Ed Wilton, soon back from Japan, took up residence in one of the labourers' cottages and joined me in the enterprise. We used the name Linguarama (invented one night by my wife), which though not sounding very academic, was easy to remember. We thought it certainly had the edge on Inlingua.

Inlingua and Berlitz, with their respective empires, were now our rivals. With such large numbers of schools, probably neither one felt unduly threatened. What I felt, however, was that only the Japanese Berlitz schools and mere handful in Europe were actually dealing with executives. Berlitz America did, but we had no immediate ambitions in the US market. Most Inlingua schools concentrated on large numbers (as Berlitz Portugal had done). Consequently, I saw our competition in Europe as being, if not minimal, hardly strong.

In the event, we set up 30-odd schools over the next 15 years in major cities such as Madrid, Barcelona, Milan, Hamburg, Frankfurt, Munich and Paris. In many of these centres we became market leaders in our special field, and our rivals were forced to imitate us in order to maintain a presence in the executive market. The Linguarama story is a long one and my memoirs would never be completed if I were to try to describe every initiative, adventure, success, disappointment or failure. I worked with many outstanding and reliable people. I encountered the usual quota of indifferent performers and unfortunately no small number of con men, phonies and stab-in-the-back artists. The language business is people-intensive, widespread and fiercely competitive. It is a business where clients often grope in the dark with regard to their own requirements and school directors or salesmen are often able to cut corners, use unsuitable staff or make untenable claims as to future progress. The public justifiably regards with some suspicion advertising which says "you can speak any language fluently inside three and a half weeks" – such ads are common – but what training officer really knows what is involved in sending a trainee to learn Arabic or Chinese, or the respective differences and difficulties inherent in tackling Rumanian or Bulgarian?

As far as language teachers are concerned, quality varies enormously. I have engaged a couple of thousand or more in my career – there are very few hard and fast rules. Young teachers are inevitably peripatetically inclined and many become footloose, wandering from school to school across Europe or Asia, going private now and then, returning to an employer when pickings are scarce. Basically Europe is busy in winter, closed in summer. English in England booms in June, July and August and hibernates in winter. I have always found that teachers who were seriously involved in sport were more reliable and student-friendly than the average. Young teachers (often female) who were accompanied by one or more parents at the interview usually turned out well. Husband-and-wife teams sent abroad in most cases brought problems. Some nationalities fulfil contracts more faithfully than others. New Zealanders and South Africans generally top the list for steadiness. People who let you down are frequently the ones who were least qualified to do the job in the first place. University graduates with good degrees in languages or education usually think of their career and build in two or three years of language teaching abroad as a useful and enlightening component. They are nearly always correct in the performance of their duties. It is a mistake to listen to some sob story and take on somebody (often local) who is not fully qualified but needs a job. Not infrequently the appointment goes to their head, they try to lord it over more qualified staff and more often than not confide their personal problems to clients whom they later try to steal.

*   *   *   *   *

One of our outstanding school directors was a Frenchman named Robert Sirabella whom we sent to run Madrid, later to open further schools in Barcelona, Pamplona and Seville. Born in Algeria, he was an ex-parachutist and lived dangerously. Though a controversial figure, he was an excellent marketing man as well as a fully qualified pedagogue. He eventually became a partner in our Spanish operation and helped in the setting up of Paris in 1980. He left the organisation in 1988, bought a yacht and sailed solo half way round the world, before disappearing mysteriously from his boat (presumed drowned) in 1990.

At Riversdown, Steve Allison, Sue Roby, Pat Dowdell and John Ordish carved out reputations for themselves as brilliant teachers over a period of several years; Karean McGowan was an exceptional secretary and personal assistant, Sheila Troke a versatile and inspired chef.

In France Elizabeth Péres-Ross has completed 25 years of diligent service and still acts as adviser for Richard Lewis Communications. Other brilliant linguists who worked for us were Warwick Terry from New Zealand, Stella Kenway from England and Eleanor Kalmanasch from Canada. The last named – quadrilingual and of Rumanian extraction – ran our school in São Paulo for ten years until she was held up at gunpoint in the school office at noon and nearly relieved of the cash in her desk drawer. She loved Brazil, but decided to call it a day and currently works for us at peacable Riversdown.

*   *   *   *   *

The Brazilian venture is a story in itself. In the mid 1970s the country seemed ripe for a language boom. Some Portuguese acquaintances of mine had fled the revolution; one of them, Fernando Mota, was anxious to participate – he lived at that time in Rio de Janeiro. I flew out via Recife and checked into the Hotel Gloria at the northern end of the Copacabana. After a few hours sleep I met Fernando for lunch. He had to work in the afternoon so he invited me for dinner at his home that evening.

After lunch I decided to spend a few hours on the famous Copacabana beach. I left all my valuables in the hotel safe, for I knew Rio's reputation for thieves and pick-pockets, and strolled down the beach wearing only a short-sleeved shirt and a bathing costume, carrying an extra pair of shorts to change into after swimming. The beach was not too crowded and I found a suitable spot near the middle to set up base. I swam for 10 minutes leaving my shirt and shorts on the sand near where I entered the water. There were about $50 and a credit card in the pocket of the shorts and I kept my clothes clearly in view as I swam. After swimming I lay on my back on the warm sand with my shirt under my head and my shorts a foot from it. I decided my bathing suit would soon dry.

After a few minutes, a negro bearing an incredible resemblance to Pele came up to me and asked me the time in Portuguese. I told him it was 4 o'clock – he seemed reasonably satisfied and wandered off. I was beginning to feel jet lag a bit, but decided not to sleep, as it might be too risky. Though basically awake I must have dozed for a moment or two, for suddenly I noticed that my shorts had moved a few inches further away. I checked the pockets – the money and credit card had gone.

Looking around I saw Pele's double striding steadily away from me. He was only 10 yards away so I started walking after him. The distance between us did not decrease, so I began to jog. When I started jogging, he started jogging and still the distance remained constant. Finally, when I ran, he ran too. I shouted after him, but he did not turn his head. After half a mile, I gave up; he was about 25 years of age and used to the sand, I guess. When I plodded back to my shirt and shorts, there they were – gone, as the Welsh say. I sat down and had a rest.

After about half an hour, Pele came back. I told him it was 5 o'clock and asked him who had taken my money. He was very friendly and said he didn't know. I got friendly too and told him there would be a reward for anyone who might return my American Express card to the Hotel Gloria. You never know, one of his friends might find it on the beach. He nodded brightly and said he would ask around. I told him I was off to cancel the card, so the police would arrest anyone who might try to use it. This is actually a laughable remark in Brazil, but I thought I would try it anyway.

Back at the Gloria I put on one of my remaining shirts and got some more money out of the safe. At 8 pm Fernando picked me up and took me to his place – an impressive 6th floor apartment overlooking the very spot where I had been relieved of my apparel. We were halfway through dinner when his phone rang. On answering it, he indicated that the call was for me – somewhat surprising, as I knew nobody in Brazil. On the other end of the line a man speaking Brazilian Portuguese informed me that he had found "*os documentos*" on the beach. What documents, I asked. A credit card with my name on it and a visiting card with Fernando's name, address and telephone number. He had rung Fernando's number on the off chance that I might be there. He hadn't found any banknotes among the *documentos* by any chance? No sir, only the cards. I told him to come by to collect his reward.

Ten minutes later the door-bell rang and Fernando, taking no chances, opened the door six inches on the chain. What might have been Pele's brother flashed my Amex through the gap. I grabbed it quick and gave him $10 *à contre-coeur*. He seemed crestfallen at the amount but I was not in a charitable mood and Fernando slammed the door shut, almost amputating his fingers.

"You're in trouble" Fernando told me as we downed a banana *caipirinha*. They know your name, you're a foreigner and you told the guy on the beach you were staying at the Hotel Gloria. A big mistake, that. I agreed. Once they get their clutches into you like that on the Copacabana, they never let go. They could also wait for me outside Fernando's apartment and encourage me to up the reward by a few thousand.

We left his flat at midnight via the basement garage, with car doors locked. They didn't know his car and I kept low down anyway. Fernando dropped me 50 metres from the Gloria, surrounded at that time of the night by a horde of unsalubrious characters on the look-out for greenhorns like me. I slipped across the marble-floored lobby behind a bunch of noisy Argentinians, but the numerous shadowy figures lurking in the foyer did nothing to augment my confidence in the integrity of the establishment itself. At one in the morning I picked up my bags and lugged them to the reception desk, where I asked for the bill. An astonished clerk eventually produced it and restituted my cash and camera which I had deposited earlier in the hotel safe. Dollars stuffed into inside pockets, I threaded my way through a rapidly thickening retinue to the front door, where I bundled my suitcases onto the back seat of a hovering taxi and ordered the driver, in a loud voice, to take me to the Hotel Miramar. This did not go unnoticed by my entourage and another taxi followed mine to the Miramar, also located in the central part of the Copacabana. On arrival, I paid and tipped the driver, scuttled through the revolving door of the hotel, belted straight across the foyer and out through the back door, where another line of taxis awaited. I took the first one to the Ipanema beach, adjacent to Copacabana, where I quickly checked in at the Hotel Kramer, German-managed. I had no problems during the rest of my stay in Rio. It seemed that I had shaken my tail and I was careful not to visit Fernando at his apartment. The Copacabana-Ipanema area is the most densely-populated place in the world after Macau, so the teeming crowds covered my tracks for the few days I remained in the beautiful city.

In São Paulo I soon found a suitable building and we ran a lively and sizeable school there for over a decade. It was, however, a continual source of problems and, in the end, not worth the hassle. In the first place, none of our teachers could get work permits. In theory, these can be obtained through the normal channels, that is to say, that we applied for them through the Brazilian Embassy in London. The embassy staff were invariably friendly, cheerful and optimistic. The permits would be granted by the Ministry of Justice in Brasilia and the London Embassy would be duly informed. This suited us fine and we paid insignificant fees to have the applications sent off. Six weeks was the estimated waiting time; this posed no problem for us, as it was a long term project. When ten weeks or three months had passed, the embassy staff, apologetic, encouraged us to send telegrams, helpfully worded by them, to the authorities in Brazil. We paid further insignificant expenses and waited patiently. Nothing ever happened. Eleanor Kalmanasch, our manager in Brazil, was now screaming for teachers, as she had concluded several large contracts with São Paulo firms. We flew a couple of men out on tourist visas and they worked clandestinely for the 6 months they were allowed to stay. After that they flew to Ascención, Paraguay, where they stayed two days and renewed their tourist visas for another 6 months. Several of them taught for us in this manner for five years or more. In the 10 years we ran a school in Brazil, not a single teacher ever obtained a work permit through the Brazilian embassy in London, though we played it by the book with every applicant. The only person in the whole decade who got a permit was Eleanor Kalmanasch, for whom we paid $5000 to our Brazilian lawyer, who then engineered it. All our teachers paid taxes on their salaries in the correct manner. They were all working illegally – the authorities were fully aware of their activiies as they were taxing them. No teacher was ever approached, accused or deported.

We made a lot of money in Brazil, but we were only allowed to change 10 percent of the profit into pounds or dollars to repatriate to the UK. You could take as many Brazilian *cruzeiros* out of the country as you could carry in a suitcase, but the exchange rate in the UK or the US was abysmal. I got sick of carrying the suitcases. When the inevitable hold-up guy walked into the school one day and pointed his gun at Kalmanasch, she, and soon after ourselves, decided to call it a day. The thief did not succeed in getting away with the loot, as Kalmanasch screamed and all the students came pouring out of the classrooms to see what was going on. The gangster fled without our cash, but when we eventually closed Brazil, our lawyer found ways of keeping it all anyway. We put it down to experience.

*   *   *   *   *

In 1977 the US publishing firm, Encyclopaedia Britannica, were interested in buying Linguarama and I had several discussions with them in Chicago, where their HQ was located. Charles Swanson, their President, was a most pleasant person to deal with, and Tom Gies, the President of the International Division, was anxious to incorporate us into his operation. In the end the acquisition did not take place – our company needed a few more years of development to attract the right price – but the result of our deliberation was that we set up a join venture with EB in what was then the German Federal Republic. EB contributed $300,000 start up capital and we provided the know-how. Shares were held in equal proportions by the Americans and ourselves.

Linguarama Britannica prospered in due course, as we set up 6 schools in major German cities. The first two or three years proved enormously difficult however. EB, against our advice, had provided an MD for Germany out of their Chicago office. He was a very personable Cuban – an ex-diplomat who had sought refuge in the United States after the Cuban Revolution. Well-dressed and bilingual, he gave a very good first impression and seemed to have done reasonably well in Chicago. He had not been long in our German HQ (based in Munich) before I detected that he was not all he seemed to be. Although business was bad in the first year, Chicago seemed quite pleased. As the Cuban was doing the reporting, I began to scrutinize the reports more carefully. He was reasonbly adept at keeping books and could shuffle figures round with the best of them. By deferring this and that and using the odd euphemism here and there, he was painting a rather rosy picture for Charles Swanson of a business which was definitely struggling at the time. I also noticed that he had virtually hived off three rooms on the top floor of the school (one being his office) and that he resented my occasional intrusion into that area. His secretary – a German woman newly-appointed by him – also looked distinctly unhappy each time I hove into view. As I did not think there was any hanky-panky going on, I was somewhat puzzled by the whole thing. A few months later, when I had had a heart-to-heart chat with Charles Swanson about the Cuban's imaginative reporting, our ex-diplomat was summarily fired by EB (who had been paying his wages) and I gained access to his closely guarded chambers. The cupboards, always kept locked when I had been around, were all stuffed with hundreds of air purifiers. Our Caribbean friend, who promptly absconded with the company car and sued EB for unfair dismissal, had been running another business on the side.

*   *   *   *   *

Hugh Howse, Head of English by Radio and Television, seems to have been reasonably friendly with Robert Maxwell, who was gradually edging into the language business through his publishing interests and ultimately the purchase of Berlitz itself.

In the mid 1980s, when Hugh and I set up a BBC Club in Tokyo, one of Hugh's associates, Andrea Charman, mentioned that a sizeable language school which Robert Maxwell had set up in Hong Kong was losing half a million a month and needed looking at. She arranged for me to meet a Maxwell executive in London – Dobbs I think his name was – to see if the situation could be remedied.

I met Dobbs in due course and agreed to spend a couple of days in Hong Kong on my next trip to Tokyo, take a look at the ailing establishment and send back a report with my recommendations.

In December of the same year, one of the pleasant months in the Colony as far as climate is concerned, I was due to read a paper at the Institute of Education there run by an old friend Dr Werner Bickley whom I had known in his British Council days in Tokyo. I combined this activity with my inspection of the Maxwell School of Languages, situated in a prime location in the Wanchai district, where I met Li Peng, the manager, a sharp young Hong

Kong Chinese of around thirty years of age. Together we went through the accounts and discussed the general position.

Drawing on one hundred years experience, the Berlitz people in America had, by the end of the 1970s, refined a formula which would ensure profitability in a language school operation, as long as it was strictly adhered to, and barring major accidents. I knew it by heart! Thirty three percent of turnover for teachers'salaries, thirty three percent all other expenses and thirty three percent profit. In practice a twenty percent contingency fund would wipe out so much profit, but that still left a healthy 13% for the school owner, or more if he/she achieved volume. It was important that the 33% "other expenses" be carefully controlled, so that rent should be 8-10%, advertising settling at 8-10% (after the first year) and office staff 3-4%.

These are sensible and pragmatic business guidelines, almost rules if you want the operation to pay. I quickly found out that Maxwell was breaking every rule in the book. To begin with, his rent was 70% of turnover! He had taken out a lease on two floors of quite a large building in Wanchai – I think he had something like 2000 square metres (about 20,000 square feet). At that time rents in Hong Kong were sky high – they usually are – but his lease was concluded at the height of a particularly promising property boom and had several years to run. Teachers were paid at a normal rate, but there were too many of them, all on fixed salaries, whether students appeared or not. His administrative staff, including Mr Peng, cost about 20% of turnover. I was not able to figure out what most of them did. Neither could Peng, who had had no previous experience in the field. As students were slow in materializing, Maxwell had authorized a lavish advertising campaign, which had some effect, but which used up about 30% of the first year's turnover. There were probably about a steady 1000 students in the school, plus a couple hundred more unsteady ones. The problem was that with the Maxwell formula in operation, every lesson given incurred a substantial loss. The rent and advertising costs were still going up in the particular economic situation at the time, so that even greater volume would not achieve profitability or stem the sizeable monthly deficit. It was a business with no plan, no sense, no hope.

I could see that Peng, an intelligent young man from a good business family and US-educated, was quietly appalled at the state of affairs. Neither he nor I could understand how a so-called business big-wheel like Maxwell could make such elementary mistakes in a business which he was clearly interested in. It was not just a sideline for Maxwell; when he bought Berlitz and its various publishing arms, he acquired the largest language business in the world.

As Peng was able to draw on apparently unlimited credit from Maxwell's banks, he had no liquidity problems and was well satisfied with his own substantial salary. But no self-respecting Chinese (certainly not a Hong Konger) likes to run an irremediably losing business in a growth market. What would his family say if he continued his association with a venture which required him to go to the bank every month for another half million? What was his CV going to look like?

It did not take me long to explain to Li Peng that the various contracts which Maxwell had entered into made the school non-viable this year, next year, forever. He knew it already. At that time Maxwell's bankruptcy was several years in the future, but it was clear for anyone with common sense to see that Maxwell was a peerless phoney, only kept in place by the shortsightedness and gullibility of bank managers (the ones who write snivelling little letters to honest citizens who are £100 overdrawn); they screamed loud enough when the bubble burst.

After Maxwell's suicide, the Japanese Fukitake group was anxious to take one hundred percent control of Berlitz, in which they had already acquired a minority stake. My former employee Jacques Meon was still managing director of Berlitz Japan, by far the most profitable arm of the organisation. The buying price was a reported $236 million, which was not bad considering I had started up Japan with $55,000. Unfortunately for Fukitake, with cash in hand, the Berlitz shares **could not be found**. Maxwell had pledged them (somewhere) against badly needed credit. When they finally did turn up, two Swiss banks disputed their ownership. Fukitake managed to sort it out in the end and now run the Berlitz empire (on which the Rising Sun never sets.)

I concluded my Hong Kong trip with a couple of pleasant days spent with my former employee and good friend, Hans Peter Franklin, who, going to Hong Kong a few years earlier, had started a tennis school with his bare hands, as they say, and developed it into the Sportathlon Group worth several million a the time of writing. Hans could have run Maxwell's school all right – besides being a super tennis player he could also add up.

Maxwell never paid me, of course.

*　　*　　*　　*　　*

In 1982 I toured some parts of Latin America, planning a marketing trip in Mexico, Venezuela, Colombia, Ecuador, Peru, Chile and Argentina. Brazil and Mexico were familiar; I was surprised to notice many differences in the other Spanish-speaking countries. Venezuela, though Latin America, seemed to face the United States. Cars, highways, signs and police uniforms all reflected their northern neighbour. Most rich Venezuelans bought retirement properties in Florida. Colombia, by contrast, seemed essentially Hispanic. I was impressed not only by the quality of the coffee, but by the ultra-polite, gentle manner of the people, seemingly at odds with the country's alarming reputation for violence. Staying at the Hilton, I was warned by the doorman to turn left, not right, if I ventured out through the front door for an evening walk.

Ecuador – I went to Quito – felt quaint and basically safe, but Peru was a different matter. One of my friends, the daughter of a Peruvian Ambassador, had given me the name of her cousin as a contact. Eduardo – he was an eminent lawyer – insisted on picking me up personally at the hotel and deposited me safely there after dinner. Peru was going through a particularly bad time and violence, burglary and kidnappings were rampant. When we arrived at his home, a huge portcullis of a gate, operated electronically from within his bullet-proof car, rose to admit us. His security consisted of a 12-foot concrete wall (with barbed wire and broken glass on top) surrounding his large garden, plus a bearded guard with a sub-machine gun and a huge Alsation dog. He told me that the only one of the three he trusted was the dog.

Chile was a lot better. I stayed with my old friend Philip Ray and his charming family just outside Santiago. I had an interesting five days seeing a little of this very European-style capital and the nearby attractive coast. I was due to leave for Argentina on the Saturday morning and checked into the downtown Hilton on the Friday night. At 2 am I was awakened by a telephone call. It was from the British Embassy.

"Mr Lewis?"

"Yes"

"We believe you are booked on the British Caledonian flight tomorrow morning to Buenos Aires".

"That's correct. Is this an early call?"

"Not exactly. The aeroplane will not be coming to Santiago, as it was held up two hours ago in Brazil. Argentina has just invaded the Falkland Islands. We are technically at war with Argentina."

"Can I take an Aerolineas Argentinas flight?"

"You can, but we advise you not to. We don't know yet how the situation will develop. It is possible you might be interned."

The hotel was buzzing at breakfast. I expected the Chileans to show Latin American solidarity with the Argentinians, but it was just the opposite. It appeared that Argentina had her eyes on a couple of Chilean islands in the Beagle Channel. The waiters and hotel staff blurted out how pro-British they were and urged me to tell Maggie to give them hell. I had little influence with the Prime Minister at the time, and felt a bit sorry for the Argentinians (who really like the English), but she gave them hell anyway.

Fortunately, the nasty affair is now well behind us and Jane and I are planning a trip to Buenos Aires, where she was born. If anyone there asks me how to solve the problem of sovereignty, I shall propose that Britain keep the Falklands, but give Argentina the Malvinas.

*   *   *   *   *

The time came when repeated shows of interest in our company from the City indicated that it was time to sell. In 1986-7 mergers and acquisitions were becoming all the rage. There was a lot of cash around and the institutions were anxious to place their surpluses in anything which would produce more than ten to fifteen per cent. Language schools, especially those in chains of more than 30 outlets, were seen as a good investment in a growth market. The recession had not yet started and Japanese businessmen, among others, poured into England in their thousands each summer.

Going public is a long and protracted business with many audits, consolidations and "doing diligence". I will not bore the reader with all the tedious details. Suffice it to say that our various companies were consolidated and that the shares were eventually put on the Stock Exchange by merging with a publicly listed company – City and Foreign – run by Lord Stevens, the Chairman of the Daily Express. All the shareholders of Linguarama divided the selling price. Wilton and I retained a considerable number of shares in the public company, which appreciated substantially when the newspapers revealed the acquisition. I was asked to sign a 5-year contract to run the new company and I duly obliged. Not unsurprisingly, in true City fashion, I was forced out after just over a year and some bookkeeper was made Group Managing Director. I sold the rest of my shares in due course and took a year off. I had had the foresight not to include any property in the sale of the company, so that Riversdown and its land remained at my disposal.

In 1989 Wilton, I and one or two friends set up a communication skills organisation bearing my name (at the suggestion of some of the partners). At the time of writing (1997) we have about 30 outlets in the UK, France, Germany, Finland, Sweden, Italy, Spain, Russia, Denmark and Hong Kong. Though we teach any language, we specialize in communication techniques and cross-cultural issues. More of this in a subsequent chapter.

Chapter 19

Courses and Students

Summer Courses

Italians say that the difference between an English winter and an English summer is that the rain is warmer in summer. Be that as it may, hordes of Italians attend English language courses every summer in the UK. Spaniards, Arabs and Japanese, in order to escape from their own summer heat, do likewise. Diligent Nordics and Germans often spend a full month of their holidays brushing up their skills in English while even the French, though reluctant to concede the dominance of English over French, arrive in no small numbers.

English in England in Summer is consequently a multi-million pound industry. Language schools, bursting at the seams from June to end of August, are unable to cope with this seasonal influx on their own premises. Universities and colleges are therefore hired the length and breadth of the British Isles to provide both teaching space and food and accommodation for the invading aliens. Tens of thousands more, taught in village halls, YMCAs, Scout Huts, chapels, fire stations and portakabins, are housed with a vast army of professional or amateur landladies in south coast resorts stretching from Folkestone to Bournemouth.

We used only colleges and universities, in particular the University of Kent in Canterbury, Bishop Otter College in Chichester, St Mary's in Twickenham, Shoreditch College in Englefield Green, and Matlock College in Derbyshire.

These establishments varied in size, price, quality of accommodation and food, teaching facilities, and the attitude of their governors towards foreigners. It was a fair bet that two hundred and fifty non-indigenous students containing a liberal sprinkling of youngish Arabs, Spaniards and Italians, if allowed to go on a rampage, could wreck the joint. This happened not infrequently over the years, though whether they did any worse damage than that inflicted by British university students in term time is questionable. We were fairly fortunate in that most of our inmates were mature executives whose idea of a rampage was making spaghetti in the college kitchen at midnight.

Another feature of these summer courses was that we simultaneously held teacher training courses to provide us with instructors for Europe in the following winter. As our organisation grew, we trained as many as sixty teachers on one "method course". These method courses lasted seven days, during which time we unveiled the secrets of the Direct Method. The trainees were accepted on the basis of already possessing a university degree or teaching diploma (P.G.C.E.) Some of the trainees took the course in order to qualify them for other jobs or simply out of interest.

*   *   *   *   *

In the mid-1970s when the enrolment for such courses was at an all-time high, we were using Shoreditch College. In early August one year we were running a course for 150 foreigners of all nationalities as well as a method course for 60 Brits. The method course leaders were Mathias Wallen, an experienced New Zealander called Pete Adolph and myself. Ten other instructors taught the foreigners. All was going smoothly, the weather was hot and many of the classes were taught out of doors. Shoreditch had exceptionally beautiful grounds with a large number of majestic cypresses and cedars, fine rose-bushes and an extensive area of attractive shrubs.

Suddenly we were presented with a serious complaint by the college authorities. One of the lecturers, doing research, was spending the summer, with his wife and 8-year old son, in two of the college rooms. One morning in mid-week, the young boy was playing alone in the grounds, when he was attacked by "a large man". After being grabbed, the boy managed to free himself and ran into the maze of shrubbery, where he was chased by his assailant. The attacker managed to get his hands several times on the boy, but was unable to pin him down and, after several rough encounters, the youngster managed to flee to his parents' quarters.

The incident bore all the signs of an attempted sexual assault, though the boy, in his innocence, did not recognize it as such. It was to be expected that our poor foreigners were instantly indicated as the chief suspects. The last thing I wanted was for them to be grilled individually by the local police. Fortunately the lecturer concerned was dead against involving the constabulary. He felt that a police investigation would only serve to heighten the traumatic shock that the boy was already experiencing. He preferred that we should solve the problem internally and simply remove the offender from the premises.

I had a feeling from the start that our foreigners had not been involved. All their enrolment sheets had a photograph attached and the boy, on perusing these, was unable to identify his attacker. A check on the class attendance registers that morning confirmed that all the foreign students had been in class and the instructors were sure that nobody had absented themselves.

That left us with the method course. Again the boy scrutinized the photographs and this time he recognized his assailant. Let us call him Smith. His enrolment sheet showed him to be an unmarried man of 42 years of age, a former grammar school teacher, Cambridge degree in History, hobbies hiking and birdwatching. He had paid for his course and wished to find a job in Italy or Greece.

The 60 method trainees were divided into three classes of 20 each. He was not in my class. I checked with Mathias, who said he was not in his class either. We examined Peter Adolph's register. He was not included. Then where was he? Our ten instructors looked at his picture and declared he certainly did not attend their classes with the foreigners, though one or two said he looked familiar. Mathias took one more look at the picture and then remembered seeing him enrol on the first day and pay his £1 as deposit for his room key. But he had not attended any classes. Mathias recalled him as being quite huge; the lecturer's son confirmed this. No-one saw him that day, even though thirteen of us kept our eyes wide open. The lecturer fretted at our tardiness in finding him.

At dinner time we saw him. Five minutes after everyone else had started tucking in, he sneaked in through a side door and sat down at a table full of Italians. He ate his meal with head down and talked to nobody. After eating dessert, he got up and left by the side door, as everyone else took coffee. We had already located his room, which had been left empty all day. Now we saw a light in the window and under his door. We informed the lecturer and asked him what he wanted us to do.

It was Wednesday evening. The method course was due to end on Saturday at noon. The lecturer did not relish the idea of a police arrest and a subsequent court case at which his son would have to testify. We could have of course evicted him there and then, but the lecturer, contemplating the possibility of violent resistance, advised against this, too. The best solution, he felt, would be to do nothing and let the man depart on Saturday. He would keep the boy indoors; we would "mark" Smith, monitoring all his movements. This was not as easy as it sounds. There was always one of us off duty, but keeping track of him was difficult. After breakfast one of us followed him at a respectable distance. He traipsed the college grounds constantly the whole morning, frequently disappearing into the shrubbery and emerging often much later from a point far from that of entry. We hid behind cedars, bent low behind hawthorns and scratched ourselves frequently on the thorns of the rose bushes. He seemed never to be still, plodding resolutely with head down, hunched shoulders, hands deep in pockets, muttering unheard comments or obscenities when he glimpsed us following him. At no time did he let on that he had seen us; we swapped shifts like minders in LA Law. He came in for lunch and dinner, not for the coffee breaks. He went to his room only at night and stayed there till he put his light out around eleven. We supposed he went to bed early.

The minding continued throughout Thursday and Friday. Smith was cunning in keeping a low profile. He never sat at the same table twice; he conversed with nobody. As he had never attended a method class, Mathias, Peter and I had assumed he was a foreigner. Our ten instructors of foreigners assumed he was on a method class. The foreigners assumed he was one of our instructors or a method trainee. To the cooks, he was one mouth out of 300.

He was an unattractive, though academic-looking, hulk of one hundred kilos. Mathias and I were already planning high noon on Saturday. When method courses ended, the routine was for the trainees to stand in line and come up to Stella Kenway one by one to return their key, collect their deposit of £1 and simultaneously receive their certificate of attendance which graded them according to ability. There was no way I was going to give Smith any certificate, except one which would have committed him to an institution. We anticipated a difficult moment if the man was as quirky as he looked. Mathias and Peter Adolph were the biggest of our instructors – eighty-odd kilos anyway. We decided that the three of us would stand right behind Stella and be ready to jump on him if he turned nasty. We were by no means relishing the idea and hoped that he would simply make off with his key and ignore the ceremony.

He appeared, however, and stood in the queue, about number fifty out of sixty. As Stella dished out the certificates he shuffled forward, key in hand. After ten minutes or so he was near the desk. He had seen the three of us and no doubt weighed up the situation. First he glared, then sneered, then glared again. You could hear his heavy breathing from ten yards. His turn came. A trembling Stella grabbed his key and gave him a quid. He stood there, waiting, looking at the next certificate which had a name nothing like Smith on it. His head moved from side to side, as if in wonderment.

"Next one!" snapped Stella courageously. He came out of his hunched posture as if stabbed. He now sneered openly and contemptuously at the lot of us, threw his pound on the floor, turned on his heel, stuck his hands into the pockets of his dirty mack and marched off, briskly, out of our lives, on to perhaps another summer course. It was a long, hot summer.

*　　*　　*　　*　　*

For several years we held the summer courses for foreign students and trainee teachers in the University of Kent in Canterbury. The university authorities there were considerably less strait-laced than others we had known and we were allowed to use most of the facilities and common areas until quite late at night – which suited the habits of the large number of Italians and Spaniards who were regular attendees.

Normally we would have as many as 15-20 different nationalities in the college. In the evenings we had to dream up all kinds of social activities to keep them amused after their lessons and discourage the thirsty Nordics from devoting their entire evening to the consumption of alcoholic beverages.

One of the most popular events was the weekly International Song Contest, which never lacked participants in quantity, though one could not always say that of the quality. Entrants were allowed to sing, (solo or with others) dance or play an instrument. Usually they sang in groups. In fact, the standard varied enormously and we never quite knew what we were getting next. In general – and perhaps surprisingly – the Spaniards and Italians usually came last. Their "choirs" were often too big, uncoordinated and frequently raucous. They enjoyed themselves perhaps more than anyone else, but rarely won any prizes. The Arabs wailed away monotonously and often at length – they never won either. Ireland, Scotland and Sweden often triumphed. England, France and Germany were kind of middling. Ladislav sang "Il Sole Mio" in Czech week after week and usually got third prize. But the best, on the whole, were the Japanese.

Japanese people at parties, whether at home or abroad, show no hesitation in contributing musical numbers when they are asked to. With them it is a kind of collective social obligation. They are not all particularly talented, but they always put on a good show. Also they hate to lose. One night we had double-headers – that is to say that each country contributed two numbers. It was known that the Spaniards had an excellent flamenco singer who was bound to score good points in the second round. Spain also started with a fine guitarist in the first round. The Japanese, who were the only ones with a chance of beating the Spaniards, countered with an elegant fan dancer in round one and an exquisite trio singing impeccable close melody in the second round. The flamenco singer did her stuff and after two rounds Japan and Spain were exactly equal with 18 1/2 points each.

When this happened, we used a tie-breaker, where each tying country was allowed to put on one more number to decide the issue, with a different performer. Everyone knew that the Spaniards had a fine baritone singer left and he thrilled the audience – and the judges – with some Aragonese ballad which nearly lifted the roof off. Surely that was it!

A slender, willowy Japanese girl, unnoticed before, shyly took the stage. She sang a song in Japanese. We had never heard anything like it on our courses. Her voice was mellow magic, her body pliant and appealing, her eastern features angelic. It was clearly a love song. The judges could not understand the words, but that was of little import. They knew class when they heard it. She got 10 out of 10 and Japan won. What intrigued me about the whole thing was the oriental subtlety of the plot. The girl was a well-known professional night club singer back in Tokyo. The Japanese, banking on the first two rounds ending in a tie, had held her back for the *coup de grâce*.

*   *   *   *   *

One year we had a lot of good volley ball players and three strong teams were formed to play a world series. Italians, French and Portuguese made up the Latins. Germans, Swedes and Danes were northern Europe. Tokyo medical students – fine athletes all – represented Japan. Ladislav Moudry was appointed referee.

The Latinos beat northern Europe 15-12, 15-13. The Japanese beat northern Europe 15-9, 15-10. The "final" – between the Latinos and Japan – resulted in a 15-13, 15-12 win for the Japanese. They exulted in their modest way; they were very proud of themselves. Ladislav, after presenting the trophy, suggested that Czechoslovakia play the winners in a special challenge match. The Japanese were most willing and looked around for the Czech team.

"It's me," said Ladislav. They made special rules, where Ladislav, playing alone against them, was allowed to knock the ball up twice before striking. The Japanese confidently agreed and served the first ball at the lone Czech. Ladislav, diving low to his left, just managed to knock up the ball a couple of feet from the ground. His second knock propelled it about 10 feet in the air, nearer the net. He then leapt up like a cat after a sparrow and smashed the ball between two of the surprised Japanese. They naturally fought back strongly. Ladislav beat the lot of them 15-9, 15-6.

*   *   *   *   *

The summer courses held on the college campuses boomed for a 15-year period between 1973 and 1988. Many executives attended these courses, but others came from all walks of life and the variety of types we encountered was enormous. We rarely accepted anyone under 16, as courses for very young people require a different kind of supervision. Our school was popular with engineers, technicians, lawyers, bankers, teachers and clerical staff from many European countries who traded with the UK. Younger people tended to come from Japan (those in the gap year between high school and university) and the Arab countries (particularly the Gulf) whose inhabitants flee the scorching heat of the Middle Eastern summer. We dealt with various sons of sheikhs and rulers, most of them quite intelligent, though sometimes hard to discipline.

A special case arose in the summer of 1978, when a British company from Huddersfield ran into problems in Libya. This firm sold sewage works to various overseas entities and had contracted with the Libyan government to set up a huge sewage plant near Benghazi. The normal procedure was to send out a dozen Yorkshire engineers to see to the building of the plant, to supervise the first 6 months of its operation and to train about 60 local staff for its future maintenance. Communication was obviously a problem, but the Yorkshiremen had managed fairly well in some countries where French or Spanish was spoken or where there was a reasonable level of English among the locals.

In Libya the difficulties of communication were compounded by several cultural and linguistic factors. In the first place, people living in oil-rich states had got used to the idea of never doing any manual work or menial labour of any kind. The activities to be carried out at sewage plants entailed no small amount of drudgery, while the olfactory ambience left much to be desired. It proved therefore impossible for the Libyans to recruit staff from cities such as Benghazi or Tripoli, where a certain level of pseudo-sophistication had been adopted by urban dwellers. In fact the only men they could find to do the job were 60 camel-boys from the desert. They did not have urban pretensions and were used to dealing with large piles of camel dung.

I have to tell you, dear reader, that Libyan camel-boys aged 16-19 who have spent all their short lives in the desert, who know little of city life or even the terms to describe it, who can barely read or write their own language (Arabic) and who have never experienced contact with a foreigner or a foreign tongue, hardly represent the cream of the cream when it comes to learning English. Even the Arabic they spoke was a relatively obscure Bedouin dialect not fully understood by Benghazi clerics, so that matching up this language gem with Huddersfield English was clearly going to be no piece of cake.

It might have been easier to teach 10 Yorkshiremen Arabic, but after a few weeks out there the engineers from the Pennines strongly refused to undertake the task. It would have taken a long time, they would not even speak real Arabic at the end of it, and – they hated the place. The company bit the bullet and asked us to organize instruction for the camel-boys. They had thought at first of a summer course, but 2 months (the period the colleges were free) was clearly too short a time to achieve any result. We set up a 6-month course to be given in rented premises in Huddersfield.

I will not go into all the details of the Yorkshire sojourn of these young Libyans. Suffice it to say that their studies were punctuated by episodes of shop-lifting, student strikes, fires lit in metal wastepaper baskets in their bedrooms, endemic truancy and, in many cases, zero progress in their learning. Teetotallers at home, they indulged in the offerings of the local pubs, often collapsed on their beds fully dressed and not infrequently had to be dragged out of bed at noon to attend their lessons. Good bacon and egg breakfasts were of no use to them (Muslims don't eat pig-meat); many of them had little experience of eating vegetables, either.

Well, in the end it wasn't so bad. About one third of them learned to communicate in Huddersfield English and, in due course, this helped to set up the plant (a little behind schedule). Nobody starved to death and there were no suicides, though with some of our teachers and landladies it was a near thing.

The poor boys themselves were in no way to blame. The episode only serves to show that, in many instances, cultural barriers often outweigh linguistic ones during the acquisition of a second tongue.

On another occasion I had to organize an 8-week intensive course for group of 5 young Arabs from the U.A.E. They were from oil-rich Abu Dhabi, were well educated and impeccably dressed. The course was held in the north of England and we had an excellent teacher, who handled the small group impeccably. Progress was good, but one problem persisted: the youngest Arab, a 15-year-old named Abdullah, frequently took off – on his own – to Manchester or Liverpool. The fact that he missed a lot of lessons was not so serious in itself, as he was easily the sharpest of the class, but we were naturally worried about a boy of this age wandering round the streets, restaurants, pubs and (we suspected) the night clubs of these two cities. I was supervising the course closely and I had several run-ins with Abdullah, who was small, neat, invariably impeccably dressed. During my stern lectures, he glowered at me fiercely, but he was clearly well-brought up and did not interrupt my sermons, though he obviously resented them deeply. The problem was that they seemed to have little effect and his absences continued.

Finally, after a couple of days truancy, he returned from London, of all places, so I really had to let fly at him. I had him on the carpet for half an hour, in front of his slightly older compatriots, to make sure they got the message too. In essence, I told him the next misdemeanour of any variety would result in my packing him off on the next plane to Abu Dhabi. After that, the sorties ceased and he learnt a lot of English, though I did not get another friendly look or word from him for the rest of the month.

Fifteen years passed. One day my telephone rang at Riversdown and a firm of English contractors asked for me. I had had no previous contact with them, but they were doing big business in Abu Dhabi and English instruction needed organising for 200 trainees in that country. Their conrtact was with ADNOC – the Abu Dhabi National Oil Company – by far the richest firm in a very rich country. The director of ADNOC, who felt personally involved in the ambitious training scheme (2 years) had insisted that it must be organized by me. I asked who my unknown backer might be. His name was Abdullah al-Badi, one of the most affluent and influential figures in the kingdom. Apparently he had known me as a 15-year old, not long after he had lost his father, and had so much appreciated the "parental care" bestowed on him that he wished to recognize it in the current situation.

Some weeks later I went out to the Emirates and did the job for Abdullah, now a charming, fiercely energetic and successful executive, as well as a good husband, caring father and breeder of some of the fastest camels in the Gulf. Only the Maktoum family beats the Al-Badis in the Dubai classic camel races, which I attended with my former pupil. We have remained firm friends ever since – Abdullah, intelligent, conscientious, loyal, of impeccable manners and morals, is a splendid representative of his part of the world.

The second time I went to Abu Dhabi I shared an unusual and memorable occasion with him. The Al-Badi family own several fine houses in the old capital of Abu-Dhabi, Al-Ain, which is situated in the middle of the desert, not far from the frontier of Oman. Abdullah invited me to stay there overnight and see some of the desert in the process.

Like many sheikhs, he drove a Mercedes, and he had just taken possession of a brand new scarlet 560. In this we streaked along the excellent road to Al-Ain, he and I in the front and a huge bodyguard called Ali in the back. I have always been interested in the Islamic religion and the way in which it dominates the behaviour of its adherents. Abdullah, on several occasions, was kind enough to explain the various precepts of Islam, which, in many ways are strikingly similar to those of Christianity. Abdullah, devout believer, has great didactic talent and he succeeded in imparting to me the depth of feeling, sincerity and conviction experienced by strict Muslims. On the way to Al-Ain he developed the theme once more.

About half way through the journey he drove off the tarmac surface of the high road, going off at a tangent across the firm, flat sands. In about half an hour, close to a picturesque escarpment, we came across a camel farm, which he owned. We spent an hour inspecting the fine animals – they had impressive pedigrees and were bred to win races in Dubai. There were some lovable baby camels – Abdullah told me how much they were worth – I remember there were a lot of zeroes in the figures. Around 5 o'clock he and the bodyguard climbed fifty yards or so up the escarpment, knelt down facing Mecca and prayed, while I took pictures of the animals. Had I known what was going to happen next, I would have said a little prayer myself.

Abdullah said good-bye to the camel keepers (they seemed devoted to him) and informed me that we were now in a bit of a hurry, as dinner awaited us at his brother's home in Al-Ain. As his brother, General Mohammed Al-Badi, was the Abu Dhabi Chief of Staff, more punctuality was required than is usual around those parts. Abdullah explained to me that instead of returning to the high road he would drive as the crow flies straight across the desert. The sand was hard for 20 miles, but might get a bit softer after that. In any case, not to worry – it was quite safe.

We fastened our seat belts and took off on screeching tyres and flying sand. I am used to Stags and Jaguars myself, but I can tell you that a 560 pushed almost to the limit by a race-minded young Arab with no traffic to worry about takes a lot of catching, if by any chance you want to catch it. Sand spurted six feet high from our rear wheels as we poured the desert in front of us down our radiator at 220 km an hour. When we got to the softer sand the plumes on either side behind us rose to a height of thirty or forty feet at least and must, like the pyramids, have been visible from space. The sun turned crimson and, as sunset approached, Abdullah asked me if I would mind if he went through the hundred-names-of-God routine. I had heard of this custom, but never experienced it from close up. Apparently Allah has 99 other names;

a devout Muslim must know them all and on occasion demonstrate his knowledge. For some reason this was one of those occasions. It is not a quiet ceremony. Still firmly clutching the steering wheel, Abdullah began to screech at the top of his voice, in those tremulous, wailing tones that only Arabs and Turks can produce. As Abdullah got into it – I suppose he was in the fifties and sixties – his decibel count offered valiant competition with the strident, piercing whine of the Mercedes 12-cylinder engine doing 250 k.p.h. and the resoundingly sibilant hiss of the twin plumes of sand being projected heavenwards. As the magnificent sun dipped below the horizon, the desert took on hues of indigo and gold and Abdullah switched on his powerful headlights, illuminating large turquoise cacti and scattering small desert creatures. My initial feeling of apprehension gave way to a sense of exhilaration engendered by the magic of the evening sky, the emerging stars, the passioned prayer and the sheer speed across the empty stretches. It was a driver's paradise – no speed limits, no policemen, no traffic or traffic lights, no annoying intersections, no road, in fact. For me it was a once-in-a-lifetime experience, though old Ali in the back seemed quite used to it.

I relate this event without any cynicism and can only admire Abdullah, fine driver as he is, who got all three of us alive to Al-Ain and in time for supper. I just wish I could have videoed the desert ride.

*   *   *   *   *

I once ran a summer language course in Bishop Otter College in Chichester. Among the 150 students (all adults) were 28 Italians. Both in and out of the classroom they were quite a handful, what with their tardiness, volubility, appetite for jesting and general uncontrollability. For all these reasons I placed them in the charge of a middle-aged friend of mine noted for his powers of organisation and unflappability. His name was Bill Strange and as far as their classes went, he did a splendid job. The problem was the excursions. Every Wednesday the Italians wanted to go to Oxford. This was not problematic in itself, as we had a nice 36-seater bus at our disposal and the journey was quite manageable. The trick was to come back with the same number of Italians that you went out with. Once let loose in Oxford, they tended to make themselves scarce. The first Wednesday that Bill led the expedition, taking 23 Italians with him, he came back with 21, even though he had been assured on leaving Oxford that the Italian party was complete. Two irate Italians were left stranded in Oxford and had to be brought back, expensively, by private car.

The second Wednesday Bill counted 20 of them carefully as they entered the bus on departure, missed two as they scrambled in late and came back with 20 instead of 22. More irate phone calls from the University City.

The third Wednesday saw 18 Italians get into the bus, double-counted religiously by Bill Strange. On his return that evening he had more than his worried look, as he had brought back 21. We were still trying to sort this out when the usual phone call from Oxford announced that five had been left behind. Early that morning, eight Italians had gone to Oxford under their own steam. Seeing our bus in its usual place, they naturally piled into it for a free ride back. As Bill found it hard to distinguish one Italian from another, he had sanctioned departure. After that we put him in charge of the German bird-watching group and he was untroubled for the rest of the summer.

Chapter 20

Here and There in Europe

The Wizard of Dribble

Summers are the busiest time of the year in the UK language market, for not only do large numbers of foreign students come on summer courses at universities and colleges, but our own schools catering for executives have virtually full occupancy in June, July and August. Accordingly Jane and I plan most of our holidays in spring or autumn, often heading for the Mediterranean when it is relatively uncrowded.

In the autumn of 1977 we visited Malta for the first time and found it charming. This tiny island – about 18 miles long and 9 miles wide – does not have breathtaking scenery, such as is possessed by Tahiti or Bora Bora, but it is one of the coziest places imaginable. Strategically located in the centre of the Mediterranean, this little archipelago has played a vital role in the struggle of a succession of powers for domination of the area. In recent times, their greatest moment of glory was in 1565 when the Knights of St John, aided by 6,000 Maltese infantry, withstood the Ottoman siege of Suleiyman the Great, who deployed a task force of around 25,000 men. The capital, which was thereafter re-named Valletta, became a town of splendid palaces and unparalleled fortifications. In the Second World War the Maltese, fighting on the side of the Allies, showed such fortitude and stamina, that the whole island was decorated – hence Malta G.C.

Jane and I spent a lovely week exploring old Malta and getting to know the friendly, humble, tenacious inhabitants. At that time the most famous foreign resident of Malta was not a noble or diplomat or film star, but the uniquely talented English footballer from Stoke-on-Trent, Sir Stanley Matthews. Arguably the best footballer of all time, Matthews, knighted a few years before on account of his services to British sport, was living quietly with his Czech wife in the picturesque fishing village of Marsaxlokk. I had been fortunate enough to see Matthews play often during the war, not only in nearby Blackpool, but in various internationals. He could dribble a football like no man before or since, often beating two or three men "on a sixpence". Even Pele, whom I was to meet a few years later in Thailand, rated him the best winger that had ever lived.

He lived in a pink house on top of the barren hillside, overlooking Marsaxlokk Bay. Jane and I walked up the hill and I knocked on the front door. Matthews himself opened it. I recognized him of course, but felt I should go through the proper routine.

"Excuse our calling unannounced, but would it be possible to have a few words with Sir Stanley Matthews, if he is at home".

"Speaking. What can I do for you?"

"Well, you have given me so much pleasure on the football field, as I grew up, that I felt I could not pass your house without at least bringing you some English tea."

I gave him a big tin of Twinings Breakfast. He smiled readily and looked over my shoulder at Jane, who hugged the garden gate. His Staffordshire accent was warm and friendly.

"Won't you come in?"

He introduced us to his wife, a former Czech beauty and sportswoman, and we sat down to reminisce together. I recalled his dazzling displays of wizardry against Portugal, Hungary, the Rest of Europe and many other teams.

"Do you remember the night when you played for Stoke against Manchester United and somebody tripped you up and you staggered into the penalty area before you fell? The crowd booed you for half an hour?"

"I know they did, but I was desperately trying to keep my balance, not looking for the area."

"I agree – I thought the booing was disgraceful."

"You have a good memory."

"Some things stick in your mind."

His wife busied herself making sandwiches – salmon, chicken and lettuce on brown bread with lots of capers which Sir Stanley swore by. Most athletes have an obsession with some kind of food. With Pele it was fish, with Mimoun pure water, with Matthews capers on lettuce. He was still quietly handsome and fit at 62 years of age and played football weekly for the Malta Post Office. In England he had played with distinction in the First Division till he was over 50.

I asked the living legend how he did in the Malta League.

"Well, I can still dribble – beat a man – even centre and shoot properly. But I don't have my old balance any more. When they tackle me hard, I go flying. It's embarrassing."

We stayed a couple of hours and enjoyed the calm, the Maltese sunshine, the cosy atmosphere. Sir Stanley and I corresponded for a few years – he went on to coach in Canada and, at the time of writing, enjoys good health at the age of 82. There will never be another like him.

*   *   *   *   *

The Disappearance of Luis Rueda

My friendship with Luis Rueda, the smiling Spaniard from Zamora, continued over the years. When driving from Paris to Lisbon along the Bordeaux-Biarritz-San Sebastián-Burgos-Salamanca route, I nearly always stayed overnight in Zamora, where Luis was one of the best-known citizens. Sometimes I went with him to support Zamora Football Club. His best friend, José Cobas, was the captain and star goalkeeper. Once he introduced me to the young bull-fighter Miguel Baez Litri, who gave me an autographed photograph. Zamora is a rather small, provincial capital on the Castilian plateau with a wonderful old cathedral and a plethora of magnificent Romanesque churches. It also has a creditable number of bars and I enjoyed many an evening drinking the strong red wine of nearby Toro and hobnobbing with *zamoranos* of all ages. Luis, a complete teetotaller himself, knew everybody in town and everybody knew him.

Luis' wife, Nines de los Ríos, came from a large family. She and Luis had two children only – Luisito and Mila. Mila was never far from home, even after marrying. Luisito by contrast was a great wanderer and roamed the Mediterranean. He was very handsome as a young man and worked as a model in Italy and the Balearics, eventually settling in Ibiza. At one time he had an unfortunate liaison with a call girl and they produced an offspring – a boy – whom neither of them wanted. Luisito's constant travelling precluded his keeping the boy and his lady of the night had no taste for the joys of motherhood. One day she rang Luis Rueda's doorbell in Zamora and dumped the infant into his grandfather's arms. Luis gratefully accepted and brought up the child, also called Luis, as his own son. Luis Rueda always looked far younger than his years. The latest Luis was an exact replica of Luisito. Consequently when one visited the Ruedas in the 1980s one had a strong sense of *déja vu* – the scene was that of the late 1950s, with an energetic, whooping Luis Rueda playing football outside his house with his chubby youngster.

I exchanged letters with Luis two or three times a year. He was a good correspondent and always replied promptly. Then in the spring of 1986 his letters stopped coming. In the summer, still without reply, I got a little worried; I phoned him up – nobody answered. I wrote again, I telephoned several times, there was never anyone at home. I assumed they had gone on their holidays and I stopped calling, but in the autumn I tried again. The phone worked all right, but the house was empty. I sent a telegram – there was no reply.

By now I was quite worried. Luis had never left his house for more than a month since 1949. If he had changed address, he would undoubtedly have told me. We were best friends and he sent me a crate full of oranges every Christmas. I began to phone two or three times a week. I checked his phone with the Spanish telephone company; they assured me there was nothing wrong with it.

At the end of October I drove to Lisbon. The mystery would soon be unravelled. As I planned to go via Zamora, I had written a week earlier to say I was coming, just in case. I arrived in front of his house at sunset; it was shuttered and empty. I knew the neighbours on either side – not very well, but at least they would recognize me. I knocked on the door of the one on the left. They were out. As I went to try the one on the right, a young man in ragged clothes came up the street and beat me to the front gate. He went to the door of Rueda's neighbour and knocked on it. The old lady who lived alone there asked who it was. He gave a name and asked for alms. She told him to go away. He insisted for a while, but she was adamant and her tone became more irritable. Eventually he gave up and left. At no time had the old lady opened her door. It was my turn, so I went and knocked on it. She told me to go away. I explained, in my best Zamora Spanish, that I was not looking for monetary assistance, but wished to talk to her. Very funny, she said, now go away. Like the impoverished young man, I argued a bit. She said if I didn't go away she would ring for the police.

I went round to the house of Nines' brother. There was nobody at home. Neither was her sister – the neighbour told me she was in Madrid. She didn't know where the Ruedas were. She gave me the phone number of Luis' niece. She and her husband were certainly at home. I rang a dozen times without getting a reply. It turned out later to be the wrong number. I went to the home of a friend and was told he had emigrated to Germany. Another one, Gallego, had moved to Santiago de Compostela. The person who lived in his house had no idea where the Ruedas were. Had not seen them for months.

By now it was getting late. I checked into the *parador* where I had a shower and a sandwich and then went to a couple of bars. The owners knew Luis well but said they didn't know where he was. Then one of the customers said to me that he had heard that the police were after him.

If someone had told me that the police were after the Pope, it would have surprised me considerably less. Luis Rueda was an eminently respectable citizen of Zamora, the boundaries of which he seldom crossed. His family had been brought up good Catholics, he had (like many Spaniards) at least 2 good jobs, he never touched alcohol, he was faithful to his wife, he helped out with the Fire Brigade, he swore only occasionally – in short he was the epitome of probity and reliability. And the police were after him. I asked for more details, but the whole bar clammed up.

After trying the niece's dozen times, I went round to her house, which I found with difficulty. There was a light – I knocked. The door opened – it was midnight – when she saw me, she dragged me in. They had opened my letter to Luis and had been waiting all evening for me to ring. Where the hell is Luis, I asked. Hiding from the police, she whispered back. As her husband poured me a brandy, the story came out in hushed tones.

A few months earlier the call girl from Ibiza – the mother of Luis' grandson – had made a sudden appearance on the Rueda threshold and demanded that her son be returned to her. Luis Rueda naturally refused to turn over the boy, who had no recollection of his mother. The Ruedas had borne the costs of his upbringing – he was now eight and in the middle of his schooling – he looked upon Luis and Nines as his parents. The slovenly appearance of the call girl, moreover, gave little confidence in her ability to take care of her child. So an indignant Luis bundled her off.

She was not long in returning, this time with a lawyer. It appeared that she had legal rights to the custody of the child. This was subsequently confirmed when Luis consulted a Zamora solicitor. He had two weeks to hand over his grandson, who would be carted off to Ibiza. The Zamora police, sympathetic to Rueda, told him they would be obliged to collect the boy the following Saturday but one. There was great consternation in the Rueda household – a weeping Nines had to pack the boy's clothes for departure, Mila came in daily to share the sobbing. As the days went by, an agitated Luis shuttled between the boy's school, the lawyer and the police station. There was no legal loophole and the fateful Saturday loomed up. On the Friday evening the whole Rueda family disappeared.

The police arrived the following morning to find the house closed, shuttered and abandoned. The neighbours had seen the Ruedas drive off at midnight – they had no idea to which destination. Mila, Luis' daughter, professed to be shocked, burst into tears and had to be comforted by an embarrassed policeman. The numerous members of Nines' family – the Los Ríos – were equally uninformed. Maybe Luis had taken the family to his cousin's in San Sebastián, where they went every year. The police investigated the theory; they were not there.

The weeks went by and mail, including mine, piled up in the Rueda letter box. Every now and again Mila came round, opened the envelopes which seemed to contain bills, and paid them. The other mail she could not forward since, as she kept telling the police, she did not know where to send them. The Zamora constabulary went through the motions of hunting a wanted man. Rueda's home was visited twice weekly, notices were put up in police stations, Mila was questioned periodically, mail to her own home was in theory scrutinized for tell-tale postmarks, the call girl's lawyer served the usual papers on the usual recipients. Rumours flew around that the call girl might be willing to renounce her rights if a certain amount of financial compensation were to be considered. This amount, according to rumour, reduced steadily as time passed. The friendly police shrugged their shoulders at all and sundry, were careful to warn Mila of their "raids" on the Rueda home. All Zamora buzzed with the conspiracy – it was a very Spanish situation.

Rueda's niece told me all this while her husband poured me cognacs. I was more than relieved to hear my friend was still alive and well. Naturally my close friendship with him meant that I was now part of the conspiracy. Lowering her voice and eyeing the walls, the niece gave me instructions in a sealed envelope. They would tell me how to find Rueda. I thanked them for their confidence (and liquor) and went back to my *parador*. In the privacy of my room I slit open the envelope.

In the rugged mountains of north-west Castile, secondary and tertiary roads go off into the hills, revealing further tributaries which lose their tarmac surface and become no more than wide, sandy paths along which only one vehicle at a time can proceed. Some of these paths, surrounded by woodland, lead to the lesser-known shores of Lake Sanabria – a summer retreat where knowledgeable and well-heeled Spaniards seek refuge from the city heat and bury themselves for a few months in rural solitude. There are secluded villas along some of these wooded shores, invisible from the road and hardly seen from the lake. In winter these villas are closed, mute and shuttered, for these months are cold, dreary and unhospitable at an unfriendly altitude. The sparsely-scattered shops that serve victuals and other summer necessities in the hot season are closed in winter. The freezing region is abandoned by hikers, swimmers, boat people and retired septuagenarians. There are no skiers, for jagged rocks jut out through the thin covering of crispy snow. Even the birds have left for warmer climes; those animals that have not hibernated – foxes, wild boar and hares – are occasionally to be glimpsed scurrying away in the dark refuge of the leafless forest. In these dismal, dreary surroundings, in a disused, nigh-invisible, dilapidated cabin owned by his cousin Arturo, Luis Rueda had holed up with his wife and grandson for the winter.

My envelope contained a hand-drawn map whose faint paths, arrows, crosses and diverse cryptic symbols would have made a worthy prop for a filming of "Treasure Island". There were no names, numbers or readily identifiable clues. The main road to Sanabria I knew; after departing that, my progress depended on an accurate reading of turn-offs, signs, twists and turns, wooden bridges and loops and forks. I left Zamora at 7 am. It took me three hours to find the cabin. There was nobody in it. I banged on shutters and shouted my name in English and Spanish. I denied any connection with the authorities. There was only silence, apart from the gentle lapping of miniscule waves on the gravelly shore of the nearby lake.

I was disappointed, and hungry too. The nearest village, with a shop and café, was seven miles away. I drove there and had coffee and a *chorizo* sandwich in the café. I daren't ask about the Ruedas. The shop next door said they were doing little business. A Señor Gonzalez had been in that morning with wife and a youngster and had bought supplies for at least a week. That gave me hope; I returned to the cabin. They were there. Luis' car was hidden among the bushes. I could smell surreptitious cooking; I hammered hungrily on the shutters. My name served as a password – in moments a door was whipped open and I was pulled inside. It was like an American movie – no-one had followed me? Who had given me directions? Was I hungry? Minutes later we were relaxed, laughing and chattering. It was the first time I had ever heard the garrulous Nines speak in a low voice. We gorged quickly on ham, onions, red and green peppers. The cabin was in semi-darkness, light coming in only through one un-shuttered window facing the grey waters of the lake. The boy, unconcerned, played with toy soldiers.

Using only candles at night, combating the cold with dozens of blankets, buying food and supplies under the name Gonzalez, the Ruedas led a spartan existence for many months, taking no chances with the possibility of discovery. There they would remain until summer, when the influx of holiday-makers would force them to seek another hideout. I was anxious to play my part in the drama. I offered Luis retreats in northern England, fast cars, piles of tinned food and funds a-plenty. He chuckled madly and refused them all, albeit touched by my fidelity. *"No te preocupes, amigo"* he assured me. "We'll handle this in the Spanish manner. They'll only find me when I want to be found."

Zamoranos stick with *zamoranos* and that included the police, the magistrates and the rest of the municipality. I never quite figured out how it was solved in the end, but Luis' self-imposed exile came to an end in the summer, which he spent in San Sebastian; in the autumn he returned to Zamora and the Ibiza girl and her threats went out of his life for good. Luis resumed his role as the most respected moral citizen of Zamora and continued to reply to my mail and send me oranges every Christmas, until he died, of natural causes, in 1995.

*   *   *   *   *

Down the Danube

As Charles Berlitz used to say, there's no business like the language business. It is, however, a hard one, imposing considerable demands, both in terms of time and effort, on those who embrace it as a career. To say it is people-intensive is putting it mildly. Teachers, pursuing an important, rewarding, often frustrating profession, can demonstrate great stamina, patience and brilliance. Frequently they are themselves extremely sensitive, periodically moody, and in the case of the vagrant type, unstable and unsure of their own goals. When one employs several hundred such people of twenty-odd different nationalities, one cannot escape involvement in many of their personal problems and aspirations. Students are far more numerous and one has to pay constant attention to their needs too (especially in the case of residential schools). They can be more difficult to handle than staff, yet often are more amenable. In general, they become less exigent when they get good lessons.

The necessity to rub shoulders on a daily basis with both customers and staff means that a language school director – if he or she takes things seriously – works a 50 or 60-hour week. If one is involved at group level, that is to say with a chain of 30-odd schools to manage, it is much longer than that. Day-to-day people problems arise so frequently that only week-ends are left for planning courses, strategies and new ventures. In my own case, I do not regard an 84-hour week as particularly onerous and still work at this tempo in my mid-sixties. Successful managers in many professions have told me they do the same thing.

However, nobody can, or should, work with such intensity unless they are completely enthusiastic about what they are doing. I have loved language study since I was six years old; the variety, riches, and idiosyncrasies of the world's tongues reflect, for me, the fascinating, intriguing, unpredictable, and greatest wonder of creation – the labrynthine human mind and personality. The wise Chinese scholar, the reindeer-herding Lapp, the Portuguese negotiator, the honest Finn, the Japanese salaryman, the Taos Navajo have looked at me through different eyes, judged me by different standards, engaged me in conversation with a diversity of strategies. In return I have responded and reacted, and no doubt shown them a plethora of subtly adapted Lancashire attitudes. It takes two to tango; no two dances are ever the same.

The jewelled variety of world views and wildly differing grammar-grooves and thought channels have been rewarding enough, but in addition, my particular job has allowed me to dip into, in a sense, the activities and challenges of other professions. Sales, marketing, personnel training, writing, publishing, broadcasting, scriptwriting, advertising, negotiating, lecturing and counselling have been some of these. It is difficult for me to quantify what measure of success I have met with in all these areas, but they sure beat the hell out of painting gasworks and cleaning out railway carriages. My school friends, long ago retired, say: But how do you find time to do all these things? How can you work like that at your age? Well, if you get up early you can achieve a lot, but the fact is that I have never neglected another important aspect of life, and that is holidays. It has been my good fortune that my family has shared my love of people and places and, at least for a couple of decades, we went round the world together in cars, jeeps and planes, more often on skis, yachts and bicycles. During these trips – which often lasted one month or more – we encountered situations and personalities that have enriched our experience, given us an extra dimension in language and human reaction.

It is perhaps on bicycle trips that one comes into closest contact with indigenous communities and their way of life. For several years the five of us cycled down rivers, for not only did they frequently set the scene for a variety of human occupations, but they also flowed **downwards** towards the sea, a factor which alleviated considerably the often arduous nature of the exercise. We cycled through tunnels, over mountains, around pot-holes but always, whenever we didn't lose it, by the banks of a fast-flowing waterway. We started in Northumbria, then the Yorkshire dales, then the Test and the Ex. Later we graduated to rivers in Jersey and Menorca, to savage torrents in Finland and down the mighty Rhône to the Camargue. Eventually we met the challenge of the Danube and the Yangtse-Kiang. We might have done more, but fifteen hundred kilometres of the Yangtse finished us.

Our trip down the Danube was one of the most enjoyable and certainly the most varied, as it is perhaps the most international river on the globe. We began in Vienna and biked through Austria, Czechoslovakia, Hungary, Yugoslavia, Bulgaria and Rumania before finally splashing in among the jellyfish in the Black Sea. It was 1984 – George Orwell's year of doom – and indeed some of the countries we cycled through no longer exist. All of them, with the exception of Austria, still laboured under the communist yoke, and if any of my children were entertaining notions of workers' paradises, they must have been somewhat dispelled by the austere living conditions, spartan dwellings, turgid bureaucracies, savage Alsatian border dogs, unremarkable cuisines and stultifying personal apathy that we encountered as we went along. It says a lot for the beautiful, history-laden Danube and the latent vitality and variety of the diverse cultures that people her banks – especially the peasants and villagers – that our sojourn remained unspoiled by political dogma and official pesterings. We were snapped at by hounds in Bratislava, short-changed swapping currency in Hungary, waited four hours for a meal in a Bulgarian restaurant, bribed guards not to throw our bikes off the train in Yugoslavia, but it was the People's Republic of Rumania which reserved for us the supreme, shining example of socialist officialdom.

After nearly a month of hard pedalling in hot weather we had finally reached Bucharest, the Rumanian capital. We had lived on ice cream and beer for two days, for roadside restaurants did not exist in Rumania at that time and there was nothing in the shops to buy. Cafés were aplenty along the route, but do not think for a moment that café in this country signified the provision of coffee, or nice pastries, or anything of that ilk. Café proprietors shrugged their shoulders at our modest requests, served up more beer and ice cream and offered us mountains of *lei* to purchase our bikes. These sturdy Austrian machines were in fact all that stood between us and total helplessness. We clung to them. In view of the aforementioned shortages (and other amusing hardships) we had decided that the final 500-kilometre lap along that flat, uninteresting and wooded stretch of the Danube which constitutes the border between Bulgaria and Rumania, offered little to us in the way of scenery or cultural reward. Accordingly we had diverted our route to Bucharest, where we intended to put our cycles on the train to Constanza and pedal along the Black Sea to Mamaia.

We wallowed in luxury overnight in the Bucharest Hilton – I have never been so reluctant to check out of a 5-star establishment as I was the next morning – and we glided over town to the railway station – quite a sizeable, ornamented one in the Central European tradition. The officials were ornamented too, with shabby-smart, red and grey uniforms reminiscent of those worn by border guards chasing Sean Connery over sparsely vegetated hills. For those readers who are familiar with the cosy routines of eastern European countries of the era, I will not go into too much detail about the tedious and time-consuming procedures mandatory for the obtaining of rail tickets. Suffice it to say that you do not buy train tickets in such *régimes* in the train station, or anywhere remotely near it. Instead you go across town and enjoy yourself for three and a half hours in Bucharest's state-run (and only) travel bureau where the screeching, milling crowd besieging the counters make a horde of Manchester United lager louts look like a clutch of choirboys at the vicar's tea party.

Starting early, while the kids guarded the bikes back on Platform One, Jane and I emerged from this melée at noon with tickets for five people and five cycles to Constanza.   Fortunately trains to this coastal town from Bucharest were relatively frequent, so we had chances on the two o'clock, the four o'clock and the seven o'clock trains. We eagerly greeted the first of these transports only to be told, ten minutes before departure, that they would not take our bikes. This was somewhat of a setback, as we did not have time to check them into left luggage – another alternative. In the two hours remaining before the next train I went to see the station master. She was a woman –mid-forties, stiff-backed, pudding-faced, bemedalled, bespectacled – an ideological devotee contemptuous of anyone who was not related to Ceausescu, was not a Hero of the Soviet Union or who had not accompanied Mao on the Long March. Yes, we had tickets for 5 bikes to Constanza but we could not put them on passengers' knees, could we? Passengers' knees in Rumania usually had other passengers sitting on them. Yes, there were goods vans on Rumanian trains, but they were for priority goods like cabbages, sacks of flour and squawking chickens, not for shiny articles of luxury. There was a left luggage department in the station, but that was for honest suitcases. We couldn't put bikes on shelves, could we? Then what should we do? She looked away in disdain and busied herself saving the *régime*. She would not even take a bribe, like all the men did. The four o'clock train came and departed, passengers hanging out of the windows looking like the next load for Auschwitz.

Things were now getting serious. If we didn't make the seven o'clock, even our lousy passenger tickets would be useless. But what to do with the bikes? At about half past five, after buttonholing everyone who could speak English, French or German, I discovered that there was another stationmaster – one who controlled freight – and this time he was a man. A couple of packets of Kent got me into his office where he sat chewing gum and doing a crossword under a sizeable portrait of Ceausescu.   He was a small, timid-looking individual, a kind of Balkan Woody Allen. Still masticating, he motioned me to take a seat. Putting another pack of Kent on his desk, I poured out my troubles and probably went over the top in intimating what I thought about the bemedalled bitch in the office next door. He seemed to like it and soon started nodding sympathetically. When I had finished my diatribe he took the chewing gum out of his mouth and addressed me in impeccable English. He had studied a couple of years in England, was an ardent Arsenal fan and had served four years as Rumanian consul in Tel Aviv. He seemed completely westernized, obviously relished the opportunity to practise his polished English and chatted away merrily for half an hour, apparently forgetting the dire situation that had brought me to his door. When I dared mention it again he beamed down his big nose at me, flicked his right hand gaily towards the wall beside him and assured me that he had already worked out a solution.

"Don't take your bikes to the Black Sea", he advised, "they'll steal them for sure!"

"So what do we do with them?"

"Where are you going after your stay in Rumania?"

"Vienna. Then by plane to England."

"OK. What you do is this: you send the cycles by rail freight to Belgrade. Left luggage does not take bicycles, but our goods department does. I personally will see to it that they leave for Yugoslavia in two or three days time. They will sit in the goods yard in Belgrade railway station and await your collecting them. You use your rail tickets to Constanza, have your Black Sea holiday, then come back by train to Bucharest and Belgrade. When you've got the bikes, you go by train to Vienna with the cycles in the guard's van. No problem."

"How do I get the tickets for the bikes?"

"I give them to you now. Five bikes to Belgrade is a pittance. Don't bother getting a refund for the others – it will take a month."

Woody was a gem; he didn't even smoke, though he accepted a few packets of Wrigleys for future use. Accompanying us to the freight department, he stuck little red "export" labels on the handlebar of each bike while we attached white ones with "Lewis, Belgrade" inscribed on them. He shook hands genially with all of us and sent his warmest regards to George Graham, Frank Mclintock and Terry Neale. As we clambered aboard the pathetically overcrowded seven o'clock, I mentally said goodbye to our precious Austrian cycles for ever. But a week later at six o'clock in the morning they were waiting for us in a remote, unsupervised siding of Belgrade railway station, tied together with string in the morning mist, with labels intact, unharmed, unpunctured, unguarded and, miraculously, unstolen.

*   *   *   *   *

To Rome by Stag

Once I unwisely drove a Korean friend of mine, as well as our Japanese cook, to Rome in a Triumph Stag. It was a splendid, rather flamboyant, canary-coloured open roadster with a wickedly spluttering muffler which tended to irritate customs officials who were stuck in sedentary jobs on the frontier. They gave us a lot of unwelcome attention, searching our cases and so on, but the real problem was not the car, but the Korean. The son of one of the wealthiest families in Seoul, he was handsome enough, in his prime at 30, but his rugged good looks were those of a domineering gangland mobster. He was one of the kindest of souls, but looked every inch a hired assassin. We had had some trouble with the French officials, who tried to convince us that Seoul was in North Korea and that Kim was a visa-less Commie. Only my atlas settled the question, but by that time our cases had been ransacked and our three lives dissected. I suspected the Italian customs would be worse and I was right. Kim was grilled at the frontier like O.J. Simpson and accused of much worse than a mere double murder. It appeared he had been sent by Kim Il Sung himself to penetrate the Italian world-wide drug ring while he was in Rome. For an hour my Italian verbs were put to the test. The cook was body searched, the car underwent the same kind of attention they get in the Ferrari mechanics' pit. The officials in gleaming uniforms paraded up and down like attorneys-general, their oratory was magnificent, their arguments swift and penetrating, but in the end they had to let us go. Even they were not able to move Seoul.

Our three or four days in Rome passed pleasantly, but unfortunately our kind Italian hosts gave me a splendid departing gift: a Peruvian fertility charm in the form of an eight inch silver fish, bejewelled with rubies, hanging from a chain necklace. It was beautiful, worth a few hundred dollars, but hardly a national treasure.

The border inspector at Ventimiglia – sadly a different frontier from that where we had entered – was very proud of his gold-braided uniform and had considerably greater powers of oratory than his colleagues at our point of entry. He had a field day with North and South Korea, Japanese *Yakuza* terror and suspicious Englishmen with a yellow Stag, a Finnish driving licence and supposed to be born in Wigan. He attracted a large crowd of passers-by, not to mention a snorting line of French motorists concertina-ing up behind us. When my atlas again won the day, he flung an imperious, bad-tempered arm at the boot and said "Open it up!"

My friends had carefully wrapped the silver charm in intricate layers of packaging and the end result was a sizeable brown cardboard box, sealed with red wax and tied with string.

"*Che cosa è?*" thundered the official. At this point my Italian, which had done reasonably well up to then, suffered a temporary breakdown. A description of my Peruvian fertility offering was now beyond me. Weakly, I uttered the only word that came into my head:

"*Una pesca.*"

"*Una PESCA?*" screamed the customs man incredulously.

"*Si, una pesca.*"

"*APRA!* Open it up!"

When we eventually got to the contents, he held up the charm, glistening in the sunlight for the long line of motorists and admirers to see.

"He calls this a FISH!" he sneered loudly.

We were taken to see the *Commandante*, a gentleman in even more impressive attire, in a sumptuous office a minute's walk away. Kim hung his head like a convicted felon. Tanaka maintained his idiotic fixed grin and I tried to look like a decent, well-brought Englishman, albeit contemplating a *lire* fine in the billions. The official explained the circumstances to the *Commandante* mentioning Pyongyang and the Italian national heritage at least twice. The *Commandante,* a man with a magnificent head of white hair and an impressive moustache, listened to it all, eyed me coldly and contemplated in silence. What a sense of timing, I thought.

He turned his gaze to the official. "*ESCA, IDIOTA!* " he bellowed. He turned to me and my Asian retinue, addressed us in impeccable English. "Gentlemen, I apologise for the behaviour of this imbecile whom I have the misfortune to employ. He is miserably paid, but too much in any case. I hope you enjoy the rest of your holiday. Good afternoon."

They say that all Italians are great actors, except the ones in the films.

*   *   *   *   *

On the Volga

In 1991 I was approached by two Russians from Volgograd who wished to set up a language school in that city in conjunction with Richard Lewis Communications. One was Alexander Kosov, an assistant professor at the University of Volgograd, the other was Antonina Zilin, a member of the Russian Parliament and a lady of considerable means who seemed quite capable and willing to provide any necessary capital.

It was not in RLC's interest to get involved with the rouble economy – we all knew what a state of confusion Russia was in at that time – but I was certainly interested in a school which could teach Russian in Russia, the fees for which would be collected in hard currency in the west. Basically, we were not interested in teaching English to Russians in Russia.

As both Alexander and Antonina proved reliable, I was willing to pursue the project; Kosov subsequently came to Riversdown, took some training in the RLC method and, with my help, wrote an RLC manual in modern post-Soviet Russian. I had indicated to our Russian colleagues that if we were to send western businessmen to Russia on immersion courses, the actual teaching would be the least of our problems; the success of the venture would depend largely on the quality of food and accommodation we provided. There are many intensive courses in Russian offered in the universities of Moscow and St

Petersburg; university hostel accommodation is, however, completely unsuitable for executives.

I told Alexander and Antonina that they must find 4 or 5-star rooms in Volgograd and guarantee excellent food; I did not consider it likely that they would succeed.

They did, however, in an unusual manner. When Eisenhower became President of the United States, he expressed a wish to visit the battlefield of Stalingrad which, as we all know, witnessed one of the major turning points of the Second World War. The municipal authorities in Stalingrad (now called Volgograd) prepared for his visit by building a private villa, in a compound with 8 suites (for Eisenhower's retinue), a reception room and cooking quarters. Each suite, luxuriously appointed, contained a bedroom, a study, a large kitchen and a bathroom with toilet.

In the end Eisenhower changed his mind and did not go. Nobody quite knew what to do with the building, so it was used in an *ad hoc* manner by a variety of dignitaries when they passed through the lower Volga region. These had included Khruschev, Brezhnev, Charles de Gaulle, Fidel Castro, Presidents Najibullah and Nazarbarjev, Princess Anne and Elizabeth Rehn, the Finnish Defence Minister! Most of the time it remained empty.

When Alexander Kosov proposed this as the school location, I thought I was being exposed to a Russian sense of humour. He was, however, quite serious and when I found out that it could be rented for $500 a month, so was I. The following January, I flew down to Volgograd and inspected the building, which was in good shape. After some discussion with our friends, I decided the best way to solve the food question was to send them part of the fee paid in hard currency and entrust three or four Russian housewives to buy what was needed in the markets and cook it at home. Students would eat one or two meals a day in Volgograd families. Russian women, if they are given the ingredients, can produce really tasty repasts; in practice the system worked fine. We subsequently sent various executives from the UK, Sweden, Finland and Germany to Volgograd. Kosov did a good job and we were able to satisfy our clientele.

The volume of our Russian business is fairly small, but I write of this venture on account of some of the interesting insights that I was given into the state of affairs in Russia in the period of the Soviet break-up. There was for instance the question of ownership. Who owned our building, who fixed the rent and to whom was it paid? Even Alexander Kosov, who had to pay it, was a little woolly about it. Up to Gorbachev, the villa had been Soviet property. When the Soviet Union was dissolved, Soviet assets reverted to the various states so that in theory it was administered by the Russian state. As committees were changing fast, the link between Moscow and far-off properties tended to get lost, especially in cases where regular rents were not being collected. The

Communist Party got into the act wherever they could, but as they were in the process of being smashed by Yeltsin, administering empty buildings in Volgograd was low on their list of priorities. The city council was in the picture somehow, but did not possess any title to the villa, which continued to be well maintained by a caretaker and a cook, possibly his wife, who laid on meals for the pair of them in the presidential kitchen. Volgograd was heaving with Russian, Georgian and Armenian entrepreneurs, but they had bigger fish to fry. Nobody could buy the property as nobody knew who owned it. A communist who had been around when the last dignitaries visited had since disappeared. It was unclear who was paying the caretaker and the cook, who also did the gardening.

In these ephemeral and unballasted cirumstances the calculation of rent seemed to be up to Kosov and me more than anybody else. I know that we arrived at the figure of $500 a month with considerable ease. We only had the caretaker to discuss it with and he kept nodding so hard I thought his head would drop off. Rent in advance? Of course not. What if it took us a while to rustle up students? The landlords would be understanding. Who were the current landlords? The answer was so nebulous and protracted that even Dostoievski would have had trouble with it. Who would collect the rent? He, the caretaker would. He would pass it on through the proper channels. Yes, Mr Kosov would get a receipt. Yes, hard currency would do nicely.

Alexander was quite satisfied with these arrangements. We collect students' fees in say, pounds. We forward two thirds of these to Alexander who pays rent, teachers and Russian housewives. The executives comment on the high quality of the teaching and food. In six years we have never had a hiccough.

*   *   *   *   *

Antonina remained very much on the periphery of these negotiations, though she certainly took good care of me personally while I was in Volgograd. The temperature was minus 20 degrees and a bitingly cold easterly whistled in every morning from the steppes and over the frozen Caspian. It was good to have well-heeled friends with a warm flat, though I could not complain about Eisenhower's bed. The caretaker served the same breakfast every morning – champagne and caviar on toast. I thought at first that he was trying to impress me, but Alexander explained to me that such things were easy to come by. Champagne – Russian variety – is not expensive and does not taste too bad. Caviar comes from that region – the Caspian Sea and the river itself. All caviar is the property of the state and there are severe penalties for fishermen who do not turn over the sturgeons they catch to the local authorities. However human nature is human nature and at that time the "authorities" were in pretty bad shape. Alexander showed me a photo, taken by a fishing friend, of a sturgeon which had been opened up to reveal 20 kilograms of caviar in its ample stomach.

My Russian friends showed me Volgograd. In spite of the freezing conditions, I managed to get about quite a lot, though sights worth seeing are few, since the town was blown to pieces in the prolonged struggle with the Germans. The buildings are consequently post-war – ponderous square and oblong blocs thrown up by unimaginative Soviet constructors. The town possesses, however, the largest statue in the world – Mother Russia – a huge bronze effigy of a very Slavic lady looking down from the heights over the broad Volga. It is very impressive, either in spite of or because of its sheer bulk and expresses the strong bonds that most Russians feel for their homeland.

Worth seeing, too, is the war museum. Murals occupy 360 degrees of wall space – one can get quite dizzy spinning round to take it all in. The various stages of the battles for Stalingrad are vividly depicted in striking colour. The message is of course a little one-sided, but the artistry is commendable and conveys clearly the suffering, bravery and sheer desperation of the soldiers and civilians involved in this momentous and bitter struggle.

Antonina's husband, Boris, ran a sizeable factory producing industrial components of some kind. He was the prototypical Russian, hearty, boisterous, hospitable, spoke no English and had a great moustache. It was clear, however, that Antonina was the powerful one. The good quality of their clothes and the warmth and opulent furnishing of their flat left you in no doubt as to the considerable resources that the family possessed. I asked Alexander where the wealth had come from. Again the situation was very Russian, at least typical of the particular transition in which Russia found itself at the time.

Antonina had been very active in the local Communist Party and had gradually worked her way up the system, eventually becoming one of the movers and shakers in the local council. This position did not bring any money in itself, but officials latch on to certain privileges, not uncommon in a variety of régimes. One day, in the Brezhnev era, Antonina was made responsible for the distribution of 150 vacuum cleaners of surprisingly good quality, to the citizens of Volgograd. Anyone familiar with the workings of the Soviet system, will know that goods tend to become available in large batches, after perhaps many months or even years of scarcity. They are then distributed, in some weird fashion, in Soviet townships whereupon they are immediately gobbled up by a starved public with millions of unused roubles in the bank. The cost of the article, officially fixed at a low level by the command economy, presents no problem. How to get your hands on it is the trick.

Volgograd had a population of well over a million, so that 150 vacuum cleaners would not go very far. Antonina suddenly acquired many friends and

admirers with dusty floors. Who would get the machines? The first personage
to get one was the Rector of Volgograd University where one of Antonina's
daughters had been trying to get in for some time. Other citizens who had an
in on the procurement of cars, building sites or machinery or who had access
to special avenues of political influence, also became hoover families. By
cunning and very leisurely bartering, Antonina joined the class of new Russian
millionaires. Some of her wealth she may have used to become a Member of
Parliament. Boris got his factory.

The Zhilins were very generous and kind-hearted hosts. There was no
way you could obviate the 5-floor climb up the concrete stairway of their
apartment bloc (in the dark after 7 pm) for Soviet architects put in lifts only if
buildings had 6 floors or more, but once in their home nothing was denied to
a Zhilin guest. Their furniture, household appliances and gleaming American
style kitchen were reminiscent of what we imagine graced the *dachas* of
Khruschev, Breshnev, Gorbachev and their buddies. Dinner was delicious.
Even the conversation, conducted largely by virtue of the fluent English of the
two attractive, university-educated and elegantly-attired Zhilin daughters, was
nothing less than sparkling.

Russians, often curt and brusque in public on account of their
unfortunate and oppressive history, are openly benign and engaging in their
own homes.

The following summer Antonina and Boris came to Riversdown for one
month's English each. She, with her outgoing personality, learnt a tremendous
amount. Boris absorbed a bit less, but enjoyed himself, while his steppe
masculinity and handsomeness allied to his unfailing joviality compensated for
the occasional shakiness of his embryonic grammar. The Zhilins transferred to
the bank £20.000 more than the amount corresponding to their fees. This
they blew in one hour and a half in an Edinburgh fashion shop, to the
considerable annoyance of Mrs Nakanishi, wife of a Japanese billionaire, who,
on accompanying them on their shopping expedition, felt obliged to spend
£25,000 so as not to be outdone.

Another ephemeral figure who floated in the background of our activities
in Russia was another *nouveau* very *riche,* Vladimir Verbitzki, who pulled
strings in Minsk but had gone to school in Volgograd. He was a good-looking,
clean-cut thirty-five year old of impeccable dress and manner who bought me
a big dinner at MacDonalds in Moscow (only the best people go inside, the
rest buy hamburgers on the street) and was generally helpful in orientating us
as we passed through the capital. He later brought his third wife to
Riversdown for a language course and used to carry thick wads of crisp one
hundred dollar bills in his back trouser pocket, peeling them off when required
in the manner of a Texas oil-man. He told me he made his money selling
advertising space on (former Soviet) Russian satellites, apparently there are a

lot of under-used ones whizzing around. Vladimir, though he did not seem to be very close to the communists, promised to introduce me to Gorbachev or Yeltsin any time I had an hour to spare. He said President Nazarbayev of Kazakhstan was very interested in meeting me and he would line something up when he lunched with him the following Friday. He left his wife a few days longer than she expected at Riversdown, (his first two marriages had been of fairly short duration) but he eventually showed up, to her (and our) great delight, muttering something about malfunctioning helicopters, yet beaming all the while.

Our experience with the Russians has indicated that Russian academics are extremely competent and reliable – it is very much to their credit, as at the time of writing they unfortunately do not enjoy adequate remuneration or social standing in the new, turbulent society.

*   *   *   *   *

Athletes

Modern athletes, with the unrivalled opportunities they have in recent years of making huge sums of money as they perform around the globe, often take intensive language courses. These are usually in English though Ludmila Engquist, the Russian-born gold medallist running for Sweden, took a 4-week total immersion in Swedish in order to be able to conduct better television interviews. This intensely dedicated athlete, ruthlessly dominant on the track, exhibited great charm and humour in the classroom.

Dossena, the Italian World Cup footballer and Yannick Dalmas, the French racing driver, also took courses at Riversdown. Certainly the most famous athlete to study with us was the 4-times gold Olympic medallist, Lasse Virén. Lasse, who won gold medals in Munich (5,000m. and 10,000 m.) and then repeated this outstanding feat 4 years later in the Montreal Olympics, came to Riversdown to brush up his English around the age of 40. He and his wife Päivi are also close friends of ours. Myrskylä – Lasse's home village – is a few miles from Pukaro and Päivi was actually born in Lapinjärvi, located between the two.

Lasse improved both his English and his pheasant shooting while at Riversdown, besides going for numerous runs, with local athletes, in the surrounding countryside. In his last week of study he was asked to write an essay entitled "The Story of my Life". He dutifully completed 5 pages and his teacher marked them carefully. I asked her what she thought of the essay. "Oh, it was quite good and very interesting", she replied. "Just one funny thing though." "What was that?" I asked. "He never mentioned running."

Chapter 21

Down the Yangtse

Having conquered the Danube, or at least having cycled down 6-countries-worth of it, my family decided we had just about enough energy and enthusiasm for biking left in us to tackle just one more river. The Volga was too long and bug-hater David refused to go anywhere near the Nile or the Amazon, so in the end we settled for the Yangtse, or the Yangtse-Kiang, to give it its full title. This seemed suitable for several reasons: We wanted to see China; Deng had lessened the xenophobia in that country; and we were assured that in April the cool, sunny climate in north and central China would be insect-free and pleasant cycling weather. They did not tell us about the rats, which are particularly perky in the spring, but that is another matter.

China is not only the world's most populated country, it also boasts the planet's oldest civilisation – an agriculture-based society formed on the Yellow River 5000 years ago. During this long period – practically all of recorded human history – China, essentially an isolated country, cut off from other peoples by a vast ocean to the east, jungles to the south, towering mountain ranges to the west and freezing steppes to the north, has never formed a lasting, friendly relationship with a distant country. For two millennia the Chinese Empire was its own universe, sucking in Korea, Vietnam and other neighbours, while exacting tributes from others, including Japan. Its unbroken culture spread itself over many centuries throughout East Asia, where its ifluence is manifest in music, dance, paintings, religion, philosophy, architecture, theatre, societal structure and administration and, above all, language and literature.

Westerners who see China as a Third World, relatively backward nation in terms of crude technology, sparse infrastructure, appalling hygiene, rampant pollution, outdated politics and inadequate communication fall into the trap of misjudging, underestimating and misunderstanding the power and impact of the Chinese people on their neighbours and, in another sense, the world at large. China sees herself as *Chung-Kuo* – the Middle Kingdom – the centre of the universe and venue of the world's oldest lifestyle. A visitor from the Tang Dynasty (China's golden age) would see its legacy intact in the streets and fields of China today. The Chinese, a billion strong, see no diminishment of their moral authority – exercised with such power for thousands of years – and their sense of cultural superiority is greater than even that of the Japanese, whom they civilised. Foreigners in the eyes of Chinese are inferior, corrupt, decadent, disloyal and volatile, frequently hegemonistic, barbaric and, in essence, 'devils'.

They did not make these assumptions lightly. In the 'Opium Wars' between 1839 and 1860 Britain forced Bengal opium on the Chinese, annexed Hong Kong and claimed enclaves in several Chinese ports, including Shanghai. France, Germany and Russia soon followed the British, while the Japanese, imitating the West as usual, smashed China in the war of 1894-5 and annexed Taiwan. This proved merely a prelude to a full-scale invasion of the mainland, followed by civil war after the Japanese withdrawal, culminating in victory for Mao's forces in 1949. The foreign 'devils' had to abandon their profitable ghettoes in Shanghai and other cities, leaving only Hong Kong in alien hands.

That xenophobia might be an understandable reaction to the events cited above can be readily perceived; whether the Chinese actually possess cultural superiority over the rest of us is another matter. They believe they do.

Where they feel particularly superior is in the area of moral and spiritual values. In as much as most nations feel that their norms are the correct ones – that their behaviour alone is truly exemplary – this is not surprising in itself. The Chinese, however, like the Russians and the Muslims, combine their sense of moral righteousness with fierce criticism of western societies. The large European nations of former imperial glory – Britain, France, Spain and Portugal – they see in decline, decay and spiritual disintegration. They see the American culture as having begun to decline before it reached its peak. The Japanese, once earnest students of Chinese philosophies and precepts, have succumbed to materialism and consumerism. Russia was never admired.

What are these superior Chinese values? They are not slow to tell you. They list them as follows:

modesty

tolerance

filial piety, courtesy, thrift

patience, respect for the elderly

sincerity, loyalty, family closeness, tradition

trustworthiness, stoicism, tenacity, self-sacrifice, kindness

moderation, patriotism, asceticism, diligence, harmony towards all

resistance to corruption, learning, respect for hierarchy

generosity, adaptability, conscientiousness

sense of duty, pride (no losing face)

being undemanding, friendships

gratitude for favours

impartiality, purity

gentleness

wisdom

A westerner, ploughing through this list of self-ascribed values, might wonder about modesty and impartiality, but, in the main, the Chinese do go about their daily lives, especially at the individual level, exhibiting many of those characteristics. Whatever they might think of us, we can hardly fail to see them as hard-working, conscientious, patient, undemanding and thrifty. They seem generally to be in harmony with each other (good team members) and towards us they are usually courteous and compliant.

Cognizant of the unrivalled durability, resilience and opulence of Chinese civilisation, as well as the accumulated wisdom and composure of her people, I was nevertheless intensely curious to see for myself what actually happened on the ground. In 1985 China was in a particularly acute stage of transition (there have been many in her past). When Mao triumphed in 1949 and the foreign 'devils' were forced to abandon all enclaves on Chinese soil save Hong Kong, the new leader imposed on China a political, ideological and economic structure (Maoist communism) which seemed to fly in the face of all that China stood for. The Emperors had gone, it was true, but the hierarchical mentality of the Chinese, embedded since Confucius in the 3rd century B.C., could not evaporate in a sudden change of dogma. Nobody in the Middle Kingdom believed in equality of society for 2000 years, and nobody does today. Social discipline (essential in a sprawling, multi-ethnic country like China) was based on inequality – a comforting, familiar inequality where the rights one possessed on one's particular rung on the social ladder were unquestionably guaranteed. And what was all this about the primacy of the state? Chinese had always been collectivist in behaviour – they had to be to survive – but one's first loyalty was to the **family** where the unequal relationships between father and son, husband and wife, siblings, already provided a sound structure for a secure future and a cared-for old age. Would bureaucrats in Beijing take care of the old folk in Xinkiang or even Canton? What prosperity had ever existed in China came from the hard work of the farmers and the ability to sell their produce on the best terms available, or, in more modern times, from small family businesses, especially in that vast beehive of activity south of the Yangtse. What about the strength of the great, extended Chinese families who lived and worked not only in China, but also prospered in London, San Francisco, Vancouver, Hawaii, Singapore and throughout the peninsulas and archipelagos of South East Asia? Were the Wongs, the Zhangs, the Lees, the Yehs now to fade into insignificance, collectively pledging their obeisance to this un-Sinic-like structure – the Party – deriving not from any line of revered ancestors, but in existence only for a blip in China's history and conjured up, in all places, in barbarian Russia?

If the Party maintained its ideological grip o the Chinese in unrelenting fashion from 1948 to 1986, it speaks more for the utter ruthlessness of Mao and some who followed him than for any compatibility between a command economy and the innate Chinese entrepreneurial spirit. Mao knew how many millions of lives had been sacrificed in Russia and the Ukraine to keep Stalin in power; if there was one place in the world where life was cheaper than in Russia, it was China. Nearly a billion people suffered the yoke of complete totalitarianism for one decade after another. A brilliant Prime Minister, Chou-en-Lai, gained favour with Mao and found meaningful dialogue with the west; unfortunately he died in his prime and, with the Great Leap Forward, premature and ill-planned industrialisation plunged China into an abyss of failure, despair, near-starvation and discontent. When wise men began to speculate, Mao smashed the intelligentsia with the inappropriately named Cultural Revolution, when, in 1966, teachers, professors, doctors, lawyers and all manner of non-manual workers were exiled to the countryside for 5,10 or 12 years' hard labour, thereby teaching them the true meaning of revolution.

Chinese civilisation had rarely sunk to such a low. After Mao's death, the Gang of Four, led by his wife, equalled him in cruelty and myopic vision. Only the rising star of the dimunitive octogenerian Deng Xiao Ping saved the country from further self-destruction. In 1978 he rescued the intelligentsia, liberalised the economy and, while keeping the party in sole command, gave the green light to capitalism wherever a Chinese could find it. The people found plenty and soon started making money for themselves instead of surrendering eveything to the collective. Deng declared "it was glorious to get rich" and even allowed foreigners to come into China to show people how to do it. In 1985, as we prepared to depart for China, this was the climate which awaited us. We would still be regarded as barbarians or foreign devils, but the word was out that we should be treated civilly, at the very least. What better way to get to know the Chinese than to cycle in their midst?

*   *   *   *   *

We flew out to Beijing with the national airline of the People's Republic – CAAC. The only thing I can say in favour of this airline is that if you go with them it lessens the cultural shock on arrival. At first sight, the air hostesses seem to resemble the black-haired, brown-eyed beauties of JAL, MAS and Singapore Airlines, but one was quickly disabused of that notion. Taught to smile, they had been taught little else – certainly not the art of catering to passengers' needs. On the first 5 1/2-hour leg to Sharjah, various travellers sought to obtain a cup of coffee; they were served tea – quite good it was – though sugar and milk did not make an appearance. Coffee miraculously surfaced on the second leg. Those who tasted it then asked for tea, which made our oriental girls think that westerners were very strange creatures. It took one hour exactly to get a blanket, though if you could read Chinese, newspapers were no problem. On the credit side, the attendants didn't give a damn whether you fastened your seat belt or not and you could walk around the plane as much as you liked in all kinds of turbulence.

Our eventual party consisted of nine: five in our family, Mathias Wallen, Diane Creedon from the USA, Kimi Morizane from Japan and Anna Mattila from Finland. My daughter Caroline and Anna took the Moscow-Beijing Trans-Siberian train and would meet us in the Chinese capital. The rest of us flew out together. The plan was to have a couple of days in Beijing, then fly to Chungking, way up the Yangtse, then cycle down the mighty river to Shanghai. That is how it worked out, more or less.

I was not without contacts in China. Encyclopaedia Britannica had arranged for 3 worthy Chinese colleagues to meet us at the airport. These were Xu Wei Zung, the editor of the encyclopaedia in Chinese, Shongjie Hiang, editor of the Encyclopaedia of Knowledge and Zhou Gou Yuang, the inventor of Pin-Yin and China's foremost linguist. Later we were to visit Chun-Chan Yeh, one of China's most eminent professors and a famous novelist in his own right. (We knew his son in London).

Peking Airport was as phlegmatic as the cabin crew had been. Luggage took one hour and a half to clear, the forbidding customs declarations took another 45 minutes, then were stamped in 10 seconds by officials who showed no inclination to read them, or, for that matter, to look at our luggage. We might have been Dover fishmongers going on a day trip to Calais.

Our three encyclopaedic friends greeted us with wide smiles and firm, western-style handshakes. They had lined up 3 taxis for the 40-minute ride into town. Peking stands on a flat, dusty Loess plain of great magnitude and the highway along which we sped was wide, straight and well-surfaced. I thought our convoy was going pretty fast. After 5 minutes we heard the wail of a police siren and a police car caught up with the first taxi, pulled it in and fined the editor of the Encyclopaedia of Knowledge 4 yuan. The two other taxis stepped on the gas so the police couldn't catch them and we were soon approaching the city centre. Up to now the ride had reminded me of my entry into Pyongyang 6 years earlier – the impressive width of the carriageway combined with the lack of traffic gave one an exhilarating feeling of breakneck speed and vehicular freedom. Reforestation-plan silver birches on either side soon gave way to lonely grey and white apartment buildings. Then people began to appear. In North Korea everybody had walked but here they walked and cycled too.

Soon we were cutting through columns of bicycles. As flat as Milan, Peking is a cyclist's paradise. Its broad, smooth-asphalted avenues permit riders to cruise along ten or twelve abreast at a leisurely pace of their own choosing. Indeed everybody seemed to be pedalling at exactly the same speed – that of people who had a long way to go, but were bent on getting there. At intersections, columns of bikes crossed other columns at right-angles, but I saw no collisions. Traffic manners were impeccable. Cars, trucks and buses gave cycles a wide berth, often crossing the white line completely and using the full width of the left hand side. In light traffic this is often feasible and seems to be safer for all concerned. During the many hours that we cycled in China, I do not remember a four-wheeled vehicle coming nearer than 3 metres from us.

Suddenly we saw the wide acres of Tiananmen Square on our left. We proceeded to the Beijing Hotel, where Anna Mattila and my daughter anxiously awaited us in the company of a well-dressed, 25-year-old Chinese named Zhang, who had a wide smile on his face and two hotel rooms in his back pocket. These were good tidings indeed, as decent accommodation is a scarce commodity in China. Zhang had also laid on a Toyota minibus, so our entire group piled into this, paying off the taxis. Zhang guided us to the Min Zu (all nationalities) Hotel, where the rooms were booked.

During the next couple of hours we found out what travelling around China was all about. Caroline and Anna already had accommodation in a hostel, so there were seven of us for the 2 rooms. By the time we got to the Min Zu one room had already evaporated, but Zhang quickly secured the remaining one on our behalf and made us take possession of it by putting all our luggage into it. It contained two beds. What to do with the other five? Zhang – a versatile young man whose life seemed to consist of addressing a long list of problems and solving them one by one, did not seem unduly concerned. We suggested Jane and Diane might use the two beds right off, but Zhang said a better policy was for all nine of us to occupy armchairs in the hotel lobby facing the reception desk. We managed this eventually, as chairs kept being vacated, and sat in a weary line. Zhang then went to work, that is to say, he parked himself opposite two female reception clerks and fixed them with a constant, unwavering smile. They ignored him most of the time, but his gaze never left them. Every ten minutes or so he exchanged pleasantries with one or the other. I thought his elbows might wear out, but I knew little of the depth and breadth of Chinese patience. No, there weren't any more free rooms and yes, the hotel was massively overbooked, but he would wait.

Occasionally he gave his elbows a rest and came over to cheer us up with stories of Americans who had slept in the streets or been given rooms out near Manchuria, but mainly he manned his station at the reception desk, laughing and joking and puffing at one "Viceroy" after another and after a couple of hours he and the receptionists were as thick as thieves, so they bounced a Canadian late arrival and awarded us another room with 2 beds and that was that.

Zhang and the encyclopaedia men came for dinner at 7:30 after we had had a few hours' snooze. We had a convivial evening – Chinese food of course – the bill was 300 yuan (about $75) – more or less what we would have paid for 12 people in London. When our other guests had left, Zhang stayed behind to make plans for the morrow. Caroline and Anna really had him in tow and I sensed that he was a man who could get things done, in spite of his relative youth. The minibus he had retained to take us to the Great Wall and then to Professor Yeh's home in the evening. That was the easy part. What about our 9 tickets to Chungking the day after that? I had booked them, was my my naïve reply. He gave one of his hollow laughs. Did I have physical possession of them? No? Then we should have to present ourselves bright and early the next morning at CAAC. Apparently in China a ticket in the hand is worth nine in the rush at the booking office.

The next morning, coffee was a bit slow in the hotel, but Zhang was there with his white bus and he and I entered the CAAC booking office – a dark, roomy space – at 8:15. The queues were already fearsome, as hordes had rushed in when it opened at 8. Zhang, undeterred, pushed his way forward through the throng till he found the right window. The girl there told him that our 9 tickets had been re-sold, since we had arrived too late to claim them. Zhang agreed with her and laughed his head off. He told her an amusing story about some silly foreigners who had dallied over 2 cups of coffee in their hotel, thereby losing their tickets, and having their whole holiday ruined. She screamed with glee and they both wagged their dark heads in unison for 5 minutes and she gave him the tickets. We all had another good laugh when we found out I had no money on me to pay for them. Zhang pushed me through the crowds back to a money-changer and, once the dollars had begot yuan, violated all the queues again to pay the ticket clerk. The whole thing was sewn up by 8:40 – we made our exit under the baleful glares of lines of Americans and Outer Mongolians. If Zhang had stuck around to offer his services he could have got rich in one morning, but for some reason he latched on to us, for which we were by no means ungrateful.

The Great Wall of China is no disappointment. It took us about an hour and a half in the minibus across a dusty, brown plain. The monotony of the ochre landscape was relieved by the manifold activities of the Chinese populace which can be observed at the roadside. All China seems to be working, constantly. For 30 miles the road was being widened – goodness knows why, (it was wide enough) – and we witnessed thousands, perhaps tens of thousands of shovellers – most of them seemingly left handed, digging deep into the brown soil in steady, rhythmic unison. They seemed less intent than German workmen, less regimented than Japanese. One felt that if they fell behind schedule, they could always call up another million shovels.

One assumes that these workers were digging for the state, though at least they had the air of getting paid for it, unlike the zombie Friday labourers of North Korea. Interspersed among the shovel gangs, one discerned thousands of China's new entrepreneurs. Farmers wheeling barrows or standing at makeshift stalls sold pigs, hens, chickens, sweet potatoes, spinach, bamboo shoots, beans, mushrooms and long, pale green cabbages. Women peddled basketwork, pottery, pairs of spectacles, thimbles, lace, cheap jewellery and T-shirts (I've climbed the Wall). Other women knitted frantically or deep-fried maize dough in oil, which they sold in tubular strips not unlike Spanish *churros* . Nobody was immobile, most women and younger people beavered away restlessly at one thing or another. Multiply that person's energy by one billion, I thought, and who will stop China, one day?

We enjoyed the Wall. Mathias bought a Mao hat with a red star on it, puffed out his cheeks and posed as a Mao look-alike, while David took his picture. A dozen Chinese onlookers giggled with glee, some of them glancing over their shoulder. Zhang explained which side of the wall had been China and which side had harboured the oncoming Mongol hordes. We were well able to imagine Genghis Khan's warriors streaming out of the morning mist on our left, storming and breaching the fortifications, bribing the sentries, subjecting all of China to a 100-year occupation. The wall itself is still awe-inspiring. It is said that it is the only man-made structure visible from space, apart from the Egyptian pyramids. Built around the 3rd century BC, it is 6000 kilometres long and ranks, in my estimation, with the Grand Canyon and Angkor Wat as one of the world's three great tourist attractions.

*   *   *   *   *

That evening all nine of us visited the home of Professor Chun-chan Yeh, reputedly one of the ten most distinguished scholars in the whole of China. This precious invitation to his home came by way of his son who lived in London and whose wife taught Chinese in our school. Professor Yeh, an absolute authority on the Chinese language, spoke perfect English, as did his charming wife. He looked about 70 years of age, his spouse a little less. Grey-haired, wide cheek-boned, of average European height, they were an extremely handsome pair dressed simply, but elegantly. His charisma knew no bounds: essentially Anglophile, he knew English literature and institutions better than most Britons; he himself was a well-known novelist in China and his most famous work, "A Mountain Village" had been, along with others, translated into English. He kindly presented us with a copy for our Yangtse reading.

His house stood around 4 sides of a traditional, old Chinese courtyard, though he and his wife now only occupied two sides. It appeared that they had been obliged to cede the other two wings at the time of the Cultural Revolution. Given his profession and eminent position, it occurred to me that he might have suffered a far worse fate and, as our discussion became more meaningful and intimate, I was able to touch delicately on the subject. He nodded slightly in recogition of my tentative query. "I was better connected than some of my more unfortunate fellow-professors", he muttered. I did not pursue the subject, but later in the evening, as he and his wife gave us a tour of what remained of his house (four or five rooms), I noticed a slightly fading sepia photograph, simply framed, on one wall. It seemed to be a group of professors, or wise men, all in their mid-sixties or seventies. Professor Yeh sat in the middle of the front row. On his right was seated Mao-Tse-Tung and on his left was the handsome Premier, Chou-en-Lai. Yeh noticed I had noticed, but made no comment. That's Chinese humility, I thought.

*   *   *   *   *

The next morning we vacated our precious accommodation at the Min Zu and piled our bike-bags and Norwegian sleeping bags into the minibus for Zhang to whisk us off to the airport. Prices were reasonable, especially when nine of us shared the cost of 2 rooms. We tried to tip the driver of the minibus who had transported us royally during our stay, but Zhang said it was not necessary. He did accept a couple of fountain pens – a sign of status in China in 1985. On most occasions when we tried to give people tips or presents, we found them energetically refused. Apparently it was the current government line that Chinese needed no favours from foreigners – their service and hospitality were for free. I found this situation very refreshing after years of weighing up one's chances with French waiters, but it was hard to see genuinely poor people go unrewarded.

Zhang himself took no emolument – he was much more interested in obtaining a place in an English university – and I vowed to help him on our return. We arranged to meet up in Beijing in just under a month's time.

China, in spite of being the 3rd biggest country in the world, has only one time zone. Chungking lies 1500 kilometres southwest of Beijing, which means that in spring it is dark in the capital around 6 pm, while the cities of the upper Yangtse enjoy daylight till 10 or 11 pm. We flew for 4 hours over brown plains, rugged mountains and ubiquitous rice paddies. The huge sprawl of Chungking seemed endless from the air. I remembered it as the war-time capital of China – the refuge of Chiang-Kai-Shek's High Command as Japanese armies spread across east China. No-one really knows how many people live in Chungking today. Officially listed at 5 million souls, its labrynthine conglomeration of shacks, huts and lean-tos in the countless suburbs defy any accurate census. The inhabitants of the city tell you with conviction that they are over 16 million.

Be that as it may, we arrived in brilliant sunshine, though it was already five in the afternoon. China International Travel Service (CITS) met us regally at the airport and the two guides, a young man and a young woman, both speaking creditable English, helped us and our bags into a rickety green-and-white bus for the one-hour ride to the Chungking Grand Hotel. We rattled through innumerable suburbs – rural rather than urban in nature. Pigs and chickens were everywhere, cats and dogs in suspiciously short supply. Even the outlying districts seemed thronged with people – astonished brown faces peeped out at us from every alleyway, window and hole in the wall. Foreigners are a common sight in Beijing and Shanghai; in 1985 they were a rarity on the upper and middle Yangtse.

On coming into what appeared to be the city centre, our guides asked the bus driver to stop the vehicle. The male guide flung out his right arm over a valley-like park and indicated a palatial-looking building, two hundred yards long, on the other side.

"That, ladies and gentlemen, is the Grand Hotel – your hotel for tonight" he intoned proudly.

We were impressed. Not only did it rival the Escorial and the Mafra Palace in length, but it was of the classic architecture of Chinese antiquity. In fact, as realised later, it was a carbon copy of the Palace of Heaven in Peking. We thanked the CITS for providing us with such sumptuous accommodation, bearing in mind our cramped quarters in the Min Zu. Our vision of royal apartments to wallow in luxury was, of course, both naïve and short-lived. At the check-in desk we were assigned 2 rooms, though one of them was, we were told, quite sizeable. Six and three was the split. What to do with 5 men and 4 women? The clerk was surprised at our lack of invention: one woman would go in with five men, naturally.

Of course Jane joined us males – at least there were 4 beds – and Caroline, Diane and Anna took the other room, which already had one inhabitant – a young English university student back-packing her way through China. The two rooms were both on the front of the hotel and were at opposite ends of the 200-yard terrace with its magnificent balustrade. They were dingy in the extreme, but the huge columns of the balustrade reminded us of past imperial glory.

Chungking is the capital of Szechuan province, noted for its wonderful, very spicy cuisine. After settling in, we went to a restaurant recommended by our guides and had what turned out to be the very best meal we encountered in China. It was the local speciality – a monstrous river fish cooked in a variety of spices and then coated from head to tail in brown chocolate! There were lots of piquant side dishes, too, but that huge fish lives in my memory. Nine of us could not finish it off.

We wandered round the streets and side-alleys of Chungking until midnight. The houses were small, often one or two stories, the great majority were wooden or corrugated iron lean-tos against supporting brick walls. People beckoned us to inspect the interiors. I really am not sure why. Either they wanted to shame us (for living so well, when they lived so humbly) or they were simply being friendly and had man's natural inclination to invite people into his home. In most cases they lived 6-10 in the only room, with a few animals thrown in. They washed their babies and small children in enamel basins full of tepid brown water, usually out on the street in front of their dwelling. At 11 pm nobody seemed to be in bed, children, grown-ups and animals milled around. In some houses twenty or thirty people gathered around TV sets, volume turned up to maximum.

I will not dwell further on the poverty, the inhuman overcrowding, the smells, the unbelievable absence of any pretence of hygiene. These facts are often mentioned when one describes China. Suffice it to say that it is far more demeaning that one can imagine (at least in cities like Chungking), yet these people bore themselves with dignity, often with gentleness. In everyone's eyes – miraculously – one detected a glimmer of hope.

We all went to bed around 1 am, weary from sensory overload, sensing the throbbing pulse of rural-urban China, her enormous problems, her 16-hour-day-long energy, her compulsive industriousness, her age-old wisdom and perceptiveness, her invincible durability. The hotel rooms were dark, for electricity was cut off around midnight – it saves money. We groped around for our beds and belongings, soon hit our respective pillows. After half an hour, the six of us were rudely awakened by terrified female screams and the thudding of feet. Our door, carefully fastened for security, was battered on frenziedly. Kimi, nearest to it, opened it, dizzily. Caroline, Anna and Diane, silhouetted in the pale moonlight, came stumbling over the threshold.

"Rats!" they yelled.

We fumbled for our torches, finally threw some light on the events occurring in the other room. The girls had been woken up after a few minutes' sleep by rodents crawling over them. Anna thought it was Caroline giving her a friendly paw and touched a warm rat in the dark. There were plenty of others.

The girls were definitely not going back, not even to collect their belongings. I am no great rat-tamer myself, but somebody had to go and check things out. I took the biggest of the torches and walked the length of the balustrade to Room 9. The door was still wide open and, as I poked my torch through the opening, the beam illuminated a dozen rodents scampering up and down on the three empty beds. On the fourth bed, snoring soundly and with not a care in the world, was the young woman from Nottingham University, one rat perched on her chest and two others strolling round her. I didn't see any point in waking her – she obviously could handle things in China. I swept my beam here and there and grabbed rucksacks and sleeping bags which I threw out on the balcony. A dozen pairs of beady rat eyes, reflecting luminous red in my direction, watched me contemptuously. Not one animal showed any fear of me – they were dead right. Few men would have tackled a dozen of them with one torch. I was not one of them.

We were now 9 in a room – that is to say, at least, for whether or not we were also co-habiting with rodents in Room 2 had yet to be established. Nine powerful torches swept over every nook and cranny. Nobody seemed sleepy any more. Mathias, Jane and I were the only ones who had ever seen rats before – he on the farm, Jane in the suburbs of Buenos Aires and I running along the railway lines in Wigan station. We finally decided Room 2 was OK, though Mathias put his two apples in the pockets of his anorak, which he hung up on a hook to make sure no rodents got them. We all had an undisturbed night – nobody saw or heard a single rat or mouse. But the next morning Mathias' pockets contained only apple cores.

The next morning I decided to test some of the Chinese qualities which the inhabitants of the Middle Kingdom said they possessed. On check-out I asked for our combined bill and, on receiving it, asserted I would only pay half. The clerk looked me in the eye uncomprehendingly.

"Why only half?" he queried.

"We were only nine. There were at least eighteen of us in Rooms 2 and 9 – perhaps more."

"Eighteen, sir?"

"Rats. They shared our rooms."

"Rats, sir?"

I thought he was playing the hypocrite, but then he reached for his dictionary and I held my fire.

"L-A-T, sir?"

"No, R-A-T."

"I see," he found the word. He avoided my eye, but nodded quietly and went off to find the manager, who soon appeared. They exchanged views quickly in voluble Szechuanese. The manager looked at me apologetically and smiled gently:

"It's all right, sir – you can pay half."

Honest people, I thought. Maybe some of the nice things Chinese say about themselves were true. In fact, we encountered no dishonesty while we were in China, though their enigmatic behaviour in many other respects could prove extremely irritating to westerners. I guess that's what cross culture is all about.

*   *   *   *   *

The famous and spectacular Yangtse Gorges are located between Chungking and Wuhan; this leg of our trip we planned to do by boat, since not only did the gorges look most striking from the water, but there were few, if any, roads following the river bank. We spent another day exploring Chungking as well as procuring 9 downriver tickets on the steamer which left every evening. These vessels have 4 classes with differing standards of accommodation. In any other country these would be 1st, 2nd, 3rd and 4th class, but in communist China, "1st class" had unpleasant connotations, so the classes were called "Special 2nd", "2nd", 3rd and 4th. We were well-advised to travel Special 2nd. This time we got three cabins with 3 beds in each. They were appointed in a spartan manner, but at least had been half-cleaned and there were no animals under the beds. We were, of course, located on the top deck, the other classes descending in order. During the two-day trip we had occasion to visit the other classes, the lowest decks very briefly. The second class was packed and smelly; on the third deck people slept in every inch of corridor space as well as in the cabins. On the lowest deck there were no cabins and it was here where the majority of passengers travelled. One had no fears about the boat capsizing through having too high a centre of gravity. Again, one does not wish to be critical of states which are doing their best to develop, but it was not easy to comprehend how a country which had enjoyed nearly 5000 years of relatively unbroken civilisation could end up with conditions of transport for humans inferior to those enjoyed by cattle elsewhere. The stench and squalor on the fourth deck, where tightly-packed bodies lay night and day amid the debris of malodorous victuals and greasy personal belongings, had to be seen (and smelled) to be believed. So there are one billion people in China and they are overcrowded, but so are the Dutch and the Japanese, two of the cleanest countries on earth. The population density of China is 127 people per square kilometre. In Japan it is 331, in Holland 380, even in the UK it is 239! Large parts of China are uninhabitable, you say, but so is most of Japan and parts of Scotland are pretty cold in winter. The Chinese people have done may things very well in their history. They have excelled in philosophy and literature, calligraphy, painting, architecture, pottery, sculpture, music and theatre, even religious teaching. There is no doubt that they have a profound understanding of food. At certain times they have shown genius in military strategy, intensive agriculture and industrial organisation. Overseas Chinese have shown, and continue to demonstrate, their unrivalled business acumen. Yet they have failed dismally, at the end of the 20th century, to solve their problems in three vital areas – transportation, accommodation and hygiene.

All foreign visitors to China are impacted by this. The Japanese do not forgive them their lack of cleanliness easily. Tokyo commuters are packed like sardines every morning in the underground, but they still show up neat and proper at the office and the trains are cleaned constantly. For westerners the transport-housing problem is even more menacing. In China it is no use having a hard-earned ticket from A to B if (i) you have no roof over your head in B and (ii) you cannot get from B to C, or even back to A! Many tourists have to miss out on attractive spots like Xian, when they are faced with the prospect of a two-day cattle ride (by train) from Xian back to Peking.

Organized groups of tourists are provided with a limited number of hotel rooms at premium prices, but the individual traveller (foreign or Chinese) moving around China in areas unremarkable for tourism finds himself/herself subjugated to primitive conditions of shelter in small-town hotels which would fail to be acceptable at hostelry level even in such poverty-stricken nations as Madagascar, Vietnam or Brazil.

The Gorges of the Yangtse rank, along with the Great Wall and the Xian warriors, among China's great tourist attractions. We went through them in misty weather (it was actually chilly out of the sun) and the crew wrapped large red blankets round those special II class passengers who leaned over the rail. The fog enhanced the mysterious, rugged beauty of the cliff faces, though the river was a dirty brown on dull days. In the sun it was almost yellow, fast-flowing, fed by the April melting snow further up. The CITS were happy to have all 9 of us on board: this meant that for 2 whole days they knew where we were. Once let loose on bicycles we were off their radar, though officially they scheduled every nightly stop. We spent our time on board taking in the sights, reading books on China, playing cards in front of a thronged saloon full of curious Chinese and, on the last evening, even dancing. The recorded music alternated Chinese and Western melodies; the onlookers gawked at our foxtrots and jive, then joined in, timidly at first, probably wondering what the Gang of Four would have thought about it all.

We got off the boat at Wuhan, a rambling, industrial city of three million people. We were now in non-tourist territory and the primitive conditions in our hotel as well as the astonished stares of the town's inhabitants, gave us a foretaste of what was to come. We met by accident (we think) a young man in the bar who spoke halting, but reasonable, English. He was a Wong, around 30 years of age and very anxious to be of service. He told us he had a day off on the morrow and would help us to buy bicycles. He was as good as his word and, after an indifferent breakfast, we set off in his company to the Wuhan Cycle Shop. It appeared that Wuhan bikes were famous throughout China, there being only one other make, the details of which I do not remember. The shop was full of bicycles, all spanking new. Choosing a bike was not a difficult task as they were all one-geared, black, heavy and had wheels 28" in diameter. They were modelled on the English Raleigh bikes which I had ridden as a boy in the 1930s. They had thick tyres and big bells that went jingle jingle instead of ding ding. They all had cross bars, as most women in China wear pants when cycling. They were £50 each – I didn't haggle.

The procedure of getting a bike ready was pretty much the same as elsewhere: saddles were adjusted to the individual's height, tyres were pumped up and kicked, brakes were tested, chains were oiled, we each had a spin up and down the street to see if all was well. There were, of course, one thousand Chinese massed outside the bike shop by now. Once we were all satisfied I paid my £450 and got my receipts. Our panniers had been strapped on, pumps had been fitted, sleeping bags were tucked under the saddle – we were ready for the road, except for one thing: we needed registration plates. The documentation I had already filled in had been substantial; I feared we would lose more valuable time over the plates. The shop could not provide them, we had to go to the police station. Wong took us there, paid a small sum, we filled in new forms, a policeman stamped them, put them in a drawer and told us that we could come and collect the plates in about a month.

Fortunately we had left the bikes in the shop during this operation. They were receiving their final polish when we got back. We gave a surprised Wong two fountain pens and a London tee-shirt, grabbed the bikes and lit out of town, direction east, as fast as we could go. An amazed green-clad policeman gaped as we whizzed past him at one of Wuhan's crossroads. He had never seen bikes without registration plates before, but he had never seen Martians before either; he remained rooted to the spot as we waved hysterically at him and pedalled off into the midday sun. All other bikes we saw in China possessed plates – it was obviously strictly illegal to ride without them – yet the subject was never brought up by the numerous policemen we cycled past. We were hauled in for various other offences, but the bikes seemed sacrosanct. After all we had boosted the Wuhan economy – the bobbies were perhaps secretly pleased that we were not flaunting Cannondales. Perhaps riding those single-gear monsters was seen as a suitable punishment in itself. But none of us had a single puncture during the entire trip, in spite of the pebbles, rocks and pot-holes which lay in wait for us.

It would be too tiresome for the reader to accompany us every mile of our long trek along the Yangtse, though one or two generalisations might be of interest. In the first place, the mediaeval state of the roads led to our falling pathetically short of our planned daily mileage. If Mao's men had failed in their Great Leap Forward, so did we in the Great Push. Secondly we found that we could not follow Chinese maps – we were not always sure which way was up. We relied heavily on Kimi who could recognize Chinese characters, as they are similar to Japanese *kanji*, but even he had us going backwards at times. Thirdly – and most seriously – we frequently lost the river, as the roads did not always sensibly stick to its banks. Now, we knew that the only way we were ever going to get to Shanghai was to follow the course of the Yangtse. Whenever the river disappeared we felt panic. One day we lost it for 4 hours, going round in circles, asking people to let us in their top flats, to see if we could get a glimpse from on high. Mainly, people did not comprehend. "Yangtse" sounds quite different in Chinese, neither Kimi nor ourselves could pronounce it sufficiently to be recognized. They knew we wanted something and obligingly took us to Post Offices, bike repair shops, restaurants and public toilets. The police were no better. After 4 hours' searching we were finally stymied, moreover surrounded by about 300 Chinese on bicycles. They were fascinated by us and probably didn't want us to find the river. They stared at our wristwatches and western clothes and the bolder men touched Caroline's (blonde) hair. They did it so gently and kindly that she never felt threatened or uncomfortable. After an hour of immobility, an elderly man with soft, intelligent features threaded his way to us through the throng. He said:

"I speak English."

Without further ado I said:

"Where is the river?"

He digested the remark and replied quietly:

"Follow me."

The crowd parted to let him lead us and he biked off slowly and steadily. In twenty minutes we were on the familiar banks of our beloved Yangtse.

"Where did you learn your English?" I asked him.

"Follow Me" he answered.

*　　*　　*　　*　　*

The part of the Yangtse which flows between Wuhan and Shanghai runs through one of China's most densely populated regions. This is to be expected, as the irrigation benefits afforded by the great river facilitate intense cultivation of rice to support a large population. At that time nearly 800 million Chinese were still peasants and we pedalled past a goodly number of them. The spectacle of millions of land workers toiling 12 hours a day to feed the nation inevitably makes a deep impression on westerners. In order to maximize utilisation of the daylight hours, Chinese in agricultural areas go to bed and rise with the sun. They are a special breed of human being, conditioned by many centuries of unremitting toil. Men and women are entirely focussed on rice cultivation, they live in hermetic ignorance of any world outside China. Most of them spend the whole of their lives within one or two miles of their home and have their hands and feet under water for a large proportion of the day. They have rarely, if ever, heard a non-Chinese language, never seen a lampshade or a proper toilet seat, never ridden in a private car. They are short in stature, sharp-eyed, dark-skinned. This is not entirely due to their exposure to the sun, but genetic, as even the schoolchildren are of the same hue. Their diet – mostly rice and vegetables – is monotonous but healthy. We saw many octogenarians of both sexes. Food in humid south China is rarely transported out of the region, so that beef is rarely seen in the south, though it is in evidence in northern provinces.

The fields are vast and fenceless. Besides rice, crops were grown, often two at a time, e.g. squash or sweet potatoes could be grown with maize. No weeds are allowed to grow in China – there are many hands for weeding. As they bent over their tasks, peasants rarely bothered to look up at us – the impossibility of communication probably discouraged them – though they were friendly enough if we addressed them. In the cities it was quite different: we were invariably scrutinized from close quarters by curious yet amicable throngs. Between Wuhan and Shanghai, only the towns of Soo-chow and Nanjing are used to tourists. Elsewhere, people employed both in agriculture and industry have never seen foreigners. This applied also to the staff of the so-called hotels that we stayed at in the industrial areas. "Tourist hotels" in places such as Beijing and Soo-chow, though inadequate by our standards, are at least specially geared to Western needs in terms of food and sanitation. Normal Chinese hotels cater for Chinese commercial reps and lowly officials who have very modest demands on hotel services. We were not supposed to stay in these hotels at all. The only reason why we were allowed in was that often we would show up late at night, lost, frequently hungry and with nowhere else to go. Nine round-eyes congregating with nine unregistered bicycles at 11 pm in the dimly-lit lobbies of these primitive establishments was enough to give any provincial hotel manager a fit, not to mention the hapless young girls on reception.

Yet the Chinese have such an innate sense of hospitality that it was impossible for them to turn us away. They were inevitably on the horns of a dilemma: we were certainly not authorized to be where we were; but they had been directed to be nice to foreigners. Though obviously afraid of their own police, they invariably slipped us room keys, often after an hour's hesitation and voluble discussion amongst themselves. The police found out about us an hour later and usually came round to question us. Once, we were all hauled out of bed at two in the morning and interrogated in our pyjamas. As the police could not speak English, the poor English master of the local school also had his slumbers disturbed to act as interpreter. We felt sorry for him, since many of our answers were pretty inane. The grilling usually took the same course:

> "Where did you stay last night?"
> "We don't know for sure, but here is the hotel receipt."
> "This is not a tourist hotel."
> "Isn't it?"
> "No, why didn't you phone the CITS to book your accommodation?"
> "We did, but they couldn't understand our English."
> "Which route did you take today?"
> "Here is our map. The route is pencilled in."
> "It is not a direct route."
> "Unfortunately not. We got lost 3 times."
> "Where are you headed tomorrow?"
> "Wuxi."

"Then the CITS must book you into the Tourist Hotel there."

"Thank you."

"What is the purpose of your visit to China?"

"To see the wonderful sights of your beautiful country."

"What are your impressions of China?"

"We are struck by the kindness of the ordinary people, the staff of the CITS and the police and other officials."

"Do you assure us you will book the Wuxi Tourist Hotel and stay there tomorrow night?"

"Of course."

"We wish you good night." (it was now 3 am)

"Good night."

They usually saluted as they withdrew.

We would never reach Wuxi, of course. Wuxi was one hundred kilometres away and while this would have been a doddle in England or even Wales, the obstacle course of the scarred highways along the Yangtse meant that we would do fifty or sixty at the best.

Which brings us to another feature of our Chinese Odyssey: our dependence on the kindness of truck drivers. Though we started early, our morning progress would be hindered by hundreds of Chinese fellow-cyclists who seemed to feel it their duty to escort us out of town. This attendance would last for nearly an hour, when they would finally drop off one by one. The bush telegraph would have informed the inhabitants of the next town that the aliens were on their way, and they would cycle out about an hour to meet us and escort us in. Unintended meanderings and slowly-served meals would delay us further. The result was that most evenings, as dusk fell, we would be anything from 20 to 40 kilometres from our destination, well out of reach of accommodation for the night. We soon found out that we had the utmost difficulty in cycling in the dark. Bikes and lorries did not use lights. The dark-blue Mao-suits of the cyclists rendered them and their black bikes invisible. So were the pot-holes. We could barely read the maps, even in daylight. Consequently about eight each evening, as twilight gathered around us, Anna Mattila did her party trick. By the simple expedient of standing in the middle of the road, she would stop empty lorries. She then asked them in fluent Finnish – a sonorous language – to take us to the next town. Paralysed like rabbits in the glare of our torches, they almost invariably acceded to our request. With a little practice, we learnt how to load lorries with nine people and nine Wuhan bikes in 60 seconds flat. The drivers, most of them simple souls, were quite terrified, but they had hearts of gold and drove us on to our destination. It was noticeable that they always unloaded us in dark, quiet, outlying suburbs of the towns – there was no point in asking for more trouble than they already had. On the two occasions when the police discovered this practice, the hapless drivers were harangued mercilessly and we felt guilty, as indeed we ought to. We tried to compensate them after the police had gone with money, cigarettes and fountain pens. Usually they were too terrorized to accept anything save a few fags. The trucks themselves were frequently in an abject state of repair with patched-up bodies, worn tyres, atrocious wheel slack and several layers of grime and grease. To save fuel, drivers would cut off the ignition when going downhill or even on the flat, freewheeling sometimes for half a mile or so.

The provincial hotels had rat-infested cell-like rooms, with dirty grey walls, innocent of any form of decoration. The blankets and pillows were the same colour as the walls, there were no sheets or pillowcases. Lighting consisted of one bare bulb (40 watt) hanging from the ceiling. Electrical wiring was invariably stuck on the surface of the wall after it had (many years ago) been painted. There were no bathrooms as we know them. These hotels would have two large rooms, one for men and one for women, which consisted of bare concrete walls, with a pipe along all its length. This pipe would have about 20 holes punched in it. When the tap was turned on, 20 jets of steaming hot water would spurt from the pipe. Twenty naked men, or women, would take a hole each and "shower" simultaneously. A bit primitive, but quite effective – there was no hanging around waiting for someone to quit the bathroom. Food was largely of poor quality, the breakfasts, particularly, proved very difficult for us. Quails' eggs floating round in insipid fish soup got us off to a bad start to the day. We had some good meals in Shanghai and Beijing as well as in the Jin Ling Hotel in Nanjing, but in general (apart from Szechuan) the standard of Chinese food in China is far inferior to that of Chinese restaurants in Hong Kong, Europe or America. The thousand-year eggs, black, weren't bad and we had some reasonable pieces of duck and pork. Meatballs were watery, almost tasteless. Long, green cabbage was ubiquitous, had a boring, slightly bitter taste. The quality of the fish varied enormously. All water had to be boiled, even the Chinese dare not drink it otherwise. Wine is not really wine (more like cordial); orange and other bottled soft drinks taste very strange indeed. We cleaned our teeth in Coca-cola. Most of us had tummy trouble at some time during the trip, though to be fair to China, their variety is far less devastating than Mexico's Montezuma's Revenge. The pollution of the industrialized areas leads to all foreigners developing very sore throats after 10 days or so in China. We were no exceptions.

*   *   *   *   *

Our progress along the river was slow but sure and there was something new to see every day. The roads themselves presented kaleidoscopic variety. There were few cars, but many overloaded, rattling trucks. The most interesting vehicles were improvised by the peasants themselves. Some had carts, often pulled by 3 donkeys, two in front and one behind the other two. The loads they could move were colossal – oil-drums, boxes and containers, even whole tree-trunks. Other workers began with a bicycle, tricycle or small 50cc motorbike and built round them plywood frameworks or platforms upon which they could transport an unbelievable amount of merchandise. One man had 15 huge baskets, full of we know not what, all tied on with string. Another had a plywood platform, with a foot-high rail all round, fencing in 8 geese which hissed at every cyclist they saw. Another had 6 baskets with two piglets in each. Kimi ascertained how they had managed to coax a squealing piglet into a basket little more than its own size. Apparently they give the animals generous swigs of vodka till they get quite drunk and they then pack them into the baskets while they are sleepy. Others transported bales of hay or garden produce or huge piles of compressed dung. Those with 50cc engines chugged away at a faster pace than the cyclists. Diane and Mathias, our less strenuous members, often grabbed the rear of one of the motored contraptions and let themselves be dragged along, especially up inclines. The drivers seemed to take no notice whatsoever, or gave a casual, acquiescent nod. Continually we were given such pieces of evidence of the phlegmatic, passive attitude of Chinese people. Try hanging onto the back of a German cart sometime.

One could not really ascertain what these rural Chinese thought of us. Though peasants, they are aware, just as much as city-dwellers, that they inhabit the Middle Kingdom – that is to say, the centre of the world. This is where it all happens and they are daily witnesses. We, devils or not, have come from afar, we act and look strange and we are temporarily sharing the 5000-year-old Chinese experience: the peasant does not, basically, feel inferior to us. We revolve round China, not the other way round. Mathias and I felt this attitude towards us and debated its validity. They are one billion and invented paper in the 2nd century AD, when northern Europeans were still wiping their bottoms clean with sycamore leaves. Paper was not introduced into northern Europe until the 13th century. Printing was common in China by the 8th century, movable type was used in the 11th. This technology only reached Europe in the 15th century!

Who are the isolated, provincial ones? Of course the Chinese acknowledge and envy our technology, but technical know-how can be transferred. What about culture? We met some Chinese-Canadians in Shanghai.

"The culture is all here", they told us. "All we have is money."

Being convinced of their centrality, most Chinese have no great desire to travel and show little interest in other civilisations. Some businessmen, and those government officials involved in international trade or diplomacy acknowledge the necessity to learn English as a means of communication, but their interest does not extend to any great extent to the literature, arts or philosophies of the English-speaking nations.   Professor Yeh and our Britannica friends excepted, few people recognized any western writers beyond Shakespeare, though it was possible to see one or two books by Hemingway, Steinbeck, Dickens, Balzac and Dostoievski in the bookstores of Shanghai. All the art we saw in China consisted of copies or reproductions of the classical scrolls of antiquity or garish political posters. It is possible that the nature of the Chinese language instils in the Chinese a lust for symbolisation. Be that as it may, there seemed to be little correlation between art and private inspiration. It was as if the very concept of personalized art sat uneasily with their collective spirit.   Museums and art galleries were invariably housed in dark, gloomy buildings and explanations in English were few and far between. The Chinese evinced no great eagerness to share or explicate their paintings, pottery, porcelain or calligraphy with barbarians. Even the few English-speaking guides and attendants we found had little to say except the obvious. Interestingly, when we toured the Shan Juan Cave near Yixing, the young guide commented at length on the usual array of stalactites and stalagmites in the cavern. What fascinated Mathias and myself was that, seen through Chinese eyes, the geological formations represented different things from those we saw. Mathias envisaged Polynesian dancing girls on surfboards and female skiers with ski-poles in hand at the starting gate. Our guide saw seated Buddhas, a panda climbing a tree, a tiger about to leap, a pond covered in lotus blossoms. One felt that in China, the past inevitably overwhelms the present, perhaps partially blinding her people to current deficiencies and paradoxes. Yet one always feels the strength of their poetic traditions – the unerring instinct for beauty and spatial arrangement.

We had few chances to discuss politics with the Chinese, owing to the language barrier and possibly on account of their wariness in practising their new-found freedoms. It was glorious to make money, they could be nice to foreigners, but the communist government controlled the country and their lives and debate was not the same as dissent. Newspapers, apparently, never reported negative news and we had seen police snap viciously at common people on several occasions. On one of our bus trips to a tea plantation, however, Mathias was able to have a frank discussion with our CITS guide, a 39-year-old who spoke fluent English and was unusually talkative. He described his own experiences in the Cultural Revolution (1966-76), which had always fascinated Mathias on account of its unexplained, utter idiocy. Huang, now a state employee, had done very well in English at school and had graduated in the subject from the University of Beijing in 1967. He got caught up almost immediately in the Cultural Revolution and was arrested, arraigned, brought to a People's Court of teenage young Revolutionaries and sentenced to 12 years' hard labour. His crime? He had a degree in English, wore glasses, and looked very intellectual. He served his first 2 years on an agricultural commune sharing a "shack" (his word) with a fellow prisoner. He was given the hardest and most menial tasks, spreading pig-dung and cleaning out cesspools. His hands developed perennial sores, he wrecked his back and lost his glasses. It took him another year before they let him have another pair, when he was transferred to a ball-bearing factory for "good behaviour". With the fall of the Gang of Four, he was set free and given his present job as a guide-interpreter with the CITS. As this organisation has an age limit of 40, he expected to get a job as an English teacher the following year. He had heard of Professor Yeh and marvelled that we had met him. He showed some bitterness at his cruel sentence, though in a muted Chinese fashion which obviously incorporated some fatalism and acknowledgement of life's ambiguity. Truth, in China, is never in a straight line.

*   *   *   *   *

Most of the Chinese with whom we were able to converse blamed the current ills and problems of the country on the depredations of the Gang of Four, rather than on Mao himself. The Cultural Revolution had been an assault on reason at a time when Chou-en-Lai's sensibilities and popularity were beginning to create a cosier image of communism. It had seemed that the Chinese model might abandon the remaining vestiges and excesses of Stalinist ruthlessness and develop along the lines of the Czech and Hungarian versions. And then this madness – millions of youngsters waving Mao's little red book – Chou-en-Lai himself a victim. The intellectuals, who suffered most, are still at a loss to explain the phenomenon and how it could have caught on with such vindictiveness. Mass hypnosis, as occurred in Nazi Germany? The 800 million peasants were less affected; they could not be punished in the same fashion, as they were already in the place where people were sent for punishment. In 1985 we were left to marvel at Chinese resilience: there was obviously no massive civic demoralisation. The Cultural Revolution was another tragic blip in Chinese history, but in China the past is long and the future is, too. Chinese identity, subject to so many onslaughts over the centuries (including those from the West) was again being re-formulated in terms of the continuing elements of Chinese culture.

*   *   *   *   *

Our sojourn down the Yangtse was not all hardship. It is much easier, both on the eye and on the stomach, to cycle down the Rhône or the Loire. But it was not only the tourist sights of China that interested us. We wanted to experience the real, everyday slog of Chinese life and get to close quarters with people other than CITS guides. Westerners cannot achieve this (on a bike, at any rate) without some physical discomfort. We saw many beautiful things as well. The Yangtse flows through countryside of original and staggering loveliness, even apart from the Gorges. Elegant, classical temples appeared at every turn. The garden city of Soo-chow (Suzhou) is exquisite in its tranquillity and design. The Sun-Yat-Sen memorial in Nanjing is breathtaking in its conception. Kimi, with visions of the Rape of Nanjing in his head, had been wary of entering this city, where, he had heard, Japanese were hated and unwelcome. In fact one of the most intimate evenings we enjoyed with Chinese teenagers centered round Kimi in a Nanjing bar.

We decided to sell the bikes in Soo-chow – only an hour's train ride from Shanghai – rather than tackle this sprawling metropolis from the saddle. The cycles were all in good condition, we figured that if we offered them at half the price we had paid for them, we should get ready takers. This turned out to be true, though we were not sure how we should go about the business. The CITS guide wanted nothing to do with it, as he was not sure of the legal position. We hummed and hawed a while; finally I lined them all up outside a jeweller's on one of the main streets and shouted "bicycles for sale". In the space of two minutes we were surrounded by inquisitive passers-by. Once the word had got around that we were selling bikes, people started producing money. The price of a new bicycle represents many months of salary for most Chinese, so the chance to get a near-new one at half price meant there was no haggling. It took people about half an hour to assemble the cash, then one bike went, then a second, then a third and a fourth. I was stuffing wads of dirty banknotes into my pockets till they could hold no more – we were soon going to need a suitcase. Just when the business was going well, the police arrived – at least one constable did. The crowds parted to leave a corridor for him. He strode quickly forward, grabbed a bike by the handlebars, wheeled it round in a circle, looked for the registration plate which wasn't there, then addressed me sharply in sing-song Shanghainese. I nodded dumbly. Then he bought the bike and pedalled off on it.

There was pandemonium in the crowd over the last 4 bikes. The jeweller and his son dashed out of their shop, grabbed two of them, wheeled them into the shop and beckoned me inside. He took me to the till and emptied it spreading the money over the glass-topped counter. There was not enough – the day's takings could only buy one bike and a half. He gave me various messages in Shanghainese and sign language and his son high-tailed it out of the shop in order (as I understood) to fetch the remaining cash. Other people were now waving money at me through the glass door, which the jeweller kept firmly locked. After 10 minutes his son came back and completed the purchase. Mathias and the boys were trying to hang on to the remaining two bikes, but in the milling throng two young men seized them and pedalled off with them. We shouted at them irately in several languages but they disappeared in the dusk. The crowd laughed uproariously: we felt pretty sick at this point, but stuffed our money deeper into our pockets and made sure nobody picked them. We were just about to beat a retreat back to our hotel when the two young men returned with the bikes and a pile of cash in a plastic bag which they handed to us. The business was done – the whole operation took three quarters of an hour.

*　*　*　*　*

The next day we took the train to Shanghai. Again we were special II class, which meant that we were put in a separate waiting room at Soo-Chow station. On the Chinese side the commuters were packed like sardines, but we had a scented armchair each and there were artificial flowers on a low table. The arrival of the train was announced in English and we were escorted along the platform by a nice young lady in a blue uniform. Once aboard, we found ourselves in a special compartment which did not resemble those in English trains. We sat in a kind of alcove where armchairs were arranged around two low tables. We were served green tea throughout the journey, which lasted one hour and fifteen minutes. Hundreds of sardines peeped at us through a glass partition.

In Shanghai the CITS had instructed us to go to the Peace Hotel where a message would await us regarding our accommodation. At the station – a mad-house – we could not get a taxi. Feeling the loss of our bikes, we prepared to cross the city on foot, but were soon accosted by rickshaw boys who pulled little carts behind their cycles. We piled into four of these and had a hair-raising ride across Shanghai where the bustling traffic resembled that of a western city. In fact Shanghai had a decidedly western look about it – the Victorian style buildings being a legacy of the "colonies" set up in the city by the British, French, Germans, Americans and Russians.

We were pleasantly housed in the quiet Da Hua Hotel on the outskirts of the city. Shanghai had quite a different atmosphere from that of the other cities along the Yangtse and was unlike Peking, too. The people seemed sharp-eyed, alert, seemingly going about their business in a brisk, purposeful manner. It was a city with its own agenda – one felt that the mandarins of Beijing were far away and, to some extent, ignored. Shanghainese have a *rapport* with westerners that other Chinese in the PRC do not have. They were relatively smart in their dress. Blue jeans were ubiquitous, but instead of the blue smock so common at that time in most of China, most girls wore brightly coloured tops and their make-up was noticeable.

Business was being done everywhere. In the museums old ticket sellers were allowed to charge you one penny for passing from one room or courtyard to the next. In one department store, girls took a penny from peasants to ride on the escalators, though we were permitted to go free. On the streets we saw young people from the surrounding countryside peddling the surplus food from their communes. Everybody seemed to be employed in Shanghai. We walked along the famous Bund, window-shopped in Nanjing Road – the most fashionable and expensive street in China – and visited the Old Town built in Chinese Tudor style. Nearby we took a look at Chou-en-Lai's former house – tasteful and tranquil, like the man himself. Finally our boys found entertainment in the Jing Jang Club (formerly used by western colonialists) where one can still play snooker on genuine Riley tables from Liverpool.

*   *   *   *   *

It was not easy to get tickets back to Peking, but we managed it. Zhang and the same driver awaited us with the white minibus and took us to the Min Zu, where he had secured two rooms. One had a sense of Chinese *déjà vu* . There were still things to see in the capital and we ploughed through the sights in the three days that remained to us. Of these the most awesome was the Forbidden City, an almost overwhelmingly vast compound of palaces and great halls with their impressive examples of sculpture, screens and scrolls. The Imperial collection of clocks, watches and glockenspiels must be the most extensive on earth.

The Yehs were kind enough to arrange a lunch for us on our return and we once more had the pleasure of visiting their charming wooden house. Mrs Yeh was a wonderful cook and specialized in Beijing dumplings, which were delicious. I think Mathias had about twenty. Her husband had invited two people to meet us – the Head of the Department of Foreign Languages of a nearby university and one of his professors. They had 600 full-time students in their department, 400 of whom studied English, 150 Japanese and 50 Russian. These were the languages they were majoring in. Most of them were taking German, French or Spanish as their minor language. They exchanged 8 post-graduate students a year with the University of South Carolina and planned to set up a similar scheme with Japan. It was just a drop in the ocean, of course, and we talked about the stubborn monolingualism of the People's Republic and the huge task confronting educators in this respect. It was mainly a matter of numbers, as well as antiquated rote-learning methods and an inadequate infrastructure for national education. Where would the teachers come from to teach the hundreds of millions? Many of the teachers of English had never met an English-speaking person and could barely speak the language themselves. I concurred, having seen the same problem in provincial cities in Japan.

My pioneering days with the BBC and "Walter and Connie" had been followed by several English language teaching films. I had been consulted over some of these and knew Hugh Howse, who had succeeded Christopher Dilke as Head of English by Radio and Television, very well indeed. He had visited Riversdown and we had shared a two-day seminar for FIAT a couple of years before. The latest BBC production was called "FOLLOW ME". It was a mammoth programme – 60 lessons as opposed to "Walter and Connie"'s 39 and it had just hit China. We had even seen it one night on TV as we peeped through the door of a home in Chungking, where twenty or so 'guests' had their eyes glued to the screen. I had followed Hugh Howse's negotiations with the Chinese government with respect to the rights of screening the programme in China. "FOLLOW ME" ran eventually in over 60 countries; in general the BBC were not overly concerned with the price at which they sold the programme; they made most of their money selling the booklet which the viewer needed to follow the course. This cost a couple of pounds and sold in large numbers in Germany, France and so on. The Chinese laughed at this price and pointed out (quite rightly) that the ordinary Chinese could not pay it. Hugh Howse negotiated the price down in classic fashion, but even when he was well below one pound it was becoming fairly obvious that the book would not sell. I knew something about the price and quality of English language text-books I had fingered in such places as Taiwan and Indonesia and I advised Hugh to authorize the Chinese to print in their own fashion (it would be on paper resembling that we use in the toilet) and go for a royalty. He followed this route for a while and the royalty percentage grew smaller and smaller, all to no effect. In the end the Chinese offered a flat rate of one English penny (1p) per book. It was the BBC's turn to laugh their heads off, but I suspected that that was what they would get in the end (and that proved the case). Hugh signed the agreement under duress and amidst great wailing and gnashing of teeth. The programme started in China one Wednesday night and the book was put on sale in the shops on the previous Monday. They sold 6 million copies on the first day: it was £60,000 for the BBC in twenty-four hours – the best deal they had ever done.

The very size of a one billion plus population affects everything that happens in China. Though such a number is hard to visualize, one is constantly reminded of the people factor as one moves around the country. One sometimes has this impression in Japan, but there are 10 Chinese for every Japanese. We visited a modest pottery at Dingsu on the Yangtse where they made teapots for the famed tea from the Taihua mountains. The director told us this was the best tea in China; he also said that they employed 50 senior craftsmen (designers) who came up with about 50 new models each year. Two thousand different lines were being produced: 8 million pieces a year. Professor Yeh had thrown other staggering statistics at us: in its drive for industrialisation the government was planning to move 200 million people from rural reas to the cities in the space of five to six years. In theory, housing was planned for them too, though it was well known that one million people slept on the streets in Shanghai, Guangdong and other big cities in the south. Everything in China is designed on a big scale. Like the Americans, they think big and, their humility notwithstanding, they love the grandiose. They will soon be one in four of the earth's people. In the middle of the 21st century they will be the biggest market and probably the leading producers in the world. Their drive to restore their age-old identity and Asian hegemony will be unstoppable, as will the emergence of a 500 million-strong middle class. Accepting the inevitability of all this, I only wondered, as we approach the end of our century, if the techniques of democracy are within their grasp.

*   *   *   *   *

On the evening we left China, at Peking airport with the ever-present Zhang in attendance, 6 of our 8 tickets to London were bounced (Kimi was going the other way). Richard was due to start university the next day, so he and I went home alone leaving Jane, Mathias, Diane, Anna, David and Caroline on Chinese soil. CAAC showed little remorse (they invariably overbook) and it took the others four days to get on a plane home, via Paris as it turned out. This was achieved, according to Mathias, by the airline throwing 6 Frenchmen off the flight.

Zhang did his Min Zu act for our stranded group and was rewarded in due course by my getting him into an English university. He now lives permanently in England, has a Chinese wife and is the happy father of two in Milton Keynes.

Chapter 22

When Cultures Collide

In the 1950s and 1960s language teachers of the world were busy teaching languages. Nazi-occupied Europe had missed out on several years of schooling in English and the gap was to show 10-15 years later when these people entered commercial life. In eastern Europe a whole generation was obliged to learn Russian – a language of scant use in international dealings – and the adjustment to English, as well as German and French, did not take place until 1985-90.

Teaching a language meant, in the Berlitz world at least, teaching a living, changing thing – a subject which displayed a variety of facets that depended largely on the personality of the instructor. One played down the importance of grammar, with its hard and fast strictures, in an attempt to encourage spontaneity and modest fluency in the learner. Scandinavian and Dutch students, used to imitating catchy phrases in pop songs, went along well with this approach. Grammar, nevertheless, continued to loom large for other nationalities. Germans and Finns, thinking in highly-inflected languages, always had a tendency to seek the grammatical how and why. The French regard mastery of grammar as an essential cornerstone of their intellectual make-up. The other Latins, taught in a hopelessly antiquated fashion in their schools, chanted rules and exceptions like parrots.

Such learners, especially those with low levels of proficiency, saw the English language as a finite task – one that could be confronted and after a certain period of suffering completed. To achieve this end, one needed a grammar book which guided you through the maze in 50 lessons over 250 pages covering 50 vital verbs, structures (duplicated in the Passive Voice), a couple of tricky procedures called the Causative and Reported Speech, no Subjunctive worth losing sleep over and little else of grammatical challenge. This was the process of "learning the language", to which most students applied themselves with diligence. It normally took two or three years for adult learners to satisfy themselves that they knew their English grammar. At that point, of course, they began to perceive that English, far from being a finite thing, starts to uncover its idiomatic riches, its multiplicity of forms, its intriguing codes, its dialectal, regional and national varieties, and stretches in all directions – a vast sparkling sea of subtlety and nuance, towards a far-off shimmering horizon that one may never reach.

By the beginning of the 1970s English learners in the northern half of Europe had, in the main, completed the task of learning the language. They spoke English, at least in correct form and with reasonable speed. But when they entered business life they found that the linguistic tool they had acquired, while perfectly adequate and extremely useful amongst themselves – German to Finn, Swede to Italian, etc.) felt distinctly sterile or awkward when they used it with a native English speaker. Their range of expressions was thin on the ground, they lacked the variety of registers for politeness or curtness, they missed out on English nuances or sarcasm. At meetings they were disadvantaged. This was no illusion – it was a real situation which English and American people could exploit.

Thus it was that in the 1970s language teachers spent an increasing portion of their time teaching not English, which most students had already learnt, but **communicative skills** which was, as our American friends say, a whole new ball game. Communicative skills are required in one's own language and environment, both in social and business situations. Some of us are better than others in pleasing or convincing our interlocutors, as the occasion may demand. To be able to do this in a foreign language adds another dimension of difficulty. Communication often has to do with function. Our German businessman may have to give presentations of his company or product to English-speaking customers. Negotiating is another function which occurs frequently. Chairing a meeting is another, report writing is another. Personnel officers must master the function of interviewing, often in another language.

For all these functions, English has a set of phraseologies, a progression of techniques, a variety of registers, an observance of certain coded niceties, which would never have been covered in a "grammatical" language course. Such linguistic skills can be honed in 100-200 hours, depending on the number of functions practised. It is, in a sense, Stage Two of learning language proficiency. The correct use of English for social occasions is also covered in this process. Scandinavians, Dutch, Germans, Finns and some Latins spent the seventies acquiring these skills. Few English-speakers did (in foreign languages). British, American, Australian and New Zealand people are, with some outstanding exceptions, still struggling (if they bother) with Stage One.

By the early 1980s our valiant northern Europeans, especially Dutch, Swedes, Danes and Finns – and many Germans too – had completed Stage Two – the acquisition of communicative skills in English. They could sell, buy, argue, influence, cajole, stall, persuade and earn sympathy in this very useful *lingua franca* called English. They were, and remain, impressive. They are one or two decades ahead of the Anglos in these abilities.

But in the mid-1980s, Stage Three was born. What is Stage Three? What skill remains beyond their reach? It is, in essence, the management of cultural diversity – what you have to do when cultures collide. Let us take a simple example. A German sales director has just completed a course in communicative skills given by British teachers. Because of his job, he has naturally taken great care to master the art of giving a convincing presentation of his company's products in English. He possesses the necessary vocabulary in full, grammatical errors have been eliminated, his visual aids are perfect, his teachers have seen to it that his sales pitch includes some user-friendly idioms, one or two subtle selling points and possibly a flash or two of British humour. He delivers his presentation in England and his customers smilingly congratulate him on his competent performance.

But as sales director, he has to do the same thing in the United States and Japan. He cannot help but notice that he has been less effective than before. The feedback is different, his hard-won confidence begins to ebb, even while he is speaking. What has he done wrong? The answer is nothing; it is simply a matter of listening habits. His British instructors coached him in the art of pleasing a British audience. Just as people use speech in different ways, they also listen in different ways. There are good listeners and bad listeners, easy-going and demanding audiences. In this particular case the German's own factual, rather laboured style of address would have been softened, lightened and manipulated to suit humour-seeking, laid-back Brits. A typical Japanese audience would perceive this style as lacking in seriousness, possibly in detail, difficult to comprehend because of some clever phraseologies. The humour would be opaque to them, the speaker not courteous enough. He looked at the younger Japanese present too much instead of addressing his remarks to the senior (old) ones.

The Americans heard and saw it differently. The British soft-sell – so welcome to the Japanese – came across as unconvincing and lacking in product-confidence. The "old-fashioned" English hinted at out-of-date merchandise. We are cross-century executives, this is not a Victorian parlour. And why go on so long? Just give us the bottom line. The humour was OK, but what did the guy really say?

Audiences composed of other nationalities would have different expectations again. Nordics want everything shining new, presented succinctly with a touch of dry humour. French audiences wait for a tribute to their own intellectuality and then plenty of *panache*. Italians have other things to think about while you are talking, though they do not miss good deals. You must make Spaniards like you before they will buy – they couldn't give a damn about your thorough presentation. Most Asians want you to be polite and deferential – they will decide to buy much later (if you behave properly at the social events). Germans and Swiss want facts, figures and information and don't mind how long you bore them.

The interaction of cultures – in this case a British trained, honest German trying to influence hard-nosed Americans and inscrutable, reactive Japanese – is fraught with possibilities of misunderstanding and faulty assumptions. A *gaffe* at a party can be redeemed over the next cocktail. A cultural miscalculation or unintended slight among sensitive, high-flying executives can cost billions. Big business is slowly coming to grips with this phenomenon, though the surface is only just being scratched. It is in the area of negotiation where most is at stake. Negotiating across cultures takes place every day at thousands of places around the world. Negotiation itself is an art (or science) thousands of years old and such people as the Chinese are not going to do or see things your way just because a negotiating course manual written 10 years ago by an American spells it out in a certain manner. The hard sell and cynical approach which are the hallmarks of most US "art of selling" courses describe in some detail techniques which are **guaranteed to upset Asians.** And remember where the big consumer markets of the 21st century are going to be!

And so, in my middle age, I gradually relinquished my direct involvement in teaching languages in order to concentrate first on the teaching of communication skills in the business area, and now, since the mid 1980s, on the acquisition of cross cultural skills, of multi-culturalism, of global competence or whatever you want to call it. The multicultural or culturally sensitive executive is of incalculable value to his/her company. A multinational conglomerate like IBM, Unilever or Motorola not only sell to people of all nationalities, but they are involved in mergers and acquisitions, partnerships, joint ventures, huge contracts of all kinds. They have to manage foreign work forces and, quite often, the managers who manage them. The number of psychologies, mindsets and world views they are dealing with is staggering in its variety. The much sought-after standardization of procedures to achieve convergence of worldwide policies in accounting, reporting, personnel schemes and so on is challenged and frequently defeated by the stubborn divergence of local cultures. Sales bonuses go down well in the US and Britain, but cause more trouble than content in Indonesia and Taiwan.

Managing cultural diversity is a subject of infinite depth and width. Few people can teach it, especially when we deal with the business community. University professors and psychologists can write their books and publish the results of their research, but theorizing often has little to do with what actually happens in the business arena. In order to give meaningful advice to executives who may have to make a series of key decisions with Japanese, Germans, Chinese and Italians in quick succession, one has to have had hands-on experience. A cross cultural adviser should be at least 40, preferably 50. He or she should actually have lived in the countries they advise on for a minimum of 2 years, preferably more. They should, moreover, have been involved in business and made the mistakes which all newcomers do. The most careful drivers are the ones who have survived serious accidents. There is no substitute for experience in international business.

At the age of 50, I had made all possible mistakes in more than a dozen major economies. My academic studies in French, Spanish and Italian, including the literatures and philosophies in these 3 languages, had given me certain insights into the workings of the Latin mind. My 5 years in Portugal had deepened these insights. Two years working shoulder to shoulder with German broadcasters and journalists had familiarized me with a completely different mindset. A total of 7 years spent in the Nordic countries allowed me to see things through Scandinavian and Finnish eyes. I had enjoyed 5 years of closeness to Japanese people from many walks of life and my own world view had been conditioned through a knowledge of their language and observance of their calm, thoughtful behaviour. My frequent forays into Korea, China, Hong Kong, Indonesia and Thailand, not to mention Vietnam, Cambodia and Laos, had rounded off my understanding of Asian mentality and attitudes. Last but not least, my reporting to 2 sizeable US corporations over 6 to 7 years had given me a thorough understanding of how Americans saw the rest of the world, how they ran their foreign subsidiaries, what they regarded as important or vital and what they failed to perceive about cultures other than their own.

On the practical side, I had had to set up more than 30 different companies and subsidiaries in a score of different countries. At various times I had controlled over 90 establishments of learning in activities ranging from language instruction, management training, film and video production, editorial and publications, as well as teacher training on a large scale. For over 25 years I had had to sell, buy, rent, negotiate, present and address a multiplicity of deals, plans and crises – all this apart from the teaching of skills in which I have been trained. I have never received a subsidy from any government, municipality or public body. It has all been very much private enterprise, starting from scratch. Though they are not easy, I do not regard these achievements as having been particularly difficult. If you get up early in the morning and have a lot of common sense, you will always be hard to beat. The other way is to be born with a lot of money and use your connections among the rich. I was lucky enough not to have had this easy route, so I was able to enjoy fully the struggle with which most of us are faced. I was determined to make money (to compensate for lack of it in the early days) but I resolved to make it in the field for which I had been trained. I would not have been happy spending money earned from selling soap powder or second-hand cars. The rich world of language-and-culture was my business as well as my life. I stuck to what I had been taught.

Since 1971 we have had a living cross-cultural workshop being held daily at Riversdown House, 358 days a year at 14 hours per day. More than 20,000 businessmen and women from 63 different countries have shared this existence. From my own point of view, and that of my staff, it has given us the opportunity of getting to know nationals of some countries which we have not visited. Uzbeks, Tajiks, Azerbaijanis and Kazakhs are some examples, while others from African states such as Côte d'Ivoire, Zaire and Gabon have made significant cultural contributions. Vigorous interaction between our Germans, French, Italians, Latin Americans, Arabs and Japanese is of course a daily occurrence. As far as trends in intercultural business behaviour are concerned, there is little that my staff and I cannot predict. Apart from this intriguing microcosm of activity taking place before our eyes, we have the additional experience of running our own foreign staff, numbering about 700 individuals in 15 countries.

*   *   *   *   *

The advent of the 1990s brought with it an acceleration of the procedures destined to further European integration and in 1994 the EC accepted the membership of 3 new states – Sweden, Finland and Austria. Norway and Switzerland, after some deliberation, had opted out, at least for the time being.

There had been several months of agonizing in both Sweden and Finland where national referendums were held to decide upon the issue of entry. The Finnish referendum was held first – this in itself of interest, since the result would also have an effect on Swedish voters. In the event, 57 per cent of Finns approved entry, followed by Sweden squeaking in with 52 per cent in favour. It is difficult not to surmise that Finland's decision was motivated less on economic grounds than on political. The shadow of her big eastern neighbour had been long and often dark. The post-Gorbachev disarray in Russia and the ultimate collapse of the Soviet political system left her former citizens facing a confused and unpredictable future. The brittle but durable security pact between Finland and the Soviet Union, so often quoted by the Soviets, was now without any meaningful substance, (if there had ever been any). Chaos on her eastern border allowed and encouraged Finland to join a club – a friendly one, whose members shared with her a millenium of common western European cultural heritage.

The accession of both Finland and Sweden to the EU had been planned over a period of several years. Denmark had been an EC member since 1973 though she, like Britain, dissented on many issues. In economic terms, Finland and Sweden too, faced problems, particularly in the field of agriculture.

Cultural considerations also came into play. While the European pedigree of the two new Nordic members was beyond question, Finns and Swedes were well aware that they did not know one group of their new partners very well. Nordics – Swedes, Norwegians, Danes, Icelanders and Finns – normally get on well together. They have a splendid resource they fall back on to settle their disagreements – common sense. Though common sense is by no means very common among peoples (interpretations of it vary wildly) Nordics find that their version of it sits comfortably with the English, German and

Dutch versions. South of Paris, things begin to change. In the many Brussels committees of the EU (now each with 15 members) Finns and Swedes found that Latin exuberance, volubility, rhetoric and disinclination to stick to agendas presented unforseen challenges to their calmer more disciplined style and seriously upset the comfortable rhythm of their usual approach.

In my book "Finland, Cultural Lone wolf" (Otava, 1992) I had pointed out that the intense interest in cultural relativism displayed by Finns stems largely from their Asiatic traits, particularly in the area of communication. They have a dilemma inasmuch as their style of communication sits badly with their clear-cut western European values. What do I mean by this?

Western values (American, British, Anglo-Saxon and western European) are strong, clearly-defined, rarely compromised, and entrenched in various long-standing institutions such as Protestantism, (or Christianity in general) parliamentary government, rule of law, etc. Such values – generally undiscussable – are social justice, equality for women, human rights, democracy, freedom of speech, self-determinism, protection of the environment, to name but a few. Americans, Germans, French and other Westerners have a clear-cut, forceful style of communication corresponding to the clearly-defined values. These they express well with communication gambits such as truth before diplomacy, lively, forceful delivery, thinking aloud, extroverted, overt body languge and frequent interruptions of other speakers.

Asian values are in essence, different from western ones. Instead of being clear-cut, undiscussable, confidently held, frank and unambiguous, they are rarely absolute, but softer, mitigated and qualified, contextual, peripheral, malleable and in most cases ambiguous. These soft, situation-oriented values and beliefs suit the nature of some Asiatic languages (e.g. Japanese) and especially the pan-Asian style of communication which is courteous, modestly uttered, reluctant to dominate, shunning aggression or even undue persuasion (no hard sell) and employs silence as a form of conversation when the timing is appropriate.

Asians rarely meet western standards in terms of democratic systems, human rights, treatment of women, ecological awareness and so on, but see these issues in a mistier, more ambivalent light than westerners and describe them in appropriately less exact terms.

Finns, with their shy, undemanding communication, find themselves unable to impose their views and sound proposals when faced with Latin or Greek loquaciousness and rhetoric. Swedes are not much better, if at all. Though their communication style is more western, their inherent shyness, lack of familiarity with southern Europeans and dislike of verbal confrontation, results in their being as muted as their Finnish colleagues.

The Finns, though slow speakers, are quick starters when it comes to action. In view of the fact that they were due to assume the EU presidency for a 6-month period in 1999, they began to lay plans for its smooth execution. In the early 90s I had already delivered cross-cultural seminars to the Danish Ministry of Education and Norway's Ministry of Environment as well as the Norwegian Research Council. The Finnish Ministry of Finance asked me to hold an experimental workshop to be attended by delegates from a dozen Finnish ministries. The attendees were people due to represent Finland in Brussels, ultimately to be committee chairmen and vice-chairmen in 1999. They were well aware of the problems of communication described above. The prospect of modest, unassuming, fair-minded, Finnish chairs dealing with rampant French intransigence, Italian oratory, Greek wheeling and dealing, Portuguese circumlocutions and Spanish vehemence (all at the same time) loomed large.

Together with Michael Gates, the RLC country manager in Finland, I prepared a series of seminars to train Finns in the awareness of various cultural phenomena common in the Latin and Mediterranean societies. Even the non-Finnish characteristics of Germans, Dutch, Belgians and British had to be included, as well as the less serious differences between Finns, Swedes and Danes. Self-awareness plays an important part in such workshops. Michael and I devised materials and exercises to show Finnish civil servants how they seemed in the eyes of others. Many admirable Finnish qualities – honesty, determination, fair play and modesty – would often be viewed as naïvete, obstinacy, indecision and opacity by more charismatic, volatile Latins.

Another factor which puts Nordics at a disadvantage when working on international committees is their aversion to gossip – a word which has rather negative connotations in northern ears. Yet gossip proves far more important to us than we would at first admit. It is a vital source of information in business circles in many countries. In cultures like Spain, Italy, Brazil and Japan, gossip quickly updates and bypasses facts and statistics, provides political background to commercial decisions, and facilitates invaluable debate between people who do not meet officially. The Italian *chiacchiera* or Spanish *paseo* may be largely limited to women and youngsters, but the late night cafés of Madrid and Lisbon overflow with businessmen, Japanese executives make momentous decisions every evening from 6-10 pm in the bars of the Ginza, and the whole of Central and South America 'networks' merrily until one or two in the morning.

The corridors of power in Brussels, where European business and political legislation are inevitably intertwined, reverberate with gossip. European countries which do not have access to this hot-house exchange of information will be severely disadvantaged. When I ask Finns whom they have lunch with between committee sessions in Brussels they invariably answer "the Swedes". Why, I ask them. Because they are nice quiet people, like us. The Swedes reply in a similar manner – they always lunch with the Finns and the Danes. I often tell the Finns not to eat with the Swedes, as they don't know any more than they do. Mix in the corridors and cafés with the Italians and the Greeks! They will tell you what is going on and who is going to vote with whom.

Swedish and Norwegian ministries, after a somewhat slower start, emulated the Finns in taking our seminars, which we strengthened by bringing in Belgian Brussels-insiders on certain days. The Swedes are due for the presidency in the year 2001; the Norwegians, though not yet in the EU, attend many other international committees. One seminar I gave took place up in the remote Lofoten Islands where we practised a "Norway Spring Herring" simulation, participants including delegations from the EU, Finland, Sweden, Norway, Iceland, Russia, Denmark and Portugal!

Though appropriate and necessary, it is somewhat ironic that the northern nations are taking the lead in examining cross-cultural problems in international governmental deliberations. That they do so indicates their acute awareness of the problem and their general interest in other cultures. The nationalities who in fact are in most need of such seminars are the Latins themselves, particularly the French, Spanish and Italians. While the Portuguese and Greeks have long sea-faring, trading, cosmopolitan traditions, the larger countries, especially France, are often unaware that there are world views very different from their own. Their rhetoric and love of charisma blinds them to the calmer judgements and rationale of others. Their relative lack of language skills compounds the problem. The Nordics very often query "Who should adapt to whom?" At least they ask the question. The Frenchman, who does not, is nevertheless quite sure of the answer.

In 1995 I was asked to hold a cross-cultural workshop for Crown Princess Victoria of Sweden and her class in the Stockholm Enskilda Gymnasium (high school). The headmistress, Ms Thérèse Burenstam-Linder, was well aware of Swedish shortcomings in international relations and had wisely included a course in the curriculum for teenage students. The mixed class of about twenty youngsters was extremely receptive (I suppose the school is one of the best in Sweden) and we had a lively day with lots of interaction and frank discussion of some controversial issues.

The Crown Princess, a pleasant and refreshingly natural girl, dressed in a chequered shirt and blue jeans, is the great-great granddaughter of her namesake Queen Victoria, wife of Gustav V, herself named after Queen Victoria of England. The current princess, whose mother Queen Silvia is German, has every reason to be interested in multicultural matters. Born on July 14, the anniversary of the storming of the Bastille, she is said to have conceived intense admiration for Jean-Baptiste Bernadotte who left his French homeland, married Désirée of Sweden, became King Carl XIV Johan and adapted completely to the Swedish culture. The many French words that exist in Swedish were imported during his reign.

Victoria had an amusing cross-cultural anecdote to contribute to the seminar. Her father, King Carl Gustav XVI, had recently visited Japan, where they were hosted by the Japanese Imperial Family and attended various ceremonies while in Tokyo. One of these was a visit to a well-known temple where the Swedish Royal couple would be met at the top of numerous steps by the Japanese Prime Minister. This procedure, as with most state visits, had to be carefully timed, so that no party had to hang around waiting for another.

The meticulous Japanese, wishing to leave nothing to chance, had rehearsed the logistics the previous day: Swedish Royal car stops here, 86 steps along the flat to the foot of the steps, 42 temple steps to climb, total 128 steps. One of the Japanese officials went through the actual motions three times and they confirmed that the whole procedure took 2 minutes and 35 seconds. The Japanese premier, coming from inside the temple, would time his walk accordingly and meet them, on the split second, at the entrance.

He did his bit all right, but the Japanese officials had failed to take into account one vital factor – the length of the Swedish King's legs. He needed far fewer steps along the flat bit and arrived a quarter of a minute early.

The best laid plans of mice and men .....

*   *   *   *   *

In March 1997, I had the honour to be knighted by President Ahtisaari of Finland. It appeared that the award had been recommended by several eminent Finns, including Johannes Virolainen, former Prime Minister, Elizabeth Rehn, ex-Minister of Defence, Tauno Matomäki, Finland's best-known businessman, Eero Vuohula of the Bank of Finland and Eero Leivo, Vice-President of Valmet and British Consul in Jyväskylä.

The Knighthood, 1st class, is of the Order of the Lion of Finland. The actual medal I received from Ambassador Pertti Salolainen at the Finnish embassy in London. All my family were present, as well as Kaj and Mary Wallen, Ed and Marja Wilton, Bob and Lois Bradley, Reg and Jean Latham and Geoff Mason. After the ceremony, Ambassador Salolainen and his charming wife, Anja, drove with us to Riversdown House, where we had dinner with all teachers and students. Salolainen is a committed Anglophile, speaking fluent English with great humour and enthusiasm. He exudes warmth and humanity and I felt it was most fitting that I should receive my decoration from a man who typified the staunch, loyal soul of that bleak northern territory for which I have conceived so much affection and admiration.

*   *   *   *   *

Cultural diversity is not something that is going to go away tomorrow, enabling us to plan our strategies on the assumption of mutual understanding. It is in itself a phenomenon with its own riches, the exploration of which could yield incalculable benefits for us, both in terms of wider vision and more profitable policies and activity. People of different cultures share basic concepts, but view them from different angles and perspectives, leading them to behave in a manner which we may consider irrational or even in direct contradiction of what we hold sacred. We should nevertheless be optimistic about cultural diversity. The behaviour of people of different cultures is not something willy-nilly. There exist clear trends, sequences and traditions. Reactions of Americans, Europeans and Asians alike can be forecasted, usually justified and in the majority of cases managed. Even in countries where political and economic change is currently rapid or sweeping (Russia, China, Hungary, Poland, Korea, Malaysia, etc.) deeply rooted attitudes and beliefs will resist a sudden transformation of values when pressured by reformists, governments or multinational conglomerates. Post-*perestroika* Russians exhibit individual and group behavioural traits strikingly similar to those recorded in Tsarist times – these had certainly persisted, in subdued form, in the Soviet era.

By focusing on the cultural roots of national behaviour, both in society and business, we can foresee and calculate with a surprising degree of accuracy how others will react to our plans for them, and we can make certain assumptions as to how they will approach us. A working knowledge of the basic traits of other cultures (as well as our own) will minimise unpleasant surprises (culture shock), give us insights in advance, and enable us to interact successfully with nationalities with whom we previously had difficulty.

It is now a source of unending pleasure for me to feel that the knowledge I have acquired of many peoples of the world and their fascinating, ever-recurring cultural characteristics will enable me to bring people closer together, to save some companies a lot of money, but to stress finally that diversity is good for us. We should strive to avoid irritants, we should recognize pseudo-conflicts for what they are, we should laugh at some of our own foibles, but at the end of the day, we should remain faithful to our true selves. After half a bottle of wine, I make a good Frenchman; on a company-organized picnic, I make a good Japanese "salaryman." I can give a reasonable imitation of a silent Finn and a theatrical Spaniard, but I am at my best when I am being English – not just any Englishman mind, but that particular breed hailing from the west of the Pennines – just down the Road from Wigan Pier, in fact.